M000166053

Costa Rica Handbook

Peter Hutchison

> **66 99**
> In Costa Rica, carters sing.
> Men on the roads with mandolins,
> and ox-carts bright as parrots.
> And oxen with coloured ribbons,
> bells, and flowers on their horns.
> At coffee-harvest time in Costa Rica
> when all carts are heaped high with
> coffee beans

Ernesto Cardenal, Carters Sing

Footprint story

It was 1921

Ireland had just been partitioned, the British miners were striking for more pay and the federation of British industry had an idea. Exports were booming in South America – how about a handbook for businessmen trading in that far away continent? The Anglo-South American Handbook was born that year, written by W Koebel, the most prolific writer on Latin America of his day.

1924

Two editions later the book was 'privatized' and in 1924, in the hands of Royal Mail, the steamship company for South America, it became The South American Handbook, subtitled 'South America in a nutshell'. This annual publication became the 'bible' for generations of travellers to South America and remains so to this day. In the early days travel was by sea and the Handbook gave all the details needed for the long voyage from Europe. What to wear for dinner; how to arrange a cricket match with the Cable & Wireless staff on the Cape Verde Islands and a full account of the journey from Liverpool up the Amazon to Manaus: 5898 miles without changing cabin!

1939

As the continent opened up, The South American Handbook reported the new Pan Am flying boat services, and the fortnightly airship service from Rio to Europe on the Graf Zeppelin. For reasons still unclear but with extraordinary determination, the annual editions continued through the Second World War.

1970s

Many more people discovered South America and the backpacking trail started to develop. All the while the Handbook was gathering fans, including literary vagabonds such as Paul Theroux and Graham Greene (who once sent some updates addressed to "The publishers of the best travel guide in the world, Bath, England").

1990s

During the 1990s the company set about developing a new travel guide series using this legendary title as the flagship. By 1997 there were over a dozen guides in the series and the Footprint imprint was launched.

2000s

The series grew quickly and there were soon Footprint travel guides covering more than 150 countries. In 2004, Footprint launched its first thematic guide: *Surfing Europe*, packed with colour photographs, maps and charts. This was followed by further thematic guides such as *Diving the World*, *Snowboarding the World*, *Body and Soul escapes*, *Travel with Kids* and *European City Breaks*.

2008

Today we continue the traditions of the last 87 years that has served legions of travellers so well. We believe that these help to make Footprint guides different. Our policy is to use authors who are genuine experts who write for independent travellers; people possessing a spirit of adventure, looking to get off the beaten track.

Title page: Red-eyed tree frog, Salve Verde. **Above:** Volcán Poás.

For tropical paradise, beach life and a sense of adventure Costa Rica is hard to beat. This country may be tiny but it packs an all-natural punch. A loose line of volcanoes running the country's length erupt and simmer, rainforests are perennially drenched, and nature loves it – singing back a triumphant chorus of celebration. A couple of Pacific peninsulas are quite similar in shape but one is dowsed in annual rains, while the other suffers periodic droughts. In the Central Highlands, orderly lines of coffee bushes rustle in the gentle breeze while on the Caribbean a thin strip of nature reserves and newly opened beaches attract visitors with their wild beauty. From chilled-out beaches to high-adrenalin adventure activities, and all stops in between, your biggest challenge is simply choosing what to do.

↘ 7 Planning your trip
8 Where to go
10 Itineraries
12 Costa Rica highlights & itineraries
14 Six of the best surf breaks
16 Six of the best spas and eco-lodges
18 Six of the best nature experiences
20 When to go
21 Rainfall and climate charts
22 Sport and activities
25 National parks
30 How big is your footprint?
32 Costa Rica on screen and page

↘ 33 Essentials
34 Getting there
39 Getting around
44 Sleeping
47 Eating and drinking
48 Festivals and events
49 Shopping
50 Essentials A-Z

↘ 67 San José
76 Sights

NORTHERN REGION

Caribbean Sea

GUANACASTE

CARIBBEAN LOWLANDS

NICOYA PENINSULA

SAN JOSE

CENTRAL HIGHLANDS

CENTRAL PACIFIC

SOUTHERN REGION

Pacific Ocean

GOLFITO & OSA PENINSULA

Contents

↘ **117 Central Highlands**
120 Alajuela and around
135 Heredia and around
145 Cartago and around
153 Turrialba and around

↘ **159 Northern Region**
162 Puerto Viejo loop
170 Ciudad Quesada, Fortuna and Lake Arenal
186 North of Fortuna
190 Monteverde and Santa Elena

↘ **205 Guanacaste**
208 North to Liberia
217 North of Liberia

↘ **227 Nicoya Peninsula**
230 Northern beaches
238 Northwestern beaches
250 Santa Cruz to Nicoya
253 Western beaches
262 Southern peninsula

↘ **277 Central Pacific**
280 Puntarenas to Quepos
295 Quepos and Manuel Antonio
308 Southern costanera

↘ **315 Southern Pacific**
318 South to San Isidro
329 South of San Isidro

↘ **339 Golfito & the Osa Peninsula**
342 Sierpe and Bahía Drake
347 Around Puerto Jiménez
356 Golfito and the beaches

↘ **363 Caribbean lowlands**
366 Highway 32 to Puerto Limón
375 North Caribbean
386 South Caribbean

↘ **409 Background**
410 History
421 Modern Costa Rica
424 Culture
428 Land and environment
452 Books and websites

↘ **455 Footnotes**
456 Basic Spanish for travellers
461 Index
466 Complete title listing
469 Advertisers' index
469 Acknowledgements
471 About the author
472 Credits

Planning your trip

↘ **8**
Where to go

↘ **10**
Itineraries

↘ **12**
Costa Rica highlights & itineraries

↘ **14**
Six of the best surf breaks

↘ **16**
Six of the best spas and eco-lodges

↘ **18**
Six of the best nature experiences

↘ **20**
When to go

↘ **21**
Rainfall and climate charts

↘ **22**
Sport and activities

↘ **25**
National parks

↘ **30**
How big is your footprint?

↘ **32**
Costa Rica on screen and page

M. COHEN/SUPERSTOCK

Costa Rica's toucans are among the most flamboyant of all Central American birds.

Where to go

Choosing where to go in Costa Rica is tantamount to being a child in a huge sweet shop – the choice is daunting and you want to do it all … immediately. Given all the options, it's worth doing a bit of planning. Obviously, the more time you have the better, but one of the great things about Costa Rica is its diversity-to-size ratio. Even with just a few days, you would have time to visit a couple of highland spots and a beach before heading home.

Most people arrive in **San José**, the capital, where you can spend a couple of days sightseeing. It's really the only place in the country with any significant cultural attractions, so if you like museums, art galleries and cerebral fodder you should allow a couple of days here. Beyond the capital, the **Central Highlands** are a tidy mosaic of volcanic hills dotted with towns and coffee plantations, most within reach of a national park. Typical day-trips from the capital take in the craft town of Sarchí and a steady climb up the huge crater of Volcán Poás. A tour of the

scenic Orosí Valley is easily followed by a haul up to the steaming vents of Volcán Irazú. Or take a ride on a ski lift through the rainforest canopy in Parque Nacional Braulio Carrillo, just 90 minutes from the capital.

North of San José, **Volcán Arenal** leaves onlookers trance-like on night trips as the glowing lava crashes down the mountainside. Nearby, the world-famous cloudforest of **Monteverde** provides a brief insight into the magnificent diversity of the highlands.

Guanacaste, to the northwest, draws visitors to its volcanic landscape and the bubbling mudpots of Rincón de la Vieja, the birder's wetland paradise of Palo Verde and the Tempisque river basin, the dry forests of Santa Rosa and the cultural landscape of the *sabanero*, Costa Rica's very own cowboy.

Beach lovers and surfers can pick pretty much any spot from the northern **Nicoya Peninsula** down the **Central Pacific** coastline and they will find a personally

Opposite left: Arabica-quality coffee beans on a plantation near Volcán Poás.
Opposite right: The green church in Sarchí is especially attractive at sunset.
Above: Central America's most active volcano, Arenal, is an easy trip from nearby Fortuna.

tailored version of paradise with lively resorts and quiet hideaways catering for all budgets, tastes and energy levels.

Southern Costa Rica is a tougher option. Travelling overland down the mountainous spine of the country, **Chirripó Grande** is the country's highest peak and a serious

North of San José, Volcán Arenal leaves onlookers trance-like on night trips as the glowing lava crashes down the mountainside.

challenge for the trekker. Further south, on the **Osa Peninsula**, the pristine Parque Nacional Corcovado is a moment of magic for both the adventurer and wildlife lover.

The **Caribbean** divides neatly in two halves. North of Puerto Limón, the canals of Tortuguero are likely to provide quiet moments of awestruck contemplation as you encounter the wildlife and vegetation of this aquatic inland waterworld, while on the coast turtles nest on the beaches as they have for millions of years. South of Limón, the carnival capital of Costa Rica, the discerning traveller can find a blend of upmarket retreats offering top-quality service with a price to match, and quiet undeveloped beaches that are perfect for the budget traveller.

Itineraries

Ten days

Seeing a cross-section of Costa Rica in 10 days could be tough. Space it out and it could be ideal. After a day in San José or a nearby town of the Central Valley, it's a short trip north to Fortuna taking in the craft capital of Sarchí, and the topiary creations of Zarcero en route. A couple of days in Fortuna allows plenty of time to see the Arenal volcano and the nearby waterfall, and still have time for a day trip north to the wetlands of Caño Negro Wildlife Reserve close to the Nicaraguan border, before heading round Lake Arenal to Santa Elena for a couple of days exploring the delights of the cloudforest in the Monteverde area.

Heading further north you could have a few days' adventure at one of the lodges close to Rincón de la Vieja hiking through the national park, or simply taking it easy.

With just a few days left, head out to the Nicoya Peninsula and find a beach that takes your fancy. Tamarindo is a lively spot, while Playa del Coco is a good budget option. Sámara and Nosara are slightly pricier but offer peace and quiet. Enjoy some genuine rest and relaxation, with the occasional local excursion, before heading back to San José (40 minutes by plane or half a day overland).

Ten active days

Many options in Costa Rica have been packaged to create two-, three- or four-day trips. By mixing and matching, you create a tailor-made trip to match the pace you want. A suggested itinerary might include: two or three days' whitewater rafting on the Pacuare or Reventazón rivers near Turrialba, followed by a flight down to Palmar Sur or Puerto Jiménez for some trekking through Parque Nacional Corcovado before heading to Drake for some relaxing diving.

AGE FOTOSTOCK/SUPERSTOCK

Two weeks

A few extra days couple would allow you to tag on a trip to Parque Nacional Tortuguero on the Caribbean to the suggested itinerary, above. Alternatively after visiting Arenal and Monteverde, you could head out to Tortuguero National Park before going south to relax on the quieter beaches and at one of the secluded homely lodges.

Two weeks is long enough to consider doing a fly-drive option. Take the first week to acclimatize yourself to Costa Rica, seeing a couple of places that you can't reach in a private vehicle, and then head out on your own to explore and enjoy the freedom of going left, right, straight on or backwards whenever you please.

Three weeks

You are now moving into the realms of really being able to explore. After a brief foray through the Central Valley exploring the delights of the region, head out to Arenal and Monteverde and make your way slowly south down the Pan-American Highway through San Isidro de El General. Hikers can stop off

Opposite page: Statues at the entrance of the Banco Central de Costa Rica museum in San José.
Top: Sculpted bushes in Zarcero form an archway leading up to the church.
Above: Conchal Beach, Nicoya Peninsula.

for a few days to knock off Chirripó, while others can explore the quieter options of this forgotten region. Continue south through the scenic Coto Brus Valley to San Vito and finally to Golfito, where you can step out to explore the coast or tramp through the rainforest of Parque Nacional Corcovado.

Awestruck and amazed, head up the coastal road slowly taking in Dominical, Jacó or Manuel Antonio – depending on whether you like deserted, busy or popular – to enjoy the beach before heading back to San José.

Costa Rica highlights & itineraries

See colour maps in centre of book

Lago de Nicaragua

La Cruz

Los Chiles

Parque Nacional Santa Rosa

Upala

Santa Rosa National Park & La Casona

Historic site that repelled the invasion of US filibuster William Walker in 1856, page 218.

Refugio Nacional de Vida Silvestre Caño Negro

Parque Nacional Rincón de la Vieja

Cordillera de Guanacaste

ALAJUEL

Liberia

Guayabo

Rincón de la Vieja National Park

Steaming and spluttering volcanic geothermal activity on the Old Lady, page 217.

Tilarán

Vol Arenal (1633m)

Laguna de Arenal

Tanque

Cañas

Fortuna

Salinas

GUANACASTE

Cordillera de Tilarán

Reserva Biológ Bosque Nubo Monteverde

Nicoya

Isla Chira

Hojancha

Carmona

Golfo de Nicoyo

Esparza

Puntarenas

Playa Grande & Tamarindo

Two of the Nicoya Peninsula's many beautiful beaches, pages 239 & 240.

Peninsula de Nicoya

PUNTARENAS

Cóbano

Montezuma

Jacó

Monteverde Cloud Forest

Misty magic in the mountain highlands, page 192.

Montezuma, Malpaís & Santa Teresa

Fast-growing beach hangout for surfing, yoga and nature, pages 263 & 266.

Ten days ●➡

Ten active days ●➡

Two week extension ●➡

Three weeks ●➡

Pacific Ocean

Manuel Antonio National Park

Rainforest wilderness and beautiful beaches side by side, page 299.

N

20 km

20 miles

Dominical

Budget beach life and surf-cool heaven with whale watching to the south, page 308.

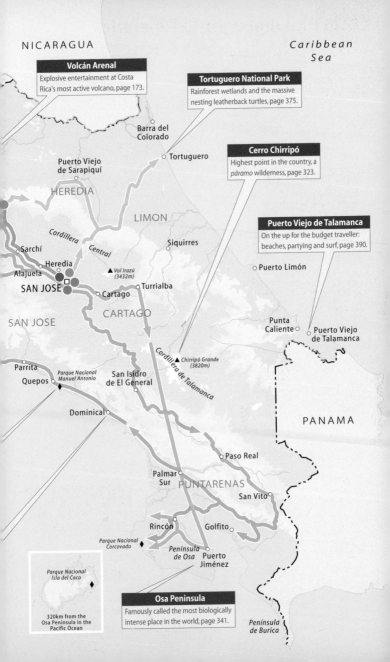

NICARAGUA

Caribbean Sea

Volcán Arenal
Explosive entertainment at Costa Rica's most active volcano, page 173.

Tortuguero National Park
Rainforest wetlands and the massive nesting leatherback turtles, page 375.

Cerro Chirripó
Highest point in the country, a *páramo* wilderness, page 323.

Puerto Viejo de Talamanca
On the up for the budget traveller: beaches, partying and surf, page 390.

Barra del Colorado

Puerto Viejo de Sarapiquí

○ Tortuguero

HEREDIA

LIMON

Cordillera Central

Sarchí

Heredia

Alajuela

SAN JOSÉ

Siquirres

▲ Vol Irazú (3432m)

Turrialba ○

Cartago

○ Puerto Limón

Punta Caliente ○

Puerto Viejo de Talamanca

SAN JOSE

CARTAGO

Cordillera de Talamanca

▲ Chirripó Grande (3820m)

Parrita ○

Quepos

Parque Nacional Manuel Antonio

San Isidro de El General

Dominical ○

PANAMA

Paso Real ○

Palmar Sur ○

PUNTARENAS

San Vito ○

Rincón ○

Golfito ○

Parque Nacional Corcovado

Península de Osa

Puerto Jiménez

Parque Nacional Isla del Coco

320km from the Osa Peninsula in the Pacific Ocean

Osa Peninsula
Famously called the most biologically intense place in the world, page 341.

Península de Burica

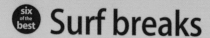

Surf breaks

Pavones

Hidden away on the south Pacific coast, Pavones is a legendary left point break that rides for up to 800 m on a good swell. It's the longest ride in Costa Rica, and being a fickle fiend, it's also the longest wait; when there's no swell its popularity can lead to a crowded line up. However, as luck would have it, there are a number of other left handers around the point and also a beach break which can be bigger than the point itself. And Pavones is just the right sort of laid-back town you'll want to wait in on quiet days.

Salsa Brava

Over on the Caribbean side, offshore of Puerto Viejo de Talamanca, Salsa Brava reef break is known for its size and power. It's the biggest wave in Costa Rica, and definitely not for novices (the powerful wave breaks over coral – you may need to pack a spare board for this one). It needs a swell to work; the best time of year is from December to April. This is one of the most up-and-coming beach spots in Costa Rica.

Witches' Rock

At the northernmost point of the Nicoya Peninsula, *Peña Bruja*, mistakenly translated in the 1980s as 'Witches' Rock' is a famous break, with fast, hollow rights, and good lefts when it's smaller. A beautiful, remote and picturesque spot, the wave is off Playa Naranjo, in Santa Rosa National Park. Access is by 4WD during dry season (boat during the wet) and camping is available at the park ranger's station.

JIM WILEMAN/ALAMY

Opposite page: Playa Grande. **Above:** Santa Teresa, Nicoya Peninsula.

Playa Hermosa

Just south of Jacó (itself a great surf spot, well suited for the novice), Playa Hermosa provides a powerful and consistent beach break, with a hollow peak that could be compared to Puerto Escondido in Mexico. Sticking out into the Pacific, the spot is assured reliable swell. At times it's perfect. Playa Hermosa is your laid-back surf base, while Jacó provides a lively party atmosphere.

Playa Grande

Playa Grande, a short trip across the estuary from Tamarindo, provides one of the most consistent breaks in the country, with lefts and rights of good size (it's the most westerly point of Costa Rica and can get swells from the north, south and west). There's almost always something happening at Playa Grande except at the bottom of the tide. A few hotels in Playa Grande and lots in Tamarindo make it a good base from which to explore and take side trips.

Malpaís

Slowly and reluctantly emerging into the spotlight Malpaís, on the southwest tip of the Nicoya Peninsula, provides one of the best all-round surfing experiences in the country. There are several breaks up and down a short stretch of beach, with good transport for moving between them. There are courses for beginners, and a good mix of lefts and rights for all levels of surfer. There's plenty going on in the area, and enough services to make it a good spot for a surf crowd, or a family looking for more than one activity by the beach.

Spas and eco-lodges

Estudio Los Almendros

www.somaritmoscostarica.com

This rustic retreat, at the tip of the Nicoya Peninsula, is set in the environs of the Cabo Blanco National Park. Classes take place in the studio or by the beach, combining somatic movement with the use of giant gym balls, creating stretches and positions that feel both relieving and invigorating. Accommodation is basic, spread around the tropical garden that sprawls from the forested hillside down to the sea. There's a natural pool for swimming, while nature trails, snorkelling trips and the bars and cafés of the picturesque village of Montezuma are all close at hand. Prices start at US$30 per room per night.

Nosara Yoga Institute

www.nosarayoga.com

Run by Leading kripalu teacher, Don Stapleton, and his wife, Nosara is a renowned yoga teachers' training centre, but also runs regular workshops and retreats, drop-in classes, and a popular 'surf yoga' programme twice a year aimed at those who know yoga and who want to learn to surf (Nosara is a major surf spot). Yoga is practised in the Rancho Pavilion, which has an imposing thatched roof and open sides to let in both light and colours from the garden. There's also a smaller studio, Tree Tops, positioned high on a hill overlooking the sea. There is no accommodation at Nosara Yoga Institute but the Stapletons will recommend a handful of neighbouring hotels to suit your budget. Prices start at US$968 per course (seven to eight days).

Panacea

www.panaceacr.com

The Panacea philosophy is total detachment from your everyday life, and its secluded mountain setting overlooking the Pacific Ocean makes this instantly achievable. Yoga classes are held daily in a palm-thatched *rancho* with polished teak floors. Gentle moves (mainly iyengar) involve plenty of breathwork and can be tailored to suit individual needs. Water aerobics classes in an infinity pool on the side of the mountain are an invigorating complement to yoga. Try the aromatherapy tub, where water circulates while diffusing the oils into the air. Accommodation is in six rustic terracotta-tiled *cabinas* (bungalows), at staggered levels on the mountainside. Food is vegetarian (with some fresh seafood) using locally sourced ingredients, served in the simple dining room, which opens out to the pool and views of the mountains. There are meditation gardens, a walking labyrinth and a small drumming circle. Prices start at US$715 per person for seven nights.

Opposite page: Panacea. Above: Samasati Nature Retreat.

Rancho Pacífico

www.ranchopacifico.com

This boutique-style retreat combines jungle, mountain and ocean with sheer indulgence (guests are invited to sip champagne during spa treatments). Each villa has its own spa garden and soaking tub, so treatments can be taken in complete privacy, while the rooftop spa offers breathtaking views of the rainforest and Pacific. Massages range from lymph drainage, trigger point therapy to hot stone and four hands. Products are made from natural resources, such as coffee, chocolate, coconut, volcanic lavender, ginger, rainforest flowers and mud. There's also a sweat cave, infinity pool and an outdoor stone jacuzzi. Food is locally sourced sumptuous Caribbean fusion with grilled meats and fish. Prices start at US$1325 per person for seven nights.

Samasati Nature Retreat

www.samasati.com

Samasati nestles in lush green jungle on Costa Rica's little-visited Caribbean coastline. Yoga, yoga philosophy and teacher-training workshops are offered, as well as meditation, shamanic dance, and wellbeing weeks. Bungalows, restaurants and yoga studios are hidden amongst the foliage, and the smell of the jungle is energizing. The wooden yoga platforms are protected by mosquito nets but open to the forest and the sounds of warbling birds, monkey howls and the hum of a million insects. Spa treatments include deep-tissue and Swedish massage, chakra balancing, reflexology, fruit scrubs, aromatherapy and Bach flower treatments. Most of the products are hand-made and water is from an on-site spring. The 10 en suite bungalows and two fully equipped cottages with open verandas are beautifully constructed from reforested wood. Prices start at US$125 per person per night.

World Family Yoga

www.worldfamilyyoga.com

This not-for-profit organization donates a percentage of its income to supporting local children. It runs a regular yoga trip for families to the remote and pristine Osa Peninsula, accessible only by boat. Guests stay in private bungalows, and wake up to screeching howler monkeys, scarlet macaws flying overhead, and the sweet smell of ylang-ylang trees. Yoga is taught by experienced anusara- inspired teachers who focus on alignment in transformative, heart-centered sessions. Families can choose to go, surfing, dolphin watching, horse riding, snorkelling and hiking through Corcovado, Costa Rica's premier rainforest reserve. Prices start at US$1250 per person per week.

Nature experiences

Tortuguero National Park

If creeping along the coast in the middle of the night, with no torch, wasn't exciting enough, imagine seeing a massive leatherback turtle coming ashore to nest at Tortuguero National Park. Laboriously dragging itself up the beach to beyond the high water mark, it digs a deep hole to incubate the leathery eggs, and returns exhausted to the restful world of the ocean. See www.tortuguerovillage.com.

Marino Ballena National Park

Marino Ballena National Park, www.marino ballena.org, in the southern central Pacific coast just doesn't make sense. Every December to April migrating northern hemisphere humpback whales visit, and from August to October their southern hemisphere cousins drop by. Add dolphins and turtles, and it's a veritable natural zoo. And yet barely anyone visits. True, you're not guaranteed a sighting, but when you do get one, it's a truly unforgettable experience. The area is less developed than much of Costa Rica, so the best accommodation is the rustic Hotel Canto de Ballenas, www.turismoruralcr.com.

Monteverde Cloud Forest Reserve

Whether you're with a guide, or exploring alone, Monteverde Cloud Forest Reserve, www.monteverdeinfo.com, offers the chance to discover a great wilderness. Wander the quieter trails passing trees cloaked in moss and epiphytes, drenched by passing clouds. Catch a glimpse of an exotic bird, spider or brightly coloured frog. Take a nocturnal tour to see tarantulas and other creatures of the night. Then get up early to experience the rainforest as dawn breaks. You can happily spend a day enthralled by the jungle, but for real adventure, head deep into the reserve and spend a few days at one of the field stations.

Opposite page top: Costa Rica's cloudforest is home to thousands of species of insect.
Opposite page bottom: Each year leatherback turtles migrate hundreds of miles to nest.
Above: The beaches and bays of Manuel Antonio National Park are surrounded by luscious rainforest.

Mount Chirripó

In their eagerness to provide good service and a warm welcome, Costa Ricans have taken much of the work out of exploration. However, you can't avoid the tough stuff if you want to climb Mount Chirripó in the central Talamancas. The trip starts from San Gerardo de Rivas (www.sangerardocosta rica.com), easily reached from San Isidro de El General. Allow at least one day up and one day down – more if you have the time. It's not a technical climb, more of a steady plod, but you have to keep moving. As you climb through the different ecosystems, from cloudforest to alpine páramo, you'll see plenty of birds – and hear even more. Listen out for the rriikkk-rriikk-rriikk of the toucans. It's a great trek, and leads to the highest point in Costa Rica.

Volcán Arenal

Volcán Arenal is another casualty of the nature documentary. Having peered down the crater of an explosive volcano at home on TV, could anything match that drama in real life? Probably not, but if you can find a spot to sit, rest and watch Arenal, it is mighty impressive. By day, a steady gentle puff of smoke rises from the crater, while the occasional line of dust and debris is disturbed as something rolls down the perfectly symmetrical slope. At night, the dust trails reveal themselves to be molten lava, drawing a bright orange line crashing, smashing and splitting down the volcano. It might seem a long way off, but it can be deadly. Enjoy a geological spectacle.

Manuel Antonio National Park

Why does Costa Rica have so many national parks? Because there's so much to protect. For convenience and beauty, head for Manuel Antonio National Park, which has stunning beaches and rainforest side-by-side. Cahuita National Park on the Caribbean also has a forest-fringed beach, with clear waters and some of the best corals in Costa Rica. For challenging hiking, steaming mudpots and waterfalls head up to Rincón de la Vieja, a little to the east of Liberia. Choosing a favourite national park is like having to choose a favourite child. You can't – just love them all.

When to go

High season

If your trip is about beaches, clear blue skies and bare flesh head to the north and central Pacific coast between December and April (high season). During this time almost no rain falls in the Central Highlands and the Pacific regions. Christmas and New Year in particular are very busy with Costa Ricans and international visitors looking to enjoy some time away from home. Easter week is also very busy: banks and public services close, and many buses stop running. Outside these months rain falls steadily, and is heaviest in September and October. On the Caribbean slope (everywhere east of the continental divide), rains fall more consistently throughout the year, the drier months being February to June, with a small summer (*veranillo*) window in September and October.

Green season

Outside the high season, rainfall normally occurs in bursts lasting a couple of hours and travel is still possible in the vast majority of places. This rainy season has been renamed the 'green season' by some marketing wag at the Costa Rican Tourism Institute – and with good effect. The green season is an increasingly popular time to visit as the country tends to be quieter and discounts are often possible. A word of warning: some places do close for a break or remodelling and a few, very few, become inaccessible in normal green-season conditions. Check before travelling.

Best of the festivals

While Costa Rican festivals don't rise to the country-stopping levels of some Latin nations, there are several dotted throughout the year that are worth joining in if you get the opportunity. As a general rule, find out if there are any national holidays while you are in Costa Rica; changing cash can be very difficult.

The biggest festival is probably **Carnival**, held in the week leading up to 12 October, commemorating the Spanish discovery of the New World. **Independence Day** (15 September) is also a lively celebration, while the **Virgin of Los Angeles** (2 August) is a solemn religious occasion in Cartago attracting pilgrims from throughout Costa Rica and Central America.

Costa Rica

Activity	J	F	M	A	M	J	J	A	S	O	N	D
Birdwatching (breeding season)			★	★	★							
Diving in the Cocos Islands					★	★	★	★	★	★	★	
Diving off the mainland	★	★	★	★								
Turtle watching (Playa Grande)	★	★	★									
Turtle watching (Tortuguero)				★	★	★	★	★	★			
Whitewater rafting	★	★	★	★	★	★	★	★	★	★	★	★
Windsurfing/kitesurfing	★	★	★	★								★

Rainfall and climate charts

San José

Month	Average temperature in °C max-min	Average rainfall in mm
Jan	24 - 14	15
Feb	24 - 14	05
Mar	26 - 15	20
Apr	26 - 17	46
May	26 - 17	229
Jun	26 - 17	241
Jul	25 - 17	211
Aug	26 - 16	241
Sep	25 - 16	305
Oct	25 - 16	300
Nov	25 - 16	145
Dec	24 - 14	41

Limón

Month	Average temperature in °C max-min	Average rainfall in mm
Jan	31 - 20	317
Feb	31 - 20	211
Mar	31 - 21	234
Apr	31 - 22	276
May	31 - 22	282
Jun	31 - 22	296
Jul	31 - 22	427
Aug	31 - 22	312
Sep	31 - 22	145
Oct	31 - 22	206
Nov	29 - 21	391
Dec	31 - 21	445

Quepos

Month	Average temperature in °C max-min	Average rainfall in mm
Jan	31 - 21	72
Feb	31 - 21	36
Mar	32 - 22	60
Apr	32 - 22	167
May	32 - 22	392
Jun	31 - 22	433
Jul	31 - 21	461
Aug	30 - 22	478
Sep	30 - 22	528
Oct	30 - 22	644
Nov	30 - 22	388
Dec	30 - 21	169

Montezuma

Month	Average temperature in °C max-min	Average rainfall in mm
Jan	26 - 21	69
Feb	27 - 20	36
Mar	28 - 21	30
Apr	29 - 21	48
May	29 - 22	162
Jun	28 - 21	238
Jul	27 - 22	329
Aug	28 - 21	307
Sep	28 - 21	388
Oct	27 - 21	385
Nov	26 - 22	272
Dec	26 - 21	192

Tortuguero

Month	Average temperature in °C max-min	Average rainfall in mm
Jan	31 - 20	317
Feb	31 - 20	211
Mar	31 - 15	204
Apr	31 - 22	276
May	31 - 22	282
Jun	31 - 22	296
Jul	31 - 22	427
Aug	30 - 22	312
Sep	31 - 22	145
Oct	31 - 22	208
Nov	29 - 21	391
Dec	31 - 21	446

Volcán Arenal

Month	Average temperature in °C max-min	Average rainfall in mm
Jan	28 - 20	192
Feb	29 - 20	132
Mar	30 - 20	92
Apr	31 - 21	95
May	31 - 22	262
Jun	30 - 22	414
Jul	30 - 22	509
Aug	30 - 22	437
Sep	30 - 22	412
Oct	30 - 21	435
Nov	29 - 22	308
Dec	28 - 21	259

Nicoya

Month	Average temperature in °C max-min	Average rainfall in mm
Jan	33 - 21	05
Feb	34 - 22	11
Mar	36 - 22	24
Apr	36 - 23	69
May	33 - 23	274
Jun	33 - 22	325
Jul	33 - 22	244
Aug	32 - 22	305
Sep	31 - 22	399
Oct	31 - 22	407
Nov	31 - 22	316
Dec	32 - 21	25

Puntarenas

Month	Average temperature in °C max-min	Average rainfall in mm
Jan	36 - 22	07
Feb	36 - 22	06
Mar	35 - 23	05
Apr	35 - 23	31
May	33 - 24	192
Jun	32 - 23	228
Jul	33 - 23	159
Aug	33 - 23	229
Sep	32 - 23	298
Oct	32 - 23	273
Nov	32 - 23	120
Dec	33 - 22	30

Palmar Sur

Month	Average temperature in °C max-min	Average rainfall in mm
Jan	33 - 21	50
Feb	33 - 15	53
Mar	34 - 22	97
Apr	33 - 22	225
May	32 - 22	422
Jun	32 - 22	408
Jul	32 - 22	370
Aug	31 - 22	414
Sep	31 - 22	495
Oct	31 - 22	597
Nov	31 - 22	350
Dec	32 - 22	106

Sport and activities

Birdwatching

ⓘ **Birdwatch Costa Rica**, Apdo 7911, 1000 San José, T2228-4768, www.birdwatch costarica.com. **Cheesemans' Ecology Safaris**, 20800 Kittredge Rd, Saratoga, CA 95070, T800-527-5330 in the US or T408-867-1371, www.cheesemans.com. **Field Guides**, 9433 Bee Cave Rd, Building 1, Suite 150, Austin, TX 78733, T800-728-4953 or T512-263-7295, www.fieldguides.com. **Wings**, 1643 N Alvernon, Suite 105, Tucson, AZ 85712, T888-293-6443 or T520-320-9868, www.wingsbirds.com.

With more bird species than the whole of North America or Europe (875 at the last count) Costa Rica is undoubtedly a birdwatcher's paradise. Thousands of birders visit every year to see some of the most magnificent birds in the neotropics: resplendent quetzals, three-wattled bellbirds, bare-necked umbrella birds, violaceous trogons, scarlet macaws, chestnut-bellied herons, turquoise cotingas, sunbitterns and hundreds more species.

Two of the best-known birding spots are **La Selva Biological Station** in the Caribbean lowlands (part of the Organisation for Tropical Studies, www.ots.ac.cr), which runs birdwatching courses, and the world-famous **Monteverde Cloud Forest Reserve**.

Once out of the towns and cities of the Central Valley you'll find a tremendous diversity of habitats: lush cloudforests, dry deciduous woods, rainforests and even subalpine *páramo* in the Cerro de la Muerte highlands. A typical birdwatching trip might include **Villa Lapas** (bordering Parque Nacional Carara), **Tiskita Lodge** on the south Pacific coast (near Punta Banco), **Monteverde**, **Tortuguero National Park** on the Caribbean coast, and a visit to **La Selva Biological Station**.

Bungee jumping

ⓘ **Tropical Bungee**, www.bungee.co.cr.

OK, so you can bungee jump anywhere in the world. But why not try it in Costa Rica? Who's to say you won't find it a bizarrely unnatural, life-affirming experience? In theory, you shouldn't jump off bridges, even if it is down into a scenic river gorge with a small stream gently flowing below – instinct and self-preservation create a huge stop sign. But for some reason, with a few hefty bits of rubber attached to your ankles, it's OK. You don't have to do anything physical yourself, yet afterwards we guarantee that you'll be exhausted. It's wonderfully pointless and, if your body's up to it, something you should try. Try Tropical Bungee, near Grecia.

AGE FOTOSTOCK/SUPERSTOCK

The magnificent and elusive quetzal.

The diversity of Costa Rica's eco-systems on land are matched by its abundance of underwater creatures; you might find yourself swimming with manta rays up to 6 m long.

Canopy tours

ⓘ www.monteverdeinfo.com/
canopy/tour.htm, www.canopytour.com.
Canopy tours cost from US$8 up to
around US$75.

The rainforest canopy is where most of the wildlife action takes places and there are now a multitude of ways of getting you up there for a bird's-eye view. The calmest way to experience the canopy is by exploring on a suspension bridge, strung out along the trees where you are free to walk at leisure or with a guide. Main suspension tours are **Santa Elena**, **Fortuna** and **Rainmaker** near Quepos.

An equally calm way through the canopy is on an aerial tour, using adapted ski lifts to carry you through the trees. Try the famous (and expensive) one near **Braulio Carrillo National Park**, or the less-impressive option in **Monteverde**. There's also the good old-fashioned option of climbing a tree. A couple of places, in particular **Hacienda Barú** (near Dominical), and **Selva Bananito Lodge** (near Puerto Limón), let you use tree-climbing ropes.

Finally, for the adventurous, there's the **zip wire** option (see page 29).

Diving

ⓘ The cost of diving starts at around US$35 for a beach dive on the south Caribbean, rising to around US$50-85 for a 2-tank dive. A **PADI** Open Water course out of Playa del Coco costs about US$295. Diving trips to the Cocos Islands on live-aboard boats start at around US$2700 for an 8-day trip, with 6 full days' of diving.

Costa Rica gets a bit of a hard time on the diving front primarily because of poor visibility (at around the 30-50 ft in the wet season). It's best from May to November when there is less rain and you can enjoy the warm waters. The northern Pacific coast around **Playa del Coco** is a local diving hotspot with trips out to nearby islands. Further south, **Drake** is a popular base from which to visit Isla del Caño, where you're almost guaranteed sightings of sharks. On the Caribbean side, the dive action is centred around the coral waters off the coast of **Cahuita National Park** and further south in the **Gandoca-Manzanillo National Wildlife Refuge**. If you're looking for truly world-class diving, the clear waters of the **Cocos Islands**, 550 km southwest of Costa Rica, offer

KORIAN SCHWAB/SHUTTERSTOCK

excellent opportunities. For experienced divers, live-aboard boats provide phenomenal encounters with schools of hammerhead sharks, as well as white-tipped sharks, whale sharks and manta rays.

Fishing

ⓘ Deep-sea fishing starts at around US$600 for one day, inland waterways can start at as little as US$250 for the day. For more specific information and updated fishing reports contact **Jerry Ruhlow**, T1-800-308-3394, T2282-6743, www.costaricaoutdoors.com. Also look at lodges in the main fishing areas.

Fishing doesn't get any better than this, with tarpon and snook off Costa Rica's Caribbean coast; marlin, sailfish, dorado, tuna and other species on the Pacific and trout, rainbow bass (*guapote*), bobo, machaca and more in inland lakes and rivers.

The peak time of year for fishing varies, but when it is at its best, good boats and beach accommodation are often hard to find, so book ahead. See also box, page 232.

Mountain biking

ⓘ **Coast to Coast Adventures**, T2280-8054, www.ctocadventures.com, offers bespoke trips, providing all gear including bike, water bottle and helmet. From a general hire company, mountain bikes cost US$5 an hour.

Pedal power has taken over in parts of Costa Rica. You can rent a bike for a couple of hours, a day or even a couple of weeks. Joining a tour is often the best way to get to some of the best off-road sites. Guanacaste is ideal for hugging the coastline, providing fantastic views and a challenging ride. Several two-day trips out of San José give you the chance to get seriously muddy, ending up in places like Manuel Antonio, or combining the biking with paddling down white water.

Surfing

ⓘ **Alacran Surf Tours**, 100 m north of Banco Interfin in San José, T232-9597, toll free on T1-866-252-2726, www.alacransurf.com, offers trips from 1 day to a fortnight. Beginners should head for Dominical or Malpaís which both have good surf schools: **Pura Vida Adventures**, Malpaís, south Nicoya, in the US on T415-465-2162, www.puravidaadventures.com; **Green Iguana Surf Camp**, T2787-0033, www.greeniguanasurfcamp.com. **Del Mar Surf Camp**, Playa Hermosa, T2643-3197, www.costaricasurfing chicas.com. www.surf-costarica.com and www.crsurf.com if you just want to surf the web.

Costa Rica offers world-class waves in beautiful surroundings with air and water temperatures averaging in the high 20°s C. The best conditions are December to June.

National parks

With so many national parks and protected areas, natural attractions are Costa Rica's biggest draw: turtle watching in Tortuguero and Las Baulas National Park; dolphin and whale spotting around the Osa Peninsula; birdwatching through the protected areas throughout the country. The 26 national parks and many more biological reserves, wildlife refuges and other protected areas protect 25.4% of the national territory according to MINAE (Ministerio de Ambiente y Energía), who have overall control of managing the parks. For information about a specific park, see the relevant text throughout the book. For details on the national park system see Background chapter, page 431.

Entrance to all national parks costs US$8-10. Entrance times vary, while a handful (Manuel Antonio, Rincón de la Vieja, Braulio Carrillo, Guayobo and Cabo Blanco) actually close for a day or two to relieve pressure on the areas and for maintenance.

Most parks can be visited easily and conveniently simply by turning up. If you have a specific enquiry or want to book in advance, contact the **Fundación de Parques Nacionales**, C 23-25, Av 15, Barrio Escalante, San José, T192 or T2257-2239, www.minae.go.cr, which has information on

Two top nature retreats

▸▸ **Selva Bananito**, www.selva bananito.com. Hidden deep in the Talamanca mountains on the Caribbean, Selva Bananito is a pristine eco-lodge, one of the best in the world. Mostly constructed from reclaimed wood, it's an all-natural kind of place. Stilted cabins offer great comforts, privacy and views into the forest. Tree climbing, canopy observation, waterfall and cliff rappels keep you busy in the day, and as night falls, all you can hear is the sound of the forest.

▸▸ **Lapa Ríos**, www.laparios.com. Tucked away on the south side of the Osa Peninsula is this sanctuary of calm and tranquillity. Thatched-roof bungalows sit perched on small ridges, with clear vistas searching out to the Golfo Dulce. You could happily hide away in your rooms, popping out only to eat in the spacious open-air restaurant with more jaw-dropping views from the roof-top viewing platform. But wait, there's a jungle out there to explore, so strike the right balance between rest and adventure.

some of the protected areas and is growing to encompass the whole network.

Opposite page: Fishing the incoming tide. **Above:** Female green basilisk in Tortuguero.

You can rent a board or even take classes at many of the more popular destinations. If you can already surf, there are more than 30 established breaks across the country.

Pacific coast

One of the towns most associated with surfing in Costa Rica is **Playa Tamarindo**, from where there is excellent access to quality breaks. Tamarindo itself has three good breaks; *El Estero*, a long right-hander; *Pico Pequeño*; and *Langosta*, a strong, quality point wave. Just north of Tamarindo lies *Potrero Grande*. Known as *Oli's Point* (supposedly after Oliver North who had a secret base nearby), this is a fast right-hand point breaking over a reef. A southerly swell can give a quality wave of up to 7 ft. **Playa Grande** is the most westerly point of Costa Rica (see page 15). To the far north is **Santa Rosa National Park** and **Playa Naranjo**, home of *Peña Bruja*, mistakenly translated as 'Witches' Rock' (see page 14).

Heading south along the coastline of the Nicoya Peninsula, **Avellanas** is a quality beach break with a right point known as *Little Hawaii*. **Playa Negra**, 10 minutes further south, is a popular right-hand point that holds up to 10 ft on a westerly swell; but it can be crowded and dangerously shallow at low tide. Some 600 m south, **Callejones** is much less crowded. **Junquillal** offers beach breaks throughout the tidal range.

Towards the end of the peninsula and the Cabo Blanco Reserve are a number of beautiful, uncrowded beach breaks, including **Nosara**, **Sámara** and **Punta Guiones**. From here, the waves become more of a challenge to get to, with many only accessible by 4WD.

Boca Barranca, just north of Jacó, has a long, fast left-hander that breaks over a sand bottom into the river mouth. The best time to surf is early in the morning and on a good day it can hold up to 10 ft. (The river is supposedly free of crocodiles but keep your eyes peeled!)

South of Boca Barranca towards Jacó is **Puerto Caldera**, a popular left-hander best surfed on the incoming tide. Further south off the Costanera Highway is **Tivives** (a beach break offering lefts and rights and a hollow left breaking into the river mouth) and **Valor** (access by paddling across the river).

Playa Escondida, accessible only by boat, lies at the mouth of the Gulf of Nicoya. The beach offers lefts and rights and is best between mid and high tide. **Jacó**, the closest beach resort to San José, is a good base but can become quite crowded. However, there are a number of quality breaks close to the town. *Roca Loca* – not for the faint-hearted – is accessible by climbing down the cliff then across the rocks. Ten minutes south of Jacó is **Playa Hermosa** (see page 15).

On the journey south towards Quepos is **Esterillos**, a quiet, uncrowded beach break. Between Esterillos and Quepos lies the town of **Parrita**, offering both reef and beach breaks. Just north of Quepos is **Boca Damas**, by the mouth of the Damas River, which can hold a sizeable swell. **Quepos** itself offers a beach break with strong lefts. **Playa Espadilla** in Manuel Antonio needs a good-sized swell to work but can offer both lefts and rights.

South of Quepos, **Playa El Rey**, has waves similar to Playa Hermosa, while the surf town of **Dominical** offers some of the best beach breaks in Costa Rica. It also has a left- and right-reef break and the area is often frequented by pods of dolphins. Working better at the end of the wet season, the waves can be very hollow.

At the north end of the Osa Peninsula, close to the mainland, is **Bahía Drake**. Only accessible by boat, Drake is a beautiful spot. At the peninsula's southern tip is **Matapalo**, just

ANTONIO JORGE NUNES/SHUTTERSTOCK

Opposite: An old rusty vessel with a tree growing out of it, Puerto Viejo. **Above:** Irazú volcano.

across the mouth of the Golfo Dulce. The best waves are a 15- to 20-minute walk through the jungle. Three spots worth checking out are: *Back Wash*, a slow right-hander that works best on a big swell; *Pan Dulce*, a small white-sand bay with a hollow right that works well on a mid to large swell; and *Matapalo*, a powerful right-hander that can hold a sizeable swell. Across the Gulf lies **Pavones**, the longest ride in Costa Rica (see page 14).

Towards the border with Panama **Punta Banco** has a left and right breaking over a coral reef. **Punta Burica** (only accessible by boat) is the last beach before the border.

Caribbean coast

Storms in the Caribbean Sea produce swells that can become quite sizeable, and which break on the coral reefs close to the Costa Rican coast. The best waves are found from November to March. Most of the breaks are to the south of **Puerto Limón**. There are three quality breaks in Limón: *Playa Bonita*, a strong left breaking over a coral reef which can be a challenging drop; *Portete*, a hollow right-hander breaking over coral; and *Isla Uvita*, only accessible by a dawn boat from Limón, with a wave of up to 10 ft that breaks in three sections over a shallow coral reef.

South from Limón, towards Panama, **Cahuita** is a beautiful national park with great beaches and waves. Further south is **Puerto Viejo**, known as *Salsa Brava* (see page 14). Ten minutes down the coast is the fun beach break of **Playa Cocles**, which can have strong currents, and **Manzanillo**, which has good-quality, uncrowded waves.

Trekking and hiking

ⓘ **Ocarina Expeditions**, San José, T2229-4278, www.ocarinaexpeditions.com, organizes fully supported treks; day hikes start at around US$99, a 3-day trip to Chirripó costs around US$555 per person. **ATEC**, Puerto Viejo de Talamanca, www.ateccr.org, offers the coast-to-coast trek (6-15 days depending on your fitness), US$750 for 1-3 people. See also www.ctocadventures.com.

Costa Rica offers so many activities, that hiking often takes a bit of a back seat. However, beyond dashing between nature reserves and short guided walks lasting a few hours there are some excellent opportunities.

The most popular hike has to be up **Cerro Chirripó**, the country's highest peak at 3820 m. The shortest route is a steady trudge, but there are many variations that add to the two- or three-day hike.

Second on the list is hiking through the tropical wet forest of **Corcovado National Park** on the Osa Peninsula. It's hot, sweaty and hard work but very rewarding. The massive Pacific Ocean stretches out to the west, and primary rainforest – home to jaguar, tapir, howler, spider and capuchin monkeys, poisonous snakes and hundreds of birds – pushes right up to the beach. With sharks in the sea and sting rays in the tidal rivers, you're short of places to hide. But that's the joy of being out in the wild.

Less common walks head from the cloudforests of **Monteverde** down the Caribbean slope to **Arenal**, and further north trails lead through the national parks of **Rincón de la Vieja** and **Tenorio**. You can also complete a trip from **Santa María**, south of San José, down the Pacific slope to **Quepos**.

However, the ultimate trek has to be crossing the continental divide from **coast to coast**, following ancient indigenous trails. The 234-km expedition from the Pacific to the Atlantic starts from Manuel Antonio, and involves biking and hiking up to the continental divide, across the Talamancas, then biking, hiking and rafting through the diverse terrain on the other side until finally you arrive at the Atlantic.

Whitewater rafting

ⓘ A day-trip starts at around US$75-95, a couple of days cost US$250 and 3 days US$300, including all meals and transport. **Costa Rica Expeditions**, Av 3, C Central-2, T2257-0766, www.costaricaexpeditions.com. **Ríos Tropicales**, C 38, between Paseo Colón and Av 2, 50 m south of the subway, T2233-6455, www.riostropicales.com. For other operators see San José, page 105.

Rafting in Costa Rica takes you through some of the country's most spectacular scenery. One moment you're drifting through serene, green valleys, the next you're fighting for dear life as your adrenalin-pumped body is forced head-first through a wall of water. It isn't everyone's cup of tea, but it is mighty refreshing.

STEVE BLY/ALAMY

Whitewater rafting on the lower Pacuare river.

That said, you don't have to be an adrenalin junkie to enjoy whitewater rafting, just choose an appropriate trip. Rafting assesses rivers in terms of difficulty. A simple float down parts of the Corobicí or Sarapiquí is a Grade I or II – gentle and relaxing, it's a great way to see wildlife. Grade III marks the beginning of whitewater rafting, with Grades IV and above requiring previous experience. The most popular Grade III and IV rivers are sections of the Pacuare and Reventazón, near Turrialba, the Sarapiquí and General. Grade V requires more experience and specialist knowledge.

Whitewater rafting down the Pacuare river provides the ultimate natural adrenalin mix. One minute you're drifting along slowly with your buddies, primary rainforest all around, a monkey here, a toucan there; the next you are bracing yourself and dealing with a manic few seconds of barked orders and a neat cluster of boulders ahead. "Right, right back, left stop!" Listen to that oarsman – he's your ticket out. Afterwards, check you are all still on board and then get back to the scenery. Some trips include an overnight stop – waking among the mist-shrouded trees of the rainforest is worth the early-morning rise.

Ziplining through the cloudforest provides a bird's eye view of the canopy.

the western end of the lake, and **Bahía Salinas** on the Pacific to the north, with world-class kite- and windsurfing destinations.

Opportunities for novices and experts exist. Beginner courses are provided by a couple of lodges in the area, with boards, wetsuits and even money-back guarantees provided.

Windsurfing and kitesurfing

ⓘ **Tilawa**, T2695-5050, www.hotel-tilawa.com, offer windsurfing, kitesurfing, wakeboarding and a windsurfing school at their hotel. Classes from US$100 for half day, equipment rental from US$40, cheaper for hotel guests. **Kite Surfing Center**, Bahía Salinas at the Blue Dream Hotel, T2826-5221, www.bluedreamhotel.com. Half-day kite rental for experienced kitesurfers from US$45. Starter lessons US$240.

Westerly trade winds blow across northern Costa Rica between December and April. Reluctantly, the air is pushed up and over obstacles before being forced through the corridor that is **Lake Arenal**. The most reliable winds in the northern hemisphere provide

Ziplining

ⓘ **Sky Trek**, www.skytrek.com.

These are high-tension cables strung out between forest giants, offering a combination of great views, high speed and heart-pumping adrenalin. Sky Trek near Monteverde is one of the most memorable. Consisting of 4 km of cable, the longest section is around 800 m and you can reach speeds of up to 40 mph. There are also nine observation platforms with great views although with all the cloud around, it can be a leap of faith that the cable disappearing into the distance actually goes somewhere!

How big is your footprint?

Costa Rica has undergone a phenomenal transition in recent decades: from a slash-and-burn culture of deforestation, to one of the planet's leading exponents of nature tourism and ecotourism. And, increasingly, visitors are keen to be involved. The problem lies in deciding what conserves the environment and what does not.

The **Costa Rican Tourist Board (ICT)** has introduced an environmentally based classification system that could help travellers a lot when choosing between hotels. The **Certification for Sustainable Tourism (CST)** (www.turismo-sostenible.co.cr) rates hotels on the degree to which they comply with a sustainable model of natural, cultural and social resource management. Hotels are awarded a level rating from 0 to 5 (5 being the most sustainable). It isn't perfect, but it is a good effort and useful if you want environmental considerations to be a primary factor in choosing where you stay.

In essence, it comes down to the individual to make choices and informed decisions. In the US contact **The International Ecotourism Society (TIES)** 1333 H St NW, Suite 300E, Washington, DC 2005, T202-347-9203, www.ecotourism.org, for a comprehensive breakdown of the issues. TIES has links with several Costa Rican organizations that share an interest in promoting ecotourism.

ERICK N/SHUTTERSTOCK

Organizations like **Conservation International** in the US on T1-202-912-1000, www.ecotour.org, and **Tourism Concern** in the UK on T020-7133-3330, www.tourismconcern.org.uk, work hard to raise awareness of the responsibilities of tourists and have begun to develop and promote eco-tourism projects and destinations. Additionally, organizations such as **Earthwatch**, in US and Canada on T1-800-776-0188, in the UK on T01865-318838, www.earthwatch.org, offer opportunities to participate directly in scientific research and development projects.

While the authenticity of some ecotourism operators' claims need to be interpreted with care, there is clearly both a huge demand for this type of activity and also significant opportunities to support worthwhile conservation and social-development initiatives.

AGE FOTOSTOCK/SUPERSTOCK

Travelling light

▸ Where possible choose a tour operator or hotel with a proven ethical and environmental commitment – if in doubt, ask.

▸ Consider staying in local accommodation rather than foreign-owned hotels – the economic benefits for host communities are far greater, and there are many more opportunities to learn about local culture.

▸ Spend money on locally produced (rather than imported) goods and services and use common sense when bargaining – your few dollars saved may be a week's salary to others.

▸ Use water and electricity carefully – travellers may receive a preferential supply while the needs of local communities are overlooked.

▸ Learn about local etiquette and culture – consider local norms, behaviour and dress appropriately for local cultures and situations.

▸ Protect wildlife and other natural resources – don't buy souvenirs or goods made from wildlife unless they are clearly sustainably produced and are not protected under CITES legislation (CITES controls trade in endangered species).

▸ Do not drop any litter, used matches or cigarette butts; this not only increases fire risk but also some animals will eat whatever they find.

▸ Always ask before taking photographs or videos of people.

▸ Make a voluntary contribution to counter the pollution caused by international travel. **Climate Concern** calculates the amount of carbon dioxide (CO_2) you generate, and then helps to offset your CO_2 by funding projects that reduce this major greenhouse gas. Visit www.co2.org. The author has offset CO_2 emissions from both air and car travel used in researching Footprint *Costa Rica* through Climate Care's CO_2 reduction projects.

TIMUR KULGARIN/SHUTTERSTOCK

Opposite page: Mushroom in the cloudforest. **Above:** The magenta-throated woodstar.

Costa Rica on screen and page

Books to read

Costa Rica lacks the traumas, battles, leaders and tragedies that inspire great literature. Not for this nature-packed republic, the oeuvres and passion of Brazil, Mexico, Cuba or even Nicaragua. The most productive period for *Tico* literature was the 1940s. Carlos Fallas wrote *Mamita Yunai* in 1941, one of the country's most important works of literary fiction about the appalling conditions on the banana plantations of the United Fruit Company. Joaquín Gutiérrez chose the conditions of blacks, racism and life on the Caribbean as the subject for novels, short stories and essays.

María Isabela Carvajal, writing under the pseudonym of Carmen Lyra was also critical of the impact of the fruit companies on Costa Rica. Her first book *En una silla de ruedas* (*In a Wheelchair*) was published in 1918, followed by a collection of folk stories *Cuentos de mi Tía Panchita* (*Tales of My Aunt Panchita*) in 1920. As a political activist, *Bananosy Hombres* (*Bananas and Men*) was written shortly after the banana workers' strike of 1934. Her image appears on the 10,000 colones note. More recently Ana Istarú has taken on the feminist role, attacking machismo in her poetry.

Films to watch

While Costa Rica has been in more natural documentaries than you can count, its presence on the big screen is, well, lacking. Its primary role is as a film set for other locations – a role it performs very well indeed.

Ridley Scott's *1492: Conquest of Paradise* (1992) was shot in the Central Pacific around the Jacó, Punta Leona and Herradura beaches. *Congo* (1995) was shot at Volcán Arenal, Pacuare river and Braulio Carrillo National Park. *Spy Kids 2* (2002) was shot at Volcán Arenal, Manuel Antonio National Park and La Paz waterfall. Mel Gibson's *Apocalypto* (2006) was filmed mainly in Mexico, with scenic shots including Volcán Arenal, Braulio Carrillo National Park, La Selva Biological Station and Tapantí National Park.

Costa Rican actor Mauricio Amuy was, at one stage, thought to be lined up for a leading role in *Apocalypto* but ended up playing the role of a Maya chief. (Gibson's passion for things *Tico* was confirmed with the news he'd purchased a ranch property in Guanacaste.)

Other smaller films shot in Costa Rica include *El Dorado* (1988), *Carnival in Costa Rica* (1948), *Mowgli* (1998), *100 Days in the Jungle* (2002), *Mariposa Azul* (2004) and *The Vivero Letter* (1998).

Contents

34 Getting there
34 Air
37 Boat
37 Road

39 Getting around
39 Air
39 Boat
39 Road
44 Train

44 Sleeping

47 Eating and drinking

48 Festivals and events

49 Shopping

50 Essentials A-Z

Footprint features

35 Packing for Costa Rica
38 Border crossings
40 Domestic flights in Costa Rica
high-season schedule
45 Accommodation price codes
47 Eating price codes
54 Language schools
60 Phone number changes

Essentials

Getting there

Travel to Costa Rica is usually straightforward. Direct flights from the US are common, and also possible from some European countries.

Air

UK and Ireland
There are no direct flights to Costa Rica from the United Kingdom or Ireland. Flights will take from 14 to 22 hours depending on the connection. You will have to make at least one stopover. **American Airlines**, **Continental**, **Delta** and **United Airlines** connect through Miami, or any of their direct services from the US. Alternatively you can link through a European agency. **Iberia** flights connect through Madrid. **Martinair**, a subsidiary of KLM, connects through Amsterdam. **Condor** connects through Frankfurt. You can also go via Bogotá, Colombia, with **Avianca**. **Prices** vary from £440 in the low season, up to £700 in the high season. The low season price corresponds roughly to the winter months in the northern hemisphere.

From Europe
Direct options from Europe are varied. **Iberia** have direct daily flights from Madrid. The standard economy fair is around €2000. **Martinair** have direct flights from Amsterdam which get as low as €500 and **LTU** have flights six days a week from Dusseldorf. The frequency of the Martinair and LTU flights varies every year. From Germany, **Condor** have flights twice a week.

From North America
Daily flights leave various locations in the United States and Canada for Costa Rica, taking three to eight hours. There are direct daily flights from Atlanta, Charlotte, Chicago, Dallas/Fort Worth, Detroit, Houston, Los Angeles, Miami, Newark, New York, Oakland, Phoenix, Philadelphia, San Francisco and Washington with **American Airlines**, **Continental**, **Delta**, **Grupo Taca**, **Martinair**, **NorthWest**, **United Airlines** or **US Airways**. Scheduled flights from Canada leave Montreal and Toronto going via Havana and San Salvador, before eventually arriving in San José. **American Airlines**, **Continental**, **Delta** and **US Airways** have regular flights to Daniel Oduber Quirós International Airport in the northwestern province of Guanacaste, near Liberia. There are also charter flights from the US and direct from Canada and increasingly from the US in the high season. Try **Air Transat** or **North West**.

Flight **prices** vary but seasonal offers get as low as US$200 from Miami. The full economy fare from Miami in high season is around US$650.

Australia, New Zealand and South Africa
Routes from Australia and New Zealand go via Los Angeles, picking up connections with one of the North American airlines. Flying with **Qantas** to Los Angeles costs from Aus$3000 return. From South Africa the situation is even worse with flights going via Europe and possibly the United States or Mexico before touching down in San José. Via London and the US return, fares start at R$14,000.

Packing for Costa Rica

As far as clothes are concerned, it's simplest to think through what you'll be doing before you pack. Starting at the lower altitudes you'll need beach-wear, sunglasses, a sun hat (which you'll probably need everywhere) and sun cream. When venturing on trails, shorts and a light shirt are ideal. If you're a bug magnet lightweight long trousers are perfect – even better if you can find ones that unzip above the knee. The same lightweight approach works wonders for the Central Highlands with a light sweater or jacket for the evenings when there may be a slight chill in the air. At higher altitudes you'll need something a bit thicker. Don't bother taking a raincoat unless going on very long treks. Otherwise buy an umbrella locally and use that for critical short journeys or sit the rain out. Bring comfortable shoes appropriate to your chosen activity be it hiking, horse riding or pool tiding, as well as a change if they get wet.

Invaluable personal items worth taking if you're travelling independently include: a penknife, torch (head torches as used by climbers are particularly useful), camera, wash bag, alarm clock, strong cord, sewing kit, water bottle, wet wipes, insect repellent and the eternally useful universal sink plug. Spectacle and contact lens wearers should take a spare pair or sufficient supplies to last the trip – although it is possible to get most items in Costa Rica.

If you have personal medical requirements make sure you enough to last your trip and seek medical advice before leaving home if you have any reason to be concerned.

As ever, specialists will want to take items particular to their speciality. A good pair of binoculars is useful. Birders and nature lovers will want to take field guides – they're available in some of the better lodges but it's better to have your own if possible. Divers and keen snorkellers may want to consider taking their own mask, and experienced anglers may want to travel with the lucky lure.

All this should be packed in a strong bag, the lighter the better, and ideally one that can be locked with a removable padlock that can be used on dodgy doors and lockers if the need arises in cheaper hotels. Most mid- and upper-range hotels have safe boxes.

It is equally important to mention what not to take. Although the vast majority of people travel without losing anything, the possibility always exists. So, just in case your bags do go missing, it is probably best to leave any specially prized or sentimental possessions at home.

Latin America

Regular daily flights are available from Panama and Nicaragua with **Grupo Taca**. Further afield there are daily connecting flights with every Latin American capital with Grupo Taca.

Airlines

Airlines
Air Transat www.airtransat.com
American Airlines www.aa.com
Avianca www.avianca.com
British Airways www.ba.com

Condor www.condor.com
Continental Airlines www.continental.com
Delta Airlines www.delta.com
Grupo Taca www.grupotaca.com
Iberia www.iberia.com
Martinair www.martinair.com
North West www.nwa.com

Quantas www.qantas.com.au
United Airlines www.united.com
US Airways www.usairways.com

Discount flight agents

North America
EXito, 108 Rutgers St, Fort Collins, CO 80525, T1-800-655-4053; worldwide T970-482-3019, www.exitotravel.com.
STA, with over 80 locations in the USA and hundreds worldwide, T1-800-781-4040, www.statravel.com.
Tico Travel, T1-800-493-8426, www.ticotravel.com. Digs out some very good deals on just flights.

United Kingdom
Journey Latin America, 12-13 Heathfield Terr, Chiswick, W4 4JE, T020-8747-8315, www.journeylatinamerica.co.uk.

STA, 6 Wrights Lane, London W8 6TA, T08701-600-599, www.statravel.co.uk.
South American Experience, Welby House, 96 Wilton Rd, Victoria, London SW1V 1DW, T0845-277-3366, www.southamericanexperience.co.uk.
Trailfinders, 215 Kensington High St, London W8 6BD, T020-7938-3939, www.trailfinders.com.

Australia, New Zealand, South Africa
STA Australia (T1300-733-035) and New Zealand (T0508-782-872) share the same website at www.statravel.com.au.
STA South Africa, T021-418-6570, www.statravel.co.za.
Trailfinders Australia, 8 Spring St, Sydney, NSW 2000, T1300-780-212, www.trailfinders.com.au.

Airport information

Juan Santamaría International Airport is 16 km northwest of San José on the southern outskirts of the town of Alajuela, information T2441-0744 or T2443-2622. For arrivals the airport is simply laid out with immigration, baggage reclaim and customs following naturally one after the other. After customs, but before leaving the customs hall, there is a tourist desk which can provide maps and information, as well as book hotel accommodation and transport to San José and other areas. In the same area is a branch of Banco Nacional, which opens to meet international flights, and a line of car rental desks where you can pick up or arrange vehicle hire. Outside, the swarms of greeting taxis will compete for your business. US$15 is the standard fare to downtown San José. If you're looking for something a little cheaper it's a short walk to the bus stop where buses leave every 10 minutes for the 40-minute, 200 colones (US$0.70) trip. Head out to the main road following the short airport access road, and join the queue opposite the petrol station.

Accommodation at the airport The closest hotel to the airport is **L-AL Hampton Inn**, T2436-0000, hamptoninn.hilton.com. Handy if you want to get in or get out quickly with the minimum of fuss, made easier with a courtesy pick-up and drop off. The price includes continental breakfast, free local calls, free stay for kids and the third and fourth adult sharing the same room. Add the free-form pool and this could be the starting or finishing post you're looking for. ▸▸ *See also page 88.*

Airport departure tax Departure tax of US$26 is payable at the check-in desk.

Daniel Oduber Quirós International Airport, in the northwest of the country 13 km from Liberia along Highway 21, is a much smaller airport. The expanding modern terminal has full customs and immigration services, a small café and a branch of Bancredito. A good spot if you want to head straight for the beach. Transport from the airport is limited to readily available taxis – ask around to get the best price.

Boat

Cruise liners stop at **Puntarenas** on the Pacific coast and **Limón** on the Caribbean coast before passengers disembark to be bussed cross country for a whirlwind tour of a couple of places. A good way of seeing lots of different places, but not the best way to see Costa Rica unless you can arrange to leave the vessel.

Road

Travelling overland to Costa Rica is possible and distinctly enjoyable from North America and all countries in Central America. Whether travelling by bus or private vehicle, you should allow plenty of time for the journey, however. Although you could do the journey in a manic week, taking a few weeks to travel slowly through Mexico, Guatemala, Honduras and Nicaragua would be a far more rewarding experience. If so, Footprint's Mexico and Central America Handbook will take you every step of the journey, guiding you through the interesting sights of the region. Changing money at border posts may seem risky, but it is rarely that bad. Try to get an idea of what your money is worth from another traveller before asking a money changer. Given that you are in a buyer's market, you are unlikely to get the best deal, but at least you can avoid being totally ripped off.

By private vehicle

Travelling overland is fairly simple with a degree of advance planning and a vehicle that can make the journey. You will need vehicle registration documents, your driver's licence and an international driver's licence (not essential but can be useful) and insurance. On entering Costa Rica you will be required to buy compulsory insurance (US$30 for three months) and road use tax (US$10 per month). Although there are no charges for entering any Central American country with a vehicle, it would be wise to check with embassies before setting out.

The journey itself is certain to involve wildly varying experiences. Drive with caution: pot-holed roads, hazards, animals – domestic and wild – and people are some of the many problems that may stop you in your tracks. Avoid driving at night unless totally essential and take utmost care when choosing when to pull up and where to park your car.

Naturally enough a good map is essential – while GPS and satellite nagivation systems are useful, they can lead to additional problems in Costa Rica. An excellent series of maps covering the region and each country is published by **International Travel Maps** (ITMB) ① *345 West Broadway, Vancouver BC, V5Y 1P8, Canada, T604-879-3621, www.itmb.com*, most compiled with historical notes by the late Kevin Healey.

By bus

The bus journey is equally challenging. You can drift through the countries one by one using local buses or take an international bus and see the countries through the window – missing opportunities all over the place, but needs must when someone else drives. The most direct service is with **Ticabus** ① *11 C 2-74, Zona 9, T502-331-4279, www.ticabus.com*, leaving Tapachula in southern Mexico at 0700 daily, US$80, 48 hours.

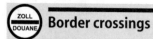

Border crossings

Peñas Blancas–Nicaragua On the western side of the isthmus, Peñas Blancas is the only road crossing between the two countries. It is simple and straightforward taking the traffic of the Pan-American Highway. After completing formalities at the new immigration office on the Nicaraguan border (open 0600-2000, Monday-Friday, 0600-1800, Saturday and Sunday), head to the Costa Rican border post. Pedestrians need to fill out an immigration card and then get both stamped and checked. If travelling by international bus, the driver will wait for all passengers to go through immigration. If making your own way, buses going to **La Cruz**, **Liberia** and **San José** stop just outside the immigration offices. If driving, once you have completed immigration and customs you will need to buy compulsory insurance and road use tax at the border if the car is not registered in Nicaragua or Costa Rica: US$30 a month. All cars are fumigated. Bear in mind the last fuel stop in Nicaragua is in Rivas, 37 km from the border. The first fuel stop in Costa Rica is in La Cruz, 19 km from the border. See page 223.

Los Chiles–Nicaragua Inland, to the southeast of Lake Nicaragua, there is a daily boat service along the Río Frío, from San Carlos to Los Chiles, US$6, 45 minutes. Departure formalities must be completed in San Carlos, including payment of departure tax. Immigration in Los Chiles is open daily from 0800-1600, usually closing for lunch. The crossing post, which is actually 4 km north of Los Chiles, is reported to be less straightforward than Peñas Blancas due to the high number of Nicaraguans that use the border crossing. It is not possible to cross this border by vehicle. See page 186.

Barra del Colorado–San Juan del Norte, Nicaragua There is no immigration post on this route but, in theory at least, it is possible to cross the border from Nicaragua to Barra del Colorado in Costa Rica by taking a boat from San Carlos down the Río San Juan to San Carlos del Norte. From there you can catch a boat to Barra del Colorado and work down the coast to Limón. The cost of such a journey is likely to be prohibitive, and you should visit immigration as soon as possible in Limón – where you are likely to be treated with a degree of suspicion. See page 380.

Paso Canoas–Panama On the western side of Costa Rica, Paso Canoas marks the border with Panama as the main road crossing and the route of the Pan-American Highway. Entering and departing is straightforward. Immigration and customs are open 24 hours on the Panama side, Costa Rica provides services 0600-2200. Bus services on the Panamanian side take you to and from **David**, the nearest town of significance to the border, with connecting services further south. On the Costa Rican side, there are cheap hotels, restaurants and buses heading inland to **Ciudad Neily**, **Golfito** and **San José**. See page 332.

Río Sereno–Panama A short distance from San Vito, at the head of the Coto Brus valley, the crossing of Río Sereno is handy if you are heading to or from the Chiriquí Highlands in Panama, but the crossing is closed to vehicle traffic. See page 333.

Sixaola–Panama At the far southeastern corner of Costa Rica. Either side of the creaking rail bridge that connects Panama and Costa Rica, the immigration posts check people crossing the border, and the odd vehicle that inches along the sleepers stands out a mile. It all seems very *ad hoc* but it works, with Costa Rican immigration open from 0700-1700, in Panama 0800-1800 (the same hours given the time difference). All formalities are completed as with other borders but with a more gentle laid-back approach. It doesn't take long, but don't come this way if you're in hurry. See page 393.

Getting around

Transport within Costa Rica is simple and straightforward by air or road, whether in a private or rented vehicle or on public buses. In an ideal world, judicious use of hotel-provided transport to get to out-of-the-way places like Tortuguero or Corcovado National Park, combined with a rented vehicle, provide the freedom to explore a bit of the country going at your own pace.

If public buses are more your style, there is an efficient and generally effective network of buses to get you to all major destinations and most smaller towns. You may find that occasionally you have to go via one town to make a connection, but the extra time taken is rarely excessive.

Air

Two companies provide a scheduled service from San Jose to 16 destinations throughout the country. **SANSA**, T2221-9414, www.flysansa.com and **NatureAir**, T2220-3054, and www.natureair.com. SANSA have also developed a mini-hub around Liberia with flights to Tamarindo, Arenal and Tambor.

SANSA fly out of the domestic terminal at Juan Santamaría Airport near to Alajuela. Flights are in Cessna Caravans. Flights must be paid for when you make the reservation, which can be done online, and tickets are non-refundable. They occasionally have an airpass offering favourable prices for buying in bulk. NatureAir operates out of Tobías Bolaños airport, in Pavas, 5 km west of San José. They use 19-seater Twin Otter Vistaliner and seven-seater Britten-Norman Islanders. In addition to domestic flights NatureAir have a service to Granada in Nicaragua and Bocas del Toro in Panama Reservations can be made in advance online. Children under two years travel free, from two to 12, there is a 25% discount. Weight allowances are minimal at 12 kg (25 pounds) with a US$0.45 surcharge for every pound.

Charter flights

Paradise Air T2231-0938, www.flywithparadise.com, provide an air charter service with 7-seater Gippsland Aeronautics GA8 Airvans and 12-seater Cessna Grand Caravans. Working out of Puerto Jiménez on the Osa Peninsula is **Alfa Romeo Aero Taxi**, T735-5353, www.alfaromeoair.com, operating mainly between the capital and the southwest but covering other destinations countrywide as well.

Boat

Ferry services are available to both the **Nicoya Peninsula** and the **Osa Peninsula**. Vehicle and passenger ferries are available between Puntarenas and Playa Naranjo and Paquera to the south and between Puerto Nispero and Puerto Moreno at the mouth of the Río Tempisque. The passenger-only ferry service to the Osa Peninsula leaves from Golfito for Puerto Jiménez.

Road ›› *For information on maps, see page 55.*

The road network throughout Costa Rica is generally very good and most destinations of interest are accessible by paved road. As a rule the roads are better than most in Central

Domestic flights in Costa Rica – high-season schedule

Destination	NatureAir		SANSA	
From San José	Frequency	Cost	Frequency	Cost
Arenal/Fortuna	Daily	US$87	Two daily	US$65
Barra del Colorado	-	-	Daily	US$72
Coto 47 (Ciudad Neily)			Daily	US$89
Drake Bay	Two daily	US$120	Daily	US$91
Golfito	Two daily	US$117	Two daily	US$89
Liberia	Four daily	US$117	Two daily	US$89
Limón	Five a week	US$90		
Nosara	Two daily	US$117	Daily	US$89
Palmar Sur/Dominical	Two daily	US$106	Daily	US$81
Puerto Jiménez	Five daily	US$120	Two daily	US$89
Punta Islita	Daily	US$120	Daily	US$89
Quepos	Four daily	US$66	Four daily	US$53
Sámara-Carrillo			Daily	US$89
Tamarindo	Three daily	US$117	Seven daily	US$89
Tambor	Two daily	US$87	Five daily	US$71
Tortuguero	Daily	US$96	Daily	US$72
From Liberia				
Arenal/Fortuna	-	-	Daily	US$65
Nosara	Daily	US$89	-	-
San José	Daily	US$79	Daily	US$65
Tamarindo	Two daily	US$51	Daily	US$45
Tambor	-	-	Daily	US$55

Note Not all flights are direct. Services are reduced in the low season.

America, but still liberally doused in potholes – not always big, but sometimes unbelievably deep. The majority of roads in the Central Highlands are paved, creating a warren-like network of poorly signposted confusion. Beyond the highlands, paved roads link most regions in the country, apart from the northeastern lowlands.

Moving between major destinations is easy but as soon as you want to deviate slightly, the roads deteriorate from well packed stony roads which allow a fair speed, if a somewhat juddering ride, to wash-board bone-shakers, loosely packed sandy shales which become quicksand in the rain or rocky roads more like dry-stream beds. You don't know the quality of a road when you start out, so the only solution is to take advice from locals – and do listen – and be flexible about your travel plans.

Car hire
Renting a vehicle in Costa Rica is extremely popular. Even so, it's worth being aware of the negative possibilities: minor road accidents; mechanical breakdown; new road rules; speeding tickets. Even worse there's something about being behind a wheel in a foreign

country that makes the impossible possible. You could end up with an empty fuel tank and a seasonally flooded river between you and the next gas station, or, worse still, be in a serious accident. However, the vast majority of people who rent a vehicle return it to the rental company without so much as a scratch or the slightest hiccup and if you've got the budget, and can face the new challenges it's definitely worth considering.

If you do rent, make sure you are going to use the vehicle. In some locations you won't need it and it is pointless to have the thing sitting around doing nothing. You can get round this problem to a certain degree by arranging drop-offs and pick-ups from different locations around the country. There is normally a charge for this service but it works out cheaper than driving back to the original rental office.

What vehicle? Think about where you are likely to want to go – the general recommendation is to get a 4WD with high clearance, but if you only intend to stay on good roads and visit the main areas then you'll be paying for more than you need. If you are thinking of travelling around the quieter areas of the Nicoya Peninsula, heading for Santa Elena/Monteverde or the Osa Peninsula, driving in the rainy (green) season, or just striking out to see where a road goes then 4WD is almost a must.

Vehicles available for hire are normally Japanese: mainly Toyotas with some Suzukis and other makes, ranging from simple sedans like the Toyota *Corolla*, through mid-size 4WD like the Toyota *Terios* or *Rav 4*, up to the beefy Toyota *Land Cruisers*. Most cars will have a/c, a good radio and locking system.

To drive in Costa Rica you have to be over 21 (although some hire companies insist on your being over 23) have a full driving licence from your home country, your passport and be able to pay a deposit (normally put on a credit card, deductable) of up to US$1500 against any possible damage.

Prices vary starting at around US$22-37 a day for the cheapest cars. A *Terios* is around US$40, a *Rav 4* US$48 and a Toyota *Land Cruiser* from US$95. The weekly rate is normally priced at six days for the price of seven. The monthly rate is the week rate by 3.5. To this you need to add insurance which ranges from US$12 to US$30 a day. All fuel in Costa Rica is unleaded. As of August 2008, regular was US$1.15/litre, super US$1.20 and diesel US$1.10. A few roads, mainly in the Central Highlands, have road tolls with minimal charges.

Car rental companies There are more than enough car hire firms in San José to choose from (see page 112). The main international companies have offices in the city and at the airport, or you can go with a local company, or even companies that specialize in using not A-1 quality vehicles – reliable but not so precious. Beyond San José, there are few rental companies with maybe just one company in the popular Pacific Coast towns.

Most companies are fair with you if you are fair with their vehicle. When checking the vehicle out, stay with the assistant and agree on paint chips, dents and damage. Check the amount of fuel in the tank. Likewise when returning it stay with the assistant and agree on any charges to be paid before you leave the office. Also make sure the fuel tank is filled to the agreed level – you will be charged heavily if the company has to fill the vehicle. If the car is exceptionally dirty, it may be worth getting it cleaned for a few dollars before returning it to the hire company.

Driving in Costa Rica
It has been argued that Latin Americans are some of the best drivers in the world – how could they survive the road conditions with so few accidents if they weren't. Labelling

Costa Rican driving as good or bad is unfair for obvious reasons. The only good rule is that *Tico* drivers are observant – which is the best advice for any prospective driver. Look out for other drivers, for pot holes, poorly sign-posted roads, be wary of unmarked speed restrictions and aspire to develop a sixth sense. Beyond that, here are a few tips.

Signposting around the country is generally appalling. Most people start their journey in San José, and often end up driving round the city for a couple of hours before they get anywhere.

Driving in the rain clearly has an added danger, especially in torrential downpours. Be especially careful when roads are drying out. Overhanging trees mean roads dry out in patches – particularly in and approaching the Central Highlands where twisting roads make driving dangerous at the best of times. Moving away from populated areas, be aware that some vehicles do not always have lights. Don't drive at night unless it is essential. **Gas stations** in parts of the country are few and far between. Fill up when you get the chance. Driving **off-road** creates new hazards, apart from the fact that your rental company may stipulate you are not allowed to drive off-road. If you've ended up in difficulty unintentionally, retrace your route and find another way through. If you come across a landslide, mudpools or a fjord, get out and walk the route first – if you can't walk through, round or over the obstacle it's unlikely the vehicle will make it in good condition.

Rules and regulations

Speed limits On highways and secondary roads 80 kph; in urban areas 40 kph; around schools, hospitals and clinics 25 kph. Driving under the influence of **alcohol** and/or **drugs** is strictly prohibited. Wearing a **seatbelt** is a legal requirement. You must **pull over** if requested to do so by a police officer. Your personal **documents** and the vehicle registration are private property and may not be retained by a police officer for any reason. If the police officer insists on retaining your documents ask him to escort you to the nearest police station to clear up the problem. If you believe a police officer has acted inappropriately call T2257-7798 ext 2506. If you are involved in an **accident**, do not move your vehicle until a police officer has arrived and prepared a report. The accident can be reported on 911 or direct to the transport police on 117. You should also call the car rental company. If you are fined for an **infringement** of the law, do not give money directly to the police. Pay the fine, which is subject to 30% tax, at the nearest Banco Nacional. Driving on **beaches** is prohibited everywhere, except when there is no other path connecting two towns.

Motorbike rental

You can rent good quality off-road bikes, Suzuki DR 250s and 350s, from **Wild Rider Motorcycles**, T2258-4604, www.wild-rider.com, in San José for one-day guided tours or just head out on the open road from US$60 a day. A one-day guided tour of Irazú, Cartago, the Orosí Valley and Ujarrás – roughly 180 km – will cost you US$159 (four riders). If you want to travel out in a little more style, then **Rent-a-Harley** in San José, T2289-5552, www.mariaalexandra.com, is a service provided by Apartotel Maria Alexandra. Day and multi-day tours available. Rental starts at US$70 a day, all gear included.

Bus travel

Bus travel is by far the most popular mode of travel in Costa Rica – for Costa Ricans at least. You can get anywhere in the country by catching a bus or two. Buses range from comfortable cushioned and air conditioned highway cruisers to chicken buses that crawl along stopping every 10 m to pick up passengers.

San José is the main hub of the service with most buses, with a few regional exceptions, starting or finishing in the capital. Nationwide services are provided by a couple of dozen private companies that are dotted around the city in clusters. A few services have clustered together and the **Coca-Cola Terminal** is the centre for Central Highland services with a few offices in surrounding streets and to the north providing many other services. All Caribbean destinations are neatly served from the **Gran Terminal del Caribe**.

Beyond the capital a few towns act as a point to change direction. To the west **Puntarenas** is a good stop-off point acting as a transport hub for the west coast Central Pacific region, so avoiding the need to return to the highlands and linking to services down the Pacific coast and up to Santa Elena and Monteverde. Further north **Cañas** is the point to break from the Pan-American Highway and head inland to **Tilarán** and from there to **Fortuna** or **Monteverde**. **Liberia** offers similar, but lesser opportunities with links to the Nicoya Peninsula. Heading south, **San Isidro de El General** is a useful place to change buses, as is **Palmar Norte**, where you can link with the southern section of the coastal road (*costanera*) and travel north to **Dominical**, **Quepos** and **Manuel Antonio**. On the Caribbean, **Limón** is the main transport hub, but it is possible to get buses travelling all the way down the coast from San José so you don't have to change unless you're stopping over.

Buses tend to depart promptly so it is best to arrive on time, and the service tends to be reliable if the weather and conditions have been kind to the road. The cost of travel is cheap, working out at roughly between US$0.80 and US$1.40 an hour. The longest journey in the country is currently that between San José to Puerto Jiménez on the Osa Peninsula (eight hours), and will set you back around US$7. Local buses exist in the larger towns but tend to be of limited use to the passing visitor outside San José.

Private bus

A few companies provide a very useful private shuttle service. Zipping around the country in tidy minibuses, this is a great way to get from one place to another quickly and efficiently. The **Fantasy Bus** operated by **Grayline**, T2220-2126, www.grayline costarica.com, have several daily services. Starting from San José, buses go to and through Arenal to Liberia, Rincón de la Vieja, Tamarindo and Playa Hermosa. Heading south, buses go to Jacó and Manuel Antonio. Heading east, buses travel through Limón to Cahuita and Puerto Viejo de Talamana. Most buses start from the Hotel Best Western Down Town. Buses also leave Jacó linking to the northern destinations. Each journey costs US$35-45 depending on distance. **Interbus**, T2283-5573, www.interbusonline.com, offer a similar service with 52 regular routes covering all the popular spots and a few out of the way places as well. Daily routes from San José linking to Arenal and Fortuna; Jacó, Quepos and Manuel Antonio; Limón, Cahuita and Puerto Viejo de Talamanca; Monteverde; Flamingo and Tamarindo. Prices start at US$25 rising to US$35. If you are travelling in a group (up to six people), you could rent a bus from **Coach Costa Rica**, T2229-4192, www.coachcostarica.com. Rates are for destination on a daily basis, or for US$150 a day with chauffeur, if booked for more than three days.

Taxis

Taxis are usually the easiest mode of transport in San José and many of the larger towns. They are a surprisingly affordable way of putting together your own tour if you are in a group of four. In San José taxis have a list of tariffs for long-distance journeys. Taxis can be hailed in the street or booked in advance – your hotel will have a number for a local firm.

Cycling

Costa Rica is generally 'cyclist friendly', with less traffic than in neighbouring Central American countries. However, paving is thin and soon deteriorates, especially at the shoulders, so look out for cracks and potholes, which bring traffic to a crawl. The prevailing wind is from the northeast, so if making an extensive tour, travelling from Panama to Nicaragua is slightly easier. The Nicoya Peninsula is particularly bad for cyclists – a mountain bike is recommended for the terrain and the poor road state.

Recommended reading for all users: Bill Baker's *Essential Road Guide to Costa Rica* (1995), with detailed strip maps, kilometre by kilometre road logs, motoring information plus San José map and Bus Guide.

Hitchhiking

If you like hitchhiking Costa Rica is as safe a place as any – with normal and sensible precautions you will undoubtedly have some of the most enjoyable, honest and open conversations while sharing a couple of hours with the temporary friend. The inverse traffic rule applies – where there is less traffic you're less likely to find a ride, but if a vehicle passes it will quite often pick you up. Likewise, busy roads tend to be far too anonymous – the Pan-American Highway is a particularly difficult place to catch a ride.

Train

The train line which once linked Puntarenas on the Pacific and Limón and the Atlantic have steadily fallen into disrepair and there are no regular passenger services.

A tourist train runs from San José to the Pacific at weekends, departing from Estación del Pacífico, 600 m south of Parque Central, at 0600, travelling to Caldera with a stop in Orotina, returning at 1500. Tickets (US$39 return) must be purchased Monday-Wednesday for following weekend. The tours are in refurbished 1940s German wagons. Contact **America Travel** ① *T2233-3300, www.ticotraintour.com.*

Sleeping

Accommodation options cover all styles and budgets and in Costa Rica the variety and diversity is spectacular. Eccentric and purist designs perched on a hillside providing respite for mind and body, quiet hotels in secluded private reserves, beachfront properties and glorious romantic hideaways, down through steady steps of luxury, comforts and services to the simplest, most basic rooms. The level of service also varies fantastically.

The good hotels fill up in the high season (and some in the green season as well) and booking in advance is advisable. Mid- and upper-range hotels will require a deposit in advance. Lower budget hotels will also accept reservations and while you may not be able to secure the room, do what you can to check the booking is being honoured. If you plan to arrive late in the evening, let the hotel know.

While a few companies may have two or three hotels in the country, there are not really any chains as such beyond Best Western, which has around 20 hotels throughout the country in the main tourist areas. A number of hotels have grouped together, one of particular note is the **Small Distinctive Hotels of Costa Rica**, www.distinctivehotels.com, which has seven small hotels providing excellent service.

Accommodation price codes

LL US$150+	L US$100-149	AL US$66-99
A US$46-65	B US$31-45	C US$21-30
D US$ 12-20	E US$ 7-11	F Under US$6

LL-L Hotels in these categories focus on providing exceptional service in natural surroundings and unique opportunities. They may have full comforts and services or they may make a virtue out of silence being golden. You will be pampered, spoilt, well tended and want for nothing.

AL-A This price bracket has slipped slightly from the 'exclusive' to the very comfortable. You should expect a wide range of services – many that you will probably never use including a pool, sauna, gym, jacuzzi, restaurant, bar and safe box. There is often a casino, depending on the style and location of the place.

B Hotels in this category should provide more than standard facilities and a fair degree of comfort. Many include a good breakfast and offer extras such as a colour TV, minibar, a/c and a swimming pool. Internet access and WiFi is quite common at this level and above. As a rule they accept credit cards, and in many cases children under the age of 12 are allowed to stay for free if they stay in the same room.

C-D Hotels in these categories range from very comfortable to functional and there are some real bargains to be had – although there is a tendency to drift towards floral bedspreads, plastic flowers and ornamental lighting. You should expect your own bathroom, constant hot water, a towel, soap and toilet paper. There is sometimes a restaurant and a communal sitting area. In tropical regions you may have the option of a/c but may have to pay extra.

E-F Hotels in these categories are often extremely simple with bedside or ceiling fans, shared bathrooms and little in the way of furniture. While rooms may not have been painted for quite a few years, standards of cleanliness are generally OK with some notably pleasant surprises around the country. A window in the room can make all the difference – ask to see rooms first.

The high season generally runs from December to April. Outside of these months it is the green season. Discounts at this time are common and can be as much as 50%. They vary greatly from location to location – some places choose not to discount at all, others prefer to close rather than operate at a reduced capacity. Many of the mid-range hotels and above allow children under 12 to stay for free or a fraction of the full adult rate. Ask when making reservations.

Out of town In general, away from San José the better establishments are outside the main town. These hotels and lodges tend to have their own restaurant or at least comfortable snack options. Services vary greatly as some aim for a pure ambience devoid of external influences, while others have options for all forms of sport, pampering and relaxation. Although not essential, it is often useful to have your own transport.

In town Cheaper accommodation tends to be in or close to the centre of town or at least easily accessible to public transport routes. Options range from very comfortable family-run hotels to penny-pinching flea-pits.

Taxes, discounts and children Hotels are subject to an intriguingly precise 16.39% sales tax. The more expensive hotels tend not to include this in the quoted price, so make sure you know whether the price you are quoted includes tax or not. Tax is included in the prices quoted in this guide – see box, page 45, for breakdown of what to expect in each category.

Food Many hotels provide food but at an extra cost. The typical cost of meals at an **AL** category hotel might be US$6 for breakfast, US$10 to US$8 for lunch and dinner. While this system is ideal if you want to move around and eat in different places, when you are stranded in an isolated place, meal costs can mount up so be sure to budget accordingly.

Business hotels Costa Rica has cottoned on to the opportunities for business travel and provides some of the best business hotels and conference facilities in Central America for capacities of up to 1200 delegates. Service levels start at the very height of luxury down to more rustic settings, with nature as the backdrop.

Bed and breakfast Setting out with a filling breakfast inside you is easily the best way to travel. The **Costa Rica Bed & Breakfast Group** ① *c/o Pat Bliss, Interlink 978, PO Box 025635, Miami, Florida 33152, T2229-8638, www.catch22.com/~vudu/ bliss2.html*, is a network of small B&Bs offering smart and friendly sleeping options throughout the country. In addition to a reservation service, they also provide itinerary planning to get you between the 200+ inns and hotels in their directory.

Long-term rentals Rentals of rooms or apartments are popular with people staying in the country for a month or two. The discounts are considerable – some places will even give a discount for stays of over three nights. Ask about discounts when making a reservation.

Youth hostels Three hostels and lodgings are affiliated to the **International Youth Hostelling Federation** throughout Costa Rica. Prices fall within our **B** to **D** categories. While they do not all offer discounts for membership, you will find a clean bed and a friendly face. For information visit www.hihostels.com. Hostels are mentioned throughout the text.

Ecotourism – Cooprena At the rustic end of the scale Cooprena heads a network of co-operatively owned lodges and houses that provide accommodation throughout the country in rural settings. Conditions are normally basic, but are in excellent positions for experiencing rural Costa Rican home life and with opportunities for activities nearby. Close to the ideals of ecotourism, the impact of visitors is minimal; sustainable use of the environment primary, and the money goes to the local community. **Simbiosis Tours** ① *PO Box 6939-1000, San José, T2248-2538, www.turismoruralcr.com*.

Other companies are evolving, a couple that have been developing slowly are **Vacaciones con Familias Campesinas** ① *T2354-6047, www.costaricaruraltours.com*, covering northern Costa Rica; and **Rural Costa Rica** ① *T8858-5588, www.ruralcostarica.com*, a women's group in Santa Fe, north Costa Rica.

Camping Camping in Costa Rica is very much on the decline in all but the most out-of-the-way places. Given the difficulties of getting to quiet secluded spots on public transport, it is probably better to camp in Costa Rica as a preferred style of sleeping rather than a way of saving money and getting to quiet hideaways. There are, of course, exceptions. If you do camp, normal rules apply to take all your rubbish with you – even if that is contrary to local habits.

Eating price codes

ŸŸŸ over US$20 ŸŸ US$10-19 Ÿ US$9 and under

Prices refer to the cost of a meal for one person with a drink.

Eating and drinking

Few people return from Costa Rica raving about the national dish. The food is simple, relying heavily on the staples of rice and beans. Mixed with shredded beef, chicken or sometimes fish, served with a couple of warmed tortillas and you have the dish of **casado** that fuels the majority of the country's workers. Only you will know how long you can enjoy the pleasures of rice and beans day after day. One way of spicing up the food is with liberal helpings of *Salsa Lizano* which is always somewhere near the dinner table.

If you want to try national dishes the best place to head for is the central markets. While general advice is to avoid markets, fairly good food hygiene and food sold so quickly it barely has time to go off make most markets in Costa Rica a safe bet. You can tell if the food is good by the number of people waiting. The market is also a fairly good place to pick up fruit and salad if you want to prepare food yourself. Naturally you will need to clean it, but the produce is often fresher than it is in supermarkets – and a fraction of the price.

Restaurants

Courtesy of the influx of nationalities from around the globe, dining in Costa Rica is tantamount to culinary globetrotting. You have the freedom to explore national delights one day, and more familiar dishes from around the globe the next.

Local restaurants tend to do most of their business at lunch times when *comida típica* (typical food) is served at a cost of a few dollars. More upmarket restaurants improve the level of service, atmosphere, food and, naturally, augment the price. You'll find almost anything your palette desires in San José – French, Italian, Asian, Pacific fusion, seafood – and in the more popular locations round the country. Further afield you can enjoy regional specialities and menu limitations.

Drinking and bars

Being a fairly conservative nation, Costa Ricans don't indulge heavily in drinking. On Friday and Saturday nights the streets are not filled with people struggling from one bar to another – but the bars are lively. Once you've tapped into the local happening bar, beer is the lubricant of choice with *Imperial* and *Pilsen* being the most popular lagers and *Bavaria* a darker malty option. The spirit of choice and convenience is rum (*ron*). Other spirits and good wine find their way to the tables of bars and restaurants as the price rises. How much do you need a gin 'n' tonic? The sugar-cane, falling-over juice found in dive-bars hidden down poorly lit alleys and best kept there is *Guaro* – guaranteed to provide a sore head and a night you won't forget, even if it is only for the headache the following day. *Café Rica* is a caffeine-based liquor, true to the country's coffee origins.

Festivals and events

Bank holidays are cause for celebration everywhere and Costa Rica is no different. On national holidays, banks, government offices and stores close down so make sure you have enough money. National holidays are listed here, regional and local festivals are listed in the relevant chapter. Large festivals tend to go big on processions, costumes and traditional marching bands, but find a small town and you'll get horse racing, bull-friendly bull fighting (where the lucky beast leaves the ring exhausted but alive) and a chance to rub shoulders with the townsfolk at a more intimate gathering.

The main holiday period is Christmas and New Year, and Easter week, when much of San José decants from the highlands to the beaches. Book accommodation well in advance at this time of year.

Festival calendar

January
1 Jan New Year's Day.

March
Mar (2nd Sun) National Oxcart Day with colourful processions and music in Escazú.
Mar/Apr Maundy Thursday and Good Friday, Easter Week.

April
11 Apr Juan Santamaría Day, celebrating the victorious Battle of Rivas against William Walker in 1856.

May
1 May Labour Day, which apparently heralds the President's State of the Nation address, cricket matches and a day off.

July
25 Jul Annexation of Guanacaste, celebrating Guanacaste's decision to stay with Costa Rica rather than Nicaragua in 1824.

August
2 Aug Virgin Mary Queen of Angels, Patron of Costa Rica celebrated with religious pilgrimages to the Basilica in Cartago.

15 Aug Day of the Virgin Mary's Assumption to Heaven and Mother's Day.

September
15 Sep Independence Day, with parades and marching bands through the streets of San José.

October
12 Oct Spanish discovery of the New World, celebrated with particular energy and flair in Limón and the Caribbean.

November
2 Nov All Souls' Day, the Day of the Dead, showing respect to those who have passed on.

December
Dec 25 – Christmas, celebrations build before and continue in the week after, particularly in San José but also on a smaller scale throughout much of the country.
31 Dec, 1 and 2 Jan La Danza de los Diablitos, a festival with traditional masks, costumes, music and dancing in the Indian village of Boruca.

Shopping

There is certainly no shortage of souvenirs to buy in Costa Rica. Items range from small collectibles, fridge magnets, knick-knacks and T-shirts of the anthropomorphized gaudy-leaf frogs and "My Uncle went to Costa Rica and…" genre, to genuinely well-made wooden furniture and decorative pieces. Haggling is not entered into as a rule but you may find the occasional opportunity to flex your negotiating might.

If you want to buy a few gifts, it's worth having a look at some shops in San José early on in your trip – then, as you travel round, you'll know what is available at the last minute and can make an informed choice.

Don't buy any archaeological artefacts or items made from endangered species including turtles, animal skins and coral.

What to buy

With row upon row of carefully decorated gifts sitting in neat rows it's easy to think Costa Rica is only full of mass-produced items. Look a little closer and you'll see the quirky touch and character of the hand-painted items.

The main place to buy gifts – for some the only place – is **Sarchí** in the Central Highlands. The town has become the artisan centre of the country, churning out creations of colourful, hand-decorated *carretas* (ox-carts). Given that oxen are rarely used by visitors to Costa Rica, time has seen the carts evolve and shrink to become garden ornaments, drinks cabinets and jewellery boxes. Don't worry about getting them home – they can be flat-packed and shipped if required, as can the sturdy wood and leather rocking chairs sitting on porches and balconies throughout the country. You can relax even further laying back in a hammock.

But if you can't get to the densely packed one-stop shop that is Sarchí, don't worry. You can buy gifts throughout the country. **Wooden carvings** are popular with decorative and functional pieces including bowls, trays and carvings, as well as recycled wood from coffee plants used to create figures and animals. Lightweight balsa is often carved into tropical wildlife creations.

Jewellery sets semi-precious jade in gold and silver, and jade, copper and bronze are used to create **pre-Columbian replicas**. Indigenous pieces are available in a few select places, including the deep red **ceramics** of the Chorotegas in Guaitil, the **masks** and **woven goods** of the Boruca, or the **carved gourds** or *jícara* of the Guaymi and Bribrí in the far south.

Textiles provide plenty of options beyond the simple T-shirt, with mats, table cloths and napkins evoking memories of Costa Rica when you're having a meal back home several months later. Although they're from Panama, vividly colourful *molas* (brightly coloured appliqués) are available in some parts of the south of the country.

Contemporary, traditional and religious **art** hangs off the walls of galleries dotted around **San José** and **Escazú**. A personal favourite is the vibrancy of Patricia Erickson – but look around, you'll find something you like. Ceramic creations are no more distinctive than in the colourful and slightly humourous pieces of Cecilia Figueres.

Music makes a good gift and brings back memories faster than a hypnotist in a clock factory. For folklore you won't get a broader swatch than *Costa Rica Pura Vida*, sold in market squares and record shops. Less manic on the *marimba* is the ambient jazz feel of *Editus* who, with Panamanian Rubén Blades, won a Grammy for their album *Tiempos*.

Finally fill any spare space in your bag with freshly roasted **coffee**, **liquors** or **paper** and **envelopes** recycled from banana leaves.

Essentials A-Z

Accident and emergency

For all emergencies dial T911 – operators will guide you to the correct service, including ambulance, police, fire and traffic accidents.

Children

Travelling with children and as a family is quite possible in Costa Rica at any age, but check you're all going to get something from the experience. As a relatively easy country to travel around, and good levels of health, you should have fun. To add to the bonus, many of the mid-range hotels welcome children under 10 for free.

After the flight, the travel distances shrink considerably. Choose an itinerary that breaks the journeys down into manageable chunks, or where the travel itself is an adventure.

Food can be a problem if the children are not adaptable. It is easier to take biscuits, drinks, bread, etc with you on longer trips than to rely on meal stops where the food may not be to taste. Avocados are safe, easy to eat and nutritious; they can be fed to babies as young as 6 months and most older children like them. A small immersion heater and jug for making hot drinks is invaluable.

On long-distance buses children generally pay half or reduced fares. For shorter trips it is cheaper, if less comfortable, to seat small children on your knee. Often there are spare seats which children can occupy after tickets have been collected. In city and local excursion buses, small children do not generally pay a fare, but are not entitled to a seat when paying customers are standing. On sightseeing tours you should always bargain for a family rate – often children can go free. Note that a child travelling free on a long excursion is not always covered by the operator's travel insurance; it is advisable to pay a small premium to arrange cover. All airlines charge a reduced price for children under 12 and less for children under two. Double check the child's baggage allowance – some are as low as 7 kg. In hotels try to negotiate family rates. In the better hotels in more commercial resorts, it is quite common for children under 10 or 12 to be allowed to stay for no extra charge as long as they are sharing a room.

Conduct

Politeness and courtesy, even a little ceremoniousness, prevails in all situations – in fact, even the traffic police give tickets in a rather pleasant manner. Being flustered, rushed and hurried simply doesn't fit in with the way of doing things in Costa Rica – a common trait throughout Latin America. Equally common is the sometimes extended process of introductions – a good greeting invariably leads to a good meeting. Likewise when departing, take the time to say goodbye.

Visitors should keep to appointed times – or as it is known the *hora inglesa*. With just a tinge of sadness, the mañana culture of tomorrow so characteristic of Latin society is taking a back-seat in many areas that affect the tourist. Tours leave on time, private bus services tend to leave promptly and restaurant reservations should be honoured accordingly. Get involved with the government and bureaucracy and it's a different world. To be fair, governments and councils worldwide have their procedures and things take time, but sometimes the frustrations mount and the sheer volume of paperwork required is frightening. Keep a fair degree of patience and a healthy dose of tolerance to hand if dealing with officials. And always be polite.

Customs and duty free

The duty free allowance is 500 cigarettes and three litres of wine or spirits. No customs duties are charged on personal luggage, including items for personal and professional use as long as they are not in sufficiently large quantities that could suggest commercial use. As at all immigration posts, your bags may be searched on entering the country. In the case of families, one declaration can be filled out for the whole family.

Disabled travellers

It would be fair to say that Costa Rica is opening up to – rather than open to – the disabled traveller. Some hotels and restaurants have gone out of their way to include ramps, lifts and bathrooms for guests in wheelchairs and some popular sights are easily accessible. For the hearing and visually impaired, there is no reason to expect problems or difficulties if you can provide guidance on your special requirements.

Vaya con Silla de Ruedas (Go with Wheelchairs), T2454-2810, www.gowith wheelchairs.com, is a specialist organization that works primarily to provide day tours for passengers on cruise ships, but can also plan other trips.

Dress

Most Costa Ricans devote a great deal of attention to their clothes and appearance. How you dress is how people will judge you, particularly in the business arena. Beyond business, smart, clean clothes are always appreciated. In beach communities, wear at least a sarong and a shirt when walking round town or if you're away from the beach.

Drugs and drink

Drinking is a part of life, but drunkenness is fairly uncommon. Yes, walking through San José, Limón or other cities and popular areas in the early hours of Saturday morning you will find a few individuals the worse for wear, but nothing excessive.

Drugs too are frowned upon, although their presence is increasing as Costa Rica is used as a transhipment port for cocaine travelling up from South America. All the usual drugs are illegal in Costa Rica with a jail term being the penalty for possession.

Embassies and consulates

Costa Rican embassies abroad
Austria, Wagramer Strasse 23, Stiege 1, Etage 1, Top 2 y 3 A-1220 Viena, T263-3824, embajadaaustria_costa.rica@chello.at.
Australia and New Zealand, Consular Services, PO Box 205 Spit Junction NSW 2088. Postal address: PO Box 205, NSW 2088 Sydney, T2-9969-4050, congenrica@gmail.com.
Belgium, 489 Av, Louise, Boite 13, 1050 Brussels, T640-5541, www.costaricaembassy.be.
Canada, 325 Dalhousie St, Suite 407, Ottawa, Ontario, K1N 5TA, T2613-562-2855, www.costaricaembassy.com.
Denmark, Consular services, Landemarket 10 1119 Copenhague K, T3343-3100, mmj@norsker-jacoby.dk.
France, 4 Square Rapp 75007, Paris, T1-4578-9966, www.ambassade-costarica.org.
Germany, Dessauer Str 28-29, D-10963 Berlin, T30-2639-8990, www.botschaft-costarica.de.
Israel, Abba Hillel Silver St 14 Mail Box 38 Beit Oz, 15th floor Ramat Gan, 52506 , T3-613-5061, emcri@netmedia.net.il.
Italy, Vía Liegi 2, Int 8 Roma, costaricaroma@yahoo.it.
Japan, Kowa Building No 38 9 FL 901 4-12-24 Nishi-Azabu Minato-Ku Tokio, 106-0031, T3-3486-1812.

Netherlands, Laan Copes Van Cattenburg 46, 2585 GB, La Haya, T70-354-0780, embajada@embacr.nl.

New Zealand, see Australia, above.

Norway, Skippergat 33, 8th floor 0154, Oslo, T2242-5823, embajada@costarica.no.

Nicaragua, Las Colinas 2da entrada, Calle Prado Ecuestre 304, Managua, T276-1352, infembcr@cablenet.com.ni.

Panama, C Samuel Lewis, Edificio Plaza Omega 3rd floor, contiguo Santuario Nacional, Panama City, T264-2980, embajadacr@cwpanama.net.

Spain, Paseo de la Castellana 164, 17-A, 28046 Madrid, T91-345-9622, embajada@embcr.org.

Switzerland, Schwarztorstrasse 11, 3007 Berne, T31-372-7887, embajada.costa.rica@thenet.ch.

UK, Flat 1, 14 Lancaster Gate, London W2 3LH, T020-7706-8844, costarica@btconnect.com.

USA, 2114-S St, NW, Washington, DC 20008, T202-234-2945/6, www.costarica-embassy.org.

Consular offices: Atlanta, 1870 The Exchange, Suite 100 Atlanta, GA 30339, T770-951-7025.

Boston, 300 First Av, 3rd floor Needham, Massachusetts 02494, T781-449-3030.

Chicago, 203 N Wahash Av Suite 1312, Chicago, IL 60601, T312-263-2772.

Dallas, 7777 Forest Lane B-445, Dallas, Texas 75230, T972-566-7020.

Denver, 3356 South Xenia St, Denver, Costa Rica 80231, T303-696-8211.

Houston, 3000 Wilcrest Suite 112, Houston, TX 77042, T713-266-0484.

Los Angeles, 1605 West Olympic Blvd, Suite 400, Los Angeles, CA 90015, T213-380-6031.

Miami, 1101 Brickell Av Suite 704-5, Miami, FL 33131, T305-871-7485.

New York, 80 Wall St, Suite 718, New York, NY 10005, T212-509-3066.

San Francisco, Callier Place, Freemont, CA 94536, T510-790-0785.

Gay and lesbian travellers

A vibrant and lively gay scene exists in San José and various places throughout Costa Rica. Attitudes to gay and lesbian people fit in with the non-confrontational approach to life in general – live and let live. However, that said, public displays of affection should be avoided in the street – best left to the bars, clubs and meeting places. Information on the internet is available at ww.gaycostarica.com.

As a first point of contact in San José the **Joluva Guesthouse** is a gay-friendly hotel which will share information on the vibrant gay scene in San José and throughout the country. **Gente 10**, C 3, Av 5-7,T2258-4561, www.gente10.com, has listings of hotels, restaurants, bars, clubs and events in the gay circuit. **Triángulo Rosa** and the **Rainbow Group** are both involved in raising awareness of HIV and other issues. Look at www.gay costarica.com to get the latest developments. For a broader view visit www.iglta.org (International Gay and Lesbian Travel Association).

Health

Health risks

No vaccinations are specifically required to enter Costa Rica, however, it is recommended that you are up to date with basic immunization (see below). The major risks posed are those caused by insect disease carriers such as mosquitoes and sandflies, especially during the wet season and along the Caribbean coast. The key parasitic and viral diseases are **malaria**, South American **tyrpanosomiasis (Chagas disease)** and **dengue fever**. You are always at risk from these, and dengue fever is particularly hard to protect against as the mosquitoes can bite throughout the day as well as at night (unlike those that carry malaria and Chagas disease); try to wear clothes that cover arms and legs and also use effective mosquito repellent. Mosquito nets dipped in permethrin provide a good physical and chemical barrier at night.

Some form of **diarrhoea** or intestinal upset is a possibility, the standard advice is to be careful with drinking water and ice; if you have any doubts about the water then boil it or filter and treat it. In a restaurant buy bottled water or ask where the water has come from. Food can also pose a problem, be wary of salads if you don't know whether they have been washed or not.

Vaccinations

Confirm primary courses and boosters are up to date. Beyond ensuring that you have protection against tetanus, you should have a vaccination against hepatitis A and typhoid. If staying for an extended period or in a rural area rabies and hepatitis B should also be considered. (Vaccination against rabies and diphtheria may also be advised.) A yellow fever certificate is required if coming from an area with a risk of transmission. It is paramount that you take the latest advice before travelling.

Further information

www.btha.org British Travel Health Association.

www.cdc.gov US government site that gives excellent advice on travel health and details of disease outbreaks.

www.fco.gov.uk British Foreign and Commonwealth Office travel site has useful information on each country, people, climate and a list of UK embassies/consulates.

www.fitfortravel.scot.nhs.uk A-Z of vaccine/health advice for each country.

www.numberonehealth.co.uk Travel screening services, vaccine and travel health advice, email/SMS text vaccine reminders and screens returned travellers for tropical diseases.

Insurance

Travel insurance is essential. If you are cutting back on costs, don't cut back on insurance and make sure that it at least covers medical accidents and emergency repatriation. Luggage, delay, flight company collapse and theft should also be covered if possible. If you are taking items of high value (binoculars, cameras, videos or laptops) make sure they are covered – some policies do not cover goods over a certain value unless declared in advance. Insurance companies vary in their requirements relating to claims and payments. The bare minimum requirement is a police report – for more details you should read the small print in your policy. If you have had a theft and did not have travel insurance, it is possible that your house insurance provides cover.

Internet

Internet access is widely available in Costa Rica. There are several internet cafés in San José, but fewer services in the smaller towns. However, enterprising individuals and organizations are setting up small offices in out of the way places like Puerto Viejo de Talamanca and Ciudad Neily. Prices vary, but expect to pay between US$1 and US$2 an hour, although some places will charge a fortune if they can get away with it. Connections are normally good and getting better. Many of the budget places targeting backpackers have a machine or two for free use, making it reasonably easy to stay in touch.

Language

Spanish is the official language. If you want to learn there are schools in San José (see pages 54 and 115), up in the mountains of Monteverde and at several Pacific beach locations (see also Language school listings in Directory sections throughout the book). A grasp of the basics will help greatly in showing willing to communicate even if you can't quite get the finer details sorted out. **English** is spoken well in many of the popular

Language schools

There are over 40 language schools throughout Costa Rica providing a mix of Spanish courses. Classes normally last for four hours, given in the morning or afternoon (some people just can't study in the mornings), five days a week. Although one week is helpful, longer stays are encouraged for real progress. Conventional wisdom suggests that one-to-one classes create the optimum learning conditions, but some people don't like the intensive focus. More commonly, classes are in groups of two to six people. Good schools provide an activities programme, with trips to attractions and national parks and complementing classes, and some also provide academic credits.

If you're serious about learning Spanish, choosing a **homestay** is the best option because you avoid contact with English speakers. A homestay is literally staying in the home of a *Tico* family. By taking classes and living with Spanish-speaking people you maximize the opportunities for learning and practising your new language skills. This so-called "immersion technique" can be pretty tough, but it does work.

Beyond San José there are schools in several parts of the country. You can hang out at the beach in Flamingo or down in Montezumo, take classes in the cloudforests of Montverde or relax in the Orosí Valley while you practice your verbs. No one ever said learning a language was easy, but it can be easier in a beautiful place.

Prices vary considerably. The **Centro Panamericano de Idiomas** (www.cpi-edu.com), who have schools in Flamingo, Monteverde and Heredia, charge US$660 for two weeks of four hours a day. **Amerispan** in the US (www.amerispan.com), offer classes at nine different locations, and charge a weekly fee starting at US$270 for group classes. **Institute for Spanish Language Studies** in the US (www.isls.com), has schools in Costa Rica, offering innovative and flexible programmes. **Spanish Abroad**, in the US (www.spanishabroad.com), are also worth checking out. See San José (page 115) and other destinations' directories for schools in the capital and throughout the country.

resorts and destinations, as well as the main services – vehicle hire, hotels and tour operators – that you will normally encounter. In Limón a **creole** dialect derived from English is spoken, which is just about understandable to English speakers after a couple of beers. Several thousand also speak **Chinese** as a first language. Indigenous languages are still spoken with **Bribrí** and **Cabecar** in the southern Caribbean being the most widespread.

Laws

At the cutting edge of social change, the broad tolerance that is Costa Rican society prevails. You can do more or less what your heart and body desires as long you're not harming someone or something else.

If you're looking for an official line on what is acceptable, the US State Department produce *Tips for Travelers to Central and South America* which can be obtained through the US Government Printing Office, Washington, DC 20402 or via the Bureau of Consular Affairs at www.travel.state.gov.

Maps

General maps of the country are available on arrival. Several companies provide very good maps of the country. **International Travel Maps**, published by ITMB in Canada (www.itmb.com), produce an excellent 1:330,000 travel map (6th Ed) which is widely available in stores throughout the country, and internationally in good book stores.

The **Instituto Geográfico Nacional de Costa Rica**, at the Ministry of Public Works and Transport (MOPT) in San José (see page 103), sells good 1:50,000 topographical maps.

Media

Newspapers

Of the 6 daily national newspapers the most popular and oldest is **La Nación** (www.nacion.co.cr) which tows – or creates – the establishment line. It also has the best arts and listings section and recognizes the significant expatriate community in Costa Rica with an online Week in Review English version at www.nacion.com/ln_ee/english/. **La República**, www.larepublica.net, is the main competition, slightly slimmed down in content and style. Bringing up the from the rear – or the gutter – is **Al Día** which tends to have a more frivolous approach to events but good sports coverage. **La Prensa Libre**, www.prensalibre.co.cr, is a good evening paper. **Rumbo** is the main weekly news magazine of the three which also include **Triunfo** and **Perfil**. **La Gaceta** is the official government weekly paper.

English-language readers are treated to the **Tico Times**, www.ticotimes.net, with a gentle mix of national and international issues. They also publish the densely informative **Exploring Costa Rica** which stuffs everything you need to know about Costa Rica into a few hundred pages. **Costa Rica Today** is a free general interest weekly found in the better hotels and restaurants. Free regional magazines in Jacó (**Jacó**

News), Quepos (**Quepolandía**, www.quepolandia.com) and Tamarindo (**The Howler**) provide local information.

Television

There are, at the last count, 13 local television channels which carry a mix of imported drama, sport and news. The main station is **Channel 7**, which competes with strong growth in the uptake of cable and satellite services importing a staggering array of programmes. If you time it right, you can watch the **Discovery Channel** documentary on Monteverde Cloudforest after walking through the area.

Radio

Over 100 radio stations are available on the FM band – a few of which broadcast in English. **107.5 FM** provides a heady mix of good driving music, and **Radio Dos**, on 99.5 FM and on the internet at www.radiodos.com, plays a similar mix of hits. Once you've had enough of living the past, explore the wavelengths with the search button. You'll find Jazz on **Echo 95.9**. Outside the Central Highlands reception is patchy.

Money

**Currency → ** *US$1=551.45 colones (Oct 2008)*
The unit of currency is the colón, consisting of 100 céntimos. Gold coloured coins are minted for five, 10, 25, 50 and 100 colones. Public telephones use older silver five, 10 and 20 colón coins. Notes in use: 50, 100, 500, 1000, 2000, 5000 and 10,000 colones.

Dollars cash are widely accepted but don't rely on it outside most popular destinations. Always have a stash of colones.

Cash, traveller's cheques (TCs) and credit cards

Ideally, take all 3. Cash should be taken in US dollars – it is by far the easiest currency to change. It is possible to change other currencies but the rate is normally reduced and you may have to walk around several banks. It is possible to change euros, but the rate is better for dollars.

TCs have added security because they are replaceable if they are lost or stolen. Take dollar TCs and make sure they are a well known names like American Express, Citibank or Thomas Cook. Keep the original purchase receipt separate from the cheques – for added security make a photocopy.

Credit cards are widely accepted in hotels and restaurants in San José and the more established resorts, but may be difficult to use beyond these areas. Check with hotels in advance when making reservations. The real value of a credit card is for obtaining cash advances easily from ATMs and banks. Visa and MasterCard are widely accepted with Visa probably having the edge. American Express and Diners Club are accepted in business hotels but shouldn't \be relied upon outside the business setting.

Banks and changing money

Getting some 'first day' money before departure can prove difficult, although you may be able to get some in Miami if you are catching a connecting flight. There is a bank and ATM, just after customs, at the Juán Santamaría International Airport in San José which opens to meet arriving flights so you can change money immediately on arrival if you needed.

Banks are the easiest place to change money. Branches of the state banks **Banco Nacional** and **Banco de Costa Rica** are most common throughout the country. Service varies wildly – it can be incredibly slow or surprisingly fast. Banks in areas where processing TCs and credit cards is a rare occurrence may take a little longer but even this isn't a golden rule. Commission rates tend to be around 1%. Charges against credit cards vary – it may be as much as 5% when buying goods or tours. Check beforehand and avoid using a card if you have the option.

The black market in Costa Rica has largely disappeared, and the few street changers that hang around the central area are used for convenience as much as anything. In general it's best to avoid changing money on the street unless you are totally relaxed with the idea. Don't flash large amounts of money around. Know how much money to expect before asking. While you may show your dollars to the changer in advance, don't hand over the money until you have counted the money you are to receive.

Cost of living and travelling

Budgeting for a trip is clearly dependent on your tastes, styles and mode of travel. Annual income per head of population is around the US$4980 mark, but this varies widely throughout the population. Basic rented accommodation starts at around US$300 a month and rises according to the level of comforts and services.

Planning for day to day travel is difficult. At the bottom end of the scale you could manage on US$20 to US$25 a day to cover accommodation, hotels and travel by bus. But this would leave very little for comforts, trips and tours. Moderately comfortable travel is found in the US$45 to US$70 range. This will cover reasonable accommodation – allowing for regional differences – and pleasant meals. Beyond US$70 things start to get very comfortable with attention to service levels, design and decor. The cost of a room for two people is normally only 25% higher than for a single. The cost of adding a third person is often only a small increase and this will bring the daily budget per person down considerably. There are two extra costs that should be considered. Renting a vehicle will set you back around US$350 a week. Likewise, tours are an extra cost ranging in price from US$45 for a day trip up to US$200 for a two day all-inclusive whitewater rafting or Tortuguero wildlife trip. As a very rough guideline, bus travel works out to be between US$0.80 to US$1.40 per hr of travel. The longest possible single journey in the country is eight hours, although three to five is more common. Inflation always has an impact on cost of living. A relative drop in numbers of visitors has kept prices fairly stable in recent years. With numbers starting to pick up again, prices could well rise, especially with a lengthy period of high oil prices.

National parks

SINAC (Sistema Nacional de Areas de Conservación), Apdo 10104-1000, San José, Costa Rica, T2234-0973, www.sinac.go.cr, administer the national park system. For information, write in advance or contact **Fundación de Parques Nacionales**, 300 m north and 150 m east of Santa Teresita Church, C 23, Av 15, Barrio Escalante, San José, T2257-2239, open 0800-1200 and 1300-1700, Mon-Fri. In reality you can pay to enter most parks at entrance stations. **InBio Parques**, T2507-8100, www.inbio.ac.cr, is also a good resource for national park information (see page 136).

Opening hours

Banks 0900-1500, Mon-Fri. Some banks open longer and on Sat morning.
Commercial offices 0800-1800, Mon-Fri.
Government offices 0800-1600, Mon-Fri.
Shops 0800-1800 Mon-Sat. While the tendency to close for lunch is becoming a thing of the past, service is often reduced at lunchtimes. See also Conduct, page 50.

Post

The Costa Rican postal system (*correo*) is slow and unreliable. Parcels often go missing, whether being sent or received, so think twice before sending anything of value. Post takes about 10 days to North America, and 2-3 weeks to Europe. Sea mail, which is generally only used for large packages can take up to three months. Postal rates are affordable. If sending a package overseas, don't seal the bag before you go to the post office as it needs to be cleared by customs first. Packing materials are available at post offices in San José and Limón.

Post can be sent to the *Lista de Correos* of your local post office if you wish to receive mail. For San José, the address would be: Your Name, Correo de Costa Rica, Lista de Correos, San José, Costa Rica, Central America. There is a nominal charge of US$0.15 to collect each item.

Courier services are also available from San José. **DHL**, Paseo Colón, C 34, Edif Elizabeth, 1st floor, T2210-3838, www.dhl.com. **Federal Express**, World Service Center, Paseo Colón, 100 m east of the León Cortés statue, San José, T0800-052-1090, www.fedex.com. **UPS**, 50 m east of Pizza Hut, Pavas, San José T2290-2828, www.ups.com.

Religion

While 90% of Costa Ricans are nominally Roman Catholic, the number that actually attend church on a regular basis is far less. This should not be confused with a lack of respect for the church however.

Safety

In general Costa Rica is an extremely safe country. While long term residents say crime has increased, it is still very low in comparison with most countries. The majority of crimes can be avoided by being aware of the risks. Government authorities have committed to increasing the police presence with the introduction of a Tourist Police Corps in many popular tourist centres.

Protecting money and valuables

If you can trust your hotel, leaving your valuables at reception or in a safe box in your hotel is the safest way of protecting them. If you need to carry cash around, keep it in a safe place about your person, preferably somewhere under your clothing so it is concealed. Do not walk around with highly visible bags which might as well have, 'this is precious to me, please steal it', printed on them. If you are carrying a camera, make sure you have your hand on it or the bag at all times. Avoid walking through dark areas on your own at night.

Dangerous places

Bus stops and stations are notoriously busy places where confusion and bewilderment are likely to be the main feelings of the first time visitor and therfore perfect conditions for the bag-lifter to relieve you of your belongings. Remain calm at all times. Try not to appear unnecessarily rushed or lost. If you need to get your bearings, sit down, gather your bags and thoughts together. If you need to ask directions, avoid leaving one person in charge of more bags than they can physically hold.

The Coca-Cola Terminal and surrounding area in San José has a reputation for crime. A police office has opened in the terminal area and some locals say that crime is now falling. Nevertheless, take utmost care – don't show obvious signs of wealth, don't flash around a camera or other expensive items, don't bring anything so precious you can't afford to lose and don't put yourself at risk.

Con tricks

To say there is less creative theft in Costa Rica than in neighbouring countries is little consolation once you've had your pockets emptied. Be wary of various scams or tricks that attempt to distract you or take advantage of a lapsed moment of concentration. A common trick is to throw shampoo or mud on you, a helper clears it off while a third relieves you of your possessions. Other tricks involve dropping money and asking if it is yours. In the ensuing conversation with your guard dropped, your pockets are pilfered.

Driving

Rental cars are commonly the target of theft and normally rich pickings if you're carrying all your holiday gear. The tourist number plates that used to be on rental vehicles and stuck out like a sore thumb have now gone. However, your vehicle will still obviously be a hire car – not many Costa Ricans drive 4WDs. Do not park in the street – use hotel parking or find a parking lot. Do not leave valuables in the car at any time and if you have no choice, do your best to put them out of sight. Do not park on the roadside in popular quiet spots – your car will be seen. Regular letters to the *Tico Times* report the highly organized scams that operate close to the Río Tárcoles bridge, between Jacó and Orotina (see page 283).

Women

The risks for women travelling in Costa Rica is no different to the risks in your home country. Common sense should see you through most situations. Avoid alcohol and drugs if you are likely to be on your own. Avoid accepting alcohol and drugs from anyone that you can't trust 100%. See also page 65.

Violent crime

Violent crime in Costa Rica is extremely rare – if for any reason you are subject to violent crime do not put your life at risk in defence of your possessions.

Swimming and rip tides

The hypnotic beauty of some of Costa Rica's beaches hide the very real threat of riptides – currents which pull you out to sea. If you know what you are looking for, it is possible to see rip currents which are given away by a noticeable difference in water colour, have a gap in the breaking waves and foam or other objects floating out to sea. Apart from Manuel

Antonio, there are no lifesaving programmes in Costa Rica and you will often only have local advice to go on, if that. Dangerous beaches popular with tourists are: Playa Jacó, Playa Esterillos, Playa Palma, Playa Espadilla, Playa Bonita and Playa Cahuita.

If you get caught in a rip tide the first advice is don't panic – 80% of ocean drownings occur in rip tides when people panic and try to fight the current. Swim at a manageable pace parallel to the shore until you are clear of the current – the waves at either side of the rip tide will take you back to the shore. If you cannot break free of the current, let it take you out beyond the breakers, then swim diagonally toward the shore. Trying to swim against the current will result in exhaustion and ultimately could prove fatal.

Sex tourism and sex workers

Prostitution for women over 18 is legal in Costa Rica. Prostitutes are supposed to carry health cards which indicate when they last received a check-up. The line of tolerance has created a sex tourist industry which is easily accessed if you are interested, and equally easily avoided. One area that has caused concern, however, is the growth in child prostitution. This is illegal and government authorities come down heavily on offenders.

Student travellers

An **International Student Identity Card (ISIC)** is very useful in Costa Rica. You get discounts on entry to some museums, cinemas, events and even at some hotels. It'll normally only be a couple of dollars off, but it all adds up over a few weeks. You can obtain an ISIC from your college or university at home. Student status also entitles you to very good discounts on flights. The best student travel agent is **OTEC**, C 3, Av 1-3, T2256-0633, www.otec.co.cr, with stupendous discounts

(up to 50%) off flights for students, teachers and others who can convince staff that they are in education. It's almost enough to make you change career!

Tipping

Once a reward for exceptional service and attention to detail the tendency to tip at the drop of a hat is taking over in Costa Rica – this is, in essence, the different approach to tips between Europe and the US. In the better restaurants, a 13% sales tax and a 10% service charge is automatically added to your bill. You are welcome to contest paying the service charge if you wish. The general consensus is that bellboys and chamber-maids receive tips of between US$0.50 and US$2 per item or day. Taxi drivers are not tipped but if the service is exceptional then why not? Tour guides can be tipped as you see fit – again, it is recommended that the tip reflects the degree of personal service and attention rather than an assumed payment.

Telephone

Costa Rica has the dubious honour of having the highest number of land and mobile telephone lines per head of population in Central America. This is all very well if you have your own phone, but the majority of visitors will be subjected to hotel telephones, which attract a hefty surcharge, public telephones which rarely work, or using an expensive roaming mobile, or phones over the internet.

For all the modern technology a public phone is still the most convenient, if it works. Those that take cash, accept small change of five, 10 and 20 colones. Simply dial the number and feed in the money. Rates are cheap but it's a good idea to have plenty of change handy. To get the international operator or to make collect calls dial 116.

The network is provided by the state-owned telecommunications company **RACSA**, with competing services provided by **ICE-tel**, a subsidiary of the national power company ICE which also happens to be the sole owner of RACSA.

Phone or **calling cards** are very useful. There are 3 systems in operation in Costa Rica, the most useful is **Viajera Internacional 199** which permits national and international calls from any telephone. Available in values of 100, 200, 500, 1000 and 3000 colones. After scratching off the security patch, dial 199 and then follow the instructions. It can get rather tedious tapping in the 20-digit security code – to make a follow-on call hit the hash key (#). **Colibrí 197** provides a similar national service but their permitted number of lines are often busy. The **CHIP** cards work from blue public phones.

Mobile phones are widely used and available in country. International roaming is also possible, contact your phone service provider to get the service set up and while you're there get a run down of prices. You pay to make and receive calls, for text messages and voice mails, irrespective of whether you pick them up. Rates can be as high – around US$4/min for some networks. The cheapest option is to buy a local SIM card and put that in your phone – make sure your phone is not locked by your service provider as part of any contract.

Internet call services (such as Skype) can be useful, particularly if the business or person you are calling has a Skype account. They may have so ask.

In San José you can send and receive **faxes** (US$0.30 receiving up to 5 pages) and make credit card calls from the **RACSA Telecommunications Centre**, office at Av 1, C 5, T287-0087. They also have a (pricey) internet service. Many hotels, even at the cheaper end, have fax machines and may be happy for you to receive faxes for a charge.

Phone number changes

In March 2008 Costa Rican numbers shifted from 7 digit to 8 digits. Landlines get an extra '2' in the front of the original 7-digit number, so T234-5678 becomes T2234-5678. Mobile phones get an extran '8', so T876-5432 becomes T8876-5432. The changes are being put in place due to the increase in demand for both landlines and cell phone lines. The technology behind the change will be sorted very quickly but websites, business cards and other literature is likely to be updated much more slowly. So if you're dialling a 7-digit number, stick a 2 or 8 in front to make it work.

Time

GMT -6, equal to Central Standard Time. No daylight saving time.

Tourist information

Costa Rican Tourist Board (Instituto Costarricense de Turismo or ICT), PO Box 777-1000, San José, Costa Rica, Central America, contact them on T2299-5800 in Costa Rica, or toll free from the US and Canada on T1-800-COSTA RICA, www.visitcostarica.com. The ICT also has several offices in the US and Europe. There are various ways of getting in touch, the easiest is via the website which, although tiresome to navigate, is packed with useful information once you find it.

Tourism is now so important in the country that the ICT can largely take a back seat as private industry works on all levels to promote various attractions, hotels and rstaurants. Guides are readily available at nature attractions but if you are looking for a specialist guide you should book through a tour operator or travel agent in advance.

The country is a popular destination and information is fairly easy to get hold of, both in libraries and in your national press or via the web. If you want more streetwise information look up the weekly English-language newspaper the *Tico Times* (www.ticotimes.net). You can also arrange a 6-month subscription, from US$34 (hard copy in the US), US$33 (PDF worldwide), look on the internet or write to Apdo 4632, San José, Costa Rica, T2258-1558, or in the US c/o The Tico Times-SJO 717, 1601 NW 97th Av Unit C-101, PO Box 025216, Miami, Fl 33102-5216.

Bimonthly *Costa Rica Outdoors* has good information on outdoor activities, T1-800-308-3394, in Costa Rica on T2282-6260, www.costaricaoutdoors.com.

Tour operators

Costa Rica is sufficiently developed for tour operators to be able to provide complete packages, or just to sort out a couple of time-crucial events while you're in the country. If there is something you simply have to do, or somewhere you just have to stay, it is worth trying to make arrangements in advance.

North America
Abercrombie & Kent, 1520 Kensington Rd, Suite 212, Oak Brook, Illinois, 60523-2156, T1-800-554-7016, www.abercrombie kent.com. Luxury tours based on nature, adventure or family vacations.

Costa Rica Experts, 3166 N Lincoln Av, Suite 424, Chicago, IL 60657, T1-800-827-9046, www.costaricaexperts.com. Endless variety for bespoke or off-the-shelf holidays. Good prices without skimping on quality.
Elderhostel, 11 Av de Lafayette, Boston, MA 02111, toll free on T1-877-426-8056, from outside the US and Canada call T1-978-323-4141, www.elderhostel.org. Trips for the over 55s with gentle and useful pursuits like 'An Introduction to Birdwatching' and 'Energizing Bodies and Minds'.
GAP Adventures, 19 Charlotte St, Toronto, Ontario, M5V 2H5, toll free on T1-800-708-7761, www.gapadventures.com. Good tours at good prices.
Holbrook Travel, 3540 NW 13th St, Gainesville, FL 32609-2196, toll free on T1-800-451-7111, www.holbrooktravel.com. Everything from specialist nature tours and family trips through to full-on adventure, also owners of the Selva Verde Lodge near Puerto Viejo de Sarapiquí, see page 167.
LADATCO Tours, 2200 S Dixie Highway, Suite 704, Coconut Grove, FL 33133, www.ladatco.com, T1-800-327-6162. Reliable short trips from an operator that's been working in the region a long time.
Mila Tours, T1-800-367-7378, www.milatours.com. Experienced operator.
Sunny Land Tours, 21 Old Kings Rd North, Suite B-212, Palm Coast, FL 32137, toll free on T1-800-783-7839, www.sunnylandtours.com. Build your own bespoke tour or just pick a couple of trips from their itineraries.

Tara Tours, 12002 SW 128 CT, Suite 209, Miami, Florida 33186, T1-800-327-0080, www.taratours.com. Good selection of 7- to 12-day trips.

Tico Travel, toll free on T1-800-493-8426, www.ticotravel.com. Very cheap flights (US$220 Miami-San José return in the green season), and good deals on other trips including surfing and fishing.

Wildland Adventures, 3516 NE 155th St, Seattle, WA, 98155-7412, T1-800-345-4453, www.wildland.com. Soft adventure trips, some family friendly.

UK and Ireland

Condor Journeys and Adventures, 2 Ferry Bank, Colintraive, Argyll PA22 3AR, T01700-841318, www.condorjourneys-adventures.com.

Exodus Travels, Grange Mills, Weir Rd, London, SW12 0NE, T020-8673-0859, www.exodus.co.uk.

Galapagos Classic Cruises, 6 Keyes Rd, London, NW2 3XA, T020-8933-0613. www.GalapagosCruises.co.uk. Tailor-made tours to Costa Rica.

Geodyssey, 116 Tollington Park, London, N4 3RB, T020-7281-7788, www.geodyssey.co.uk.

Journey Latin America, 12-13 Heathfield Terr, Chiswick, London, W4 4JE, T020-8747-8315, www.journeylatinamerica.co.uk. The best deal on flights from London also with bespoke and adventure tours.

Last Frontiers, Fleet Marston Farm, Aylesbury, Buckinghamshire, HP18 0QT, T01296-653000, www.lastfrontiers.co.uk. Tailor-made travel to Latin America. Private tours, family holidays and honeymoons.

LATA, www.lata.org. Lists tour operators, hotels, airlines, etc.

Reef & Rainforest Tours, A7 Dart Marine Park, Steamer Quay, Totnes, Devon, TQ9 5AL, T01803-866965, www.reefandrainforest.co.uk and www.familytours.co.uk. Specialists in tailor-made and group wildlife tours.

Select Latin America, 3.51 Canterbury Court, 1-3 Brixton Rd, Kennington Park Business Centre, London, SW9 6DE, T020-7407-1478, www.selectlatin america.co.uk. Quality tailor-made holidays and small group tours.

South American Experience, Welby House, 96 Wilton Rd, Victoria, London, SW1V 1DW, T0845-277-3366, www.southamerican experience.co.uk. Flights and pick'n'mix bespoke tour options.

Steppes Travel, 51 Castle St, Cirencester, Gloucestershire, GL7 1QD, T01285-885333, www.steppestravel.co.uk. Tailor-made and group itineraries throughout Costa Rica and the rest of Latin America.

Sunvil Latin America, Sunvil House, Upper Square, Old Isleworth, Middlesex, TW7 7BJ, T020-8568-4499, www.sunvil.co.uk. Fully supported trips for a week to a fortnight or longer fly-drive options.

Trips Worldwide, 14 Frederick Pl, Clifton, Bristol, BS8 1AS, T0117-311-4403, www.tripsworldwide.co.uk. Tailor-made trips to Costa Rica with 15 years' experience in the region.

Germany

Die Reisegalerie, Grüneburgweg 84, 60323 Frankfurt, T069-9720-6000, www.reise galerie.com. Trips to Costa Rica or just the flight with LTU if you want to go alone.

Armo Tours, Balthasar Straße 50, 50670 Cologne, T0221-729-430, www.armo tours.com. German-based office of a Costa Rican tour operator.

Holland

Thika Travel, T0346-242526, www.thika.nl. Providing flights through Martinair and working with *Ecole Travel* in San José. Also offices in Belgium, T03-451-1400, www.thika.be.

Switzerland

Helvetic Tours, Neue Hard 7, CH-8010 Zürich, T1-277-4200, www.helvetictours.ch. Good for the last minute and the tour market.

Kundert Travel, Fähnlibrunnenstrasse 8, 8700 Küsnacht, Zurich, T01-910-9969, www.kundert-travel.ch. Will make arrangements or organize flights.

Australia, New Zealand, Japan

The Adventure Travel Company, 224 Clarendon St, South Melbourne, VIC 3205, Australia, T1-800-238-368 or T03-9696-8400, www.adventure-travel.com.au; and in New Zealand at 1st floor, Lambton Square,

Lambton Quay, Wellington, T04-494-7180, www.adventuretravel.co.nz.

Costa Rica Tourist Board Japanese website, www.costarica.co.jp.

South Africa

STA, Level 3, Leslie Social Sciences Building, Cape Town, T021-685-1808, www.statravel.co.za.

Visas and immigration

Citizens holding valid passports from most western European nations, the US, Canada and Japan are permitted to stay in Costa Rica for 90 days without a visa. Visitors from the United States should note that they are required to have a passport to re-enter the USA as part of the US's Western Hemisphere Travel Initiative. See www.rree.go.cr for the latest information on entry requirements.

Citizens holding valid passports from Australia, New Zealand and South Africa are allowed to stay in Costa Rica for 30 days without a visa.

Citizens of all countries not listed above must obtain a visa from a Costa Rican embassy or consulate before travelling, at a cost of US$20.

Visa extensions

A *prórroga de turismo* can be obtained at Immigration in San José; the office is in Uruca on the road from the capital to the airport. Contact telephone numbers for this, and regional offices, are at www.migracion.go.cr. You will need 4 passport photos, an airline or bus ticket out of the country and proof of funds (for example traveller's cheques); you can apply for an extension of 1 or 2 months at a cost of 625 colones per month. The paperwork can take up to 3 days but travel agents can arrange all extension and exit formalities for a small fee. Alternatively, you can leave the country for 72 hrs and get a new 30- or 90-day visa when you re-enter. If entering overland an onward ticket is sometimes requested. A bus ticket can be bought close to the border immigration office which can then be refunded in San José if required.

Residency

If planning on taking up residency, the process requires a degree of administration. There are a number of options for retired and investing individuals. Essentially you need to prove that you have a regular income in excess of US$600 per month, or that you are going to invest over US$50,000 to create a regular income. For assistance in understanding and tackling the process contact the **Association of Residents of Costa Rica**, Casa Canada, Av 4 and C 40, PO Box 1191-1007, Centro Colón, San José, Costa Rica, T2233-8068, www.arcr.net (a useful website for residents).

Voltage

Voltage 110 volt, 60 cycles AC with US flat-pin plugs.

Women travellers

For the vast majority of women, visiting Costa Rica is likely to be a trouble-free and enjoyable experience. The status of women continues to evolve and for those seeking a professional career and education, opportunity is widely available. However, although certain sections of society acknowledge the desire to take gender out of business relations don't be fooled. Across the country as a whole, the reality is that the domain of the woman is still that of wife and mother at home – even if the woman does go out to work.

As in any country, women, especially those travelling alone, should exercise a degree of caution. In general, Costa Rica is much safer (in terms of violent crime against women) than the USA or Europe, and rape and muggings are uncommon.

However, there have been some well publicized incidents in which female tourists have been attacked and even killed, and you should exercise the normal caution you would anywhere in the world.

Women will be judged by the clothes they wear, and while skimpy tops and short shorts are acceptable around beach areas, you should be aware that white women attract more attention than a *Tica* in the same clothes. In towns and cities, you should avoid short skirts or shorts, and try to dress more as the locals do: you will notice they dress more formally away from home.

You should bear in mind that machismo is a strong element in Costa Rican culture, and you should expect to be hissed or whistled at when you pass men. In general, these appreciative responses to your presence are best ignored – simply walk on and try not to let it bother you. If you are being seriously pestered, simply say, *"no me moleste, por favor"*, or more strongly, *"déjeme en paz."*

You can greatly reduce the risk of getting into dangerous situations by avoiding getting drunk when you are out by yourself or with a group of girls, and by bearing in mind that most people who invite you for a stroll on the beach are not motivated by a desire to practice their English.

Working in the country

Working in Costa Rica is not a problem – getting paid for it could well be. However, with the right skills and qualifications it is possible to arrange a job after arriving in the country. The skills that are most in demand, and consequently the best paid, are for qualified English teachers – employed with a proper school you will get you the best pay. Alternatively you may be able to get work in the tourism industry where service and English is much appreciated – but don't expect to get paid much.

Technically you should get a work permit from immigration if you are planning to work. If the job is above board, you will receive support from your employer in tackling the process (which is long and drawn out, taking as much as 4 months). In reality, most people cross the border every three months to refresh their visa, or just pay the fine when leaving. A word of warning, however: government authorities have let it be known they intend to crack down on so-called permanent tourists.

Volunteering

Volunteering to help with environmental and conservation work is very popular in Costa Rica. If your idea of volunteering is turning up and showing willingness to help sometimes when you're not going to the beach then forget it. Volunteering in Costa Rica is well developed, organized and you normally have to pay for food and sometimes lodgings. (Charges usually vary from US$75 to US$150 a week.) The workload and type varies enormously. You may be building and maintaining paths, recording information about plant and wildlife populations, clearing out animal cages or have general administration duties. What you do will depend partly on what you can do and what you're prepared to do.

Most volunteers organize a placement before arriving. The first stage is to complete the application process successfully. The most popular places are often filled more than 6 months in advance. Once working you will normally work a shift pattern with 2- to 4-day breaks for travel.

Volunteering at national parks can be organized through **ASVO**, the Asociación de Voluntarios para el Servicio en las Areas Protegidas, T2258-4430, www.asvocr.org.

You can also contact organizations direct. Look in the text for **Hacienda Barú** near Dominical (page 308), **Zoo Ave** in the Central Highlands (page 123), **Caño Palma Biological Station** in Tortuguero (page 382), **Pacuare Nature Reserve** close to Limón (page 368), **Aviarios del Caribe** (page 394), **ANAI** (page 387) and the **Talamanca Dolphin Foundation** (page 393) on the south Caribbean coast close to Puerto Viejo de Talamanca, the **Children's Eternal Rainforest** in Monteverde (page 195), the **Delfín Amor Eco Lodge** (page 345) and **Campanario Biological Reserve** in Bahía Drake (page 345), and **Rara Avis** near Puerto Viejo de Sarapiquí (page 162). This is not a comprehensive list – just a series of pointers.

It is also possible to organize volunteering through intermediary companies in your home country. The cost or level or commitment required is normally higher but the degree of support is usually greater. In the US try **Peace Corps** T1-800-424-8580, www.peacecorps.gov. In the UK **World Challenge Expeditions**, Black Arrow House, 2 Chandos Rd, London, NW10 6NF, T020-8728-7200, www.world-challenge.co.uk, provide a volunteer program. Also try **i-to-i** Woodside House, 261 Low Lane, Leeds, LS18 5NY, T0800-011-1156, www.i-to-i.com.

Contents

    70   Ins and outs
    75   History

76 Sights
    76   Central San José
    83   Outside the centre
    84   Escazú and western
          suburbs
    85   Easy trips from San José

88 Listings
    88   Sleeping
    96   Eating
  100 Bars and clubs
  101 Entertainment
  102 Festivals and events
  103 Shopping
  105 Activities and tours
  107 Transport
  113 Directory

Footprint features

68 Don't miss …
71 24 hours in San José
78 Churches

San José

At a glance

⊝ **Getting around** This is easiest on foot, otherwise take a cab unless you're really keen on the local buses.

◉ **Time required** 2 or 3 days will give you enough time to see most of what San José has to offer.

☼ **Weather** Nov-Apr is driest.

☻ **When not to go** May-Oct can be a bit grim and grey at times, but the rain doesn't last long.

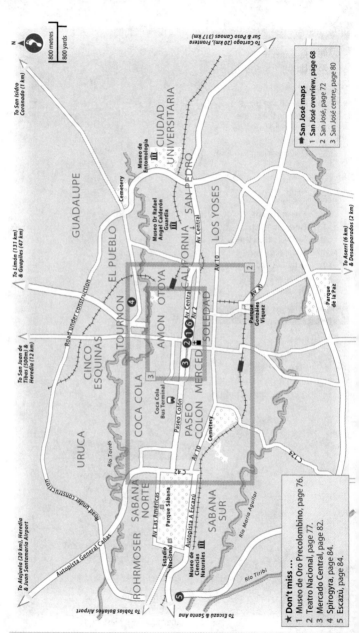

N

800 metres
800 yards

To Alajuela (20 km), Heredia & Juan Santamaría Airport

To San Juan de Tibás (500m) & Heredia (12 km)

To Limón (131 km) & Guápiles (47 km)

To San Isidro Coronado (1 km)

URUCA

ROHRMOSER

SABANA NORTE

Autopista General Cañas

Road under construction

Río Torres

CINCO ESQUINAS

GUADALUPE

Cemetery

EL PUEBLO

TOURNON

Road under construction

CIUDAD UNIVERSITARIA

Museo de Entomología

To Cartago (20 km), Frontera Sur & Paso Canoas (317 km)

CALIFORNIA

SAN PEDRO

Museo Dr Rafael Angel Calderón Guardia

Av Central

LOS YOSES

AMON

OTOYA

Av Central

Av 2

COCA COLA

Coca Cola Bus Terminal

SOLEDAD

MERCED

Paseo Colón

PASEO COLON

Cemetery

Av 10

Parque Gonzáles Víquez

AV 10

Parque de la Paz

To Aserrí (6 km) & Desamparados (2 km)

SABANA SUR

Río María Aguilar

Río Tiribí

To Escazú & Santa Ana

To Escazú A Escazú

Autopista A Escazú

C 42

Av Las Américas

Parque Sábana

Estadio Nacional

Museo de Ciencias Naturales

To Tobías Bolaños Airport

C 124

★ San José maps
1 San José overview, page 68
2 San José, page 72
3 San José centre, page 80

★ Don't miss ...
1 Museo de Oro Precolombino, page 76.
2 Teatro Nacional, page 77.
3 Mercado Central, page 82.
4 Spirogyra, page 84.
5 Escazú, page 84.

Few visitors to Costa Rica return home with gasp-inducing tales of the beauty of San José. The reasons are simple enough: it is not particularly beautiful, and any sharp intake of breath will probably have more to do with an attempt to avoid the pollution. By day the city streets are packed with traffic as heavy buses barely moving beyond second gear crawl through the streets and keen-eyed kamikaze taxis look for the raised arm hailing business. At street level a general theme of clutter and chaos prevails with vendors selling fruit, cigarettes and other daily necessities as an endless stream of immaculately dressed *Ticos* scurry to and from work. By night, streets lit by the rhythmic flash and glow of neon slowly empty as the *Josefinos* hurry home or out to bars, restaurants and clubs.

After almost two hundred years as capital, the city still seems unwilling to take the lead. Attractions and activities awaiting the visitor come across as reluctant suggestions rather than vibrant 'must-sees'. With San José you may have to put in a little more effort and imagination than with many cities but love at first sight does happen and some are certain to become infatuated with the city after a couple of days exploring its understated secrets.

Getting there → *See also Getting there in Essentials, page 34.*

Air San José's modern **Juan Santamaría International Airport** (T2441-0744 or T2443-2622) is 16 km northwest of the city centre on the outskirts of the town of Alajuela. The airport has international and domestic connections. After baggage reclaim and customs a tourist desk (open 0900-1700 daily) has supplies of basic maps and a selection of brochures. The desk can book accommodation and arrange transport to the city if required. There is an ATM machine, and a small bank for changing currency and travellers' cheques and several car rental agencies. Airport services close to check-in and the departure area include currency exchange, bank ATMs, a few small shops, a café and a restaurant. Beyond passport control there are a few cafés, a newsagent, a well-stocked perfumery and drink store. There are also a couple of well-stocked gift shops.

Transport for the 30-minute journey to San José downtown is easiest with one of the red taxis that greet international flights fixed fare, pre-payment from the booth (US$15). You can book in advance if you're really keen at www.taxiaeropuerto.com. A cheaper option is to take one of the regular local buses from the main road outside the terminal building just beyond the line of taxis. The 40-minute journey is 200 colones (US$0.50). Buses leave every 10 minutes through the day and slightly less frequently at night. If you don't know exactly where your hotel is or if you arrive at night the simplest and safest option is to get a taxi. If travelling on your own, look for other travellers who may be happy to double up and share the cost.

Bus San José has very good local, national and international bus connections. National buses provide connections throughout the country, serving most popular destinations directly. International buses link the whole of Central America from Panama to Mexico. The standard of bus varies greatly ranging from the shell of a bus with plastic seats to a comfortable air-conditioned luxury 'liner', sometimes fitted with TV and video. If your destination is off the main routes, expect to travel in a beaten up old vehicle. ➤ *See Transport, page 107, for further details.*

Car The capital is served by roads on all sides that twist and turn round precipitous drops, affording both driver and passengers spectacular views and equally dramatic opportunities for accidents. Approaching San José from the west, traffic is channelled down Paseo Colón – the city's main thoroughfare which leads to Avenida Central. From the northeast, the route follows the potentially dangerous road through Parque Nacional Braulio Carrillo, complete with natural distractions. From the south, the Pan-American Highway (called Highway 2 in Costa Rica) travels through the Talamanca Mountains descending quickly to skim west of Cartago approaching the capital from the southeast. *Ticos* believe that of the three routes, the last is the most dangerous due to large amounts of heavy goods traffic, but in reality there is little difference. Parking in the city during the day is not that difficult with several *parqueos públicos* dotted around the city. 24-hour parking is available but may be more difficult to find. One specific word of warning. Most car rental firms are along Paseo Colón, one of the busiest and fastest stretches in San José, and it is a test to start your driving career in the city here. Added to that, traffic flows change at rush hour, weekdays between 0630 and 0830, when the road becomes one-way, heading into the centre of town. ➤➤ *For further information, see also page 112.*

24 hours in San José

If you want to see the city wake up, you'll have to be ready by 0600 (there's a crisp chill in the air most days so take a jumper). Head for the **Mercado Central** where the collective rubbing of eyes happens under a flurry of activity and occasional song. You can breakfast on *empanadas* or *tortillas* and have a coffee at one of the many stand-up bars (or take a more leisurely sit-down option). You'll have to be early to catch the butchers and fishmongers stocking up.

After breakfast, stroll north to the **Centro Costarricense de Ciencias y Cultura** and then continue on foot or by taxi out to the **Spirogyra** butterfly farm. Grab a coffee in the café here or at El Pueblo across the road. You can do a bit of shopping if places are opening, but don't worry, you'll be coming back here later in the evening.

Get a taxi (approximately 700 colones) to the Alianza Francesa building on the corner of Avenida 7 and Calle 5 and from here explore the colonial splendour of Barrio Amón before walking down to the Plaza de la Cultura where you can lunch on the streetside café of the Hotel Gran Costa Rica.

Refreshed and revived, take in the attractions of the Plaza de la Cultura including the eloquence of the **Teatro Nacional** and the underground **Museo de Oro**, and head east along Avenida Central to the **Museo Nacional**.

Return to base for a refreshing nap in preparation for an evening ahead out in **El Pueblo** enjoying a meal – there are several options to suit all tastes and wallets. After dinner, walk off the meal exploring the small alleys, streets and stalls of the village.

Getting around

Central San José conforms to the extended grid system building outwards from two main streets that cross in the centre of the city – Avenida Central and Calle Central. Avenues run west to east, with the odd numbers (Avenida 1, Avenida 3, etc) north of Calle Central and even numbers (Avenida 2, Avenida 4, etc) to the south. Likewise, the streets or *calles* are numbered odd to the east of the city and even to the west.

On foot Central San José is easy to explore on foot – most places of interest are close to the centre. Joining the general mêlée, you can bump and grind your way through the chaos or stroll at leisure. With the simplicity of the street layout, if you're lost just head back towards the lower numbered streets and you end up in the centre.

But hazards do exist. The streets of capital cities are rarely paved with gold, but in parts of San José they are barely paved at all. This is not a warning to watch out for the occasional raised or cracked paving slab, it is serious advice about looking where you are walking. Slabs stick up at shin-cracking angles and in some places they're missing completely, revealing precipitous drops to the drainage system below. Keep your eyes down while walking and stop when you want to look around (look on it as good training for jungle walks).

A second hazard, not that peculiar to San José, is the traffic. Crossing the roads is safest at pedestrian crossings which conform to the standard green man code (you'll be pushing your luck if you leave the kerb on anything but green). A complicated one-way system adds to the confusion, so when crossing roads the simple rule is to watch the vehicles, even if it is a pedestrian crossing. While courtesy does exist, few drivers at the lights hang around unnecessarily.

Bus An extensive service covers the surrounding districts and suburbs of the city (cost 80-225 colones – try and have change ready). While buses can be a handy way of travelling longer distances around the city, snail-like paces are common, especially at rush hour. Once you get the hang of a few basic routes, judicious use of buses can be very convenient, but as a general rule unless weighed down with luggage, or late for an appointment (in which case consider a taxi), it's probably worth walking any distance up to 20 blocks or so.

② San José

➡ San José maps
1 San José overview, page 68
2 San José, page 72
3 San José centre, page 80

300 metres
300 yards

Sleeping 🛏
Aranjuez **1** A6
CACTS **2** B2
Costa Rica
  Backpackers **15** C6
Costa Rica Guesthouse
  16 C6
D'Raya Vida **4** A6
Galileo Backpackers'
  Hostel **13** B1
Gaudy's **3** A1
Grano de Oro **5** B2
Green House **17** D5
JC Friends Hostel **6** B1
Kap's Place **7** A6
Musoc **8** B3

Petit Victoria **9** B2
Rosa del Paseo **11** B2
Villa Tournón **12** A5

Eating 🍴
Boudsoq **3** B2
El Cuartel de la Boca
  del Monte **1** B6

As ever, warnings related to busy places hold true. Pickpockets and bagsnatchers love cramped settings so take care.

Taxi With over 7500 cabs cruising the streets, taxis are a quick and efficient way of moving around the city. Official red cabs are marked with a yellow triangle on the side and equipped with meters or *marías* that should be used for all journeys within the

La Bastille **2** *B2*
La Cocina de Leña **4** *A5*
Machu Picchu **5** *B2*
Shakti **8** *C5*
Soda Tapia **6** *B1*

Buses 🚌
Alajuela & Airport
  Buses **1** *B3*
Heredia Buses **2** *B3/B4*
Liberia Buses **3** *B3*
Panaline Bus **4** *B3*
San Isidro Buses **5** *D4*
Sirca Bus **6** *C5*

Ticabus **7** *B2*
Transnica Bus **8** *B3*
Terminal Alfaro **9** *A3*
Terminal Atlántico
  Norte **10** *A3*
Terminal Caribe
  (Sixaola) **11** *A4*
Terminal Cartago **12** *D5*

Terminal Coca Cola **13** *B3*
Terminal Los Santos **14** *D6*
Terminal Puntarenas **15** *C3*
Terminal Turrialba **16** *C5*

metropolitan district. Although meters are generally used if you're travelling with a *Tico*, visitors on their own often find them 'broken'. But taxi drivers know their patch and once you've made friends, they're an invaluable asset. On the whole, drivers are fair but get a rough idea of the cost before setting off. The meter starts at 405 colones and advances 10 colones every 500 m or so. A cross-town journey will be in the region of 600-1000 colones (US$1.20-US$2). ▸▸ *See also page 113.*

Orientation and information

Centred on the **Plaza de la Cultura**, San José has little by way of geography or history to help newcomers get their bearings. The most useful locator is **Avenida Central** which for the course of its length draws a neat horizontal line through the city map. En route it guides you by, or pretty close to, the majority of the city's attractions from the streetwise banter of the **Mercado Central** in the west to the formal governmental chaos of the **National Assembly** to the east.

A little further afield, the districts of **Barrio Amón** and **Otoya** to the northeast transport you to a world built on coffee wealth where once-common colonial splendour now stands more as a monument to grand living and architectural extravagance.

The **ICT (Instituto Costarricense de Turismo)** ① *daily 0900-1700 (the ICT also has a good website www.visitcostarica.com packed with hotel, tour operator and transport information)* has an efficient and helpful tourist office below the Plaza de la Cultura (in addition to the information desk at Juan Santamaría International Airport). The staff can help with general information and maps, and assist with specific inquiries and problems. Other good sources of information are the numerous tour operators scattered throughout the city. While some may give you the hard sell, others are happy to provide the latest information on availability and accessibility.

Best time to visit

The best time to visit San José is from December to April when you are guaranteed clear skies and very little rain. At other times of year, trips out to the surrounding volcanoes may be eerie but ultimately disappointing because the peaks are often completely covered in cloud if you don't make an early start. The capital enjoys a comfortable climate throughout the year with temperatures fluctuating around the 20°C (68°F) mark by just a few degrees. The mildest time of year is January and February (15-23°C/59-73°F). By May the hottest weather is on its way but the temperatures have tweaked only slightly higher to 18-26°C (64-79°F). In essence you may want a jumper for early mornings, evenings and late nights, but by day a shirt is ideal. Rainfall, however, which becomes a regular occurrence from May to November, changes the situation dramatically. The rainfall is rarely permanent, and tends towards intense, torrential downpours that last a few hours. *Josefinos* prefer the umbrella to the raincoat as protection – vendors of cheap *paraguas* come out of the shadows when the rainfall begins. Get one and join in!

Festivals and celebrations (see page 102) are held throughout the year in the Plaza de la Cultura but the single greatest festival in the capital is 15 September, Independence Day, when costumed parades move down the street, to the rhythm of marching bands.

History

For much of its colonial history Costa Rica, with Cartago as its capital, was on the fringes of the New World. Most of the isthmus was governed by the Audiencia de Guatemala which, ruling from southern Mexico in the north down to modern day Costa Rica in the south, barely mustered interest in the distant trading outpost. To the south, Panama much preferred wealthy trade with the riches of South America.

Left alone with little colonial meddling, a slow and sometimes painful growth saw a string of communities build up in the central highlands, among them San José (1737), Heredia (1706) and Alajuela (1782). In the mid-18th century San José was a ramshackle collection of farms but by the end of the century, a monopoly in tobacco trade had given the city a slight prominence over other towns of the region, fuelling the development and early signs of civic pride. When news of Guatemala's independence from Spain in 1821 finally reached Costa Rica – delivered with such indifference that the news took over a month to arrive – the citizens of San José, with the shoots of a promising coffee industry beginning to appear, were confident of their ability to assume the status of capital.

The emerging agricultural elite, combined with the entrepreneurial spirit of the time, created conflict between the emerging towns, pitting the youthful, energetic and independently minded cities of San José and Alajuela against the more traditional forces of Cartago and Heredia who favoured annexation to a Central America Federation. The dispute was settled in 1823 at the Battle of Ochomongo but skirmishes continued for a further 20 years as the four towns fought for ascendancy of the Central Valley.

The victorious outcome for San José set a path for the nation's growth. Forced by necessity to enter the world economy, a flurry of activity promoted trade in mining and lumber, but it was coffee from the Central Valley that provided a stable and reliable market. As growth of the golden bean was promoted, *cafetaleros* (merchant classes) developed to take advantage of new opportunities. They controlled the export and processing of coffee as well as the credit going to family farms, getting rich in the process and quickly becoming the most influential players in the early development of the young republic.

The wealth provided by a coffee elite which sold directly to Europe quickly brought return trade in European tastes to the capital. Infrastructure improved through the mid to late 19th century with the introduction of two-storey buildings, street lamps and cabs. The cultural landscape shifted with the introduction of language classes, Shakespeare, operetta and cockfighting. The University of Santo Tomás opened in 1843 and by 1897 the Teatro Nacional (National Theatre), financed by a coffee tax, stood at the centre of the capital as monument to the extravagant wealth, style and tastes that now dominated the lives of rich *Josefinos*. Although coffee cultivation spread throughout the Central Valley, the strength of the coffee oligarchy ensured San José remained in control.

The air of opulence was considerably dampened by the depression of the 1930s and as the country spent a couple of decades drifting through depression, economic and social reform and civil war, the capital's stylish extravagance became a distant memory. However, when economic growth stimulated expansion in the late 1950s, industrial development fuelled new prosperity in the capital and San José grew at the expense of the surrounding rural communities as people flocked to its bright lights. The rapid growth of the city, in the absence of urban planning, quickly destroyed its European charm, replacing it instead with blocked streets and increasing pollution. Today *Josefinos* are broadly indifferent about their capital. However, like a close family member, the city's weaknesses are not an area for public discussion – certainly not by foreigners.

Sights

Few come to San José to see the sights. But there is something about Costa Rica that encourages diversity and the capital is no different. In among the chaos of the streets, you can find somewhere to sit and wonder about the madness of it all. Between unimaginative high-rise blocks – some of which are exceptionally ugly – odd, solitary gestures to architectural style stand out. The numerous parks and plazas dotted around the city are often so cluttered with monuments and benches, winding paths and flower beds that few people pass through them, leaving them strangely empty and peaceful even at the busiest times of day.

On the museum front, San José has its fair share. Compact and numerous, the museums are not daunting even if coverage is a little patchy. While the specialist may find them wanting, if you are after a brief insight into Costa Rican culture and history you'll be more than happy. Of the many options available, if time is limited, the underground **Museo de Oro Precolombino** (Pre-Columbian Gold Museum) is impressive in content and presentation and the **Museo de Jade** (Jade Museum), with the largest collection of jade in the Americas, is a source of pride for all *Josefinos*. The **Museo Nacional** (National Museum) now occupying Bellavista Fortress stands monument to the changing fortunes of the city and country.

While there may be no such thing as a normal city, San José seems less normal than most. Without the romantic legacy of Paris, the classical weight of Rome or the frightening chaos of some of the larger Latin cities, San José is manageable and, approached without too much expectation, almost refreshing.

Central San José

Around the Plaza de la Cultura

At the heart of the city the Plaza de la Cultura is a vibrant hub of pedestrian activity on Avenida Central and Calle 3-5. The Plaza itself, just a few uncomfortable benches, clusters of telephones and queues of frustrated *Josefinos* patiently waiting for access to one that works, holds little of architectural interest. But it's worth spending a while watching the constant flow of people from all walks of life and basking in a bit of the *Josefino* style. Where perfect people-watching conditions prevail you can usually find a street café and sure enough the Hotel Gran Costa Rica's **Café Parisienne** offers a perfect vantage point for the urban anthropologist.

Buried like hidden treasure below the Plaza, through a rather daunting gated entrance on the eastern side, is the **Museo de Oro Precolombino** (Pre-Columbian Gold Museum) ① *C3-5, Av Central-2, T2243-4202, www.museosdelbancocentral.org, daily, 0930-1700, US$7, students US$4; bags must be stored when visiting, secure cloakroom service provided; there is an audio guide to the room that can be rented from the cloakroom.* Delicate figurines of frogs, spiders, raptors and other creatures glisten in the museum sponsored by the Banco Nacional. Plotting the development of metallurgical techniques in the Diquis region of southwest Costa Rica, the pieces demonstrate a fine degree of skill and craftsmanship. Gold work grew steadily from around 500 AD, marking a move away from the Mayan influences of the north which preferred jade, to the southern influences of Panama and Colombia which placed greater importance on gold.

Within the same three-storey underground complex the small **Museo Numismática** (Numismatic Museum) displays a selection of bills, coins and *boletos de café* reflecting Costa Rican history from the 16th century to the present day. An open area is used for temporary exhibitions displaying part of the Banco Nacional's large collection of fine arts and archaeological exhibitions. While you're here, you can pop into the **ICT Tourist Office** and pick up any extra information you may want.

Back at ground level, on the southern side of the plaza is the iconic and neoclassical **Teatro Nacional** (National Theatre) ① *Av 2, C 3, T2221-9417, www.teatronacional.go.cr, Mon-Sat 0900-1600, US$5, guided tours are available, see La Nación or Tico Times for performances.* This is one of the most impressive buildings in the city, and a source of considerable pride, it was funded by a coffee tax in the late 19th century when the country's social elite realized the city was lacking a theatre suitable for world-class performances. Construction of the theatre called on the skills of European artisans including Belgian architects and Italian artists. The colonnades of the exterior are complemented by a lavish interior with a balance of extravagance and detail in the mahogany furniture, crystal chandeliers, gold-leaf murals and paintings, including the well-known image of *Marielitos* smiling out of the dockside scene *Alegoría a Las Exportaciones*. The stylish café is a fitting tribute to the paymasters of the theatre and definitely worth a visit.

Around Plaza de la Democracia

Head east down Avenida Central from Plaza de la Cultura for half a dozen blocks and you reach Plaza de la Democracia. Created in 1989 to celebrate the centenary of Costa Rican democracy, the bare plaza looks rather like a vast tiered waterfall without the water and there's a bronze statue of **José Figueres**. A small craft market selling hammocks, pictures and wood items lines the western side of the plaza.

On the plaza's eastern flank is the **Museo Nacional** (National Museum) ① *C 17, Av Central-2, entrance on plaza is often locked, T2257-1433, www.museocostarica. go.cr, Tue-Fri 0830-1630, Sat, Sun and holidays 0900-1630, US$4,* housed in the converted barracks of the Bellavista Fortress which still shows the bullet scars of battle from the 1948 civil war, a mixed bag of displays looks at indigenous life pre-colonization and the introduction of Catholicism in Costa Rica, with a few rooms given over to art and lifestyle in the colonial era. Downstairs, a small exhibition leads through the quarters and prison cells of the fortress explaining events leading up to the civil war. Signs are mainly in Spanish and exhibits are changed from time to time. The exhibition rooms border a pleasant courtyard overlooking the city and the Plaza de la Democracia below.

One block north is the **Palacio Nacional** ① *C 17, Av Central-2, Mon-Fri from 1600, ID required,* where the Legislative Assembly sits. Catch up on government business and brush up your Spanish at the same time while listening in on sessions.

Around Parque Nacional

The Parque Nacional covers a couple of blocks one block north of the Palacio Nacional. It's an extensive parkland densely packed with trees and palms where secretive couples hide in the shade and anyone with a bit of time to kill can be found adding to the laid-back atmosphere. Overseeing all the activity is the **Monumento Nacional** with its grandiloquent statue representing the five Central American republics ousting the North American filibuster William Walker and the abolition of slavery in Central America. A statue of national hero **Juan Santamaría** donated by the Sandinista Government of Nicaragua stands in the southwest corner of the park.

Churches

San José has a good variety of churches drawing inspiration from many sources. But lovers of ecclesiastic architecture often leave San José a little disappointed.

Frustration knocks with locked doors: churches often only open on service days and then possibly only for a few hours. In Barrio México, for example, northeast of the centre, the large dome of a church stands high above the surrounding buildings. The fine masonry work and detail look more suited to a city cathedral, but in this quiet, run-down corner of town north of the Coca-Cola terminal, the church remains locked, bolted and beyond the eyes of visitors and worshippers alike.

Throughout the Central Valley spectacular churches dominate central plazas not only by their sheer size but also in their attention to detail. They stand as monuments to more than just the faith of the region. Many of the churches must have been way beyond the financial means of the small villages and it is difficult to imagine that faith alone fuelled their construction. There must have also been a fair amount of motivating community rivalry.

Whatever the case, the lover of fine architecture, churches in particular, will have more joy renting a car and drifting through the towns of the Central Valley – take a journey out to San Ramón, San Rafael de Heredia, San Isidro or head south to the Route of the Saints – than in San José itself.

On the north side of the park, the **Biblioteca Nacional** (National Library) ① *Av 3, C 15, Mon-Fri, 0800-1830, open to non-nationals with ID,* hides behind a starkly modern exterior. In addition to several current periodicals, the archives hold national newspapers dating back to 1833. At the northwestern corner of the park in the old liquor factory is the **Museo de Arte y Diseño Contemporaneo** (Museum of Contemporary Art and Design) ① *Av 3, C 15, T2257-9370, www.madc.ac.cr, Mon-Sat 1030-1730, closed Sun, US$1, free Mon,* along with the offices of the Ministry of Culture. There are changing displays with works by national artists.

Northeast of Parque Nacional

If you like trains, head for the former **Museo Nacional de Ferrocarril** (National Railway Museum) in the old Atlantic Railway station behind the library. The station was the final stop of the San José to Limón line that linked the Central Valley to the Caribbean lowlands. When the trains stopped running in 1990, the station quickly fell into disrepair. There's still no official train museum, but you can have a look around. Taking its place is the **Museo de Formas, Espacios y Sonidos** (Museum of Forms, Space and Sounds) ① *Av 3, C 21, T223 4173, www.musarco.go.cr, Tue-Fri 0930-1500.* The old restored stagecoaches contain interactive displays and a photographic history of the train line along with a random assortment memorabilia.

A little further out of town **Museo Dr Rafael Angel Calderón Guardia** ① *Av 11, C 25, T2221-1239, musecal@racsa.co.cr, Mon-Sat 0900-1700, US$0.50,* has displays on the life of the reformist president who laid the foundations for the Costa Rican welfare state in the early 1940s. Set in the old Calderón mansion, there are also temporary art exhibitions and a small library.

Around Parque España and Parque Morazán

From Parque Nacional heading west down Avenida 3 is the southern side of **Parque España**, a refreshingly verdant square with an air of calm. On Sunday there is normally an outdoor market in the square. Directly north of the square is the INS or Instituto Nacional de Seguros which houses on the top floor the **Museo de Jade Fidel Tristan** ① *Av 7, C 9-11, 11th floor of INS building, T2287-6034, Mon-Fri 0830-1530, Sat 0900-1300, closed Sun, US$2.* In addition to the largest collection of jade carvings in the Americas with literally hundreds of smoothly fashioned pieces, there are displays of pre-Columbian art, pottery and sculpture. Renovated in 2000, the museum demonstrates the significance of jade to the Maya and Aztec and provides an excellent view over the city.

From Parque España you can clearly see the ornate **Casa Amarilla** to the northeast which holds Costa Rica's Ministry of Foreign Affairs and, reportedly, a piece of the Berlin Wall. The building is not, however, open to the public. To the west, the simple yet bizarre structure of the **Edificio Metálico**, designed in Belgium and shipped from France, is still a school today (as it was in the 1890s when first welded together).

Crossing Calle 9 leads west to **Parque Morazán** which is overshadowed by the 17 or so storeys of the Aurola Holiday Inn (with excellent views from the top floor casino). The park's namesake General Francisco Morazán briefly tried to reunite Central America using Costa Rica as the military base in 1842 – the General was executed shortly after in the Parque Central. The largest of the green spots in the centre, the park is remarkably quiet for most of the day and an ideal spot to rest and meet up after exploring the (relatively uninspiring) gift shops on the south and west side of the park.

Behind the two parks the historic districts or *barrios* of **Amón** and **Otoya** lead to the north. This was once the residential district of the coffee elite and wealthier classes and single storey architecture of the colonial period abounds with low slung eaves shading broad balconies. Today the tiled courtyards, lush private gardens and patios are enjoyed by guests, diners and employees of hotels, restaurants and some of the more style-conscious embassies who stepped in with renovation plans just in time to stop the complete destruction of the district. Some of the most accessible examples are the **Alianza Francesa** building on the corner of Avenida 7 and Calle 5, which has a fine exterior, **Hotel Britannia** on Calle 3 and Avenida 11 and the beautifully restored **Hotel Alóki** on Calle 13, Avenida 9-11. Other treasures can be found in the area, including **El Castillo** on Avenida 11 and Calle 3 where the defensive turrets and religious themes merge in the home of a former bishop. Along Avenida 9 between Calles 3 and 7 the walls lining the street are decorated with colourful ceramic tiles depicting rural scenes.

At the limit of comfortable walking distance is the **Parque Zoológico Simón Bolívar** ① *Av 11, C 7, go north on C 7 until you reach Av 11, Mon-Fri 0900-1600, Sat-Sun 0900-1700, US$3, donations welcome,* where you can see many of Costa Rica's mammals, including monkeys, big cats and tapirs as well as caiman and several species of birds. The zoo is popular especially at weekends with young *Josefino* families. While the zoo is not the best kept place in the world, as part of Costa Rica's overall conservation and awareness strategy it plays an important role. Conditions are improving slowly.

Around Parque Central

Parque Central is a couple of blocks west of the Plaza de la Cultura and distinctive for the grandiose but rather ugly bandstand in the centre bordered by Avenida 2 and Calle Central. There is little to endear you to the plaza, but the park is a major thoroughfare of the city, and makes for good people-watching. Even if there is no street café you can

➡ **San José maps**
1 San José overview, page 68
2 San José, page 72
3 San José centre, page 80

N

100 metres
100 yards

Sleeping 🛏
Aurola **4** *B4*
Balmoral **5** *C4*
Best Western
  Downtown **7** *A2*
Bienvenido **8** *B1*
Boruca **9** *B1*
Boston **10** *D3*
Britannia **11** *A4*
Capital **12** *B2*
Casa Ridgeway **13** *D6*
Cinco Hormigas
  Rojas **14** *A6*
Clarion Amón
  Plaza **6** *A4*
Cocori **15** *B1*
Compostela **17** *B2*
Costa Rica Morazán **19** *C4*
Del Bulevar **20** *C3*
Del Rey **21** *C5*
Diana's Inn **22** *B4*
Diplomat **23** *C2*
Don Carlos **24** *A5*
Doña Inés **25** *D5*
Doral **26** *C2*
Dunn Inn **2** *A4*
Europa **29** *B3*
Fleur de Lys **30** *D5*
Fortuna **31** *D2*
Gran Hotel
  Centroamericano **32** *C2*
Gran Hotel Costa
  Rica **33** *C3*
Gran Imperial **34** *B2*
Hemingway Inn **35** *A5*
Hostal Pangea **40** *A4*
Joluva Guesthouse **38** *A4*
Kabata Hostel **3** *A5*
Kekoldi **39** *A4*
La Posada de Don
  Tobías **41** *A1*

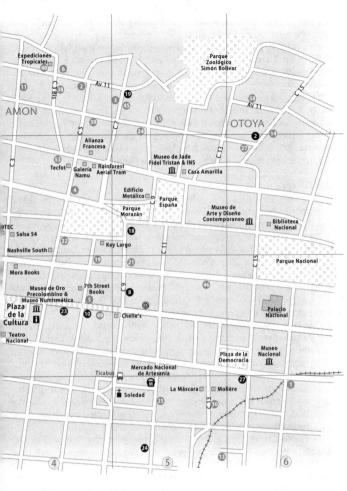

Marlyn **42** *A2*
Nuevo Alameda **43** *B1*
Nuevo Central **44** *B2*
Nuevo Johnson **37** *C2*
Pensión de la Cuesta **46** *C5*
Pensión Otoya **47** *B3*
Plaza **48** *C2*
Posada de la Museo **1** *D6*
Presidente **49** *C4*
Príncipe **50** *D3*
Realto **51** *B3*
Rincón de San José **27** *B6*

Santo Tomás **53** *B4*
Talamanca **55** *C1*
Tranquilo
  Backpackers **45** *A5*
Vesuvio **58** *A6*

Eating 🍴
Bakea **19** *A5*
Café Bohemia **9** *C3*
Café Mundo **2** *B6*
Café Parisienne **3** *C3*
Churrería Manolo **6** *C3*

El Balcón de Europa **8** *C5*
Gran Diamente **12** *B2*
La Puriscaleña **5** *B3*
La Vasconia **20** *B3*
Musmanni **13** *C3*
News Café **10** *C4*
Nuestra Tierra **27** *D6*
Pio Pio **16** *C2*
Pollo a la Leña **21** *B3*
Soda El Parque **22** *D3*
Soda Nini **26** *B3*
Spoon **23** *C4*

Tin Jo **24** *D5*
Vishnu **25** *B3/D3*

normally pick up an ice cream. At weekends, Sundays in particular, this is a popular spot with *Ticos* who seem to slow down to saunter and meander through any temporary stalls and general happenings that may be occurring. To the east is the slightly cramped **Catedrál Metropolitana** visited by Pope John Paul II in 1983 on his first visit to Central America. Recently renovated, the lines are clean and crisp if a little uninspiring. Gone are the polluting sooty candles replaced instead with a neat line of electric ones.

North of the plaza on Avenida 2 is the **Teatro Melico Salazar** ① *see press for details or call T2257-6005,* which, after the Teatro Nacional, is Costa Rica's most important theatre and the newly opened **Café La Bohemia** tempting you with more coffee, cakes and a menu that explains the historic scenes depicted on the ceiling in black and white photographs. Performances and shows at the Melico have a broader appeal ranging from pop and jazz concerts through to ballet and orchestral works.

Western Central

Within the boundaries of the central walking district, the pedestrianized Avenida Central heads west for a few blocks towards the **Banco Central**. Most banks have a branch close to the area and there are several ATMs nearby. Bustling with the busy chaos of people rushing around, the shops, banks and department stores make this one of the main arteries of the city. Three blocks west of the Plaza Cultura, a right up Calle 2 leads to the elegant façade of the **Correo Central** (Central Post Office). Understated and often overlooked, the building seems perfectly balanced in proportion and setting. Inside, the halls of postboxes are a bit daunting, but upstairs is the interesting **Museo Postal** (Post Museum), **Telegráfico Filatélico de Costa Rica** ① *C 2, Av 1-3, T2223-9766, Mon-Fri 0800-1630, free.* The **Café Teando** is a splendid café that retains some period pieces and serves excellent coffee and cakes.

A few blocks further west along Avenida 1 bustling heart of the city comes to the fore with the **Mercado Central** taking up a whole block bordered by Avenida Central-1 and Calles 6-8. The covered market is a noisy, colourful and in places rather smelly affair selling everything from cheese, spices, fruit, vegetables, dried and fresh flowers through to leather sandals, saddles, bridles and simple tourist gifts. The honey is particularly recommended and if you're looking to set up a business you can buy one of the small boxes used by the boot boys to hold polish and brushes and get shining some shoes. Restaurants and juice bars serve good, cheap food and drinks which is generally cleanly prepared with a turnover so quick it doesn't have time to go off. Go for the ones with lots of customers.

Parque Braulio Carrillo also known as 'Parque La Merced' borders Avenida 2 sharing Calle 12 with **La Merced Church**. Eclectic-Gothic in style the church looks tired, weary and confused but there is enough detail to keep the eye amused for a few minutes. On the roof, ornate ironwork decoration contrasts disappointingly with iron panelling of the corrugated variety. Entering from the north, the nave appears fresh and airy, yet from the west the church seems cramped and cluttered. Built and rebuilt over a period of 80 years that ended in 1894, the current round of renovations should see the church back to its former glory. On the western side of the Parque is vast San Juan de Dios Hospital.

Paseo Colón and west of the centre

West of town the six-lane Paseo Colón feeds and drains the city centre of traffic. The pavements are lined with offices, car rental companies, garages, restaurants, fast-food outlets and the odd hotel and supermarket. It's a chaotic road that is daunting to the pedestrian and motorist alike and you will probably travel along it at least once while in San José. If you need to walk, there are several pedestrian bridges spanning the road.

At the western end of Paseo Colón is **Parque Sabana**. Until the middle of the 20th century the area was the city's airport but the transformation has created a vast parkland of trees and greenery just 30 minutes' walk or a short bus ride from central San José. On the western side is the **Estadio Nacional** (National Stadium) where the national football team plays in front of capacity crowds of 20,000, valiantly attempting to qualify for the finals of the World Cup after making it to the last two championships. There's a running track, sports centre with a swimming pool and a lake but most will travel out this far for the **Museo de Arte Costarricense** (Museum of Costa Rican Art) ① *C 40, Paseo Colón and Av 2, walk west down Paseo Colón for a 30-min walk, T2222-7155, Tue-Sun 1000-1600, US$5, US$3 for students, free on Sun, buses for Sabana Cementerio leave from Av 2,* in the old terminal building. There's a small but interesting collection of 19th- and 20th-century art and sculpture by national and international artists forming the most representative collection of Costa Rican contemporary art exhibited chronologically and according to themes and ideas. The collection changes every two years with a couple of rooms for temporary exhibits. The pleasant sculpture garden demonstrates pieces by Franciso Zúñiga (1912-1998) and Hernán González.

At the southwestern corner is the **Museo de Ciencias Naturales** ① *Colegio La Salle, T2232-1306, Mon-Sat 0800-1630, Sun 0900-1700, US$2, buses marked Sabana Estadio run close to the museum, ask the driver where to get out for Colegio La Salle,* which has a huge collection of mounted, stuffed and stored animals which should help you recognize animals when you're out in the wild.

Outside the centre

A few places of interest exist just beyond the realm of a comfortable walk. If you like to walk then striking out is not a problem, but taking a cab will leave you with enough energy to explore.

North of centre

The Disneyesque façade of the **Centro Costarricense de Ciencias y Cultura** (Costa Rican Centre of Science and Culture) ① *at the northern end of C 4 beyond Av 9, T2258-4929, www.museocr.com, Tue-Fri 0800-1630, Sat-Sun 0900-1700, US$2, US$1.30 children, US$2.50 and US$1.75 at weekends, join C 4 and head north, or catch a cab, see La Nación newspaper for performances and exhibits,* hides a fascinating mix of art, history, study and fun. Turrets and fluttering banners entice you towards the cells, wings and corridors of the former penitentiary. Photographs show the extent of the restoration work that began in 1992. The **Museo de Niños** (Children's Museum) is, judging by the amount of noise at least, a lot of fun with games and activities using up a couple of wings. The **Galería Nacional** (National Gallery) uses the vaulted ceilings and stark spaces to display a mix of permanent and temporary exhibitions. This leads to the **Biblioteca Carlos Luis Sáenz** (Carlos Luis Sáenz Library) where a few cells and prisoner accounts report conditions of life in the prison. Completing the eclectic mix, the **Auditorio Nacional** is a performance venue with plays, occasional orchestral performances and other events. There's lots to do and explore in this carefully restored building, and if the weather is good, you can sit outside on the lawns.

In **Barrio Tournón**, north of the River Torres, is the **Centro Commercial El Pueblo** shopping centre. The warren of paths and alleyways set out like a small colonial village comes alive at night. A wide variety of souvenir shops sells everything from colonial art, delicate wood carvings, fine ceramics and T-shirts. Although prices overall are higher than shops in the downtown area, you won't find so many shops in the same place anywhere else in the city. As night falls, the place comes alive as cafés, restaurants and bars open and the finery of San José decants here from the centre. As with the shops, some of the best restaurants in the city are in El Pueblo, but you can also just take a snack or a drink. Nightclubs will keep the dawnraiders going until the early hours. Some shops and restaurants open from mid-morning, most from mid-afternoon. Nightclubs stay open until early morning. You can walk to El Pueblo, some 20 minutes from the centre. A taxi (strongly advised at night) will cost around US$2 from central San José; agree fare beforehand.

Also in Barrio Tournón, one block east and south of El Pueblo, is **Spirogyra** ① *T2222-2937, www.butterflygardencr.com, daily 0800-1600 (last tour around 1500), US$6 adults, US$3 children*. This butterfly farm, some 20 minutes' walk from central San José, is in one of the last truly natural green areas of the city. The experience consists of a short video followed by a 45-minute guided tour of the exuberant botanical garden which is home to the 20 or so species of butterfly bred for export. Several species of hummingbird also visit the gardens. After the tour, you are welcome to stay as long as you like poking around looking under leaves for hatching larvae and watching the butterflies feed. There is a small café at the garden. If you're walking, head north out of the city along Calle 3, turning right at Highway 108 passing Hotel Villa Tournón, turn right at the main road opposite El Pueblo; a taxi from downtown San José is around US$2.

South of centre
Close to the centre, but not easily included within a walking route is the delightful **Iglesia Soledad** (Soledad Church). Often overlooked, the yellow church sits slightly elevated above the traffic, enjoying a rare spot of calm and solitude.

Eastern districts and San Pedro
Beyond the Museo Nacional, Avenida Central heads east through the residential districts of **Los Yoses** and **La California** to **San Pedro** and the vast campus of the University of Costa Rica. Los Yoses and La California achieve the magical act of being calm residential areas just a few blocks from the city centre. Hardly surprising, then, that this is home for some of the wealthier residents of the city, as well as some comfortable hotels and a few embassies.

Crossing the city's ring road leads to San Pedro, and the **University of Costa Rica (UCR)**. As you'd expect it's lively with student life, cafés, bookstores and a general feel of vitality. While you're here visit the **Museo de Entomología** (Insect Museum) ① *T2207-5647, Mon-Fri, 1300-1700, US$3, buses travel from Av 2 out to San Pedro, ask the driver to drop you at the C Central in San Pedro from where you can walk north a couple of blocks. A taxi out to San Pedro will cost around US$3.* Located, rather bizarrely, in the basement of the **Artes Musicales** (School of Music) there are hundreds of insects to gawp at so you'll be familiar with the thing climbing up your arm on the jungle treks.

Escazú and western suburbs
Outside the western boundaries of the city, the fashionable suburb of Escazú made a break for independence several years ago. Away from the chaotic traffic and noise of the city, it slowly creeps up the hills to the south and has the charm and feel of a small village.

Hotels and restaurants make the most of the setting on the lower slopes affording spectacular views across the Central Valley. Many expats living in Costa Rica would not dream of spending a night in the capital, choosing instead to stay in Escazú, carrying out their business with a series of 20-minute commutes by bus or taxi and keeping the capital's contamination to a minimum. First-time visitors to Costa Rica should spend at least some time in the capital but if you're returning, you'll know that Escazú has much to offer.

In keeping with the Central Valley way of things, each of the three smaller towns that make up the Escazú experience – **San Rafael**, **San Miguel** and further up the hill **San Antonio** – has a church. Up in San Antonio de Escazú the bustle of the lower slopes has gone, and just enough adobe houses exist around the central plaza to create the effect of a village settlement. Facing the square, the modest church of San Antonio de Escazú has a beautiful setting overlooking the valley of San José, even if the bright green of the church is a little painful on the eye against the rusty-browns and natural-greens of the village.

A couple of things draw Escazú out of itself. **Día del Boyero** (Day of the Oxcart Driver), on the second Sunday of March, is one of the country's largest festivals. It fills the sleepy streets with colourful oxcarts accompanied by music on *marimbas* (a kind of xylophone) and dancers in traditional dress. Another is the **wooden carvings** of Barry Biesanz ① *T2289-4337, www.biesanz.com*. Using a mix of dark and light woods, Biesanz has created a distinctive style. The fine bowls are beautifully simple in shape and form with a lightness and fineness that seems almost unnatural. The boxes – be they humidors, jewellery boxes or simply what Barry calls for "small things" – are exquisite. You don't have to trek up to the workshop to buy a Biesanz piece, they are available in good souvenir shops in San José and in the El Pueblo commercial centre.

Easy trips from San José

There are many tour operators in San José (see page 105) that offer all-inclusive trips in the city, the surrounding area and throughout the country. Ranging in length from half a day to two or three days, here is a summary of the general offerings. Prices and details are intended to give an idea of cost and options, start and duration times are approximate. It is possible to do most of the activities independently by public transport or using a private vehicle. Few, however, are possible within the same time frames if travelling by public transport. As always with set tours, the disadvantage is a fairly strictly adhered-to itinerary.

San José city tour ① *US$28, half day, am and pm, 4 hrs*. The aim is to give you an overview of the city by exploring some of the urban areas, museums and architectural and historical sites of San José by bus, but itineraries vary. Make sure that anything you want to see is included. The core elements normally include a drive through Sabana Park, a walking tour of the historic Teatro Nacional (National Theatre), a visit to the Museo Nacional (National Museum), the Corte Suprema (Supreme Court), and the Universidad de Costa Rica (University) in San Pedro. Tours often end with a stop in Moravia to pick up souvenirs from the many craft shops in the northeastern suburb.

Pueblo Antiguo ① *US$45, day or night tour, 0900 or 1700 start, 3 hrs. Price includes entrance ticket, dinner and show*. A chance to appreciate the variety and history of Costa Rica all in one place. Pueblo Antiguo is not actually an old town, but a cultural amusement park which uses actors and architecture to recreate the customs and traditions found throughout Costa Rica. Both trips include shows; the night trip includes dinner.

Irazú Volcano ① *US$36, 0830 start, 5 hrs. Take: sweater, binoculars and comfortable shoes. See page 147*. Trips climb to the windy and often cloudy summit of Irazú volcano for a view of the massive crater. On a clear day you can see both the Atlantic and Pacific oceans. After visiting the volcano, trips visit the old capital of Cartago stopping at the ruins of the old church and the pilgrimage Basilica of the Virgen de los Angeles.

Lankester Gardens and Orosi Valley ① *US$42, less without lunch, morning start, 6 hrs. Take: sweater, binoculars, walking shoes and raincoat. See page 147.* This trip heads southeast of San José to Lankester Botanical Gardens, followed by a ride through the understated beauty of the Orosi Valley, around the lake created by the Cachi Dam. It includes lunch at a lakeside restaurant, a visit to the country's oldest colonial church and to the carving workshop of the Dreamer's House.

Irazú/Orosi/Lankester Gardens ① *US$58, 0830 start, 9 hrs. Take: sweater, binoculars, comfortable shoes and raincoat.* Combines the Irazú Volcano and the Lankester Gardens and Orosi Valley tours. Makes for an impressive combination of scenery, history and botany.

Poás Volcano National Park ① *US$36, 0830 start, 5hrs. Take: sweater, binoculars, comfortable shoes and raincoat. See page 124.* Tours begin with a pleasant drive through the lush coffee plantations and flower farms of the northern Central Valley to Poás Volcano, one of the world's largest geysers. The volcano is active, but completely safe for viewing. Trips usually include a short hike in Poás National Park.

Grecia and Sarchí (Oxcart factory) Town ① *US$29, 1100 start, 5 hrs. Take: sweater, binoculars and comfortable shoes. See page 125.* Heading north, the trip drives through coffee and sugar cane plantations before arriving at Grecia, famous for its metal church, and then moving on to the craft factories of Sarchí where the colourful oxcarts that are almost a national symbol are built and decorated.

Poás Volcano/Grecia/Sarchí ① *US$68, slightly less without lunch, start 0830, 8 hrs. Take: sweater, comfortable walking shoes and raincoat.* Combines a trip to Poás Volcano National Park with a visit to Grecia and Sarchí.

Carara National Park ① *US$76, 0800 start, 9 hrs. Take: sun hat, suntan lotion, walking shoes, swimsuit and towel and binoculars. See page 284.* A short ride west for a couple of hours, the reserve is the best day trip to the rainforest from the capital.

Braulio Carrillo National Park ① *US$36, 0715 start, 4 hrs. Take: comfortable walking shoes, sweater, raincoat and binoculars. See page 139.* A trip over the continental divide and through the Zurquí Tunnel is followed by a walk through the Braulio Carrillo National Park, one of many important rainforest reserves in Costa Rica. Some companies tag on another half-day activity such as a river trip in Sarapiquí, or a ride on the aerial tram.

Rainforest aerial tram ① *US$84, 0800 start, 6 hrs. Take: light clothing and shoes, raincoat, insect repellent and binoculars. See page 140.* Ingenious in the extreme, the Rainforest aerial tram on the borders of Braulio Carrillo National Park has spawned many imitations but this is the original.

Butterfly farm and coffee plantation tours ① *US$55-80, 0800 start, 5-8 hrs. Take: comfortable walking outfit.* Visit two of Costa Rica's typical exports in one. Trips round coffee plantations are popular, and Café Britt has developed the experience into an art form. Butterfly farms, in particular Costa Rica's largest La Gúacima (see page 122), and the smaller but no less enjoyable Spirogyra both export butterflies throughout the world. The farms offer a fascinating insight into their life cycle.

The Best of Costa Rica (Four in One) ① *US$82, early morning start, 11 hrs. Take: hat, light jacket, raingear, walking shoes, insect repellent and binoculars.* A pretty quick journey through a cross-section of Costa Rica, heading first for the vast crater of Poás Volcano, before going north to see La Paz waterfall with a drop of some 50 m and spending a couple of hours floating down the Río Sarapiquí before lunch and heading back to San José in a sweeping loop that brings you through Braulio Carrillo on the return to the capital. It is a lot to pack in one day but manageable.

Isla Tortuga – Pacific Island Cruise ① *US$89, 0630 start, 11 hrs. Take: sweater, binoculars, swimsuit, sunblock and towel. See page 263.* Take a boat trip on a luxury yacht visiting the pristine white sand beaches and crystal clear waters of Isla Tortuga off the southern Nicoya Peninsula. Meals include a seafood buffet served on the beach. Good opportunities for snorkelling and seeing marine life.

Whitewater rafting ① *US$ 75-95, 0600 start, 10 hrs. Take: sandals, sunscreen, towel and change of clothing. See page 105.* If you've been whitewater rafting before you won't need convincing; if you haven't, a one-day trip may be just right. One-day trips up to Class III for beginners and beyond for experienced rafters are possible on the Ríos Sarapiquí, Reventazón and Pacuare. The scenery is unbelievable, and all equipment is provided. But it is better to go for longer if you can.

Canopy Tour ① *US$77, 0800 start, 8hrs. Take: outdoor gear, insect repellant and sunblock. Includes lunch.* There are lots of canopy tours in Costa Rica but you can take a day trip from San José, sliding from platform to platform, flying through the trees and stopping off to explore the tropical forest en route.

Arenal Volcano by Night and Tabacón Hot Springs ① *US$99 (1-day), 1035 start, 11hrs; from US$180 (2-day, excluding overnight accommodation). Take: swimsuit, towel, comfortable walking shoes, sweater, insect repellent and binoculars.* A one-day trip that's possible, if tight for time. As one of the most active volcanoes (see page 173) in the Americas, the trip is subject to change depending on volcanic activity. But expect to get a good view of lava flows and possibly hear eruptions and the sound of the lava cascading down the volcano slopes. Later you visit thermal springs, relaxing in the soothing warm waters of the beautifully kitsch baths of Tabacón Resort (see page 173). Often includes dinner and stops along the way, possibly at Sarchí.

Two-day options are also available, incorporating a trip north to Caño Negro Lagoon travelling along the Río Frío by boat and observing the wetland birdlife of the region (see page 176). The second day involves a choice of horse riding, canopy tours or mountain biking.

Tourist train to the Pacific A tourist train runs from San José to the Pacific at weekends, departing from San José Central Station at 0700, travelling to arrive in Caldera at 1115, return journey departs at 1600. Tickets (US$39 return) must be purchased 48 hours in advance. The tours are in refurbished 1940s German wagons. Contact **America Travel**, T2233-3300, www.ticotraintour.com.

Tortuguero Canals ① *US$75-190 (1-, 2- or 3-day options), 0620 start. Take: raincoat, comfortable walking outfit, insect repellent and overnight bags if required. See page 375.* Visiting Tortuguero National Park in one day is a long 13-hour trip, and it is far better to take two or even three days. Only take the one-day option if time is really tight. On Costa Rica's north Caribbean coast, the turtles' nesting beaches and the inland waterways are justifiably revered as a nature paradise. Transport to the area is by bus, then by boat through canals that lead through secondary and primary rainforest. After arriving, trips incorporate quiet journeys by boat through the National Park before heading home. If staying overnight, trips include a beach night walk looking for nesting turtles and an early morning boat trip or hike.

Monteverde in a day? ① *See page 190.* Although logistically possible, a visit to Monteverde in just one day is unlikely to be enjoyable. The road is unpaved, the journey tiring and you'll arrive at midday – not the best time to see birds. Some people and companies would like to see the road paved, giving access to day-trippers. For the time being at least, however, this is not going to happen. Anyway, the place deserves more than just a cursory glance, so with luck Monteverde in a day will continue to be impossible for a long time to come.

⊙ San José listings

Hotel prices

LL over US$200	L US$151-200	AL US$101-150
A US$66-100	B US$46-65	C US$31-45
D US$21-30	E US$12-20	F US$7-11
G US$6 and under		

Restaurant prices

₸₸₸ over US$30   ₸₸ US$15-30   ₸ under US$15

See pages 44-47 for further information.

⊖ Sleeping

Accommodation in San José is as wide and varied as you would expect in the capital, with a surprising number of options in the middle price bracket. Hotels range in size and style from the chains of Holiday Inn and Best Western, to more stylish affairs that build on the history or architecture of a building or district. Lower down the price range there are many good choices before things start to fray a little at the edges. A number of good budget hostels targeting backpackers have greatly improved the options, providing cheap, clean and pleasant budget accommodation. These places will be full of international tourists, have food, internet and a range of other services. Budget accommodation is found dotted around the heart of the city. There are a number of options around the Mercado Central area and the Coca-Cola Bus Terminal. Both areas are lively and enjoyable but safety can be a problem and there have been reports of muggings. Police are aware of the issue and while security has been stepped up, if you choose to stay in here you should take appropriate precautions, including avoiding going out at night alone – both men and women.

Many expats living in Costa Rica prefer to stay in the quiet western suburb of Escazú or Alajuela close to the airport rather than face the congestion of the capital. If you plan to stay in the capital for a week or so, consider the **Apartotel** option, see page 96.

Near the airport
LL Ramada Plaza Herradura, 10 mins from the airport, T2209-9800, www.ramada herradura.com. The 234 elegantly furnished rooms have a/c, cable TV, telephones and the

full range of business services. A couple of restaurants offer Mediterranean dishes at the Tirrenia and relaxed dining at the café restaurant Tropicala. High-tech conference spaces accommodate up to 2000 people.
LL-L Costa Rica Marriott, 10 mins from Juan Santamaría airport, San Antonio de Belén, T2298-0000, www.marriotthotels.com. More an experience than a hotel. Built in the style of a coffee plantation inside and out, every detail of this divine hotel is a joy. Tiled floors and heavy wooden beams lit with ironwork chandeliers fill the reception and set the tone throughout. The 276 fully equipped rooms and suites are spacious and most have balcony views. Four restaurants offer the very best cuisine in settings from formal dining to poolside snacks. A couple of pools, driving range and full health club complete the list. A good choice in the luxury end.
AL Best Western Irazú, La Uruca, next to San José 2000 shopping centre, T2290-9300, www.bestwestern.com. After a major renovation, the modern and dependable Best Western on the outskirts of San José is ideally situated along the Autopista General Cañas. 214 rooms with private bathroom all have a/c, cable TV and telephone, and most with balcony overlooking the pool and nearby hot tub. Children under 12 are free. Full service tour operator in the hotel. There are a couple of restaurants including a Denny's service, a 24-hr casino, and an exercise room and sauna.
AL Hampton Inn, T2436-0000, www. hamptoninn.com. Closest hotel to the airport, handy if you want to get in or get out quickly with the minimum of fuss, made easier with a courtesy pick-up to both terminals (see Alajuela 'Sleeping' for more details).

Central San José *p76, maps p72 and 80*
LL-L Aurola, Av 5, C 5-7, T2523-1000, www. holiday-inn.com. Newly renovated with 200 comfortable rooms varying in size with all the services expected of a Holiday Inn. The 17-storey building is a San José landmark with a spectacular view from the top floor casino.

LL-AL Presidente, Av Central, C 7, T2222-3022, www.hotel-presidente.com. 100 rooms, in crisp, modern decor with cable TV, a/c, telephone, room service, safebox, laundry, business centre, sauna and jacuzzi, popular News bar with international newspapers, café and restaurant (mid-range), Fiesta casino, travel agency and parking. Great sense of style to the place, comfortable without being overbearing.
AL Balmoral, Av Central, C 7-9, T2222-5022, www.balmoral.co.cr. Classic decor, in 112 well appointed rooms with congenial service.
AL Del Rey, Av 1, C 9, T2257-7800, www. hoteldelrey.com. Standing proud on a busy corner in a fine blaze of pink and white the Del Rey is almost part of San José legend, looking as it does like an iced cake. As the advert on Radio 107.5 FM says, "you don't have to stay at the Del Rey, to play at the Del Rey". The large rooms are a bit shabby. What draws the crowds is the lively casino downstairs and the sports bar, a renowned hang-out for professional sex workers. Join the queues like moths to the flame, or avoid at all costs.
AL Gran Hotel Costa Rica, Av 2, C Central, T2221-4000, www.granhotelcr.com. Just over 100 newly remodelled rooms with cable TV, fan, telephone, security box, laundry and room service. Mid-range restaurant and 24-hour street Café Parisienne, open to non-guests, provides some of the best people-watching in the city. A great San José landmark, it is one of the oldest purpose-built hotels in the capital. Lives up to the Grand name without being too ostentatious. Used by John F Kennedy on his visit to Costa Rica in 1963.
A Best Western – Downtown, Av 7, C 6, T2255-4766, www.bestwestern.com. Private bathroom, TV, a/c, telephone, email services, safeboxes, pool, free breakfast and coffee, parking and free airport transfers. Makes good use of a small space with airy rooms, poolside restaurant and helpful staff. An oasis in the city.
A Costa Rica Morazán, C 7, Av 1, T2222-4622, www.costaricamorazan.com. Rooms

vary but all have private bathrooms, TV and telephone. The central location and big casino make it popular. Parking and airport shuttle service.

A Doral, Av 4, C 6-8, T2233-9410, www.hotel doralcr.com. Private bathroom, TV, telephone, ceiling fans, safebox, laundry, restaurant and drinks service. Big rooms with strange colour combinations, some with balconies, and some, on the inside, that are quite dark. Cheaper without breakfast.

A Europa, Av 5, C Central, T2222-1222, www.hoteleuropacr.com. San José's oldest hotel with 67 spacious rooms, fully equipped with TV, telephone, fan and a/c, safebox, bathroom, minibar, tiled bathrooms with bath tub, 24-hr room service and outdoor pool. Crisp decor in a relaxed and professional hotel. The international restaurant is expensive, but the hotel is excellent value.

A-B Plaza, Av Central, C 2-4, T2257-1896, www.hotelplazacr.com. TV, radio, telephone, private bath, room service, laundry services, safeboxes and parking. Central location with pleasant friendly staff. Some rooms a bit cramped and bathrooms could do with a refurb.

B Del Bulevar, Av Central, C Central, T2257-0022. Private bath with tub, telephone, TV, a/c, room service, restaurant and bar. Big rooms, some spacious enough for 4. Friendly and central, with bar overlooking the lively C Central – good place to stop for a couple of quiet drinks.

B Diana's Inn, Av 3, C 5, perched on the southwest corner of Parque Morazán, T2223-6542, dianas@racsa.co.cr. There's a friendly family feel in this central B&B. Former home of a Costa Rica president, it has 7 rooms with TV, private bathroom and hot water.

B Talamanca, Av 2, C 8-10, T2233-5033. Private baths, hot water, a/c or ceiling fan, cable TV, telephone, minibar, restaurant with balcony, fine bar with excellent views on the 9th floor. Quite small rooms but good service. Stylish decor throughout, the reception is decorated with replicas of pre-Columbian Huetares ceramics.

B-C Pensión de la Cuesta, Av 1, C 11-15, T2256-7946, www.pensiondelacuesta.com. A little piece of eccentricity always brightens the day as does the lurid pink canopy over the entrance to the hotel. But inside, this old colonial home has smart and clean rooms and apartments. Shared bath and use of the kitchen.

C Diplomat, C 6, Av Central, T2221-8133. Not much to shout about apart from being very central and reasonably priced. 29 rooms with private bath and hot water.

C Fortuna, Av 6, C 2-4, T2223-5344. Simple rooms and tired decor in a very functional atmosphere. TV, telephone, credit cards accepted.

C Gran Hotel Centroamericano, Av 2, C 6-8, T2221-3362. 45 rooms with private bath, self-service restaurant, telephone and laundry. Clean, small rooms, although some a little dark, very helpful staff.

C-D Nuevo Alameda, Av Central, C 12, T2233-3551, www.hotelnuevoalameda.com. Private bathrooms, some shared, some with TV, a/c which sometimes works. Spacious rooms at the front, and a few cheaper rooms available but you'll have to ask. Popular.

C-E Gran Hotel Imperial, Av 1-Central, C 8, T2222-8463, www.hostelgranimperial.com. Just refurbished with a good selection of rooms of all sizes with shared and private bathrooms. This was the original backpacker hang-out, and after years of neglect is making a much needed push into the light. Good range of services, great location for central San José and bus stations. Breakfast, laundry, internet and social area.

D Bienvenido, C 10, Av 1-3, T2233-2161. One of the best hotels near Coca-Cola bus station. Clean, hot showers, good restaurant, near centre and airport bus.

D Capital, Av 3-5, C 4, T2221-8497. Private bath, hot water, fan, cable TV, laundry service. Pleasant clean rooms, ask for one facing the street for more light. Beautiful selection of 1920s railroad photographs in reception.

D Compostela, Av 3-5, C 6, T2257-1514. Hot water, most rooms with private bath. Rooms a little dark.

D La Posada de Don Tobías, Av 7-9, C 12, T2258-3162, www.costaricasmallhotels.com. Private bath, hot water. Spotless and smart with well lit rooms. Not the best location in San José but ideal for an early morning bus.

D Nuevo Central, Av 3, C 4-6, T2222-3509, www.nuevohotelcentral.com. Telephone, private bath, hot water, credit cards accepted. Good, efficient and friendly service, but rooms a little on the dark side.

D Nuevo Johnson, Av Central y 2, C 8, T2223-7633, www.hotelnuevojohnson.com. Old-time favourite struggling in the competition of backpacker spots. Private bathrooms, telephones in rooms, bar/restaurant. Friendly and helpful staff. Good value for the price, but get a room with a window. Good choice if you're looking to avoid the backpacker circuit.

D Realto, Av 7-5, C 2, T2221-7456. Basic rooms close to the centre of town, a bit tatty, but some rooms well lit and spotlessly clean.

D-E Cocori, Av 5, C 16, T2233-0081, hotelcocori@racsa.co.cr. Private bathroom, very clean, high standards and helpful owner. Ideal for early buses and just 100 m from Coca-Cola bus terminal.

D-E Principe, Av 6, C Central -2, T2222-7983. Basic rooms, but good for the price especially on the top floor. Most rooms with private bath and hot water. Safe, secure and friendly.

E Boston, Av 8, C Central-2, T2221-0563. TV, private bath, hot water, laundry service, telephone in reception. Friendly service, but nothing makes it stand out. Several cheapies nearby if you're having no luck.

E Marlyn, C 4, Av 7-9, T2233-3212. Rooms are small and a bit dark. Hot showers, good security, will store luggage, parking for motorcycles (just). Some rooms with bath.

E Musoc, Av 1-3, C 16, big pink building at the eastern entrance to the Coca-Cola terminal, T2222-9437. Private bath, hot water, well maintained. Well run even if the rooms are a little cramped. Perfect for early morning buses, or if you arrive in the city late.

E-F Pensión Otoya, C 1, Av 3-5, T2221-3925. Close to the centre, clean, friendly and popular. Hot water throughout and some rooms with private bath. Luggage store, telephone, internet access, English spoken.

G Boruca, Av 1-3, C 14, T2223-0016. Basic place with simple rooms, shared bathroom, a bit dark, but the owner is friendly and helpful.

Paseo Colón and west of the centre
p82, maps p72 and 80

The business end of town, handy for getting out of town quickly.

L-AL Grano de Oro, C 30, Av 2-4, T2255-3322, www.hotelgranodeoro.com. Exquisite, lavish and warmly welcoming, this hotel enjoys the finest colonial architecture of an early 20th-century stately mansion with absolute luxury in a wide range of rooms. 40 rooms and suites, each uniquely decorated, all provide complete comfort. The wrought ironwork of the beds set off rooms with the usual comforts of cable TV, jacuzzi or sundeck spa, minibar and ceiling fan. A luxuriant garden patio is full of heliconias, orchids and palms. The excellent restaurant offers differing moods in the dining room, the sunroom or out on the tropical patio where the quiet murmur of conversation continues amid top-class, attentive service.

AL Rosa del Paseo, Paseo Colón, C 28-30, T2257-3225, www.rosadelpaseo.com. A boutique hotel close to the centre of town. Private bath with tub, cable TV and tropical breakfast. A Victorian colonial home until 1992, the refurbished house has been beautifully restored incorporating original features while extending the hotel to include a small, quiet landscaped courtyard. Great building.

A-B CACTS, C 28-30, Av 3 bis No 2845, T2221-2928, www.hotelcacts.com. Nothing terribly original about the decor but 25 spotlessly clean, bright rooms equipped with private bath, ceiling fans, telephone and cable TV. A little out from the centre of town, the hotel is quiet and safe. The staff can arrange tours and airport pick-ups. Discounts for students, families and groups. Internet access, free luggage storage, German, English and Spanish spoken. All this and breakfast included.

B-C Petit Victoria, Av 2, C 28, 100 m south from Pizza Hut on Paseo Colón, T2221-6372. Private bath, cable TV, parking, laundry service, car rental, bar and restaurant, room service, includes breakfast. Charming colonial house, now fully restored. Rooms are smartly decorated to provide service without spoiling the atmosphere. The covered patio restaurant serves traditional food, and welcomes non-guests for *almuerzo*. Steeped in tradition, the Petit Victoria was the former family home of Oscar Arias Sánchez, former President and Nobel Peace prize winner and was used as campaign HQ for his victorious presidential elections in the 1980s. English and French spoken.

D JC Friends Hostel, C 34 y Av 3, Casa Esquinera, Paseo Colón. Blue painted and recently established, JC is owned by an extremely well travelled *Tico* who has bucketloads of local information to impart. Communal kitchen, lockers, a/c and internet access. Tuasa bus stops opposite. Also have a hostal in Tamarindo.

D-E Gaudy's, Av 5, C 36-38, No 3636, T2258-2937, www.backpacker.co.cr. Friendly option providing dormitories and double rooms. Kitchen facilities, free internet, Wi-Fi zone and coffee. Has an intimacy that many of the larger backpacking places lack.

E Galileo Backpackers' Hostel, 100 m east of SodaTapia (see Eating), T2248-2094. Friendly place and faces, charming property with dorm beds, free internet. Good, quiet spot.

Around Parque España and Parque Morazán *p83, maps p72 and 80*

This region around Barrios Amón and Otoya is home to historic houses and comfortable hotels – prices reflect the quality of hotels and the history of the barrio.

L Clarion Hotel Amón Plaza, Av 11, C 3 bis, T2523-4614, www.hotelamonplaza.com. A large 87-room hotel with all the comforts for the modern business traveller in the stylish district of barrio Amón. A 24-hr bar, conference centre, Wi-Fi, gym and sauna. Lavish in the extreme: you could be anywhere – it just so happens you're in San José.

L-AL Britannia, Av 11, C 3, T2223-6667, US toll free T1-800-263-2618, www.hotel britanniacostarica.com. A historic landmark, in a mansion dating back to the days of the coffee boom. After careful restoration the hotel keeps its character while providing first-class service. Rooms offer all expected comforts with ceiling fans and large tiled bathrooms. The traditional courtyard reception continues downstairs to the converted wine cellar, now a restaurant. A city landmark, with a range of packages.

L-AL D'Raya Vida, Av 11, C 15, T2223-4168, www.rayavida.com. An upmarket B&B/boutique hotel option with just 4 fine, individually decorated rooms. The house has several moods, and includes a lounge (with baby grand piano) and a small patio complete with fountain and pewter reliefs, all finished off with original artwork. Discounts for longer stays.

L-AL Santo Tomás, Av 7, C 3-5, T2255-0448, www.hotelsantotomas.com. In a district of good-quality hotels, the cavernous rooms of this turn-of-the-century coffee plantation home stand out. Relaxed and professional service in a homely atmosphere, each of the 20 rooms has queen-size beds, private bath, cable TV and telephone. The garden patio is relaxing and a charming spot for your tropical breakfast, evening drinks and cocktails and now includes a small pool.

AL-A Don Carlos, C 9, Av 7-9, T2221-6707, www.doncarloshotel.com. A family-run hotel with 33 big rooms each with private bath, cable TV, room safes and secure parking. Littered with art throughout, the pre-Columbian restaurant and cocktail lounge is overlooked by masks and sculptures. The best piece is the exquisite 272 hand-painted tile mural of San José in the early 1900s created by Mario Arroyabe.

A Castillo, Av 9, C 9, T2221-5141, www.hotel castillo.biz. Comfortable, restored mansion house in the Otoya district of town. All rooms have bathroom, TV, and many have good views looking out across the city. Breakfast served in pleasant garden and there's a pool table to while away the afternoons. Discounts for longer stays.

A Kekoldi, Av 9, C 5-7, T2248-0804, www.kekoldi.com. An absolutely delightful hotel designed and elaborately decorated by English artist Helen Eltis with fresh, breezy use of pastels. Drapes and trompe i'oeil windows painted in corners and on walls throughout the 10 rooms, each with private bathroom and telephone. German management and English spoken. Linked to Kekoldi Beach Hotel El Dorado Mojado in Manuel Antonio.

A Rincón de San José, Av 9, C 13-5, T2221-9702, www.hotelrincondesanjose.com. Hidden behind a rather austere looking exterior is a quaint B&B of 42 rooms with hardwood floors and a stylish tropical garden patio bar. All rooms have private bath, ceiling fans, TV and telephone, with connecting rooms available for families. English and German spoken, and continental breakfast included.

A-B Dunn Inn, Av 11, C 5, T2222-3232, www.hoteldunninn.com. Rooms and suites use wood panelling in some rooms to retain a sense of atmosphere in this late 19th-century house. Wall-to-wall carpets, cable TV, private bath, ceiling fan and telephone add to the comfort in the rooms. La Palm restaurant and bar offers international food with a Peruvian flair.

B Cinco Hormigas Rojas, C15, Av 9-11 bis, T2257-8581, www.cincohormigasrojas.com. A serene B&B in the heart of Otoya with 6 charming and comfortable rooms. Filled with pictures by the artist owner Mayra Guell. Wonderful eccentricity in an increasingly predictable world.

B Hemingway Inn, Av 9, C 9, T2221-1804, www.hemingwayinn.com. No great surprise that the B&B is filled with photographs and references to the author. 17 simply decorated rooms in a house full of twisting corridors and character. The rooms, named after authors, vary greatly in size so ask for a big one. Each room has private bath and cable TV. There is a small patio restaurant for breakfast and access to a kitchen if you want to prepare a meal yourself. Discounts for weekly and monthly rates. English spoken.

B Vesuvio, Av 11, C 13-15, T2221-7586, www.hotelvesuvio.com. Clean, efficient, no great frills for the area, but good, helpful service. 20 simple rooms with TV, private bath, hot water and ceiling fan. Good, popular mid-range Italian, seafood and international patio restaurant.

B-C Joluva Guesthouse, Av 9-11, C 3 bis, T2223-7961, www.joluva.com. A relaxing and welcoming gay-friendly hotel. Rooms vary greatly in size but all are clean and well looked after with cable TV and many with private bathroom. Continental breakfast, served on a quiet patio, included. Exclusive tours and information available for guests.

C-D Hostel Pangea, Av 11, C 3 bis, T2221-1992, www.hostelpangea.com. Friendly, clean spot, use of kitchen. Good local information, with free coffee, internet and breakfast, good spot and TV/lounge room with big TV. Claims to have the only rooftop bar in San José.

C-D Tranquilo Backpackers, C 7, Av 9-11, T2223-3189, www.tranquilobackpackers.com. Dormitory accommodation in a relaxed atmosphere – slightly more chilled than Pangea. Usual mix of services including internet, movies, bar, pool, small library and good information board. Check them both out and see which suits your style.

D-E Kabata Hostel, C 7, Av 9-11, across the road from **Tranquilo**, T2283-2000, www.kabatahostel.com. Dormitory and private accommodation, internet, use of kitchen. OK, but doesn't have the community spirit of other budget places.

North of centre *p83, maps p72 and 80*
AL Villa Tournón, on Highway 108, 150 m west of El Pueblo shopping village so a little away from the centre, T2233-6622, www. costarica-hotelvillatournon.com. A spacious and modern hotel with excellent service. All the normal treats and comforts, complete with pool and jacuzzi. Also wheelchair access. Eclipse Tours has an office in the hotel.

South of centre *p84, maps p72 and 80*

L-AL Fleur de Lys, C 13, Av 2-6, T2223-1206, www.hotelfleurdelys.com. This restored Victorian mansion is an absolutely delightful place with 31 uniquely decorated rooms, each named after a native Costa Rican flower. Each elegant room has a bathroom, hair dryer, telephone and cable TV. A French restaurant and a bar will mean the only reason you have to leave the hotel is to visit the Museo Nacional one block away.

A Doña Inés, C 11, Av 2-6, round the back of Iglesia de Soledad, T2222-7443, www.donaines.com. A peaceful courtyard makes for a calming influence in this quiet Italian-run hotel. Rooms have TV, private bath, internet and telephone. The hotel is quiet, safe and has parking and 24-hr security.

A-B Posada del Museo, Av 2, C 17, T2258-1027, www.hotelposadadelmuseo.com. Beautiful Victorian house, with very comfortable rooms and a family-run restaurant of the same name in the basement. Great location away from the chaos of the central downtown area.

C-D Green House Hotel, Plaza González Viques, C 11, Av 16 y 18, T2258-0102, www.greenhousehostel.altervista.org. New very clean hostel with both private and shared rooms come with hot water bath, free breakfast, communal kitchen, Wi-Fi, cable TV, not close to the centre but OK otherwise.

C-E Casa Ridgeway, C 15, Av 6 bis (between Av 6-8), T2233-6168, www.amigosparala paz.org. A friendly and quiet spot fitting for a small guest house operated by the Friends' Peace Center. Private and dormitory rooms, along with a communal kitchen and patio dining area add to the sense of calm. Good range of services. Exceptional value for money as well as being a pleasant place to stay.

Eastern districts and San Pedro *p84, map p72*

L-AL Boutique Hotel Jade, Paseo Rubén Darío, C 41, 275 m north of Autos Subarú, Los Yoses, T2224-2455, www.hotelboutiquejade.com. Queen-size beds, cable TV, minibar, telephone, internet, safebox, room service, gym, parking, laundry, car rental, Jurgen's restaurant. A very comfortable hotel in an ideal setting for business or pleasure visits.

A Ara Macao, Barrio California, 50 m south of Pizza Hut, C 25 bis, Av Central-2, Barrio California, T2233-2742, www.aramacao inn.com. A small, quiet hotel with 12 smartly decorated rooms, 8 with kitchenettes. Private bathroom, cable TV and fans in all rooms, with a small patio for relaxing.

A Don Fadrique, Los Yoses, C 37, Av 8, T2224-7583, www.hoteldonfadrique.com. A stylish and family-run hotel with one of the country's finest private collections of artwork adorning the walls it combines the amenities and services of a big hotel with the intimacy and personal attention of a traditional Spanish inn. 20 rooms, each with bathroom and hot water, all with views over the garden or the peaks of the Central Valley.

A-B Costa Rica Guesthouse, Av 6, C 21-23, T2223-7034, www.costa-rica-guesthouse.com. Good mid-range option without being overly precious. Internet, social room, excellent beds and access to all services of Costa Rica Backpackers across the road.

B Aranjuez, C 19, Av 11-13, T2256-1825, www.hotelaranjuez.com. One of the cheaper options up in Barrio Aranjuez, but still filled with style in this 1930s house with a pleasant garden. Shared or private bathroom with hair dryers, splendid breakfast and free coffee all day. Friendly English-speaking staff, clean, well kept, bag store, recommended. Visa accepted.

C-D Costa Rica Backpackers, Av 6, C 21-23, T2221-6191, www.costaricaback packers.com. Top billing (with a pool at these prices), but also with good dormitories and rooms, kitchen and laundry services, free coffee and internet. Parking possible.

C-D Kap's Place, C 19, Av 11-13, T2221-1169, www.kapsplace.com. A popular mid-range option, with tastefully and colourfully decorated rooms.

D-E Casa Yoses, Av 8, C 41, 250 m west from Spoon in Los Yoses, T2234-5486, www.casayoses.com. Popular hostel in restored mansion with relaxing gardens. located near the trendy San Pedro Mall. Breakfast and internet are gratis.

E Hostel Toruma, T2224-4085, Av Central, C 29-31, www.hosteltoruma.com. With links to Hostel Pangea, this crowded former Youth Hostel is waiting for a revamp. Good points include: restaurant, clean rooms, hot water, lockable compartments in each room, safe deposit box, credit cards accepted. The place is going to grow.

Escazú *p84*

LL Alta, heading west out of Escazú on the old road to Santa Ana, T2282-4160, www.thealtahotel.com. This beautiful Mediterranean-style hotel has 23 rooms, each with a balcony overlooking the Central Valley, fully equipped with private bath, cable TV, a/c and telephone. Stylish hardwood furniture sits beautifully on the terracotta-tiled floor and contrasting maize-toned stucco walls. There's a glass-tiled pool in the landscaped gardens and massage and reflexology is also available. Dining is at the stylish La Luz restaurant.

LL-L Camino Real Próspero Fernández Highway, Multiplaza Mall, Escazú, T2208-2100, www.interconti.com. A mega-hotel that impresses from the moment you enter. Costa Rica's nature theme transfers to the rooms which have natural names as opposed to numbers. The rooms are fully equipped and suited for both business leisure. The 3 restaurants serve good international cuisine.

L Posada El Quijote, Bello Horizonte de Escazú, T2289-8401, www.quijote.co.cr. Renovated colonial house with modern art collection and fantastic view over the Central Valley. Private bathrooms with hot water and cable TV in 8 rooms, and 2 new studio apartments. The breakfast is legendary and the garden patio relaxing. 10 mins from centre, 15 mins from airport. Airport pick-up available.

L San Gildar, San Rafael de Escazú, 250 m west of Costa Rica Country Club, T2289-

8843, www.hotelsangildar.com. Each of the 27 rooms overlooks the swimming pool and lush tropical gardens. The rooms have private bath, television and telephone. The Terraza del Sol restaurant which also overlooks the garden and pool has excellent service and the size of the hotel makes it a popular choice.

AL La Casa de las Tías, 100 m south of Centro Comercial El Cruce, San Rafael de Escazú, T2289-5517, www.hotels.co.cr/casatias.html. 5 rooms in a large Victorian-style house, decorated with paintings from throughout Latin America. Price includes breakfast, each room has private bath and fan. Airport pick-up available.

A Pico Blanco Inn, San Antonio de Escazú some 3 km up in the hills, T2228-1908, www.hotelpicoblanco.com. All 20 rooms have balconies and great views of the Central Valley. Also has a couple of self-contained cottages and a pool. Airport pick-up can be requested which will make finding the place easier. Price includes breakfast. Recommended.

A-B Costa Verde Inn, 300 m south of the cemetery, T2228-4080, www.costaverdeinn.com. A secluded and charming country home with a dozen imaginatively decorated rooms – a popular choice away from the centre of town. Tropical gardens surround a swimming pool, and in the evenings you can sit round the fireplace.

A-C Villa Escazú B&B, 1 km southwest of Escazú, T2289-7971, www.hotels.co.cr/vescazu.html. 6 comfortable rooms which share 3 bathrooms in this Swiss-chalet style home rich in Costa Rican hardwoods. Good views from the garden patio, price includes breakfast. Ask for Inéz or Mary Ann who are known to be especially attentive and helpful hosts.

B Tapezco Inn, 25 m south west of San Miguel church, Escazú, T2228-1084, www.tapezco-inn.co.cr. Close to the main square, the simple rooms all have private bath with hot water. There's a jacuzzi, sauna and price includes breakfast.

Apartotels

Apartotels should provide all the comforts of living at home with the services of a hotel -- but they are generally only an option for people staying for a week or so.

LL Apartotel Villas de Río, San Rafael de Escazú, 25 m before Costa Rica Country Club, T2208-2400, www.villasdelrio.com. 64 luxury apartments fully equipped with kitchenettes, including cable TV, VCR/DVD players and smoke detectors. There is also a gymnasium, a couple of pools, sauna and transportation to city centre. Very secure and very smart.

L-AL Apartotel Maria Alexandra, in San Rafael, T2228-1507,www.mariaalex andra.com. Comfortable apartments and townhouses accommodationg 2-5 people, all with fully equipped kitchenette. The apartments have a laundry room, a/c, telephone and cable TV, and there's a swimming pool and sauna. Discounts for longer stays. Very good value if you can put a group together.

AL-A Apartotel El Sesteo, 200 m south of McDonald's, Sabana Sur, T2296-1805, www.sesteo.com. Some double apartments with kitchenettes and living rooms, some simple rooms with ceiling fans, private bath, cable TV and telephone. Topped off with a tropical garden, swimming pool and secure parking.

B Apartamentos Scotland, C 29, Av 1 (eastern suburbs), T2223-0033, www.hotels.co.cr/scotland.html. Weekly (US$250-350) or monthly (US$650-900) for comfortable, furnished apartments with, full-service and kitchenettes.

---

❷ Eating

Traditional feasting in Costa Rica tends to be on a steady supply of rice'n'beans, a little on the heavy side perhaps, but definitely worth trying. Beyond *Tico* food, however, inspiration comes from as wide a source as the capital's denizens. Italian, French and Chinese restaurants are many but there are plenty of other national dishes to be found. Fine restaurants tend to be in or near good hotels, with one or two notable exceptions. Consequently, the best restaurants are generally west of the town centre, on or around Paseo Colón and Parque Sabana, or to the north in the districts of Amón, Otoya and further east in the residential suburbs of Los Yoses. Escazú also has some memorable dining options (see page 99). Many of the good hotels also have exceptional restaurants open to non-guests. (The more upmarket ones add a 10% service charge and a 13% tax. Tips over and above this occasionally shocking pair of surcharges are only expected if the service is exceptional.)

A local dining habit peculiar to San José and Costa Rica includes the omnipresent *soda* which is the national version of a fast-food outlet found on many street corners. Varying greatly in style, you can have a bite to eat with a hearty midday *plato del día* or *casado*, which start at around US$2.

The markets also provide a good choice of simple dishes and turnover of food is so fast that the health and hygiebe risks are minimal.

The city also has a good number of cafés and bakeries where you can stop for a bite to eat and get coffee or refreshment before heading out to explore the streets again.

Breakfast tends to be a non-starter in the city so head to one of the markets or grab some fruit if your hotel doesn't provide breakfast. Lunch is the main meal of the day, when *Josefinos* stream from office blocks and pack the tables and chairs of the more affordable *sodas* and restaurants. For the end of the day, dinner options are as wide and varied as your tastes and budget.

San José *p76, maps p68, p72 and 80*
⊞ Grano de Oro, in the hotel of the same name (see page 91), T2255-3322. As elegant and stylish as the hotel. Dining inside or out on the garden patio, the ambience is intimate and warm. Inspiration for the menu draws on national and French dishes.
⊞ Jurgen's, C 41 and Paseo Rubén Darío, 250 m north of Auto Subarú, Los Yoses, T2283-2239. First-class service and an excellent

international menu in a sophisticated atmosphere. Recommended. Open Mon-Fri 1200-1430, 1800-2200, Sat 1800-2300.

La Bastille, Paseo Colón, C 22, T2255-4994, www.la-bastille-restaurante.com. Stylish French food in elegant surroundings. Fine range of dishes from seafood to beef, chicken and pork. Closed Sun.

La Cocina de Leña, in El Pueblo Commercial Centre to the north, T2223-3704, www.lacocinadelena.com. A rustic ambience with all sorts of homely paraphernalia hanging on the walls. The excellent menu is considered by many to be the best *Tico* food in the capital with tasty and filling dishes like *tamales* and creole stew, and some seafood and vegetarian food. The service is spot on: good but laid back. Recommended. Open daily from 1100.

Le Chandelier, 100 m south and 100 m west of the ICE building in Los Yoses, T2225-3980. One of San José's best restaurants, blending local dishes with French cuisine, in a beautifully restored mansion. Closed Sun.

Tin Jo, C 11, Av 6-8, T2221-7605. Asian influences from several countries. It's popular, the atmosphere has enough authenticity without overflowing into the realm of tack and the food's great. Open Mon-Thu 1130-1500, 1730-2200, Fri and Sat 1130-1500, 1730-2300, Sun 1130-2200.

Bakea, C 7, Av 11, Barrio Amón, T2221-1051, www.restaurantebakea.com. Stylish decor in a traditional colonial home. Blends of French, Mediterranean, Asian and Caribbean flavours. Excellent value *menú del día*. Open Mon 1200-1600, Tue-Fri 1200-2400, Sat 1700-2400.

Café Mundo on Av 9, C 13-15, opposite Hotel Rincón de San José (see page 93). T2222-6190. The place for the chic, smart and suave to see and be seen. The old mansion has been tastefully restored with great use of colours and space. Good salads, great pasta and bread to die for. Mon-Thu 1100-2300, Fri 1100-2400, Sat 1700-2400.

El Balcón de Europa, C 9 and Av Central-1, T2221-4841. A well known Italian place near the centre of town. The photos and anecdotal quotes covering the walls make it popular, but some dishes rather small and tasteless. Mon-Fri 1100-2230, Sat-Sun 1430-2300.

El Chicote, 400 m west of the ICE building on the north side of Parque Sabana, T2232-0936. A traditional steak house, serving good, filling steaks in an easy-going atmosphere. Open daily 1100-2300.

El Cuartel de la Boca del Monte, Av 1 and C 21-23, east of the centre, T2221-0327. Doubles up serving good food that is popular with locals in the day, before the musicians tune up and play to equally packed rooms in the evening. Open Mon-Fri until 0100, Sat until 0200.

Machu Picchu, C 32, Av 1-3 west of the centre, T2222-7384. Good Peruvian restaurant, which despite the rather sparse decor serves tasty seafood dishes.

Nuestra Tierra, Av 2, C 15, directly south of the Museo Nacional, T2258-6500. Open 24 hrs and a completely genuine Tico experience with great food, used by tourists and locals alike.

Pizza Metro is at Av 2 and C 5-7. Good Italian place, small and cosy with pizza and pasta. Not that cheap but recommended.

Bar México, north of the Coca-Cola district in Paso de la Vaca. Dead by day but comes alive at night with a flurry of music and good Mexican food, and the occasional *mariachi* band. See also page 100.

Antojitos. A Mexican chain with branches on Paseo Colón, Pavas Highway west of Sabana and in Centro Comercial Cocorí. Excellent food at moderate prices.

Choza del Sabor, on the corner of C Central and Av 5. Has good, local *comida* with a couple of gestures to decor but the *menú del día* is a good and tasty bargain.

Comedor, beneath 'Dorado' sign, C 8, Av 4-6. Very cheap.

Gran Diamente, Av 5, C 4-6. A lively kitchen where you can watch the food being prepared. One of several cheap options down Av 5 that you'll find if you take a stroll.

¶ La Puriscaleña, on the corner of C Central and Av 5. Local spot with good, staple food, mainly takeaway with a few places to perch while you eat. Nothing flashy – the real appeal is its being open 24 hrs.

¶ Mercado Central. A lively spot with a large number of eateries to choose from – pick one with lots of people, and the food will almost certainly be OK.

¶ Pollo a la Leña, C 1, Av 3-5. Has seriously cheap chicken, popular with the locals.

Cafés and snacks

¶¶ Boudsoq, Av Central, C 30, east of centre. Good French bakery with croissants and pâtisserie to die for.

¶¶ Café La Bohemia, in the Teatro Melico Salazar. Fine café in an easy-going, but traditional ambience. Black and white photos on the ceiling plot the history of San José.

¶¶ Café La Bohemia, C Central, Av 2, next to Teatro Melico Salazar. Pastas and meats as well as light lunches such as quiches and crêpes.

¶¶ Café Parisienne, Plaza de la Cultura. The street café of the Gran Hotel Costa Rica. As sure as night follows day, you will at some point take a meal, snack or at least a drink here. Food is a little overpriced and the quality is hardly a highlight, but that is not the point: this is where to watch the world go by.

¶¶ News Café, Av Central, C 7, T2222-3022. American-style sports bar-restaurant that pulls in the gringos and has just had a complete refurb. Dependable downtown option for a leisurely, satisfying lunch or a cool beer in the sociable bar. Open daily 0600-2200.

¶ Bagelman, Paseo Rubén Darío (Av Central), C 33, just east of Hostal Toruma. Smart and tasty fast food/bagel heaven.

¶ Café del Teatro, Av 2, C 3, in foyer of National Theatre. Bit pricey but worth it for the sheer style and sophistication of the belle epoque interior. Popular meeting place for poets and writers, always busy. Mon-Sat.

¶ Musmanni. Several outlets throughout the city serving bread and pastries. Best early in the day.

¶ Spoon has a central bakery at Av Central, C 5-7, where you can have good coffee and pastries to take out or eat in. There are several others throughout the city.

Vegetarian

¶ La Mazorca, in San Pedro, near University of Costa Rica (Rodrigo Facio site). Vegetarian and health foods.

¶ Macrobiótica, C 11, Av 6-8. A health shop selling good bread.

¶ Naturama Uno, Av 1, C 3-5. Health food shop opposite Omni Cinema building, cheap.

¶ Shakti, C 13, Av 8, weekdays only. Vegetarian options throughout the day, with good *menú del día*.

¶ Vishnu, Av 3, C 1/C3, with several branches in the city. Good quality, cheap, excellent *plato del día* and sells good wholemeal bread. Veggie burgers to gladden the heart of even the most carnivorous client. Open daily, 0800-2000 – just about early enough for breakfast. The best known vegetarian fast-food outlet.

¶ Whapin, C 35, Av 13. Excellent Caribbean restaurant with authentic rice and beans and fried plantains. Live music occasionally.

Sodas

Churrería Manolo, Av Central, C Central-2. Good spot for people-watching with simple, quick food (good sandwiches and hot chocolate) or takeaway options.

La Vasconia, Av 2, C 5. Lively place serving good food throughout the day. Walls draped in football memorabilia: imagine a low-budget, *Tico* version of 'Cheers'.

Pio Pio, Parque Central. The menu of fried chicken is OK, the service is poor, and the waiters will stitch you up with a flurry of fingers over a calculator, but it is open 24 hrs.

Soda El Parque, C 2, Av 4-6. Open 24 hrs and a popular spot for business people by day and worse-for-wear party-goers by night.

Soda Magaly, a little closer to town at Av Central and C 23, near Hostel Toruma. Good and cheap.

Soda Nini, Av 3, C 2-4, just north of the centre. Cheap and cheerful.

Soda Tapia, C 42, Av 2-4, east side of Parque Sabana. A classic stopping place for *Josefinos*, with good food, served quickly.

Fast food

Fast food *Tico*-style is best from the stalls in the Mercado Central (C 6-8). Stop here for a quick breakfast or lunch. None are open in the evening.

Corona de Oro, Av 3, C 2-4 (next to **Nini**) is excellent.

Soda Flor de Costa Rica, northeastern entrance in the flower pavilion, very good and cheap meals, very clean, open 0700-1800.

Galería complex, Av Central-2, C 5-7 has several snack bars. Try **Chicharronera Nacional**, Av 1, C 10-12, very popular, or **Popular**, Av 3, C 6-8, good *casado*. El **Merendero**, Av 6, C 0-2, cheap local food.

Escazú p84

♦♦♦ **Cerutti**, T2228-4511. Smart restaurant in a 100-year-old house in Escazú. Rated as one of the best Italian restaurants in Costa Rica. Decorated with antiques and candles, the restaurant's speciality is 'high Italian'. Open lunch and dinner every day except Tue.

♦♦♦ **La Luz**, in Hotel Alta on the old road to Santa Ana, T2282-4160. Serves a California-Costa Rica fusion menu. Wrought iron chandeliers and heavy wood beams set the atmosphere and the valley view is superb. In the restaurant's own words: "Dining at La Luz pushes every corner of the culinary envelope"! Daily 0700-1500 and 1800-2200.

♦♦♦ **Le Monastère**, in a restored monastery in the hills, T2289-4404, www.monastere-restaurant.com. The international menu is served as "ritual, a celebration of life and a combination of mysticism." Add the twinkling lights in the valley below and this truly is memorable dining. Mon-Sat 1800-2300.

♦♦♦ **Tiquicia**, south of Escazú, T2289-5839. Quite an adventure to get here, the views are unbeatable day or night. Traditional

fare is served in a positively rustic setting. Tiquicia is an institution and would be more so if the hours weren't so erratic (Mon-Fri 1700-midnight, Sat 1100-midnight, Sun 1100-1800, if they feel like it! Call first and check). Get a taxi or a 4WD if going after rain.

♦♦ **Chango**, on the outskirts of central Escazú, T2228-1173. Does a good trade in steaks and grills, with live music and small screen entertainment.

♦♦ **El Che**, just to the south of San Rafael, T2228-1598. Serves up the traditional Argentine *parillada* experience: meats grilled before your eyes.

♦♦ **Il Capriccio**, San Rafael, T2228-9332. Serves up a good Italian menu with a fine wine selection.

♦♦ **La Cascada**, just off Autopista Próspero Fernández, San Rafael, T2228-0906. A long-time seafood and steak house favourite with *Ticos* and visitors alike. It's simple, popular and the food will fill you up.

♦♦ **Los Anonos**, 600 m west of Anonos bridge, T2228-0180. Serves traditional Costa Rican meat dishes and is justly popular.

♦♦ **Taj Mahal**, from the Centro Comercial Paco in Escazú go 1km West on the old highway to Santa Ana, T2228-0980. Indian food for a change and if you're craving a curry you'll be happy here.

♦♦ **Villa Rey**, C Vieja toward Santa Ana, San Rafael, T2289-5028. Chinese restaurant with traditional *cantones* dishes.

♦ About your only option on the cheap front here – other than the usual globally encompassing fast-food chains – are several eateries in the various shopping malls.

Cafés

Bagelman's, Galerías San Rafael, T2228-4460. 10 kinds of bagel for 30 cents each. Sun-Thu 0700-2200, Fri and Sat 0700-2300.

Deli Mundo, Plaza Colonial, San Rafael de Escazú. Serves light dishes to Jewish recipes, fresh juices and sells bagels.

La Chocolatería, across the way from Bagelman's. Hand-made chocolate and cakes, quiet and elegant atmosphere, cosy.

Il Panino, in Multicentro Paco 2 km west of Escazú on the old road to Santa Ana. The best café in town serving a smart, sharp and well-dressed crowd. Italian coffee or local brews. Surprisingly affordable, with great selection of Latin, Arabic, Italian and Turkish music. Sometimes shows classic silent movies. Open until 2300 in the week, 0100 Fri and Sat.

⊙ Bars and clubs

It is hardly surprising that a cosmopolitan city such as San José should have such a wide and varied nightlife. If you know where to look you can find all sorts of nocturnal entertainment. There are plenty of simple bars where you can hunker down with a friend and a beer. Live music is also popular (cover charge of around US$4). Music may be a head-thumping new rock band, a *Tico* Brillcream boy-band or something a little more suave. The tendency is to just turn up and see what happens. Clubs too are popular and cover music from techno and garage, to reggae, jazz and salsa. Entrance is normally between US$2-US$6. If you want a particular group look in the listings section of *La Nación* on a Thu, or in the *Tico Times*.

Josefinos are almost always well dressed so it would be surprising if they didn't dress to impress when hitting the town but smart jeans or a skirt will get you in to most clubs. Note: you may well need photo ID.

Below is a list of the permanent happening places but, as is always the case, the fashionable venues change from day to day.

Central San José *p76, maps p72 and 80*
Bars
Bar México, Av 13 and C 16-18, up in Barrio México. You are unlikely to stumble across this place, but the trip may be worth it. *Mariachis* occasionally make it up this far and when they do the bar comes alive.
Chelle's, C 9 and Av Central. Never closes, great if you can't or simply don't want to

sleep. Gets progressively more entertaining as the night wears on. A wonderful selection of hardened drinkers roll up, slightly more concerned with getting a drink than fussing over furnishings and delicate mood lighting.
El Cuartel de la Boca del Monte, Av 1, C 21-23, towards Barrio California. Where the young bohemians hang out – it's a lively spot in an understated way. There's a comfortably dark but not oppressive atmosphere to the place. Local up-and-coming bands often play live. The music varys greatly and there is a cover charge of US$2.
Hotel Aurora, Parque Morazán. You get a different perspective from this 17th-floor bar and casino. The drinks are pretty pricey but if you can get there for sunset and the weather is good, the view is spectacular.
Las Risas, Av Central-1 and C 1. As close to the centre of town as you can get and spread over a couple of floors with a bar and a disco, it is popular with young *Josefinos*.

There are several pubs and bars aimed at expats and tourists, many run by expats themselves, covering a few blocks to the east of Plaza de la Cultura.
Beatle Bar, Av Central and C 9. A popular spot with visitors where you can get a relatively quiet beer and exchange travellers' tales.
Blue Marlin Bar, in the Hotel del Rey, Av 1, C 9. A very popular sports bar but for most the entertainment lies elsewhere. The bar is jam-packed with foreign visitors and courtesans, hoping to make each others' acquaintance.
Nashville South, C 5, Av 1-3. A Country and Western gringo bar just off Parque Morazán where you can sit at the bar, working your way along the optics as you talk with your new-found friends. Good for food too.

Gay and lesbian clubs
Though none is exclusively gay, there are a few gay-friendly dance clubs playing a mix of techno and Latin themes, including: **Déjà vu**, C 2, Av 14-16 and **La Avispa**, C 1 and Av 8-10.

North of centre *p83, maps p72 and 80*

Bars

Centro Comercial El Pueblo, Barrio Tournón, is a great place for exploring, dipping into a couple of bars and taking a meal. Once here it'll dawn on you why the downtown area of San José is almost dead. At certain times the queues of taxis and vehicles unloading *Ticas* exquisitely dressed in their finest, and young suitors, makes the place feel like one big film première. A gentle meander round the village and you'll soon stumble across a bar that suits your mood.

Los Balcones has live music, a small terrace and no cover charge.

Clubs

Coco Loco is perhaps the liveliest club to hit with a young crowd. It moves to a broad beat from the merengue and salsa of the new world to the latest sounds sweeping the world. Very hip.

Infinito, gets a slightly older crowd and packs in 3 dance floors playing different styles so you can move from rock to reggae and finally romance before heading home.

La Plaza, outside the walls of El Pueblo. Quieter and classier, but the big dance floor does mean you can still make a fool of yourself without crashing into other people.

South of centre *p84, maps p72 and 80*

Clubs

Dynasty, south of town, in Desamparados in the Centro Comercial del Sur. Distinctive Caribbean themes of soul and reggae.

Terrau, C de la Armagua. The most popular of many clubs along this street. It's definitely the trendy place to be. The area gets going around 2300 and keeps going till dawn.

Eastern districts and San Pedro *p84, maps p72*

Bars

Jazz Cafe, Av Central, 400 m east of San Pedro church. Widely thought of as the best live music venue in the capital and probably the country. Good bar and music – including

Grammy award-winning **Editus** – and a few dishes to keep the hunger pangs at bay.

La Villa has a reputation as an academic watering hole – a good place to practise your Spanish.

Escazú *p84*

There are several bars around San Rafael and San Antonio districts which are popular hang-outs with cool young *Ticos*, including: **Fandango** in San Rafael.

🎭 Entertainment

San José *p76, maps p68, p72 and 80*

San José has no shortage of cultural activities, with a good range of permanent and changing events. For listings see the *Viva* section of *La Nación* on Thu or the *Tico Times* and look in the *Weekend* section.

Casinos

Given the number of casinos around San José you'd be forgiven for assuming that gambling was a national sport, but the driving influence is overwhelmingly foreign visitors. If you fancy being fleeced the most popular casinos are at the **Hotel Costa Rica Morazán**, **Hotel del Rey**, **Hotel Gran Costa Rica** and the top floor of the **Hotel Aurora**.

Cinemas

There are many excellent modern cinemas showing the latest releases and a couple of art movie theatres. Most films are in English with Spanish subtitles which can be useful if you're trying to improve your language skills. Most theatres have comfortable seating and have a/c. *Viva* in *La Nación* on Thu will tell you what is showing when.

Cariari 1-6, *Plaza Real Cariari*, almost in Heredia, T2293-3300.

Cinemateca at the University of Costa Rica's Abelardo Bonilla auditorium, San Pedro, shows good films at 1700 and 1900 daily.

Variedades, C 5, Av Central-1, T2222-6108.

Sala Garbo, Av 2, C 28, T2222-1034. Art-house movies.

San Pedro 1-10, Mall San Pedro, 10-screen multiplex, T2283-5716.

Theatres

A vibrant dance and theatre scene exists and you'll find everything from classy productions of opera and ballet at the Teatro Nacional to innovative contemporary comedies. Almost all productions will be in Spanish, with the exception of those produced by the **Little Theatre Group** (T2355-1623 for details or look in listings). Other theatres often have workshops, especially for children. Orchestral works, jazz, concerts and dance are also common. Prices start from around US$5, rising to US$20-plus for international performers. Seasons for the Teatro Nacional, Teatro Melico Salazar and many others start in Mar. Discounts for students at most performances. Look in press listing for 2-for-1 specials, often on Wed.

Auditorio Nacional, in the Centro Costarricense de Ciencias y Cultura, set to become an increasingly popular venue. For performances visit www.museocr.com.

Giratables, Paseo Rubén Darío, C 33, Los Yoses, T2253-6001, www.teatrogiratablas. com. Popular and lively works, often comical, and with occasional performances and workshops for children.

Teatro de la Aduana, C 25, Av 3-5, T2257-8305. Home to the National Theatre Company.

Teatro del Angel, Av Central, C 13-15, T2222-8258. Comedy, spoof and dance.

Teatro de la Comedía, Av Central, C 13-15, T2233-2170.

Teatro Eugene O'Neill, part of the Costa Rican-North American Cultural Centre, Central, C 37, Los Yoses, T2207-7500, www.cccncr.com/teatro.html. Open to all performing arts including cinema, dance, music and theatre.

Teatro Laurence Olivier, Av 2, C 28, T2222-1034. Comedies.

Teatro Melico Salazar, Av 2, C Central-2, T2257-6005, www.teatromelico.go.cr. One of the most popular venues in San José with regular performances of dance, music, theatre and orchestra.

Teatro Nacional, Av 2, C 3, T2221-1329, www.teatronacional.go.cr. San José's largest theatre and the main venue for classical performances. It sometimes stoops to jazz but whatever you see will be excellent.

Teatro Molière, Av 1, C 13, T2255-2694. Innovative improvised theatre group.

Escazú *p84*
Art galleries
Galería Klaus Steinmetz Arte Contemporáneo, T2289-5403. 2 floors exhibit and sell works of famous artists from all over Latin America. Definitely worth a look.

Café de Artistas, T2228-6045. Only foreign painters and ceramics. Tue-Sat, 0730-1830.

Cinema
Cinemark Escazú, Multiplaza, T2201-5050, www.cinemarkca.com. Latest US and European releases.

☸ Festivals and events

San José *p76, maps p68, p72 and 80*
There are a few festivals in or close to the city that are worth looking out for if you happen to be in town at the time. Unlike many Latin American festivals which revolve heavily around drink, those in San José tend to be far more salubrious.

2nd Sun of Mar Día del Boyero celebrates Day of the Oxcart Driver in San Antonio de Escazú. Parades of ox-drawn carts, with music, dancing and blessings from the priesthood.

2nd week of Mar International Festival of Culture, when musicians from throughout Central America assemble in a week of open-air performances in the Plaza de Cultura and other venues throughout the city.

19 Mar Día de San José (St Joseph's Day), honouring the patron saint of the capital.
Mar/Apr Semana Santa, Easter week parades through the streets.
2 Aug Virgin de Los Angeles, honouring the patron saint of Costa Rica with a pilgrimage from San José to the basilica in Cartago.
15 Sep Independence Day, celebrates independence in 1821. Bands and dance troupes take to the streets. Things kick off the night before.
2 Nov All Souls' Day or Day of the Dead when, as throughout Latin America, families visit cemeteries and graveyards to remember the deceased.
26-27 Dec El Tope, the annual horse parade, starts at noon on the 26th and travels along the principal avenues of San José. A carnival starts next day at about 1700 in the same area. Fairs, firework displays and bull-running (anyone can take part!) at El Zapote south of the city.

○ Shopping

San José *p76, maps p68, p72 and 80*
Book and map shops
Librería Francesa, in Curridabat, 100 m east and 25 south of Pops, www.libreria francesa.net. Spanish, French, English and Italian books, and also sells some good maps.
Librería Internacional, Barrio Dent, 300 m west of Taco Bell in San Pedro and several other branches around town, T2283-6965, www.libreriainternacional.com. English, German and Spanish titles at about 20% over US prices, special order service. Sells a good range of wildlife and travel guides including Footprint's *Mexico and Central America* and other titles.
Librería Lehmann, Av Central, C 1-3, T2522-4848, www.librerialehmann.com. Has a large selection of Spanish and English books and magazines. They also stock several maps including the 1:50,000 topographical maps produced by the Instituto Geográfico Nacional de Costa Rica (IGN).

Mora Books, Av 1, C 3-5, T2255-4136, in Omni building above Pizza Hut, www.morabooks.com. Large selection of used books at reasonable prices.
7th Street Books, C 7, Av Central-1, T2256-8251, marroca@racsa.co.cr, and a website for their publishing company www.zonatropical.net. A wide range of new and used books, maps and brochures covering nature, national parks, history and culture on many topics of interest to visitors to Costa Rica. Good range of country guides. Open Mon-Sat 0900-1800, Sun 1000-1700.
Universal, Av Central, C Central-1, T2222-2222, www.universalcr.com. Spanish books and maps, and a few titles in English.
Instituto Geográfico Nacional, Av 20, C 9-11 at Ministry of Public Works and Transport (MOPT) in Plaza González, T2523-2630. Supplies good 1:50,000 topographical maps for walkers. Open 0700-1530.

Department stores and malls
Universal, Av Central and C Central-2. A general department store with a broad range of practical items such as stationery and film.
Big shopping plazas include: **San Pedro**, on the eastern ring road; **Multiplaza Mall**, near Camino Real, Escazú; both of which have excellent shops.

Markets
Mercado Central, C 6-8, Av Central. The largest of the several covered markets dotted around San José. Sells everything from leather sandals, horse saddles and bridles and simple tourist gifts through to cheese, spices, fruit, vegetables, dried and fresh flowers. The honey is particularly good. Its restaurants and juice bars serve a wide variety of food and drink at good prices.
Vegetable Market, Av 7, C 6-8. Indoor market with a couple of good restaurants.
West of the Plaza de la Cultura, a small **street market** borders the Plaza de la Democracía selling a broad range of goods including hammocks, woven bags, wooden carvings and painted feathers.

Handicrafts and souvenirs

Mercado Central, Av Central and C 6-8. Filled with life, noise and a general chaos. Behind all the daily commerce and greetings, you'll find a few typical items for sale such as leather goods and wooden items – many without the price increases found in stores catering for tourists. You may have to rummage around, but with a bit of luck you'll find a truly memorable souvenir of your trip.

El Pueblo, north of town in Barrio Tournón, has several good shops, although prices vary greatly, so shop around. Several craft cooperatives exist including: **Mercado Nacional de Artesanía**, C 11, Av 4, T2221-5012, open Mon-Fri 0900-1800, Sat 0900-1700, with a good selection of items at reasonable prices; **Canapi**, C 11 and Av 1, a cooperative and cheaper than most; **La Casona**, C Central and Av Central-1, open daily from 0900-1900, a market of small *artesanía* shops with lots of interesting stalls to sift through.

There is also a selection of stalls on the west side of Plaza de la Democracía, which sells the full range of desirables including hammocks, paintings, wood carvings and T-shirts.

Parque Morazán (the south and west side), is non-stop shops with many selling the same things, but the odd nugget can be found.

Plaza de la Cultura and along Av Central. Impromptu stalls sprout up around here and you will always find a couple of wandering salespeople around Café Parisienne selling cigars, humidors and other souvenirs.

Galería Namu, opposite the Alianza Francesa building on Av 7 and C 5-7, T2256-3412, www.galerianamu.com. The best one-stop shop for homegrown art. Indigenous art and crafts would be the traditional phrase, but Namu has blended conventional themes of rugs, throws, textiles and mask carvings with many more contemporary developments, keeping indigenous art alive. The result is some inspired pieces which come with an information sheet so you can spread the story. If San José is at the start and end of your trip, pop in on the first day, think about what you want to buy while you travel, and then visit again to buy it all just before you leave. If you're just passing, take your credit card and give yourself more than 30 mins. Open Mon-Sat 0900-1830.

Boutique Annemarie is the souvenir and gift shop in the main lobby of the Hotel Don Carlos, C 9, Av 7-9. They guarantee the largest selection and the best prices in Costa Rica with over 100,000 handcrafted items and pieces of art on display. Open 365 days a year from 0900-1900.

For more general stores you will find most of what you want down **Av Central**.

Some 8 km northeast of San José, **Moravia** is a popular spot for souvenirs, often included in day trips from the capital. The leather rocking chairs (which dismantle for export) found in some *artesanía* shops are sometimes cheaper in Sarchí, see page 132.

The largest one-stop shop is the **Mercado de Artesanías Las Garzas** with its countless stalls to tempt and tease with all manner of colourful goods and banter. Buses leave San José from Av 3, C 5-7. Shops are open daily, slightly shorter hours on Sun.

Escazú *p84*

There are a number of modern shopping plazas on the main road running north to south. It seems a long way to come to walk through a shopping mall. But if that is where your interest lies, there are a couple along the main street of Calle León Cortés. To the north of town on Highway 27 you'll find Costa Rica's largest – the **Multiplaza**.

E-Music, in the Multiplaza, T2288-2000. Truly international music choice with Latin, Brazilian, African and Middle Eastern.

▲ Activities and tours

San José *p76, maps p68, p72 and 80*
Grab a copy of the *Tico Times* and scan the listings which have details of organizations like the Hash House Harriers (non-competitive running, T2282-6010), Ultimate Frisbee (T2337-5249), bridge clubs and more.

Bowling

Metro Bowl, next to the Multiplaza in Escazú. Open 1100-2400, Mon-Thu, until 0200 on Fri and Sat.

Football

This is the only one spectator sport that counts in Costa Rica. Saprissa home games take place on Sun mornings. Catch a local bus heading north and you can buy a ticket on the gate. International games occasionally take place in the Stadio Nacional in Parque Sabana. Watch the local press for details or visit www.saprissa.co.cr; you can get a ticket for most games if you turn up in good time.

Golf

Meliá Cariari, on the road out to the airport, T2232-8122.
Valle del Sol, in Santa Ana, T2282-9222. Recently expanded.

Hiking

Parque Sabana is a good place to stretch your legs. There's also a **swimming** pool in the park if you fancy a dip. If you're looking for a one-day hike go to **Escazú** and tackle some of the smaller hills, or head out to **Volcán Barva** and explore some of the higher trails.

Rafting

For rafting see also Turrialba, page 158.
Aguas Bravas, T2292-2072, www.aguas-bravas.co.cr. Whitewater rafting on various rivers throughout the country, with their own activity centre near Puerto Viejo de Sarapiquí. Also arrange a wide variety of other adventure activities including kayaking, horse riding, mountain biking and tailor-made trips.

Aventuras Naturales, Av 5, C 33-35, T2225-3939, www.adventurecostarica.com. Well respected adventure tour operator, specialists in whitewater rafting with their own lodge on the Pacuare complete with canopy adventure tour. Also branching out into biking, hiking – one of the untapped options in Costa Rica – and adventure tours.

Ríos Tropicales, C 38, between Paseo Colón and Av 2, 50 m south of Subway, T2233-6455, www.riostropicales.com. Specialists in whitewater rafting. Good selection of options on the Pacuare, Reventazón, Sarapiquí, General, Corobicí; also sea kayaking and a Tortuguero Jungle trip. Excellent guides, careful to assess abilities, and good food. Ríos Tropicales is one of the longest-running rafting operations in Costa Rica and is actively involved in conservation and reforestation projects. Several standard offerings, such as 1-day trips from US$99, accommodation in the company's jungle lodge and excellent food. They can organize classes in whitewater rafting or kayaking, special events and bespoke trips for the experienced. Also branching out beyond whitewater with mountain biking.

Tour operators

Service levels across the board tend to be very high. Trips and tours are sold through a number of companies but many use the same operator to provide the service so a San José city tour is likely to be the same irrespective of who you book through. Trips will vary if the package involves an overnight stay. Check the standard of the hotel used and that the guides you choose have appropriate experience and knowledge. Below is a list of some of the main tour operators in San José and a few specialist providers.
Aguas Bravas, T2292-2072, www.aguas-bravas.co.cr. See Rafting, above.
Armo Tours, C9, Av 6, T2257-0202, www.armotours.com. Highly recommended for national tours, good service, German,

English, French and Italian spoken. Has an office in Germany. Offer the flexible and independent Naturepass that allows you to travel freely, with the support of a tour operator.

Aventuras Naturales, Av 5, C 33-35, T2225-3939, www.adventurecostarica.com. See Rafting, above.

Calypso Cruises, 4 blocks north of the Toyota Agency on Paseo Colón, T2256-2727, www.calypsocruises.com. Originators of the Pacific Island Cruise with an all-inclusive day trip from US$119 – a popular trip – a several other sailing options.

Costa Rica Expeditions, Av 3, C Central-2, T2257-0766, www.costaricaexpeditions.com. Upmarket wildlife adventures taking you to popular but out of the way places in comfort and style. Very good and knowledgeable guides. Options include whitewater rafting (US$99 for 1-day trip, including lunch and transport). Owners of Tortuga Lodge on the Caribbean coast, Corcovado Lodge on the Osa Peninsula and Monteverde Lodge near Santa Elena, and has connections with over 50 other hotels. Highly recommended. Open daily 0530-2100.

Costa Rica Sun Tours, Av 4, C 36, T2296-7757, www.crsuntours.com. Regular departures on many of the normal tours departing from San José, Arenal, Monteverde, Osa Peninsula/Corcovado and Manuel Antonio. Tours can often be arranged at short notice. Warmly recommended.

Expediciones Tropicales, C 3, Av 11-13, T2257-4171, www.costaricainfo.com. The full range of 1- and 2-day tours. Staff are friendly, helpful and happy to talk through the options without the hard sell. They operate the *Four in One* tour – see page 87, that everyone now tries to copy. Rent-a-car, van or bus services are handy for groups. Daily 0700-2000.

Green Tropical Tours, C El Rodeo, Coronado, 1 km north of the church, T2229-4192, www.greentropical.com. Tailor-made tours including many normal tours and some to less widely visited areas like Guayabo National Monument and Los Juncos Cloudforest.

Horizontes, C 28, Av 1-3, T2222-2022, www.horizontes.com. A wide range of services and high standards from one of Costa Rica's most respected tour operators. Basics, including car rental and hotel reservations through to specialist trips focusing on natural history, conservation, birdwatching, photography, culture, agriculture and adventure. English, Spanish, Italian, German and French spoken. Open 0800-0530 Mon-Fri, 0900-1200 Sat from Dec-Apr. Hours may change in green season.

Original Canopy Tour, Av 9, C 3a, T2291-4465, www.canopytour.com. As the name suggests, the pioneers in Costa Rica, with 3 canopy tours around the country. Rates from US$45 per person.

OTEC, C 3, Av 1-3, T2256-0633, www.otec.co.cr. A travel agent that provides stupendous discounts on flights for students, teachers and others who can convince staff that they are in education. Almost enough to make you go back to school!

Simbiosis Tours, 150 m north and 50 m west of Torre Mercedes Benz, San José, T2290-8646, www.turismoruralcr.com. The booking arm of the Cooprena network of 8 community-based accommodation and camping options. Good options around the country, including horse riding and experiencing typical food, dances and music from the region. Probably your best bet for organized ecotourism in Costa Rica.

Swiss Travel Service, one of the biggest operators with several branches around town including Camino Real Inter-Continental, Gran Hotel Costa Rica, Meliá Cariari Hotel, and the Radisson Europa, T2282-4898, www.swisstravelcr.com. In addition to standard tours, they arrange almost anything you can imagine from birdwatching to horse riding. Good guides, with a lot of cruise experience – warmly recommended.

Tam Travel, has 4 branches, 1 in San José Palacio Hotel, T2256-0203, www.tamtravel.com. Helpful and efficient operator. Open 7 days a week, 24-hr answering service.

⊖ Transport

San José *p76, maps p68, p72 and 80*

Air

A good network of regional airports makes for quick and efficient travel around the country. Prices are reasonable and schedules are frequent enough to make it worth considering taking a flight if time is tight – certainly to places like Puerto Jiménez, Tortuguero and Barra del Colorado.

The main domestic air services are provided by SANSA and Nature Air. **SANSA**, Edif Colón, 1st floor, Office 1-31, San José, T2223-4179, www.flysansa.com, operates from the domestic terminal of Juan Santa María International Airport to the northwest of the capital. **NatureAir**, T2299-6000, www.natureair.com, from Tobías Bolaños airport, 5 km west of San José in the district of Pavas. See Essentials, page 40 for flight schedules. Tickets can be arranged direct or through most travel agents.

Charter flights are also available and reasonably affordable if travelling in a group. Most charter companies work out of Tobías Bolaños airport. See Charter flights, in Essentials, page 39.

Airline offices Aeroperlas, see SANSA, below. **Air France**, Of Ejecutivo La Sabana Edif 6, 7th floor, Sabana Sur, T2220-4111, www.airfrance.com. **Alitalia**, Paseo Colón Edificio Torre Mercedes, 2nd floor, T2295-6820, www.alitalia.it. **American Airlines**, Edif Centro Cars, Sabana Este, T2248-9010, www.aa.com. **British Airways**, www.ba.com. **Continental**, Oficentro La Virgen, Edif 2, Pavas, T0800-044-0005, www.continental.com. **Copa**, Edi Torres Mercedes, 1st floor, Paseo Colón, T2223-2672, www.copaair.com. **Delta**, 100 m east and 50 m south of Toyota, Paseo Colón, Edif Elizabeth, San José, T0800-056-2002 , www.delta.com. **Grupo Taca**, see SANSA, below. **Iberia**, Oficentro Tical, Río Segundo, Alaguela, T2431-5633, www.iberia.com. **Japan Airlines**, C 34, Av 6, T2257-4646, www.japanair.com. **KLM**,

behind Controlaría General Building, Sabana Sur, T2220-4111, www.klm.com. **Martinair** (subsidiary of KLM) – Sabana Sur, behind Controlaría General Building, T2232-3246, www.martinair.com. **Mexicana**, C 5, Av 7-9, T2257-6334, www.mexicana.com.mx. **SANSA**, Edif Colón, 1st floor, Office 1-31, San José, T2223-4179, www.flysansa.com. **NatureAir**, T2299-6000, www.natureair.com. **United Airlines**, Sabana Sur, behind Controlaría General Building, T1-800-538-2929, www.united.com.

Bus

Local San José's urban bus system is extensive and efficient enough (allowing for traffic congestion). Buses run from around 0500 until 2300 or so at night. Urban buses cost 100-140 colones (US$0.20-0.30) payable to the driver on boarding. It's a little more (225-375 colones, US$0.45-0.75) for outer lying districts such as Escazú, Alajuela and Heredia. Buses get very crowded at rush hour, and luggage space is limited at the best of times.

Bus destinations are marked on the front of the bus. In theory, buses only stop for passengers to board and alight at official stops. Far from obvious, the cunningly disguised metal posts doubling up as stops are more likely to be found through accident than design. Labelled on one side with the destination, the bus stop blends in perfectly with the pavement furniture. The clearest indication is a neat line of people patiently queuing so join the end and wait.

General routes of interest: heading west towards **Parque Sabana** down **Paseo Colón** from the centre of town, buses leave from along Av 3. Returning from Parque Sabana buses travel down Paseo Colón before joining Av 2. With these 2 routes you can move through the heart of the city. A **cheap tour of San José** can be made on the bus marked *'periférico'* from Paseo Colón in front of the Cine Colón, a 45-min circle of the city. A smaller circle is made by the

Buses from San José

Destination	Frequency	Duration	Cost
Alajuela (and airport)	Every 10 mins	30 mins	70 cents
Alajuela (and airport)	Every 10 mins, every 30 mins at night	30 mins	70 cents
Cahuita	3 daily	4 hrs	US$6.80
Cartago	Every 10 mins	45 mins	US$0.75
Ciudad Neilly	5 daily	7½ hrs	US$9.00
Ciudad Quesada (San Carlos)	Hourly	2½ hrs	US$2.50
Dominical – buses via San Isidro de El General or Quepos			
Escazú	Every 10 mins	20 mins	50 cents
Fortuna	3 daily	3½ hrs	US$3.60
Golfito	0700, 1500	7½ hrs	US$10.60
Guápiles	15 daily	1¼ hrs	US$2.00
Heredia	Every 10 mins	30 mins	50 cents
Heredia	Every 20 mins	30 mins	50 cents
Irazú Volcano National Park	1 Sat, 1 Sun 0800 in the morning		US$6.40
Jacó	5 daily	2¼ hrs	US$3.00
Liberia	15 daily	4½ hrs	US$5
Limón	22 buses between 0500 and 2200	3 hrs, 3 hrs direct	US$4.30 US$4.10
Los Chiles	2 daily	5 hrs	US$3.90
Monteverde/Santa Elena	2 daily	5 hrs	US$4.30
Montezumo – buses going to Puntarenas and then ferry to Paquera			
Nicoya (by bridge)	2 daily	4 hrs	US$5.75
Nicoya (via Liberia)	5 daily	5-6 hrs	US$5.75
Nosara (by bridge)	1 at 0500	6 hrs	US$7.10
Palmar Norte/Sur	7 daily	6 hrs	US$8.35
Santa María de Dota	6 daily	2 hrs	US$2.20
Palmar Norte/Sur	1 daily	5 hrs	US$8
Paso Canoas	5 (1 direct at 1100)	7-8 hrs	US$11.20
Peñas Blancas	5, 10 at weekends	5 hrs	US$6.60
Playa del Coco (via Liberia)	2 daily	5 hrs	US$6.00

Company and terminal	Address	Telephone
Tuasa	C 10, Av Central - 2	T2222-5325
Tuasa	Av 2, C 10-12	
Autotransportes Mepe, Gran Terminal del Caribe	Barrio Tournon	T8758-1572
SACSA	C 5, Av 18-20	T2233-5350
Tracopa, Terminal Alfaro	Av 5 and C 14	T2290-1308
Autotransportes San Carlos, Atlántico Norte Terminal	Av 9, C 12, Av 7-9, C 12	T2255-4300
Street stop	C16, Av Central – 1	
Atlántico Norte Terminal	Av 7-9, C 12,	T2255-4300
Tracopa, Terminal Alfaro	Av 5 and C 14	T2290-1308
Empresarios Guapileño, Gran Terminal del Caribe	Barrio Tournon	T2222-0610
Street stop	Av 2, C 10-12, also C 10, Av 1	
Street stop	Av 2, C 12-14	
Buses Metrópoli	Av 2, C 1-3, in front of Gran Hotel Costa Rica	T2530-1064
Transportes Jacó, Coca-Cola Terminal		T2290-2922
Pulmitan	C 14, Av 1-3	T2222-1650
Autotransporte Mepe, Gran Terminal del Caribe	Barrio Tournon	T8758-1572
Auto Transportes Caribeño		T2221-2596
Autotransportes San Carlos, Atlántico Norte Terminal	Av 7-9, C 12	T2255-4300
Atlántico Norte Terminal	Av 9. C 12.	T2258-5674
Empresa Alfaro	Av 5 and C 14	T2222-2666
Empresa Alfaro	Av 5 and C 14	T2222-2666
Empresa Alfaro	Av 5 and C 14	T2222-2666
Tracopa	Av 5 and C 14	T2290-1308
Autotransportes Los Santos Dota	Av 16, C 19-21	T2541-1326
Autotransportes Blanco Lobo	Av 9 y 11, C 12,	T8771-2550
Tracopa	Av 5 and C 14	T2290-1308
Transportes Deldu	Av 3, C 16	T2203-7162
	Av 1-3, C14	T2222-1650

Destination	Frequency	Duration	Cost
Playa Flamingo	0800, 1100 and 1500	5-6 hrs	US$6.60
Playa Panama	1 at 1530	4½ hrs	US$5.75
Poás (from Alajuela)	1 at 0915	4 hrs	US$1.70
Puerto Jiménez	1 daily at 1200	8 hrs	US$7
Puerto Viejo de Talamanca	4 daily	4½ hrs	US$7.80
Puerto Viejo de Sarapiquí	10 daily	2 hrs	US$3.00
Puerto Viejo de Sarapiquí (via Varablanca)	3 daily	4 hrs	US$3.00
Puntarenas	Hourly	2 hrs	US$3.20
Quepos	9 daily, 3 direct	3½ or 5 hrs	US$4.30/ US$5.50
Río Frío	5 daily	2 hrs	US$2.10
Sámara	2 daily at 1230 and 1815	5 hrs	US$6.60
San Isidro de El General	18 daily	3 hrs	US$3.80
San Isidro de El General		3 hrs	US$3.80
San Rafael de Guatasu	1 at 1545	4 hrs	US$4.60
San Ramón	Hourly from 0400-2200	2 hrs	US$1.15
San Vito	4 daily (1 direct at 1445)	6-8 hrs	US$9.75
Santa Cruz	8 daily	5 hrs	US$5.80
Santa Cruz (by bridge)	1 at 0800	5 hrs	US$5.80
Santa Cruz/Playa Flamingo	1 at 1530	5 hrs	US$6.60
Santa Elena/Monteverde	2 daily	5 hrs	US$4.30
Sarchí	5 daily	1½ hrs	US$1.50
Siquirres	12 daily	2-2½ hrs	US$2.50
Sixaola – buses via Puerto Viejo	4 daily	6 hrs	US$9.70
Tamarindo	1 at 1600	6 hrs	US$6.00
Tamarindo (via bridge)	1130 and 1330	5 hrs	US$6
Tilarán (via Canas)	5 daily	4 hrs	US$5.70
Tortuguero – no direct service	Daily bus (6 hrs), to Puerto Caño Blanco and boat from there to Tortuguero		2 piso,
Turrialba	18 daily	1¾ hrs	US$2
Upala	3 daily	4 hrs	US$6.50
Uvita	0530 and 1500	5 hrs	US$6.40
Zarcero	8 daily	1½ hrs	US$1.70

Company and terminal	Address	Telephone
Tralapa	Av 3, C 18-20	T2223-5859
	Av 3, C 18-20	T2221-7202
Tuasu	Av 2, C 12-14	T2222-5325
Autotransportes Blanco Lobo	Av 9 y 11, C 12	T8771-2550
Autotransporte Mepe, Gran Terminal del Caribe	Barrio Tournon	T8758-1572
Autotransporte Sarapiquí (por pista – through Gran Terminal del Caribe the Zurqui Tunnel)	Barrio Tournon	T2222-0610
Autotransporte Sarapiquí, Gran Terminal del Caribe	Barrio Tournon	T2222-0610
Empresarios Unidos	C 16, Av 10-12	T8777-0708
Transportes Morales, Coca-Cola Terminal		T2223-5567
Autotransporte Sarapiquí, Gran Terminal del Caribe	Barrio Tournon	T2222-0610
Empresa Alfaro	Av 5 y C 14	T2290-1308
Autotransportes Blanco Lobo	Av 9 y 11, C 12	T2257-4121
Transportes Musoc	C Central, Av 22-24	T2222-2422
Transnorte de Upala	Av 3 y 5, C 10	T2221-9022
Empresarios Unidos	C 16, Av 10-12	T2222-0064
Tracopa	Av 5 y C 14	T2290-1308
Tralapa	Av 3, C 18-20	T2223-5859
Empresa Alfaro	Av 5 y C 14	T2290-1300
Tralapa	Av 3, C 18-20	T2223-5859
Atlántico Norte Terminal	Av 9, C 12,	T2258-5674
Coca-Cola Terminal		T2223-5567
Any bus going to the Caribbean (Lineares del Atlántico), Gran Terminal del Caribe	Barrio Tournon	T2222-2727
Autotransporte Mepe, Gran Terminal del Caribe	Barrio Tournon	T8758-1572
Tralapa	Av 3, C 18-20	T2223-5859
Empresa Alfaro	Av 5 y C 14	T2290-1308
Atlántico Norte Terminal	Av 9, C 12	T2258-5674
Caño Blanco Marina Local 11	Edificio Las Arcadas,	T2256-9444
Transtusa	C 13, Av 6-8	T2556-5331
Transportes Upala	Av 3-5, C 10	T2221-9022
Coca-Cola Terminal		T2223-5567
Coca-Cola Terminal		T2223-5567

'Sabana/Cementerio' bus travelling along Paseo Colón out to Parque Sabana and then returning along Av 10. Pick it up on Av 2, at **Parque Morazán** or on Av 3.

Starting points for stops and destinations: Desmaparados, Av 4, C 5-7; **Escazú**, Av Central-1, C 16; **Moravia**, Av 3, C 3-5; **Sabana Cementerio**, Av 2, C 8-10; **Sabana Estadio**, Av 2, C 2-4; **San Pedro**, Av Central, C 9-11.

National Buses cover the whole country and you can get between any two reasonably sized towns with just one bus journey. If there is not a direct service, you will be able to get a more local bus from a town near to your destination. The buses vary greatly in quality. Popular routes between cities are often served by luxury coaches with a/c and occasionally TV and video. Moving off the well-driven tarmac, the quality of bus matches the terrain perfectly: the rougher the road, the rougher the bus. Experienced global bus travellers will find the Costa Rican network pretty much a dream, first timers may have to learn the fine art of dozing while your head is bounced off.

Buses tend to leave on or close to the scheduled departure time, relatively uncommon in Latin America, so don't be late. For the latest bus information you can contact the ICT office below the Plaza de la Cultura, or ask in your hotel. See also timetable on page 108.

Bus terminals and **company offices** are spread through out the capital, with a general concentration on the **Coca-Cola** district. For several years the terminal has been notorious, providing rich pickings for thieves. While the police presence has increased in the last year, it isn't round-the-clock, so keep your wits about you and don't leave bags unattended for a second. All destinations on the Caribbean coast are served by the new **Gran Terminal del Caribe** to the north of the city. For specific details of destinations and departure points see the table on page 108. In recent years there has been some consolidation in the long distance bus industry, and some companies now share offices and depots. If this continues, more locations may change.

For most bus journeys buying **tickets** in advance, even by a couple of hours, is a good idea although not essential, so visit the terminal before departure to buy a ticket. However, at holiday times, Christmas, New Year, Easter and if arrival at your destination by a certain time is important, book as far in advance as possible.

International **Nicaragua** and **Panama** are served by good international bus services. The buses are comfortable, the service reliable and it is a good way of covering a lot of ground without the expense of a flight. Although it can hardly be called sightseeing, you will see a bit more than you would from an aeroplane. Several companies provide a service. **Tica Bus**, Paseo Colón, 200 m north and 100 m west of Torre Mercedes, Nacional, T2221-8954, www.ticabus.com. Covers the whole of Central America up to Guatemala including a daily service to **Panama City**, departing at 2300, arriving in Panama City at 1500 the following day. From Panama the bus leaves at 1100, arriving in San José at 1400 the next day, US$26 one way. For **Managua** 3 buses a day, leaving at 0600, 0730 and 1230 arriving at 1400, 1500 and 2100. US$21 one way. Moving on from there involves an overnight stay, but the Tica Bus terminal in Managua does have some basic accommodation. Other international bus companies include: **Sirca Express**, **Nicabus**, **Panaline** and **Tracopa**.

Car hire
Paseo Colón is the home of the car hire firm. Practically every international and national company has an office and compound here. Most have an office at the airport as well so if you have booked in advance and want the vehicle immediately, arrange to pick it up at the airport. Office hours tend to be from 0800 until around 1800, while some companies

open as early at 0530, staying open until 2200. Check hours to ensure you don't miss the drop-off date and incur a penalty. **Adobe**, 8 branches around the country, T2258-4242, www.adobecar.com. Japanese cars and 4WD, drop-off at the beach if you fly NatureAir or Sansa, flexible insurance, drivers aged 18-21 accepted with US$1500 on credit card. **Alamo**, Av 18, C 11-13, north side of Plaza González Víquez, T2242-7733, www.alamocostarica.com. 11 locations around the country. **Avis**, main office in Heredia, T2293-2222, www.avis.com. Well known international name with offices in Hotel Melia Cariari and Hotel Melia Corobicí. **Budget**, C 30, Paseo Colón, T2255-4750, www.budget.co.cr. Open Mon-Sat 0700-1800, Sun, 0700-1600, also at international airport, Liberia, Jacó, Sámara, Tambor, Mal País and Tamarindo. **Dollar**, Paseo Colón, C 32-34, T2257-0671, www.dollarcostarica.com. Very good rates. **Economy**, Paseo Colón, T2299-2000, www.economyrentacar.com. Many branches throughout the country including Liberia, Tamarindo and Jacó Beach. **Europcar**, Paseo Colón, C 36-38, T2440-9990, www.europcar.co.cr. Good cars and helpful staff. Several offices around the country. **Hertz**, C 38, Paseo Colón, T2221-1818, www.costarica rentacar.net. **National**, C 36, Av 7, T2290-8787, www.natcar.com. About 15 offices around the country. Open daily 0600-2200 . **Payless**, C 10 Av 13-15, Barrio México, T2257-0026, www.eleganterentacar.com. Cars, jeeps, vans, minimum age 23, has branches throughout the country. **Toyota**, Paseo Colón, T2258-5797, www.toyotarent.com. Good cars, very helpful staff, also have an office at airport and in Liberia. **Tricolor**, Paseo Colón, Av 30-32, T2440-3333, www.tricolorcarrental.com. Good cars at competitive prices with friendly service and a good map.

Motorcycles

Wild Rider Motorcycles, Paseo Colón, C 32 diagonal Kentucky, T2258-4604, www.wild-rider.com. Suzuki DR 250s and

DR 350s available for rent from US$60 a day. Experience is essential not only to rent the bike, but also for your survival on the roads.

Taxis

The basic fee of 420 colones (US$0.80) plus 25 colones (5 cents) for every 100 m or so, makes most cross-town journeys affordable and efficient. There are several taxi ranks throughout the city – the main one is on the north side of Parque Central – you can hail a cab in the street or get your hotel to book one by telephone. As with taxis worldwide they're everywhere on sunny days, but when it is raining or late at night you could end up waiting forever.

Taxis also offer alternative way of exploring the highlands. With a group of 4, this becomes a remarkably affordable way to travel without the hassles of driving yourself. A cab to Volcán Irazú is around 18,000 colones, (US$35). If taking a long distance ride, you may have to pay part of the fare in advance. Red cab drivers should have a list of recommended prices for most areas if you want to consider your options.

❶ Directory

San José *p76, maps p68, p72 and 80*
Banks
If you have a credit card, you can withdraw cash from ATMs dotted around San José and found in the lobbies of some of the better hotels. TCs and dollars can be changed in many hotels and in banks where queues can be long and service slow – not particularly unique to Costa Rica but something to bear in mind. Opening hours are generally 0830-1530 with some opening a little later and on Sat. **Banco de Costa Rica**, Av Central, C 6 y 4. 0800-1900. **Banco de Crédito Agrícola**, Av 4, C Central 1/2. 0800-1530. **Banco de San José**, Av 3 y 5, C Central, 0800-1900. MC ATMs. Cash advance against

American Express, MC and Visa charging US$5 for up to US$1500. **Banco Nacional**, Av 1-3, C 2 y 4. 0830-1900. 24-hr Visa ATMs, TCs and cash changed on the 3rd floor. **Banco Popular**, Av 2, C 1. 0800-1500, Visa ATMs. **Financiera Londres**, Av 1, C Central, T2258-3003, will take TCs and change euros. **OFINTERSA**, Casa de Cambio, Edificio Schyfter, 2nd floor, 20 m north of the junction of Av Central and C2. Open 0830-1700, can be quicker than the banks when they are busy. **Western Union**, Av 4, C 9-11. Money transfer services, quicker than banks but you pay a price premium.

Cultural centres

Alianza Francesa, Av 7, C 5, T2222-2283, www.alianzafr.ac.cr. French newspapers, French films every Wed evening, friendly. **Centro Cultural Costarricense Norteamericano**, C 37, Av 1-5, Los Yoses, T2207-7500, www.cccncr.com. Good films, plays, art exhibitions and English-language library, open until 1930. **Instituto Británico**, 50 m south of Automercado, Los Yoses, T2234-9054, www.institutobritanico.co.cr. Language classes as well as reference materials. **Mexican Cultural Centre**, C 41, Av 10, T2283-2333.

Embassies

Australia , no embassy in Costa Rica. Representation in Mexico at Rubén Darío No 55, Colonia Polanco 11580, México DF. T00-525-5531-5225, www.mexico.embassy. gov.au. **Belgium**, 4th entrance to Los Yoses, 25 m south of Subarú, T2225-6633, open 0730-1600. **Canada**, Building 5 (3rd floor) of Oficentro Ejecutivo La Sabana, Sabana Sur, T2242-4400, www.costarica.gc.ca, open 0800-1630, Fri until 1330. **Denmark**, no embassy in Costa Rica, nearest representation is in Nicaragua at Bolonia De Plaza España 1C abajo, 2 C al lago, ½ C abajo, Managua, T00-505-268-0250 al 55. **France**, 200 m south, 25 m west of Indoor Club, Curridabat, T2234-4167, open 0830-1230. **Germany**, Edif Torre La Sabana, 8th floor, 300 m west of ICE,

T2290-9091, open 0715-1615. **Israel**, 11th floor, Edificio Colón, Paseo Colón, C 38 y 40, T2221-6444, http://sanjose.mfa.gov.il, open 0830-1630. **Italy**, 5th entrance to Barrio Los Yoses, T2234-2326, open 0900-1200. **Japan**, Edif Torre La Sabana, 10th floor, T2232-1255, www.cr.emb-japan.go.jp, open 0800-1200 and 1330-1700. **Mexico**, Av 7a No 1371, C 13-15, T2257-0633, open 0900-1200 and 1400-1630. **Netherlands**, 3rd floor, Edif 3, Oficentro Ejecutivo La Sabana, T2296-1490, www.nethemb.or.cr, open 0900-1200. **Nicaragua**, Av Central, C 25-27, opposite *Pizza Hut*, T2221-2924, open 0830-1630. **Norway**, representation in Nicaragua at 100 m east of El Güegüense roundabout, Managua, Nicaragua, T00-505-266-5197, www.noruega.org.ni. **Panama**, C 38, Av 7 (275 m north of Centro Colón building, Paseo Colón), T2280-1570, open 0900-1400. **South Africa**, representation in Mexico. **Spain**, C 32, Paseo Colón, T2222-1933. **Sweden**, represented in Guatemala at Octava Av 15-07 Zona 10, Guatemala City, T00-502-2384-7300, open 0900-1200. **Switzerland**, 2nd floor, Edif Colón, Paseo Colón, C 38, T2221-4829, open 0730-1600. **United Kingdom**, 11th floor, Edif Colón, Paseo Colón, C 38, T2258-2025, www.britishembassy.gov.uk/costarica, open 1400-2200. **United States**, opposite Centro Comercial, Pavas, T2519-2000, www.us embassy.or.cr. Mon-Fri 0800-1130.

Internet

Cybercafé Las Arcadas, in the basement of Edificio Las Arcadas, next to the Gran Hotel Costa Rica. Open 7 days a week, 0700-2100, very helpful staff, 500 colones 1 hr. Good machines. **Internet Café**, 4th floor, Av C, C4, open 0900-2200. A better way to spend less money at just 400 colones per hr and for each part of an hour. They have several branches around town including 2nd floor, Av Central, C Los Estudiantes, open 0900-2100, at the western end of Paseo Colón in Edifico Colón, C 38-40, and, if you just have to tap all night, there is a 24-hr café in San Pedro, close to Banco Popular.

Language schools

The number of schools has increased rapidly in recent years. Listed below are a selection of widely respected school and those recommended by readers. **Academia Latinoamericana de Español**, Av 8, C 31-33, San Pedro Montes de Oca, T2224-9917, www.alespanish.com. **Academia Tica**, out in San Isidro de Coronado and with a school in Jacó, T2229-0013, www.academiatica.com. Good chance of avoiding the crowds. **AmeriSpan**, PO Box 58129, Philadelphia, PA 19102, T1-800-879-6640 (USA and Canada), www.amerispan.com. 10 affiliated schools in Escazú, Alajuela, Heredia and throughout the country. **Centro Lingüístico Conversa**, Apdo 17, Centro Colón 1007, San José, T2221-7649, toll free on T1-888-669-1644, www.conversa.co.cr. Has 2 schools, one just off Paseo Colón and also out in Santa Ana. **Costa Rican International Language Academy**, Barrio Dent, from Autos Subarú, 300m north and 50 m west on C Ronda, T2280-1685, www.spanishandmore.com. Latin American music and dancing on top of language study and local accommodation. **Costa Rica Spanish Institute**, San Pedro district, T2234-1001, www.cosi.co.cr, with a homestay in San José or the beach programme based in Manuel Antonio. **Institute for Spanish Language Studies**, T2258-5111, in the US on T1-800-765-0025, www.isls.com, has eight schools in Costa Rica, offering innovative and flexible programmes. **Instituto Británico**, Los Yoses, T2225-0256, www.institutobritanico.co.cr, with classes in English and Spanish. **Instituto de Español Costa Rica**, A 1, C Central – C 1, Guadalupe, T2280-6622, www.professionalspanish.com. Close to the centre of San José, and complete with its own B&B (**C**). English, French and German spoken. Many offers including 2 for 1 deals. **Instituto Universal de Idiomas**, Av 2, C 9, Apdo 751-2150 Moravia, San José, T2223-9662, www.universal-edu.com. Stress on conversational Spanish. **Intensa**, C 33, Av 1-3, Barrio Escalante, T2281-1818, www.intensa.com. **Intercultura Language &** Cultural Center, Heredia, T2260-8480, www.interculturacostarica.com.

Language schools in Escazú Centro Lingüístico Conversa, T2221-7649, www.conversa.net, or ILERI – Instituto de Lenguas y Relaciones International, T2288-1687, www.ilerispanishschool.com.

Laundry

All but the very cheapest hotels will do laundry if requested. **Laundry Las Arcadas**, next to Las Arcadas internet café beside the Gran Hotel Costa Rica, daily 0800-1900, self service, US$3 per load, also dryers available. **Lavandería Lavamex**, Av Central y 1, C 8, in small shopping mall below Gran Hotel Imperial, T2258-2303. US$8 wash and dry. Book swap, very popular with travellers. More than just a laundry, Karl and Patricia offer priceless travel advice on Costa Rica and can also help if you have problems. **Sixaola**, branches in Alajuela and Sabanilla, 2-hr dry cleaning available, expensive. **Martinizing**, US franchise, at Curridabat, Sabana Oriente (by new ring road) and Escazú.

Libraries

Biblioteca Nacional, (National Library) Av 3, C 5-7, is a useful reference resource for anyone looking to research Costa Rica with several current special interest periodicals, and copies of all national newspapers dating back to 1833. No lending facilities. Mon-Fri 0800-1630, open to foreigners with identification. **Centro Cultural Costarricense Norteamericano**, C 37, Av 1-5, has a good library. **Universidad de Costa Rica** in San Pedro suburb, east of central San José.

Medical services

The standard of medical facilities in Costa Rica, and in San José in particular, is very high. Call your embassy for a recommendation. The clinic of choice for residents is **Clínica Bíblica**, C 1, Av 14, T2257-5252, www.clinicabiblica.com, which also has an emergency service and a 24-hr pharmacy. **Hospital CIMA**, 1 km east of the Multiplaza on

the Santa Ana road, T2208-1000, www.cimahospital.com is a modern hospital that opened in 2000. Fully equipped for 24-hr emergencies and pharmacy. Social Security Hospitals have good reputations (free to social security members), but few members of staff speak English.
Doctor: Dr Jorge Quesada Vargas, Clínica Internacional, Av 14, C 3-5, speaks German.
Dentist: Dra Fresia Hidalgo, Uned Building, San Pedro, T2234-2840, 1400-1800. English spoken, reasonable prices, recommended. Fernando Baldioceda and Silvia Oreamuno, 225 m north of the Toyota intersection on Paseo Colón, both speak English.
Pharmacies: widespread through the city. There are a couple on Av 2 close to the junction with C Central and several close to Hospital San Juan on Paseo Colón.
Red Cross Ambulance: T2221-5818.

Post offices
The Central Post Office takes up much of a block with the entrance on C 2 between Av 1 and 2, open 0730-1800, Mon-Fri, 0730-1200 Sat, closed Sun. If you are picking letters up from the *Lista de Correos* you can read them in the stylish Teando Café. The Museo de Filateca may also take up a little of your time. There is also a Visa ATM machine in the post office. **Courier services** are also available from San José. **DHL,** Paseo Colón, Calle 34, Edif Elizabeth, 1st floor, T2210-3838, www.dhl.com. **Federal Express,** World Service Center, Paseo Colón, 100 m east of the León Cortés statue, San José, T0800-052-1090, www.fedex.com. **UPS,** 50 m east of Pizza Hut, Pavas, San José T2290-2828, www.ups.com.

Useful addresses
Emergencies: T911. **Immigration** is on the airport highway, opposite Hospital México. You need to go here for exit visas, extensions, etc. If they are busy, you could queue all day. To get there, take bus 10 or 10A Uruca, marked 'México', then cross over highway at the bridge and walk 200 m along highway.

Key phone numbers

Juan Santamaría International Airport, T2441-0744 or T2443-2622
SANSA, T2223-4179
NatureAir, T2299-6000
Tica Bus, T2221-8954
UK Embassy, T2258-2025
US Embassy, T2519-2000
Hospital CIMA, T2208-1000
SINAC, T2234-0973

Better to find a travel agent who can obtain what you need for a fee, say US$5. Make sure you get a receipt if you give up your passport. **Judiciary,** thefts should be reported in San José to Recepción de Denuncias, Organismo de Investigación Judicial (OIJ), C19, Av 6-8, T2222-1365. **Sistema Nacional de Areas de Conservación** (SINAC, Apdo 10104-1000, T2234-0973, www.sinac.go.cr) in San José administers the National Park system. For information and permits to visit and/or camp in the Parks apply to **Fundación de Parques Nacionales** (FPN), 300 m north and 175 m east of Santa Teresita Church, Barrio Escalante, C 23, Av 15, San José, T2257-2239, www.fpncostarica.org, open Mon-Fri 0800-1200, 1300-1700. Most permits can be obtained at park entrances, but check in advance if your trip depends on gaining entrance. To contact park personnel by radio link or make accommodation reservations, T2233-4160, but good Spanish is a help (bilingual operators at National Parks can be reached by dialling 192). If you make reservations at their San José office, make sure they have made them direct with the park and that you have clear confirmation to avoid difficulties on arrival. If you want to work as a volunteer in the parks, contact SINAC. An alternative is to contact **ASVO** (Asociación de Voluntarios para el servicio en las Areas Protegidas), Av 3-5, C 36, San José, T2258-4430, www.asvocr.org.

Contents

120 Alajuela and around
122 Ins and outs
122 Sights
122 South and west of
Alajuela
124 Parque Nacional Volcán
Poás
125 Northwest of Alajuela
128 Listings

135 Heredia and around
136 Ins and outs
136 Sights
136 South of Heredia
141 East of Heredia towards
Monte de la Cruz
141 Northeast of San José
141 Listings

145 Cartago and around
145 Ins and outs
145 Sights
147 Volcán Irazú
148 Orosí Valley
149 Parque Nacional
Tapantí-Marcizo de
la Muerte
150 Listings

153 Turrialba and around
153 Ins and outs
153 Sights
156 Listings

Footprint features

118 Don't miss …
121 Coffee cup of Costa Rica
138 A day trip on Volcán Barva
148 Visiting Volcán Irazú
155 Rafting the Reventazón and
Pacuare

Central Highlands

At a glance

⊖ **Getting around** There's a
good local bus service that's
quick and efficient.

◉ **Time required** Anything from
3 to 10 days.

☽ **Weather** It's warm by day
but gets chilly at night if you're
in higher altitudes and it's wettest
May-Oct, but the clouds make the
volcanoes very atmospheric.

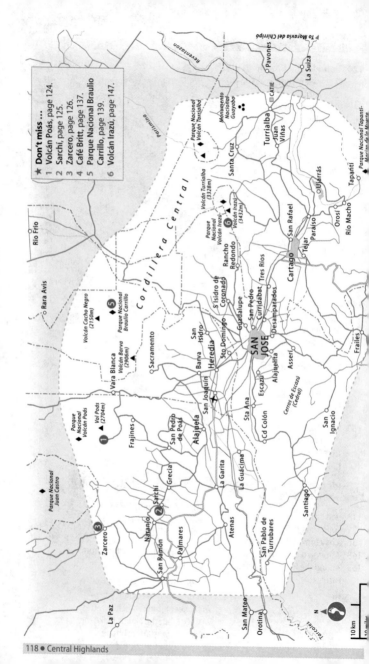

Don't miss ...

1 Volcán Poás, page 124.
2 Sarchí, page 125.
3 Zarcero, page 126.
4 Café Britt, page 137.
5 Parque Nacional Braulio Carrillo, page 139.
6 Volcán Irazú, page 147.

To Moravia del Chirripó

Pavones

La Suiza

CATIE

Reventazón

Turrialba

Juan Viñas

Parque Nacional Volcán Turrialba

Monumento Nacional Guayabo

Santa Cruz

Parque Nacional Tapantí-Macizo de la Muerte

Tapantí

Río Macho

Orosi

Ujarrás

San Rafael

Paraíso

Volcán Turrialba (3328m)

Parque Nacional Volcán Irazú

Volcán Irazú (3432m)

San Pedro

Rancho Redondo

Tres Ríos

Cartago

Tejar

Pavas

Pavas

Cordillera Central

Río Frío

Rara Avis

Volcán Cacho Negro (2150m)

Parque Nacional Braulio Carrillo

Sacramento

Volcán Barva (2906m)

Vara Blanca

San Isidro

San Pedro de Coronado

Guadalupe

San Isidro

San Domingo

Barva

Heredia

Curridabat

Desamparados

SAN JOSÉ

Frailes

Parque Nacional Juan Castro

Parque Nacional Volcán Poás

Vol Poás (2704m)

Frajines

San Pedro de Poás

Alajuela

San Joaquín

Santo Domingo

San Ana

Escazú

Cd Colón

Alajuelita

Asserí

Cerros de Escazú (Cedral)

San Ignacio

Zarcero

San Ramón

Naranjo

Sarchí

Grecia

Palmares

La Garita

Atenas

San Pablo de Turrubares

La Guácima

Santiago

La Paz

San Mateo

Orotina

Tárcoles

N

10 km

10 miles

Bordered by mountains and looming volcanic peaks, Costa Rica's Central Highlands are a curious mix of national parks, vibrant market towns and slow-paced agricultural communities. And as you travel through the region you can see that the nation's coffee heritage, evident in the neat lines of shimmering bushes that rise and fall with the contours of the lowland slopes, is very much alive and well.

Like the 'golden bean', people have flourished in the consistently temperate climate of these fertile valleys and over two-thirds of Costa Rica's population lives in the region. It's home to the towns of Alajuela, Heredia and Cartago – all of whom once fought San José for domination of the country. And although each now lives in the shadow of the capital, they all have a feel that subtly betrays an individual sense of history and purpose: Alajuela's transience, the energy and creativity of Heredia, and the shell-shocked wanderings of pilgrims in Cartago. Heavenly inspiration and coffee wealth created an impressive sense of civic pride and even the smallest towns have churches of cathedral proportions. Equally unusual are the Dalí-esque topiary creations of Zarcero and the frighteningly successful craft centre of Sarchí.

The volcanic national parks of Irazú and Poás huff and fume, keeping everyone on their toes. Braulio Carrillo National Park, a vast area of primary rainforest, is ideal for guided walks, aerial tram rides and hiking up Volcán Barva. The calm of the Orosí Valley and the orchids of Lankester Gardens are worth a few hours of your time and the more adventurous can strike out through the rainforests of the Tapantí National Park, or get soaked rafting down the mighty Reventazón and Pacuare rivers.

Alajuela and around

Capital of the province of Alajuela, and just over 2 km from the international airport, this once-quiet market town (population 53,430) reflects the realities of modern living. Walking the streets, the atmosphere is one of latent energy, a feeling of nonchalance secure in the knowledge that if the townspeople tried, really tried, they could make a world of difference. After all, the town and indeed national hero Juan Santamaría was born here and he, only a lad at the time, single-handedly saved the country from foreign invasion in the battle of 1856.

The tempo picks up at weekends when farmers converge on the town from the surrounding hills selling fruit, vegetables, flowers and dairy goods. But even so, it is difficult to believe that this is Costa Rica's third largest city – you won't be rushed off your feet. For many Alajuela is an ideal base from where to catch an early-morning flight, to collapse after a late-night arrival or as a lower-key alternative to staying in San José (the busy capital is just 30 minutes away by frequent bus). It makes a good base for exploring the craft centre of Sarchí, heading out to the Butterfly Farm in La Gúacima, the Zoo Ave bird sanctuary or up to the spectacular crater of Volcán Poás. ▸▸ *For listings, see pages 128-134.*

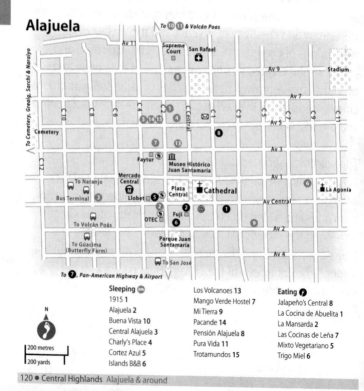

Alajuela

Sleeping
1915 **1**
Alajuela **2**
Buena Vista **10**
Central Alajuela **3**
Charly's Place **4**
Cortez Azul **5**
Islands B&B **6**
Los Volcanoes **13**
Mango Verde Hostel **7**
Mi Tierra **9**
Pacande **14**
Pensión Alajuela **8**
Pura Vida **11**
Trotamundos **15**

Eating
Jalapeño's Central **8**
La Cocina de Abuelita **1**
La Mansarda **2**
Las Cocinas de Leña **7**
Mixto Vegetariano **5**
Trigo Miel **6**

200 metres
200 yards

Coffee cup of Costa Rica

First impressions of the Central Highlands region do little to inspire – the view of the Autopista General Cañas from a bus or taxi running between the airport and San José might make it difficult to believe that there is any nature out there – but beyond the urban landscape of the freeway, the fertility of the land that makes up the Central Highlands is the foundation of modern Costa Rica. It's colloquially called the Meseta Central (central plateau). The volcanoes of Poás and Barva to the north, Irazú and Turrialba to the east and the northern limits of the Talamanca massif to the south create hundreds of rivers that have shaped and scarred the landscape. Only Turrialba sends all its rivers to one ocean, the Caribbean, the rest preferring to share the rainfall between the Caribbean and the Pacific.

After a brief foray through the region for easy pickings, the actual colonization of Costa Rica was late in coming compared to its Central American neighbours. Although Columbus first landed in Limón in 1502, it was not until 1561 that the first permanent settlement of Garcimuñoz was founded in the western Central Highlands. The founding of Cartago in 1563 marks the beginning of the country's colonization proper, with cattle ranching, mule breeding and cacao farming sustaining families despite constant and ongoing uprisings from indigenous peoples protesting against the slave system of the *encomienda* (see page 412). Fixed communities began to spring up across the fertile valley, among them Heredia (1706), San José (1736) and later Alajuela (officially 1782).

Indifferent economic growth turned into prosperity with the introduction of coffee in the early 1800s and the region rapidly grew to produce and finally export sufficient quantities of the bean to fund the development of a very vibrant middle-class. Comfortable temperatures ranging from 15-23°C, coupled with rich volcanic soils and highland sun were perfect conditions for what became known as the 'golden bean'.

Despite the vagaries of the today's global coffee market, the wealth created from these exports inspired and funded ecclesiastical architecture on a scale rarely seen. A spectacular trail of churches leads from one town to the next through the whole of the Central Highlands and ornate masonry and fine stained glasswork stand as monuments to religious priorities and wealth.

In the early 20th century, the rise of the banana in the tropical lowlands, the fall in coffee prices and greater access to education, moved the power focus away from coffee elites and the simple classification of the highlands ended. Today, the towns and cities of the area have thrived or struggled depending on their respective histories and agriculture has diversified beyond the golden bean. Economic necessity and the growth of communication has also broken down the old barriers of time and distance. But instead of breaking down to become one large amalgamation, many towns in the Central Highlands have held on to their differences, all the time watched over by the volcanic peaks that have created and shared the region's destiny.

Ins and outs ›› *Colour map 2, B2.*

Getting there
Buses from San José run every 10 minutes or so from Calle 10, Avenida Central-2 and Avenida 2, Calle 10-12, with the latter location providing a half hourly service through the night between 2400 and 0500. Buses to San José leave from the main bus terminal in Alajuela and from Avenida 4 and Calle 2-4. Both cost US$0.70. To get to the airport simply get on a bus going to San José – the bus stops outside the terminal building. From the airport, get a bus going to Alajuela. ›› *See Transport, page 133, for further details.*

Sights

Small enough to walk round, the town focuses on the **Central Plaza** shaded by huge mango trees – a clear and obvious symbol giving lead to the town's moniker as the 'city of mangoes'. When not craning your neck looking up in the trees for the mythical sloths, join in the general mêlée of underactivity with the townsfolk sitting on benches dotted through the plaza. A meander of at most 100 m, will take you to the domed **cathedral** which closed for renovation following the earthquake in 1991. Now reopened, it is one of several 19th-century buildings around the plaza, most of which suffer from general neglect. A more interesting church, in setting as much as style, is **La Agonía** five blocks to the east. A monument to Juan Santamaría, the drummer boy who torched the building in Rivas (Nicaragua) in which William Walker's filibusters were entrenched in 1856 (see page 413), thus ending his plans for domination of Central America, stands proud a couple of blocks south of the plaza. The **Museo Histórico Juan Santamaría** ① *Av 3, C 2, one block north of the plaza, T2441-4775, www.mhcjs.go.cr (website works sporadically), Tue-Sun 1000-1800, free,* tells a somewhat confusing account of the war. A collection of paintings, maps and descriptions mumble their way through events in Spanish. There's also a more modern auditorium for talks and lectures.

Ojo de Agua ① *about 6 km south of Alajuela, T2441-2808, open daily until 1700, US$1.25, children under 6 free, US$2 for parking,* is a spring-fed water park popular with *Josefinos* at weekend. There is a series of swimming pools including a children's pool, an Olympic pool for the serious swimmer, a boating lake as well as areas for picnics, playing games and generally having a good time. To get there, take a direct bus from Avenida 1, Calle 20-22 in San José or take bus to Alajuela and then on to San Antonio de Belén.

South and west of Alajuela ●● ›› *pp129-131. Colour map 2, B2.*

Butterfly Farm
① *T2438-0400, www.butterflyfarm.co.cr. Daily 0830-1700. US$15 adults, US$10 students, US$7 children under 12, includes 2-hr guided tour at 0830, 1100, 1300 and 1500. Easiest transport option is a pick-up return service provided by the Butterfly Farm. Departures from main hotels in San José 3 times a day. Price including tour US$25. Travelling independently, there is a bus for La Guácima Mon-Sat from Av 1, C 20-22, roughly hourly, last return 1700, 1 hr journey, US$0.60. At last stop walk 300 m from school south to the butterfly sign. There are also buses from Alajuela. Take bus marked 'La Guácima abajo' from Av 2 between C 8-10. Hourly service, journey 40 mins. By car, turn east toward San Antonio de Belén from the airport highway (Autopista General Cañas) at the Herradura Hotel, and follow The Butterfly Farm blue morpho road signs.*

The small town of La Guácima de Alajuela, some 20 km west of San José and 7 km from Alajuela, would be a quiet little backwater if it weren't for the buses filled with visitors arriving to see the world's second largest exporter of butterflies (the largest one being in Taiwan). The farm is a fascinating insight into the life cycle of the butterfly. After a short introductory video, a tour leads you through enclosed tropical gardens where the guide points out some of the 120 native species at every stage of development, explaining details of habits and preferences.

Set up in 1984 by Joris Brinckerhoff, a former Peace Corps volunteer, the Butterfly Farm was opened in 1990. After visiting the laboratories and completing the two-hour tour you are free to wander through the fascinating gardens and enjoy the experience at a more leisurely pace. Visiting in the morning, especially in the rainy season, is strongly recommended as the butterflies tend to take shelter when it is raining or overcast.

Zoo Ave

ⓘ T2433-8989, www.zooave.org. Open daily 0900-1700. US$1, children US$1.50. If driving, follow the signs to Zoo Ave from the Pan-American Highway heading west from Juan Santamaría International Airport. Take a bus from Alajuela to La Garita. A cab to the zoo from Alajuela will cost around US$5.

Heading west towards Atenas the road drops slightly before arriving in **La Garita de Alajuela**, with a climate perfect for Zoo Ave. Owned and operated by the Nature Restoration Foundation, this government-recognized wildlife rescue centre is set in landscaped gardens. While visitors enjoy a relaxing day learning about the animals and plants, Zoo Ave educates visitors about the importance of Costa Rican wildlife through interactive exhibits and rehabilitation and release programmes. Zoo Ave's breeding efforts are focused on threatened, endangered or otherwise sensitive species such as scarlet and green macaws, the green iguana and the squirrel monkey. Captive breeding programmes have successfully introduced macaws as part of the Scarlet Macaw Restoration Program.

While visiting you'll see over 100 species of native and exotic birds including toucans, parrots, black swans, eagles and the resplendent quetzal, as well as all four types of monkey, and other mammals and reptiles.

Atenas

Next stop heading west from La Garita is Atenas (population 6569), notorious for a consistency of climate that keeps the temperatures between 17° to 32°C a fact that has become part of local legend. A second, less well known, local story is that both the church and the main plaza of this small town lie on an earthquake fault. Whether both, either or neither are fact can be discussed while trying *toronja rellena* (local speciality: a sweet-filled grapefruit).

Parque Nacional Volcán Poás ⓘⓘ ⟫ pp130-134. Colour map 2, B2.

ⓘ *Daily 0800-1530, 1 hr later Fri-Sat from Dec-Apr. US$7. Plenty of parking available. Tours to Poás are provided by many tour operators in San José. See page 105. On a clear day with no wind you can wear shorts and T-shirts. When the clouds come in and block the sun, the temperature plummets. Add a sprinkling of rain or just being drenched by clouds and you can quickly get cold so take a rain jacket just in case. Good wheelchair access.*

At a lofty 2708 m this national park centres on the vast crater of Poás Volcano. Only 37 km north of Alajuela along gently winding roads which stop only a few hundred metres from the summit, this is easily the most popular national park in the country. The main draw is the vast crater, 1320 m wide, with its steeply sloping sides descending for a depth of 300 m. Currently filled with a simmering turquoise lake, in more active periods the crater dries out, dusting the surrounding landscape with a sprinkling of sulphur. The most notorious eruption in the 20th century blew an ash cloud skyward some 8 km. The crater erupted between 1952 and 1954, with a couple of explosions in 1989 and again in 1994. Today, volcanologists believe the magma chamber is just 400-500 m below the lake's surface. Reassuringly for most visitors, the national park guards believe it is a lot deeper. If there was any risk to visitors the park would be closed.

Beyond the drama of the volcano, 79 bird species, including quetzals and hummingbirds, reside in the park's dwarf cloud forest and a short trail of just over 1 km leads to a second crater now filled with the Botos Lagoon. Last entry on the trail is at 1430. Free rambling is not permitted for safety reasons, so stick to the paths.

A good **visitor information centre** is the final stop, from where it's a few hundred metres uphill to the look-out post. In keeping with the popularity of the park, there is road access almost to the summit. After visiting the information centre the Café Britt coffee bar provides snacks and drinks.

Alajuela to Poás

Travelling up to Poás, the road passes through good coffee country with gently undulating hills rising slowly towards the volcanic slopes of Poás. As you climb from the warmth of Alajuela, the temperature gives way to freshness and then a slight chill when you are in the shade.

There are two roads leading to Poás making for a pleasant circuit. One leads north from Alajuela towards **San Pedro de Poás**. En route the views are spectacular, shifting and changing with the light and the weather, a fact not wasted on Casa del Café, a roadside stop with a good viewing point overlooking the rows of coffee fields. Beyond San Pedro the road continues to climb to the town of **Frajines** and the nearby resort of **Laguna de Fraijanes** ⓘ *T2482-2166*. A natural lagoon is the focal point for picnics and barbecues, and there are trails through 18 ha of forest, horses for hire, fishing and some basic cabins each sleeping three people (D).

An alternative route to Poás heads northeast of Alajuela toward Carrizal following the road to the lowland town of San Miguel and bearing left just before the town of Vara Blanca. Just beyond Vara Blanca the road crosses the saddle between the summits of Poás and Volcán Barva passing on the way **La Paz Waterfall Gardens** ⓘ *5 km north of Vara Blanca, T2482-2720, www.waterfallgardens.com, daily, 0800-1700, last admission 1530, US$32.* The nature park and wildlife refuge has over 3.5 km of trails leading through the forests and five waterfalls and includes Costa Rica's largest butterfly observatory. There's also a full-service restaurant and accommodation is available at the Peace Lodge see page 130.

Just like the flora and fauna of the country, the traditional communities of the Central Highlands have sought out the best place to live and farm. A neat line of villages and hamlets huddles round the lower western slopes of Poás Volcano sitting at an altitude of close to 1500 m. Rivers have slowly carved the landscape, creating a mosaic of steep hills and deep valleys. But while this resulting countryside is scenic, it doesn't make for easy links between valleys. Before the advent of the car, each community developed almost in isolation, only coming together at market time and on special occasions.

Heading northwest from Alajuela the road leads to **Grecia**, the craft centre of **Sarchí**, the transport hub of **Naranjo**, the topiary plaza fronting the church of **Zarcero** and further down the slopes to **San Ramón** and **Palmares**. None of these towns in their own right is an absolute 'must-see', but a quiet day spent meandering through the area gives a good insight into the agricultural heartland of the highlands.

Grecia

A small town (population 17,173) just over 18 km northwest of Alajuela, Grecia adds the sweet delights of pineapple to the coffee produce of the region. A distinctive feature of the town is the red all-metal church dominating the leafy plaza and the Casa de la Cultura.

A short distance before Grecia on the road to Alajuela is **World of Snakes** ① *T494-3700, www.theworldofsnakes.com, Mon-Fri 0800-1600, US$11, children US$6, reductions for biology students*, a snake farm with over 50 species on display. You can get really close up if you want.

Sarchí

Not the once-popular advertising agency that threatened to take over the world before retiring in the Costa Rican highlands, but a craft village that owes its fame to the finely painted *carretas* (oxcarts) produced in the town, some might think Sarchí's (population 10,772) charms somewhat lacking, but as a passing stop it's worth a visit. However, you can't fail to be hit by the blatant commercialism of the place. Originally distinctive to the area and still used by some farmers, the oxcarts are now seen throughout the country, their popularity elevating them almost to the status of national emblem. If you like them, you'll love the place.

Sarchí is actually two towns – **Sarchí Sur** and **Sarchí Norte** – separated by some 3 km, set among steep hills which afford impressive vistas across the valleys of coffee bushes. The heart of the town is to the north but there are *fábricas* (factories) in both parts. In Sarchí Norte, a gently tiered plaza leads to a birthday cake church of bright lime green which positively glows at sunset. Inside, the vaulted wooden ceilings illustrate the creative individualism expressed in churches throughout the Central Valley.

The oxcarts and wooden furniture are mass-produced by hand in *fábricas* (factories) and *mueblarías* (furniture shops) and the town has done everything it can to help relieve you of your money, and why not? Visit the workshop of Fábrica de Carretas Chaverri (see page 132) and you can't help but be impressed by the craftsmanship of the artists. The brightly coloured floral and angular motifs are all hand-painted making each cart unique. A full-size cart costs between US$320 and US$360, but smaller options are available at a fraction of the price. If transport is a problem, worldwide flat-pack shipping can be arranged.

If you are still doubtful about spending your hard-earned cash the options are many. The colourful painting style is also applied to benches and cluster tables. At some time in your stay in Costa Rica you will relax in one of the sturdy comfortable leather chairs rocking on balconies and patios throughout the country. You can buy them in Sarchí and again they can be flat-packed and shipped home. Other goods available include hammocks, salad bowls, walking sticks, wallets, vases and of course coffee.

Parque Nacional Juan Castro Blanco

ⓘ *Private visits to Juan Castro Blanco have always been possible, taking a car north to Bajos del Toro Amarillo. Infrastructure is beginning to open up with simple accommodation available at the Centro Turístico Toro Amarillo. Buses leave from Grecia, passing through Sarchí.*

North of Sarchí and east of Zarcero, Juan Castro Blanco National Park (14,453 ha) protects the slopes and watersheds of **Volcán Porvenir** (2267 m) and **Volcán Platanar** (2183 m), the origin of many rivers that feed the northern lowlands. The national park has large areas of transitional rain- and cloudforest, making it a perfect, albeit hidden-away, spot for birdwatchers.

Bosque de Paz Rain- and Cloud Forest Reserve

The privately owned Bosque de Paz Rain- and Cloud Forest Reserve of around 1000 ha connects Juan Castro Blanco and Poás Volcano national parks, acting as a biological corridor. A network of 28 km of trails winds through forest ranging in altitude from 1400 m to 2450 m. The bird list is currently up to 300 species with 324 orchid counted to date.

Naranjo

The agricultural town of Naranjo (population 17,482) has an exquisite bright white church which is slowly being restored. To the side, there's a rather incongruous grotto that leads to a small altar and behind it is a little pond stocked with Koi carp. The main town plaza has a shocking post-modern pyramidal structure which just tops off the feeling that, despite being a quiet place, the desired gentle serenity of the place never quite materializes.

Back on the Pan-American Highway heading north from San José the Río Colorado is at Km 37, and is the jumping-off point for **Tropical Bungee**. After passing the Grecia turn, continue for 1 km over the river. Shortly after the river, looking to the right, you will see a large 'Tropical Bungee' sign just off the road – take the next right. Follow the signs down to the bridge. If the office is not open, look out for Carlos, whose house is the last one before the road descends. Even better, call in advance. ▸▸ *See page 133 for more details.*

Zarcero

At the northern limit of the Central Valley, Zarcero (population 3904) enjoys a fresh mountain climate where the bean gives way to the beast. After climbing the gently meandering lower slopes scaling the last few kilometres the roads adopt an obsessive winding tendency. The views are very scenic – drivers should make sure they keep their eyes on the road. Dairy cattle chewing the cud fuel the local economy. A local speciality is *palmito*, a white, moist cheese rather like mozzarella, and a range of sweet products including *dulce de leche* and the best *cajeta de leche* in the country. Fruit jams are another regional product, which can be bought in town or at any of the many roadside stalls. Heading north from Zarcero, the road falls, rapidly twisting and winding down through the western limits of the Cordillera Central and the eastern edge of the Cordillera de Tilarán.

In town, it is the bizarre topiary creations filling the main square that draw in the crowds. Travel guides and brochures go into linguistic spasms in their attempts to describe and explain these creations of Zarcero's most famous son, Evangelista Blanco Breves. Given the job of maintaining the central plaza in 1964, Evangelista set about the task with a few simple ideas that have subsequently grown, been clipped, grown and been clipped again. He has created animals, couples dancing, a helicopter, baskets and many Henry Moore-like sculptures that are still in metamorphosis. According to Evangelista, the inspiration and the idea for these naturally evolving artworks comes from 'El Maestro' – the great celestial Master who also happens to reside in the white twin-towered church at the end of a topiary double arch leading through the plaza. Within the church, colour and motifs use just a pinch of artistic guidance from the *carreteras* of Sarchí.

San Ramón

San Ramón (population 14,122), known locally as the 'City of Poets', is easily reached from the Pan-American Highway, some 76 km from San José. As the most western settlement of substance in the Central Valley, the town developed through market trading and still has a vibrant street market on Saturday mornings. The history of the stark neo-Gothic metal church which replaced the previous building destroyed by earthquake in 1924, can be viewed at the **Museo de San Ramón** ① T2437-9851, Mon-Fri, 0830-1700, free, on the north side of the church. The museum also has a smattering of local history exhibits and black and white photos.

Los Angeles Cloud Forest Reserve

① *About 20 km north of San Ramón and 40 km northwest of Alajuela. From San Ramón, follow the road to La Fortuna until the town of Los Angeles Norte. Shortly after this point you will see signs for the Villa Blanca Cloud Forest Nature Spa & Hotel, T2461-0300, www.villablanca-costarica.com (see page 131). Optional guided walks from US$26, night walks (US$26), birdwatching (US$26), coffee plantation tours (US$85), horse riding US$32 for 2 hrs and zip-lines canopy tour US$42. One-day visits from San José can be arranged direct or through tour operators in the capital, see page 105.*

This privately owned, 800-ha cloudforest reserve attracts far fewer visitors than the better-known Monteverde (see page 192). What prominence it does have is in part due to the fact that it is owned by former President of Costa Rica, Rodrigo Carazo and his wife, Estrella, who also own the Villa Blanca Spa & Hotel, see page 131. It also gives the visitor a good insight into life in the cloudforest on a day trip from San José – something which is very difficult to do with Monteverde.

The reserve has a couple of short trails, with a longer one requiring about eight hours and probably an overnight stop, passing waterfalls and good views. Guided treks are available, with horse riding and a canopy tour for those wanting a bit more buzz.

Palmares

South of the Pan-American Highway, 7 km from San Ramón, is the small town of Palmares (population: 5622). This quiet town has an exceptionally overgrown main square squashed up to a rather bleak, albeit ornate, church with a façade that belies the beauty and details of the stained-glass windows of the interior. General comings and goings give way to fiesta for 10 days in the middle of January with carnival rides, music, dancing and non-fatal bull fights.

For Sleeping and Eating price codes and other relevant information, see Essentials, pages 44-47.

● Sleeping

Alajuela *p120, map p120*

Without exception, no one knows street names and numbers. When looking for hotels, aim for the nearest landmark.

AL-B Hotel 1915, C 2, Av 5-7, 300 m north of Central Park, T441-0495, www.1915hotel. com. Beautiful old family home smartly refurbished with wooden furnishings and a stylish garden patio café. Very pleasant service. Rooms all have cable TV, minibar, telephone, Wi-Fi, some have a/c. Price includes breakfast. Parking available. There are also several apartments just half a block away sleeping up to 5 people. Best in town for the price.

A-B Los Volcanoes, Av 3, C Central-2, T2441-0525, losvolcanes@racsa.co.cr. Good place, central location. Blends high service levels with a homely feel complete with hammocks. Free airport transfers.

B Pacande, C 2-4, Av 5, T2443-8481, www.hotelpacande.com. Friendly spot although perhaps lacking some style. Good service with free internet, and well maintained, cheaper for groups in dormitory rooms.

B-C Charly's Place, a couple of blocks north of the central park on Av 5, C Central-1, T2441-0115, lilyhotel@latinmail.com. Popular place, although slightly overpriced, with 11 rooms, most with private bathrooms, cheaper without, and some with TV. Handy services for the newly arrived or just departing, use of kitchen and patio for relaxing. Breakfast in high season, parking available. Credit cards accepted.

B-C Hotel Alajuela, on southwest corner of Central Park at Av Central and C 2, T2441-1241, alajuela@racsa.co.cr. Offers 28 generally good, although fairly

standard, rooms and apartments all with private bathroom. Helpful staff and a garden patio to relax on.

A-B Islands B&B, Av 1, C 7-9, 50 m west of La Agonía church, T2442-0573, islandsbb@ hotmail.com. A small *Tico*-owned B&B with 8 comfortably decorated rooms. Rooms have cable TV, free local calls. Breakfast served in small garden patio. Airport pick-up available, very secure and 24-hr parking.

B Hotel Mi Tierra, new name, new location, same people, Av2, C 3-5 T2441-4022, www.hotelmitierra.net. Single to quad rooms, with private or shared bath. Pool, adventure tours organized on site, and parking. Popular with travellers.

B-C Pensión Alajuela, Av 9, C Central-2, opposite the court house, T2441-6251, www.pensionalajuela.com. Mixed bag of 12 simple rooms, some with private bath, some without. Each otherwise rather bare room has been painted with a nature scene. There's a small bar downstairs as well as laundry, fax and internet service.

C-D Hotel Trotamundos, 1 block north and half block west from Museo Juan Santamaria, T2430-5832, www.hosteltrotamundos.com. Cheap rooms as well as lounge, kitchen and internet. Breakfast also included.

C-D Mango Verde Hostel, Av 3, C 2-4, T2441-6330, mifloresbb@hotmail.com. 6 clean rooms with private bath and hot water, and the courtyard and communal area create a relaxing atmosphere. Use of kitchen for guests, laundry, parking available and close to the centre of town.

D-F Central Alajuela, Av Central, C 6-8, close to the bus terminal, T2443-8437. Pretty basic rooms and shared bathrooms have cold water but it is reasonably clean. Popular with *Ticos* arriving from out of town.

E Cortez Azul, Av 5, C 2-4, T2443-6145, hotelcortezazul@gmail.com. Popular spot with a handful of good clean rooms and dorms.

Outside Alajuela

LL Villas Xandari, 5 km north of Alajuela, T2443-2020, www.xandari.com. Formerly a coffee *finca*. An inspirational creation from the minds of Californian architect Sherrill Broudy and artist Charlene Broudy. More a mind and body experience than a hotel. With beautiful views and calming music from the restaurant balcony day and night, Xandari eschews *Tico* conventions of room shape and design, drawing instead on Moorish origins. Each of the 21 excessively spacious private villas has a balcony and private bathroom and is decorated with original artwork. The restaurant revels in the organic produce of Xandari's gardens. If the calming serenity is not sufficient, you can wander through 4 km of trails, take a dip in 1 of 3 pools or have a massage in the full spa. One of Costa Rica's most impressive hotels.

L-A Las Orquídeas Inn, further north on the road out to Grecía at the Alajuela, La Garita, San Pedro de Poás fork, T2433-9346, www.orquideasinn.com. Close to 30 spacious rooms and villas making the most of views of Poás volcano. The Inn also has a fine restaurant, pool and bar. Pick-ups from airport 10 mins away can be arranged.

AL Pura Vida Hotel, 2 km from town in the district of Tuetal, northwest of Alajuela T2430-2929, www.puravidahotel.com. An excellent place. Rooms and 5 *casitas* set in the beautiful gardens are equipped with kitchenettes. Garden paths lead between tropical flowers, including orcids and butterfly-attracting plants, and have distant views of Volcán Poás. Breakfast can be arranged for any time to help with the early morning airport runs. Can help with booking rental cars, excursions and arrange airport pick-ups.

A Buena Vista, 7 km north of Alajuela on the road to Volcán Poás, T2442-8605, in the US and Canada 1-800-506-2304, www.hotelbuenavistacr.com. 15 large rooms come with private bathroom and cable TV, many with balconies have views of the Central Valley or Volcán Poás. This modern, tidy plantation-style hotel has an understated charm. Services include pool, well stocked gift shop, restaurant with a good mix of international dishes and wines and a quiet bar.

Close to the airport

L Hampton Inn, T2443-0000, www.hamptoninn.com. Closest hotel to the airport and therefore handy if you want to get in or out quickly with the minimum of fuss. As with every Hampton Inn, the price includes continental breakfast and free local calls. Add the free-form pool and complimentary transportation to and from the airport and this could be the final post you're looking for.

L Garden Court Hotel, T2443-0043, www.gardencourtairporthotel.com. Again, very handy for the airport, the Garden Court has pool, restaurant, free breakfast and internet services.

A La Rosa de América, in Barrio San José on the road to Atenas, T2433-2741, www.larosadeamerica.com. La Rosa has a beautiful setting a well as being in a convenient spot. With pool, restaurant, fans in rooms and hot water. Recommended.

Zoo Ave *p123*

LL Hotel Club Martino, opposite Zoo Ave, T2433-8382, www.hotelmartino.com. Plantation-style family-run hotel with luxurious and graceful elegance throughout the 34 rooms, excellent Italian restaurant, large pool, gym, tennis courts and health spa.

AL-A Chatelle Country Resort, T2487-8282, www.hotelchatelle.com. 15 rooms with bath, some with kitchenette and all with TV. Beautiful gardens, good restaurant, pool, weekly/monthly rates, airport pick-up available at no extra charge. Opposite is an orchid nursery with a marvellous variety of blooms, run as a hobby by an enthusiastic English-speaking optometrist, who will give you a guided tour for US$3.50.

Atenas p123

AL El Cafetal Inn, out of town in St Eulalia, 4.7 km towards Grecia, T2446-5785, www.cafetal.com. Beautiful private house set among fields of coffee bushes. Large pool, 10 rooms, all well appointed, airport transport. Recommended.

A Ana's Place, only place in downtown Atenas, T2446-5019. Includes breakfast, private bathroom, weekly/monthly rates available.

Parque Nacional Volcán Poás p124

You cannot camp in the park but there are a couple of good places listed here and several places advertising cabins leading up to Poás and in the surrounding area.

L-A Poás Volcano Lodge, T2482-2194 or in UK T01420-549205, www.poasvolcano lodge.com (PO Box 5723-1000, San José). 500 m from Vara Blanca junction on road to Poasito approaching the volcano from the east. Sign on gate at El Cortijo farm where the farm road leads for 1 km to the house. 25 mins to volcano by car, 1½ hrs from San José. Merging both English and Welsh-style farmhouse stonework (indicating the owner's origins) and the openness of a ranch, this charismatic lodge has good views of the volcano and gets a large amount of return clientèle and recommendations. The 9 rooms are spacious and accommodate couples and families equally well. There is a games room, or mountain bikes and horse riding for those with a bit more energy to burn. Great food includes the Breakfast Feast which will set you up for the day. Price includes breakfast; good wholesome dinners cost between US$8-12.

D Lagunillas Lodge, T2448-5506. Simple farmhouse lodgings in a private setting 3 km before the park entrance. Good views and horses available for hire.

Alajuela to Poás p124

LL Peace Lodge, part of La Paz Waterfall Gardens, T2225-0643, www.waterfall gardens.com. Complete luxury with jacuzzi and stone fireplace in each room. You'll have the rainforest as your own private wonderland before the Waterfall Gardens open to the public.

Grecia p125

L-A Posada Mimosa, T2494-5868, www.mimosa.co.cr. Rooms, suites and a couple of fully equipped cabins and a cottage set in beautiful, tropical gardens, with great views especially from the pool, which is heated by solar energy. All accommodation has private bath and hot water. Suites and cabins have a small kitchenette, ideal for longer stays.

A-B B & B Grecia, in downtown Grecia, T2494-2573, www.bandbgrecia.com. A handful of rooms, with tropical gardens, lecture rooms, and Wi-Fi. Has links to language classes given by Harmonia Casa (www.harmoniacasa.com).

A few cheap options include: **D Cabaña Los Cipreses** and **G Pensión Quirós**.

Sarchí p125

B Hotel Villa Sarchí, 800 m north of town in San Juan de Valverde Vega, T2454-5000. 11 rooms with private bath, hot water, cable TV and pool. Difficult to find but the views are said to be good.

B Cabinas Daniel Zamora, at northern end of town, T2454-4596. Has simple box-like rooms with private bath, fan, hot water and extra blankets if the nights are cold. The rooms are bright and spotless and parking is available.

Bosque de Paz Rain- and Cloud Forest Reserve p126

LL Bosque de Paz Rain/Cloud Forest Private Biological Reserve, T2234-6676, www.bosquedepaz.com. (Infrastructure in the park is virtually non-existent – this is the closest realistic visiting point.) The lodge has 12 rooms set in the forest, each with 2 double beds, private bathroom and hot water. Pleasant touches like Costa Rican pottery are dotted round the hotel, and there is a reference library so you can explore in greater detail what you find on your forays into the cloudforest.

Naranjo *p126*

F La Bambo, down the hill by the football pitch. They may have mustered up enough energy to let you stay in one of their simple rooms.

Zarcero *p126*

B-C Don Beto, on the northern side of the church, T2463-3137, www.hoteldonbeto.com. 8 clean rooms, some with private bath and views over the plaza, in a family home.

San Ramón *p127*

A-B La Posada, 400 m north of the cathedral, T2445-7359, www.posadahotel.net. 34 comfortable rooms in a popular B&B, with private bath, hot water and cable TV. Full use of kitchen and laundry, internet available and small patio complete with rattan rocking chairs. Plenty of parking.
D Gran Hotel, 150 m west of the central park, T2445-6363. Big rooms with private bathrooms, hot water, clean. Good open TV area and friendly as well.
F Hotel Nuevo Jardín, 5 blocks north of the central park, T2445-5620. Simple, clean and friendly.

Los Angeles Cloud Forest Reserve *p127*

LL Villa Blanca Cloud Forest Spa & Nature Reserve, at the edge of the Los Angeles Cloud Forest Reserve. From San Ramón head north to Los Angeles and follow the signs, T2228-4603, www.villablanca-costarica.com. *Casitas* set a rustic tone, but the small houses are fully equipped with private bathroom and hot water.

Palmares *p127*

No cheap accommodation options here.
LL Vista del Valle Plantation, about 6 km southeast of Palmares in the town of Rosario de Naranjo, T2450-0800, www.vistadel

valle.com. A dozen guest rooms of varying size and styles, each with private bathroom and a balcony, set in beautiful surroundings on the boundary of the Río Grande Nature Preserve. Mike Bresnan and his wife Johanna have made every effort to create a sustainable operation involving the local community in tourism activities. In addition to the pool, you can wander through the grounds and discover a 100-m waterfall. Horse riding and birdwatching are also possible. Ask for directions when booking.

❼ Eating

Alajuela *p120, map p120*

❢ **La Cocina de Abuelita**. Simple buffet menu serving traditional *Tico* dishes. Open at lunchtimes daily.
❢ **Las Cocinas de Leña**, C 2, Av 6. Well established, serving grills and seafood at mid-range prices.
❢ **La Mansarda**. Good wholesome *Tico* food, nothing flashy but reasonably priced. Open daily, 1330-2330.
❢ **Mixto Vegetariano**, Av Central, C 2-4. Good vegetarian dishes with a *Tico* twist. Open Mon-Sat.
❢❢ **Jalapeño's Central**, 50 m south of post office, T2430-4027. Great Mexican food in a friendly place.

Several fast-food chains can be found on C Central leading south from Central Park.

Cafés

Trigo Miel, Av 2, C Central-2 is one of a couple of pâtisserie-style cafés in Alajuela serving divine snacks, good coffee topped off with a classy sense of style and finesse. There are also a number of *sodas* dotted round the square and down C Central.

Zoo Ave *p123*

❢❢-❢ **Fiesta del Maíz** *soda*/restaurant. Sells cheap products made only from maize; you can taste spoonfuls before you buy. Open weekends only, it's very busy as a stopping place for weekenders on their way to and from Jacó Beach.

🍴 **Mi Quinta**, a second stopping point, almost as popular.

Sarchí *p125*

🍴🍴 **Las Carretas**, run by and next to Fábrica de Chaverri in Sarchí Sur. Serves *comida típica*.

🍴🍴 **Típico La Finca**, in the north. The best restaurant, serving authentic *Tico* cuisine in a pretty garden with good views.

Naranjo *p126*

There are several *sodas* around the bus stop, one block south and west of the church.

🍴 **Restaurante El Mirador**, heading north to Zarcero. Great views over coffee *fincas* neatly leading down the slope to the Central Valley.

Zarcero *p126*

Several *sodas* and small restaurants around the plaza.

San Ramón *p127*

Restaurants dotted around town, with a few *sodas* close to the bus station.

🍸 Bars and clubs

Alajuela *p120, map p120*

Bars and clubs are limited in Alajuela. Most people choose to head into San José, but there are a couple overlooking the Central Park.

La Troja, south of town, is always popular, but ask locally for the latest hotspots.

🎉 Festivals and events

Alajuela *p120, map p120*

11 Apr Juan Santamaría Day sees Alajuela celebrate the life of the town's most famous son, commemorating the Battle of Rivas in 1856 with a week of general celebration, bands, concerts and dancing.

Mid-Jul The town's fruitful heritage comes to the fore with a Mango Festival that involves parades, public concerts and an arts and crafts fair.

🛍 Shopping

Alajuela *p120, map p120*

There's not much to splash the cash on in Alajuela but **Llobet's**, Av Central-1, C 2-4, is a local institution and a rather amusing department store selling almost everything but rather strangely nothing you really want. **Goodlight Books**, Av 3, C 1-3 T2430-4083, www.goodlightbooks.com. Quality used books, mostly English, espresso, pastries and internet.

Sarchí *p125*

Fábrica de Carretas Chaverri, T2454-4411. Established in 1903, the family-run operation has seen four generations of the Chaverri family produce oxcarts in the area. Nearby is the **Plaza de la Artesanía**, a shopping complex with plenty of souvenir shops to explore. **Taller Lalo Alfaro**, the oldest workshop, is in Sarchí Norte and worth a visit to get a more traditional line on production methods.

⛰ Activities and tours

Alajuela *p120, map p120*

The local football team is Liga Deportiva Alajuelense or more simply **La Liga**, one of Costa Rica's best league teams. Games are normally on Sun but check locally for details, see local press or just watch for everyone heading to the stadium in the northeast corner of the town on match days. Several of the hotels are getting in on the tour markets.

Tour operators

With so many tour operators in San José, Alajuela doesn't even bother trying to compete. There are the following, however.

OTEC have an office on C 2, Av Central-2, T2442-4018, and although aimed at students and those in education, they should be able to help with most problems.

Faytur, Av 3, C 2-4, T2443-4171, www.faytur.com. Provides a wide range of services, primarily hotel bookings, car rentals and flights.

Tropical Bungee, T2248-2212, www.bungee.co.cr. Drops people off an old iron bridge spanning the Río Colorado. A drop of around 80 m sends you flying with the birds in a way that no zip wire or canopy tour ever can. Operating since 1991 and with 10,000+ jumps to their name, Tropical Bungee has an unblemished safety record but, as ever, the risk is always yours. If bungee is not your style, you can also rappel down the Río Colorado and head up river for an exciting nature walk along the river gorge. Open every day, but Sat is more popular. US$65 for 1st jump, US$30 for 2nd.

⊖ Transport

Alajuela *p120, map p120*
Buses leave from the bus terminal or one of the many street stops nearby. Buses to **San José** leave from the main bus terminal and from the station at Av 4, C 2-4 every 10 mins. The latter also provides a half-hourly service between 2400 and 0500, cost US$0.70. From San José buses leave from C 10, Av Central-2 and Av 2, C 10-12 with the latter providing the 24-hr service. Regular buses to **Heredia** leave from the terminal, first at 0400, last at 2300, US$0.50.

Buses to the **Butterfly Farm** marked *'La Guácima abajo'* leave from Av 2 between C 8-10, hourly service, US$0.35. One block west of the terminal buses leave for **Grecia**, **Sarchí** and **Naranjo** every 25 mins, first departure at 0500, last at 2200. One block south of the terminal, buses depart to several small villages in the area, including **Laguna de Fraijanes**.

Parque Nacional Volcán Poás
There is a daily excursion bus to Parque Nacional Volcán Poás (right up to the crater) from the main square of **Alajuela**. It leaves at 0915 (or before if full), connecting with 0830 bus from **San José** (from Av 2, C 12-14, US$3 each way); be there early for a seat; although extra buses run if necessary, the area gets very crowded, US$1.70 each way. The bus waits at the top with ample time to see everything (clouds permitting), returning at 1430. Daily bus to **Alajuela-Poasito** at 1200 (US$1) will take you part way to the summit.

The volcano can be reached by car from **San José**. A taxi for 6 hrs with a side trip will cost about US$50-60.

Atenas *p123*
Buses to Atenas leave from the Coca-Cola bus terminal in **San José** departing every 30 mins, US$1.20. From **Alajuela** catch a bus from the bus terminal heading to La Garita. In Atenas the library on the plaza also serves as the office for the bus company, **Cooptransatenas**, T2446-5767.

Grecia *p125*
Buses to Grecia depart **San José** from the Coca-Cola terminal, every 30 mins, US$1.40. Regular buses from **Alajuela** leave every 45 mins, US$0.90, with others travelling on to **Sarchí**.

Sarchí *p125*
Several times a day to Sarchí from the Coca-Cola Terminal in **San José** at 0530, 0600 and 0630, then at 1215 and 1730, taking roughly 1½ hrs, US$1.45. Alternatively travel to **Alajuela** and get one of the half hourly buses to Sarchí, US$1.10.

Taxis from Sarchí to make quick and frequent journeys between the 2 towns if you want to look around before buying.

Bosque de Paz Rain- and Cloud Forest Reserve *p126*

The easiest way to reach the reserve is by heading north from Sarchí Sur, towards the town of **Bajos de Toro** in the corridor between the two national parks. An equally scenic alternative route leaves from east of **Zarcero** rising to the continental divide before falling again to arrive in Bajos de Toro. Contact the reserve in advance for precise directions. Pick-ups from the airport can be arranged.

Naranjo *p126*

Transportes Naranjo, T2451-3655, have buses to and from **San José**'s Coca-Cola terminal every 20 mins, US$1.40. Buses also connect to other towns and villages in the area.

Zarcero *p126*

Zarcero is the gateway to the northern lowlands with buses heading to **Ciudad Quesada** (San Carlos) and beyond. Buses from **San José** leave the Coca-Cola Terminal at 0915, 1215, 1615 and 1715, 2 hrs, US$1.45. Alternatively any bus heading for Ciudad Quesada passes through the town.

San Ramón *p127*

Heading north by car the road forks, the right leading to Zarcero (20 km) and finally to Ciudad Quesada. The left fork heads north to La Tigra and Fortuna passing the Los Angeles Cloud Forest Reserve (see above, page 127). From San José, buses heading to **Puntarenas** stop at San Ramón leaving from the Empresarios Unidos stop in **San José** at C 16, Av 10-12, 12 a day, USUS1.15. There is also a service via **Alajuela**.

❻ Directory

Alajuela *p120, map p120*

Banks Absolutely no shortage of banks to choose from and all within 3 blocks of each other. **Banco Nacional**, C 2, Av Central-1, is facing Central Park. **Banco Interfin** next door has Visa and MasterCard ATMs. **Banco Crédito Agrícola de Cartago**, C 2, Av Central-2 (one block south of Central Park). **Banco de Santa Cruz**, C 2, Av 3 (2 blocks north of Central Park), also the offices of Credomatic. **Internet** Many of the budget accommodation places have internet access. Otherwise, there are several internet places around town but none firmly established. On the south side of the main plaza an upstairs café combines internet with pool, open daily 0900-2200, 250 colones/hr. **Medical services** Emergency: T911. San Rafael Hospital, 200 m southeast of the airport autopista intersection, T2436-1000, can help in a crisis. There are several pharmacies around town. **Post office** on the corner of Av 5 and C 1, Mon-Fri 0800-1730, Sat 0730-1200.

Sarchí *p125*

Banks Banco Nacional has branches in Sarchí Sur and Sarchí Norte.
Post office services are also found in both villages.

Naranjo *p126*

Banks Banco Nacional, on north side of plaza, has ATMs taking Visa and MasterCard.

Heredia and around

On the lower slopes of Volcán Barva just 11 km north of San José, Heredia (population 30,968, altitude 1200 m) enjoys a history entrenched in the growth of coffee throughout the Central Highlands. Founded in 1706, the town fought for dominance of the country alongside Cartago against Alajuela and the eventually victorious San José at the time of independence. Today, though, the quiet town is in danger of losing its position as the fourth city of the republic to more vibrant growth areas such as Liberia and Turrialba. However, Heredians don't seem to be too concerned – traces of colonial heritage and the youthful energy of the Universidad Nacional (National University) give the town a busy grace. This 'City of Flowers' has a quiet charm that seems to say San José is welcome to the spotlight.

In the town you can explore the few sights there are in a couple of hours but there are a few respected language schools in the area, so staying longer is also an option. The town offers the best access to Volcán Barva (2906 m), the main destination for trekkers and hikers in Parque Nacional Braulio Carrillo. ▸▸ *For listings, see pages 141-144.*

Heredia

Sleeping 🛏
América **1**
Casa Ciudadela Hostel **6**
El Verano **2**
Heredia **4**
Hostel Dreamplace **8**
Las Flores **5**
Valladolid **7**

Eating 🍴
Cowboy **3**
El Gran Papa **4**
El Príncipe **5**
Fresas **6**
L'Antica Roma **7**
Le Petit Paris **8**
Vishnu **12**

Bars & clubs 🍸
Bulevar **1**

Ins and outs ›› *Colour map 2, B3.*

Getting there

Buses to and from San José leave the capital for the 20- to 40-minute journey (depending on traffic) every 10 minutes from Avenida 2, Calle 10-12 and every 20 minutes from Avenida 2, Calle 12-14 close to La Merced Church. Buses arrive on Avenida 4 and Calle Central, one block south of the Central Plaza, US0.45, and Avenida 6, Calle 1 and 3. From the airport, expect to pay between US$10-15. Buses to other destinations leave from close to the market place, three blocks south of the Central Plaza. ›› *See Transport, page 144, for further details.*

Sights

The sights of Heredia can be seen from one spot through judicious positioning in the northeastern corner of the main plaza (facing north). Over your right shoulder is the **Basílica de la Inmaculada Concepción**, with a short squat design that has helped the structure weather several earthquakes since completion in 1797. External weathering has taken its toll but the inside is a complete contrast. Starkly crisp and bright white, it's proof positive that beauty lies within. Looking north is **El Fortín** (unfortunately closed to the public), a single turret complete with gun slats overlooking a small park. On the northern side of plaza is the **Casa de la Cultura**, a beautifully restored colonial house that was once the residence of President Alfredo González Flores (1914-1917). Today in addition to being a fine example of period architecture with beautiful woodcarvings inside, the Casa de la Cultura houses exhibitions and concerts. Keep an eye out for events or just turn up and see what is going on.

Tour complete, spin round and explore the **Central Plaza** which has a light, airy feel with enough mango trees to provide shade, but not too many to block the light completely. And of course take time to join in the traditional pastime of sitting around for a while, contemplating the issues of the day, catching up with news from friends new and old, and generally doing nothing. A couple of blocks south, the market is a cacophonous hub of trading.

South of Heredia ›› *Colour map 2, B3.*

On the road to Santo Domingo is **INBio Parque** ① *T2244-4730, www.inbio.ac.cr/ inbioparque, daily from 0730-1600, US$23 in high season, under-12s US$13*, an educational and recreational centre which explains and gives insight into Costa Rica's biological diversity and the country's national parks. In a remarkably small area you can visit the ecosystems of the Central Highland Forest, Dry Forest and Humid Forest, with a couple of trails set out for bromeliads and guarumo. The construction of a wetland area has added to the localized diversity and new interactive exhibits are planned. Guides are available, and there is a rolling programme of courses and talks covering a range of subjects. Excellent for students, and interesting for the generalist. There are also restaurants, cafés and all usual amenities on site. A pick-up is easily arranged from hotels in San José or, if travelling by car, it's 400 m north and 250 m west of the Shell petrol station in Santo Domingo.

Café Britt coffee plantation

ⓘ *Head north from Heredia and follow the 'Café Britt Coffee Tour' signs. Cappuccino Coffee Tour lasts 2 hrs every day at 1100 , US$35, includes lunch and show. A shorter, but equally entertaining coffee tour runs at 0900 and 1500 in the high season, US$20, US$14 for students and children. Coffee Lover's Tour is US$65 per person. They tend to have something new every season to keep you going back for more. Tours can be booked through any tour operator in San José or book in advance on T2260-2748, www.coffeetour.com.*

Heading north from Heredia is the Café Britt coffee plantation. As one of the largest *beneficios* in the country, Café Britt is well suited to providing tours round every aspect of the coffee-making process from tending the trees and harvesting, through to processing and packaging. But the real skill comes in the making of this theatre. Professional actors guide you through the whole process and the result is informative and, judging by the look on most people's faces, very enjoyable. The success of the tour is so great that Café Britt combines the tour with several other Central Valley activities including visits to the Butterfly Farm at La Guácina and the Rainforest Aerial Tram. For the true caffeine addict there is a Coffee Lover's Tour which turns the novice coffee drinker into a connoisseur, followed by a visits to the coffee mill during harvest, so this tour only runs in the high season.

Barva

A short distance further north from Heredia the town of Barva (population 6348) has kept some historic charm. The whitewashed church overlooking the plaza surrounded by single-storey adobe and tile houses dates back to the 1700s. The **Museo de Cultura Popular** ⓘ *T2260-1619, www.ilam.org/cr/museoculturapopular, Mon-Fri 0900-1600, Sat and Sun 1000-1700, US$1.50, 500 m east of the Salón Comunal de Santa Lucía de Barva,* has some examples of the local *bahareque* adobe construction method and several exhibits paying tribute to the town's colonial heritage. Traditional food is served in the rustic setting at weekends and on weekdays with advance notice. Great opportunities for groups, like mask-making, *bahareque* construction systems and traditional pastimes.

Volcán Barva

ⓘ *T2261-2619. Headquarters open daily 0800-1600. US$8. No tour operators in San José provide this trip at present, but Ocarina Expeditions (T2229-4278, www.ocarina expeditions.com) should be able to help with arrangements.*

North of Barva the road climbs the lower slopes of Barva Volcano (2906 m) rising to the distinctly chilly and moist climate of the cloudforest. Several comfortable lodges, hotels and mountain resorts are hidden away in the pine forests of the upper slopes. From Barva the road forks creating a loop that provides access to Barva Volcano and accommodation in the area. Buses from Heredia use the following route. Taking the right fork, the road reaches **San José de la Montaña** after 6 km. For the next 5 km the road twists and turns as the temperature falls and the road climbs to **Porrosatí** at 1900 m. The route to the entrance and headquarters of Parque Nacional Braulio for climbing Barva Volcano takes a right fork leading to the town of **Sacramento** (5 km) and beyond, while the road leads downhill via Birrí and eventually back to Barva. Taking the left fork north of Barva as far as Birrí and then taking a right completes the circuit in reverse.

A day trek on Volcán Barva

Hiking the rugged slopes of Volcán Barva is a satisfying day's adventure, and despite its proximity to San José, this sector of Braulio Carrillo National Park remains undiscovered.

Starting your day in Heredia, go north to Barva, the Central Valley's first colonial town. Pass north through town (veer right at the fork after bridge) to San José de la Montaña then, climbing (veer right) to Paso Llano, turn left and continue to the park's entrance. The final 3 km, a challenging 4WD-only road, is often impassable in the rainy season.

Alternatively, take an early San José de la Montaña bus from in front of Heredia central market, leaving at 0630, 1200 and 1600. An hour's journey brings you to the final stop at Paso Llano. It's a 6.5-km hike to the park. (Coffee and a taste of local life are available at Soda El Monte or El Ranchito (open Thu-Sun).

If you're walking the last stretch, you'll pass through old oak forests and crystal streams. Quetzals, bellbirds and hummingbirds in live these misty

mountains, and bromeliads and orchids dress the giant trees. Just before Sacramento, an *artesanía* shop sells cypress wares. Sacramento is the last town. One kilometre further on the pavement ends, so it's best to park in town and hike the final 3.5 km stretch. Pay the US$6 park fee and enjoy the 1.5-km trail to the Laguna de Barva, choosing either of the two trails, which eventually converge. The laguna is a dormant crater surrounded by dense cloudforest. A lookout point over the scenic Sarapiquí area is another marked trail and both trails lead to covered platforms providing an opportunity to relax amid this incredible landscape.

Camping facilities and rustic cabins (US$2 pp, reservations T2268-1039) are available near the park entrance. Remember to bring rain gear and a warm sweater, preparing for the elements at 2906 m. If heading down the slope to Heredia by bus, catch one in Paso Llano at 0730, 1300 or 1700 and enjoy the spectacular views on the way down.

Climbing Volcán Barva Hiking to the summit of Barva Volcano (2906 m) is one of the best ways of seeing some of the less-explored parts of Parque Nacional Braulio Carrillo (see below for more details). The hike to the top passes through fine cloudforest, with moss-covered trees heavily laden with epiphytes and bromeliads. The area is popular with birdwatchers and, fortunately for them, quetzals, king vultures and the three-wattled bell bird, as well as countless hummingbirds. Monkeys, reptiles, poison-arrow frogs and the endemic, and currently endangered, *Bufo holdridgei* toad can also be seen. The summit trek offers spectacular views across densely forested valleys shrouded in swirling mist rising from the lowland valleys. Trails lead to three water-filled craters including the **Danta crater** surrounded by profuse vegetation and almost 500 m across. From the summit, magnificent views stretch across the Central Valley.

Access to Barva is difficult compared to some national parks in Costa Rica. Three daily buses travel to Porrosatí from San José de la Montaña and Heredia, from where a poorly marked trail leads to the summit and then out through the park headquarters. A more common route leaves from park headquarters, 3 km beyond Sacramento. The road is rough and if travelling by private vehicle you will need a 4WD and even then you may not make it in the wet season. Entrance fees are payable at the headquarters, from where signs lead to the summit. The 4 km takes a little over one hour depending on your condition. For the serious trekker there is a trail heading north from the top of Barva down to **La Selva Biological Station** near Puerto Viajo de Sarapiquí (see page 164). The trip takes about four days, covers about 65 km and requires proper planning.

Despite its proximity to San José, groups entering the park do get lost. News of their survival only gets out with them, so go prepared – the weather can change dramatically and getting caught in cloud is very disorientating. For all trekking in the park you should have maps, compass, food and water, and appropriate protective equipment depending on the length and duration of your stay. Camping is allowed in the park but there are no services so pack up what you take in.

Parque Nacional Braulio Carrillo

ⓘ T2261-0257, daily 0800-1530. If arriving before the rangers' station opens pay on your way out (US$8). Take any bus heading east of San José from the Gran Terminal de Caribe north of downtown San José and ask the driver to drop you off at the entrance.

Just 20 km from San José, Braulio Carrillo National Park protects some of the country's most rugged landscapes. If you're not inclined to get out and explore you're in luck, as you get a good impression of the topography from the San José–Guápiles–Limón Highway that travels through the park. Steep-sided gorges eroded by rivers hidden at the bottom of heavily forested valleys border both sides of the road. Clouds drift up the valleys, rising to the volcanic peaks of **Barva** (2906 m) and **Cacho Negro** (2150 m) where they deposit rainfall that totals around 4.5 m annually. The result is some dramatic waterfalls, most hardly ever seen by human eyes.

The 47,583-ha park was created in 1978 to protect against damage caused by the construction of a new highway to the Caribbean. Named after the republic's third president, who proclaimed himself dictator for life in 1842, the park at least commemorates his attempts to improve communications between the Central Valley and the lowlands. Today, Highway 32 is one of the country's busiest roads making the national park the most popular in the country. The vast majority passing through see the road and driving conditions as precarious, dangerous and best avoided. Some tours incorporate this journey as part of a visit to the national park. It goes without saying that you will not see any wildlife from a bus, but you can pass over the continental divide just to the south of the Zurquí tunnel.

The biological stock-take is staggering. Estimates suggest that over 90% of the park is primary forest and contains some 6000 species of plants – over 50% of the total found in Costa Rica. While the higher altitudes struggle to support life in the chilled and windy atmosphere, profuse humid rainforest dominates here, reaching its greatest diversity at the lower altitudes. Animal and bird life is equally profuse. Over 500 species of migratory and resident birds have been logged including quetzals in the higher altitudes, toucans, king vultures, the umbrella bird and the national bird: the sooty robin. Mammals include three species of monkey as well as tapirs, pacas, jaguars, pumas and ocelots. To complete the list, reptiles include two of the most deadly snakes in the world, the fer-de-lance and bushmaster.

For management purposes the parks is divided between the **Quebrada González Sector** and the **Barva Volcano Sector**. The entrance at Quebrada González is 23 km beyond the Zurquí tunnel (easy to drive past, if you get to the flag-poles of the Rainforest Aerial Tram you've gone too far). Three short trails lead from the rangers' station:

Las Palmas is a 1.6-km trail taking about 1½ hours, good for birdwatching. **El Ceibo** is 1 km and takes just an hour and leads to some fine examples of the ceibo tree. The **Botarrama** trail is an extension of El Ceibo that leads to the Río Sucio and gets deeper into the rainforest covering 3 km taking about two hours. An animal list stating regular sightings of spider, white-faced and howler monkeys, toucans, peccaries, tarantulas and snakes makes for an interesting read before and after your trek.

Rainforest aerial tram

① *T2257-5961, www.rfat.com. Daily 0630 (0900 on Mon)-1600, although most tours arrive after 0900, so travel privately if you wish to visit early. Entrance and tram ride US$55 adults, US$27.50 students with ID card and under 11s. A package from San José, including pick-up from most hotels, tram fees, hanging bridge, canopy tour, one meal and hike is US$104 for adults, US$57.50 for students and under 11s. Reservations office behind the Aurola Holiday Inn, or 150 m west of the INS building. To get there take any bus heading towards Guápiles from the Gran Caribe bus terminal north of town on Calle Central. If driving, take the San José-Guápiles Highway (32), heading northeast from the capital. Vehicles park in a secure car park and you are shuttled down to the ride. Upon returning to the boarding station, you can stop for a snack or a meal at the Rainforest Café. Rainforest Gift Shop has natural remedies covering everything from headaches and high blood pressure through to impotence.*

Moving silently through the forest at canopy level is the best way to see the complexity of the rainforest but is obviously inherently problematic for homo sapiens. Fortunately, the unique attraction of the Rainforest Aerial Tram, the brainchild of Dr Donald Perry and John Williams, gives you precisely that opportunity, however. Open-air cable cars, with protection from the sun and rain, glide slowly through the forest rising from ground level to drift below, in and above the canopy for an up-close and personal view of life above the forest floor. Each car has a bilingual guide, equipped with a radio, who will point out interesting fauna encountered on your journey. As with all good guides, their keen and practised eyes will help spot birds and animals, often long before the casual observer, and you will see the sheer density of plant life and insects found in the upper sections of the rainforest. At the half-way point a short walk leads to a vista stretching to the Caribbean lowlands with views as far as Tortuguero on a clear day. The return journey 'flies' just above the canopy, before coming back to land – an unforgettable experience. And there is now also a hanging bridge and canopy tour with zip lines if the tram has left you wanting more.

Visitors to the park should have realistic expectations. Birds abound but birdwatchers should aim to arrive as early in the morning as possible. It is possible to see monkeys, but don't expect them. Several coatis hang around the departure point, but the best chance of seeing other mammals is by hiking one of the short trails that lead through the 400-ha private reserve used for research.

In addition to being a fascinating ride, the creation of a successful green tourism experience on this scale with relatively low impact is incredible. The history of the creation and construction of the ride makes for an interesting tale explained in a video shown afterwards. It's well worth seeing.

East of Heredia towards Monte de la Cruz

A few kilometres east of Heredia, **San Rafael de Heredia** is notable for one of the most impressive churches in the Central Highlands. In a town of just over 11,000 a church worthy of any European capital city stands loud and proud; recently cleansed and purified, it beams in brilliant white. Sadly for the residents who would like to see visitors stay a little longer, it provides only passing interest.

Not far from San Rafael, however, and above Los Angeles is **Galería Octágono** ① T2267-6325, www.galeriaoctagono.com, showing handmade textiles created by a women's community cooperative. It's also a B&B run by informative and friendly owners and provides other meals (at additional cost), as well as transportation and hikes.

North of San Rafael, Highway 113 leads up the slopes of Barva Volcano eventually reaching **Monte de la Cruz**. The refreshing climate makes this a popular mountain retreat for the better-off families of the Central Highlands, and private homes and mansions border the road, some hidden behind imposing front gates. It is also possible to hike in the region but trails are limited and poorly marked.

Northeast of San José

Running northeast of San José, but south of the main highway, the road runs to **San Isidro de Coronado**. A dramatic grey church stands starkly bereft of paint despite its Gothic splendour. While the town is a popular summer resort, San Isidro owes its place on the map largely to the Instituto Clodomiro Picado snake farm. Sadly watching the snake-feeding is no longer an option, but those interested in medical research can visit.

From San Isidro the road goes on through fine countryside to **Las Nubes** (32 km), a village on the boundaries of Parque Nacional Braulio Carrillo with good opportunities for almost solitary walking and hiking and a great view of Irazú.

To the north, a road leads to **San Jerónimo** and onto the valley of the Río Hondura. The century-old stone road now seriously degraded was originally built in the 1880s to transport coffee from San José to the Caribbean coast.

◉ Heredia and around listings

For Sleeping and Eating price codes and other relevant information, see Essentials, pages 44-47.

◉ Sleeping

Heredia *p135, map p135*
AL-A Valladolid, C 7, Av 7, T2260-2905, www.hotelvalladolid.net. 11 spacious and smart rooms, all with a/c, bath, telephone and cable TV. Some rooms and suites have microwave and fridge. The 5th floor has a sauna, jacuzzi and the Bonavista Bar with its fine views overlooking the Central Valley. There's also a travel agency to help organize tours. The best option in town.

A-B Apartotel Vargas, Apdo 510-3000, Heredia, 800 m north of Colegio Santa Cecilia and San Francisco Church, to the west of the town centre, T2237-8526, apartotelvargas@ yahoo.com. 15 large, well-furnished apartments with kitchenette, bathroom, hot water, laundry, TV, internet and enclosed patio. Garage with ample parking and nightwatchman, English-speaking staff and collection from the airport can be arranged with Sr Vargas. Excellent value for money. Recommended for language students.
A America, C Central, Av 2-4, T2260-9292, www.hotelamericacr.com. The style and grandeur of Hollywood greets the guest in

this former cinema now converted into a hotel. Sadly the 42 rooms don't match the splendour but each has a private bathroom, hot water and telephone with cable TV. Handy for the centre of town and there's an ATM in the lobby.

B-C Heredia, C 6, Av 3-5, T2238-0880, www.hotelamericacr.com. 12 rooms, some quite dark, but all have private bath and hot water. A simple hotel with helpful staff and new owners.

C Las Flores, Av 12, C 12-14, T2261-8147, www.hotel-lasflores.com. Each room with private bath, hot water and parking available. A friendly place, regularly recommended.

C-E Casa Ciudadela Hostel, Av 7, C Central-1, T2263-5578, www.casaciudadela. com. Easy-going hostel with dorms and private rooms, use of kitchen, Wi-Fi. Just north of town, good base if staying in town.

D-E Hostel Dreamplace, Av 2, C 3-5. T2560-1111, www.costaricatravel.ch. Dorm and private rooms, and good selection of services and information.

F El Verano, on west side of the market square, T2237-1616. Basic, friendly budget option, acceptable for the price.

Out of town

LL Finca Rosa Blanca, 1.6 km from Santa Bárbara de Heredia, to the north of Heredia, T2269-9392, www.fincarosablanca.com. An absolutely divine hotel, on a bluff overlooking the Central Valley. 10 deluxe suites in an architectural orgasm of style, romance and exclusivity at the very extremes of imagination. Total relaxation continues at the pool, and the body is cared for with fruit and vegetables from the hotel's organic garden and the spa. Probably one of the most divine independent hotels in the world.

LL-AL Bougainvillea, Santo Tomás de Santo Domingo, 9 km east of Heredia and just 10 mins out of San José, T2244-1414, www.hb.co.cr. An exquisite and warm hotel with 81 large rooms each with a desk, cable TV, a/c. Crisp lines and fine classic decor lead to balconies looking out onto the Central

Valley. The blue and white tiled bathrooms even have hairdryers. The hotel is decorated with local art and has 5 ha of gardens replete with bougainvillea attracting hummingbirds and butterflies. If relaxing in the gardens and by the pool isn't hard enough work for you, there are tennis courts. Free shuttle service to San José.

L The Treehouse , at The Ark Herb Farm, T2269-4847, www.arkherbfarm.com. Incredible treehouse to spend the night in with spectacular views of the Central Valley. Includes transport and breakfast. Also tours through medicinal plant gardens US$12.

Volcán Barva *p136*

AL-A El Cypresal Hotel, above Birrí, T2266-1090, www.elcypresalhotel.com. Fireplace in all rooms, Italian restaurant, great view of central valley,

A-C Monte Campana Quality Inn, T2269-7086. Mountain cabins and rooms, pool, restaurant, hiking, tennis, good value.

A Las Ardillas, heading uphill from Birrí, T2266-1003. A well hidden resort within the pine forest. 18 *cabinas* each with private bathroom, hot water and kitchenette. Wooden floors and beams create a warm ambience in the restaurant which serves international and traditional cuisine. There's a sauna and jacuzzi, hypnosis, massage and beauty treatments.

Rainforest aerial tram *p140*

LL Rain Forest Lodge, T2257-5961, www.rfat.com. 10 cosy bungalows, all with balcony looking out to the forest. Cabins include 2 single beds, private bathroom with hot water. Rate includes unlimited tram rides as well all meals.

East of Heredia towards Monte de la Cruz *p141*

LL Hotel and Villas La Condesa, just above El Castillo, T2267-6000, www.hotella condesa.com. Exclusive hotel retreat part of the Occidental Hotels group. Almost 100 rooms and suites and a selection of villas sleeping 4-8 people, all with excellent views over the Central Highlands. Large standard rooms have tiled private bathrooms with bath tub, cable TV and minibar and the suites are suitably luxurious. 4 restaurants provide a range of dining options. Patio de Los Condes, complete with waterfall, serves breakfast on an informal patio, Miramonte serves light dishes and Florencia offers the very best in European cuisine. La Cava del Conde is a bar and disco with live music at weekends. Sports facilities and several meeting rooms make this an ideal conference hotel in the week and a refreshing mountain retreat at all times. **AL Chalet Tirol**, T2267-6222, www.tirolcr. com. The final stopping place for most visitors to the region down a mystical avenue of moss-clad pine trees that block and diffuse the light to create an ethereal corridor. At a lofty 1800 m and set in 15 ha of private cloudforest, this piece of Alpine Costa Rica is authentic in almost every detail. 20 or so chalets and suites are hidden within the forest offering unrivalled privacy. In addition to the expected homely comforts, each room has a heater to fend off the winter cold. The French restaurant is strongly recommended. Activities include hiking on trails close to the hotel or taking a guide to Parque Nacional Braulio Carrillo through virgin cloudforest. The hotel is also host to the Whitten Entomological Collection of more than one million forest insects and arthropods, and hosts an annual International Music Festival. It's quite a long way up but you won't need to go down until you leave.

🍴 Eating

Heredia p135, map p135
🍴🍴 **Cowboy Restaurant**, C 9, Av 5. A grill option where the Mid West meets Costa Rica. It's not all meat, but probably best avoided by vegetarians. Lively bar in the evenings and credit cards accepted.
🍴🍴 **El Gran Papa**, C 9, Av 3. Has a gentle buzz and gets the bulk of lunchtime business trade, but without being stuffy. There's a

good range of *bocas*, pastas and cocktails along with international and national dishes.
🍴 **Banco de los Mariscos**, 500 m west from the central plaza in Santa Bárbara, T2269-9090. Great seafood.
🍴 **L'Antica Roma**, C 7, Av 7, T2260-2905. A formal decor but friendly service with a good mix of *comida típica* and international dishes.
🍴 **El Principe**, C 5, Av Central-2. Truly international menu ranging from Chinese to pasta and local dishes.
🍴 **Fresas**, C 7, Av 1, T2237-3915. Diner-style restaurant serving everything you could possibly want including snacks, sandwiches, breakfast, full meals, fresh fruit juices and strawberries. Will also deliver.
🍴 **Le Petit Paris**, C 5 and Av Central-2. A little piece of France in the heart of Heredia. Amid Doisneau photographs and 1930s posters of 'gay Paree', the ambience shifts between the bar, restaurant and patio café. Live music on Thu, usually jazz.
🍴 **Vishnu**, C 7, Av Central-1. Good whole-some vegetarian served fast-food style.
🍴 **Entrepanes**, above Pop's on Central Park, fine coffee and pastries.

Volcán Barva p136
All hotels listed have restaurants and welcome non-guests.
🍴 **Auxilladora**, in Sacramento, north of Porrosatí heading to the National Park headquarters. A basic menu.
🍴 **Sacramento**, next door to Auxilladora. Has a little more on offer, serving *comida típica* and a well-stocked bar to keep the cold at bay.

🍸 Bars and clubs

Heredia p135, map p135
Bulevar Bar, Av Central, C 5-7. One of Heredia's happening places, a fact that becomes blatantly obvious as soon as you're within one block of it. Fast food and *bocas* available.
Le Petit Paris, C 5, Av Central-2. Stylish French bar and café-restaurant.
Océano, C 4, Av 2-4. A popular student bar.

⊕ Transport

Heredia *p135, map p135*
In **San José** buses depart from Av 2, C 10-12, every 10 mins between 0500-0015, then hourly through the night until 0400, US$0.50. Through the day buses also leave from Av 2, C 12-14, every 20 mins. Buses from Heredia to the capital leave from Av 4, C Central-1. Local buses leave from Av 8, C 2-4 by the market. Buses to **Barva** leave every 30 mins, US$0,30. To **San José de la Montaña**, every 30 mins, US$0.40, and to **Porrosatí/Sacramento** at 0630, 1230 and 1600, US$0.50 for the 1-hr journey.

Taxis are widely available.

Volcán Barva *p136*
Buses leave **Heredia** from the market place at 0630, 1230 and 1600 taking 1 hr for the journey to **Porrosatí** where the bus waits for 1 hr before departing at 0730, 1300 and 1700. Some buses continue to **Sacramento**, reducing the walking time.

ⓘ Directory

Heredia *p135, map p135*
Banks Branches of several banks dotted around town. **Banco Nacional** has a branch on the corner of Av 6 and C 6, **Banco de Costa Rica** is at Av 6, C1, and **Banco Popular** is east of the church at Av Central, C 3.
Cultural centres Casa de la Cultura, facing the northeastern corner of the plaza at Av Central and C Central, T2262-2505, has a good schedule of events covering all the performing arts and a few of the observational ones. **Internet** Several around town, one of the long-standing reliables is **Internet Café**, Av 2, C 5-7, Mon-Fri 0830-2130, Sat 1000-2000, Sun 1200-1800, US$2 per hr, 15 mins US$1.

Language schools Centro Panamericana de Idiomas, in San Joaquín de Flores, T2265-6306, www.cpi-edu.com. Also has schools in Monteverde and Playa Flamingo. Intensive classes of 5½ hrs a day focusing on grammar and conversation, with supportive oral and written work. Maximum class sizes of 4 covering all levels. Full range of cultural activities, tours and a volunteer programme. University credits available. Also has a seminar programme on special subjects. 4 hrs a day, US$465 with homestay, US$315 without, 5½-hr day, US$580 and US$430. **Instituto Profesional de Educación Daza**, T2237-1801, www.learnspanish costarica.com. Founded in 1984, multiple levels with maximum class sizes of 6. Wide range of cultural activities support the classroom studies. Homestay strongly encouraged. US$370 a week with homestay, US$240 without. **Intercultura**, Centro de Idiomas, Av 4 and C10, T2260-8480, www.interculturacostarica.com.
Language tuition in small classes covering all levels from beginner to advanced, with a good varied cultural activities programme and options for homestays and a volunteer programme. Also has a school in Sámara on the Nicoya Peninsula if you want to move around. University credits also available. Prices from US$270 a week without homestay, US$394 with.
All schools offer discounts for more than 1 week. **Laundry** Sol y Mar, Mon-Sat, 0830-1900, Sun, 0830-1400. Wash 5kg for US$3 and dry it for another US$3. **Medical services** San Vicente de Paul Hospital, Av 8 and C 14, T2261-0091. **Red Cross**, on the corner of C Central and Av 3. Several pharmacies can be found on the streets between the market area and Central Park. **Post office** On the north side of the plaza, next to the fort. **Useful addresses** Emergency: T911.

Cartago and around

The massif of Volcán Irazú dominates the skyline from Cartago, the provincial capital and gateway to the southeastern corner of the Central Valley. Once the ruling quarter of Costa Rica, today the province has a distinctly rural feel. It's dotted with macadamia nut plantations on the lower slopes, the less exotic products of potatoes and onions on the volcanic slopes, and the dependable presence of coffee where conditions allow.

Exploring the town, it is difficult to see how this quiet spot once mustered up enough energy to lead the nation. Listless and without direction the town continues apparently unaware of, or at least with only limited interest in, its historical legacy. Volcán Irazú is a highly visible reminder of the forces without and within, last erupting in dramatic style to coincide with the arrival of President Kennedy in 1963. The orchids of Lankester Gardens, and the fine views of the Orosí Valley, make pleasant, relaxing trips; while the more adventurous can hike in Tapantí-Macizo de la Muerte National Park, or whitewater raft on the Pacuare and Reventazón rivers close to Turrialba. The Guayabo National Monument, to the north of Turrialba, is the country's most important pre-Columbian archaeological site.▸▸ *For listings, see pages 150-152.*

Ins and outs ▸▸ *Colour map 2, C3.*

Getting there

If driving, it's a simple car ride of just over 20 km from San José. From Avenida 2, head east and follow the signs. SACSA buses leave from Calle 5 and Avenida 18-20, every 10 minutes, 45-minute journey, US$0.75. Transtusa buses stop at Cartago en route to Turrialba with 15 buses a day leaving from Calle 13 and Avenida 6-8.▸▸ *See Transport, page 152, for further details.*

Getting around

The two areas of interest are only 1 km apart – a gentle stroll unless it is raining. If so, there are plenty of cabs around Las Ruinas and the streets surrounding the Basilica.

Best time to visit

Pilgrimages to the Basilica take place throughout the year, but 2 August is the most important date in the pilgrims' calendar.

Sights

Sprawling at the foot of Irazú volcano and surrounded by mountains, Cartago was founded in 1563 by Juan Vásquez de Coronado who also conquered much of the Central Valley. The city's dominant position was frequently tested, and finally faltered in 1823 when San José acquired the capital seat after a series of minor civil scuffles. Since then, nature has challenged the city with many tremors and two devastating earthquakes first in 1841 and again in 1910, finally finishing off the architectural heritage of the town.

When tried to the limits of physical endurance, faith often comes to the fore and Cartago has one of the finest churches in the country, and certainly the most popular with many thousands completing a personal pilgrimage to the Basílica de Nuestra Señora de Los Angeles.

With the old city destroyed by earthquakes the town's architectural sights are limited to two. **La Parroquia**, locally known as *Las Ruinas*, was once the seat of the first parish of Cartago founded back in 1575. Frequent tremors meant the church was reconstructed several times. Almost completely destroyed in 1841, it was rebuilt only to be destroyed again in 1910, in an earthquake estimated to measure around 6.4 on the Richter scale. What stands now is what remained then. A small ornamental garden fills the space within, but is closed for much of the time. In front of the ruins, the Central Park is a large expanse of pavement, but despite the blandness, it makes for good people-watching, and if you're lucky you may see busking and street performances *Tico*-style. Small signs of civic pride are appearing with some of the older buildings undergoing simple restoration – hope for better things to come.

A couple of blocks north of Central Park, the **Central Market** builds daily to a noisy, smelly, chaotic bundle of trading. Cleaner than it looks, it does have a rough edge that is missing from many of Costa Rica's markets, and so common in other Latin countries.

One kilometre to the east, the **Basílica de Nuestra Señora de Los Angeles** is what the crowds have come to see. To be more specific it is the diminutive **La Negrita**, an indigenous image of the Virgin Mary less than 15 cm high, that draws pilgrims from throughout the country, and from all over Central America, because of its supposedly great healing powers. Having arrived at the Basílica, pilgrims take to their knees, inching their way down the aisle towards La Negrita. In all the excitement, it's easy to overlook the finery of the Basílica itself. Destroyed by earthquake it was rebuilt in 1926 in Byzantine style. The interior is ornately decorated with gold leaf, fine carvings and

Cartago

N

200 metres
200 yards

To San José
To Irazú
To Paraíso & Turrialba
To Aguacalientes

Plaza
Old Train Staton
S Banco de Costa Rica
Mercado Central
Club de Cartago
Banco Interfin Mercatur
Pali Supermarket
S Banco Nacional de Costa Rica
Parque Central
La Parroquia
Fuji
Plaza
S Banco Popular
Basílica de Nuestra Señora de Los Angeles

AV 6
AV 4
AV 2
AV 1
AV 3
AV 5
AV 7

Sleeping	Bars & clubs	Pitaya, Aguacalientes &
Dinastía **1**	Metropolis **2**	Lourdes **4**
Los Angeles Lodge		San José **5**
B&B **2**	Buses	San Juan de Chichúa **6**
	Cachí via Ujarra &	Tierra Blancas/San
Eating	Paraíso **1**	Gerardo **7**
Puerto del Sol **6**	Orosi/Rio Machi **2**	Turrialba **8**
Soda Apolo **1**	Paraíso **3**	

always with fresh flowers. To the side of the church, pilgrims fill La Negrita-shaped plastic containers and *refresco* bottles with holy water so that they can take a little of her curative powers back home.

About 4 km southeast of Cartago, and a short bus ride beyond Tejar, is **Aguacalientes**, a warm-water *balneario* (spa) ideal for picnics.

Jardín Botánico Lankester

① T2552-3247, www.jardinbotanicolankester.org. Open 0830-1630, visitors must leave by 1730, except bank holidays. US$5, free for under-6s. The gardens are 5 km east of Cartago on the road to Paraíso. There is no direct bus service. From Cartago take a bus towards Paraíso, asking the driver to let you off at the entrance to 'Jardín Botánico Lankester' and from there walk south for 500 m, turning right at the sign. Most tour operators in San José provide tours (from US$42) to the gardens, normally as part of a trip to Irazú and/or the Orosí Valley.

An overgrown 'hobby' founded by the British naturalist Charles H Lankester in the 1950s, Lankester Botanical Garden has grown to be an internationally renowned collection of epiphytic flora, in particular the orchid, of Costa Rica. The gardens have around 800 species of national and exotic orchids laid out in the 10.7 ha of tranquil gardens. These showy flowers come in a great variety of colours and reach peak blooming between February and May when temperatures are highest and rainfall lowest.

Beyond the orchids, the gardens also have many examples of bromeliads, ferns and cacti as well as heliconia, palm and bamboo. Nature plays its part with over 100 birds visiting the gardens. It's positively calming, and respectful noise levels are requested, nay expected.

For the orchidophiles and botanists there are short courses covering care and cultivation of orchids, plant recognition and nature photography to name a few topics. Contact the gardens for details.

Volcán Irazú 🌐🔵 ▸▸ pp150-151. Colour map 2, B3.

① Daily 0800-1530. National Park entrance of US$10 plus US$2.50 to park if you are driving. Most tour operators in San José have day trips to Irazú costing around US$36 per person. Buses Metropoli (T2530-1064) have daily services leaving at 0800 from Av 2, C 1-3, in front of Gran Hotel Costa Rica, returns at 1230, US$6.50. There are buses from Cartago going regularly to Tierras Blancas, and one a day even further up the slopes as far as San Juan de Chicúa, which leaves a refreshing but enjoyable 10 km hike uphill to the summit. A taxi is also a possibility with a group, and the recommended price is 10,000 colones (US$22) plus entrance. At the summit there is a small café serving snacks and coffee, as well as a few souvenirs of baseball caps, T-shirts and coffee table books covering Costa Rica's exploding volcanoes.

On a clear day, the silhouette of Irazú looms above Cartago, on a cloudy day the peak and much of the lower slopes are stuck in the clouds – at 3432 m it is the highest volcano in Costa Rica. With a road reaching to within a few hundred metres of the dramatic lagoon-filled craters, this is one of the country's most popular national parks. Whether buffeted by freezing winds, or basking in glorious sunlight, the volcano is definitely worth visiting.

This 'mountain of quakes and thunder', named after the nearby indigenous village of Iztarú which once existed on the volcanic slopes, has a lively history. The first documented eruption was recorded by Diego de la Haya Fernández, the governor of Cartago at the time, in 1723. Violent eruptions began in 1963 damaging the crater and sending volcanic material down the western slopes to flood the Río Reventado and the community of

Visiting Volcán Irazú

If you're uncertain whether to visit Irazú and risk being clouded over, heed the words of one traveller who writes: "In the afternoon the mountain top is buried in fog and mist or drizzle, but the ride up in the mist can be magical, for the mountainside is half-displaced in time. There are new jeeps and tractors, but the herds of cattle are small, the fields are quilt-work, handcarts and oxcarts are to be seen under the fretworked porches of well-kept frame houses. The land is fertile, the pace is slow, the air is clean. It is a very attractive mixture of old and new. Irazú is a strange mountain, well worth the ride up."

Taras. This eruption showered Cartago and the capital San José with ash – a dramatic welcome for President John F Kennedy who was visiting at the time.

As recently as 1994 a sudden explosion in the north wall of the crater sent a landslide down the Río Sucio to within sight of the bridge over the main highway connecting San José and Limón. Today, fumaroles, small lava flows and light tremors are proof that the mountain still quakes and thunders.

Once at the top, the landscape is bare, covered in desolate grey sand which looks like the surface of the moon but for pockets of fragile vegetation slowly colonizing the harsh climate. The temperature range of -3°C to 17°C and the poor soil supports a hardy low scrub with thick leaves and stunted growth to cope with the fierce winds and sudden temperature changes near the summit. There are five craters in total, three of which can be easily visited. The **main crater** is a cube blown out of the earth, 1050 m wide, with vertiginous walls 300 m deep and complete with a sulphurous green lake at the bottom. The **Diego de la Haya crater** is slightly smaller. **Playa Hermosa crater**, slowly being colonized, is a good spot to see the ubiquitous *volcano junco* bird but otherwise little wildlife and few plants survive in this hostile desert.

The views, however, are stupendous. (The summit is often shrouded in cloud but your best chance of a clear view is in the morning.) Even if the lower slopes are cloudy, it is quite possible that the summit is above the clouds. The rainy season is from May to December, but take warm clothing and a wind-proof jacket as protection all year round.

Orosí Valley ●❼● ›› pp150-152.

From **Paraíso**, 8 km southwest of Cartago, the road falls away heading east and south on a circular route revealing the hidden secrets of the Orosí Valley. The valley floor is flooded by the waters of the artificial Lago Cachí created by the Cachí Dam which blocks the river before flowing out to the Reventazón river popular for whitewater rafting. Surrounded by steep-sided mountains rising up to cloud level, occasionally dressed with the fashionable costume of neatly lined, green coffee bushes, the 30-km road makes a pleasant day trip with restaurants providing scenic opportunities for meals along the way. Longer stays are possible at various hotels catering for all budgets.

East of Paraíso

Following the northern shore, the road drops past a look-out post leading to the small community of **Ujarrás** and the ruins of the country's first colonial church built between 1570 and 1580. Legend has it that in 1666, English pirates, including the youthful Henry

Morgan, were seen off by the citizens of Ujarrás aided by the Virgin. This miraculous protection is celebrated annually on April 16, or the closest Sunday, when the saint is carried in procession from Paraíso to the ruined church. The grounds surrounding the ruins are a popular picnic spot with *Josefino* families. Over the road are a couple of pools that are positively heaving at weekends. The **Charrarra Tourist Complex** is a 30-minute walk from Ujarrás (there are direct buses at weekends leaving one block north of Cartago ruins). There is a restaurant, swimming pool, boat rides on the lake and a good campsite.

Continuing east, the **Presa de Cachí** (Cachí Dam) is not particularly impressive in scale or detail, unless it's releasing water, but makes for a natural stopping point before heading along the southern shore and the compulsory stop at the **Casa del Soñador** (the Dreamer's House), where Hermes and Miguel Quesada carve figurines and faces using twisted old coffee plant roots and driftwood (some are for sale), continuing a sculptural tradition started by their late father, Macedonia Quesada.

South of Paraíso

Heading south of Paraíso the views are equally impressive as the road twists and descends into the valley passing hillside pastures, flower farms and the inevitable coffee plantations. From high up on the hillside you can rest and refresh yourself at Sanchiri Mirador & Lodge (see page 151). Rolling down the hill a few hundred metres is an ICT-owned mirador (lookout) complete with picnic spots and kiosk selling drinks and snacks.

Orosí

A rising star of the valley, Orosí is best known for the 18th-century **Parroquia de San José** built by Franciscan missionaries. Recently restored, the church has weathered the trials of countless earthquake tremors, a fact that is clearly apparent in the strained pitch roof that has warped over the centuries. Across the cloister, the **Museo de Arte Religioso** ① *Mon-Sat 1300-1700, Sun 0900-1700, church open every morning, US$2.50,* displays religious artifacts and artwork in the former monastery living quarters.

In town there are **hot springs** next to Orosí Lodge, and a second set in Los Patios a short distance south of town. Ask locally for directions, but both are very crowded at weekends.

South of Orosí

A short distance south of Orosí the road splits, the left fork crosses the Río Orosí to the Río Palomo. The right fork leads towards Tapantí-Macizo de la Muerte National Park some 9 km from the main road and a number of interesting local sights en route. **Monte Sky** is a private reserve covering 536 ha and bordering the national park. Over 590 bird species have been counted to date and the number is growing (see also page 150).

Parque Nacional Tapantí-Macizo de la Muerte

① *Local contact details T2771-3155. Official park hours through Tapantí are 0700-1700 daily. US$6. Camping is not at present permitted within the park but there are plans to build a campsite and facilities. Restrooms and drinking water are available. There is a small information centre with trail maps and a simple slide show. To get to the park by car, simply follow the directions to Orosí and follow the road to the park headquarters. Buses only run as far as Río Paloma from where it is a 9-km walk uphill. Alternatively take a taxi from Orosí. Several tour operators in San José can arrange trips with guides. It is also possible to reach Tapantí Macizo from the Pan-American Highway.*

Tapantí Macizo de la Muerte is the country's newest national park and one of the wettest parts of the country, some parts reportedly receiving as much as 8 m of rain a year. Approached from Orosí and just 30 km from Cartago the national park is surprisingly easy to reach and packs in the interest.

Covering 58,323 ha, Tapantí-Macizo includes the former Tapantí National Park and much of the Río Macho Forest Reserve. The park protects the Río Orosí basin which feeds the Cachí Dam hydro power plant. Strategically the southern boundary of the park joins with the Chirripó National Park extending the continuous protected area that makes up La Amistad Biosphere Reserve. The park incorporates a wide range of life zones from lower montane wet forest to montane rainforest with altitudes rising from 1220 m to over 2560 m at the border with Chirripó. The diverse altitudes and relative seclusion of the park has created an impressive species list which is currently incomplete due to the recent creation of the park. Tapir, pacas, racoons, and white-faced monkeys make up some of over 45 species of mammal found in the area as well as the elusive jaguar and ocelot. The quetzal nests in late spring and can be found on the western slopes near the entry point, with the black-faced solitaire, countless hummingbirds and oropendolas contributing to some 260 species of birds recorded so far. The wet conditions are ideal for lizards, snakes – including pit vipers – and frogs.

Until 1992 Tapantí was a wildlife refuge and the elevated status has increased interest but visitor numbers are still quite small, depite the fact that it is reletively easy to get here. Three trails lead off the principal road providing walks ranging from 30 minutes to two hours but don't forget the raincoat or umbrella. There are several waterfalls that are good for swimming and some good picnic spots.

◉ Cartago and around listings

For Sleeping and Eating price codes and other relevant information, see Essentials, pages 44-47.

▣ Sleeping

Cartago p145, map p146
There is a dearth of accommodation and eating options in the centre of town. If visiting, it is probably only worth a brief stop before moving on.
A-B Los Angeles Lodge B&B, Av 4, C 14-16, just north of the Basilica, T2591-4169. Open despite looking permanently closed. Rooms are clean and pleasant and there's a good restaurant.
D Dinastia, C 3, Av 6-8, at the *Las Ruinas* end of town, T2551-7057. The rooms (slightly more expensive with private bath) are pretty small and definitely basic, and generally better with a window although noisier because they are just north of the central market. Credit cards accepted.

Volcán Irazú p147
C Hotel Gestoria Irazú, on the road leading up to the summit in San Juan de Chicuá, T2224-9814, gestoria@racsa.co.cr. The rooms are simple with private bath, hot water and extra blankets to help you get through the cold winter nights. The *comida típica* is meant to be some of the best around.

Orosí Valley p148
A Orosí Lodge, Orosí, T2533-3578, www.orosilodge.com. A beautiful European-style café with a small balcony greets guests at this carefully maintained lodge. 7 rooms all with balcony overlooking the valley towards Volcán Irazú, have orthopaedic beds, private bath, hot water and kitchenette constructed to European standards. The owners Andreas and Cornelia provide just about everything you could want. Divine home-baked cookies, mountain bikes, kayaks and horses for hire and an internet service. Credit cards accepted.

A-B Cabañas de Montaña Piedras Albas, 1500 m east of the church in Cachí, T2577-1462. A pair of fully equipped cabins high in the hills close to the Río Naranjo. Good if you are looking for a quiet spot to stay for a few days. Getting up here needs a 4WD, but the views are incredible and you'll have the 4 trails leading through the forest pretty much to yourself. Excellent birdwatching, telescope for star gazing.

A-B Monte Sky, T2228-0010, www.intnet. co.cr/montesky. Space sleeping up to 20 people with basic accommodation, ideal for students and groups, with set programmes provided or you can make your own. Need to pay US$8 entrance into the private reserve.

A-B Sanchiri Mirador & Lodge, south of Paraíso, T2574-5454, www.sanchiri.com. The mid-priced restaurant, serving local and international food is in a rustic open cabin, precariously balanced on a bluff and has the best views of the valley. Half a dozen cabins, each with private bath and hot water, also have very good views.

B Kiri Lodge, 2 km east of Purisil trout farm, T2533-2272, www.kirilodge.net. There are good trails leading through the lodge's ground to the national park. 6 excellent cabins and breakfast included. Peaceful and very friendly.

B Hotel Reventazón, Orosí, T2533-3838, www.hotelreventazon.com. 7 rather stark and characterless rooms, with telephone, TV, fridge. But clean and friendly service, and good local knowledge. Internet and credit cards accepted.

C-D Río Palomo, south of Orosí, T2533-3128. Simple rooms, with private bath, a pool, and a well thought of local restaurant.

C-F Montaña Linda, Orosí, if dialling locally call T2533-3640. www.montanalinda.com. A classic backpackers' place, with a good range of options. B&B, dormitory rooms and options for camping using their tents if you haven't got your own. The owners Toine and Sara are friendly and know their patch very well. Trips to local waterfalls, Tapantí Macizo de la Muerte National Park, Purisil trout

fishing, and any other local sights are easily arranged and mix perfectly with the Spanish classes at the **Montaña Linda Language School** which uses local teachers trained by the school to get you *hablando español*. And if you want total linguistic immersion – the best way – there is a homestay option.

⑦ Eating

Cartago *p145, map p146*
Food options are as uninspiring as the accommodation.

🍴 **Puerto del Sol**, Av 4, C 14-16, is just north of the Basilica at the eastern end of town.

🍴 **Soda Apolo**, on west side of La Parroquia. Serves simple fast food *Tico*-style, open 24 hrs.

Several branches of international fast-food chains are on or close to Av 4, C 1-3. Many *sodas* in and around the Central Market.

Supermarkets Pali Supermarket, corner of Av 4 and C 6. Macrobiótica, Av 6, C 2-4.

Volcán Irazú *p147*
🍴🍴 **Restaurantes Linda Vista**, San Juan de Chicuá (a little further uphill from Hotel Gestoria Irazú see above). Spectacular views and apparently good food and drinks. But most people stop to post, stick, pin or glue their business card, or any other personal item, to the wall. Join in, you're in good company. The Dalai Lama popped by but sadly didn't leave a card.

Orosí Valley *p148*
🍴🍴 **La Casona del Cafetal**, right on the southern shore of Lake Cachí, T2577-1515. A very popular weekend dining destination open every day, but with an all-you-can-eat buffet on Sun for US$13. The à la carte menu starts at around US$6. It's a beautiful setting. After lunch you can take a horse-drawn carriage round the coffee plantation before heading east towards the town of Orosí.

☊ Bar and clubs

Cartago *p145, map p146*
Metropolis Bar, on the south side of La Parroquia. The best-looking place to stop for a drink.
Club de Cartago. A glorious building that has struggled through the town's historic challenges. Sadly it only holds private functions, but it's worth a look to see if there is an impromptu opportunity.

☻ Festivals and events

Cartago *p145, map p146*
2 Aug Pilgrims from throughout Costa Rica and Central America arrive to pay tribute to **La Negrita**, see page 146.

☉ Transport

Cartago *p145, map p146*
If travelling by car, roads lead north to Irazú for a pleasant and occasionally cloudy drive to the volcano summit. To the southeast Orosí is along Highway 10, from where a good road leads round Cachí Lake. In Paraíso the road peels off to the right leading to Turrialba. An alternative route to Turrialba takes Highway 233, following the contours of Irazú's misty slopes, taking in several quiet rural villages on the way.

A good service supplies the surrounding area. **San José**, from Av 4, C 2-4, every 10 mins, 45 mins, US$0.75. Arrives and departs San José from C 5, Av 18-20. **Orosí/Río Macho**, every 30 mins from C 6, Av 1-3, 40 mins, US$0.70. **Turrialba**, every hr from Av 3, C 8-10, 1 hr direct, 1 hr 20 collectivo. **Cachí**, via Ujarrás and Paraíso from C 6, Av 1-3, every 1½ hrs, 1 hr 20 mins. **Paraíso**, every 5 mins

from Av 5, C 4-6. **Aguacalientes**, every 15 mins from C 1, Av 3-5.

Closest bus for **Irazú** rides to **San Juan de Chicuá**, still 10 km from the summit. The bus leaves Cartago from north of the central market, Av 6, C1-3, at 1730, returning at 0500 the next day, so in reality you have to spend at least 2 nights on the volcano or in a hotel if you can't get a ride. There are also buses to **Tierra Blancas**, closest regular bus travelling towards Irazú, every 30 mins from C 4, Av 6-8. If travelling by public transport the best bet is to take the weekend bus from San José.

To visit **Volcán Turrialba** take a bus from C 4 y Av 6 to the village of **San Gerardo**.

Orosí Valley *p148*
Buses to **Cachí**, via **Ujarrás** and **Paraíso** leave Cartago from C 6, Av 1-3, every 1½ hrs, taking 1 hr 20 mins for the journey. Ask in Cartago or Paraíso if a bus that circuits the lake has started up. The demand for one is growing and improved road conditions on the southern shore make it quite likely. From **Cartago** to **Orosí/Río Macho** from C 6, Av 1-3 every 30 mins, 40 mins, US$0.55.

☻ Directory

Cartago *p145, map p146*
Banks Banco de Costa Rica has an ATM on Av 4, C 5-7. Banco Interfin, on the corner of Av 2, C 2, neighbouring Central Park has Visa and MasterCard ATMs. Banco Nacional on Av 2, C 1-3, has a Visa ATM. **Internet** New place on C 1, Av 3-5, just south of Parque Central. **Medical services** Hospital Dr Max Peralta, entrance on C 3, Av 7, T5550-1999. **Pharmacies** can be found along Av 4 between C 1- 6. **Useful addresses** Emergency: T911.

Turrialba and around

A lively local shopping hub that has expanded to fill the flood plains of the Río Turrialba, the otherwise forgettable town of Turrialba (population 33,411) appears in the spotlight not through its own merits but rather by a collection of associations. With the Reventazón and Pacuare rivers nearby, the town is the Costa Rican centre for whitewater rafting and kayaking, it's the nearest place of any size to the Guayabo National Monument archaeological site, the world famous CATIE tropical research station is just down the road, and Volcán Turrialba National Park offers a quiet, high-altitude hike for those who like to walk to the top of a volcano instead of driving. ▶ For listings, see pages 156-158.

Ins and outs ▶ Colour map 2, C4.

Getting there

By car, Turrialba is easily reached from San José via Cartago. Coming from the Caribbean a wonderfully scenic Highway 10 rises and falls through the mountains and coffee fields from Siquirres on the San José-Limón Highway. By bus, there are hourly buses to Turrialba from San José between 0500 and 2100 with Transtusa (T2556-4233), leaving Calle 13, Avenida 6-8, 1¾ hours, US$2.10. There are buses every two hours from 0600 to 1800 from Siquirres, 1½ hours, US$1.70. ▶ See Transport, page 158, for further details.

Getting around

Turrialba is small enough to walk round, but to keep you on your toes the *calles* start from the Parque Central as with most Costa Rican towns, but the *avenidas* take the railway as the dividing line. For trips to outer lying areas you will have to take a taxi or explore bus options from the central bus station.

Best time to visit

If whitewater rafting, the higher water makes for better rapids, so visit between May and Nov. However it is quite possible the water level could be too high at this time of year and it is possible to raft all year round and, naturally, you may prefer not to go rafting in the rain. Temperatures are comfortably warm at around 22°C year round.

Sights

At the confluence of the Turrialba and Colorado rivers, 62 km from San José, the town is a bridge between the Central Highlands and the Caribbean lowlands and was a former stopping point on the old Atlantic railway between Cartago and Puerto Limón. (The disused train tracks to Limón run right through town.) Despite the loss of transport links, the streets are busy with villagers from surrounding communities stocking up before heading home. Sights in the town are almost nil – even the trailer loads of kayaks that periodically rumble through the town barely turn heads.

Out of town is **Lake Angostura**, once hoped to be a centre for watersports, which is currently suffocating under dense beds of water lilies. Further along the road to Siquirres in Tres Equis is **Parque Viborana** ① *T2538-1510 (call in advance), US$5*, with 25 species of snakes from Costa Rica on display including the Bushmaster, Jumping viper and boa constrictors.

Parque Nacional Volcán Turrialba → *Colour map 2, B4.*

ⓘ *Volcán Turrialba is the least visited and smallest of the Central Highland volcanoes to merit its own national park. Established back in 1955, the lack of interest means there is no entrance fee – or at least no one to collect it, officially you get a permit in San José – and no services provided.*

At 3328 m, the volcano sits on the easternmost flank of the Cordillera Central, next to Volcán Irazú and on a clear day can be seen from the San José–Limón Highway. Three craters show evidence of lava flows, but while the volcano is partially active with fumaroles and slight seismic activity, the last reported eruptions occurred in 1864 and 1865. Vegetation is characterized by tough, twisted branches and small trees. Mammal populations of armadillos, porcupines, pumas and oncillas are believed to be very low, and recorded bird species, including the black-faced solitaire and several species of hummingbird, number 84.

There are a couple of routes to the volcano. From Cartago a bus runs from Calle 4 y Avenida 6 to San Gerardo north of Turrialba, you then walk or hitch a ride to **Finca La**

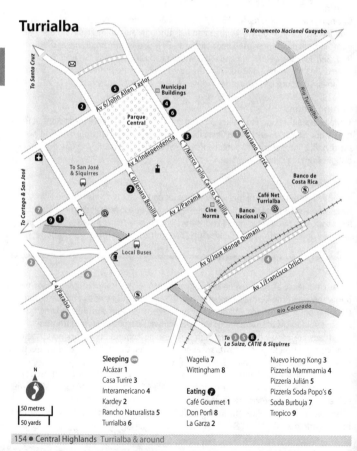

Turrialba

To Monumento Nacional Guayabo

To Santa Cruz

Av 6/John Allen Taylor
Municipal Buildings
Parque Central
Av 4/Independencia
Rio Turrialba
C 3/Mariano Cortés
C 1/Marco Tulio Castro Cardilla
To San José & Siquirres
C 0/Jennaro Bonilla
Av 2/Panama
Cine Norma
Banco Nacional
Café Net Turrialba
Banco de Costa Rica
To Cartago & San José
Local Buses
Av 0/José Monge Dumani
Av 1/Francisco Orlich
C 4/Paraíso
Rio Colorado
To La Suiza, CATIE & Siquirres

N

50 metres
50 yards

Sleeping
Alcázar 1
Casa Turire 3
Interamericano 4
Kardey 2
Rancho Naturalista 5
Turrialba 6
Wagelia 7
Wittingham 8

Eating
Café Gourmet 1
Don Porfi 8
La Garza 2
Nuevo Hong Kong 3
Pizzería Mammamia 4
Pizzería Julián 5
Pizzería Soda Popo's 6
Soda Burbuja 7
Tropico 9

Rafting the Reventazón and Pacuare

A short distance from Turrialba the Pacuare and Reventazón rivers crash and thunder down the valleys leading from the eastern slopes of the Talamanca Mountains. Organized trips lasting one to four days run Class III, IV and sometimes V rapids roaring through pristine primary rainforest. This is some of the best scenery in Costa Rica with sheer-sided gorges draped in finely woven natural green cloth. Seeing toucans, sloths and spider monkeys is virtually guaranteed (unless it is raining, in which case the river will be higher and you'll be paddling too hard to look for animals).

Full equipment is provided and for novices, safety training is given. Any reasonably fit person should be able to handle up to Class IV with good supervision and instruction.

Several organizations run trips in the area, see Activities and tours, page 158.

Central which sits in the saddle between Irazú and Turrialba. From Turrialba, take a bus to Santa Cruz and walk up to Finca La Central. Day trips can be organized through tour operators in San José. If you want to stay overnight you can camp. Alternatively 2 km from Finca La Central is **Volcán Turrialba Lodge** (see page 157).

Monumento Nacional Guayabo → Colour map 2, B4.

① T2569-1220. Mon-Sun 0800-1530. US$6. From Turrialba there are buses at 1100 and 1500 (returning 1230 and 1600), and an additional bus on Sun at 0900, returning 1700. Check times locally. (If you miss the bus it is quite difficult to hitch as there is little traffic.) If you cannot get a bus all the way to Guayabo, several buses each day pass the turn-off to Guayabo; the town is a 2-hr walk uphill.

Despite being the country's premier archaeological site, Guayabo National Monument is often overlooked – many maps don't even show its location. Still barely explored, the indigenous ceremonial centre lies 4 km from the town of Guayabo, and 19 km from Turrialba.

Over 3000 years old, the site was occupied from 1000 BC to 1400 AD and flourishing around 800 AD, the period from which many of the stone structures still standing remain. Stone roads stretch for considerable distances interrupted by mounds of different sizes and heights that were used for construction of housing. Petroglyphs have been etched on to many of the stones, their meaning still undeciphered, and centuries-old aqueducts still carry water to the reservoirs.

Underfunded and visited by few, excavation only began in 1968 despite the site having been discovered at the end of the 19th century by Anastasio Alfaro. The protected area covers 232 ha, only a very small fraction of which has been excavated. Little is known about the people who lived here beyond the broad notion that the community was multi-skilled and ruled by a *cacique*. The economy was based on agriculture, hunting and fishing, but the reason for the site's location and its abandonment in the 1400s, remains a mystery. If you are looking for ruins of majestic proportions don't visit. Guayabo does not compare with the great ruins of Guatemala, Mexico or South America. (Archaeologists call this part of the Americas the Intermediate Area lying between those two larger civilizations.) If, however, you want to visit a spot where you can let your imagination run wild – with no one around to tell you different – while exploring some trails and enjoying plenty of birds, wildlife and impressive waterfalls, then it is worth making the effort.

CATIE → Colour map 2, C4.

ⓘ *About 4 km southeast of Turrialba, T2558-2000 ext 2275, www.catie.ac.cr, open daily 0700-1600, US\$5 or can be booked in advance or through an agency in San José.*

The Centro Agronómico Tropical de Investigación y Enseñanza is an international, non-profit organization whose main purpose is research, higher education and outreach in agricultural sciences, natural resources and related subjects in the American tropics.

Created in 1940 in response to an acknowledged need to share research and experiences in tropical agriculture across the Americas, the Costa Rican government donated 2500 ha to CATIE's forerunner, the Inter-American Institute of Agricultural Sciences. Today, 11 Latin American and Caribbean nations support CATIE's work carried out by a staff of 120, including 40 with doctorates and 50 with masters' degrees.

CATIE's philosophy is to 'produce while conserving and conserve while producing'. Contributions to such broad goals are, by their own admittance, difficult to measure, but CATIE has made significant developments in agroforestry, integrated pest management and management of tropical crops and tropical nature forests. It also maintains a genetic resource bank of several crops and produce. In short, CATIE is of great interest to tropical agronomists and researchers, it has one of the largest fruit collections in the world as well as an important library on tropical agriculture.

For less academic visitors it is the landscaped gardens and trails leading through the ecologically varied zones that attract birders in particular. Visits are welcome, and easily arranged directly or through many of the hotels in the Turrialba area. If you want to stay or organize a group trip, a wide range of accommodation options are available including student dormitory rooms, apartments and a few guesthouses prices **AL-L**. There is also a gym and a couple of restaurants.

Moravia del Chirripó

In the village of Moravia del Chirripó, east of Turrialba, guides and horses can be hired for an excursion into the trackless jungle homeland of the Talamanca people, with their legends of lost goldfields. The bus from Turrialba takes four hours, only certain in dry season; in wet season go to Grano de Oro, from where it's a one-hour walk. No accommodation in Moravia, stay put at the *pulpería* (tavern) in Grano de Oro. Trips can be arranged to the Chirripó Indian Reserve of **Alto Pacuare**, east of Turrialba; the reserve is a 2½-hour hike from Río Vereh, and is good for serious naturalists and hikers.

◉ Turrialba and around listings

For Sleeping and Eating price codes and other relevant information, see Essentials, pages 44-47.

◉ Sleeping

Turrialba *p153, map p154*

AL Wagelia, Av 4 at the entrance to Turrialba, T2556-1566, www.hotelwagelia. com. The best hotel in town, if a little overpriced. 18 rooms (with fan or a/c) surrounding a central courtyard each with private bath, telephone and safebox, some

also have TV. Also has a restaurant and bar and a tour operator with good local tours.

B-D Interamericano, Av 1, facing the old railway line, T2556-0142, www.hotelinter americano.com. According to the North American couple that run the hotel, it's "nothing fancy but we do guarantee it's clean." The rooms are indeed spotlessly clean, bright with natural light and have good beds. Doubt-less this modesty, a keenness to help and excellent local knowledge is one reason people keep coming back. There's also a small bar,

social area and noticeboard, internet access and storage of kayaks is free for guests (small charge for non-guests). Even if you're not a guest you can bring your queries here.
C Alcázar, C 3, Av 2-4. Clean, tidy, efficient and just a few too many plastic flowers. Small terrace upstairs and each room has cable TV, telephone, fan and private bath with hot water. A classic of this price bracket, rumoured to be closing down so call ahead.
C Kardey, C 4, Av 2-4, T2556-0050. 20 rooms, with a communal kitchen.
D Turrialba, Av 2, C 2-4, T2556-6654. Clean simple rooms with private bath, hot water and TV. There are also a couple of pool tables and soft drinks for sale.
F Wittingham, C 4, Av 0-2, T2556-8822. 7 fairly dark but OK rooms, some with private bath. An option if other places are full.

Out of town
LL Pacuare Lodge, on the banks of the Pacuare River, www.junglelodgecostarica. com. Stunning rooms in a spectacular setting. The Honeymoon Suite has it's own hanging bridge access. Go and chill out, or try some of the adventurous activites. You can arrive by road or on a rafting trip.
LL-L Casa Turire, 14 km southeast of Turrialba, T2531-1111, www.hotelcasaturire. com. Comfort and elegance in an idyllic tropical setting. With a plantation-style ambience and personal service, Casa Turire is one of the celebrated five 'Small Distinctive Hotels'. 12 luxury rooms with bath and 4 suites are fully equipped with every comfort. The restaurant is Mediterranean-style, and there is a spring-fed pool, library and parlour games room. The arrival of Lake Angostura now makes Casa Turire a lakeside hotel.
L Rancho Naturalista, south of the town of La Suiza, T2430-0400, www.rancho naturalista.net. 11 rooms, most with private bath. Reservations essential (the spot is very popular with birdwatchers). Price per person includes gourmet meals, horse riding, guided tours, transfers from San José and airport. Programmes organized for birdwatchers

and naturalists to surrounding area and CATIE.
A Turrialtico, turning east on the road to Siquirres, T2538-1111, www.turrialtico.com. Clean, with private bath, comfortable and friendly with small restaurant. Set on a hilltop with spectacular panoramic views.
A pp Volcán Turrialba Lodge, 2 km from Finca La Central, T2273-4335, www.volcanturrialbalodge.com. Accessible only by 4WD and well signposted if you're driving, but the lodge can also arrange transport. 22 homely rooms with private bath and stove. Some excellent tours including treks and horse riding to the crater floor so you could easily stay for several days. Wholesome Costa Rican food cooked over an open fire.
E San Agustín, in Vereh, some 25 km south-east of Turrialba, take the bus via Jicotea, www.costaricabackpacker.com. Truly isolated for real rural Costa Rica experience. Candle-light camping, river bathing, hiking and horse riding in surrounding area. The kind of wilderness experience people were travelling to find 25 years ago.

Monumento Nacional Guayabo *p155*
C-D Albergue y Restaurant La Calzada, T2556-0465. Has a few rooms and a small restaurant. Best to make a reservation. Camping is reported to be allowed on the site. Drinking water and toilets are provided.

🍴 Eating

Turrialba *p153, map p154*
Several cheap restaurants and *sodas* are dotted around the main square.
🍴 **La Garza**. Good local food.
🍴 **Nuevo Hong Kong**, facing the Parque Central, on the corner of C 1 and Av 4. Serves good cheap Chinese.
🍴 **Pizzería Julián**, on the north side of the square.
🍴 **Pizzería Mammamia**. Fast-food-style café.
🍴 **Pizzería Soda Popo's**. Similar to Mammamia.

Soda Burbuja. Popular family-run place open to the street with big portions of local dishes, very good value.

Cafés
Café Gourmet, opposite Hotel Wagelia on Av 4. Serves excellent coffee indoors or on the tiny patio just big enough for 2 to watch the world meander by.
Trópico, next to Café Gourmet. Serves 100 natural fruit juices.

Out of town
Don Porfi, on the road south out of Turrialba. Locally popular, with good seafood and international menu.

Monumento Nacional Guayabo *p155*
There are a couple of small cafés in the town of Guayabo.

▲ Activities and tours

Turrialba *p153, map p154*
Costa Sol Rafting, C1, Av 6-8, T2293-2150, www.costasolrafting.com. Based in Heredia, many of the standard trips, and a few specifically aimed at beginners.
Loco's Tropical Tours, T2556-6035, www.whiteh2o.com. Not the biggest rafting operation in Costa Rica but, they claim, the friendliest. *Tico*-run, and with a fair amount of experience. Custom rafting trips on the Reventazón and Pacuare rivers, 2-day trips, family river trips to Río Pejiballe, horse riding. Prices from US$55 to US$125 a day.
    A couple of smaller operations include: **Rainforest World**, T2556-2678, www.rforestw.com; and **Ticos River Adventures**, T2556-1231, www.ticoriver. com. Both offer 1-day trips around Turrialba and a few multi-day trips further afield, also kayak hire and kayak school.
Rafting operations in San José like **Costa Rica Expeditions** and **Ríos Tropicales**, see page 105, also have trips that you can meet up with in Turrialba.

Serendipity Adventures, T2558-1000, www.serendipityadventures.com. Provide hot-air balloon tours in the Turrialba area, or to the north around Naranjo or Volcán Arenal. Whichever one you choose it is certain to be a stunning adventure. Serendipity also arrange a variety of adventure and nature tours.

🚍 Transport

Turrialba *p153, map p154*
Buses to **San José** and **Siquirres** leave from Av 4, C 0-2. Services to San José run from 0500 until 2100 every ½ hr, 90 mins, US$1.55. To Siquirres they depart every 2 hrs, taking 1½ hrs, US$1.30. Buses to local destinations leave from the terminal on the corner of Av 2, C 2.

🏢 Directory

Turrialba *p153, map p154*
Banks Several banks mostly along C 3 between Av 2-4 generally open from 0830-1530. **Banco de Costa Rica**, Av 0 and C 3, has Visa and MasterCard ATM. A little to the west is **Banco Nacional**, Av 0, C 1-3, ATMs. **Internet** Internet café on C 2, Av 2-4, close to the San José/ Siquirres bus stop. **Language schools** Adventure Spanish School, T2556-4609, www.adventurespanish school.com, US$315 for a week of 4 hrs a day, add US$125 for homestay. With locations in Arenal and Playa Dominical. **Spanish by the River**, T2556-7380, www.spanishbythe sea.com, have set up on the outskirts of Turrialba. Good chance to meet fewer English speakers in relative isolation. US$130 for 4 hrs a day with group tuition, add US$85 if you want to stay with a local family. **Medical services** The local hospital is on T2556-1133, several pharmacies found around the centre of town. **Post office** The post office is north of the Parque Central on C 0 just past Av 8. **Useful addresses** Emergencies: T911.

Contents

162 Puerto Viejo loop
162 Ins and outs
162 Anticlockwise loop
166 Listings

170 Ciudad Quesada, Fortuna and Lake Arenal
170 Ins and outs
171 Ciudad Quesada (San Carlos)
171 Fortuna
173 Parque Nacional Arenal
175 Around Lake Arenal
177 Listings

186 North of Fortuna
186 North to Nicaragua via Upala
186 North to Los Chiles
187 Refugio Nacional de Vida Silvestre Caño Negro
188 Listings

190 Monteverde and Santa Elena
190 Ins and outs
192 History and background information
192 Reserva Biológica Bosque Nuboso Monteverde
196 Reserva Biológica Bosque Nuboso Santa Elena
198 Listings

Footprint features

160 Don't miss ...
172 Pocosol – the power of nature
175 La Fortuna or Monteverde?
192 What is cloudforest?

At a glance

Getting around Locations are spread across different bus routes so be patient on buses. Take the jeep–boat–jeep route between Fortuna and Santa Elena.

Time required 4 days, but you could stay longer.

Weather Clear skies in the lowlands through to cloudforest at Monteverde.

When not to go Monteverde is good throughout the year, but the rains just don't stop around May-Jul.

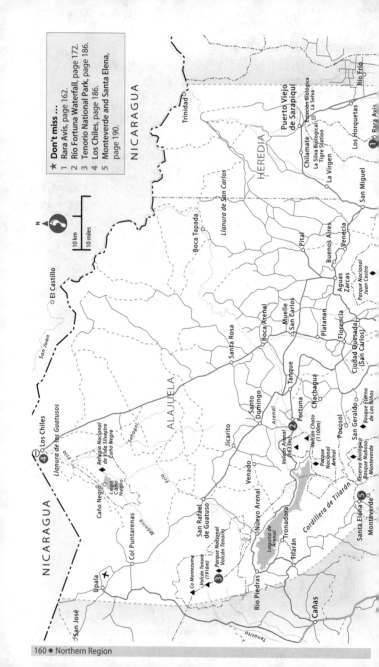

Don't miss...

★
1 Rara Avis, page 162.
2 Río Fortuna Waterfall, page 172.
3 Tenorio National Park, page 186.
4 Los Chiles, page 186.
5 Monteverde and Santa Elena, page 190.

NICARAGUA

NICARAGUA

El Castillo

San Juan

Upala

San José

Col Puntarenas

Caño Negro

Lago Caño Negro

Refugio Nacional de Vida Silvestre Caño Negro

Río Frío

Llanura de los Guatusos

Los Chiles ④

① Los Chiles

Monico

Río

San Rafael de Guatuso

Cerro Montezuma

Volcán Tenorio (1916m)

Parque Nacional Volcán Tenorio ③

Río Piedras

Tronadora

Tilarán

Cañas

Tenorito

Laguna de Arenal

Cordillera de Tilarán

Santa Elena

Monteverde ⑤

Reserva Biológica Bosque Nuboso Monteverde

Bosque Eterno de Los Niños

San Geraldo

Pocosol

Bosque Nacional Arenal

Volcán Chato (1100m)

Volcán Arenal (1633m)

Fortuna ②

Chachagua

Tabacón

Nuevo Arenal

Venado

Jicarito

Sebogal

Río

Santo Domingo

Tanque

Boca Arenal

Santa Rosa

Muelle San Carlos

Platanar

Florencia

Ciudad Quesada (San Carlos)

Parque Nacional Juan Castro

Aguas Zarcas

Buenos Aires

Venecia

Pital

Boca Tapada

Llanura de San Carlos

Llanura de San Carlos

San Miguel

San Carlos

ALAJUELA

HEREDIA

Trinidad

Puerto Viejo de Sarapiquí

Chilamate

Estación Biológica La Selva

La Silva Biológica Tigre Station

La Virgen

Los Horquetas

Río Frío

① Rara Avis

Rara Avis

N

10 km

10 miles

160 • Northern Region

Sweeping northwest from San José, the mountains of the Cordillera de Tilarán and Central create a number of irresistible opportunities. The Puerto Viejo de Sarapiquí loop takes in good scenery, a host of outstanding wildlife opportunities where you can get muddy and mucky, and adventurous pursuits. Volcán Arenal, overshadowing the small town of Fortuna, is the perfect symmetrical volcano, standing clear and tall against the horizon, puffing fumes, exploding against a fine blue sky (if you're lucky), with the expansive Lake Arenal in the foreground. Among the lowland towns to the north, Los Chiles close to the Nicaraguan border stands out with the profuse wildlife of the Caño Negro Wildlife Reserve nearby. A few hours south of Lake Arenal or heading east from the Pan-American Highway bumpy roads climb through simple dairy communities to the cloudforest reserves of Monteverde and Santa Elena and a search for the resplendent – but elusive – quetzal.

Puerto Viejo loop

If you're looking for a short trip from San José, the Puerto Viejo loop takes in the impressive diversity of Costa Rica in a simple drive or bus trip. Climbing over the continental divide before sinking down to the Northern lowlands, the scenery is impressive. If you have time you can tramp through rainforest, get on the river for whitewater rafting, or enjoy the several waterfalls in the area.
▸▸ *For listings, see pages 166-169.*

Ins and outs ▸▸ *Colour map 2, B3.*

Getting there and around

This is neither a recognized district nor a geographical region, but a road (Highway 4) that can be travelled as part of a round trip. It leaves the San José-Limón Highway at Rancho Roberto's restaurant at the edge of Braulio Carrillo National Park, then heads north, looping through Puerto Viejo de Sarapiquí, passing biological stations, ecolodges and adventure centres. The final leg of the circuit goes across the saddle between Volcán Barva and Volcán Poás directly north of San José. The circular route is particularly scenic in the section from Varablanca to San Miguel. You can make the journey in one day – a popular choice for tours from San José – or travel at a more leisurely pace stopping off as you wish.

Travelling by bus is easy, with frequent hourly, services taking the route clockwise and anticlockwise from the Gran Terminal de Caribe in San José. However, be aware that some of the places of interest are not on the main road so you may find yourself walking a short distance or hitching a ride. ▸▸ *For further details, see Transport, page 169.*

Anticlockwise loop ⬤⬤ ▸▸ *pp166-169.*

Rara Avis

ⓘ *Booking accommodation in advance is strongly recommended, especially in the dry season, T2764 1111, www.rara-avis.com. Reached through Las Horquetas, around 16 km north of the San José-Limón road, Rara Avis is a privately owned reserve with accommodation close to the lower slopes of Braulio Carrillo National Park. It was developed to show the that rainforest can be economically productive and consequently to save it from destruction. Once visited, few would doubt the success of the place which provides guests with an intimate experience of the rainforest.*

Perched on the eastern flanks of the park at an altitude of 700 m, the diversity of the reserve is staggering. Some 367 birds have been recorded including umbrella birds and the green macaw. You will probably see monkeys, coatis and anteaters, and the really lucky may occasionally get to see spotted tapirs and jaguars – or at least their footprints.

At the reserve itself – reached by a bone-shaking 15-km, three-hour adventure in a tractor-pulled cart (see Transport below, page 169) – an extensive network of trails leads through primary forest. Some are quite rough and muddy so go prepared. You can hike them with a guide or enjoy the solitude and absolute silence by breaking out on your own, sneaking off to the double waterfall for a swim at its base.

Several ongoing projects at Rara Avis are proving the rainforest can be economically productive (since its creation in 1983, Rara Avis has managed to return a slight profit).

Firstly, the lodges bring in a reliable source of income. Other natural projects include a butterfly export programme, cultivation of the rare and endemic stained glass palm ornamental plant, and research into the sustainable use of orchids.

Parque Nacional Braulio Carrillo
& Puerto Viejo loop

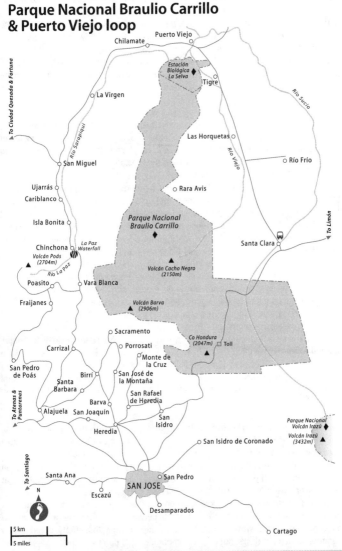

Heliconia Island B&B

ⓘ T2764-5220, www.heliconiaisland.com. Open daily but call ahead to be sure. US$10. If driving, Montero is 8 km south of Puerto Viejo de Sarapiquí. Look for the right turn 1 km south of Río Isla Grande bridge and the Isla Grand petrol station. A right turn, followed by another right turn leads down a grassy track which should be signposted. If travelling by bus, ask the driver to drop you off at Montero.

In the thoroughly missable hamlet of Montero, close to the Río Isla Grande bridge, is the pleasant surprise of Heliconias Island, a fantastic collection of 70 types of heliconia from all over the world. Rarely will you get the chance to see such variety and diversity in such a small area. New Dutch owners have added a few rooms (**AL**), keeping it intimate and personal. The 5-ha island garden is a joy to visit, and you can rest with refreshments in the impressively high, thatched bamboo hut restaurant.

Estación Biológica La Selva → *Colour map 2, B3.*

ⓘ T2524-0628, www.esintro.co.cr. The station is open every day, and begins life at dawn – around 0600. Entrance, including the guided walk is US$28. The station is just 3 km south of Puerto Viejo de Sarapiquí. There is a sign but you'll probably miss it a couple of times if driving yourself. Buses from San José to Puerto Viejo will drop you off at the junction from where you can walk the kilometre or so to the entrance.

Joining Braulio Carrillo National Park at its northernmost boundary, La Selva Biological Station is an internationally renowned research station. The species diversity is spectacular and for both the specialist and general interest visitor, La Selva is a natural playground. The figures are bewildering. The place is drenched with an average of 4 m of rain a year. Over half (436) of the bird species found in Costa Rica have been sighted on the 1600 ha – just over 6 sq miles – of old growth and disturbed tropical wetforests. Toucans, parrots, trogons, hummingbirds, monkeys, peccaries, agoutis and coatis are regularly seen by visitors. There's even a rather touching warning to keep an eye out in particular for seven of the 56 venomous snake species found at the station.

Owned and operated by the Organization for Tropical Studies (which also runs Palo Verde in Guanacaste and Las Cruces in southern Costa Rica), the station is first and foremost a research station and focuses on that role. But natural history visitors are welcome and usually visit as part of a day trip from San José or Puerto Viejo de Sarapiquí. **Guided tours** leave at 0800 and 1330, US$28. There is also an Early Bird walk at 0530, a night walk starting between 1800 and 1900, and an introductory full day birdwatching course at 0800 on Saturdays. All courses require advance notice. There are also several other courses to choose from and access to local tours and trips.

Puerto Viejo de Sarapiquí → *Colour map 2, B3. Population: 9864. Altitude: 70 m.*

On arriving, it's difficult to believe that Puerto Viejo de Sarapiquí is the largest town in the northwestern lowlands and was once a flourishing port moving people and produce northwards down the Sarapiquí River to join the River San Juan and from there to the Caribbean. There are still possibilities for river travel but you will need time, plenty of cash and a fair amount of patience if you want to make it to Tortuguero. For the moment at least, the opportunity to jump on the banana boat has long gone.

Today's Puerto Viejo de Sarapiquí is a couple of roads linking the small riverside dock with the bus station and not much of interest in between. You enter town at the junction a few hundred metres west of town. The town limps along in that empty, bored way so common of defunct docks. But it isn't as though people don't visit the area – the road west to La Virgen and the road south to the main highway are littered with ecolodges, private reserves and river rafting opportunities. River trips on the Sarapiquí can be organized from, or near, Puerto Viejo – upstream is whitewater trips, downstream float trips – but most people book from San José.

Tours to agricultural centres come and go. The Banana Plantation tour may reopen again soon, but you could always try a Pineapple Tour. Mainly aimed at groups, explore the options at www.agritourscr.com or www.sarapiquicostarica.com.

West to La Virgen and San Miguel

Go west young man (or woman) and you'll find several **lodges** ideal for relaxing in, birdwatching, adventure or messing about on the rapids of the Río Sarapiquí lining the road from Puerto Viejo to San Miguel. There are plenty of places to choose from, we've selected a few – see page 167.

Set in 200 ha of lowland rainforest **Selva Verde Lodge**, is a popular stopover for the day or, if time allows, for a few days. Adjoining Braulio Carrillo National Park and La Selva Biological Station, it's a great little spot for birding, nature tours and river trips. There's a short self-guided tour through the grounds, or you can go on longer guided trips along the multitude of trails – focusing on botany, birding, orchids or butterflies – with a resident bilingual naturalist. The River Sarapiquí, which runs through the property, makes for a scenic and gentle boat journey or, further upstream, an adrenalin-pumping challenge.

Next door, the **Sarapiquí Conservation Learning Centre** ① T2766-6482, www.learningcentercostarica.org, works to ensure that the local community gets to learn about, and benefit from, the secrets of the rainforest. Extending education about the rainforest to the local community is an essential link if the desire to reduce deforestation is to be effective at a grass roots level. A good library is available in the Learning Centre, and there is a volunteer programme teaching English.

Continuing west, a rainforest museum, botanical gardens and the 330-ha **Tirimbina Biological Reserve** ① T2761-0055, www.tirimbina.org – part of Centro Neotrópico Sarapiquí – provide ample space for exploring the lowland Caribbean rainforest. The area incorporates a suspension bridge and suspended canopy walkway, making it a great place to relax, learn and be challenged physically and mentally. Behind the scenes sustainable eco-perspectives employ local people and use solar energy to provide electricity. There's also a biological waste-water treatment plant. All in all, it's proof positive that environmental consideration doesn't have to compromise comforts and service levels. Knowing when they're onto a good thing, a chocolate tour is one of several offered.

Next door is the **Serpentario Snake Garden** ① US$6, with a good selection of the Costa Rican reptiles; there are over 50 snakes and frogs to observe including a 29-ft anaconda. It's a good opportunity to get close, safely.

La Virgen and San Miguel

The small town of La Virgen, with a few facilities (see page 168), 9 km north of San Miguel, suddenly appears and disappears along the roadside. West of the town are a couple of activity centres (see page 168).

Continuing south, the road reaches San Miguel, which has a couple of *sodas* simply marked La Mirador. Behind the scruffy-looking façade is a simple restaurant serving traditional dishes with incredible views down into the valley and across to a waterfall. If the beauty of the spot isn't enough, hummingbirds buzz and zip round the balcony performing aerial displays in a frenzy of disputes around the hanging honey birdfeeders. From here the road climbs the scenic **Sarapiquí Valley** with several stopping places, including the popular and impressive **La Paz waterfalls**. In 2008, American extreme kayaker Pat Keller decided to drop off the edge, taking the 120-ft drop (36-m) in a plastic boat. He emerged with nothing more than a broken hand.

West and north from San Miguel

From San Miguel a road that alternates between bad and OK reaches **Venecia** which has an interesting church, one clean and cheap hotel (F) and Restaurant El Parque, near the church, providing good local food. Nearby are the **pre-Columbian tumuli of Ciudad Cutris**. A good road goes to within 2 km of Cutris, from where you can walk or take a 4WD. The ruins, which are of limited interest to all but the most devoted, are on private property and you need a permit from the local *finca*.

West of Venecia the road continues to follow the contours of Platanar Volcano arriving at **Aguas Zarcas**, at which point the road splits. Heading west the road leads to Ciudad Quesada (San Carlos) (see page 171). Heading north then west is a slightly more direct route to Fortuna (also page 171). North of Aguas Zarcas is a lowland agricultural region. You can stay at a cooperative lodge at **La Gloria de San Carlos de Aguas Zarcas**.

Heading north then west via **Pital**, the road descends to the rainforest lowlands, reaching the Río San Carlos after 40 km, and the town of **Boca Tapada** a remote wilderness destination with accommodation.

◉ Puerto Viejo Loop listings

For Sleeping and Eating price codes and other relevant information, see Essentials, pages 44-47.

◎ Sleeping

Rara Avis *p162*
A number of accommodation options are available. All prices include transport, 3 daily meals (traditional country-style Costa Rican fare served family-style in the open-air dining room) and guides.
LL River Edge Cabin. This secluded choice is ideal for birdwatchers and couples. The lodge has a couple of double bedrooms, hot water, private bath and solar-powered lighting. Hammocks on the shared balcony look across to the forest.
LL Waterfall Lodge. Has 8 rooms, each with a private bath and balcony, in a comfortable but rustic lodge. It's just a couple of hundred metres from the waterfall – hence the name.
AL Casitas. The cheapest option, with 2-room cabins sleeping up to 4 people,

sharing a cold water shower. Special rates are available for student groups and researchers.

Estación Biológica La Selva *p164*
AL per person in dormitory-style accommodation, with 3 meals a day. Rates are reduced for researchers and students.

Puerto Viejo de Sarapiquí *p164*
In town
A-B El Bambú, in a blaze of floodlights on the north side of the football pitch, T2766-6005, www.elbambu.com. 30 rooms with a/c, TV, telephone, hot water and private bath. Small pool and smart restaurant looking out to the garden. No great surprise, but there's bamboo furniture throughout. Best in town, but still overpriced.
A-B Posada Andrea Cristina, on the western outskirts of town, just left of the main junction, T2766-6265, www.andrea cristina.com. Small, comfortable cabins, set in tropical gardens in a Costa Rican family-run B&B. Good local knowledge and tours.

C-D Mi Lindo Sarapiquí, on the west side of the park, T2766-6074. 15 spotless rooms with hot water, private bath and fan. Nothing flashy but a good deal.

F Cabinas Laura, behind Banco Nacional, T2766-6236. All rooms have private bath. Clean enough, best budget option in town.

G Hospedaje Gonar, on the road to the dock above the hardware store, T2844-4677. Basic rooms, the ones with windows are better, but they're all pretty grubby. An option if Cabinas Laura is full.

Out of town

A-B El Gavilán Lodge, southern bank of the Río Sarapiquí, best reached by taxi from town, T2234-9507, www.gavilanlodge.com. 13 tidy rooms with tiled floors and simple wooden furniture sleeping 2-4 people all with hot water private bath and a/c. Well tended gardens beside the open-air restaurant serving international and Costa Rican dishes. The 75-ha private reserve has 3 trails round the hotel where you can see spider, capuchin and howler monkeys, and a bird list currently standing at over 100.

C Ara Ambigua, turn right after the cemetery 1.5 km from Puerto Viejo, T2766-7101, www.hotelaraambigua.com. Low-key set-up of 13 clean rooms and rustic lodges –some with flagstone flooring, all with private bath, and Wi-Fi. 3 small lakes and a few trails make it a pleasant stopover, with a restaurant and bar littered with old farming tools.

F pp Cabinas La Trinidad, north in Trinidad, reached by boat down the Río Sarapiquí on the San Juan River, T2381-0621. Simple cabins in a quiet spot, meals included. Boat from Puerto Viejo leaves at 1330, US10.

West to La Virgen and San Miguel p165

LL-L Selva Verde Lodge, Chilamate, T2766-6800, www.selvaverde.com. 40 rooms and 5 bungalows in a dozen clusters connected by a network of covered walkways, all have tiled private bath, hot water and wooden flooring.

What separates it from other lodges is the ease of access and the very clear attention to detail and service. A hint of Sarchíesque decor adds a pleasant touch to the simple rooms which are raised off the ground to understorey level. Buffet-style Costa Rican dishes are prepared by local women making the most of local resources. There's a small gift store, and rubber boots are available for a range of jungle hikes and excursions. Many careful touches are clearly designed to make your stay unforgettable.

L-AL Centro Neotrópico Sarapiquí, T2761-1004, www.sarapiquis.org. The Centro is a model project for sustainable development but without scrimping on comforts. The 12 standard and 24 deluxe rooms all have hot water and private bath, ceiling fans and telephone, in 3, 18-m high thatched roof *palenques*. Neither comfort nor the environment is compromised here and the magnificent central *palenque* is home to the buffet-style restaurant and bar with stunning views to the mountainous highlands. The design and layout is based on a pre-Columbian 15th-century village. Pre-Columbian tombs have been found on site.

A La Quinta Sarapiquí, 4 km from La Virgen, 12 km from Puerto Viejo, T2761-1300, www.laquintasarapiqui.com. A small country inn on a curve along the Sardinal River, the 23 rooms are pleasantly spacious, clean and all have private bath with hot water, silent fan (good for trying to sleep) and a shaded porch with chairs. The open-air bar and restaurant serves home-made food with a view out to the rainforest. The place is a good little secret with an impressive bird list of over 115 species, a small poison arrow frog trail and a butterfly garden and museum. You can stop by and stay for the night, or just pop in if travelling the Fortuna–Puerto Limón route.

E Cabinas Yacare, not far along the road from Puerto Viejo de Sarapiquí, T2766-6691. 11 simple and rather tired rooms. An OK budget choice.

La Virgen *p165*
E Rancho Leona, T2841-5341,
www.rancholeona.com. Rooms and
dormitory accommodation, with shared
bathroom, are rustic and clean and
decorated with stained glass created by
owners Leona and Ken. The main attraction
is kayaking on the River Sarapiquí from
beginner to advanced level with 2 nights'
accommodation included in the all-inclusive
price of US$75. There's a quiet patio so
you can read in the truly lush gardens, an
Indian-style sweat lodge, excellent local
knowledge of nearby attractions and musical
instruments for jamming sessions. All this
fuelled on a healthy but filling menu of
dishes served in the open-air restaurant.
They also sell top-quality and home-made
gifts including T-shirts and, of course, their
fine stained glass pieces, which don't come
cheap. In the truest sense of the phrase,
Rancho Leona is low-key and homely –
a good choice.
F-G Sarapiquí Outdoor Centre, T2761-
1123. Offers a range of full- and half-day trips
down the Sarapiquí, Toro and Pacuare rivers
and has cheap rooms or you can camp.

West and north from San Miguel *p166*
AL-A La Laguna del Lagarto Lodge, Boca
Tapada, T2289-8163, www.lagarto-lodge-
costa-rica.com. The lodge has 20 rooms
with hot water and ceiling fan, a couple
with shared bath. The open-air restaurant,
with daily meals working out at around
US$25, looks directly out to the unspoiled
rainforest and private 500-ha reserve. Over
350 bird species, including the great green
macaw have been recorded on the property.
You can roam through over 10 km of trails
with locally trained guides or head out on
your own. Beyond the sheer comfort of the
place, you can take canoeing trips on a
couple of nearby lagoons, a boat trip to
the nearby San Juan River on the border
with Nicaragua or go horse riding. Lagarto
is constantly recommended by the great
and the good.

🍴 Eating

Hotels and lodges all have restaurants.
Check meals are included in the price.

Puerto Viejo de Sarapiquí *p164*
🍴 **Mi Lindo Sarapiquí**. Serves a wide
selection of cheap dishes and super-
cold beer.
🍴 **Soda La Isquinita**, close the river.
Good, cheap food, handy when hanging
round dock.

▲ Activities and tours

Puerto Viejo de Sarapiquí *p164*
A fledgling chamber of tourism is promoting
the charms of the region, but the unified
approach is yet to arrive. Several stores
offer tourist information.
Oasis Nature Tours, T2766-6108, www.oasis
naturetours.com. Offer 2-day, 1-night tours to
Tortuguero including transport, lodging at
Ilan Ilan (see page 381), meals and jungle
walks. US$195 per person, with a minimum of
4 people, or 3 days and 2 nights for US$295.

La Virgen *p165*
Aguas Bravas, T2292-2072, www.aguas-
bravas.co.cr. General outdoor adventure
tour operator that focuses mainly on river
trips down the Sarapiquí River, but also
offers biking, safari, horse riding, hiking
and canopy tours. The put-in upstream of
La Virgen is Class III+, lower down, the river
is a beautifully scenic float. Most of their
trips are organized direct from San José,
but if you're passing they can usually work
something out.
Hacienda Pozo Azul, T2761-1360,
www.pozoazul.com. Multi-activity centre
including horse riding, whitewater rafting,
canopy tours, mountain biking and
rappelling. Good combinations and
some safer trips for younger kids.
Prices from US$10-120.

⊝ Transport

Rara Avis *p162*
Catching an early bus from San José you should be able to get to the hut in **Las Horquetas** in time to catch the tractor-cart which leaves around 0900, or go for the 1400 departure. The journey takes 3 hrs. The return journeys leave around 0800 and 1400 arriving in Las Horquetas at 1800 in time to catch a bus back if needed.

Puerto Viejo de Sarapiquí *p164*
Boat Tours and trips down the Sarapiquí where you will see howler monkeys, iguanas, caiman and many birds, can be arranged from Puerto Viejo de Sarapiquí. Boats can be hired from the dockside, US$30/hr for 1-3 people, US$10pp/hr for 4 and above. You can also go to **Tortuguero** for US$350 and include a night there while the boatman waits. A boat to the frontier with **Nicaragua** to the **La Trinidad** complex costs US$160 return. There is also a daily launch service to **Trinidad** on the San Juan River, leaving at 1330, returning at 1700, US$10. Contact Juan Guzman Mena, T2353-3001, if there is no boat at the dockside.

Bus Almost hourly buses connect with **San José** from the Gran Terminal del Caribe with **Empresarios Guapileños**, T2221-2596. Buses take 2 routes: 4 daily heading north from the capital through **Heredia** and **Vara Blanca**, 4 hrs, US$3; 7 daily buses head directly east through **Braulio Carrillo National Park** and **Las Horquetas**, 2 hrs, US$3. Regular buses also go to **Guápiles, Horquetas** and **Río Frio**. Also to **Ciudad Quesada**, 5 daily, 2½ hrs, US$2.25.

Car Following the San José–Limón Highway, after passing over and through the Braulio Carrillo National Park, Highway 4 turns north at Rancho Robertos for 33 km. A more scenic, but longer, route heads north through Heredia and Vara Blanca, heading east through La Virgen and on to Puerto Viejo.

❶ Directory

Puerto Viejo de Sarapiquí *p164*
Banks Banco de Costa Rica and Banco Nacional have branches in town.
Internet Internet Sarapiquí, is on the road into town, at the western side of town, open 0800-2200, US$1 per hr. **Post office and telephone** The post office and ICE telephone office are on the road towards the dock at the eastern end out of town.

Ciudad Quesada, Fortuna and Lake Arenal

Leaving the fertile soils of the Central Highlands where coffee is king, the roads passing through San Ramón or Zarcero quickly descend to the northern lowlands where citrus groves and ranching dominate. Small towns along the way can make an interesting stopover for a few hours, or maybe overnight. Fortuna, basking in the igneous glow of Arenal volcano and the vast waters of the lake, offers a wide range of excursions and activities for the adventurous. ►► *For listings, see pages 177-185.*

Ins and outs

Getting there
Travelling by road, all routes to Fortuna are very scenic. From the south leaving the Pan-American Highway near San Ramón, a good road leads north, passing through Chichagua, for 73 km. An alternative and longer route passes through Zarcero and Ciudad Quesada. Arriving from Tilarán to the west, a pot-holed and deteriorating road follows the north shore of Lake Arenal with great views across the lake to the volcano. Buses to Fortuna depart from all the places mentioned above and from San José. Travel between Fortuna and Santa Elena/ Monteverde is now easier with a taxi–boat–taxi option. ►► *See Transport, page 184, for further details.*

Getting around
Fortuna is small enough to stroll around. Those with the energy and inclination can take canopy tours, whitewater rafting trips, hire mountain bikes, horses or even quads to explore further afield. For shorter local journeys there are plenty of taxis.

Best time to visit
If seeing the volcano is the main reason for your visit, the skies are most reliably clear between December and April. Otherwise take into account greater rain between August and November – the waterfall will be more impressive, but walking trails will be muddier.

Tourist information
There is a tourist information office in Fortuna on the south side of the main square. Sunset Tours on the main square or Aventuras Arenal, on the main road heading east, are also worth visiting. www.arenal.net has a selection of local, but not comprehensive, information.

Ciudad Quesada

Sleeping	Eating
Del Norte 3	Coco Loco
Del Valle 1	Steak House 1
Diana 4	Cristal 2
Don Goyo 5	Los Geranios 3
El Retiro 6	Pollos Jeffry 4
Fernando 7	
La Central 8	

Ciudad Quesada (San Carlos) ⊕🄵🄿🄾🄻🄲 ➤ pp177-185. Colour map 2, B2.

Just 24 km from Zarcero and the continental divide, Ciudad Quesada – also known as San Carlos, as capital of the local canton of the same name – is the main transport hub for the northern lowlands. While the town is of limited interest for the traveller, you may find yourself passing through or even needing to stop the night as it is a natural junction when travelling between Fortuna, Los Chiles and Puerto Viejo de Sarapiquí and to San José. If driving, watch out for the one-way system.

By Costa Rican standards Ciudad Quesada is a fairly large town (population 34,875), but even so it has a distinctly small-town, country feel, the leathery faces of the workers and the occasional stetson affirming this genuine link with the land. There is really little need to move more than a block or two from the main plaza, which is densely packed with trees and palms. To the east is a cavernous church with an impressive sculpture of Christ hanging above the altar inside.

Fortuna ⊕🄵🄿🄾🄰🄼🄱🄲 ➤ pp177-185. Colour map 2, B1.

Fortuna (population 7658) is one of the most popular destinations in Costa Rica, the draw being the active volcano which attracts a steady stream of humans to the glowing lava of Arenal like moths to a flame. Once a sleepy backwater, Fortuna is now a lively hive of tourist-focussed activity and a flurry of tour operators will scrabble to sign you up for a trip to the volcano when you arrive. In addition to the volcano, you can head out to the spectacular waterfalls, explore the lake and national park by foot, horse or bike, visit the nearby caves and, of course, go and watch the lava flows on the volcano. And, with so much volcanic activity, there are also some thermal baths to relax in.

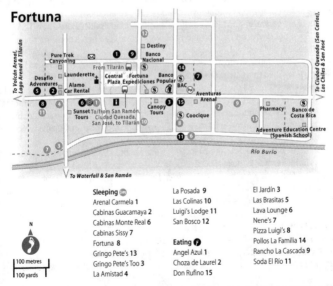

Sleeping 🛏	La Posada 9	El Jardín 3
Arenal Carmela 1	Las Colinas 10	Las Brasitas 5
Cabinas Guacamaya 2	Luigi's Lodge 11	Lava Lounge 6
Cabinas Monte Real 6	San Bosco 12	Nene's 7
Cabinas Sissy 7		Pizza Luigi's 8
Fortuna 8	Eating 🍴	Pollos La Familia 14
Gringo Pete's 13	Angel Azul 1	Rancho La Cascada 9
Gringo Pete's Too 3	Choza de Laurel 2	Soda El Río 11
La Amistad 4	Don Rufino 15	

Pocosol – the power of nature

Pocosol, south of Fortuna on the Tilarán mountains' Atlantic slope and home to the Children's Eternal rainforest, is threatened by a proposed hydroelectric project. A private company, Conelectricas RL, plans to divert waters from the Peñas Blancas and Aguas Gatas rivers, to produce electricity for an international power grid.

If the project goes ahead it will alter forever Pocosol's unique habitat and threaten all life forms depending on the rivers for survival. Tourism will also be adversely affected as the pristine landscape is damaged.

Despite opposition from local residents, the Monteverde Conservation League and environmental groups, plans continue to move ahead and illegal work has begun without permits.

The Pocosol 26 megawatt hydroelectric plant is one of over 40 hydroelectric projects being considered by the Costa Rican Electricity Institute (ICE) many of which are in Protection Zones and Forest Reserves.

For Costa Rica it's another example of the dilemmas of having to protect their resources and meeting a growing demand for electricity.

Sights in and around Fortuna

By far the most popular excursion is to see the lava flows and eruptions of Arenal – see below. But there are several other options to entertain. Heading south, **Río Fortuna waterfall** ① *US$8*, plunges 70 m from lush forest to the pool below creating a swirling hazy mist. From the entrance it is a steep and sometimes slippery path down to the falls, so wear good shoes. A short distance below the falls there are a couple of good swimming spots. You can easily walk to the falls from town following the road for 1.7 km before taking a 4-km bumpy road through yucca and papaya plantations. If you don't want to walk there are several options. You can drive, but 4WD is advisable. Bicycle hire (US$3 per hour, US$20 per day) is one option and hard work, or you can hire a horse for the day at around US$25.

Two to three hours' climb above the falls is the crater lake of **Cerro Chato**. The top (1100 m) is reached through mixed tropical/cloudforest, with a good view (if you're lucky) but beware of snakes on the path. A guide, if you need one, will charge US$13.

A couple of kilometres west of town is a small **snake farm** with a collection of 40 specimens found throughout Costa Rica. A little further west the Albergue Ecoturístico La Catarata has a small **butterfly farm** ① *US$5 for visitors*, and medicinal plants which are free for guests.

Hot baths in the area offer the chance for some serious rest and relaxation. Closest to town is **Baldi Termae** ① *daily 1000-2200, US$26, 4.5 km north of town you can walk there, and take a taxi back when you're fully relaxed for US$3.80*, which has a number of pools starting at a comfortable 33°C rising to an egg-poaching 67°C. Considerably more fancy are the baths at **Tabacón Resort** ① *daily 0700-2200, US$85 with lunch, US$70 after 1800 with lunch, 12 km from Fortuna, taxis charge US$9 for the trip, see also below*, with its pools, waterfalls, wet bars and utter self-indulgent luxury. Across the road is the cheaper **Fuentes Termales** ① *Mon-Fri 1000-2130, US$24, Sat-Sun 0800-2130, US$10*. For a completely natural experience follow the road for 1.5 km to **Quebrada Cedeña**. It can be difficult to find as there are no signs, but it's completely free – look for local parked cars.

The day trip to **Río Celeste Waterfalls** includes a rainforest hike en route to the swimming pool. Tours can be arranged through agents in Fortuna, US$35.

About an hour from Fortuna the small community of **Venado** is home to **limestone caves** dripping with stalactites, dried out river beds, small tunnels you can get stuck in and of course bats. Be prepared to get wet and dirty. Local entrance to the caves is US$4, with hard hats, rubber boots, torches and guides available for hire. All-inclusive trips from Fortuna cost around US$45. Buses to Venado and Guatuso leave from Ciudad Quesada. A dirt road leaves the north shore of the lake heading to Venado. An alternative route heads north from Tanque heading west close to Jicarito.

Tabacón Resort

① *Daily 0700-2200, US$85, US$70 after 1800. Massages and canopy tour are extra.*

Someone has got seriously carried away with Tabacón Resort. The focus is on a series of mineral pools that vary in temperature offering soothing relaxation and while the thermal-heated waters are 100% natural, the rest is pure kitsch. Soft lighting illuminates the hazy mist that settles over the resort at night as guests take a drink at the wet bar, supposedly falling hopelessly in love as the romance of the place washes their troubles away. Enjoy the waters, take a meal at the surprisingly reasonable restaurant and relax. The **Iskandria Spa** has a daunting array of treatments and massages which are certain to have you leaving the resort feeling like a new body. And if all this relaxation is just a little too much, take to the air with the canopy tour.

Heading towards Arenal Observatory leads to the south shore of Lake Arenal. While more cut off than most of the area the views across the lake are fantastic. It's also a good spot for mountain biking.

Parque Nacional Arenal

Dominated by the conical cone of the volcano, Arenal National Park covers an expanse of 12,124 ha. Upgraded from a reserve to a national park in 1994, the park protects the valuable watershed that maintains water levels in Lake Arenal and the microclimate created by the volcano.

Ins and outs

The park is open daily, 0800-1600. US$10. Heading west from Fortuna follow the signs to Arenal Observatory Lodge. While trekking solo is permitted and, subject to current advice, safe, hikes and treks can also be arranged through tour operators in Fortuna. Trips to the volcano can also be organized in Fortuna, US$30. Add the entrance fee to Baldi Termae or Tabacón if visiting after your hike, and a possible meal, and the price can easily rise to $95. Take torch, good shoes, rain and swimming gear including towel.

Volcán Arenal

Trips to see the lava flows and eruptions of Arenal Volcano are always popular. While there are variations on a theme, most leave in the late afternoon to get you to the best viewing spot for dusk. As darkness cloaks the region, the barely visible dust plumes that skirted down the bare slopes through the day reveal themselves to be glowing lava tumbling, crashing and smashing down the volcano slopes in a spray of natural fireworks. The sight is spectacular and the sound decidedly eerie in the dark of night.

Arenal was a sleeping giant until 1968 when a massive eruption devastated the western flank of the volcano killing 78 people. Since 1968 Arenal has been erupting almost continuously. A major eruption in August 2000 resulted in the death of two people who, allegedly, went beyond the advised limits. In September 2003, part of the wall of one of the active craters collapsed sending four pyroclastic avalanches down the north-west face. The National Park was evacuated for three hours as a precaution. Viewing the volcano is safe; however, the greater extent of lava flows has seen a more cautious approach to volcano viewing put in place.

Arenal is a classic Stromboli-type stratovolcano, creating a symmetrical cone formed by layers of volcanic material. It is the youngest of the stratovolcanoes in Costa Rica with no rock dating back more than 2900 years. Research by OVSICORI at the Arenal Observatory Lodge has produced a wealth of data including the mind-boggling notion that the magma chamber that feeds the eruptions is just 5 km below the surface.

You will be permitted to visit safe areas – the current spot used by groups is at El Silencio, 2 km west of Tabacón Resort – but take advice and listen to your guide; some of those who have chosen not to have not returned alive. After viewing the volcano, groups usually head down to one of the nearby thermal baths for a relaxing soak before returning to Fortuna around 2100.

Beyond the volcano the park has five interesting (and safe) **walking trails** starting at the national park entrance. The trails range from 25 minutes to a couple of hours in length and provide good opportunities to see heliconias, birdlife and howler monkeys. Las Coladas involves a bit of scrambling over old lava flows but gives good views of the lake and the extinct Volcán Chato.

Volcán Arenal

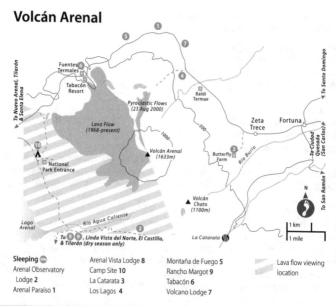

Sleeping
Arenal Observatory Lodge **2**
Arenal Paraíso **1**
Arenal Vista Lodge **8**
Camp Site **10**
La Catarata **3**
Los Lagos **4**
Montaña de Fuego **5**
Rancho Margot **9**
Tabacón **6**
Volcano Lodge **7**
Lava flow viewing location

La Fortuna or Monteverde?

From Tilarán, deciding whether to head for La Fortuna or Monteverde can be a dilemma, especially in the green season when clouds may obscure views of the volcano. And it's little consolation when you realize that at the same time, Monteverde and Santa Elena may be equally shrouded in cloud. In reality, the decision is best based on your interests and consideration of what is on offer rather than the weather. The weather changes rapidly at this time of year and taking local advice about recent weather is of limited value. But bear in mind that you can also make the journey between La Fortuna and Monteverde by foot or horse.

The good news is that transport between the two is getting better with a jeep-boat-jeep service connecting La Fortuna and Monteverde. Maybe you should do both.

Adventure trips → *See also page 184.*

Fortuna has developed as a base for a number of adventures to such an extent that at times they appear to compete with the volcano as the main attraction. **Guided hikes** head through the safe areas on the lower slopes of Arenal Volcano (from US$30), the five-hour hike to the extinct volcano of **Cerro Chato** (US$65) or all the way to Monteverde (US$65). **Arenal Hanging Bridges** is a 3.1 km trail heading through humid forest, using bridges to span the river valleys (US$45). **Mountain bikes** are also available for hire by the hour for a few dollars, or you can take a guided trip in the national park (US$45). **Arenal Paraiso Canopy Tour** has zip wires covering 12 platforms over 350 m (US$45). Other options for a totally unnatural buzz include **waterfall rappelling** and **ATV tours** (All Terrain Vehicles or quad bikes) (US$75 to US$100).

According to the Costa Rica **rafting** guide by Mayfield and Gallo, the **Peñas Blancas**, south of Fortuna, is "one of the recently discovered whitewater gems of Costa Rica". Other rivers opening up to rafting are the **Río Toro**, with options for safari float tours and kayaking. Half- and one-day trips from Fortuna cost between US$45-85. Conditions vary greatly depending on rainfall, with the best months being from July to September and occasionally through to December so check for local information.

Around Lake Arenal ⊖⊕⊙⊗⊕ » *pp180-185. Colour map 1, B5.*

Formed in 1974 to provide hydroelectric power for the country, the lake flooded the Arenal valley. While the wall damming the River Arenal, which flows east to the northern lowlands, is at the eastern end of the lake near Fortuna, the generating plant is at the western end at Tronadora close to Tilarán, where water flows through Guanacaste irrigating lowland areas before reaching the Nicoya Gulf. Trips on the lake are easily arranged through tour operators or by going down to the northern end of the dam and talking to local boatmen. Sport fishing on the lake for rainbow bass (*guapote*) and *machaca* is possible throughout the year, the best months for bass being between March and July. Prices start from US$200 all inclusive for two people for a half day, US$350 for the full day. Trips can be arranged with operators in Fortuna.

Closer to Fortuna is **Ecocentro Danaus** ① *3.5 km on road to Ciudada Quesada, T2393-8437, www.ecocentrodanaus.com, open daily 0800-1600, US$5,* a butterfly farm and tropical garden. Not only are there butterflies, but also poison arrow frogs, caimans and sloths in their natural habitat. The centre is working to develop a programme of sustainable conservation.

Around the shores of the lake

From Fortuna in the east to Tilarán at the western end of Lake Arenal the road is scattered with a number of good hotels offering trails and adventure sports, or seclusion and quiet privacy. A number of comfortable options sit on the lower slopes of the volcano – most on the north side – with good views of the eruptions. A dirt track which one day may become a road struggles along the southern shore giving access to a few comfortable hideaways but the majority of places line the road that heads around Lake Arenal's north shore. The views are great and it makes for a fine leisurely drive if you have the time. The lakeside road has improved greatly in recent years, but some sections are still unpaved, with some car-swallowing, suspension-smashing potholes. There is plenty of good accommodation around the north shore, mostly in the higher price brackets.

With only a couple of buses a day, and limited traffic, getting off the bus for a look will almost certainly delay you for a day. But if you can stop between Fortuna and Nuevo Arenal, an excellent café for a meal and drink in a prime spot over the lake is **Toad Hall**. It is also one of the best souvenir craft shops in the country – some items are modern, some traditional, many desirable (see also page 183).

Nuevo Arenal is a small but rapidly growing town with not much to see. Why 'nuevo'? Because the old one lies deep below the surface of the lake. The population moved prior to the flooding of Arenal in 1974.

Moving towards the western end of the lake, the predominant winds channelled through the region make this a world-class spot for **windsurfing**. Consequently, many lodges and hotels target that market and offer deals for longer stays. There's a flurry of development going on so expect to find new places popping up.

Tilarán → *Colour map 1, B5.*

Tilarán is a small agricultural community (population 9526) in a fairly modern town, which is largely indifferent to the visitors coming and going from all directions. In reality, as far as most travellers are concerned, the town's importance lies in its role as the transport hub linking Cañas on the Pan-American Highway, with Santa Elena and Monteverde Reserve to the south and Lake Arenal, the volcano and Fortuna to the east.

Caño Negro Wildlife Reserve → *See also p187.*

US$45-60. Organized through tour operators in Fortuna. It's a 1½-hr bus journey to Los Chiles and the boat trip lasts about 4 hrs. You can visit independently if you prefer.

Just under 50 km north of Fortuna, Caño Negro Wildlife Reserve close to the town of Los Chiles at the border with Nicaragua is a popular day trip. The wetlands are host to many waterbirds and you are certain to see monkeys, sloths and caimans.

For Sleeping and Eating price codes and other relevant information, see Essentials, pages 44-47.

⊙ Sleeping

Ciudad Quesada (San Carlos)
p171, map p170

C Don Goyo, just south of the main plaza, T2460-1780. 13 clean, well lit rooms, with private bathrooms. Restaurant and bar serving a good selection of dishes. Best value in town and hidden in a quiet little corner.

C La Central, on the plaza, T2460-0301, www.hotellacentral.net. Popular but slightly tacky hotel with rooms with bath, hot water and TV. Some rooms dark and cramped.

D El Retiro, also on the plaza down a small dirt road, T2460-0463. Clean and comfortable rooms, with bath and hot water. Nothing flashy but popular with migrant workers.

D-E Hotel Del Norte, 1½ blocks north of the main plaza, T2460-1959. Clean and secure rooms with fan and colour TV. Rooms with shared bath have more natural light.

E Del Valle, Av 3, C 0-2, T2460-0718. OK budget hotel with reasonable rooms, clean bathrooms and extremely helpful staff. Parking available.

F Several basic pensiones along Av 1 between C 2-4, around corner from Banco Popular, including **Diana**, T2460-3319, and **Fernando**, T2460-3314, probably the best of the bunch.

Out of town

LL-AL Melia Occidental El Tucano Resort and Thermal Spa, 8 km east along a bumpy road at Aguas Zarcas, T2460-6000, www.occidental-hoteles.com. 87 luxurious rooms and suites. Total comfort resort with a large pool, jacuzzi, sauna, horse riding and tennis. Hot mineral and sulphur pools and a host of beauty treatments, all with the background of exuberant tropical forest. Complete indulgence hidden away from the crowds. Open to day guests for a small fee.

D Hotel La Mirada, 4 km on the road to Fortuna, T2460-2222. Sitting on the bluff with incredible views of the northern lowlands and Arenal volcano, this is an excellent option if you have wheels. The rooms are clean and comfortable with a private bath and hot water. Parking available. Excellent value.

Fortuna *p171, map p171*
Bear in mind that while the cheapest accommodation is in Fortuna itself, you will have to pay in the region of US$25 to get to the volcano. In the green season some of the hotels in this area may well be within your budget. Also if you have a car, it's definitely worth looking at the accommodation on Lake Arenal's north shore.

Centre

AL Luigi's Lodge, a couple of blocks west of the church, T2479-9636, www.hotelluigis.com. 20 comfortable rooms with private bath, tub, hot water and coffee machine. Internet, a/c, cable TV. Small balconies overlooking a pool, with good views of the volcano and now a casino.

AL-A Cabinas Monte Real, 1 block southeast of the main plaza, T2479-9243, www.monterealhotel.com. Big rooms with private bath and hot water, a quiet spot next to the river. Ample parking.

AL-A San Bosco, T2479-9050, www.hotel sanboscocr.com. Quiet spot, clean, friendly, gardens with terrace, pool, jacuzzi and view of the volcano, excellent service and attention to detail. All rooms with private bath, slightly less without a/c. Also rents out a few houses. Best of the bunch in town.

B Cabinas Guacamaya, T2479-9393, www.cabinasguacamaya.com. 8 good-sized rooms sleeping 3 or 4, all with private bath and hot water, fridge and a/c. Clean and tidy, with plenty of parking. Close to town but away from the busy area.

B Hotel Arenal Carmela, on the south side of the church, T2479-9010, www.hotelarenal

carmela.com. 12 rooms with private bath, hot showers, floor and ceiling fans, fridge and pool. Very central, good tourist information. Apartment available sleeping 5, **E** per person.

C Hotel La Amistad, T2479-9364, www.hotellaamistadarenal.com. Clean, friendly with hot water and hard beds.

C Las Colinas, at the southeastern corner of the central park, T2479-9305, www.lascolinas arenal.com. 20 tidy rooms, with private bathroom, some with excellent views. Friendly management, with good local knowledge, discounts in the low season, internet access. Has just completed renovations – should be even better (and maybe more expensive).

AL-A Fortuna, 1 block southeast of the central park, T2479-9197, www.lafortuna hotel.com. Completely renovated, with 44 modern rooms, with bathroom, a/c, TV and most with volcano views.

D-F pp Cabinas Sissy, office is 100 m south and 100 m west of church, T2479-9256. Quiet spot beside the river, with a number of options. Basic rooms with private bathroom, some with shared bath, others with access to a kitchen and camping spaces (US$2 per person). Simple, friendly and clean.

G pp Gringo Pete's, T2479-8521. Brightly coloured and welcoming, the natural backpackers' choice. Dormitory and private rooms, lounge and garden for relaxing, well-equipped kitchen and excellent noticeboard.

Gringo Pete's Too, beside the bridge on the south side of town, is opening soon – slightly more upmarket with private rooms.

G pp La Posada, a couple of blocks east of the central park, T2479-9793. 4 simple, but spotless rooms with fan, shared bath with hot water. Small communal area out front, and the friendly owner, Thadeo, is very helpful. Popular and often full.

West of town, towards the volcano
Note that places are listed in the order that you come across them heading out of town.

C-D Arenal Backpackers,1 km from town, T2479-7000, www.arenalbackpackers.com.

Great views from the swimming pool, with a selection of tidy dormitory and private rooms. Bar and restaurant to get the party going. Good choice.

AL La Catarata, 1.7 km from town down a rough road, T2479-9522, in San José on T2290-8646, www.cataratalodge.com. 21 rooms with hot water and laundry. There's also a small butterfly farm.

AL La Pradera, T2479-9597, www.lapradera delarenal.com. Has 20 rooms and cabins with private baths and a restaurant.

B Albergue Vista Arenal, 700 m west of town, T2479-9808. 12 spacious cabins, in a quiet spot with private bath, a/c, hot water and TV. Breakfast is served on a small terrace outside, ideal for sitting around in, but you'll have to move elsewhere for food and drink.

B-C Hotel Las Flores, a couple of kilometres beyond Zeta Trece, T2479-9307. Clean, basic but a little overpriced.

B-C Hotel Arenal Rossi, in the community of Zeta Trece where there is a rash of hotels, bars and restaurants, T2479-9023, www. hotelarenalrossi.com. 25 neat rooms, most with a/c, internet and private bath. Volcano views from the garden, horses for hire, good value. Also runs the Mirador Steak House Restaurant 6 km up the road.

East of town
B Cabinas Villa Fortuna, 500 m east of the bridge, 1 km from the central plaza, T2479-9139. 10 bright and tidy wooden cabins, sleeping 2 or 3, with neat bathrooms, fans or a/c, nice pool, jacuzzi and simple gardens with a poolside café.

South of town
L Chachagua Rain Forest Hotel, 10 km south of Fortuna near Chachagua, up a very bumpy road, T2239-6464, www.chachagua rainforesthotel.com. 22 wooden cabins, complete with balconies and swinging hammocks set in tropical forest. A working ranch, with plenty of landscaped gardens, a couple of trails to nearby waterfalls and 64 species of birds counted so far. Spectacular

service throughout with fine dishes in the restaurant and barbecues in high season. You'll need a 4WD to get there, and probably won't use it when you arrive, so a package from San José is a good idea.

AL Arenal Country Inn, T2283-0101, www.arenalcountryinn.com. Once a working hacienda now with 20 large, fully equipped *cabinas* spread out among tropical gardens. Unimposing decor, tiled bathrooms, safebox, a/c. Complimentary breakfast is served in the open-air dining room – once a cattle-holding pen – and you can rest by the pool before exploring. The atmosphere in the family-run inn is calm and the service excellent.

F Hotel Dorothy, a few hundred metres south of town over the Río Burío, T2479-8068, www.geocities.com/costaricafuntours. Simple, friendly place, on quiet side of town.

Volcán Arenal *p173, map p174*

The hotels and restaurants are listed as you encounter them from Fortuna – if arriving from Tilarán, start at the end of the section (see page 180) and read backwards!

L Los Lagos, 5 km north of Fortuna, T2479-8000, www.hotelloslagos.com. Once the universally favoured spot for viewing the lava flows, it is still a very comfortable option with great views. The grounds cover a wide area and include a couple of lakes (the flows of August 2000 reached within metres of one), camping areas and several trails with currently restricted access. A selection of large rooms and villas sleep 2-4 people, with kitchenette, a/c, cable TV, bathroom and hot water. There's also a swimming pool and waterslide, thermal pools, a butterfly garden and a crocodile zoo – and all in the shadow of Arenal. A spectacular place to stay. Day tickets available.

AL Volcano Lodge, 6 km from Fortuna, T2479-1717, www.volcanolodge.com. Comfortable option with 65 spacious rooms each with private bathroom, a/c and stunning views from the balcony. For a change, take to the pool or jacuzzi which have equally good views of the lava flows.

Popular with groups, there is also a good open-air restaurant with a spectacular fish pool. The food is surprisingly cheap and if you sit on the right side you can watch the volcano while you dine. The best of the strip as far as views are concerned.

L-AL Arenal Paraíso, 1 km north, T2460-5333, www.arenalparaiso.com. 20 wooden cabins and suites with bath, a/c and balcony. Good views of the volcano, now with a canopy tour, and all local tours arranged.

L-AL Montaña de Fuego, 8 km out of Fortuna, T2460-1220, www.montanade fuego.com. 66 full-service bungalows and rooms, all with views of the volcano set in lush gardens. Next door is the expensive but elegant Restaurant Acuarelas, serving a fine mix of international and *Tico* dishes in a stylish setting.

LL-L Hotel Tabacón, T2277-8291, www. tabacon.com. A choice of 114 spacious rooms with large bathrooms and a small balcony (not all with volcano views) and full-service suites. Guests have full access to the spa and thermal pools.

West of Volcán Arenal

G pp Camp site. On the northwestern side of the volcano, 4 km after El Tabacón, a signposted gravel road heads towards the lake where there's a camp site opposite the national park entrance, with cold water and hook-ups for trailers. Excellent views of the volcano.

AL-B Arenal Observatory Lodge, T2695-5033, www.arenalobservatorylodge.com. 4WD recommended along this 9-km stretch (taxi-jeep from Fortuna, US$12). With origins dating back to 1973, the observatory was once purely a research station for the Smithsonian Institute and the presence of the volcano looms over every thing. The Lodge now has 43 rooms, 6 fully equipped for disabled travellers. Rooms vary from cabins with bunk beds and bath to newer ones with queen size beds. All use the proximity of the volcano (which is frighteningly close) to provide stunning views across the Río Agua

Caliente valley and Lake Arenal. There are several trails in the observatory's grounds through the pine forest and options for trips to Cerro Chato crater lake. While no comfort is spared, recycling is strongly encouraged where possible. Recommended.

L-AL Linda Vista del Norte Lodge, T2692-2090, www.hotellindavista.com. A selection of comfortable rooms and suites sleeping 2-4 people with hot water and stunning views over the lake. Set in a 250-ha *finca* (farm), there are a number of good, unspoilt trails through the forest, with opportunities for horse-riding tours and trekking. Recommended.

AL-B Arenal Vista Lodge, reached after fording the Río Piedras Negras, T2221-0965, www.arenalvistalodge.com. 25 funky, angular rooms sleeping 2-4 people, each with bath and hot water, make the most of the views providing a small balcony. There's a small pool and bar overlooking the lake and boat trips, riding and hiking. Rooms are considerably cheaper for 4 people.

L-AL Rancho Margot, T2479-7259, www.ranchomargot.org. Bungalows and bunkhouses on an ecological and adventure ranch. Wide range of ranching and activities, as well as great rooms.

Around Lake Arenal p175
North shore
Listed as you travel round the lake from Fortuna towards Tilarán.

L-AL Arenal Lodge, 400 m north of the dam wall and 2.5 km up a very steep road, T2290-4232, www.arenallodge.com. At a higher altitude than any other accommodation around the lake the lodge has glorious views south to the volcano and north to the lowlands. While the volcano is some distance away, you'll be able to see the lava flows. A selection of chalets and suites provide complete luxury but not all have the views. As you go up in price rooms have views and kitchenettes. The excellent but expensive restaurant has fine views of the gardens. Also provides a full range of tours and activities.

A Hotel Los Héroes (Pequeña Helvecía), T2692-8012, www.pequenahelvecia.com. A wonderful blend of idiosyncratic *Tico* hospitality and Swiss patriotism – if Costa Rica is the Switzerland of Central America, Los Héroes is its Geneva. 15 good rooms have private bath, a couple of apartments have space for 6, some have a terrace. Constantly evolving, there's now a rotating restaurant, the *Rondorama* serving *fondues*, *wiener schnitzels* and other Swiss classics, but no credit cards accepted. On top of this, there's a 60-cm gauge railway that travels up the hillside crossing two bridges and going through a couple of tunnels for 2 km (US$3, three times a day), and a small yet beautiful private family chapel. Day trips are possible starting from San José, US$28, travelling, of course, in a Swiss double-decker bus.

LL La Mansión Marina & Club, T2692-8018, www.lamansionarenal.com. 17 gloriously elegant split-level bungalows offering different levels of luxury and colourfully decorated with original paintings. The spectacular, tiled pool appears to flow directly into the lake and there's a strong emphasis on relaxation – all rooms come with a CD player and you can borrow discs from the hotel. Price includes luxury breakfast, with champagne if you wish, served in your room or on the terrace restaurant which specializes in European cuisine. Horses and canoes are available for guests to hire for a small charge.

B La Alondra, T2692-8036. Simple basic rooms sleeping up to 4 provide the cheapest option at this end of the lake. Great views, friendly *Tico* owners.

AL La Ceiba, overlooking Lake Arenal 6 km east of Nuevo Arenal, T2692-8050, www.ceibatree-lodge.com. *Tico*-owned and run, good, helpful, great panoramic views, spectacular ceiba tree in front of the lodge, good breakfast.

L-AL Villa Decary, T2694-4330, www.villa decary.com. The last option east of the village. Great secluded spot, with good views of the lake. 8 rooms and bungalows, each with a private bath and some with balcony; stylishly decorated with Guatemalan fabrics and Chorotega ceramics, and set in beautiful gardens. Breakfast of fruit and home-made breads included. Set on 3 ha of a former coffee farm, the grounds have a troop of howler monkeys and over 400 species of bird.

(Nuevo) Arenal

A-B Arenal Inn, in the centre of town by the soccer pitch. Lake views from the rooms, breakfast included. The rooms are a little overpriced, but you do have direct access to the liveliest (karaoke) bar in town (popular with locals). Visa and MasterCard accepted.
C-D Cabinas Catalina, opposite the gas station on the road into town, T2819-6793. Great place to stop if passing through. Clean, crisp decor. Ample parking.
E pp Cabinas Rodríguez, almost next door, the cheapest place in town. Basic but clean, with private bath and hot water.

West of Nuevo Arenal

L-AL Tilawa, 8 km north of Tilarán, T2695-5050, www.hotel-tilawa.com. With an ancient Greek-themed decor, the Tilawa is a multi-activity resort and the list of options is slightly daunting. Rooms with garden and lake views have a pair of queen-sized beds, private bath and ceiling fan while the suites, sleeping up to 4 people, have fully equipped kitchenettes. The open-all-day restaurant serves *Tico* and international cuisine. Activities include fishing, boat tours to Tabacón hot springs and the volcano using the hotel's catamaran, and trips to the botanical gardens. Tilawa's forte is anything that combines wind and water – windsurfing, kitesurfing, wakeboarding – and recently included a skatepark. If you're a beginner the windsurfing school will get you up on the board – and if it's not fun, it's free. You can explore the hotel grounds on foot, horse or mountain bike, watch birds, play tennis or take to the pool. Throw in a Spanish school and even a microbrewery and there's little reason to move too far from the resort.

AL Lake Coter Eco Lodge Resort, a few kilometres west of Arenal, winding up a misty 3 km road backing onto Tenorio National Park, T2289-6060, www.ecolodge costarica.com. An eco-lodge popular with birdwatchers and adventure seekers. Activities include hiking along 18 km of trails, canoeing, mountain biking, horse riding, and all the usual regional tours as well. There's also a good canopy tour open to non-guests (US$55, 2½ to 3 hrs). 22 standard rooms in the lodge have private bathrooms and there are another 14 much brighter cabins with balcony views of nearby Lake Coter. Generous meals are served in the buffet restaurant with an open fire and a games room nearby.
A Mystica Resort, T2692-1001, www. mysticalodge.com. Quiet, intimate spot, with 6 lodgings in comfortable wooden cabins (sleeping up to 4 people), each with a bathroom and veranda. The pizzeria has a spectacular view across the lake and the tropical breakfast – included in the price – is a fine way to start the day. Windsurfing, mountain biking and horse riding trips can also be easily arranged.
A-B Chalet Nicholas, 2 km west of Nuevo Arenal up a flower-festooned driveway, T2694-4041, www.chaletnicholas.com. Breaking out from the flowers, the beautiful chalet sits in a clearing with fine views over the lake and bathes in a family atmosphere. 3 rooms have orthopaedic mattresses, private baths and plenty of hot water. Run by New Yorkers Cathy and John Nicholas, the day starts with an American-style breakfast prepared using fruits grown on the property. You can hike trails or ride horses on the property and trips to the surrounding area are easily arranged. No-smoking rooms only.
A-C Vista Inn, 700 m east of Río Piedras, T2661-1840. Clean and tidy rooms sleeping 2-5 people, with a balcony set in quiet gardens. In the hamlet of Río Piedras there's a couple of small stores and a café.
C Hotel El Cielo, T2694-4290, hotelelcielo@ racsa.co.cr. Simple but good option, with great views of the lake, great place for groups.

Tilarán *p176*

There are a few reasonable options in town.
C Guadalupe, a block south and east of the church, T2695-5943, www.hotelguadalupecr.com. 25 pleasant rooms with bath, hot water and TV. Gym and parking. Recommended.
C Naralit, on the south side of the church, T2695-5393.
D Cabiñas El Sueño, 1 block north of bus terminal/central park, T2695-5347. Clean rooms around central patio, hot water, fan, TV, friendly and free coffee. Good deal.
D Hotel Restaurant Mary, south side of church, T2695-5479. Small pleasant rooms with bath. Recommended.
E Central, round the back of the church, 1 block south, T2695-5363. Rooms with shared bath, noisy.

Eating

Ciudad Quesada (San Carlos)
p171, map p170

¶¶ Coco Loco Steak House, on the western side of the plaza. Complete with wild west swing door. Evenings only.
¶¶-¶ Los Geranios, Av 4 and C 0. A hip bar and restaurant serving good *bocas* at US$2, the place to be seen in Ciudad Quesada whether young or older.
¶ Pollos Jeffry, Av 2 and C 3. Serves good basic food; although the decor is all plastic, there's a friendly atmosphere to the place.
¶ Restaurant Cristal, on the northern side of Plaza Central. Sells fast food diner style, with snacks, ice cream and good fruit dishes.

Fortuna *p171, map p171*

¶¶-¶ Choza de Laurel, west of the church, T2479-9231. Serves typical food in a rustic open-air setting with occasional visits from passing hummingbirds. Breakfast, lunch and dinner available.
¶¶ Don Rufino, Bar-cum-restaurant, serving Italian dishes, in a welcoming setting.
¶¶ Lava Lounge, south side of the church. Smooth open-air café-restaurant serving

excellent coffee and reasonably priced, good food. Travel agency on site for any questions. Definitely worth a visit.
¶¶ Pizza Luigi's. Formal open-air restaurant with distinctly Italian pretensions and a good wine list.
¶¶ Rancho La Cascada, on northern corner of main square. Cannot be missed with high conical thatched roof. Good *bocas*, films shown in evenings.
¶ Angel Azul. Good, cheap vegetarian food in a café atmosphere. Open all day.
¶ El Jardín, on the main street opposite the gas station. Good varied menu with a mix of local and fast food, *menú del día*. It's a good place to watch the world go by but success seems to have jaded the personal service and raised the prices.
¶ La Fortuna, see Sleeping, above. Open-air restaurant in the hotel of the same name, serving good, simple food, quiet spot but nothing special.
¶ Las Brasitas, west of town on the main drag. Open-air restaurant at the western end of town serving Mexican dishes, with a fair selection of tequilas.
¶ Nene's. Good food, pleasant service, not expensive. Recommended.
¶ Pollo La Familia, simple fried chicken with a selection of side dishes. Fast food *Tico*-style.
¶ Soda El Río, just on the river. Quiet spot, serving fruit, yoghurt and traditional *Tico* dishes.

West of Fortuna

A few generally mid-range restaurants have gathered just over 500 m towards the volcano.
¶¶ La Vaca Muca. Grill-bar with a mixed menu of fish and meat dishes, and a bar area popular with locals.
¶¶ Steakhouse Arenal. A steak house with Texan decor, and a few other dishes to keep the options open.
¶¶-¶ Vagabondo. The most laid-back on the strip, serving pizza and pasta.

Volcán Arenal *p173, map p174*

¶¶ Restaurant Mirador Arenal Steak House, east of Fortuna, T2460-8353.

Fine steaks and food in a great setting just in front of the volcano.

♥♥ **Kioro Mirador**. Cheekily perched on the northern flanks of the volcano, an open-air restaurant that looks directly at the volcano and says 'entertain us'. Food looks good too.

Around Lake Arenal *p175*
North shore

♥♥-♥ **Toad Hall**, T2692-8020, www.toadhall-gallery.com. Daily, 0730-1700. Café and gift shop serving a heady mix of California-style food with home-grown salads, tropical fruit juices and divine chocolate and macadamia nut brownies. The views of the lake and volcano are heavenly and you won't find a better place to stop for a break. The gift shop is a hot-spot of modern *artesanía*.

♥ **Lajas**, 2 km west of Nuevo Arenal, T2694-4780. Open daily 0800-2100. A fairly standard road-side restaurant selling *Tico* dishes. Cheaper than Toad Hall but no views. **Tycoon** souvenir shop next door.

(Nuevo) Arenal

♥♥ **Gingerbread**. High-style and high-class restaurant, that claims to be the best in the region. Range of dishes to choose from including fish and pastas.

♥ **Pizzería e Ristorante Tramonti**. Italian cuisine, excellent food and very friendly.

♥ **Típico Arenal**, T2694-4159. Good local dishes with seafood and vegetarian options. They have a large room upstairs (**C**) with private bath and hot water. The best mid-price place in town.

♥ **Tom's Pan**, 300 m south of the gas station, T2694-4547. An oasis of awesome bread and cakes – the plum tart is divine.

West of Nuevo Arenal

Caballo Negro, T2694-4515. The best restaurant for miles serving vegetarian, Swiss and seasonal fish dishes with organic salads. Warm family atmosphere in an isolated modern-day rancho. No credit cards.

Lucky Bug Gallery, close to Caballo Negro. Has built up a good reputation as a place to buy crafts and paintings, some by the owner's triplet daughters. Also provides healthy dishes of pastries and salads, and has a few rooms to rent out as well.

Equus, continuing towards Tilarán. Unassuming bar and restaurant that erupts at night in a frenzy of barbecue grills, music and drinking. *The* place for lively nightlife.

Tilarán

♥ **La Carreta**, round the back of the church. The place to go and relax if you have a couple of hours to spare. Excellent pancakes, coffee, Italian dishes and good local information – good value.

♥ **Stefanie's**, out of the bus station to the left on the corner of the main plaza. Good and quick if you need a meal between buses.

♥ **Restaurant Hotel Mary**, on the main plaza, does a steady trade.

🍸 Bars and clubs

Fortuna *p171, map p171*
A range of new places are opening up in town, ask locally. Many of the restaurants tend to have bar areas.
The only club as such is the **Las Agilas**, 4.5 km north of town next to Baldi Thermae hot pool. It is supposedly open Wed-Sat from 2000-0300 but ask locally before heading out or call on T2479-7616.

🛍 Shopping

Ciudad Quesada (San Carlos)
p171, map p170
Mercado de los Artesanías on the main plaza, sells a selection of souvenirs. Opening hours are erratic and it's oversized for the region, but you may find a bargain.

Fortuna *p171, map p171*
Several souvenir shops dotted around town sell a selection of T-shirts, carvings and postcards.

Lunática, Av Central, T2479-8255. Good collection of art and crafts, with some indigenous pieces.
House of Hammocks, 500 m west of town. Place to go if you're looking for a hammock, sitting and lying, starting at US$13.

▲ Activities and tours

Fortuna *p171, map p171*
Tour operators
All tour operators can provide the basic trips to the volcano, waterfall, caves and Caño Negro Wildlife Reserve. Travelling to Santa Elena and Monteverde is more problematic. The road route is tiresome, so many take a trip across the lake and then by horse or jeep to Monteverde. Reports suggest that horses are being overworked and trips often change at the last minute due to unforeseen problems. Be prepared for this and seek assurance from your operator and guide. Prices tend to be fairly consistent across operators.
Arenal Bungee, T2479-7440, www.arenal bungee.com. Bungee jumps, rocket launches, night jumps, water touchdowns. If it involves a bit piece of elastic you can probably do it.
Aventuras Arenal, on the main street, T2479-9133, www.arenaladventures.com. The main tour operator in town and one of the few with a national presence. Reliable information on the local area and they can advise on trips to other parts of the country and will make bookings where appropriate.
Canoa Aventura, T2479-8200, www.canoa-aventura.com. From gentle floats, to full-on whitewater, as well as the usual selection of regional tours.
Canopy Tours, southwest of the main square, T2479-9769, www.crarenalcanopy. com. A number of short trips in the area involving horse riding, mountain bike and quad tours. As the name suggests, a canopy tour is also possible starting with a horseback journey to Monteverde from Fortuna, US$65.
Desafío, behind the central church, T2479-9464, www.desafiocostarica.com. Full range

of tours, also an office in Monteverde.
Eagle Tours, 1 block east of the park, T2479-9091, www.eagletours.net. Helpful tour operator, with usual array of options.
Sunset Tours, behind Rancho Casado and on eastern corner of the central park, T2479-9415, www.sunsettourcr.com. Reliable, long-standing company with a good selection of tours, including fishing on Lake Arenal.

Around Lake Arenal *p175*
Nuevo Arenal
Arenal Adventure Tours, next to Tom's Pan, T2694-4445. A long-overdue requirement for the north shore, can arrange tours in the area so, if stopping in Nuevo Arenal, at last there is someone to help you out.

Several places rent fishing tackle, but if you want a boat, guide and full package contact **Aurora Inn, Arenal Adventure Tours** or **Chito** on T2694-4320 who is used by local hotels. He supplies snacks and tackle but bring your own if you have it. US$250 a day for 2 anglers, T2649-4320. Try also:
Rainbow Bass Fishing Safaris, T2229-5550 (Dave Myers.)
Tico Wind, T2692-2002, specialist wind surfing and kitesurfing operator.

⊖ Transport

Ciudad Quesada (San Carlos)
p171, map p170
The bus terminal is about 1 km north of the plaza. **San José** buses hourly from 0500 to 1830, 2½ hrs, US$2.50. (Buses from San José leave from the Atlántico Norte Terminal, Av 9, C 12, T2255-4300.) To **Fortuna** at 0600, 1030, 1230, 1530, 1715 and 2000, 1 hr, US$1.25. To **Tilarán** (also pass through Fortuna), at 0630 and 1600, 4hrs, US$3. To **Los Chiles** every hour between 0430-1915, 2 hrs, US$2.75. Heading east, buses go through **Aguas Zarcas**, **La Virgen** and **Chilamate** to **Puerto Viejo de Sarapiquí**, 5 a day between 0500 and 1730, 2½ hrs, US$2.25.

Fortuna *p171, map p171*

Whether travelling by bus or car, it is possible to get from Fortuna to **Santa Elena** and **Monteverde** (via **Tilarán**) in a day, but set out early to make your connection with the 1230 bus in Tilarán and to avoid driving in the dark.

An alternative, and the quickest route, is a taxi-boat-taxi option between Fortuna and Santa Elena. About 3 hrs in total, US$25. Pick up is around 0800 and takes you to the hotel of your choice (within reason). Contact your hotel for details.

The alternative route to Monteverde involves travelling overland first up to Lake Arenal, then climbing up through the Cordillera de Tilarán to Monteverde by horse. It's a full day travelling, costing between US$65 and US$120.

Daily buses from **San José**, from Terminal Atlántico Norte, via **Ciudad Quesada** at 0615, 0840, 1130, 3½ hrs, US$3.70, return at 1245, 1445. 6 buses a day from Ciudad Quesada, 1 hr, US$1. 2 buses a day to **Tilarán**, 0800 (connecting to 1230 bus Tilarán–Santa Elena/Monteverde and 1300 bus Tilarán-Puntarenas) and 1700, 3 hrs, US$2.80. Daily to **San Ramón** at 0530, 1300 and 1600, US$2.60, making connections to Puntarenas. Subject to demand, normally daily in the high season, there are direct minibuses to **Monteverde**, leaving at 0600, US$17 to US$25, and **Tamarindo** (US$25 per person, minimum 6 people) with Grayline and Interbus. Can connect to Moctezuma in a day – change at San Ramón, then Puntarenas. Book through your hotel.

Alamo have a car hire office in town, T2479-9090, www.alamocostarica.com.

Taxis in the area do their best to over-charge. Agree on price before travelling.

Tilarán *p176*

Direct buses from **San José**, from Terminal Atlántico Norte, 5 daily, 4 hrs, US$5.60. 2 daily buses to **Ciudad Quesada** via **Fortuna** at 0700 and 1230, US$5.60. To **Fortuna**, 3 hrs, US$2.80. Daily to **Santa Elena**

(for Monteverde), 1230, 3 hrs, US$1.40, return 0700 daily. To **Puntarenas** at 0600 and 1300, 3 hrs, US$1.80. To **Cañas** at daily 0500, 0730, 1000, 1230 and 1530, 40 mins, US$0.50, for buses heading north and south along the Pan-American Highway. If you get the 1230 **Tilarán-Liberia** bus, you can get from Liberia to the **Nicaraguan border** before it closes.

① Directory

Ciudad Quesada (San Carlos)
p171, map p170
Hospitals T2460-1176. **Internet** Café Internet, on Av 5, C 2-4, US$4 per hr, Mon-Fri 0800-2100, Sat 0800-1800. **Medical services** There are several pharmacies close to the centre of town. **Post office** Av 5, C 4-6.

Fortuna *p171, map p171*
Banks Banco Nacional and Banco Nacional de Costa Rica have ATMs and will change TCs. Banco Popular has a Visa ATM as does Coocique (open Sat mornings 0800-1200). **Internet** Prices quite expensive and connections poor. If desperate ask round for the best current operator. **Language schools** Adventure Education Center, eastern end of town, T2248-0147 in San José, www.adventurespanishschool.com. US$315 for a week of classes, 4 hrs per day, US$440 with homestay. Also with schools in Turrialba and Dominical. **Laundry** Lavandería La Fortuna, 0800-2100, Mon-Sat. US$6.50 wash and dry 4 kg. **Pharmacies** Farmacía San Gabriel, east down the main street, Mon-Sat 0800-2100. **Post office** North of the church.

Around Lake Arenal *p175*
Nuevo Arenal
Banks Banco Nacional, beside the football pitch.

Tilarán *p176*
Banks Banco Cootilaran, a couple of blocks north of the Central Park, and there is also a Banco de Costa Rica in town.

North of Fortuna

Across the expansive northern lowlands, small communities farm citrus fruits and raise cattle in a world without tourists. The road to Upala offers little in the way of attractions, but much for the visitor wanting to travel rarely visited regions. Close to the border with Nicaragua, Los Chiles is the gateway to the Caño Negro Wildlife Reserve and the spectacular bird and wildlife of the region ›› *For listings, see pages 188-189.*

North to Nicaragua via Upala

A quiet route to the north leads from Fortuna to **San Rafael de Guatuso**. You can come back to the lake either by turning off before San Rafael through Venado (for the caves) or from San Rafael itself. There is some basic accommodation. The roads are in fairly good condition and go through lovely countryside with beautiful views, especially approaching the lake.

Three kilometres from **Colonia Río Celeste**, 20 km west of San Rafael de Guatuso is Montaña Magil Forest Lodge is set in 240 ha in the foothills of the 1916-m **Tenorio Volcano**. The volcano is part of the 12,871-ha **Tenorio Volcano National Park** with thermal waters, boiling mud and unspoilt forest. (It is best visited from Bagaces, see page 210.) It's an increasingly popular place to visit with the spectacular **Río Celeste Waterfalls** and a clear blue plunge pool for swimming. It's reached after a 1½-hour hike through rainforest, making for a great day out. Tours can be arranged in Colonia Río Celeste, T2479-7062, www.costaricaruraltours.com, or from Fortuna (approx US$35).

A reasonable road continues north for 35 km towards the **Nicaraguan border** and the agricultural community of **Upala**. It's a small town with a population of just over 13,000. There's little to see or do, but a road leading out west to La Cruz, and a couple of roads heading southwest to the Pan-American Highway via Bijagua or to Bagaces make for an interesting journey. There is also a poor road leading east to Caño Negro, with a bus service, when conditions allow.

North to Los Chiles → *Colour map 1, A6.*

From Ciudad Quesada, a paved road quickly drops to within a 100 m of sea level and runs northwest to Florencia (service station), with accommodation at Platanar and also at Muelle San Carlos.

Heading through the northern lowlands, a good road carves through rich red laterite soils in an almost straight line for 74 km through the Guatuso Plains, where the shiny leaves of citrus fruit plantations shimmer in the bright tropical sun. If coffee is king in the highlands, citrus wears the crown in the lowlands of the north. Just short of the Nicaraguan border is **Los Chiles**, the departure point for boat trips through dense, tropical vegetation into the 10,171 ha Caño Negro Wildlife Refuge (see below). Birdwatchers flock to the northern wetlands to see the amazing variety of birdlife which feasts at the seasonal lake created by the floodwaters of the Río Frío. Even non-twitchers will enjoy the birds, not to mention the countless other animals including sloths, caiman, and several species of monkey that inhabit the rainforest and wetlands.

Los Chiles itself is a small town (district population 10,013) on the banks of the Río Frío, a few hundred metres west of Highway 35. Close to the border, it sees a lot of Nicaraguans passing through looking for seasonal agricultural work and the townspeople reflect the merging of the two nations. The central plaza, with an unassuming modern church on its eastern side, is also a football pitch – a seamless blend of fun and faith. Most places of interest are within a block or two and the days pass slowly as children chuck themselves off the dockside into the Río Frío, a couple of blocks to the west, in the heat of the afternoon sun.

Refugio Nacional de Vida Silvastre Caño Negro

ⓘ *T2470-0100 in Upala, or T2257-8563 in San José. Most people take the tour from Fortuna, which costs around US$45-60, lasting around 8 hrs in total. Tours organized from Los Chiles are cheaper at US$20 and pick-up can be organized with tour operators in Fortuna. Alternatively you can make up the numbers in town although this may be more difficult in the green season.*

Covering 10,171 ha Caño Negro National Wildlife Reserve draws birds and wildlife to one of Costa Rica's most important wetland regions and visitors flock to the Reserve. At its heart is Lake Caño Negro, a shallow seasonal lake no more than 3 m deep covering 800 ha, that completely disappears towards the end of the dry season in April and May. Swamps, gallery forest and marshes attract a wide range of migratory birds to the area, many of which are endangered. The reserve is home to the largest nesting colony of neotropical cormorants in the country and is the last permanent refuge in the country of the Nicaraguan grackle. The roseate spoonbill with its mildly humorous spatulate bill is a common sight, and you may catch a glimpse of the huge jabirú standing almost 1.5 m tall – Central America's largest bird. Travelling in a covered canoe chartered from Los Chiles, the floating safaris follow the Río Frío through primary forest taking three to four hours for each trip. With luck you'll see three of the four Costa Rican monkeys – the howler, spider and white-faced – along with sloths and reptiles including caiman.

Fishing

Freshwater fishing is an option from Los Chiles with 25 kg tarpon often taken from the Lake Caño Negro. This is world class fishing, and landing one of these silver kings is unforgettable. You can try your luck for tarpon, snook and rainbow bass on a trip from Los Chiles for around US$350 for two people, tackle and refreshments included, or organize a trip from San José which will set you back a little more.

For Sleeping and Eating price codes and other relevant information, see Essentials, pages 44-47.

🛏 Sleeping

North to Nicaragua via Upala *p186*
L Montaña Magil Forest Lodge, 3 km from Colonia Río Celeste, 20 km west of San Rafael de Guatuso, T2221-2825. Price includes meals. 10 rooms with private bath. It is reportedly difficult to find – call in advance.

L-AL Tilajari Resort Hotel, Muelle San Carlos, 13 km of Platanar, T2469-09091, www.tilajari.com. 76 luxurious rooms including 16 suites and 4 family rooms, all with a/c and comfortable private bath. It's a popular place, quiet and off the main track, and a good choice for families and groups, providing a range of activities including tennis courts, 3 pools, sauna, bar and restaurant, horses, boat trips and other excursions organized.

AL Hotel La Garza, Platanar, 8 km north of Florencia, T2475-5222, www.hotel lagarza.com. Has 12 charming spacious and airy bungalows with bath and fan, constructed from local hardwoods, with balconies overlooking the peaceful Platanar River, set in beautiful but not overtended gardens. It's a great spot, hidden and secluded – ideal for a genuinely quiet getaway – with good views of Arenal. The 230-ha hacienda is still a working dairy and cattle ranch owned and run by the Cantillo family since 1947. While very comfortable, the family is keen to welcome people with an interest in the realities of hacienda life rather than simply being an 'adventure park'. Excursions to nearby sights easily arranged and a number of original options including climbing up the inside of the 800 year-old strangler tree.

D-E Albergue Tío Henry, San Rafael de Guatuso, T2464-0211. Simple accomodation option.
F Buena Vista, Upala, T2470-0186. Has simple rooms with food available.

North to Los Chiles *p186*
Los Chiles
B Rancho Tulipán, one block west of the central park opposite the immigration office, T2471-1414, www.ranchotulipan. Com. 10 big, clean and well appointed rooms with ceramic floors, bath and hot water, the most comfortable option in town – there's even a small desk and a lamp in most rooms, not that common in Costa Rica. Good thatched ranch-style restaurant serves breakfasts and dinners, with parking at the back. Tulipán is a good source of information on the region, and can arrange tours in the area including river safaris and fishing trips and have advice on travelling north to Nicaragua.
E Cabinas Jabirú, 100 m from the bus stop, a few blocks east of central park, T2471-1496. A good budget choice with rooms decorated with tropical motifs on the walls, private bathrooms, fan, some with TV. Parking, postal service, internet, fax and laundry and a range of interesting tours. You can sort out the cheapest option to Caño Negro here (US$20 per person, minimum 3 people).
G Carolina, close to the main highway, T2471-1151. Best of the budget range with small, fairly dark rooms and a few blocks from the centre but very clean and well maintained.
G Onassis, on the southwest corner of main plaza, T2471-1001. The best bet out of the strip facing the football pitch. Basic rooms, clean, shared bath and a fan if you ask nicely.

South of town and Los Chiles
AL Hotel de Campo, in Caño Negro, reached from the main route to Los Chiles, or via Upala, T2471-1012, www.hoteldecampo.com. Comfortable rooms, all with balconies and

lake views, set in fine gardens provide a comfortable base for a good range of tours. Also with a pool and jacuzzi.

B Albergue Caño Negro, 17 km south of Los Chiles on a rough dirt road ideally suited for 4WD, T2460-0124. Rustic rooms on the banks of the Río Frío.

B Caño Negro Lodge, T2471-1000, www.canonegrolodge.com. Just over 20 rooms, with a strong focus on sustainable tourism, a/c and private bath in each, international restaurant on site, and a pool.

🍴 Eating

Los Chiles *p186*
In addition to **Rancho Tulipan** and **Cabiñas Jabirú**, try:
† **Restaurant El Parque** on the main plaza. Good home cooking.
† **Los Petates**, on the road running south of the central park. Has cheap food with large portions.

⛰ Activities and tours

Los Chiles *p186*
Local trips
Ask about guides at Rancho Tulipán, Cabinas Jabirú, or Restaurant Los Petates, if you want to organize your own trip to Caño Negro. Local prices vary greatly depending on demand but start at around US$20 per person for a minimum of 3 people, down to US$15 for groups of 4 or more. Oscar Rojas at Tulipán can help organize trips to **El Castillo** and **San Juan** in Nicaragua and could help with arrangements for travelling down the Río San Juan to the Caribbean. In Fortuna **Aventuras Arenal** and **Sunset Tours** run trips to **Caño Negro**, for between US$45-US$60 including transport.

🚍 Transport

North to Nicaragua via Upala *p186*
Buses to **San Rafael de Guatuso** leave **San José** at 1545, returning at 1000, taking 5 hrs, from Av 3-5, C 12, US$4.50 (Transportes Upala, T2221-3318). Also at 0500 and 0840 from C 12, Av 7-9, with **Transportes San Carlos**, US$4.50, 4½ hrs. Local services are available from **Ciudad Quesada** and **Fortuna**.

There are daily buses to **Upala** from San José, Av 3-5, C 12 at 1015, 1500 and 1715, taking about 4 hrs, US$6.50 (**Transportes Upala**, T2221-3318). Several buses make the 1¾ hr trip from **Cañas**.

Los Chiles *p186*
There are 3 daily boats to **San Carlos** on the Río San Juan, 1-hr, US$7. From San Carlos you can take a boat down the Río San Juan travelling to Trinidad or further downstream to Greytown but there is no border crossing from Costa Rica.

Direct buses leave from **San José** Terminal Atlántico Norte at 0530 and 1530, 5 hrs, US$4, returning to the capital at 0500, 1500. There is an hourly service between **Ciudad Quesada (San Carlos)** and Los Chiles, 2 hrs, US$2.70. If travelling from **Fortuna**, take the bus to San Carlos, alighting at Muelle – ask the bus driver to drop you off – and wait for a bus heading towards Los Chiles. You may feel stranded, but it'll shave at least an hour off your journey.

ⓘ Directory

Los Chiles *p186*
Banks Banco Nacional, with ATM, on central park. **Immigration** Half a block up from the dock, open 0800-1600 every day. **Post office** Postal services available at Cabiñas Jabirú.

Monteverde and Santa Elena

With its head often shrouded in mist, the appalling roads leading to Monteverde Cloud Forest Reserve will keep you (literally and figuratively) on the edge of your seat as you anticipate the experience of seeing one of the world's premier nature destinations. Milk churns stacked at the roadside awaiting collection give clues to the real identity of this agricultural community that hides, cut off on all sides, from the rest of Costa Rica. But this isolation has preserved something special in the surrounding hills: the seed of Monteverde Reserve has germinated to create a host of natural experiences that encapsulate the very essence of Costa Rica – diversity, seclusion and at times exhilaration. The secret that was Monteverde Reserve in the 1970s when it was founded may now be well known but, true to the uniqueness of the reserve, and despite the visitors, there is still a rough charm to the area.

Santa Elena, the supply town for the local areas of interest, is a scruffy place of barely three streets and much more appealing for the way it seems to trundle along, like nature, in a state of organized chaos. The settlement of Monteverde sits along the bumpy road that leads uphill to the reserve. ▸▸ *For listings, see pages 198-204.*

Ins and outs ▸▸ *Colour map 1, B6.*

Getting there

Monteverde is at the end of the single road leading up from Santa Elena, which in turn is only reached along a number of bone-shaking roads. If driving, there are a number of options. From the Pan-American Highway at Km 149, turn right at Yomale south of the Río Lagarto. Continue for about 40 km on mostly gravel road (allow 2½ hours) to Santa Elena. Parts of the road are quite good, 4WD is recommended and essential for the rough parts in the rain – make sure your car rental agreement allows you to travel to Monteverde. A shorter route is to take the Sardinal turn-off from the Pan-American Highway north of the Río Aranjuez. At the park in Sardinal turn left, then via Guacimal to the Monteverde road. You can also drive from Tilarán, which links with Cañas and Fortuna, along an equally poor road – a journey that takes a couple of hours. En route, 11 km from Tilarán on the road to Monteverde, you can visit the four **Viento Fresco waterfalls** ① *T2661-8193, www.viento fresco.net, US$15, or US$55 for a 3-hr horse-riding tour,* the largest at 75 m.

From San José buses for Santa Elena leave at 0630 and 1430, five hours, US$4.30. A couple come from Puntarenas via the Km 149 route leaving at 1300 and 1400, three to four hours, US$2.30. A bus leaves Tilarán at 1230, 3 hrs, US$1.80, linking with Fortuna and Volcán Arenal, and Cañas on the Pan-American Highway. There are also services with Interbus and Grayline.

An alternative, and the quickest route is a taxi-boat-taxi option between Fortuna and Santa Elena. About three hours in total, US$25. Pick up is around 0800 and takes you to the hotel of your choice (within reason). Contact your hotel for details.

Getting around and entry to the Reserve

The main focus is the small town of Santa Elena. A 5 km road leads up to the Monteverde Cloud Forest Reserve. Walking is by far the simplest way of getting there, and is certainly feasible from Santa Elena. A bus also makes the journey from Santa Elena through Monteverde to the reserve leaving town at 0600 and 1100, getting workers and independent travellers up the hill. Taxis are available from Santa Elena charging around US$5-6 for the journey. The smart choice is to get transport up the hill and walk down enjoying the views.

The second main area of interest is Santa Elena Cloud Forest Reserve, just over 7 km to the north. A shuttle bus leaves at 0700, US$2. A taxi will cost around US$7-8. Trips to activities in this area often include the cost of transportation. Of course, if you have your own vehicle moving around is a lot simpler.➤➤ *For further details, see Transport, page 203.*

Entrance to Monteverde Reserve is US$15 (students with ID half-price) valid for multiple entry during the day, cannot be purchased in advance. Office open 0700-1630 daily; the park opens at 0700 and closes at 1600.

There is a limit on the total number of visitors allowed in the reserve at any one time, so be there before 0700 to make sure of getting in during high season. If you want to book a guide, hotels will book a place for the following day. Alternatively you can just turn up and see if there are spaces on any tours.

Best time to visit

The driest months are from January to May, with the best months for birdwatching being February, March and April. This also coincides with lower rainfall, the wettest months being September to November. As this is cloudforest, remember that mist is common and rain can occur throughout the year. Some travellers feel aggrieved that they have not seen much wildlife but as with all nature experiences, be realistic in your expectations.

Tourist information

A tourist office has opened on the main street in Santa Elena. Information is very general, as the town has survived so long on its own merits. For all reserve information, guided tours and refuge reservations contact the reserve offices on T2645-5122, www.cct.or.cr – a very useful, if at times confusing, website that now includes trail maps.

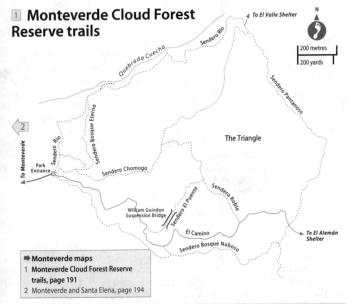

1 Monteverde Cloud Forest Reserve trails

➤ **Monteverde maps**
1 Monteverde Cloud Forest Reserve trails, page 191
2 Monteverde and Santa Elena, page 194

What is cloudforest?

Simply put, it's forest that spends much of the year blanketed in cloud creating conditions of high humidity. In Monteverde, trade winds from the Atlantic force moist air up the Tilarán Mountains, cooling the air as it rises which condenses to create clouds.

An almost magical place, like the forests of fairy tales, here there is an abundance of plants, with tree trunks and branches covered in dense blankets of mosses and lichens, twisting vines, fallen trees and giant tree ferns. Take away the path and imagine how quickly you could get lost.

History and background information

Monteverde owes its formation to the pursuit of ideals. Back in 1951, a group of Quakers from North America left the USA to avoid the draft. Buying land in Monteverde and clearing the forests for dairy farming, the community soon realized that the forest cover was essential to protect the watershed of the area, and created a protected area of 541 ha. In 1972 George Powell and his wife, after a period studying the birds of the cloudforest, set out to protect more of the region, joining forces with the long-time resident Wilford Guindon to promote the creation of a reserve. Combining the Quaker reserve with a further 328 ha, the Monteverde Cloud Forest Reserve was created in 1972.

Tedious though the facts and figures may be, those ideals have grown with the size of the reserve. Without the backing of large environmental organizations, Monteverde moved from individual passion to global awareness through the medium of rumours and television nature documentaries. Slowly, the notion of ecotourism began to reap rewards, and the Reserve spawned a myriad of reserves, protected areas and conservation projects in the region and across Costa Rica.

A visit to Monteverde or any of the many other private reserves is an opportunity to see nature in grand profusion. Plants grow on every available space, insects breed, birds feed and mammals loiter and stalk. Without a trained eye nearby, you may see only insects and hear a bird take flight, but the experience is no less enjoyable. Strike out on your own, or explore with a guide – just remember to shut out the big busy world and absorb the magic of the cloudforest. And bear in mind that even with a guide you'll be lucky to see mammals.

Looking ahead, there is much discussion about the future of Monteverde and other reserves in the area. Some residents want to see the appalling roads upgraded to improve access. Others think a better road would be the beginning of the end for Monteverde and want to restrict the potential damage that may be caused, believing that development has already reached unacceptable limits. You can decide for yourself whether visiting Monteverde is about quality or quantity but anything worth having is worth working for.

Reserva Biológica Bosque Nuboso Monteverde

Straddling the continental divide, the 10,500-ha Monteverde Cloud Forest Reserve is privately owned and administered by the Centro Científico Tropical (Tropical Science Centre) – a non-profit research and educational association. The reserve is mainly primary cloudforest spending much of the year shrouded in mist, creating stunted trees and abundant epiphytic growth. It contains over 400 species of birds, including the resplendent quetzal (best seen in the dry months between January and May, especially near the start of the Nuboso trail), the three-wattled bellbird and the bare-necked umbrella bird. There are over 100 species of mammals, including monkeys, Baird's tapir and all six endangered cats found in Costa Rica – jaguar, jaguarundi, margay, ocelot, tigrillo and puma – reptiles and amphibians. The reserve protects an estimated 500 species of butterfly, 2500 species of plants and more than 6000 species of insects. The entrance is at 1530 m, but the maximum altitude in the reserve rises to over 1800 m. Mean temperature is between 16° and 18°C and average annual rainfall is 3000 mm. The weather changes quickly – if you want to see why climb up to La Ventana and watch the Atlantic and Pacific weather systems collide over the continental divide – and wind and humidity often make the air feel cooler so take a light jacket and rain gear in case.

Ins and outs

Trails and treks There are 13 km of paths in the reserves spread across ten trails, one of which includes the Wilford Guindon Suspension Bridge. The commonly used trails are in good condition and there are easy, short and interesting walks for those who do not want to hike all day. The shortest is just 300 m, the longest 2 km. The longer walks only take about two hours but you could easily spend all day just wandering around. Trails may be restricted from time to time if they need protection. There is a trail northwards to Arenal volcano that is increasingly used, but not easy. Free maps of the reserve are available at the entrance along with an excellent self-guided Nature Trail with a guide booklet. Follow the rules and sign the register, indicating where you are going in case you get lost. Stay on the paths, leave nothing behind and take no fauna or flora out.

Equipment Recommended equipment includes: binoculars (which are available for rent at the entrance); a good camera; insect repellent; sweater and light rainwear. Rubber boots or good walking shoes are a must for the longer walks at all times of year but especially in the rainy season, and can be hired at the park office or at hotels. Note that no radios or tape recorders allowed in the reserve.

Guides A guide is a good idea if you want to see wildlife – the untrained eye misses a lot. Natural history walks with licensed biologist guides leave from near the entrance every morning and afternoon, three to four hours, US$20 (children half price). Advance reservations can be made at the office or through your hotel and are strongly recommended particularly between Jan and May. There are about 30 guides to choose from with varying specializations and experience. If you use a private guide you must pay his entrance fee.

There is an excellent night tour in the reserve where you will almost certainly see tarantulas as well as anything else the guide can seek out. Trips leave at 1900, T2661-1008, US$17. You will need to arrange transport to and from the reserve through your hotel or organize a taxi – don't forget to arrange for them to pick you up as well.

Volunteer work If you are interested in volunteer work, from non-skilled trail maintenance to skilled scientific assistance work, surveying, teaching or studying on a tropical biology programme, contact the reserve office at the address above. US$35 per person, board and lodging, two weeks minimum.

Donations These are welcome and can be made at the reserve office, with **Tropical Science Centre**, or online. All details available at www.cct.or.cr.

Settlement of Monteverde

Strung out along the road climbing to the cloudforest, the settlement of Monteverde – between Santa Elena and the Reserve – was founded by American Quakers in the 1950s. Without a centre as such, it started life as a collective of dairy farms providing milk for a

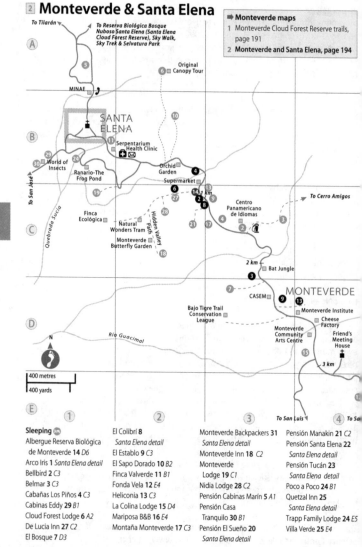

Monteverde & Santa Elena

➡ Monteverde maps

1 Monteverde Cloud Forest Reserve trails, page 191
2 Monteverde and Santa Elena, page 194

To Tilarán

To Reserva Biológica Bosque Nuboso Santa Elena (Santa Elena Cloud Forest Reserve), Sky Walk, Sky Trek & Selvatura Park

Original Canopy Tour

MINAE

SANTA ELENA

Serpentarium Health Clinic

World of Insects

Orchid Garden

Ranario-The Frog Pond

Supermarket

To Cerro Amigos

To San José

Finca Ecológica

Natural Wonders Tram

Hidden Valley Path

Centro Panamericano de Idiomas

Monteverde Butterfly Garden

2 km · Bat Jungle

CASEM

MONTEVERDE

Bajo Tigre Trail Conservation League

Monteverde Institute

Cheese Factory

Río Guacimal

Monteverde Community Arts Centre

Friend's Meeting House

3 km

400 metres
400 yards

To San Luis

To Sa

Sleeping

Albergue Reserva Biológica de Monteverde **14** *D6*
Arco Iris **1** *Santa Elena detail*
Bellbird **2** *C3*
Belmar **3** *C3*
Cabañas Los Piños **4** *C3*
Cabinas Eddy **29** *B1*
Cloud Forest Lodge **6** *A2*
De Lucia Inn **27** *C2*
El Bosque **7** *D3*

El Colibrí **8**
Santa Elena detail
El Establo **9** *C3*
El Sapo Dorado **10** *B2*
Finca Valverde **11** *B1*
Fonda Vela **12** *E4*
Heliconia **13** *C3*
La Colina Lodge **15** *D4*
Mariposa B&B **16** *E4*
Montaña Monteverde **17** *C3*

Monteverde Backpackers **31**
Santa Elena detail
Monteverde Inn **18** *C2*
Monteverde Lodge **19** *C1*
Nidia Lodge **28** *C2*
Pensión Cabinas Marín **5** *A1*
Pensión Casa Tranquilo **30** *B1*
Pensión El Sueño **20**
Santa Elena detail

Pensión Manakin **21** *C2*
Pensión Santa Elena **22**
Santa Elena detail
Pensión Tucán **23**
Santa Elena detail
Poco a Poco **24** *B1*
Quetzal Inn **25**
Santa Elena detail
Trapp Family Lodge **24** *E5*
Villa Verde **25** *E4*

cooperative cheese factory. The cheese factory, now privately owned, still operates and sells excellent cheeses of various types, fresh milk, ice cream, milkshakes to die for and *cajeta* (a butterscotch spread). Today, Monteverde maintains an air of pastoral charm, but tourism provides more revenue for the town than dairy produce ever could.

Santa Elena

El Bosque Eterno de los Niños
ⓘ T2645-5003, www.acmcr.org. 0800-1600, entrance US$8, students US$5. Contact the Monteverde Conservation League for reservations at San Gerardo (mroberts@acmcr.org) or Pocosol Field Stations (mv@acmcr.org).

Adjoining and in the past surrounding the Monteverde Cloud Forest is the Children's Eternal Rainforest, established in 1988 after an initiative by Swedish school children to save forests. Currently at 22,000 ha, the land is bought and maintained by the Monteverde Conservation League with donations from children around the world. The **Bajo del Tigre trail** is about 3 km and takes 1½ hours, guides can be arranged or you can go on a self-guided tour. There is also a twilight tour at 1730, US$22, when the forest animals are beginning to move around (T2645-5923).

For some serious adventure, trips deeper into the forest, to the **San Gerardo Field Station**, in the western part of the reserve, can be arranged. There are 7 km of trails leading through primary, secondary and regenerating forests and a spectacular view of Arenal Volcano (when clear) and the surrounding rain forest. The **Poco Sol Field Station** is at the eastern end of the protected areas near **Poco Sol Lagoon** and reached on the road from San Ramón to Fortuna. It has almost 10 km of trails visiting a beautiful waterfall and excellent opportunities for birding. Accommodation is available at both stations, B-C per person including entrance, three meals, sheets, blankets, towel, soap, and toilet paper.

Donations Donations are welcomed so that the work of the Monteverde Conservation League can continue. Children from over

Eating 🍴
Bromelia's **13** D4
Chunches **1**
  Santa Elena detail
Flor de Vida **8** C2
Johnny's Pizza **4** B2
Lucía's **6** C2
Morpho **7**
  Santa Elena detail
Seafood Marquéz **5**
  Santa Elena detail

Soda **11** Santa Elena detail
Sofía **2** C2
Stella's Bakery **9** D3
Tramonti **3** C3

Bars & clubs 🍸
Moon Shiva **14** C2

44 nations have raised money to buy land. Funds are used for purchasing additional land and for maintaining and improving the existing reserve area. Full details at www.acmcr.org.

Reserva Biológica Bosque Nuboso Santa Elena

ⓘ *T2645-5390, www.reservasantaelena.org. 0700-1600, entrance US$12, students US$6. It is a long, steep hike from the village. Day time tours leave the information office in Santa Elena at 0730 and 1130 everyday. Alternatively hire a taxi.*

One kilometre along the road from Santa Elena to Tilarán, a 5-km track is signposted to this 310-ha reserve, managed by the Centro Ecológico Bosque Nuboso de Monteverde. It is 83% primary cloudforest, the remainder being 20-year-old secondary forest at 1700 m, bordered by the Monteverde Cloud Forest Reserve and the Arenal Forest Reserve. There is an 8-km network of paths with several lookouts where you can see and hear, on a clear day, Arenal volcano. The 'canopy tour' is recommended; you climb inside a hollow strangler fig tree then cross between two platforms along aerial runways 30 m in the air (good views of orchids and bromeliads), then down a 30-m hanging rope at the end. The Centro Ecológico Bosque Nuboso is administered by the local community and profits go to five local schools. It was set up by the Costa Rican government in 1989 with collaboration from Canada. There is a small information centre where rubber boots can be hired and a small café open at weekends. The rangers are very friendly and enthusiastic and there are generally fewer visitors here than at Monteverde. Hand-painted T-shirts for sale.

Sights and excursions

While the honey-pot Monteverde Reserve is the main attraction there are many other places well worth exploring. Most of the attractions are spread over the region.

Two of the most popular adventures are found 5 km north of Santa Elena, off the road to Tilarán, **Sky Walk** ⓘ *T2645-5238, www.skywalk.co.cr, daily 0700-1600, with guided tours at 0800, 1100 and 1300, US$30, student US$24, child US$19*, using six suspension bridges, the highest being 42 m above the ground, takes you through the cloudforest at canopy level on a tour covering 2.5 km. **Sky Trek** ⓘ *T2645-5238, www.skytrek.com, daily 0700-1500, US$60, student US$48, children US$38*, is arguably even more popular and a breathtaking experience, as you fly through the air on a system of cables strung out between giant forest trees. On clear days the view from the highest tower is unbelievable and has been known to induce a fair amount of knee-wobbling in even the hardiest characters. The same company offers the **Sky Tram**, 1600 m of cable car-style ride above and with the canopy. Sold as part of a package with the Sky Trek.

Selvatura Park ⓘ *on the road out to Santa Elena Cloud Forest Reserve, T2645-5929, www.selvatura.com*, is a multi-activity park with a canopy tour (US$40), tree-top walkway (which is very stable, making it suitable for less mobile people – US$20), and a butterfly and hummingbird garden (US$10 and US$5). Discounts are available if you are taking several of the options.

The **Original Canopy Tour** ⓘ *in Santa Elena, T2645-5243, www.canopytour.com, tours leave from the office in Santa Elena daily at 0730, 1030 and 1430, adults US$45, students US$35, children US$25*, is in the grounds of Cloud Forest Lodge and gives you the chance to explore the forest canopy while zipping down steel cables between five platforms, ending up with a rappel.

If you just want to walk, from the Hotel Heliconia (see page 199) to the reserve is a steep 45-minute walk uphill (about 4 km) but there are lovely views looking towards the sea and the Nicoya Peninsula, particularly in the evening (when you are coming down and can appreciate them).

Cerro Amigos, the highest point in the region at 1842 m, reached via the Hotel Belmar, makes for a pleasant walk lasting a couple of hours. It's uphill all the way passing through forest with fine views from the top stretching across to the erupting Arenal volcano on a clear day.

Reserva Sendero Tranquilo ① *book through El Sapo Dorado on T2645-5010, daily, US$20, entry restricted to 12 people at any one time*, is, as the name suggests, a quiet reserve set on 200 ha between the Monteverde Cloud Forest Reserve and the Guacima River, near the Monteverde Cheese Factory. Tours here are limited to small guided groups.

About 100 m beyond *Hotel Sapo Dorado* is the **Orchid Garden** ① *daily 0800-1700, US$5*, with about 400 species collected by Gabriel Barboza.

Very close to Santa Elena, at the start of the climb to Monteverde, is the **Serpentarium** ① *T2645-5238, www.snaketour.com, daily 0900-2000, US$8*, with specimens of snakes and amphibians found in the nearby cloudforest.

A dirt road opposite the Hotel Heliconia leads to the **Monteverde Butterfly Garden** ① *www.monteverdebutterflygarden.com, daily 0930-1600, US$9 including guided tour, best time for a visit 1100-1300*, a beautifully presented large garden planted for breeding and researching butterflies. Entrance includes an informative and humourous guide round the four different artificial environments. Near the Butterfly Garden is **Finca Ecológica** ① *T2645-5363, 0700-1700 daily, US$5, free trail map*, which has three trails totalling around 5 km with bird lists for birdwatchers and a chance of seeing other wildlife in this transitional zone between cloud and tropical dry forest. Guides available and night tours can be arranged. Down the same path is **Natural Wonders Tram** ① *T2645-5960, daily 0700-1800, US$15*, a ski lift-style ride travelling slowly through the treetops.

Ranario – The Frog Pond ① *on the outskirts of Santa Elena town, T2645-6320, www.ranario.com, open daily 0900-2030, US$10*, is a fascinating collection of all the funky coloured frogs you've seen on postcards and in brochures. Entrance covers multiple entry so you can visit in the morning and try to find them sleeping and then return at dusk to hear the frog chorus in all its glory.

The **Bat Jungle** ① *T2645-5052, 0800-1600, US$8*, is a good opportunity to see these cute little creatures up close and personal, and also to hear them with the aid of the brilliantly named Bat Detector.

The **World of Insects** ① *300 m west of the supermarket, T2645-6859, US$7, US$5 for students*, is a collection of the creepy crawlies that you might see when exploring the cloudforest.

The **Monteverde Coffee Tour** ① *twice daily at 0800 and 1400, US$30*, enables you to see the entire production process of coffee from growing on the bush through to processing and packaging.

For Sleeping and Eating price codes and other relevant information, see Essentials, pages 44-47.

⊜ Sleeping

While accommodation in Monteverde and north of Santa Elena is somewhat spread out, there are several good accommodation options within walking distance of town.

Reserva Biológica Bosque Nubos Monteverde *p192*

Reservations are required for all reserve accommodation.

C Albergue Reserva Biológica de Monteverde, at the entrance to the reserve. Dormitory-style accommodation for up to 40.

There are also 2 refuges deeper in the reserve at Alemán and Eladios with basic facilities which provide a chance to get to some of the less well visited parts. Facilities cost US$3.50 a night for Alemán, US$5 for Eladios. In addition to paying for use of the refuge you have to pay the reserve entrance fee for each night spent in the park and a key deposit of US$5. You will need a sleeping bag, torch and food supplies.

Reserva Biológica Bosque Nubos Santa Elena *p196, map p194*

A Poco a Poco, on the cut-through road leading from the south up to the reserve, T2645-6000, www.hotelpocoapoco.com. 32 fully-equipped, comfortable rooms. A good choice close to the town.

AL-A Arco Iris, T2645-5067, www.arco irislodge.com. A mixed bag of rooms and fine cabins all with bath. There's a restaurant serving healthy breakfasts and meals in high season. Horses are available for hire and there's plenty of parking.

L-AL Finca Valverde, 300 m east of Banco Nacional up hill on road to the reserve, T2645-5157, www.monteverde.co.cr. Comfortable cabins and rooms (some with bath tub, all with bathroom) set in the forest, sleeping 2 or 4 people. Coffee is grown on the finca (which is a good spot for birdwatching) and the restaurant serves good *Tico* food.

B Pensión El Sueño, T2645-5021, www.hotelelsuenocr.com. Very friendly, with 11 small but pleasant wood-panelled rooms, some with private baths and hot showers. Meals available and parking out front.

A-B Quetzal Inn, T2645-6076, www.quetzal inn.com. Pleasant handful of smart *cabinas*, with a small bar and restaurant. Some rooms with private bath and balcony, cheaper with shared bath, more expensive with private Jacuzzi. Good choice in quiet spot.

C-E Casa Tranquilo, T2645-6782, www.casatranquilohostel.com. Selection of good rooms for mid-range and budget travellers. Small kitchen, internet service, breakfast included and good supply of information. Good choice.

C Monteverde Backpackers, T2645-5844, www.monteverdebackpackers.com. Same owners as the Backpackers in Arenal, good selection of dorm and private rooms. Communal kitchen, internet, local tours and transport options (US$18 to Arenal)

C-D Cabinas Eddy, T2645-6618, www.cabinaseddy.com. Just on the south side of town, with shared and private baths.

D-E Pensión Tucán, T2645-5017. A good, clean, budget option, some rooms with private bath, or in basic cabins with hot water shower, friendly management, breakfast and restaurant (recommended) closed Sun lunch.

E El Colibrí, up the side road opposite Chunches, T2645-5682. Clean and friendly in a timber-built house. Some rooms have balconies, others are a little cramped.

E Pensión Cabinas Marín, 500 m north of the centre past the Agricultural College, T2645-5279. Spacious rooms (no. 8 has a nice view), good breakfasts, friendly.

B-E Pensión Santa Elena, T2645-5051, www.pensionsantaelena.com. Very popular spot with backpackers and budget travellers. The rooms are clean, with simple doubles and larger rooms sleeping up to 8. The place has a lively atmosphere and a communal kitchen with a recycing system if you want to cook yourself. Excellent source of information for the area, have a look at the website.

Approaching Santa Elena from Tilarán

AL-A Mirador Lodge, 10 km north of Santa Elena, T2645-5354, www.miradorlodge.com. From May-Nov you probably need a horse not 4WD to get here down the dirt track. Rustic cabins with bathrooms set in a private reserve, popular with birdwatchers. Being so cut off, the home cooking in the restaurant is essential rather than an option.

A-B Miramontes, a couple of km north of Santa Elena, T2645-5152, www.swisshotel miramontes.com. A little piece of Switzerland, with a dozen comfortable rooms in wooden cabins, all with bath and hot water. A couple of the rooms have a veranda looking out across the forest. The Swiss-run *Spaghettería* restaurant provides cosmopolitan specialties from Italy, Switzerland, Austria, France and, of course, Costa Rica.

B Ecoverde Lodge, 6 km north of Santa Elena on road to Quebrada Grande and Tilarán, T2286-4203, www.turismoruralcr. com. 4 cabins with private bathroom, 5 with shared bathroom. Great idea, but the location is a little too far from Santa Elena to be accessible without transport.

Uphill to the reserve

A single dirt road leads up to the reserve passing through the spread-out agricultural settlement that is Monteverde. Hotels and lodges are dotted along the road, many in wonderfully secluded settings with good views. The majority are in the mid- and upper-price brackets, but there are a few exceptions. Several hotels provide **slide shows** featuring images from renowned photographers such as Michael and Patricia Hogden. Ask in your hotel for schedules. Hotels listed in order heading uphill.

L-AL Monteverde Lodge, climbing the hill a road to the right leads to this **Costa Rica**

Expeditions-owned hotel, T2645-5057, www.costaricaexpeditions.com. The spacious rooms all have bathrooms with solar-heated water. It's a graceful hotel, which impresses from the moment you arrive with its vast lobby complete with open fire. The environmental considerations extend to the solar-heated jacuzzi, bathed in natural light set in a large glass atrium. The lodge gardens, complete with running stream and a small waterfall, are relaxation itself, and there's a small lookout for viewing the surrounding forest and wildlife. Packages including meals are available, and children under 10 sharing a room go free.

AL Cloud Forest Lodge, up a right fork off the main road, T2645-5058, www.cloudforest lodge.com. 18 immaculate rooms set in 9 double cabins, each with bathroom. The lodge is up on the hill set in a private 30-ha reserve with 5 km of trails, and stunning views (on clear days) to the Pacific from the restaurant which bakes bread daily.

AL El Sapo Dorado, up a steep road left off the main road, T2645-5010, www.sapo dorado.com. The *Tico*/US owners reflect the synthesis of Costa Rican and Quaker traditions. 30 comfortable suites with bathroom and private porch entrance, surrounded by tropical gardens. You can choose from Sunset Suites, overlooking the Nicoya Peninsula, Fountain Suites or the Classic Suites, which all have an open fire. The restaurant is often recommended with international and national dishes merging vegetarian and vegan options.

Next, there is a short, flat section called Cerro Plano, with several hotels nearby. **L-AL Hotel Heliconia**, just beyond the village supermarket, T2645-5109, www.hotelheliconia.com. The hardwood chalet of the reception and restaurant is a theme reflected throughout the comfortably furnished rooms, complete with private bathroom and veranda. The restaurant serves excellent food.

AL-B El Establo, T2645-5110, www.hotel elestablo.com. After a comprehensive renovation and expansion the 155 comfortable and carpeted rooms all have private bathroom and great views to the Nicoya peninsula. There's a pool and large restaurant, Las Riendas, serving home-cooked and international dishes. Service is reported to be excellent and it's a popular choice for groups. The 50-ha farm has nature trails through the primary forest, with guides available for birdwatching, and horses available for hire at the stables.

Opposite the *Heliconia*, a gravel road leads down to several accommodation options.
AL Hotel De Lucía Inn, T2645-5976, www.costa-rica-monteverde.com. Popular hotel, building on the success of their restaurant over the road. A dozen spacious rooms all with private bath. Good restaurant and a quiet spot.
AL-A Nidia Lodge, T2645-6082, www.nidialodge.com. Another quiet, secluded option near Cerro Plano. 17 rooms set in colourful gardens – a pleasant change from the smooth operations up and down the hill.
B Monteverde Inn, close to the Butterfly Garden, T2645-5156. The rooms are basic, and could do with smartening up, but it is a quiet budget spot away from town with good views down the valley, and access to the Hidden Valley Nature Trail.
B-E Pensión Manakin, back on the main road heading up the hill, just beyond Establo, down a short road, T2645-5080, www.manakinlodge.com. 10 simple rooms, a few with bathroom, cheaper without. Filling breakfast and evening meals are available, in a family atmosphere which is great for sharing stories with other guests. Internet service available. A small balcony at the back makes for a calm place to sit and relax as the hummingbirds buzz round your ears. The Villegas are very knowledgeable about the area, and will help arrange tours and transport up to the reserve if required, and throughout Costa Rica.
L-AL Hotel de Montaña Monteverde, on the main road, T2645-5046,

www.monteverdemountainhotel.com. 42 comfortable rooms with hardwood floors, some with fireplaces. The cabin-style restaurant serves *Tico* dishes, and you can take to the jacuzzi or sauna for complete relaxation, enjoying the views out to the Nicoya Peninsula. The 15-ha gardens include several short trails and the gardens provide excellent birdwatching opportunities.
B-C Cabañas Los Piños, T2645-5252, www.lospinos.net. A selection of clean rooms with bare brick walls sleeping 2 to 6 people, all with private bath and some with kitchenettes, set in fine landscaped gardens. It's a quiet spot, and a good deal for groups and families.
C-E Hotel Bellbird, just before the gas station (look for sign that says Alberque Bellbird, T2645-5026, www.hotelbellbird.com. Selection of private rooms and dormitory-style accommodation – ideal for groups, and one of the cheapest going up the hill. It's a clean place, with a restaurant and well situated close to the Belmar for treks up the Cerro Amigos, if you don't want to be in Santa Elena.
AL Belmar, 300 m behind the service station up in the hills, T2645-5201, www.hotelbelmar.net. This Swiss chalet-style hotel perched on the hillside has spectacular views of the Nicoya Peninsula and 34 comfortable rooms with private bath and hot water, some with balconies. There is a restaurant and bar so you don't have to go down the hill for any reason. Private transport option for tours and moving on.
A-B El Bosque, T2645-5158. Set in pretty gardens are 26 low-key rooms with private bath. A good spot, with fine views. There's a short trail through the gardens, ample parking, and helpful staff are happy to help arrange tours.
A-B La Colina Lodge, T2645-5009, www.lacolinalodge.com. One of the original settlement homes complete with uneven floors, head-crackingly low doorways and a cosy fireplace decorated with agricultural antiquities. There are 14 good rooms sleeping

2-4 people with private bath, and some with a balcony. There are also 4 bunk rooms and space for camping (F) (see below). The restaurant serves the standard regional fare. The lodge also owns La Colina in Manuel Antonio and will happily arrange transport between the 2.

B-C Mariposa B&B, on the left, if you get to Fonda Vela you've gone just a little too far, T2645-5013. In a single block with 3 simple rooms sleeping up to 3 people, with bathrooms. A family atmosphere, with breakfast included in the price and dinner by arrangement make this a very relaxed place to stay even if there are no frills.

L-AL Fonda Vela, T2645-5125, www.fonda vela.com. Spread around 9 buildings are 40 beautiful rooms and suites, all with huge windows giving great views to the forest, 2 double beds and a private bathroom with hot water. Some rooms are in elevated multiplex wooden cabins. The 14-ha farm has trails leading through the forest with good birding. There are 2 excellent restaurants open to the public, a bar, TV room, art gallery and conference room and all just a 25-min walk, or a 5-min drive from the reserve. Popular with groups.

A Villa Verde, across the street from Fonda Vela, T2460-4697, www.villaverdehotel.com. A selection of rooms and suites with hot showers, shared bath and some with kitchenettes. It's a popular spot with groups, and has a large restaurant, a games room and fine views across the valley – a little too impersonal for independent travellers.

AL Trapp Family Lodge, high on a hill (without a lowly goat herd) and the closest place to the reserve, T2431-0776, www.trappfam.com. Beyond the entrance, floor to ceiling hardwoods make this a fine, elegant choice with 10 immaculate rooms, each with private bath and hot water. The upper rooms have a balcony, the lower rooms a terrace, so all you need is a comfortable chair and your binoculars for excellent birdwatching. The restaurant is open for breakfast and dinner and the friendly and helpful hosts will help arrange tours.

Camping La Colina Lodge (F), T2645-5009, www.lacolinalodge.com. Only camping option in Monteverde. OK spot, with hot water showers and shared bathroom available.

San Luis

AL-A Ecolodge San Luis, heading south on the road beside La Colina Lodge, some 40 mins' drive from Monteverde, T2645-8049, www.ecolodgesanluis.com. A research centre-cum-ecolodge owned by the University of Georgia on 66 ha of farmland and cloudforest in the San Luis Valley, bordering the Monteverde Cloud and Children's International Cloud Forest, the activities of research, farming and ecotourism are combined in the valley of the San Luis River. Set in the forest with a bird count pushing 250, and a good list of mammals which may include occasional sightings of puma and tapir, the options are wide and varied. Come just to look and learn, staying in a comfortable cabin, get your hands dirty working on the tropical farm complete with coffee, banana and fruit trees, or get totally immersed working as a research assistant. The cheaper options include staying in a bunkhouse which is ideal for large groups, or the bungalow which can sleep up to 16. Treks through the forest and horse riding are optional extras if you've got the energy.

🍴 Eating

Santa Elena p196, map p194

🍴🍴 **Morpho**, opposite the supermarket, T2645-5607. Open 1100-2130. Lively atmosphere serving very good seafood and local dishes. Justifiably popular.

🍴🍴 **Seafood Marquez**, at the northern edge of town. The atmosphere and decor may leave something to be desired, but the seafood is good and the portions filling.

Chunches, opposite Pensión Santa Elena.
A popular hangout serving good espresso
and snacks and with a pile of used books,
magazines and a laundry service at your
disposal. Set to be even better after a
recent remodelling.

Soda. The unnamed polygonal kiosk
on the main street. Open 0600-1900. Serves
seriously cheap food, nothing special, but
filling and nutritious.

Uphill to the reserve
Many of the upmarket hotels have very
good restaurants open to the public.
Try Monteverde Lodge, El Sapo Dorado
or Fondo Vela.

Johnny's Pizza, on the main road between
Santa Elena and Monteverde, T2645-5066.
Good pizzas cooked in a wood-fuel oven in
a relaxed café atmosphere. A few tables on
the balcony combine a classy touch with
precious moments for nocturnal wildlife
encounters, and after dining you can visit
the small souvenir shop.

Sofía, Cerro Plano, T2645-7017. Latin
cuisine is the buzzword here and Sofía
takes traditional dishes to a new level of
elegance.

Lucía's, down the road opposite the
Heliconia, T2645-5337. One of the best
restaurants in the area, serving a mix of
international dishes.

Flor de Vida, opposite El Establo,
T2645-6087. Open 0800-2130, earlier and
later in high season. Vegetarian restaurant
serving super-healthy food in a distinctly
chilled atmosphere.

Tramonti, the restaurant of El Bosque.
Good pizzas, a cheaper option than Johnny's.

Stella's Bakery, opposite CASEM. Has
excellent wholemeal bread, cakes and good
granola to take on hikes, or there's a small
garden café if you want to eat in.

Bromelia's. Good bookshop and café.

Bars and clubs

Santa Elena *p196, map p194*
Amigos, bar in town centre. Lively bar with
no airs and graces, serving simple beers.
Bar Taberna, on the edge of town on the
road to Monteverde. A more touristy spot.
Monteverde Sports Bar, also in town centre.

Uphill to the reserve
Moon Shiva, T2645-6270, www.moon
shiva.com. A bar and restaurant, or restaurant
and bar. Mediterranean and international
dishes. Well known for its events – sometimes
with DJs, live music and story telling.

Festivals and events

**Monteverde Cloud Forest
Reserve** *p192, map p194*
Between Jan and Apr Monteverde Music
Festival is much more than a few musicians
getting together for a jam. Classical and jazz
concerts with performances by local, national
and international musicians, performing at
sunset. Get programmes from the hotels. Has
had a few difficult years, but organizers claim
it is back up and running. Details from the
Monteverde Insisute at www.mvinstitute.org.

Shopping

**Monteverde Cloud Forest
Reserve** *p192, map p194*
Several stores in Santa Elena sell general
souvenir items. There is a small shop at the
office that sells various checklists, postcards,
camera supplies, slides, gifts and T-shirts
(the proceeds of which help towards the
conservation project). There is also a café
serving coffee and snacks which helps dust
off the morning cobwebs for those with a
problem rising so early in the day. Many
hotels have a small souvenir shops as well.

Chunches, in Santa Elena town. Completely renovated and boy do they love it. You will too. It's a good bookshop, which also sells T-shirts, general supplies, and has café and a laundry.

CASEM, close to El Bosque restaurant. A cooperative gift shop, just over half way up the road to the reserve. It sells embroidered shirts, T-shirts, wooden and woven articles and baskets. The shop next door sells genuine Monteverde coffee and you can also get used coffee sacks if they have any in stock.

Bromelias, close to Stella's Bakery. A gallery with a good selection of natural history and coffee table books.

Galería Extasis, a short distance south of CASEM. Exhibits and sells sculptures by the Costa Rican artist Marco Tulio Brenes.

Hummingbird Gallery, just before the entrance to Monteverde Cloud Forest. Open 0700-1600. Masses of different hummingbirds can be seen darting around a glade, visiting feeding dispensers filled with sugared water. In addition to artwork the gallery also sells T-shirts and other souvenirs.

Cheese Factory, about halfway up the hill to the reserve. Marks time as it has for several decades. Now privately owned, it produces and sells excellent cheeses of various types, fresh milk, ice cream, milkshakes to die for and *cajeta* – which you'll find either divine or sickly sweet depending on your taste. The shop closes 1600.

▲ Activities and tours

Monteverde Cloud Forest
Reserve *p192, map p194*
Many of the organizers of the activities in the area either have an office in Santa Elena, or you can book them direct from your hotel.

Horse riding
Several places hire out horses for short local trips, longer excursions – out to the Ecolodge San Luis to visit waterfalls 7-8 hrs, US$80 – and some travel to La Fortuna. It's a tough journey to Fortuna, and there are occasional complaints that horses are overworked.
Sabine's Smiling Horses, T2645-6894, www.smilinghorses.com, or through Pensión Santa Elena (see page 198), has a good reputation and provides a range of tours from lessons, kids' trips, day trips, 10-day riding vacations and farm stays where you have your own horse for 2 weeks.
Desafío, in front of the supermarket, T2645-5874, www.monteverdetours.com. A good reputation for horse riding trips to Fortuna, with a good range of additional services supporting travel throughout Costa Rica. Look for signs between Santa Elena and Monteverde or ask at your hotel.

⊖ Transport

Monteverde Cloud Forest
Reserve *p192, map p194*
Bus
From **San José** a direct bus runs from Av 7-9, C 12, just outside Terminal Atlántico Norte, daily at 0630 and 1430, 5 hrs, US$4.30. Return buses leave Monteverde from Hotel Villa Verde also at 0630 and 1430, picking up through town, stopping at Santa Elena bus stop. Be early. Check times in advance, Sat bus does not always run in low season.
Transportes Tilarán T2645-5032 in Santa Elena, T2222-3854 in San José for information. This service is not 'express', stops to pick up passengers all along the route, and is not a comfortable ride. Keep your day-bag with you at all times and hold onto it; several cases of theft reported, a fact acknowledged by the bus company who warn passengers by putting signs in the bus! Bus from **Puntarenas**, with Terminal Empresarios Unidos (T8777-0708), leave daily at 1400, with an occasional service at 1300 as well,

returning at 0600, 3-4 hrs, US$2.30. This bus arrives in time to catch a bus to Puerto Quepos for Quepos and Manuel Antonio. From **Tilarán** buses leave at 1230, the return bus leaving Santa Elena at 0700 (3 hrs, US$1.80). Going to Tilarán the 0700 connects with the 1230 bus to **Fortuna** and others to **Cañas** for the Pan-American Highway, **Liberia** and the **Nicoya Peninsula**.

Interbus and Grayline also provide transfers to Santa Elena and Monteverde – a good way to travel if you're looking to cover the distance more conveniently.

Car
There is a service station roughly half way between Santa Elena and the reserve open Mon-Sat 0700-1800, Sun 0700-1200. If you're heading to La Fortuna, you can avoid the rather tedious 8-hr bus journey via Tilarán by taking a jeep to Lake Arenal, then a boat, and a jeep for the last stretch. It's 2½-3 hrs, US$25 and more scenic. Most hotels can organize the trip.

Taxi
Available in the centre of Santa Elena for rides up to the reserves and other destinations. Arrange a pick-up time for the return trip. Approximate prices from Santa Elena town; US$6 to Monteverde, US$8-10 to Santa Elena Reserve.

⊙ Directory

Monteverde Cloud Forest Reserve *p192, map p194*
Banks A branch of **Banco Nacional** in Santa Elena is open 0900-1500, for changing TCs and cash advances against Visa. There is also an ATM machine for Visa in the supermarket. **Cultural centres** The Monteverde Institute, T2645-5053, www.mvinstitute.org.

An educational and cultural organization that works to blend international study and research with opportunities for the local community. The Institute organizes and promotes several projects including the Monteverde Community Art Center which provides courses for local and visiting artists. The Institute is also involved in conservation and preservation including the Boehm/ Rockwell house, where the Art Center is located, the oldest house in Monteverde. Innovative projects like the reed-bed greywater system and the construction of a composting toilet have been installed at the Art Center, which together treat all sewage and used water to reduce pollution of local rivers, and promote nutrient recycling as well. **English library**, maintained by Quakers, ask at the Friends' Meeting House. **Internet** Access is opening up in several places. Prices are still quite high, but many hostels now have access for guests. **Language schools** Centro Panamericano de Idiomas, in Monteverde on the road up to the reserve, T2645-5441, www.cpi-edu.com. Immersion language courses from 2 to 4 weeks are available. Accommodation with local families and volunteer opportunities arranged if requested. With schools in Flamingo and Heredia, you can balance study with seeing a range of places in the country. Prices from US$315 a week, reducing as the course length increases, additional US$150 per week for homestay. **Laundry** At many hotels. Chunches, in Santa Elena, provides a good service. Up the hill try **La Amistad**, just before Johnny's Pizza, open 0600-2000. By piece or weight, and can do a 1-hr turn around if required. **Medical services** Available from the Red Cross to the north of town. **Post office** At the southern end of town, at the start of the road up to the reserve. **Useful addresses** The Guardía Rural are in the centre of town.

Contents

208 North to Liberia
  208 Ins and outs
  208 Along the Pan-American
       Highway
  213 Listings

217 North of Liberia
  217 Parque Nacional Rincón
       de la Vieja
  218 Parque Nacional
       Santa Rosa
  221 Parque Nacional
       Guanacaste
  222 La Cruz and Bahía Salinas
  224 Listings

Footprint features

206 Don't miss …
219 UNESCO recognition for
    Guanacaste conservation
222 Arriving at Playa Nancite –
    safety in numbers?

Border essentials

Costa Rica–Nicaragua
  223 Peñas Blancas

Guanacaste

At a glance

◉ **Getting around** It's easy to move around by bus, but take a taxi/jeep to Rincón de la Vieja or Santa Rosa National Park.

◉ **Time required** A couple of days for Rincón de la Vieja; make it a week if going to Santa Rosa National Park as well.

◐ **Weather** Generally sunny.

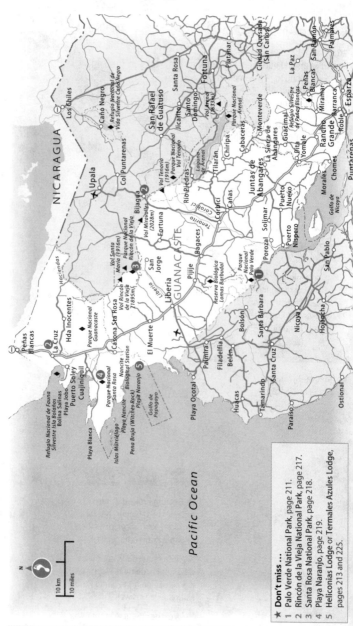

Pacific Ocean

NICARAGUA

GUANACASTE

Golfo de Nicoya

Golfo de Papagayo

★ **Don't miss...**
1 Palo Verde National Park, page 211.
2 Rincón de la Vieja National Park, page 217.
3 Santa Rosa National Park, page 218.
4 Playa Naranjo, page 219.
5 Heliconias Lodge or Termales Azules Lodge, pages 213 and 225.

N

10 km
10 miles

Los Chiles
Caño Negro
Refugio Nacional de Vida Silvestre Caño Negro
Santa Rosa
Platanar
Ciudad Quesada (San Carlos)
San Ramón
San Rafael de Guatuso
Santo Domingo
Jicaro
Vol Arenal
Parque Nacional Arenal
La Paz
Peñas Blancas
Upala
Col Puntarenas
Bijagua
Vol Tenorio (1916m)
Parque Nacional Vol Tenorio
Laguna de Arenal
Chiripa
Cabaceras
Tilarán
Monteverde
Guatimal
Refugio Silvestre de Peñas Blancas
Miramar
Esparza
Barranca
Palmira
Peñas Blancas
Vol Santa María (1916m)
Parque Nacional Rincón de la Vieja
Fortuna
Vol Miravalles (2028m)
San Jorge
Río Piedras
Corobicí
Juntas de Abangares
Rancho Grande
Morales
Chomes
Puntarenas
Robie
La Cruz
Hda Inocentes
Parque Nacional Guanacaste
Cañas Sta Rosa
La Muerte
Liberia
Pijije
Bagaces
Cañas
Corobicí
Puerto Nuevo
Puerto Níspero
San Pablo
Refugio Nacional de Fauna Silvestre Isla Bolaños
Bahía Salinas
Playa Jobo
Puerto Soley
Cuajiniquil
Parque Nacional Santa Rosa
Nancite
Playa Nancite
Pena Bruja (Witches' Rock)
Playa Naranjo
Biological Station
Islas Murciélago
Playa Blanca
El Muerte
Reserva Biológica Lomas Barbudal
Parque Nacional Palo Verde
Palmira
Filadelfia
Belén
Bolsón
Santa Bárbara
Porozal
Solimar
Nicoya
Hojancha
Playa Ocotal
Huacas
Tamarindo
Paraíso
Santa Cruz
Ostional

Toasted as the cultural heart of Costa Rica, Guanacaste's dry rolling flatlands have fed cattle since the 1600s. Although largely confined to the realms of history, the tough life of the *sabanero* – the man of the plains – has become an integral part of the regional and national identity. Moving through the territory on horseback, the *sabanero* would take his shade under the broad branches and dense leaves of a *guanacaste* – the national tree. And when the hard work is done, these people are also open, hospitable and fun-loving (if you're visiting in January and February check out one of the many fiestas in the area).

With considerably less rainfall than other parts of the country, it is easy to see why the expanses of dry, open land, broken only by the dramatic volcanic silhouettes of the Cordillera de Guanacaste, would be more appealing than the hot, insect-infested jungles covering much of the rest of the country. In the 1950s and 1960s, a boom in ranching saw vast areas of the region cleared in an attempt to increase meat exports. Only a combination of foresight and falling meat prices protected the last remaining stretches of rare dry tropical forest found in the northwest, allowing the region to join Costa Rica's growing conservation movement.

Cut off from the Central Valley and hemmed in by the mountains to the east, the region's proximity to Nicaragua has made it the site of numerous infractions between the two nations which still ripple through international relations between *Ticos* and *Nicos*. Liberia is the area's largest town but it's the national parks of Tenorio, Rincón de la Vieja, Palo Verde and Santa Rosa, with their dry tropical forests and geothermal curiosities, that pull in visitors. And for the truly independent traveller there are a few quiet, beautiful beaches in the far north.

North to Liberia

Riding the Pacific slope down from the Central Highlands north to Nicaragua is a fair old drop. You may just notice the small patchy stretch which locals claim covers cracks from tectonic activity, but beyond that it's a pretty uneventful journey. From the lowlands the road is bland, but on either side there are national parks – in particular Palo Verde and Lomas Barbudal – heaving with animals and birdlife. Make sure you drop in and visit one or two on your way north.
▶▶ *For listings, see pages 213-216.*

Ins and outs

Getting there
Air The simplest way to get to the region is to fly from San José to **Daniel Oduber Quirós International Airport**, 13 km west of Liberia. Daily flights (from US$71) with **SANSA**, T2221-9414, www.flysansa.com, and **NatureAir**, T2220-3054, www.natureair.com.

Getting around
Road Good bus services ply the Pan-American Highway from the capital and Puntarenas as far as the Nicaraguan border, although you may have problems getting to some of the more out-of-the-way national parks.

The best way of exploring Guanacaste is in your own car – you can head down the Pan-American Highway peeling off at will to explore quiet spots. From San José the road winds gently to San Ramón before beginning a meandering descent of 800 m to Esparza (31 km). There are fine views but heavy traffic and mist – particularly at night – can make conditions treacherous.

Best time to visit
Rainfall is moderate: 1000-2000 mm a year, with a long dry season from November to May. But the lowlands are deep in mud during the rainy season.

Along the Pan-American Highway ⊖❶❷❸▲❹❺ ▶▶ *pp213-216.*

Esparza → *Colour map 1, C6.*
An attractive town with a turbulent history, Esparza was once an important trading post on the Camino Real from the highlands to Nicaragua. In the 17th century the town was repeatedly sacked by pirates, belying its peaceful nature today. With grand larceny now out of favour, only the relative quiet of the place is likely to hold you.

Refugio Nacional Silvestre Peñas Blancas
ⓘ *T2460-0055. Getting to the refuge is difficult without private transport. Leave the Pan-American Highway 11 km north of Esparza heading to Miramar, where there is some simple accommodation. From here, a 14-km track leads east, then north to Peñas Blancas via Sabana Bonita. Alternatively, leave the Pan-American Highway east of Esparza at Macacona, and head north direct to Peñas Blancas. There is a trail to the refuge leaving from Peñas Blancas, but you should take a good topographical map. There are no services in the park but camping is permitted so it's a good opportunity for wilderness camping despite the denuded landscape.*

Peñas Blancas National Wildlife Refuge is one of the quieter protected areas of Costa Rica. Created to protect the regional watershed, the 2400-ha reserve has distinctive, rugged volcanic terrain and white rock deposits of diatomite – a white, porous sedimentary rock composed of algae skeletal deposits. Covering altitudes from 600-1200 m, there are areas of tropical dry, semi-deciduous and at higher elevations, premontane moist forest. The region was selectively logged before gaining protected status, but visitors still enjoy the birds and butterflies in the region, and you may even see peccaries, pacas or red brocket deer.

To Monteverde and Santa Elena

From the Pan-American Highway at **Rancho Grande**, just after crossing the Río Aranjuez, a bumpy, dramatic and at times very scenic route heads north, climbing to Santa Elena and Monteverde. Alternatively take a slightly longer, but better, road leaving the highway at Yomale (Km 149), just south of the Río Lagarto. ▸▸ *For further information, see page 190.*

Juntas de Abangares → *Colour map 1, B5.*

Crossing the provincial border and entering Guanacaste proper, a good road leads to Juntas de Abangares, a small town with a population just short of 10,000, that briefly came to fame in the late 19th century when gold finds attracted prospectors to the town. A century on, a few prospectors still mine for gold, but the main attraction, aside from basic accommodation and refreshments, is a mining museum at **La Sierra de Abangares** ⓘ *daily 0600-1800, US$2*, with mining artefacts from the boom times, including the ruins, or *mazos*, of an old stamping mill, used to crush the ore, which has a distinctly Mayan architectural style. Around the mill there are many trails providing good opportunities for seeing some of the 90 species of birds that have been identified in the area. Buses leave Cañas for Juntas at 0900 and 1400.

This also makes for a good alternative driving route (4WD strongly recommended) to Santa Elena and Monteverde for those using the Tempisque ferry or coming south from Guanacaste.

About 4 km further north of the turn-off from the Pan-American Highway to Juntas, a left turn goes to the new **Friendship Bridge**, a time-saving gift from Taiwan, cutting the travel time to the peninsula by hours.

Cañas → *Colour map 1, B5.*

Hot and dusty, the town of Cañas (population 18,136) is the first settlement of any real size heading north along the Pan-American Highway. There's a modern, but nevertheless rather grubby, church and very little else to detain you for long. The town has a deserted, windswept feel. There are several places of interest nearby, though, and for the traveller arriving from the north, Cañas is the cut-through to Tilarán inland with connections to Fortuna and Arenal volcano, and Santa Elena/Monteverde. It's also the best way to Tenorio Volcano National Park and on to Upala in the northern lowlands if travelling by bus.

Around Cañas

Rafting on Río Corobicí and Bebedero Flowing from the upper slopes of Tenorio volcano, the Río Corobicí which lower down becomes the Bebedero, is bordered with gallery forest of ceiba, palm and guanacaste trees, where you can catch glimpses of iguanas, monkeys and crocodiles. Birds are also very much in evidence: there's a fair chance of spotting parrots, aracaris, mots-mots and kingfishers and occasionally, if you are lucky, ospreys and jabirú.

The slow-running rivers are ideal for gentle floats, a more relaxing alternative to high-adrenaline whitewater river runs elsewhere, and far more conducive to watching nature. **Safaris Corobicí** ① *4 km past Cañas on the Pan-American Highway, 25 m south of the entrance to Hacienda La Pacífica, T2669-2091, greggdean@msn.com,* offer float tours down the Río Corobicí, US$37 per person for two-hour rafting, US$60 for a half day, including lunch.

Las Pumas ① *Behind Safaris Corobicí, T2669-6044, www.laspumas.org. Entrance is free, but donations are welcome and the bigger the better – details on the website. Open 0800-1700.* Las Pumas is a small private animal rescue centre specializing in looking after big cats, including margays, pumas and jaguars. As with many rescue centres in Costa Rica, the animals end up here as a result of some mishap, misfortune or tragic circumstance which would prevent survival in the wild. You may even have seen some of them before – they're no strangers to the small screen nature documentary, but we don't want to give away any of the camera tricks here.

Parque Nacional Volcán Tenorio → *Colour map 1, B5.*
① *T2695-5180. Taking a bus from San José or Cañas, 7 km north of Cañas on the Pan-American Highway, Highway 6 heads northeast for 34 km to Bijagua, in the saddle between Tenorio and Miravalles volcanoes.*
Established in 1995, Tenorio Volcano National Park is one of the country's newest national parks. With improved infrastructure since 1997, largely afforded by the development of the nearby town of Bijuagua, lying in the saddle between Tenorio and Miravalles volcanoes, the park has become a popular destination for hiking and trekking. The park protects the watershed of Tenorio Volcano (1916 m) as part of the Cordillera de Guanacaste and 12,871 ha of mixed forest including tracts of primary forest and dry tropical forest. Trails are still developing in the park, and with only basic services and lodging options available, it's a rewarding trip for the hardy. The most accessible trail leads from **Heliconias Lodge** (see page 213), but you can head for the crater lake, after taking local advice, along trails through cloudforest to the summit with views of Arenal volcano, Lake Nicaragua, and the northern lowlands. You can soak in natural hot springs, and visit the Río Celeste, with heavenly blue waters created by mineral deposits in the rock.

Bagaces and Volcán Miravalles → *Colour map 1, B4.*
Continuing along the Pan-American Highway, the small town of Bagaces (population 8000) set back from the road seems blissfully ignorant of the international traffic that thunders up and down the Highway. There's not much to see in town and the main reason to visit today is to finalize plans for a trip to Palo Verde National Park or the smaller Lomas Barbudal Biological Reserve (see below).

Three kilometres north of the road to Palo Verde National Park, a road leads to **Llanos de Cortés waterfall**, with a 10-m drop into a great swim hole – a great day trip if you've got transport. Route 164 heads north from town climbing slowly to the town of **Guayabo** with thermal pools nearby. It is a good spot for hiking to Miravalles Volcano, the highest peak in the Cordillera de Guanacaste at 2028 m. Services in the area are limited – ask at hotels for details. Continuing north, the road eventually leads to Aguas Claras and San José. The nearby **hot springs** complex of **Yoko** is popular for an evening's soak and hiking trails lead to mineral springs.

Parque Nacional Palo Verde → *Colour map 1, B4.*

ⓘ *Information from the office in Bagaces, T2671-1290 or on T2524-0607, www.ots.ac.cr. The Costa Rican National Park office is open 0800-1600. Entrance is US$10. Services are limited with most people arranging to visit through the Organization for Tropical Studies (OTS). Getting to the park is only realistically possible in a private vehicle or as part of a tour. The road leaves the Pan-American Highway close to Bagaces, from where a 4WD makes the last 28 km to the Palo Verde Station. A taxi from Bagaces is a viable option.*

At the northernmost limits of the Gulf of Nicoya, the plains of the Tempisque River are protected by Palo Verde National Park, covering 18,418 ha – an area slightly smaller than Washington DC in the United States. Subject to extensive seasonal flooding, the park has the largest concentration of waterfowl and wading birds in Central America. Add a blend of geological foundations incorporating limestone outcrops and sedimentary and volcanic deposits, and the region is one of the most diverse parks in the country. Twelve habitats have been recognized including freshwater and saltwater lagoons, marshes, grasslands, black mangrove swamp forests and deciduous and evergreen dry tropical forest.

Over 150 species of tree have been recorded in the park including the namesake palo verde or horse bean, with green leaves, branches and trunk. The bird species count of resident and migrating species is around 300, and includes herons, storks, grebes, ibis and the northern jacana. The park is the only nesting site of the jabirú in Costa Rica. Not to be outdone, land-based species also put on a pretty good show; you may well see peccaries, white-tailed deer, howler, spider and white-faced monkeys, turtles and crocodiles.

Activities in the national park are developing slowly. There are several trails with good lookout points across the Tempisque Basin and the lowlands from limestone outcrops, leading from the **Palo Verde Biological Station**, owned and operated by the Organization for Tropical Studies. You can take a half-day guided walk for US$15, or strike out on your own along the trails for nature- and birdwatching. Lodging and food, with advanced booking, is available. Boat tours (US$25), mountain biking (US$2 half day, US$5 full day) and night tours (US$29-US$22.50, depending on numbers) that seek out one of the five species of cat found in the park, can be organized with advance notice.

Reserva Biológica Lomas Barbudal → *Colour map 1, B4.*

ⓘ *For information drop in at the reserve office in Bagaces, or call T2671-1290 or T2200-0125. Donation requested for entrance to the park. The 4WD track for Lomas Barbudal is just over 10 km west of Bagaces, along the Pan-American Highway, close to the town of Pijije. The reserve administration office, with a small information centre, is 6 km down a poor road on the banks overlooking the Río Cabuyo. This road continues, eventually joining the road to Palo Verde National Park.*

Close to the northern limits of Palo Verde National Park, Lomas Barbudal Biological Reserve protects precious tree species endangered in much of the rest of the country. Around 70% of the reserve is deciduous forest and includes mahogany, rosewood and the spectacular cortez tree, which blooms in a riot of colour a few days after a rain shower in the dry season. Many of the rivers flow throughout the year creating gallery forest in addition to grassy savannahs and extremely dry forest that supports cacti and bromeliads.

Lomas Barbudal is also home to over 130 bird species including the scarlet macaw and great curassow, as well as coatis, howler and white-faced capuchin monkeys. The reserve's great claim to fame, however, is the unusual richness of its insect life. Some 250 species have been counted to date, including the Africanized bee.

Liberia → *Colour map 1, B3.*

The White City of Liberia (population 36,407), as the city is known in Costa Rica, stands out brightly just off the junction of the Pan-American Highway with Highway 21 to the Nicoya Peninsula. While it may be provincial capital, transport and commercial hub and the largest city in northern Costa Rica, don't expect high rise and hot dogs – it has evolved perfectly to survive the blazing temperatures that bake Guanacaste in the dry season.

The white, mainly single-storey buildings are designed to reflect the heat. On many of the older buildings a section of wall either side of a corner is replaced by large doors. When left open this distinctive *puerta del sol* allows warmth and ventilation to move freely through the house. Nobody ventures out at high noon, giving the town a deserted feel if you turn up around midday, but rise with the sun, or take an early evening stroll, and the streets gently swagger to life.

Liberia has just enough older buildings in the surrounding blocks to give it a colonial feel, but you won't find them around the central plaza, with its rather unattractive but impressive triangular modern church, where romantics and promenaders emerging from the shadows gather in the cool breeze at the end of the day. There's not a lot to do in town, beyond stocking up on supplies if travelling, and preparing for or relaxing after a

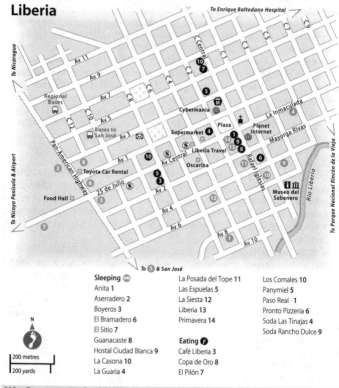

Liberia

To Enrique Baltodano Hospital

To Nicaragua

Av 11
Av 9
Av 7
Regional Buses
Av 5
Buses to San José
Av 3
Av 1
Av Central
Oscarina
Av 2
25 de Julio

Cybermania @
Plaza
Planet Internet @
Supermarket
Liberia Travel
Toyota Car Rental
Food Hall

Pan-American Highway
To Nicoya Peninsula & Airport

La Inmaculada
Mayorga Rivas
Rafael Iglesias
Rio Liberia
Museo del Sabanero

To Parque Nacional Rincón de la Vieja

Av 4
Av 6
Av 8
Av 10

To & San José

N
200 metres
200 yards

Sleeping
Anita **1**
Aserradero **2**
Boyeros **3**
El Bramadero **6**
El Sitio **7**
Guanacaste **8**
Hostal Ciudad Blanca **9**
La Casona **10**
La Guaria **4**

La Posada del Tope **11**
Las Espuelas **5**
La Siesta **12**
Liberia **13**
Primavera **14**

Eating
Café Liberia **3**
Copa de Oro **8**
El Pilón **7**

Los Comales **10**
Panymiel **5**
Paso Real **1**
Pronto Pizzeria **6**
Soda Las Tinajas **4**
Soda Rancho Dulce **9**

trip to Rincon de la Vieja National Park. South of town the **Museo del Sabanero** ⓘ *C 1, Av 6, museum and tourist office open 0800-1200, 1300-1700 Mon-Sat, closed Sun, hours very irregular*, has a rather disappointing smattering of artefacts and memorabilia in tribute to the horsemen of the plains. A privately run **tourist office** ⓘ *T2666 1606*, shares the building with the museum. The staff are helpful, knowledgeable and speak English, although the information is not always accurate and staff struggle to stay open for the hours claimed.

◉ North to Liberia listings

For Sleeping and Eating price codes and other relevant information, see Essentials, pages 44-47.

◎ Sleeping

Esparza *p208*
D Hotel Río Mar. A good choice in Barranca with bath and restaurant.
E Hotel Castañuelas, T2635-5105, hotel castanuelas@racsa.co.cr. Quiet place with a/c and the most comfortable option.
F pp **Pensión Córdoba**,
T2635-5014. Clean and modern.

Cañas *p209*
B Nuevo Hotel Cañas, C 2, Av 3, just round the corner from El Corral, T2669-0039. A popular choice with good rooms, swimming pool and a jacuzzi.
C El Corral, on the Pan-American Highway, T2669-1467. The most upmarket choice in town with a/c, private bath and restaurant.
F Cabinas Corobicí, Av 2, C 5, 200 m east of the church, T2669-0241. 11 good rooms with bath, parking available.

Around Cañas *p209*
AL Hacienda La Pacifica, www.pacifica cr.com. A working ranch with rustic rooms. A truly memorable experience, even if they are still having a few start-up teething troubles.
C Capazuri, a couple of kilometres north of Cañas on the Pan-American Highway, T2669-0580, capazuri@racsa.co.cr. Simple, uninspiring rooms, with private bath and a couple of fans, breakfast included. The place is primarily a *Tico* family resort and has a pool. Also options for **camping**, US$5 per person.

Parque Nacional Volcán Tenorio *p210*
AL-A pp **La Carolina**, 6 km north of Bijagua, take the gravel road signposting Santo Domingo and La Carolina Lodge for 6 km, T8380-1656, www.lacarolinalodge.com. Set on a 70-ha working ranch, this is the most comfortable option for visiting the Río Celeste mineral pools and trekking through the hills of Tenorio Volcano. 4 bedrooms, 3 for a couple and 1 for up to 7 people, right on the river. The price is all-inclusive, with 3 meals, guided treks, horse riding (children under 12 half price). Home cooking and juices made from the lodge's own citrus groves and dairy farm. Other local tours are easily arranged.
AL-B Heliconias Lodge, about 3 km out of Bijagua on the flanks of Tenorio. A simple lodge with 6 cabins, sleeping 2-4 people, each with bathroom and hot water, price includes breakfast. The lodge is part of the Cooprena, network, who specialize in community-based tourism, T2286-4203, www.turismoruralcr.com. Tours can be arranged to Río Celeste, Tenorio and Miravalles volcanos and waterfalls in the area.

Bagaces and Volcán Miravalles *p210*
E Las Brisas, Guayabo, T2673-0333. Simple accommodation with hot water, bath and fans.
E Parador Las Nubes del Miravalles, at Km 30, T2671-1011 (ext 280). With tents and mattresses for hire and horse riding.

Parque Nacional Palo Verde *p211*
A pp **Palo Verde Station**, T2661-4717, www.ots.ac.cr. Rustic dorm rooms.

Liberia *p212, map p212*

AL Las Espuelas, 2 km south of town on the Pan-American Highway, T2666-0144, www.bestwestern.com. With pool.

AL El Sitio, a short distance down Highway 21 towards Nicoya, T2666-1211, www.bestwestern.com. With pool.

AL-A Boyeros, on the Pan-American Highway at the entrance to town, T2666-0722, www.hotelboyeros.com. 70 rooms with balcony or terrace, a/c, bath and telephone, children under 10 free. Good restaurant, pool and ample parking.

A-B El Bramadero, T2666-0371, www.hotel elbramadero.com. 23 rooms, all with private bath, a/c and television, in a lively spot right on the Pan-American Highway – popular with business folk. Pool and restaurant.

B La Guaria, a couple of blocks east of the plaza, C 3-5, T2666-0000. Clean, tidy and central, pretty standard with a small pool at the back. Good secure parking.

B Primavera, south side of the main plaza, T2666-0464. Clean and tidy in a great location right on the main square, but set slightly off the main road, so quiet.

B Hostal Ciudad Blanca, Av 4, C 1-3, on the southwestern side of town, T2666-3962. 12 pleasant but grubby rooms with a/c, private bath, hot water and telephone. A small snack-style restaurant and bar serves local food. Fine building, but erratic service.

B-C Hotel del Aserradero, on the Pan-American Highway and Av 3, T2666-1939, abalto@racsa.co.cr. 16 spacious room in a converted old lumber mill is with private bath, fans, with some good touches. Plenty of parking, a breezy charm in the reception, reflecting the helpful nature of the owners.

B-C La Siesta, C 4, Av 4-6, a couple of blocks south of the main plaza, T2666-0678, lasiestaliberia@hotmail.com. 24 clean rooms with bathrooms, a restaurant, small pool and good service, close to the centre of town, this place stands out as a good option.

C Guanacaste, C 12, Av 3, just round the corner from the bus stations, T2666-0085, www.higuanacaste.com. Clean and friendly, simple rooms most with bath, but nothing special. Credit cards accepted. Cheap snack restaurant, money changing, parking and handy for buses. Part of the Costa Rica youth hostelling, it's a good source of information, and organizes tours to Rincón de la Vieja, including a daily shuttle service.

D-E Liberia, just a half block south of the plaza, T2666-0161. 22 basic rooms, some with private bath, in an old house, with a small café for snacks, laundry facilities and a good information board. Was once a good deal and will be again when given a new coat of paint.

D-F La Posada del Tope, C Rafael Iglesias, 1½ blocks south from church, T2666-3876. Selection of rooms of varying quality, with cold showers, and a host of useful services. Small patio ideal for resting, chatting and planning your next trip. Laundry facilities, baggage storage, good deal with Adobe car rentals and the list goes on. The owner Dennis is very helpful, has good information on visiting Rincón de la Vieja National Park and arranges transport for trips to the park. He also has a telescope for stargazing. A good budget choice.

E La Casona, Av 6, C Rafael Iglesias, T2666-2971. Rooms (those facing street can get hot) for up to 4 people with shared bath and washing facilities. It's a good choice for longer stopovers.

F Anita, C 4, Av 8, T2666-1285. Simple cheap but clean rooms. Snacks served on the tiny terrace. A little chaotic at times, but friendly. Parking available.

🍴 Eating

Esparza *p208*

Mirador Enis, a short distance beyond Esparza. A bar-restaurant that is a popular stop for tour buses breaking a journey with fruit stalls nearby, before the left turn at Barranca for Puntarenas, 15 km.

Cañas p209

Ħ-Ħ Hacienda La Pacífica, 6 km north of Cañas on the Pan-American Highway, T2669-0050. A fine restaurant decorated with ranching memorabilia, part of a former working ranch.

Central, on main square in town. One of several good Chinese restaurants.

Rincón Corobicí, on the banks of the Corobicí, T2669-0544. Clean and pleasant spot to stop with the small Las Pumas zoo and rafting down Río Corobicí with Safaris Corobici nearby.

Liberia p212, map p212

Ħ Paso Real, on south side of plaza, T2666-3455. Open 1100-2200 daily. Exquisite seafood and meat dishes, lively with a friendly atmosphere, efficient service and great food.

Ħ El Bramadero, part of the Hotel Bramadero on the Pan-American Highway. A popular spot with grills, breakfast from 0630 and a lively bar in the evenings.

Ħ Panymiel, Av Central/C8 and Av 3, C 2. Bakery, snacks and drinks.

Ħ Pronto Pizzeria, C 1, Av 4. Good food (not just pizzas) in a charming colonial house.

Ħ Copa de Oro, next to Hotel Liberia. One of several good Chinese restaurants in town, huge dishes, good value.

Ħ Soda Las Tinajas, on the west side of the Plaza, 1000-2330 daily. A great little open-air restaurant looking out on the plaza, specializing in *refrescos*. Looking scruffy, but just about staying open.

Ħ Soda Rancho Dulce, just off the main square. Pleasant outdoor *soda*, where you can watch the world drift.

Ħ Los Comales, C Central, Av 5-7. Open 0630-2100 daily. Three cheers for women's cooperatives. 25 women have got together to improve their own lives and in the process produce great traditional *guanacasteco* dishes. Good, wholesome, filling traditional food, and growing in popularity. Second branch on C 8, Av Central-1, 3 blocks east of the plaza.

Ħ El Pilon, C Central, Av 5-7, great lunch time spot, very popular with locals, and you won't have to eat again.

Ħ Café Liberia, C 8, Av Central-2, superb coffee shop, with a good selection of snacks and excellent coffee.

⊕ Entertainment

Liberia p212, map p212
CCM Cinema, in the Plaza Liberia, 2 km south of town on the Pan-American Highway. Shows current international movies.

⊛ Festivals and events

Liberia p212, map p212
25 Jul Guanacaste Day, the town celebrates annexation to Costa Rica with colourful parades, bullfights, a rodeo, music and general frivolity.

O Shopping

Liberia p212, map p212
Oscarina, C 4, Av C-2, T2666-7833. Daily 0830-1830. A good one-stop shop if you're looking for a selection of gifts, including T-shirts, ceramics and cigars.
Mini Galería Fulvia, on the main plaza. Sells the *Tico Times*, English papers and books. English spoken, and helpful.

▲ Activities and tours

Liberia p212, map p212
Liberia Travel, on the corner of Av Central and C 4, 1st floor, T2666-4772. Will confirm flights for a small fee. Most of the hotels can arrange tours to local areas including Rincón de la Vieja National Park.
Posada del Tope, C Rafael Iglesias, 1/2 block south of church. Can organize tours and assist with inquiries.

⊖ Transport

Cañas *p209*

Most buses depart from the terminal 500 m north of the centre, except for those to San José, which leave from the Pan-American Highway. Buses from **San José**, depart from C 16, Av 1-3, 8 daily from 0830, 3 hrs, US$3.30, Transportes La Cañera, T2669-0145. To **Liberia**, 7 daily from 0545, 1 hr, US$1.50. To **Puntarenas**, 7 daily from 0600, US$3.20. To **Upala**, 5 daily from 0500, 1¾ hrs, US$1.80. To **Juntas de Abangares**, 2 daily at 0900 and 1450, 1 hr, US$1.50. If going to Arenal volcano and Fortuna or Santa Elena and Monteverde, take the bus to **Tilarán**, 8 daily from 0600, 45 mins, US$1.30, and catch a connection from there. If driving, the turn-off for Tilarán is east at the filling station, no signs.

Liberia *p212, map p212*
Air

Daniel Oduber Quirós International Airport is 13 km from Liberia along Highway 21.

Bus

Buses from **San José** leave the capital from C 14, Av 1-3, with an hourly service from 0600 until 2000, 4 hrs, US$5. Buses arrive and leave for San José from Av 5, C 10-12. Local buses leave from the local terminal at C 12, Av 7-9. Liberia to **Playa del Coco**, 7 daily, 0530-1830, 1½ hrs, US$0.85. To **Playa Hermosa** and **Playa Panama**, 5 daily from 0545 to 1730, 1½ hrs, US$0.80. To **Puntarenas**, 7 daily, 0500-1530, 4 hrs, US$3.70. To **Bagaces/ Cañas**, 4 daily, 0545-1710 (but you can take any bus heading down the Pan-American Highway). To **Cañas Dulces**, 3 daily, 0600-1730. To **La Cruz/Peñas Blanca**, 7 daily 0530-1800, US$1.50. To **Filadelfia-Santa Cruz-Nicoya**, 20 daily, 0500-2020.

Car hire

Sol, T2666-2222, solcar@racsa.co.cr, and **Toyota**, T2666-7193, www.toyotarent.com. Car hire agencies offer a range of similar vehicles for roughly the same prices. A Toyota Rav 4 works out at US$60 a day in the dry season, US$48 in the green season, plus insurance (roughly US$20 a day). The weekly rate is US$320 plus US$140 insurance. If you want to cover a lot of ground, you can drop the vehicles off at other offices for an extra US$50.

Taxi

Taxis leave from the northern side of the main square and can be useful for local trips including nearby National Parks, generally US$40-50.

ⓘ Directory

Cañas *p209*
Banks There are a couple of banks in town, including a branch of **Banco Nacional**. **Post office** Next to Hotel El Corral on the Pan-American Highway.

Liberia *p212, map p212*
Banks Banco Popular and Bancrecer both have Visa ATMs. Banco de Costa Rica is on the main plaza. Credomatic, Av Central, MasterCard ATM. If all the banks are closed, try the Hotel Guanacaste for money exchange. **Hospitals** Enrique Baltodano Hospital, T2666-0011. **Internet** Ciberm@nia, north side of main plaza in the shopping mall, US$1 hr, open 0800-2200 daily. Can also make very cheap international calls. Planet Internet, ½ block south of the cathedral. Good fast machines, a/c, US$1.20 per hr, open 0800-2200. **Pharmacies** Several pharmacies close to main plaza. **Post office** At Av 3 and C 8.

North of Liberia

The Pan-American Highway continues north from Liberia to the border with Nicaragua passing a patchwork of protected reserves and parks in the heart of Guanacaste. Rincón de la Vieja National Park provides a host of geothermal curiosities for the active explorer, Santa Rosa National Park protects some of the last stands of dry tropical forest and there are plenty of smaller places to visit.
➤ For listings, see pages 224-226.

Parque Nacional Rincón de la Vieja ●● ➤➤ pp224-226. Colour map 1, A4.

ⓘ Entrance to the park is US$10. Now closed on Mon for maintenance. Check status before travelling. There are 2 routes into the park: the southern route, which has less traffic, goes from Puente La Victoria on the western side of Liberia and leads, in about 25 km, to the Santa María sector, closest to the hot springs. The northern route goes to the Las Pailas sector, turning off the Pan-American Highway 5 km northwest of Liberia, passing Cañón de la Vieja Lodge to Curubandé (no public transport on this route at present). The two sectors are linked by a trail. Beyond Curubandé, you reach Posada El Encuentro, cross the private property of Hacienda Lodge Guachipelín (US$2 for road maintenance), and beyond is Rincón de la Vieja Mountain Lodge.

Formed by the simultaneous eruption of several volcanic cones which eventually merged to become one, Rincón de la Vieja National Park now protects 14,161 ha of territory ideal for hiking, and is definitely worth visiting for a few days. The main attraction is the steaming mud pools, hot springs, steam vents and waterfalls in the area which also hosts a rewarding wildlife display in its elevated isolation. Hiking to the summit provides splendid views (on rare, clear days) across the lowlands. The massif, which rises to a height of 1916 m at Santa María volcano, is visible from Liberia when the peak is not shrouded in cloud, and the lower summit of Rincón de la Vieja (1806 m) can be reached on a two-day trek.

Meaning 'Old Lady's Corner', according to Guatuso legend an old witch living on the eastern slopes of Rincón de la Vieja sends smoke skyward whenever she is annoyed. She still gets the hump and last threw really big tantrums in 1995 and 1998, sending ash clouds as far west as Santa Rosa National Park and mudflows down the northern slopes.

Sights For the most part, the park is a calm collection of different ecosystems or lifezones, changing gradually with altitude. The park was created to protect the multitude of rivers and streams that find their source on the volcanic slopes. Four lifezones and over 250 species of birds, including the three-wattled bellbird and great currasow, as well as howler monkeys, armadillos and coatis, ticks and other biting insects are found within the boundaries.

Most places of interest are easily reached from either of the Las Pailas or Santa María Hacienda rangers' stations, which are linked by a path. A number of trails ranging from 1-8 km in length, lead from both stations with inspiring names like the 'Enchanted Forest' and the 'Hidden Falls', leading to thermal pools, mudpots and fumaroles. The area is also home to the greatest density of Costa Rica's national flower the *guaria morada* or purple orchid. Some trails to more sensitive areas may have restricted access.

Towards the summit, the windy conditions have stunted the growth of the forest. Nearby, the **Laguna Jilueros** is reported to be a good site for spotting wildlife.

Parque Nacional Santa Rosa ⊜ ⨠ p224-226. *Colour map 1, A2.*

Santa Rosa National Park holds a coveted place in the hearts of *Tico* and international visitors for its historical and natural importance. Tucked in the northwestern corner of Costa Rica, the 38,674-ha national park has grown to encompass the entire Santa Elena Peninsula and now protects, with the Murciélago Sector to the north, the largest area of dry tropical forest in Central America.

The historical significance of the region is also an essential part of *Tico* identity. As early as 1663 the land was prized for cattle raising with the founding of a ranch in the area. In the 1850s, the prying eyes of US filibuster William Walker saw the Santa Rosa Hacienda – La Casona – as an essential foothold for his imperialist ideals to take over and reunite Central America. After a brief but fierce battle at La Casona, impassioned Costa Ricans ousted Walker's forces after what was to be the greatest threat to the recently created independent republic. The park and the house have become an essential visit for every *Tico*. A more recent threat to La Casona saw the historic building almost destroyed by fire in May of 2001 – its restoration is now complete and the new building as good as the old.

Wildlife The immediate appeal of the park is the abundant and relatively easy to see wildlife. During the dry season from November to May, the mainly deciduous trees shed their leaves and the animals depend on shrinking water holes until they dry up completely. Descending from the park's upper reaches, the open dry tropical forest makes it easier to spot the fleeing white-tailed deer and the dozing howler, spider and white-faced monkeys found within the park, but keep expectations realistic. In coastal regions, mangrove swamp is the predominant vegetation. Between August and December on **Playa Nancite**, the phenomenon of the *arribada* involves thousands of Olive Ridley turtles arriving on the beach in an orgy of collective reproduction. South along the coastline, **Playa Naranjo** is one of Costa Rica's most beautiful beaches, a surfing mecca, and one of the hardest to reach – the sight of a near-deserted beach of golden sand is a just reward for a sterling effort.

To the north the **Murciélago Sector**, reached through Cuajiniquil, protects over 70 species of bat found in this part of the park.

La Casona Arching roof ridges and straining beams once took the tremendous weight of both the century-old tiles and the history bestowed upon this unassuming hacienda building that has been at the crux of Costa Rican history. First records show the property was created in 1663, but the strategic significance of the region was bought to the fore by the north American William Walker. An advocate of slavery, Walker believed the independent aspirations of Central America had strayed too far from the interests of its northern neighbour. Having walked into Nicaragua and gained the presidency, Walker's attention turned to its southern neighbour Costa Rica. His attempts to conquer Costa Rica were founded on, and floundered, at La Casona.

The Costa Ricans, under the leadership of José María Cañas, defeated Walker's band of filibusters on the afternoon of 20 March 1856. The strategic significance of the area was reinforced again in 1919 when troops marched from Nicaragua to overthrow President Federico Tinoco, and again in 1955 during the presidency of José Figueres Ferrer 'Don Pepe'. On both occasions the invading troops were defeated.

The arson attack of May 2001, by a couple of vengeful hunters angry that hunting was banned in the park, completely destroyed the collection of military paraphernalia and exhibits recording the lifestyle and events that took place at La Casona. The structure was

UNESCO recognition for Guanacaste conservation

In the world of conservation, the Guanacaste Conservation Area (ACG) is a beacon of hope and in 1999 was created a UNESCO Natural World Heritage Site. The creation of the Santa Rosa National Park in 1971 saw a shift away from ranching to conservation for the coastal region, which was complemented by the creation of the Guanacaste and Rincón de la Vieja National Parks. The creation of the Rincón Cacao Biological Corridor added the final piece of a migratory corridor that incorporates nine of the 12 Holdridge lifezones found in Costa Rica, leading from the Pacific to the 1916-m

volcanic peak at Rincón de la Vieja. Official estimates say the region protects some 235,000 species – more than in the entire of north America.

Proving that conservation is an ongoing process, work goes on to protect more of the area and add to the migratory corridor. The rainforest to the north of Rincón de la Vieja is available for purchase and the ACG is seeking support and donations. Contact them on T2666-5051, Apdo 169-5000, Liberia, Guanacaste, Costa Rica, or visit the Rincón Rainforest Campaign at www.acguanacaste.ac.cr.

reconstructed using money raised through private donations from *Ticos* outraged at such a sacrilegious act. Restoring La Casona to its former glory was an impossible dream, but the inclusion of original features such as the late 19th-century roof tiles salvaged from the flames have added a historical aura to an otherwise sterile replica. Behind the hacienda here are good views across the surrounding area.

Treks and trails A number of short trails lead out from the administration area and a detailed trail map is available at the entrance. Behind the Casona, the short **Indio Desnudo** (naked Indian) nature trail (1 km), takes a loop through fine stands of dry tropical forest with the red peeling bark of the gumbo limbo tree, with annotated signposts. The **Tierras Emergidas** trail runs parallel to the entrance road. The longest sensible one-day trek is to **Mirador Valle Naranjo**, some 6 km from the administration buildings.

Longer treks to **Playa Naranjo** and **Playa Nancite** (see box, page 222) require an overnight stay and should be booked with the administration offices. (There is a 4WD track leading to both beaches, but do not rely on being able to use it.) The trail descends gently over 12 km, moving slowly through dry tropical forest and a multitude of butterflies. By the time you've reached the lower altitudes, your eye will be well trained in spotting the iguanas, crabs and monkeys that are very much in evidence. With luck, you may even see green macaws, white-lipped pecaries, tapirs and possibly pumas, which are reported to be increasing in number in the park. A left fork leads to Playa Naranjo, the right to Playa Nancite, a restricted area that receives thousands of breeding Olive Ridley turtles. Heading south to Naranjo is the brackish **Limbo Lagoon** home to the American crocodile. The beach itself is awesome; stretching for miles around the bay and will probably be deserted. That said, it's a popular surfing spot, and out in the bay, is the surfing mecca of **Witches' Rock** – one of the oldest geological formations in Costa Rica at 680 million years old. Even so you'll still have the place to yourself. At the southern end of the Limbo Lagoon is the 6-km Carbonal trail taking in dry forest and mangroves; back on the access road to the north of the lagoon is the 3-km Los Patos trail with good panoramic views.

Murciélago Sector ① *Access to the sector is 10 km north of the Santa Rosa main entrance taking the good road heading west towards Cuajiniquil. Buses leave Liberia for Cuajiniquil a 0545 and 1530, returning at 0700 and 0430.* The annexation of the Murciélago Sector to th north incorporates the whole of the Santa Elena peninsula within the park boundaries While access to this section of the park is more difficult, it is possible to camp at the entrance to the park and there are several trails. It is possible to get out to **Playa Blanc** in the dry season in a 4WD, but at other times of year you will need permission from park authorities. This small beach with its pristine white sand is one of the most isolate and beautiful beaches in Costa Rica and is also one of the safest bathing areas in the region

Close to Cuajiniquil is the airstrip built by Oliver North during the 1980s to supply the Nicaraguan Contras. It was built on a property formerly owned by the Nicaraguan leade Somosa before it was purchased for the national park. The **Bahía Junquillal Wildlif Refuge** is also part of the national park. It's a popular spot with local families and ha

Guanacaste Conservation Area

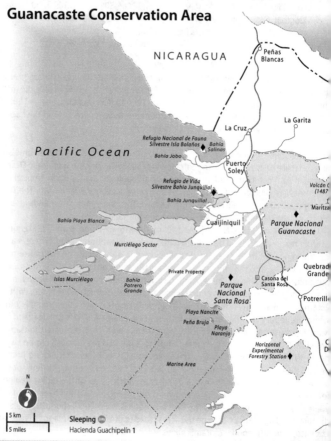

facilities for **camping**. A dirt road continues north eventually reaching the **Bahía de Salinas** – a 4WD vehicle is essential in the wet season.

Parque Nacional Guanacaste ›› *Colour map 1, A3.*

ⓘ *For all enquiries contact park administration at the Tropical Dry Forest Investigation Center, T2666-5051, www.acguanacaste.ac.cr. Entrance to the park is US$10. The park is open 24 hours, but the entrance may be barred to traffic before 0800 and after 1600. The park entrance sells maps, bird lists, a small brochure and museum guide. Entrance to Playa Nancite is carefully controlled and restricted to permit holders. Apply to the park authorities for a permit – but expect most permits to be taken by researchers during the mass turtle nestings.*

The lynchpin of the Guanacaste Conservation Area, Guanacaste National Park was created in 1991 to protect large expanses of dry and humid tropical forest. Linking two older national parks, it protects 34,651 ha, in an area covering Orosí volcano and the summit of Cacao volcano (1659 m). As with Santa Rosa National Park, the area has a history of cattle ranching but is now very conscious of the fact that ecotourists are likely to provide a more sustainable income than ranching ever could.

Lago de Nicaragua

Santa Cecilia

Brasilla

Birmania

Rincon Rainforest Reserve

ncón Cacao Biological Corridor

Seebock (895m)▲

Volcán Rincón de la Vieja (1806m)

arque Nacional ncón de la Vieja

▲ Volcán Santa María (1916m)

Colonia Blanca

Las Pailas

Santa María

avista

San Jorge

Curubande

ría

To San José

Ins and outs This is easiest by private vehicle, following the Pan-American Highway north of Liberia for 32 km, then heading west at the signpost to the park, down the 8 km entrance road. By public transport any bus travelling between Liberia and La Cruz will drop you off at the entrance, from where, with luck, you can hitch a ride with someone entering the park. If not, it's a pleasant walk, and if the road is quiet you may even see wildlife.

Services in the park are limited, with three biological stations – Cacao, Maritza and Pitilla – providing simple dormitory accommodation only with advance booking from park administration at Santa Rosa National Park. If visiting, you will probably have to take your own food unless you can make arrangements with park authorities. Trails lead from each of the stations.

Trails and biological stations Maritza Station is the most comfortable, and the closest to the Pan-American highway. Leaving the highway 10 km north of the

Arriving at Playa Nancite – safety in numbers?

Playa Nancite is treasured as the nesting site of three species of sea turtle, the largest at almost 2 m in length being the solitary leatherback and the second largest the green turtle. The smaller Olive Ridley may lose ground on size but makes up for it in numbers, arriving in thousands in an incredible natural phenomenon. At night from August to December, thousands of Olive Ridleys gather in the offshore waters, enduring a mating cycle that lasts up to nine hours. After mating, the turtles arrive in their thousands over a three- to seven-night period each depositing between 90 and 120 eggs that incubate in deep nests for 50 days. After hatching the young struggle to the surface, and cross the beach to the treacherous coastal surf. All manner of terrestrial and marine

predators feast on the young, hence the vast numbers of mating couples in one small space and the number of eggs produced, which give each individual a greater chance of survival. Estimates suggest that at the peak of the *arribadas* (arrivals) as many as 75,000 turtles may nest on the beach, before migrating as far north as Mexico and south to Peru. They return every two or three years.

Researchers at the Santa Rosa Investigation Centre have been studying the phenomenon since it was first discovered in 1972. In recent years, figures suggest the numbers of Olive Ridleys arriving at Nancite are declining – a disappointingly familiar tale – the causes of which remain unknown.

turning for Santa Rosa, opposite the turn for Cuajiniquil. It's 18 km to the station (4WD is recommended throughout the year), from where trails lead through gallery, dry and transitional dry-humid forest. The headwaters of the Tempisque river start close to the station, and to the north the Río Sapoá empties into Lake Nicaragua and eventually the Caribbean. Short trails lead to the petroglyph site close to Cerro El Hacha, you can walk to the summit of Cacao, a long day's walk, or you can hike to the Cacao Field Station.

Higher up at 1100 m above sea level is **Cacao Station**. Temperatures are lower, rainfall slightly higher and this part of the park has areas of transitional dry-humid forest and cloud-forest. Access is from the Pan-American Highway 23 km north of Liberia at Potrerillos. If you want to trek between the park's stations, bear in mind whether you want to start or end in relative comfort: Cacao station is far more basic, and doesn't have electricity.

Pitilla station may be physically close, but access is 28 km along Highway 4 from the junction with the Pan-American Highway, heading south at Santa Cecilia along 9 km of dirt road. It's a different world – the influence of the Caribbean and nearby Lake Nicaragua creating rainforest with patches of regenerating secondary forest in contrast to the predominant dry forest of the region. It is reported to be one of the best spots for birdwatching in the park, but conditions at the lodge are basic, so go prepared.

La Cruz and Bahía Salinas ●❷●❻ ►► *pp225-226. Colour map 1, A3.*

Almost at the end of the road, 19 km short of the border with Nicaragua, La Cruz (population 9412) has little to draw the casual visitor over and above a branch of Banco Popular – the only one for miles. But if you can wangle your arrival for dusk you're guaranteed one of the best sunsets this side of Ursa Minor. The town sits on the edge –

Border essentials: Costa Rica–Nicaragua

Peñas Blancas

From La Cruz it's 19 km to the border with Nicaragua at Peñas Blancas. Over and above immigration and customs, there's only a simple café/restaurant here. For arriving passengers, there is a small Costa Rica Tourist Board (ICT) office which periodically has country maps.

Border opening hours The crossing is open from 0600-2000.

Border formalities If crossing by international bus, formalities are dealt with by the bus driver. If travelling independently, hand over your passport and immigration form to be stamped. Nicaragua immigration is a walk of a few hundred metres, and is straightforward, assuming your documents are in order. There's a bank to change cash, and a bus stop for onward travel in Costa Rica near the Immigration Office.

Crossing by private vehicle Rental vehicles are not permitted to cross the border. Otherwise, just hand over the printed vehicle permit you were given on arrival and complete the necessary paperwork. If you are entering Costa Rica by car, pay your entrance stamp, then go to the **Aduana Permiso de Vehículo** for your vehicle permit (state how long you want it to last). Get insurance at the **Seguro Obligatorio**. Your vehicle is then briefly inspected and fumigated before you are allowed to depart. It doesn't take long, but don't come this way if you're in hurry. For more information, see Transport and Directory, page 226.

literally – of a west-facing steep escarpment overlooking the **Bahía Salinas** with its camping opportunities, a couple of all-inclusive resorts and Isla Bolaños Wildlife Reserve.

West of La Cruz, a good road descends rapidly – and deteriorates equally quickly – passing through old ranch land to Puerto Soley, Bahía Salinas and eventually to the undeveloped beaches of **Jobo** and **Rajada** – which locals claim are the best in the country. One of the quieter corners of Costa Rica, the roads are bad and travelling without private transport can be time-consuming.

With tours provided by the two all-inclusive hotels in the area (see below), it's a good base for families if you want to make the occasional trip. The bay also receives reliable westerly winds so, after Lake Arenal, it's the most important site for **windsurfing** in the country. You can also learn or polish up your **kitesurfing** skills at the Kite Surfing Center (see page 226).

Refugio de Fauna Silvestre Isla Bolaños Sitting in the Salinas Bay, Isla Bolaños Wildlife Refuge is a small island reserve protecting just 25 ha of stunted forest that survives on less that 1500 mm of rain a year – making this one of the driest spots in Costa Rica. But protected status is afforded to this barren land, which rises 81 m above the coastal waters, because it is one of the few known nesting sites of the brown pelican in the country (a colony of 500 or so individuals breed here) and the only known nesting site of the American oystercatcher. You will also see the magnificent and gracefully agile frigatebird. Access to the refuge is restricted – some say denied – but you can walk around the island at low tide. If you wish to visit, contact the **Area de Conservación Guanacaste**, T2666-5051, www.acguanacaste.ac.cr. Boat trips can be organized from Puerto Soley or any of the hotels and campsites surrounding the bay.

For Sleeping and Eating price codes and other relevant information, see Essentials, pages 44-47.

⦿ Sleeping

Parque Nacional Rincón de la Vieja *p217*

Southern access route

C Rinconcito Lodge, T2200-0074, www. rinconcitolodge.com. Basic rooms and cold showers, but a steadily improving option for enjoying the rustic charms of the area. Horseback and trekking guided tours, a canopy tour and trips to waterfalls. Transport can be arranged from Liberia (US$35) and the airport (US$45).

G Santa María Hacienda, 2 km inside the park. Old, spacious and basic but refurbished, only US$4 per person. Bring your own food and bedding, or **camp** (US$2). From the old hacienda you can hike 8 km to the boiling mudpots (*Las Pailas*) and come back the same day; the sulphur springs are on a different trail and only 1 hr away.

Northern access route

Leaving the Pan-American Highway 5 km north of Liberia at Cereceda the road passes through several options including the new Cañón de la Vieja Lodge.

AL Posada El Encuentro, 4.5 km up the road from the Highway, T2848-0616, www. posadaencuentro.com. 6 rooms and suites in this quiet, family-run spot. You can set out for the mountains on horseback or simply relax by the pool. Price includes breakfast served in Encuentro's restaurant.

L-A Hotel Hacienda Guachipelín, further along this road, T2256-8195, www. guachipelin.com. Seemingly in permanent expansion, now with 52 comfortable rooms all with private bath. 3 meals a day adds US$45 to the daily bill. Good range of trips including nature guides and horse riding tours to waterfalls, hot springs and mudpools, tubing, canyoning, cattle herding and

mountain biking. Includes Kazm Cañon, the next step up from a canopy tour, with rappel and Tarzan swings, from The Original Canopy Tour company. More natural adventure park than secluded wilderness hideaway. Prices around US$25-75. Transport from Liberia arranged, US$40 per person round trip).

AL Rincón de la Vieja Mountain Lodge, T2661-8198, www.rincondelaviejalodge.net. Rustic comfort in 49 rooms with private bath. The restaurant serves traditional dishes, with a small bar and a pool. You can use it as a base but most take advantage of the wide range of tours, setting out with guides, on horseback or foot, to explore the waterfalls and scenery of the area.

A Casa Rural Aroma de Campo, T2236-8100, www.aromadecampo.com. Just 6 rooms with bath, pool, and fine international restaurant. Quiet and calm is the order of the day, with the option of taking up some of the thrill tours nearby.

Cañas Dulces

Leaving the Pan-American Highway 11 km north of Liberia at El Muerto, a steep road leads to Cañas Dulces and a couple of options close to the park.

B Buena Vista Lodge, T2661-8158, www. buenavistalodgecr.com. 80 comfortable log and flagstone floor cabins, with stunning views across to the Nicoya Peninsula. You can trek to Rincón de la Vieja in the dry season. There's a mini-adventure park on your door-step in the surrounding forest including a mountain water slide, canopy tour, aerial trail, snake park, horse riding to several large waterfalls and mud and steam baths.

LL Borinquen Mountain Resort and Spa, 21 km from the Highway, T2690-1900, www.borinquenresort.com. Luxury villas and bungalows, plus all mod cons including a/c, minibar and satellite TV. Each has a private balcony looking out to the mountains and surrounding scenery. Wide range of tours and spa treatments available.

Quebrada Grande

Leaving the Pan-American Highway at Potrerillos, 23 km from Liberia, a road heads east to Quebrada Grande in the saddle between Rincón de la Vieja and the smaller Cacao.

B pp Curubanda Lodge, T2691-8177, www.curubanda.com. Seriously rustic accommodation and genuinely traditional food. You won't be seeking comforts staying here but you will have a genuine experience of Costa Rica *guanacasteco*-style. Price includes food and tours.

Parque Nacional Santa Rosa *p218*

Accommodation in the park is limited and primarily aimed at researchers.

D Dormitory accommodation available at the park administration, with a canteen providing food and refreshments.

Dormitory accommodation for up to 20 people is also available at **Playa Nancite**, but take your own food and water.

Camping facilities are available close to the park administration, where tents are shaded under the branches of a huge strangler fig. There is also a small campground at **Playa Naranjo**, take food and enough water for your entire trip as sea water has seeped into the freshwater well. Camping also permitted in the **Murciélago Sector**.

La Cruz *p222*

A Colinas del Norte, on Pan-American Highway 5 km north of La Cruz, T2679-9132. 24 rooms, with private bath, and fan or a/c. A hacienda-style hotel, using hardwood and flagstone flooring throughout. A small pool, disco, and mini golf. Will arrange horse riding tours through the nearby forest.

B Hotel La Mirada, on the road out to the Pan-American Highway T2679-9084, www.hotellamirada.com. 12 motel-style cabins, with private bath, hot water and fans. Ample parking and credit cards accepted.

C Amalia's Inn, 100 m south of the main square, T2679-96181. A mix of tidy rooms, decorated with original art by the owners, great for couples and groups of up to 6, with

private and shared bathrooms. Stunning views from the balcony out to Salinas Bay, with a small pool ideal for a quick refreshing dip. Very friendly and good local knowledge. Best option in town.

C-D Cabinas Santa Rita, 150 m south of the central park, T2679-9062. A good choice with 36 big rooms with private bath, and a/c or fan. Secure with plenty of parking. A good alternative if Amalia's is full.

C-F Hotel Bella Vista, ½ a block northwest of the plaza, close to the look out, T2679-8060. 20 neat rooms, a few in dormitories, with a pool and bar/restaurant with great views across the bay.

G Cabinas Maryfel, opposite bus terminal down a small alleyway, but without a sign, T2679-9534. 9 cabins, with private bath and parking. The rooms are dark, but clean.

Out of town

A Cañas Castilla, on the road north of La Cruz, T8381-4030, www.canas-castilla.com. A working farm, set on the banks of the River Sapoa. 4 small cabins, elegantly furnished. Plenty of light activities on the farm.

B Termales Azules Lodge, in Buenos Aires de Aguas Claras de Upala, 15 miles (24 kms) from the checkpoint on the Pan-American Highway, in San José on T2290-8646, www.turismoruralcr.com. Part of the Cooprena community tourism network. 5 comfortable rooms, with shared bath, and traditional local food. Thermal pools on site, with many tours nearby.

Bahía Salinas *p222*

Listed in the order you will encounter them from La Cruz.

LL-AL Ecoplaya Beach Resort, down a spur road about 13 km from La Cruz, T2228-7146, www.ecoplaya.com. All-inclusive resort with 88 comfortable villas, some equipped with kitchenettes, with a/c, TVs, telephones, and a patio set in colourful gardens. Seafood, *bocas* and international dishes are served in the impressive thatched restaurant where, cooled by winds from the bay, you can sip refreshing cocktails. A host of activities includes windsurfing, kayaking, horse riding, and trips to Isla Bolaños Sanctuary reserve.

B Blue Dreams Hotel, www.bluedream hotel.com. 10 small rooms in a comfortable spot. Popular with kite surfers from Nov-Jul. A range of courses from beginners to intermediate. Equipment hire available.

🍴 Eating

La Cruz *p222*
Check out the site of former Restaurant Mirador, on the escarpment edge, because something will probably open in the renovated space.
🍴-🍴 Hotel Bella Vista, on the top floor of the hotel with fine views out to the bay. Tasty combinations of seafood and typical dishes.
🍴 Thelma's, a popular choice, local dishes.
🍴 El Mercadito, at the bus terminal. Divine ice creams but don't tell everyone.
Also several *sodas* dotted around town.

Bahias Salinas *p222*
🍴 Ristorante Copal, behind the Kitesurfing Center. Seafood dishes.

🚌 Transport

Parque Nacional Rincón de la Vieja *p217*
Transport to the park is easily arranged and normally involves sharing a **taxi** from Liberia at a cost of US$30-40 per cab. Hotels in Liberia will organize the taxi, removing the hassle of arranging a return taxi. Hotel Guanacaste (see page 214), will arrange transport for US$15 per person, minimum 6 passengers, depart 0700, 1 hr to entrance, return 1700, take food and drink. La Posada del Tope (see page 214) has similar deals. You can also hitch – most tourist vehicles will pick you up.

If you take your own transport 4WD is essential, although during the dry season a vehicle with high clearance is adequate. There is parking at the Santa Maria sector.

Driving to the Las Pailas sector requires you to cross private land (US$2).

Quebrada Grande
A bus leaves Liberia at 1500 daily.

La Cruz *p222*
The bus terminal is a couple of blocks north of the central square. Buses to **San José** leave every 1½ hrs from 0545, 5 hrs, US$5.70 – more expensive at the weekend. Transport to **Liberia**, for the Nicoya Peninsula, leaves 5 times a day, 1½ hrs, US$1.30. Buses heading north to **Peñas Blancas**, leave 5 times daily, 30 mins. Buses to **Playa Jobo** west beyond Bahía Solanos leave from close to the main square at 0530, 1030 and 1500, 30 mins, US$0.30.

Peñas Blancas *p223*
There are several express and ordinary bus services a day linking with **San José**. Buses arrive and depart from San José at Av 3, C 16, 100 m north of Coca-Cola terminal, 5-6 hrs, US$5.70. Take an early bus if you want to get from San José to the border before it closes. Bus from the frontier to **Liberia**, US$1.50, 1 hr There are also buses to and from **La Cruz**, 20 mins, US$0.80.

📖 Directory

La Cruz *p222*
Banks Banco Popular, on the road to the Pan-American Highway, changes TCs, cash and has an ATM. **Banco Nacional** has ATM. **Gas station** on Pan-Am Highway. **Internet** Multiservicios, 1 block northeast of the plaza, internet access, US$1.20 per hr and fax service, open Mon-Sat 0800-2200, Sun 0900-1200 and 1930-2200. **Post office** 1 block west of the central plaza.

Peñas Blancas *p223*
Banks Branch of BCR in the *aduana*, changes cash and TCs, open daily 0700-1900. There are plenty of money changers floating around – shop around to get good rates.

Contents

230 Northern beaches
230 Ins and outs
230 The beaches
234 Listings

238 Northwestern beaches
238 Beaches north of
Tamarindo
239 Playa Grande
240 Playa Tamarindo and
further south
242 Listings

250 Santa Cruz to Nicoya
251 Listings

253 Western beaches
255 Listings

262 Southern peninsula
266 Listings

Footprint features

228 Don't miss …
231 Ins and outs of Nicoya
Peninsula
232 Fishing
263 Peninsula and Gulf islands

At a glance

◉ **Getting around** Bus services to
most beaches in the north are fine,
shuttle buses provide an handy
alternative if you're on a tight
schedule. Ferries from Puntarenas
provide access to the south, with
connecting buses heading out
to the beaches.

◉ **Time required** On Nicoya
Peninsula it's all about the beach.
How long have you got?

◗ **Weather** Sunny for much of the
year – particularly from Dec-Apr,
and even the rainy season is
tolerable. Surf's up year round if
you're looking for board action,
but the best months are Dec-Jun.
Nov-Mar is the time to see nesting
leatherbacks at Playa Grande.

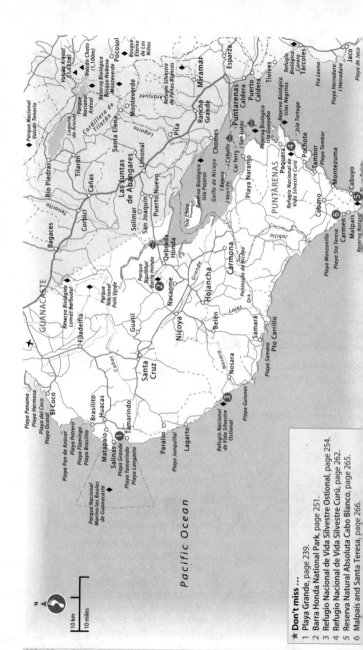

★ **Don't miss …**

1 Playa Grande, page 239.
2 Barra Honda National Park, page 251.
3 Refugio Nacional de Vida Silvestre Ostional, page 254.
4 Refugio Nacional de Vida Silvestre Curú, page 262.
5 Reserva Natural Absoluta Cabo Blanco, page 265.
6 Malpaís and Santa Teresa, page 266.

An appendage dangling off northwest Costa Rica, the Nicoya Peninsula is a fine contrast to the rest of the country. Although transport links are improving, the Gulf of Nicoya separates the region physically and culturally from mainland Costa Rica. The dry and moist forests that once dominated the landscape have been replaced by open pastures, with only the occasional guanacaste tree providing shade for grazing cattle. With a dependable dry season from December to May, conditions are ideal for lovers of sun, sea and surf.

The peninsula itself is also culturally divided. Small towns dotted along it's spinal route, Highway 21, serve as supply depots for nearby communities – some of the poorest in the country – in surrounding low-lying hills. These towns may be close, but they're a world away from the beach resorts of varying comforts that have sprung up along the coastline, pouncing on every inch of beach worth a towel, surfboard or fishing boat.

You can take your pick from bays and beaches covering the length of the western coast – to be honest if you like beaches you'll find something decent everywhere. In almost every bay there are quiet secluded villas and hotels providing mid-range comforts, as well as a couple of cheaper options and a few that are strictly upmarket.

Budget travellers using buses should head for Playa del Coco or Tamarindo, in the north, or Montezuma or Malpaís – a surfers' haven – at the southern end of the peninsula. All are served by public transport and enough visitors to keep the party going.

Northern beaches

As the beaches closest to Liberia, the northern beaches are, arguably, in Guanacaste and the most accessible part of the Nicoya Peninsula. Each resort offers something slightly different. Playa de Coco has a reputation as a party town. Heading north Hermosa has more of a family atmosphere, while Playa Panama, to the far north, is home to the all-inclusive mega-resorts. South of Playa de Coco, Ocotal hosts a number of more secluded resorts. ▸▸ For listings, see pages 234-237.

Ins and outs

Getting there and around
There's a regular bus service from Liberia and San José to Playa del Coco and Playa Hermosa. If travelling to Playa Ocotal or Playa Panama you should probably arrange transportation with your hotel. Each beach is small enough to walk round. A couple of buses travel between Playa del Coco, Hermosa and Panama. ▸▸ *For further details, see Transport, page 237.*

The beaches ⊕🏖️🍴🏨⛰️🎯🎭
▸▸ *pp234-237. Colour map 1, B3.*

Playa del Coco
A beach community with a rash of hotels and restaurants that are developing quickly, Playa del Coco is a quiet spot in the week with just enough life to keep things ticking over, without over-indulging in all-out partying. The beach is pleasant but nothing special. With good transport links to the rest of the country, the atmosphere changes at weekends and on national holidays when it becomes packed full. The town has also become one of the country's most popular dive spots, with several operators providing courses and dives at more than 30 dive sites within a 20-minute boat ride from town. Surfers use this as a departure point for Witches' Rock to the north, and it's a good base for big game fishing.

Playa del Coco

Pacific Ocean

Juice Bar Internet

Deep Blue Diving

Banco Nacional $

Rich Coast Diving

Banco Nacional $

To Playa Ocotal

N

300 metres (approx)
300 yards (approx)

To Liberia & San José
Pato Loco Inn &
L'Angoletto di
Roma Restaurant 9
Villa del Sol 10
Villa Flores 11
Vista del Mar 12

Sleeping
Cabinas Chale 1
Cabinas El Coco 2
Cabinas Sol y Mar 3
Camping Chopin 14
Coco Palms 4
Coco Verde 5
Flor de Itabo 6
La Puerta del Sol 7
Laura's House B&B 13
Luna Tica 8

Eating
Casino R 9
Jardin Tropical 5
La Rana 10

Bar & clubs
Coco Mar 2
El Bohío 13
El Roble 4
Lizard Lounge 14

Ins and outs of the Nicoya Peninsula

Getting there There are enough ways to the peninsula to keep you amused for quite a while. Domestic and international flights with American Airlines, Delta, Continental, Virgin Atlantic, Air France and increasing numbers of charter flights arrive at **Daniel Oduber Quirós International Airport**, 13 km from Liberia along Highway 21. The small, modern terminal has full customs and immigration services, a small café and a branch of Bancredito for paying departure tax (US$26). It's a good airport choice if you want to go straight to the beach although transport from here is limited to taxis (which are readily available). Ask around to get the best price. Regular domestic flights provided by **SANSA**, T2221-9414, www.flysansa.com, and **NatureAir**, T2220-3054, www.natureair.com, serve the same airport as well as the smaller airstrips at Carillo (Sámara), Nosara, Punta Islita, Tambor and Tamarindo.

There are a couple of road routes. Starting at the north of the peninsula, Highway 21 leaves the Pan-American Highway at Liberia, following the road for 108 km to Carmona towards the south and continuing unpaved to Playa Naranjo. If arriving from San José or the south, the **Friendship Bridge** spans the Río Tempisque at the north of the Gulf of Nicoya. In the far south, you can also get a passenger or vehicle ferry from Puntarenas on the mainland to Playa Naranjo at the south of the peninsula, for access to the north along a potholed road, or to Playa Tambor and Montezuma.

Getting around Apart from the main highway, roads (some paved) through the peninsula are sprinkled with varying degrees of potholes. If driving, err on the side of caution and allow plenty of time for your journey. Don't take risks crossing rivers – if it looks passable, wade across to check the depth first. It is often, although not always, possible to move between beaches without returning to the main highway but be prepared to get lost and ask directions regularly.

Public transport follows the main access routes. Buses from Liberia use the northern route and most buses from San José use the Friendship Bridge. Moving around the peninsula can be problematic. You can reach the most popular beaches with daily buses from San José or with frequent local connection from Santa Cruz or Nicoya. If moving between beaches, you will probably have to improvise with two or three buses, nipping into Santa Cruz or Nicoya to get a connection. Taxis are, of course, an option – as ever, agree the price in advance. Area website at **www.nicoyapeninsula.com**.

Playa Ocotal

Around 3 km southwest of Coco is the small beach of Playa Ocotal. Without the easy access, it's a more secluded bay than its northern neighbour and generally targeting a more upmarket clientele. The rocky headlands have developed as a dive site and fishing trips are easily arranged. Snorkelling is OK when visibility is good.

Playa Hermosa

On the main road from Highway 21 to Playa del Coco, a right spur heads north for a few kilometres leading to Playa Hermosa, a sandy golden beach spread along a broad bay that's good for swimming and other watersports. With a west-facing beach, the sunsets are impressive and cruises are a popular way to spend the twilight hours (US$60).

Fishing

Fishing just doesn't get any better than you will find in Costa Rica, with tarpon and snook on the Caribbean; marlin, sailfish, dorado, tuna and other species on the Pacific and trout, rainbow bass (*guapote*), bobo, machaca and more in inland lakes and rivers.

According to Jerry Ruhlow – who has been living, fishing and writing about fishing in Costa Rica since 1983 – it is essential to plan ahead. Peak fishing varies with the time of year and beach accommodation and the top boats are often hard to find when fishing is at its best, so book ahead. Jerry has kindly summarized the best seasons in the different parts of Costa Rica.

Pacific coast On the southernmost Pacific coast, in the **Golfito**, **Puerto Jiménez** and **Drake Bay** region, **marlin** action is best from August to December. There are **sailfish** year round, but the peak is from late November to March. It may slow from April into June then pick up again in July. If **non-stop action** is your preference and you don't have to hang a billfish to be happy, the Golfito region is your best bet. More than 40 International Game Fish Association (IGFA) certified world records have been established here and the species you can expect to catch at almost any time of year include **tuna** (sometimes to 400 pounds), **wahoo, amberjack, jack crevalle, grouper, cubera, barracuda, big roosterfish, corbina** and **snook**.

Next major fishing area heading north is **Quepos** where December to end of April is the best season for **billfish** although some **marlin** and **sailfish** are taken year round. **Dorado** and football-size **tuna** are nearly always plentiful, and they often get giant yellowfin tuna as well.

Mid-December to April are the best months for boats based in **Playa Carrillo** and the **Sámara** region as the main body of fish continue moving north. They often get there earlier and stay longer, depending on water temperature and other factors. **Dorado** and **tuna** are also plentiful these months.

A northerly wind blows from December into May in the **northernmost region**, but once the calm has returned the fishing is little short of sensational from late May or June into early September, with **marlin** peaking in August and September. There are two major tournaments in July – a few years ago one of those tournaments posted a record 1696 billfish in a four-day competition out of Flamingo Marina. Charter boats operate out of Tamarindo,

---

Other activities include diving, surfing, snorkelling and, increasingly, land-based tours. Without a main centre, the ambience is laid back and there's a mix of budget accommodation and full-service hotels and resorts.

The area is the focus of real estate developments and changes rapidly. It's still small enough to wander around and ask what's going on and what's new, and still friendly enough to have quiet, secluded moments.

Playa Panama

The Papagayo Project is the driving force behind tourism development around Playa Panama and the Bahía Culebra. The project aims to convert the scenic bay into a collection

lamingo, Portrero, Ocotal and Playa le Coco. There's always plenty of **dorado** and **tuna** in the area, and anglers working the nearby Catalina and Murcielago (Bat) Islands also score **wahoo, amberjack, cubera, roosters** and other structure fish.

Caribbean coast On the northern Caribbean coast, **tarpon** and **snook** are around most of the year, with slumps from May to mid-July when the rains are at their heaviest. Peak season is from about September through April, although late July during the *veranillo* (little summer), when rains usually stop for two or three weeks, is also excellent most years. **Rainbow bass** (*guapote*) and other freshwater species can be caught here year round in the miles of rivers and backwater lagoons. Most consistent fishing is out of the lodges near the mouth of the **Río Colorado**, but some are also caught at **Tortuguero** and **Parismina**. Northern Caribbean coast does not offer much in the way of sportfishing.

Inland waters For inland waters, **Lake Arenal** offers year-round fishing, but the quality will vary depending on wind and water level. It is a beautiful 22-mile long lake about 3 1/2 hours' drive from San José. Guides are available locally with fully equipped boats complete with

tackle. **Rainbow bass** (*guapote*) are the species most anglers go for. A beautiful fish in pastel shades of pink, rose, greens and blues, with feathered caudal and dorsal fins and a mean set of teeth, they are found only in Costa Rica and a few inland waters of southern Nicaragua. *IGFA* record is 12 1/2 lbs, taken here. Rainbow bass, **bobo, machaca, tepemechin** and other tropical species are also found in rivers throughout the country, along with **rainbow trout** in some high mountain rivers. **Caño Negro Lagoon** is a huge inland waterway that offers all of the above, plus **tarpon** and **snook**. Some waters are seasonal, and regulations often change from year to year, so check in advance.

Cost The cost of fishing varies considerably depending on the type of fishing, location, number of days and people, and accommodation requirements, to the extent that generalizing is difficult. Deep sea fishing starts at around US$600 for one day, inland waterways can start at as little as US$250 for the day. For more specific information and updated fishing reports contact **Jerry Ruhlow** on T1-800-308-3394, or T2282-6743, or at www.costaricaoutdoors.com. Also look at lodges in the main fishing areas.

of all-inclusive resorts that will dramatically change the area – and it's working. The Mexican company Grupo Situr, reported to be investing US$2.5 billion in the project, and European investment companies backing the project would like to see the area become the largest leisure city in Central America with current estimates putting up to 20,000 rooms in the bay. You don't have to be an environmentalist or biologist to speculate pessimistically on the effect that such numbers would have on the area – north of the peninsula is the Santa Rosa National Park. Not surprisingly, criticism of the project among environmentalists and ecotourists has been widespread.

On the northern side of the bay, the pre-Columbian site of **Nacascolo** may be of interest to the truly dedicated explorer of ruins.

For Sleeping and Eating price codes and other relevant information, see Essentials, pages 44-47.

ⓢ Sleeping

Playa del Coco *p230, map p230*
AL Flor de Itabo, on the road leading to the town, T2670-0438, www.flordeitabo.com. A variety of rooms, apartments and bungalows, all with private bath, a/c and cable TV, some with kitchenette, fridge and coffee machines. Hotel restaurant specializes in seafood and steaks, with a ceramic tiled pool set in colourful gardens, and a casino. Itabo specializes in big game fishing.
AL La Puerta del Sol, T2670-0195. 10 suites, all with a living room, private bath, a/c and fan, telephone and safebox – a couple of larger suites with additional comforts. Hidden down a side road to the north of town, this Italian-run gateway to the sun packs in the services and keeps a family feel to the place. Stylish furniture decorates the bright rooms, the small gym is wonderfully breezy and there's a relaxing pool. Excellent home-made pasta in the Italian restaurant.
AL-A Coco Verde, T2670-0494. 33 rooms with private bath, a/c, TV, parking lot and security guards. Good standards and clean. Has a pool, popular bar and casino.
A Cabinas Sol y Mar, entrance road to town, T2670-1111, solymar@hotmail.com. Fully equipped apartments. Nothing special, but in a quiet spot – good for families and groups.
A Villa del Sol, at the northern end of beach, T8825-0100, www.villadelsol.com. 7 rooms with private bathroom, tastefully decorated with bamboo furniture and natural woods. Pool set in gardens just a short distance from the beach, with Italian and French cuisine served in the restaurant.
A Villa Flores, T2670-0269, www.hotel-villa-flores.com. 7 rooms sleeping 2-4 people, with private bath, TV, a/c or fans – breakfast included. OK rooms set in pretty gardens, the pool has a wet bar.

A-B Laura's House B&B, T2670-0751, www.laurashousecr.net. A handful of rooms, with fan or a/c. The colour schemes are a tad garish, but there's a pool, it's set away from the busy centre, and, of course, breakfast is included.
A-B Pato Loco Inn, on entrance road into town, T2670-0145. 4 rooms and 2 apartments immaculately presented, decorated with stylish ceramics and paintings. A quiet, unassuming spot leading into town, and one of the best restaurants in town.
B Coco Palms, on the main plaza next to the soccer pitch, T2670-0367, www.hotelcoco palms.com. Comfortable rooms with private bath, set in pleasant gardens complete with pool and popular gringo and sushi bar.
B Vista del Mar, at the northern end of town, T2670-0753. 9 comfortable double rooms, a couple with ocean views and private bath, also with a/c or fan – price includes a fruity breakfast. Plenty of parking. A quiet spot with a small patio looking out to the sea. A pool and BBQ spot make it a good place for relaxing late into the evening.
C Cabinas Chale, north of town, T2670-0036. 25 double rooms and villas (sleeping up to 6 with kitchenette), all with private bath and fan or a/c, and a small terraced patio. A good choice for the active with a pool and basketball court. Villas work out as a very good deal, and monthly rentals are possible.
D Cabinas El Coco, right on the beach front just north of the pier, T2670-0110. Plenty of basic rooms, all with private bath, and basic, no-frills decor. Good sea views and the rooms at the back are slightly cheaper.
D Luna Tica, T2670-0127, luna_tica@guana castetour.com. 30 or so rooms with fan and private bath. Basic rooms are starting to look grubby so look first and check out the beds. Also has a small beachfront bar and restaurant.

Camping
G Camping Chopin. Simple services with bath and water provided.

Playa Ocotal *p231*
LL-L Ocotal Beach Resort and Marina,
southern end of the bay, T2670-0321,
www.ocotalresort.com. 59 rooms and suites,
all with 2 queen- or 1 king-size bed and a
private terrace or balcony with ocean view.
Each chic, colourful room has all the expected
comforts, and the many activities on site
include 3 pools, a jacuzzi with spectacular sea
views and a floodlit tennis court. Fishing and
diving trips can be arranged, as well as
nationwide trips and transfers.
L-A Villa Casa Blanca, set back from the
beach, in quiet seclusion, T2670-0518,
www.hotelvillacasablanca.com. 15 rooms
each uniquely decorated in a style as
individual as the service is special, set in a
charming Spanish-style villa. Colourful and
bright rooms, many with sumptuous
canopied 4-poster beds. A wholesome waffle
and pancake breakfast will see you through
most of the day. Comforts include a free-
form pool complete with wet bar, a relaxing
patio and landscaped gardens complete
with jacuzzi. You will have to venture out
for food because there is no restaurant.
A-B Ocotal Inn B&B, T2670-0835. The
cheapest option in the bay, 5 large rooms
with a/c and ceiling fan. Small pool and
excellent Peruvian seafood restaurant.

Playa Hermosa *p231*
The main road parallels the beach with
several roads giving access to it.

First entrance
A-B Hotel Playa Hermosa, T2672-0046,
www.hotelplayahermosa.com. 22 spacious
rooms, with private bath, hot water, fan and
safebox. All set in pleasant shaded gardens,
with a freeform pool that leads to the beach.
The patio restaurant has a low-key feel, with
an international and Italian menu.
L-B Villa del Sueño, T2672-0026,
www.villadelsueno.com. A mix of villas
sleeping up to 4 people, and rooms, all with
private bath, hot water and ceiling fans. An air
of Mediterranean tranquillity hovers over the

complex of rooms, each tastefully decorated
with comfortable furnishings that positively
radiate calm and relaxation. Daily and weekly
options available. Dinner is often accompanied
by live local music, and occasionally that
includes well-known Costa Rican musicians.

Second entrance
L Villa Acacia, T2672-1000, www.villa
cacia.com. 8 villas and rooms set in well-
tended gardens. The villas come with fully
equipped kitched, the rooms has balconies and
garden views. Another popular family choice.
B Iguana Inn, T2672-0065. 9 clean and tidy
rooms sleeping up to 4 people making it a
good deal for groups, in an easy-come,
easy-go atmosphere complete with use of
kitchen and laundrette. There's a small pool,
if the 100-m walk to the beach is too much,
a small bar and snack food in high season.
AL-A El Velero, T2672-0036,
www.costaricahotel.net. 22 crisply clean
rooms, with a/c, are decorated with Costa
Rican textiles. A good spot, with a pool in
the garden leading on to the beach – their
backyard so to speak! A small bar/restaurant
serves fast-food dishes with a smattering of
national influences. Happy hour – but not
too loud – every day, and barbecues on
Wed and Sun. Sunset tours arranged.

Playa Panama *p232*
There is no budget accommodation at
Playa Panama – in fact chances are you'll
be moved on unless you look the part.
LL+ Giardini di Papagayo, T2291-5859,
www.grupopapagayo.com. There's no
denying the full luxury and comfort in
this exclusive resort.
LL-AL Costa Blanca, T2672-0096,
www.costablancadelpacifico.com.
28 villas sleeping 4-6 people. In addition
to the fully-equipped villas, comforts
include a pool, jacuzzi and beach access.
LL Four Seasons Resort, T2696-0000,
www.fourseasons.com. 165 rooms and suites,
with all the comforts you could possibly wish for
whether travelling for pleasure, business or both.

🍴 Eating

Playa del Coco *p230, map p230*

🍴 **Casino R**, right on the seafront. Well-intentioned and stylish restaurant serving seafood dishes. But no casino.

🍴 **Zouk Santana**, close to the centre of town. Early evening food, moving to live music and DJs as the night moves on.

🍴-🍴 **L'Angoletto di Roma**, at Pato Loco Inn. Excellent pasta in a cosy atmosphere with Italian style and elegance – a great restaurant.

🍴-🍴 **La Rana**, on the main street. Good regular spot for a quiet beer and somewhere to sit down. Good mixed menu of seafood and fast-food style dishes.

🍴 **Jardín Tropical**. One of the cheapest eateries, with a good mix of *Tico* and snack dishes, and almost open-air.

Playa Ocotal *p231*

🍴-🍴 **Father Rooster Bar & Grill**, T2670-1246, www.fatherrooster.com. Open daily 1200-2145, sometimes a little later in high season. A great spot, right on the beach, serving seafood and meat dishes.

Playa Hermosa *p231*

🍴-🍴 **Ginger**, on the main road, T2672-0041. Open Tue-Sun. Asian and international dishes. A popular choice.

🍴 **Pescado Loco**, opposite El Velero. Simple restaurant serving seafood dishes.

🍷 Bars and clubs

Playa del Coco *p230, map p230*

Coco Mar. Popular beachfront disco, starts late, goes on even later.

El Bohío. Sedate and quiet eatery by day, brings out the karaoke machine in the evenings and it all gets very messy. Great fun, if a tad embarassing for some.

El Roble, just off the main plaza. An open-air bar-cum-disco.

Lizard Lounge, one of the many bars on the main street that rise and fall in popularity.

🛍 Shopping

Playa del Coco *p230, map p230*

Air-conditioned shops and impromptu stalls dotted around the town are more than happy to relieve you of cash in return for swimwear, beach items, jewellery and souvenirs.

🔺 Activities and tours

Playa del Coco *p230, map p230*
Canopy tours

Congo Trail, clearly signposted, take road heading southwest from Sardinal, 9 km out of town, T2666-4422, congotrail@racsa.co.cr. Truly secluded, reached from the north or the southern beaches.

Diving

Playa del Coco and neighbouring Playa Hermosa have developed a reputation as Costa Rica's main dive resorts. Dive operators offer trips to over 30 nearby sites including **Islas Catalina** to the south where you may well see manta rays, and **Islas Murciélagos**, off the Santa Elena Peninsula to the north, where bull sharks are commonly seen. None of the dive operators will deny that visibility in the area is occasionally less than perfect, but seeing whitetip reef and Pacific bull sharks, rays and mantas on a good day could easily compensate.

Most of the tours operators offer roughly the same packages. A 2-tank morning or afternoon dive is US$80, with a 2-tank trip to Catalina costing US$110, or to Murciélagos US$150. Resort courses (ie unqualified) are US$100, PADI training is also available with open water certification costing US$395. For more advanced courses contact dive operators directly. Prices include tanks, weights, guides and snacks, normally with a minimum of 2 people.

Bill Beard's Diving Safaris, Playa Hermosa. A long-running dive operation in the area, well respected, see page below.

Deep Blue Diving, beside Hotel Coco Verde, T2670-1004, www.deepblue-diving.com. Offer several packages with accommodation in local hotels.
Rich Coast Diving, T2670-0176, www.rich coastdiving.com. The only place in town that makes a conscious effort at dive conservation awareness.

Fishing
While Playa Flamingo to the south may get the main sports fishing business, Playa del Coco also has great diving facilities (see above) so is a better choice if you want to do more than just fish, fish, fish.
Flor de Itabo hotel has a good reputation and will provide all the requisite gear if you want to charter a boat. You could also try **Roca Bruja Surf Trips** (see below).

Surfing
Witches' Rock to the north of Coco is the surfing Mecca for disciples of *Endless Summer* and Playa del Coco is as good a departure point as any. Board hire and lessons are also possible.
Cabinas El Coco, on the beachfront. Can also help with getting a boat.
Costa Rica Aventuras Surf Trips, T670-1869, www.costaricaaventuras.com. Organize packages to Witch's Rock and Ollie's Point.
Roca Bruja Surf Trips, in the centre of town, T2670-1020. A bit chaotic, but can just about get their act together to provide surf trips and lessons. Also run fishing trips, half day US$250, full day US$350, up to 4, equipment provided.

Playa Hermosa *p231*
Adventure tours
Charlie's Adventures, T2672-0275. A wide range of tours on offer.
Pura Vida Adventures, T2670-1090. Mix of adventure options, surfing and fishing.

Diving
Aguasport, T2672-0050. Provide fishing and snorkelling tours for from US$20 for 2 hrs.
Bill Beard's Diving Safaris, T2672-0012, www.billbeardcostarica.com. One of the longest-running dive operations in the country, operates out of Playa Hermosa. Supplies all the normal dive options (see Diving, Playa del Coco above) and some good packages that mix blue activities (ie wet), including 7 day-trips out to the Cocos Islands, with various green options inland.

Sailing
Spanish Dancer, T2670-0058. Sunset Sailing Tours on their catamaran.
Cool Runnings, T2824-1875. Sails on 46 ft trimaran.

⊙ Transport

Playa del Coco *p230, map p230*
Buses leave from **San José** from C 14, Av 1-3, 0800 and 1400, returning at 0800 and 1400, 5 hrs, US$6.10. From **Liberia**, 6 daily buses, 0530-1815, returning 0530-1800, US$0.85.

Playa Hermosa *p231*
From **Liberia**, Empresa Esquivel, 6 daily between 0600 and 1900, US$0.90. Also on the Fantasy Bus (Grayline) route.

⊙ Directory

Playa del Coco *p230, map p230*
Banks A branch of Banco Nacional is at the entrance to town on the main road. Closed Sat. **Internet** Juice Bar Internet, on main road near the centre of town, closes around 1900. **Medical services** Nearest pharmacy is in Sardinal, 8 km east of Playa del Coco. **Post office** On the main plaza, open Mon-Fri. **Useful addresses** The police station is in the main plaza.

Northwestern beaches

Back on Highway 21 the road continues its journey to the heart of the peninsula, passing roadside stalls selling distinctive Chorotega ceramics and modern interpretations of the simple, attractive designs. About 38 km south of Liberia a fork heads west, splitting again after 24 km at a junction village called Huacas to several popular beaches, heading north, west and south. To the north, the road fringes the coastline passing the beaches of Playa Conchal, Playa Brasilito, Playa Flamingo, Playa Potrero and the distant Playa Pan de Azúcar. Apart from Brasilito and a couple elsewhere, these beaches mainly target self-catering travellers and public transport is limited.

Heading directly west – straight ahead at Huacas – the road leads to Playa Grande and Parque Nacional Marino las Baulas de Guanacaste. It's a quiet spread-out beach area, popular with surfers and also the main nesting site for the leatherback (baula) turtle in Costa Rica. Again, once in this area, public transport is limited so you'll either be happy to stay put in the area, or will have your own transport. There is daily boat transport from Tamarindo which is useful if you're planning a short visit to Playa Grande for a short visit.

Back at Huacas, most people head south, where the road leads to Playa Tamarindo, a one-time sleepy beach town that is now bursting at the seams. While surfing still attracts many, the place is moving away from such bohemian ideals and a number of mid-range hotel and restaurants, appealing to a wide range of budgets, have sprung up along the strip. ▸▸ *For listings, see pages 242-249.*

Beaches north of Tamarindo ⊜❶❷❸▲❸❻ ▸▸ *pp242-249. Colour map 1, B2.*

Playa Conchal
The white bay of Shell Beach – named for the countless tiny shells that give it its dazzling colour – is good for swimming and snorkelling. The clear waters are easily reached by meandering south along the shore from Playa Brasilito. It's definitely worth exploring Conchal on a day trip if you're not staying in the area.

Playa Brasilito
The beach at Playa Brasilito may not be particularly attractive, but good transport links, a range of other services – including more accommodation options than Conchal – and friendly, community spirit make it a useful base if you fancy exploring this part of the coast and your budget is tight. The town, no, village, is small enough to walk around and both Conchal and Flamingo are only a walk away.

Playa Flamingo
A few kilometres beyond Brasilito, Playa Flamingo is the sports fishing capital of the peninsula, with the region's largest marina providing services for trips out to sea. Once-beautiful white and grey sand beaches have suffered somewhat from a spate of development, but the small town has a good collection of services and comfortable, rather ostentatious and garish, hotels. These days, the simple charm of the area has gone although there are some quieter spots to the north at Playa Potrero – see below.

It's also worth noting that, despite the name, there are no flamingos around these parts – the name is reported to have come from a case of mistaken identity involving roseate spoonbills. If you're sailing by, contact **Flamingo Marina** ① *T2654-4203*. Costa Rica's largest marina provides full services as well as information for organizing sport fishing, sailing and scuba-diving trips.

Playa Potrero

Beyond the rocky headland of Flamingo the dark sand beach of Playa Potrero stretches north to the distance. At the end of a long bumpy road from the main highway, Potrero is at the limit of comfortable travel if you're using public transport, so accommodation favours those wanting to stay for a number of days or even weeks. If that's what you're looking for, the beach is quiet and peaceful. But enjoy the solitude while it lasts, resort developments are creeping up from the south.

In good weather, there is a back country route north through to Sardinal and Playa del Coco – ask locally for directions and conditions. A 4WD recommended.

Playa Pan de Azucar

At the end of the road, with a long grey beach, this is where the locals come to watch the sunset. It's a quite area, way off the beaten track, with just a few accommodation and restaurant options hidden away. This is probably how the rest of Costa Rica felt 30 years ago.

Playa Grande ●● ▸▸ pp242-249. Colour map 1, B2.

Back at the junction by Huacas the main road leads straight ahead to Matapalo and, after 9 km, to Playa Grande, a beach popular with surfers and leatherback turtles. Stretching like a speckled golden carpet into the distance, Playa Grande's appeal is as clear as its beach is beautiful. Along the coast of a small peninsula created by the Tamarindo Estuary, the 485 ha of beach and mangrove swamps are protected in the Parque Nacional Marino las Baulas de Guanacaste with an additional 22,000 ha covering the marine reserve.

The beach is one of the country's most important nesting sites of the *baula* (leatherback turtle, *Dermochelys coriacea*), one of the world's largest reptiles. Growing to a massive 2 m in length and weighing as much as half a ton, fully mature adults arrive at the beach between November and March, when they haul themselves up the sand to deposit between 80 and 100 ping-pong ball-sized eggs, before returning to the ocean exhausted – clearly the turtles of Ninja fame were the flap-happy juveniles.

Playa Grande is also considered to be one of the best surf spots in the country, with the beach forming the most western point of the Nicoya Peninsula and therefore receiving swells from the north, south and, naturally enough, the west.

Away from the beach, the estuarine waters protect mangrove swamps where you can see all six Costa Rican species of the total eight found in the neotropics, including white, black, the rare tea and the predominant red mangrove. From a gently drifting boat you can see a great deal of fauna including crocodiles and the colourfully pink roseate spoonbill.

With the protected beach on one side, and the mangrove reserves on the other, pressure on the land is great from all sides. Sometimes it can be difficult to know where to tread.

Around Playa Grande Turtle watching tours are most commonly arranged from, and begin in, Tamarindo, a short boat trip across the mouth of the estuary. If you are staying in Playa Grande, you will only be charged the US$10 for entering the national park.

If time allows, a visit to **El Mundo de la Tortuga** ⓘ *on the main road close to the beach, T2653-0470, open in the nesting season, US$10, the MINAE national park office is at the entrance to town, they run trips down the beach in the nesting season, US$15,* will provide answers to the endless questions surrounding the world of the turtle.

Arriving at Tamarindo at dusk, the natural response is to dump your gear or stop the car with a screech of brakes and run for the beach – the sunsets are incredible and all shades of Tamarindo society migrate in daily pilgrimage for a pagan tribute to the sinking sun. Either side of the magic moment, Tamarindo is a flurry of activity that continues to grow in all directions – rapidly – and yet the place still retains a surfy, beachside attitude.

The beach is attractive, although not stunning, and has strong tides in places so take care if swimming. For surfers there are three good breaks providing a variety of options for the surf crowd that flock to town. Beyond surf and sun, the most popular excursion is an evening trip to Playa Grande and the leatherback nesting sights. While the town is driven by surfing, there's a wide enough range of hotels and bars to make it a good beach stop – it's lively, but not overly so.

Ins and outs

Getting there There are several daily flights from San José with **SANSA** (US$89 one way) and **NatureAir** (US$117) to Tamarindo airport, 3 km north of town. Both have an office in the centre of town on the main street. There are also a couple of direct buses from San José, as well as **Interbus** and **Fantasy** bus services. ↦ *See also Transport, page 249, for further details.*

Getting around It's a small enough place to walk, with a main street running parallel to the beach. Mountain bikes, scooters and even quads are available for hire if your legs get too tired. There is an ICT **tourist office** at the north end of town, but it is rarely open.

Trips and activities

Local trips include **turtle watching** tours from November to March to neighbouring Playa Grande. Trips leave late afternoon and cost around US$30 and can be organized through most hotels. The cheapest option is direct through the MINAE office, US$15. **Jungle boat safaris** head up the mangrove swamps of the Tamarindo Estuary.

Aquatic adventures are many. If you need to buy or hire a **surf** board or equipment there are many outlets in town with short, long and boogie boards – they'll provide you with all the information or just follow the crowds.

For those who prefer to get *in* the water, **snorkelling** gear is available for hire from many outlets. **Diving** can also be organized through Agua Rica Dive Center, with courses and resort dives.

Getting back on the water, **sailing boats** leave for sunset tours and snorkelling trips. **Kayaks** are available for hire, with tours through the mangrove swamps and out to Isla Capitán. **Sports fishing** is also a popular option with half and full day trips.

Everywhere in Costa Rica has to have a **canopy tour** and Tamarindo is no different. Tamarindo Long Lines Canopy Tours zip you along seven platforms and four cables – one reaching 500 m.

Heading further afield full- and half-day tours through the hills of the surrounding area are available on **horse**, **mountain bike** and **quad-bike**.

Quick to seize an opportunity, Tamarindo is sure to develop the latest craze when the opportunity arises so keep an eye out for the latest thing. ↦ *See also Activities and tours, page 248, for further details.*

Tamarindo

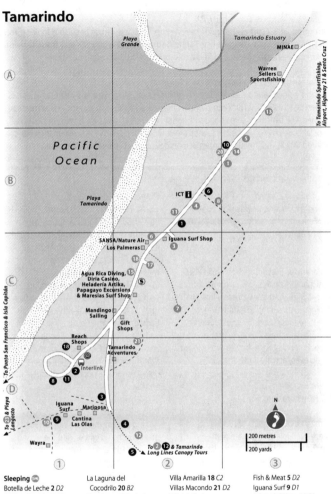

Sleeping

Botella de Leche **2** D2
Cabinas Marielos **3** C2
Cabinas Roda Mar **4** B2
Cabinas Tsunami **5** B3
Capitán Suizo **23** D1
Dolly's **6** C2
El Jardín del Edén **7** C2
El Milagro **8** B2
JC Friends Hostel **10** D1

La Laguna del
    Cocodrilo **20** B2
Pasatiempo & Pacho's
    Restaurant **12** D2
Pozo Azul **13** A3
Pueblo Dorado **14** B3
Tamarindo Diria **15** C2
Tamarindo Vista
    Villas **1** B3
Tropicana **17** C2

Villa Amarilla **18** C2
Villas Macondo **21** D2
Witch's Rock
    Surf Camp **11** B2

Eating

Coconut Café **1** B2
El Arrecife **2** D1
El Milagro **6** B2
Fiesta del Mar **8** D1

Fish & Meat **5** D2
Iguana Surf **9** D1
Johann's Bakery **10** B3
La Baula Pizzeria **11** D1
Lazy Wave **4** D2
Shark Bite Deli **3** D1
Stella's **12** D2
ZullyMar **18** D1

Playa Avellanas → *Colour map 1, B2.*

With good sand, surf and a quiet beach strip Avellanas attracts people looking to get away from the increasingly busy Tamarindo. Reached easily by taxi from Tamarindo (16 km to the north), or try and find a minibus service that might be running.

Playa Junquillal → *Colour map 1, C2.*

The long golden sand beach at Playa Junquillal about 30 km west of Santa Cruz is one of the cleanest beaches in Costa Rica and provides quiet solitude without being so deserted that you feel stranded. The beach has some good surf, and several hotels have gear for hire, but essentially it is more laid back than many other coastal areas. Behind the beach, extensive mangroves can be explored. Ask at your hotel, or contact Bernardo Sánchez at Hotel Playa Junquillal.

◉ Northwestern beaches listings

For Sleeping and Eating price codes and other relevant information, see Essentials, pages 44-47.

◉ Sleeping

Playa Conchal *p238*

LL Paradisus Playa Conchal, T2654-4502, www.paradisusplayaconchal.solmelia.com. Over 406 lavish suites with every imaginable comfort. 7 restaurants, 6 bars, reportedly the largest free-form pool in Central America, the 18-hole Garra de León golf course and 4 floodlit tennis courts. In their words, "you can do every activity under the sun".

Playa Brasilito *p238*

B-C Hotel Brasilito, T2654-4237, www.brasilito.com. 17 spacious rooms that seem to be taking gulps of cooling ocean breeze, a couple with private bath. Comfortable and friendly hotel, close to the beach, with good Perro Plano restaurant and bar. Horse riding, canopy and ATV tours trips arranged. Internet service available.
C Ojos Azules, on the main road, T2654-4343. 18 cabins, with private bath and possibly the most tasteless decor in the country.
F pp Brasilito Lodge, right on the beach, T2654-4452, brasilitolodge@yahoo.com. Big rooms, good beds and options for **camping** (**G**) in this family home budget option. Internet, email and tours provided.

Playa Flamingo *p238*

LL-AL Flamingo Beach Resort, T2654-4444 www.resortflamingobeach.com. Almost 100 a/c large rooms and suites right on the beach. A couple of bars and restaurants, large pool and tennis court. Good for arranging fishing trips and activities in the area.
LL-AL Flamingo Marina Resort, up the hill with good views, T2654-4141, www.flamingomarina.com. 30 deluxe, although a little traditional, rooms and suites, all with private bath, a/c, TV and minibar. 4 pools, a jacuzzi and the Sunrise Café and Monkey Bar.
A Mariner Inn, T2654-4081. 12 rooms with bath, a/c and the popular Spreader restaurant and bar.

Playa Potrero *p239*

Around the bay there are several resorts that flourish and wither with the season. Those listed below are listed in order that you reach them from Playa Flamingo, reaching round to the small village at the northern end of the bay.
E pp Cabinas Mayra, at the entrance to the bay, T2654-4213. Right on the beach, it's a run-down old family home steeped in charm, and a good secluded spot. Alvara Chincilla and his family have 5 cabins sleeping up to 8 people, complete with small kitchen, and you can camp on the beach. It's an absolute bargain and sooner or later someone is going to make this place an offer they can't refuse – give them a reason to stay.

A-B Cabinas Cristina, T2654-4006,
www.cabinascristina.com. A quiet spot,
with rooms sleeping 4 people, equipped
with private bath, small kitchenette and a
small pool in tropical gardens.
AL-A Cabinas Isolina Beach, T2654-4333,
www.isolinabeach.com. 34 comfortable
simply decorated bungalows with private
bath, kitchenette, set in fine shady gardens
with hammocks for relaxing in and a pool
for dipping into.
C Bahía Esmeralda, at the northern end
of the beach, T2654-4480, www.hotelbahia
esmeralda.com. Tidy rooms and villas
sleeping 2, 4 or 6, complete with private bath
and a/c or ceiling fan. Free-form pool in
tropical gardens, a short walk from the beach,
Italian restaurant and plenty of parking.

Playa Pan de Azucar p239
LL-AL Hotel Sugar Beach, T2654-4242,
www.sugar-beach.com. Bright airy rooms
with private bath and ocean views, in a
quiet and beautiful sandy forest-fringed
bay. The hotel also has a couple of beach
houses sleeping up to 10 people. Good
open-air restaurant, and fishing packages
from the hotel.

Playa Grande p239
The main road leads straight to the beach;
the left fork heading to the southern tip of the
peninsula – the closest point to Tamarindo.
G pp Kike's Place, on the road into town and
the cheapest option, T2653-0834. 8 simple
cabins sleeping up to 6 people, with a lively
bar and restaurant.
AL-A Hotel Las Tortugas, at the beach,
T2653-0423, www.lastortugashotel.com.
11 rooms each with private hot water bath,
a/c and cross ventilation. Although close to
the beach, the hotel has been constructed
to prevent light reaching the beach and
minimize impact on the area to avoid
affecting nesting turtles. Louis Wilson,
the owner, was involved with setting up
the reserve and he's also an old-time surfer,
so can help out with advice on breaks here

and along the coast. Open-air restaurant
with a tasty blend of international and
Costa Rican dishes. There's also a pool
and jacuzzi at the hotel for when your not
on the beach snorkelling or exploring the
nearby mangroves by canoe or boat. The
hotel also has the **AL-C Tortugas
Lighthouse Apartments**, with a selection
of 1- and 2-bedroom apartments with a/c,
sleeping up to 6 people, and complete
with kitchenette, available by the night
or the week.
    A left fork takes you down a pot-holed
road running through forests parallel to
the beach.
AL-A Playa Grande Inn, a short distance
from the fork, T2653-0719, www.playagrande
inn.com. Targeting the surfers, 10 very clean
rooms with hot water private bathroom and
fans. Good restaurant with local and pasta
dishes, opening onto the pool.
L-AL Bula Bula, backing onto the estuary,
T2653-0975, www.hotelbulabula.com.
Beautiful a/c rooms with extra fan, patio
and pool set in tropical gardens. Excellent
service throughout, topped off with the
surf'n'turf Great Waltini's Restaurant and
Bar. A great place, sure to make for a
memorable trip.
AL Villa Baula, at the most southerly tip of
the peninsula, T2653-0493, www.hotelvilla
baula.com. 20 stilted wooden cabins and a
handful of private bungalows provide a
truly rustic experience complete with
private bath with hot water, ceiling fan
and ocean view. German and Indonesian
food is served at the Jaguarandi restaurant,
with a couple of pools for complete
relaxation. A good selection of tours are
also available, and the have surf and
boogie boards for hire.
B Playa Grande Surf Camp, T2653-1074,
www.playagrandesurfcamp.com. A-frame
buildings and one more coventional house in
an extremely chilled gravel garden complete
with pool. Hammocks all over the place for
relaxing in but by day you'll probably be
surfing on the boards for hire (US$20).

Playa Tamarindo *p240, map p241*
Book well in advance at Christmas, New Year and Easter. Good discounts in the green season. Area websites include www.tamarindo.com.

LL-L Panacea, T2653-8515, www.panacea cr.com. Hidden in the hills behind Tamarindo, Panacea offers a luxurious retreat, with private cabinas, restaurant and infinity pool, but with the main focus on yoga.

LL-L Tamarindo Diria, T2653-0031, www.tamarindodiria.com. Over 180 very comfortable rooms with views to the ocean, the garden, or 1 of the 2 pools. All with ceiling fan and cable TV. Great restaurant leading out to a couple of pools in a tropical garden. The best hotel in Tamarindo.

LL-AL Capitán Suizo, south of town towards Playa Langosto, T2653-0075, www.hotelcapitansuizo.com. 8 bungalows, 22 rooms and 4-bedroom apartments all with patio or balcony and a/c. The bar and restaurant overlook landscaped gardens, visited by howler monkeys. Meandering paths lead to the large free-form pool. A wide range of tours is provided. Excellent service and quality, that one guest described as "simply incredible."

LL-A Tamarindo Vista Villas, near entrance to town, T2653-0114, www.best western.com. 32 villas and rooms all have a/c. Villas sleeping up to 8 have fully equipped kitchens. Waterfall-filled pool, wet bar and jacuzzi, a couple of bars and a restaurant. Internet access for guests.

L-AL El Jardín del Edén, T2653-0137, www.jardindeleden.com. Set in luxuriant tropical gardens, 32 rooms and 2 villas with private bath and views to the west and the setting sun. The restaurant is one of the best in town, with excellent seafood – expensive but worth it. A couple of pools with a wet bar and jacuzzi mean you don't even have to walk the short distance to the beach.

AL Tropicana, T2653-0503, www.tropicana cr.com. Comfortable spacious rooms, with private bath, fan, a/c and safebox. While the room decor isn't going to win many awards,

one of the 3 pools is probably the biggest in town and you can actually do lengths.

AL-A El Milagro, T2653-0042, www.elmilagro.com. 32 charming wooden bungalows with private bath, a/c or fan, small balcony and pool set in tropical gardens.

AL-A Pasatiempo, T2653-0096, www.hotelpasatiempo.com. A popular choice with 14 bungalows, colourfully decorated a/c rooms, private bath and small private patio complete with hammock. Attractive sundeck set in tropical gardens around the pool. Lively bar and restaurant making for a popular place to hang out. Recommended.

A Villa Amarilla, T2653-0038. A quiet little B&B on the main road with big, airy rooms and private bathroom with hot shower. The private garden, that has been described as a tropical Eden, backs on to the main beach. It's a quiet, homely option, and a refreshing change from all-too-predictable mid-range hotels.

A-B La Laguna del Cocodrilo, T2653-0255, www.lalagunadelcocodrilo.com. Good rooms, with terrace leading to the beach and a number of bunkbed options.

A-B Villas Macondo, T2653-0812, www.villasmacondo.com. Rooms with shared kitchen, and apartments a block back from the beach. Swimming pool, washing machine, safeboxes, fridge and friendly people too.

A-B Witchs' Rock Surf Camp, T2653-1262, www.witchsrocksurfcamp.com. Very focused on the more affluent surfer, providing, boards, coaching, information and beds for sleeping in.

B Cabinas Marielos, T2653-0141, cabinas marielos@hotmail.com. 17 cabins with private bath, fan or a/c and safebox. Shared kitchen and laundry service. Good value deals for groups of 4 or more, so often fully booked with the surf crowd. Visa accepted.

B Pozo Azul, at the entrance to town, T2653-0280. Simple but good cabins, some with a/c. Cooking facilities, clean, swimming pool. Cheaper in low season.

3 Pueblo Dorado, T2653-0008,
www.pueblodorado.com. 28 unassuming
and simple rooms, tastefully decorated with
masks, complete with hot water private bath
and a/c. There's a quiet understated charm to
the place with a behind-the-scenes efficiency.
Bigger than average pool. Good discounts in
green season.

C-D pp JC Friends Hostel, T8374-8246.
New hostel in town providing a welcome
addition to the cheaper end of the market.
Small pool, kitchen and internet.

D-E pp Botella de Leche, T2653-0944,
www.labotelladeleche.com. Spotless rooms,
good place for the backpacking crowd.
Dormitory rooms sleep 2-6 people, communal
kitchen, vast lounge with TV showing good
films, internet, laundry, use of kitchen ... pretty
much every comfort you could hope for.

F Cabinas Roda Mar, towards the northern
end of town, T2653-0109. 45 simple rooms,
with private bath (cheaper without). *Tico*-
owned with a family atmosphere. Perfectly
good budget choice.

F Cabinas Tsunami. Basic but tidy rooms,
private bath and use of the kitchen, great
value. Turn up and see if there's free space –
probably full of surfers more interested in
water than comfort.

F pp Dolly's, T2653-0017. Basic rooms,
some with bath, key deposit required.
Popular budget choice but has lots of rules
and regulations and has had mixed reports –
unfriendly if you arrive on a bad day.

Playa Langosto

LL Cala Luna, T2653-0214, www.cala
luna.com. 20 deluxe hotel rooms constructed
from tropical hardwoods, and 21 2- and
3-bedroom villas each with a private pool.
Complete luxury and stylish ambience
throughout the opulent gardens. Cala
Moresca restaurant serves regional dishes,
Italian cuisine and the traditional American
breakfast to start your day.

L Barcelo Playa Langosto, T2653-0363,
www.barcelo.com. A 4-star hotel with 135
a/c rooms. A resort-style hotel with pools,

restaurant, shopping boutique and games,
all right on the beach. All-inclusive packages
are available.

Playa Avellanas *p242*

Hotels listed in the order you come across
them from north to south.
A Cabinas Las Olas, T2652-9331,
www.cabinaslasolas.com. Well-appointed
bungalows, with fans. There's also a
restaurant and bar as well as watersports
gear for hire.
E-F Surf Camp Eureka, on the beach road.
Simple cabins for the surf crowd, and options
for camping.

Playa Junquillal *p242*

Hotels listed in the order you come across
them from north to south.
AL-A Iguanazul, T2658-8124, www.iguana
zul.com. 24 tiled-roof cabins of varying size
and locations, sleeping up to 4 people, some
with ocean and poolside views. Ceramic tiled
flooring with pleasant wooden touches finish
off the comfortable rooms, equipped with
private bath, a/c and a fan. A small pool, bar
and restaurant with a new daily menu is
perfect for relaxing in. Popular with surfers
for trips to nearby breaks, there's also a surf
school package if you want to learn. Activity
junkies will be kept happy with kayaking,
horse riding, volleyball, pool and table tennis.
B El Castillo Divertido, T2658-8428,
www.costarica-adventureholidays.com.
7 rooms, all with private bath, hot water
and fan. A funky tribute to extravagant
architecture with it's turrets.
AL-A Guacamaya Lodge, perched up
on the hill with fine views to the west,
T2658-8431, www.guacamayalodge.com.
6 immaculately maintained bungalows
and a fully equipped house. Each bungalow
has a private bathroom, with a gentle sea
breeze drifting through the airy spacious
rooms, and a small terrace. The pool is
close to the lofty Rancho bar and restaurant
that serves Swiss and other local specialities.
A good choice.

A-C Tatanka, T2653-0426, tatanka@
racsa.co.cr. 10 simple cabins with private
bath, in a line facing the pool. Stylish open-
air restaurant serving a mix of Italian, French
and *Tico* dishes.

B-C Hibiscus, just 50 m from the beach,
T2653-0437. 5 big, fresh rooms positively
basking in natural light, each with hot water
private bath and fan. Well-tended gardens
lead to the small restaurant serving seafood
and German specialities.

B Playa Junquillal, on the beach, T2653-
0432. 5 cabins sleeping up to 4 people.
Fairly basic with a refreshingly chaotic feel
to the place, but a good bargain if you are
in a group and the only place that's actually
on the beach. Simple open-air bar and
restaurant serving traditional dishes. The
manager Bernard Sánchez can organize
trips through the mangroves behind the
coastal strip.

AL Land Ho at Villa Serena, T2658-
8430, www.land-ho.com. 12 spacious
rooms and private cabins each with tiled
bathroom, a/c and fan. Early morning
breakfast room service. Piano bar next
to the restaurant that serves Costa Rican
and international dishes, *La Tortuga Bar*
down by the pool.

Camping

G pp **Camping Los Malinches**, at the
northern entrance to town, 800 m off
the main road down a signposted dirt track
after Iguanazul, T2653-0429. Spectacular
location up on the bluff overlooking the
sea. Clean bathroom and toilets provided.
Well worth the effort to get here. Bring all
your own food though.

🍴 Eating

Playa Brasilito *p238*
🍴-🍴 **Cameron Dorado**, T2654-4028. Top
seafood served at the beachside tables.
Good reputation, but reported to have
2 menus – go for the one in Spanish.

🍴-🍴 **Happy Snapper**, T2654-4413. A
popular spot serving steaks and seafood,
with occasional live music.

🍴 **Perro Plano**, restaurant in the Hotel
Brasilito. Open 0730-2200, closed Mon.
Serving tasty Thai and local dishes in the
open-air restaurant. Run by Charlie and Claire
from Ireland who decided to *Get a New Life*,
and share it with the world via the BBC.

🍴 **Pizzeria Il Forno**, a rustic setting on
the main road. Mainly pizza and pasta, with
a bit of seafood and steak for the rest of us.

Playa Flamingo *p238*
🍴-🍴 **Marie's Restaurant**. A popular
dining spot open all day serving pancakes
for breakfast, burgers and *burritos* for lunch
and a more sophisticated seafood and surf
menu for dinner, all washed down with fine
cocktails and cool beers.

Playa Potrero *p239*
🍴-🍴 **Las Brisas**, at the northern end of
the beach bay. A great spot for a beer, a
snack and shooting pool. Surprisingly
popular, given the cut-off location.

🍴 **Diablo Tun Tun**, at Hotel Villaggio Flor de
Pacífico. Italian place with great food
and music.

🍴 **Harden's Garden Bakery**. Worth seeking
out if you fancy a nibble.

Playa Tamarindo *p240, map p241*
In addition to the various hotel restaurants
mentioned above, there are many other
places to choose from. Check the *sodas* for
good breakfasts and cheap evening meals.

🍴 **Bar-Restaurant Zully Mar**, on the beach.
Serves a mix of seafood and national dishes,
in a lively setting.

🍴 **Iguana Surf**, on the road to Playa
Langosto. A lively restaurant and bar
with a great atmosphere.

🍴 **Pacho's Bar & Restaurant** or **Yucca**,
(depending on whether the mood is good
or very good) at Pasatiempo hotel. Positively
throbs with the gringo crowd ordering from
the truly international menu that squeezes

n local, Italian, Tex Mex, Thai and a few other influences. Popular, lively joint with occasional live music.

¶-¶ El Arrecife. Popular spot to hang out, for good chicken and pizzas.

¶-¶ El Milagro. An atmospheric spot that serves mid-priced surf and turf dishes among spotlighted gardens. It's a relaxed atmosphere and the service is attentive. It might cross your mind that the pool's a little too close for comfort if things start getting silly.

¶-¶ Fiesta del Mar, at the end of the road. An over-priced open-air restaurant.

¶-¶ Fish & Meat. Quiet spot with tables scattered around a plant-filled patio courtyard. Great sushi and fish dishes and, er, meat ...

¶-¶ La Baula Pizzeria. A lively spot, serving simple fare and pizzas, popular with the beach crowd.

¶-¶ Pedro's Restaurant, at the end of the road right on the beach. Good for a simple dinner of seafood.

¶ Coconut Café. Pizzas, pastries and the best fish on the beach.

¶ Johann's Bakery. A long-standing favourite selling freshly baked bread and bagels.

¶ Shark Bite Deli. Great sandwiches, cookies and biscuits and a good book swap scheme.

¶ Stella's. Very good seafood, try dorado with mango cream. Shut when we last visited but, we hope, not closing. Recommended.

¶ The Lazy Wave, T2653-0737. Menu changes daily, interesting mix of cuisine, including seafood. Only open for dinner.

Playa Avellana p242

¶ Lola's on the Beach, T2658-8097. Outdoor bar/restaurant serving lunchtime vegetarian dishes, and fruit drinks.

Playa Junquillal p242

There are many hotel restaurants to choose from.

¶-¶ La Puesta del Sol, T2653-0442. The only stand-alone restaurant in the bay, but then nothing could compete with the dishes

served up that make this a little piece of Italy. A divine garden setting. Reservations recommended.

🍷 Bars and clubs

Playa Tamarindo p240, map p241
Many restaurants double up as bars as the evening progresses. Try:
Mombo Bar, or ask locally for the current in place.
Pasatiempo has open mic sessions every Tue.

🎭 Entertainment

Playa Tamarindo p240, map p241
Diria Casino, on the main street hidden behind Heladería Artika.
Disco Noai is the place to spend the night dancing and drinking till the early hours.

○ Shopping

Playa Potrero p239
Surfside Super. If you've got a day at the beach, stock up at the supermarket by the football beach. Open 0730-2100 daily.

Playa Tamarindo p240, map p241
There are a couple of mini-malls with several shops selling everything from beach wear to beach plots. Impromptu stalls appear along the roadside in the evening selling jewellery, T-shirts, sarongs and other beachwear.
Super Las Palmeras supermarket is a one-stop shop for most things you'll want in Tamarindo. Surf and boogie boards for hire (US$6 and US$4 for ½ day), laundry (US$3.50 per kilo, min 3 kg), turtle tours to Playa Grande and the mangrove estuaries of Palo Seco.
Maresias Surf Shop, is close to the southern end of town.

▲ Activities and tours

Playa Brasilito *p238*
ATV Tours, T2654-4087, or organize through your hotel. Quad bikes for hire, US$50 for 2 hrs, US$90 for a trip out to and including the Congo canopy tour. Popular option, but beyond the budget traveller.

Playa Flamingo *p238*
Costa Rica Diving, T2654-4148, www.costarica-diving.com. Full service dive shop offering certification as well as snorkelling, sunset sailing trips.

Playa Tamarindo *p240, map p241*
Diving and surfing
Agua Rica Diving Center, T2653-0094, www.tamarindo.com/agua. 2-tank dive from US$90, resort dive US$125, full certification offered from US$390.
Iguana Surf, T2653-0148, www.iguana surf.net. Specializes in surf gear and all aquatic rentals including jet skis and hobie cats. Has a couple of offices, a small shack on the main street close to the beach, and the main office, with a restaurant, a couple of blocks inland. Also provides snorkelling tours, kayak tours of the estuary, a surf taxi and surfing lessons.
Witches' Rock Surf Camp, T2653-1262, www.witchsrocksurfcamp.com. Lessons for beginners, intermediate, established and advanced surfers. A good way to spend a couple of months. Accommodation available.

Fishing
Tamarindo Sport Fishing, T2653-0090, www.tamarindosportfishing.com. *Talking Fish* is a 38-ft Topaz Express carrying 6 people in the shade. Half day US$850, full day US$1300. Captain Randy Wilson is highly recommended.
Warren Sellers Sport Fishing, T2653-0186, www.wssportfishing.com. Also highly recommended with over 25 years' experience fishing in Costa Rica. Prices start at US$1100 offshore.

Cruises
Marlin del Rey, T2653-0700, www.marlin delrey.com. Sailing catamaran for sunset cruises (US$60), or you can charter the boat for the whole day.
Samonique, T2388-7870, www.costarica-sailing.com. Coastal cruises and sunset cruise starting at US$50 including fresh fruit and snacks. Full- and half-day tours look for dolphins and turtles with stops for snorkelling.

Land and water
Papagayo Excursions, T2653-0254, www.papagayoexcursions.com. A good selection of local tours, with others going beyond the immediate area, including Rincón de la Vieja, Santa Rosa and Palo Verde National Parks and sailing charters and sunset tours.
Tamarindo Adventures, also known as Hightide, T2653-0108, www.tamarindo adventures.net. Full range of tours and rentals including boards, kayaks, snorkelling equipment, and for transport choose from mountain bikes, scooters, dirt bikes and ATVs (All Terrain Vehicles).
Tamarindo Long Lines Canopy Tours, T2653-0939. Zips you along 8 cables on 14 platforms, with a recently introduced hanging bridge.

Turtle and nature tours
Most tour operators and hotels will be able to arrange a tour of the beach at Playa Grande, looking for nesting turtles. Trips leave just before dusk, returning around 2200. Agency rates are about US$30, or head to the MINAE office at the entrance to town where the fee is US$15.

Golf
Golfers can head out to one of 3 courses in the area. On Playa Langosto you'll find the **Hacienda Pinilla**, T2680-3000, www.haciendapinilla.com. North of Tamarindo is the **Royal Pacific** and, at the Meliá Playa Conchal Beach Resort, is the **Garra de León**. You'll be looking at the best part of US$100 for a round, with clubs.

Ə Transport

Playa Brasilito *p238*
Several buses from **San José** to **Playa
Flamingo**, jump off at Brasilito just before.
Also several buses from **Santa Cruz**. See
Playa Flamingo, below.

Playa Flamingo *p238*
A daily bus from **San José** leaves the Tralapa
terminal at Av 3, C 18-20, at 0800, 1100 and
1500 for Playa Flamingo, returning at 0245,
0900 and 1400, 5-6 hrs, US$6.60. Buses from
Santa Cruz leave every couple of hours
0600-1700, 2 hrs, US$1.60.

Playa Potrero *p239*
From **San José** take the bus to Playa
Flamingo – see above. Several buses
from **Santa Cruz** to Portero pass through
Brasilito, Flamingo and on to Portrero. See
Playa Flamingo above.

Playa Grande *p239*
There is no bus service to Playa Grande;
the nearest point of access is Huacas, from
where a taxi costs around US$8. A ferry
makes the short distance from Tamarindo,
US$1-2, from 0600-1600, arriving at the
dock beside Hotel Bula Bula.

Playa Tamarindo *p240, map p241*
A couple of direct buses are available from
San José, **Empresa Alfaro**, T2222-2666,
departing from Av 3, C 18-20 at 1130 and
1330, US$6. There is a regular service linking
to **Santa Cruz** (5 a day) and **Liberia** (6 a day).
In high season there are also services with
Interbus and **Grayline Fantasy** bus between
Jacó, **Manuel Antonio**, **Monteverde**, **San
José**, **Arenal** and **Rincón de la Vieja**,
US$29-US$38.

Playa Junquillal *p242*
Daily bus from **Santa Cruz** departs 1030,
returns at 1530, US$6.15.

Ə Directory

Playa Brasilito *p238*
Internet Café Internet Nany, wonderfully
out of place, fast machines, clean a/c office.
Open 1000-2200 daily.

Playa Flamingo *p238*
Banks There's a branch of Banco de Costa
Rica with an ATM – the only one for miles
around. **Language schools** Centro
Panamericano de Idiomas, T2645-5002,
www.cpi-edu.com, has a Spanish school in
Playa Flamingo, with additional campuses in
Monteverde and Heredia. Great choice if you
want to balance study with staying in a
variety of places in the country. Prices from
US$315 a week, plus US$150 for homestay.
Innovative programmes such as combining
PADI diving certification with Spanish
immersion courses. **Pharmacies** Open
0800-2000 daily.

Playa Tamarindo *p240, map p241*
Banks Banco Nacional, open Mon-Fri
0830-1545, with Visa ATM. **Internet**
Tamarindo Internet, open daily 0900-2200,
US$2.30 for 30 mins. Above Maresias Surf
Shop there's an internet service and others
can be expected to open up. There's also
internet access on 2nd floor of beach
shops near the turning circle. **Language
schools** Wayra Institute de Español,
T2653-0359, www.spanish-wayra.co.cr.
20-hr week-long morning or afternoon
courses from US$250, US$380 with
homestay. Discounts for longer courses. A
couple of student houses in Playa Tamarindo
or homestays can be arranged – which is
much better for your Spanish. **Laundry**
A couple to choose from with Mariposa
Laundry and Punto Limpio. **Medical
services** Pharmacy Tamarindo, open
24 hours for emergencies, T2653-0210.

Santa Cruz to Nicoya

At the economic heart of the peninsula, Santa Cruz and Nicoya are the main retail centres, linked by the vital Highway 21, and good for topping up on supplies. Nearby Guatil provides an interesting shopping trip for local Chorotega ceramics. ⟫ *For listings, see pages 251-252.*

Santa Cruz → *Colour map 1, B3.*

Heading from Liberia down Highway 21, the first town of any real size in the surrounding area is Santa Cruz (52 km), with a population of just under 18,000. Known as Costa Rica's 'National Folklore City', January is the month for the festival of Santo Cristo de Esquipulas with its colourful fiestas, dancing and regional food. (July 25th is Guanacaste Day and the town also celebrates this in some style with dancing and music.)

For much of the rest of the year, it's a quiet little town serving as a transport and supply hub. If you're heading for self-catering accommodation, Santa Cruz is a good place to stock up on basics. Activity focuses on a rather bare square called Plaza de los Mangos. While in town, take a look at the modern **church**, in the main square 600 m south, with its fine stained-glass images that spray a rainbow of colours across the congregation. The tower of the old church is monument to the earthquakes that shake the region.

Guatil → *Colour map 1, B3.*

An easy and worthwhile excursion meandering through cattle pastures and small settlements, the town of Guatil is 12 km east of Santa Cruz. The neat lines of pots and plates seen laid out along the road in parts of the peninsula are mostly produced here and the town still makes the hand-crafted and oven-baked red and black pieces. You can visit a few studios (easily found along the road), just drop in and have a look at what is on offer. If you're interested in the manufacturing process, stick your head round the back and nose around – with luck, you'll get the full low-down on techniques and plants used to make the dyes. Naturally, items are for sale as well, with prices slightly cheaper than stalls along the main road. Buses leave Santa Cruz every couple of hours.

Nicoya → *Colour map 1, C3.*

At the heart of the peninsula, Nicoya (population 25,000) is a pleasant little market town, distinguished by possessing the country's second oldest church. Like Santa Cruz, Nicoya is an important regional transport and supply centre, with links to the beach communities of Sámara and Nosara to the south, the Tempisque ferry to the east, and Playa Naranjo on the southeastern tip of the peninsula.

The church of **San Blas** has a pulpit dating back to the 16th century, while the

Nicoya

Banco Popular Ⓢ Ⓢ Banco Nacional

To Liberia

ACT Office

Av Central San Blas

Banco de Costa Rica

Chipanzo

Río

To Sámara

100 metres
100 yards

Sleeping 🛏
Jenny **2**
Las Tinajas **3**
Pensión Venecia **4**

Eating 🍴
Daniela **1**
Teyet **3**

actual building was consecrated in 1644. Looking every bit its age, the church has undergone periodic renovation over the years.

For most of the year the town beats to the gently percussive rhythm of commerce. On the 12 December, however, it lets its hair down by celebrating the Fiesta de la Yegüita, with dancing parades, fireworks, bullfights and music.

Parque Nacional Barra Honda → Colour map 1, B/C4.

ⓘ *Cost of entrance to the park is US$10, a guide costs US$35, with US$12 per person for equipment. If you wish to visit the caves you will need harnesses, ropes and guides, as entrance to the cave is from the top. To get there, first go to Nicoya, from where there are several buses a day to Quebrada Honda on the road to the Tempisque ferry (first bus 1030, last bus returns for Nicoya 1630, giving you only 2 hrs in the park). Ask the bus driver to drop you off on the road to Barra Honda (Nacaome), from where it is a 1-hr walk to Santa Ana and the park offices.*

A limestone outcrop to the west of Nicoya creates the largest cave system in Costa Rica and forms the heart of Barra Honda National Park (2295 ha). Rising to a plateau of just over 500 m, the steep sided hills are the result of fault movements. A network of 42 caves has been discovered to date but only 19 having been officially explored, making this a focus of attention for the serious spelunker.

Because access is fairly difficult, the Barra Honda caves are in excellent condition. Most people enter through the **Terciopelo Cave**, which is richly adorned with stalactites and stalagmites – formed by deposits of calcium carbonate and the trickling of water from the roof of the caves. The flutes of one, *The Organ*, provide an eerie accompaniment to the darkness, producing musical notes when gently tapped. **Santa Ana** cave descends for over 240 m, while the **Trampa** cave has the longest single vertical descent at 52 m. The musty aroma is interrupted at the **Pozo Hediondo** (Stinking Pothole) – named after the only cave with a large bat population, whose droppings produce the smell. **Nicoa cave** stands out for mention – human remains and pre-Columbian artefacts have been found here.

Above ground there are a few **trails** leading up and across the plateau with fine views across the peninsula and the Gulf of Nicoya. One trail leads to **La Cascada** – an impressive waterfall flowing over calcium deposits, but you'll need a guide to get here as the trails have been hopelessly muddled by cow paths.

ⓦ Santa Cruz to Nicoya listings

For Sleeping and Eating price codes and other relevant information, see Essentials, pages 44-47.

ⓦ Sleeping

Santa Cruz p250

A-B La Pampa, 25 m west and south of Plaza de los Mangos, T2680-0586. 25 simple rooms, some with a/c, all with private bath with *agua natural*. Good and central, plenty of parking.
B Diriá, at the entrance to town on the main highway, T2680-0080, hoteldiria@hotmail. com. Most comfortable option in town, but still a little tired. 50 clean rooms with private bath, hot water and TV. Also has 2 pools.
D Anatolia, 200 m south and 1 block west of Plaza de los Mangos, T2680-0333. Small dark rooms, with partitions and dirty bathrooms.

Nicoya p250, map p250

B Complejo Turístico Curime, 500 m south of the centre on the road to Sámara, T2685-5238. 26 bungalows and rooms, all with hot water private bath. A/c and a fridge in the bungalows, fans in the rooms. The rooms and hotel need a fresh lick of paint but there's a

curious blend of luxury options including a 3-m deep swimming pool. Price includes breakfast. The best option close to town.
D Jenny, or 'Yenny' as the sign says, T2685-5050. 24 spotless rooms with bath, a/c, towels, soap and TV. Friendly, helpful staff. Cavernous rooms – book in with a friend and play hide and seek. Recommended.
D-E Pensión Venecia, opposite old church on square, T2685-5325. Squidgy beds but good value for the price.
E Las Tinajas, opposite the bus stop to Liberia on Av 1, T2685-5081. 28 rooms with bath, modern, clean and good value.

Parque Nacional Barra Honda *p251*
E Las Delicias Ecotourism Project, T2685-5580. Simple but comfortable accommodation is available in 3 bungalows, owned and operated by the local community at the park entrance. Camping is permitted (**F**) with meals at reasonable prices, as well as guided tours.

❼ Eating

Santa Cruz *p250*
Several *sodas* dotted around town.
❙ **Coopetortilla**, 200 m south of the main square, is a local institution. A women's cooperative, cooking local dishes of *casadas* and *pinto gallo* on wooden fires. Very cheap and enjoyable.

Nicoya *p250, map p250*
There are many good, simple places to eat around the main plaza.
❙ **Café de Blita**, 2 km out of Nicoya on the road to Sámara. Has been recommended.
❙ **Daniela**. Has good breakfast, lunches, coffee and *refrescos*.
❙ **Teyet**. Good and with quick service if you're in a hurry.

❿ Transport

Santa Cruz *p250*
Buses leave and arrive from terminals on the north side of Plaza de los Mangos. Buses from **San José** leave from Av 3, C 18-20. 9 buses a day from 0700-1800, 5 hrs, US$5.80. A ½ hourly service goes to **Liberia**, 0530-1930, US$1.20, and **Nicoya**, 0630-2130, 40 mins, US$0.50. Buses to **Tamarindo** leave at 2030, USUS0.62, returning at 0645. Buses to **Playa Flamingo** and nearby beaches every 90 mins with **El Folklórico**.

Nicoya *p250, map p250*
There are 7 daily buses with **Empresa Alfaro** (Av 5, C 15, T2222-2666) from **San José**, 4-5 hrs, US$5.75. Service every 30 mins between **Liberia** 0430-2200 and **Santa Cruz** 0630-2130. To **Playa Naranjo** buses leave at 0500 and 1300, US$1.75, 2¼ hrs. There are 5 buses a day to **Sámara**, and 1 to **Nosara**.

❶ Directory

Santa Cruz *p250*
Banks Banco Nacional, with ATM, at junction with the main road. **Post office** 200 m south of Plaza de los Mangos.

Nicoya *p250, map p250*
Banks An excess of banks with a branch of Banco de Costa Rica, on the main square with an ATM, and branches of Banco Popular and Banco Nacional, a couple of blocks up C 3. **Internet** Next to restaurant Teyet, up the stairs. US$0.70/hr, open 0800-2000. Closed Sun. **Post office** On the corner of main square. **Useful addresses** The Area de Conservación Tempisque (ACT) office is on the north side of the square. While there is limited information for visitors, they can help with enquiries about protected areas and visits to nearby Barra Honda National Park.

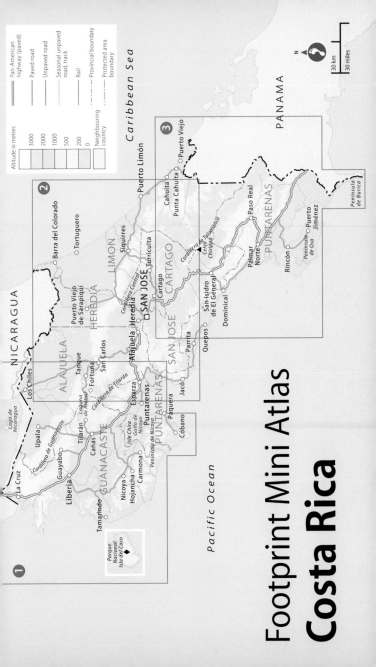

Footprint Mini Atlas
Costa Rica

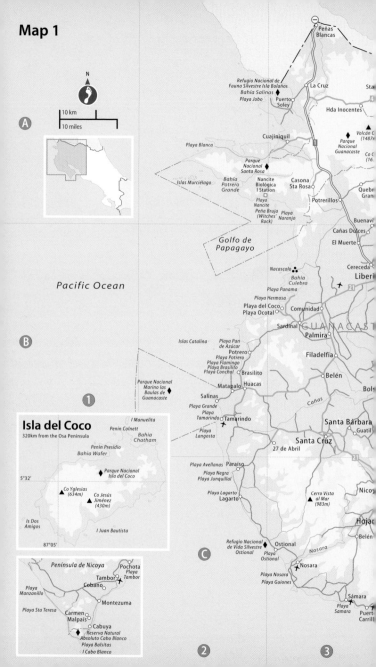

Map 1

A

N

| 10 km |
| 10 miles |

B

Pacific Ocean

1

Isla del Coco
320km from the Osa Peninsula

I Manuelita

Penín Colnett

Bahía Chatham

Penín Presidio

Bahía Wafer

Parque Nacional Isla del Coco

5°32'

Co Yglesias (634m)

Co Jesús Jiménez (430m)

Is Dos Amigos

I Juan Bautista

87°05'

Península de Nicoya

Pochota

Playa Tambor

Tambor

Cóbano

Playa Manzanillo

Montezuma

Playa Sta Teresa

Carmen

Malpaís

Cabuya

Reserva Natural Absoluto Cabo Blanco

Playa Balsitas

I Cabo Blanco

2

3

Peñas Blancas

Refugio Nacional de Fauna Silvestre Isla Bolaños
Bahía Salinas
Playa Jobo

La Cruz

Sta

Puerto Soley

Hda Inocentes

4

Cuajiniquil

Volcán C (1487

Parque Nacional Guanacaste

Co C (16.

Playa Blanca

Parque Nacional Santa Rosa

Islas Murciélago

Bahía Potrero Grande

Nancite Biológica I Station

Casona Sta Rosa

Potrerillos

Quebr Gran

Playa Nancite

Peña Bruja (Witches' Rock)

Playa Naranjo

Buenavi

Cañas Dulces

El Muerte

Cereceda

Liber

Golfo de Papagayo

Nacascolo

Bahía Culebra

Playa Panama

Playa Hermosa

Playa del Coco
Playa Ocotal

Comunidad

GUANACAST

Sardinal

Palmira

Islas Catalina

Playa Pan de Azúcar

Potrero

Playa Potrero

Playa Flamingo

Playa Brasilito

Playa Conchal

Brasilito

Filadelfia

Belén

Parque Nacional Marino las Baulas de Guanacaste

Matapalo

Huacas

Bol

Salinas

Cañas

Playa Grande

Playa Tamarindo

Tamarindo

Santa Bárbara

Guatil

Playa Langosta

Santa Cruz

27 de Abril

Playa Avellanas

Paraíso

Playa Negra

Playa Junquillal

Nico

Playa Lagarto

Lagarto

Cerro Vista al Mar (983m)

Hojai

Belén

Refugio Nacional de Vida Silvestre Ostional

Ostional

Playa Ostional

Nosara

Nosara

Playa Nosara

Playa Guiones

Sámara

Playa Samara

Puerti Carrill

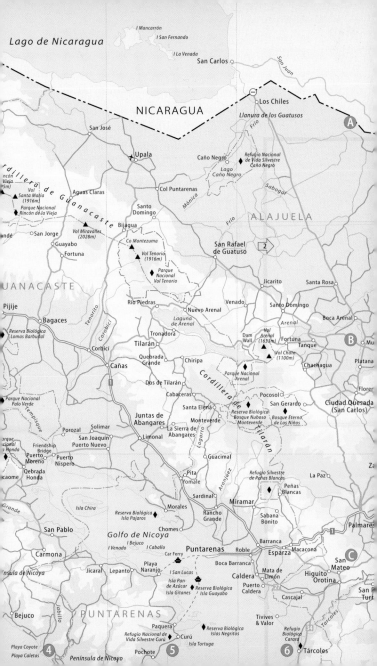

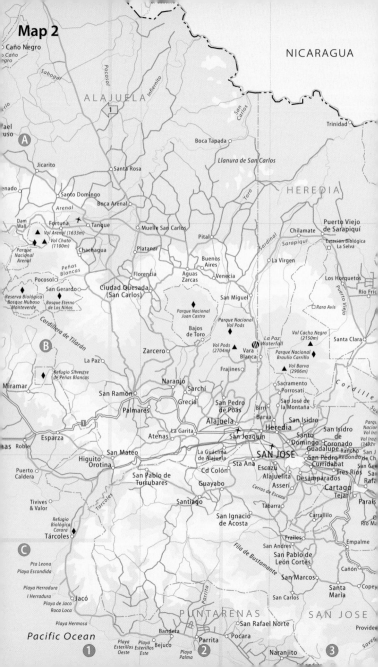

Index

A
2 B2   Alajuela

B
1 B4   Bagaces
3 B3   Bahía Drake
2 A4   Barra del Colorado
1 B3   Belén
3 B4   Boruca
3 A5   Bribrí
3 B4   Buenos Aires

C
3 A5/6   Cahuita
1 B5   Cañas
3 C3   Carate
1 inset   Carmen
2 C3   Cartago
3 C5   Ciudad Neily
2 B2   Ciudad Quesada (San Carlos)
1 A3   Cuajiniquil

D
3 B2   Dominical
3 C3   Dos Brazos
3 B3   Drake

E
1 C6   Esparza

F
2 B1   Fortuna

G
3 C4   Golfito and the beaches
2 B4   Guácimo
2 B4   Guápiles
1 B3   Guatil

H
2 B3   Heredia

I
3 C2   Isla del Caño
1 inset   Isla del Coco

J
2 C1   Jacó
1 B5   Juntas de Abangares

L
1 A3   La Cruz and Bahía Salinas
3 C3   La Palma
1 B5   Lake Arenal
1 B3   Liberia

M
1 inset   Malpaís
3 A1   Manuel Antonio
3 A6   Manzanillo
3 B2   Matapalo
2 B5   Matina
1 B6   Monteverde
1 inset   Montezuma
2 B4   Monumento Nacional Guayabo

N
1 C3   Nicoya
1 C4   Nicoya Peninsula
1 C3   Nosara

P
3 B3   Palmar Norte
3 B3   Palmar Sur
1 C5   Paquera
2 B5   Parismina
1 B/C4   Parque Nacional Barra Honda
3 A5/6   Parque Nacional Cahuita
1 C6   Parque Nacional Carara
3 A3   Parque Nacional Chirripó
3 C3   Parque Nacional Corcovado
1 A3   Parque Nacional Guanacaste
3 B4   Parque Nacional La Amistad
3 B1   Parque Nacional Manuel Antonio
3 B2   Parque Nacional Isla Marino Ballena
1 B4   Parque Nacional Palo Verde
1 A4   Parque Nacional Rincón de la Vieja
1 A2/3   Parque Nacional Santa Rosa
2 A/B4   Parque Nacional Tortuguero
2 A5   Parque Nacional Volcán Poás
1 B5   Parque Nacional Volcán Tenorio
2 B4   Parque Nacional Volcán Turrialba
3 C5   Paso Canoas
3 B4   Paso Real
1 A6   Peñas Blancas
1 C4   Peninsula Nicoya
1 B2   Playa Grande
2 C1   Playa Hermosa
1 C2   Playa Junquillal

1 C5   Playa Naranjo
1 inset   Playa Tambor
1 C3   Puerto Carillo
3 C4   Puerto Jiménez
2 B6   Puerto Limón
3 A5   Puerto Viejo de Talamanca
2 B3   Puerto Viejo
1 C5   Puntarenas

Q
3 B1   Quepos

R
1 C5   Refugio Nacional de Vida Silvestre Curú
1 C2   Refugio Nacional de Vida Silvestre Ostional
1 B4   Reserva Biológica Lomas Barbudal
1 inset   Reserva Natural Absoluta Cabo Blanco
3 C3   Rincón

S
1 C3   Sámara
2 B2   San Carlos
3 B2   San Isidro de El General
2 C3   San José
3 C2   San Pedrillo
3 C5   San Vito
1 B3   Santa Cruz
1 B3   Santa Bárbara
1 B6   Santa Elena
1 inset   Santa Teresa
3 B3   Sierpe
2 B4   Siquirres
3 A6   Sixaola

T
1 B2   Tamarindo
1 B5   Tilarán
2 A4   Tortuguero
2 C4   Turrialba

U
1 A5   Upala

V
3 B4   Valle de Coto Brus
2 B3   Volcán Irazú
1 B4   Volcán Miravalles

W
3 C5   Wilson Botanical Gardens

Western beaches

Isolated from easy road transport, and most easily reached by air, Nosara and Sámara have a reputation for being more upmarket beach destinations. But the surf is good, and a few cheaper options are opening up. You can also visit the nesting turtles at Playa Ostional. ▶▶ *For listings, see pages 255-261.*

Nosara

Rancho Congo 7
Rancho Suizo 13
Villa Mango 1

Sleeping 🛏
Almost Paradise 2
Blew Dogs 11
Cabinas Agnell 3
Café de Paris 9
Casa Romántica 4
Casa Tucán 5
Gilded Iguana 8
Harbor Reef 15
Lagarta Lodge 10
Lodge Vista del Mar 6
Playas de Nosara 12

Eating 🍴
Fooney's Mexican 8
La Dolce Vita 3
La Luna 4
Marlins Bill 9
Olga's 5
Pancho's Mexican 6
Pizza Costa Mar 11
Rancho Tico 12

Bars & clubs 🍸
Bambú 1
Disco Tropicana 2

Nosara → *Colour map 1, C3.*

Nosara is a small village about 26 km north of Sámara without much to see or do in it – which makes it ideal if you like lying around on beaches. Indeed most people come for the three unspoiled beaches which are a few kilometres from the village. **Playa Nosara** is to the north of the village across the Nosara river, and a site for nesting turtles (see Ostional, below). **Playa Pelada**, the prettiest and smallest, south of the river between rocky headlands, is a popular spot for surfers and has a bat cave at one end which is good to explore – ask locally for details. **Playa Guiones** is a long expanse of white sand backed by low dunes and forest, with good, long surf breaks. Note that it's about 5 km from Playa Guiones to Nosara village heading north – a long, hot walk. There is no bus but hitching is possible if you're prepared to do it in sections.

The roads between the main road and the beach are labyrinthine and finding the beach or your hotel can be tricky; look for signs along the main road indicating where to turn off. For Playa Pelada follow signs to Olga's Restaurant or La Luna. To get to Playa Guiones, turn off at Café de Paris and follow the road straight on to the beach.

Nosara is one of the few places where there is no development on the beach and that contributes in large measure to the appeal of the area. Much of the property backing Pelada and Guiones is owned by North Americans and Europeans, and the hills above Nosara are dotted with the holiday homes of the rich and famous. Some of the expatriate community have joined together to form the Nosara Civic Association, www.nosaracivicassociation.com, which keeps control over development and protects the habitat and wildlife.

The main local attraction is a visit to Ostional to see the mass nestings of the Olive Ridley sea turtles (see below). Other activities include hiking in the privately owned **Reserva Biológica Nosara** ① T2682-0035, www.lagarta.com/reserva.htm. Most hotels arrange horseback tours along the beaches, through hills or to a nearby waterfall. Boat and canoe trips ride into the mangrove swamps of the Nosara River. Of course fishing is possible and all beach-related equipment – surfing, boogie boards, snorkelling gear – can be hired.

Refugio Nacional de Vida Silvestre Ostional → Colour map 1, C2.
① Day and evening trips to the turtle nesting grounds are easily arranged through local hotels. If driving, Ostional is a 30-min drive north of Nosara. Visit the MINAE Ranger Station for more details. 4WD needed in rainy season if coming from Sámara. There is one daily bus at 0500 to Santa Cruz and Liberia, which returns at 1230 from Santa Cruz, 3 hrs, US$1.20.
North of Nosara is **Playa Ostional** a wide beach accessed from Nosara, protected for the natural spectacle of the *arribada* when tens of thousands of Olive Ridley turtles arrive en masse in frenzied acts of nest building. Along with Playa Nancite to the north, Ostional is one of the most important nesting sites for the *lora* (Olive Ridley turtle) in the world.

The *arribadas* – literally 'arrivals' – occur between July and November with the largest numbers arriving between August and October, at the end of the lunar cycle. Don't worry if you haven't arranged your holiday around the phases of the moon, though, you can normally see some turtle activity at any time of the month. As with humans, you'll always find one turtle that just has to be different! The beach is also occasionally used by the leatherback and Pacific green turtle.

Ostional is also interesting in that locals are permitted to harvest turtle eggs under a strict, and now well developed, programme that incorporates conservation goals with the genuine needs and requirements of the local community.

The beach is part of the wider and recently expanded **Ostional National Wildlife Refuge**, protecting 352 ha of land reserve, including Nosara beach and a marine zone of 8,000 ha. The sparse vegetation in the reserve supports mixed deciduous forest species with good populations of howler and capuchin monkeys. On the northern banks of the Río Nosara, large mangrove swamps are home to over 100 species of birds – a good spot to explore slowly by kayak.

Sámara → Colour map 1, C3. Town map p257. www.samarabeach.com.
Sámara is a smallish village that has managed to maintain some of its regular way of life alongside steady tourist development. It also has one of the best bathing beaches in Costa Rica. The place is gradually becoming more developed, but it still has a relaxed pace and, with a gentle trickle of international residents from around the world, the place is genuinely cosmopolitan and a good excuse to get away for a few days and relax by the sea.

For *Sleeping* and *Eating* price codes and other
relevant information, see *Essentials*, pages 44-47.

◉ **Sleeping**

Nosara *p253, map p253*
Hotels in Nosara charge more and offer less
than hotels in Sámara. When booking, check
whether your hotel accepts credit cards.

Playa Pelada
North section **L Playas de Nosara**, high
above Punta Pelada with amazing views over
both beaches, the ocean and the hills,
T2682-0121, www.nosarabeachhotel.com.
A very ornate and colonial-style hotel with
22 white and wooden rooms, decorated with
wall hangings, dotted around the grounds
with a pool, jacuzzi and restaurant. Trails
lead to the beach. Surf packages available.
AL-A Lagarta Lodge, T2682-0035,
www.lagarta.com. 6 pleasant rooms with
phenomenal views overlooking the ocean,
forest and hills, all with bath, hot water and
fan. Good restaurant, pool and tours offered.
A beautiful setting, the hotel owns a private
reserve and has a telescope for wildlife
viewing, making it a great choice for nature
lovers and those in search of a quiet getaway.
Also provide local hiking maps. Recommended.
AL-A Villa Mango, T2682-0130, www.villa
mangocr.com. 5 rooms in a beautiful villa
with a great, homely ambience, jaw-dropping
scenery and a pool for relaxing in. 2 kitchens,
private hot water bath in every room,
breakfast included, 8-min walk to the beach.
A Rancho Suizo, T2682-0057, www.nosara.
ch. 10 rustic bungalows with bath and fans, in
pleasant tropical gardens. Jacuzzi, swimming
pool, bar and restaurant with good food,
breakfast included. A quiet spot, not for raucous
party-goers, with eco-friendly tours, boogie
boards, snorkels, bicycles for hire. Popular
with Europeans – and children under 10.
B Hotel Almost Paradise, T2682-0173.
A rustic, pretty place in the hills above Playa
Pelada, with one fully equipped apartment

and 8 rooms sleeping 2-4 people, with bath,
hot water, fan and balcony with superb view.
A quiet hotel for people who like wildlife,
with lots of greenery, art on the walls, a
restaurant in high season, pool and bar.
Excellent value in low season. Recommended.
AL-B Lodge Vista del Mar, quite a way
north off the road, too far to walk, T2682-
0633, www.lodgevistadelmar.com. Fantastic
views from all 8 rooms over the ocean and
Nosara mountains. Rooms are simple and
pleasant with private warm water bath, there
is a communal kitchen, lap pool and
complimentary fruit and coffee for breakfast.

Middle section **AL-A Casa Romántica**,
T2682-0272, www.casa-romantica.net. A
quiet, beautiful hotel close to the beach with
10 big rooms, good for couples and families,
with hot water bath and fan. An extensive
breakfast menu is included in the price, and
there's an excellent international restaurant
managed by the Swiss owners. They have a
large pool and are just steps from the beach.
Recommended.
B Rancho Congo, T2682-0078. 2 big rooms
with bath, hot water, fans and terrace set in
natural gardens with lots of native plants. Close
to the beach, it's also good for observing
wildlife. The German owner provides a very
good breakfast for the price. Discounts for
longer stays and personalized tours.
A-E Blew Dogs, T2682-0080, www.blew
dogs.com. 3 cabins with kitchen and private
hot water bath and a flop room (or dormitory
to the rest of us), pool, bar and restaurant.
A popular spot with a great atmosphere
and a hang out for surfers. Excellent value.
A-B Gilded Iguana, T2682-0259, www.
gildediguana.com. 12 huge, airy double
rooms with bath, hot water, a/c or fan,
surrounding a pool. Owned by a gregarious
and cool gringo called Joe, good restaurant
and bar decorated with hand-painted
ceramic tiles; watersports and tours,
especially kayak and fishing.

South section AL-A Casa Tucan,
T2682-0113, www.casatucan.net. 8 units
sleeping up to 4 people have hot water bath
and a/c, some with kitchens. Attractive
outdoor restaurant and bar, there's also a
pool and tours are easily arranged. Popular
with surfers, it's also a little overpriced.
L-A Café de Paris, on the road, T2682-0087,
www.cafedeparis.net. 14 airy rooms and
some bungalows (4 with full kitchen) with
hot water bath, a/c or fan. Activity centred,
there's a pool, pool table, basketball, movies
on a big screen during high season, surf
boards and snorkelling equipment. Also
laundry, car rental, tours, flights and internet.
Also have a couple of villas with sea views for
around US$700 a week. Popular with surfers
and young groups. Families and groups
welcome. Has disabled access.
LL-AL Harbor Reef, further down the hill,
T2682-0059, www.harborreef.com. A very
big, yet unimposing resort offering standard
rooms, grand suites, apartments and houses
with private pools. Rooms are camouflaged
amid foliage – a distinguished slice of the
upper crust. The bar and restaurant are
open to all, with occasional live music.
C Casa Río Nosara, T2682-0117. 6 rustic
A-frame cabins about 2 km south of the
village, on the river, all with bath, hot water
and fan andn with use of the kitchen and
barbecue. Very friendly German owners
have 18 well looked-after horses for riding
holidays, horseback tours and river tours.
Perfect for outdoors and animal-lovers.

In the village E Cabinas Chorotega, near
the supermarket, T2682-0129. Very clean
rooms with shared or private bath, fan, bar
and restaurant downstairs, can be noisy.
F Cabinas Agnell, T2682-0142. All rooms
with bath, cold showers and fan.
Recommended.

Camping

You can camp at **Blew Dog**, in the middle
near the Gilded Iguana.

**Refugio Nacional de Vida Silvestre
Ostional** *p254*
F pp Cabinas Ostional, next to the village
shop. Very basic accommodation with bath,
clean, friendly.
F pp Cabinas Guacamaya. With bath, clean,
good food on request.
   You can also **camp** on the beach, but
ask locally for permission about where.

Sámara *p254, map p257*
L-AL (Aparthotel) Mirador de Sámara,
rising up the hill above the village with great
views, T2656-0044, www.miradordesamara.
com. 6 large, cool and comfortable suites
with cable TV, orthopaedic mattresses, bath,
kitchen, private balconies and safebox. A
restaurant serves lunch and dinner in the
tower. There's a pool, internet access, and
tours arranged around Sámara and further
afield. Groups are welcome and well catered
for and weddings can be planned here – the
friendly German owners will help arrange all
the official paper work. Recommended.
AL Las Brisas, east of town on the beach,
T2656-0250, www.brisas.net. Large, 34-
bungalow complex with bath, fan or a/c.
Italian-owned. 2 pools, jacuzzi, laundry
service. It's a little bland but with personal
touches and pleasantly landscaped. Also
has a restaurant and bar.
AL Hotel Fénix, on the beach, about 2 km
east of the village in a residential area,
T2656-0158, www.fenixhotel.com. 6 slightly
cramped double units, sleeping up to 4, with
fans, hot water private bath, kitchens, very
small pool, run by a couple from Seattle. Boat
tours and watersports offered. No restaurant,
but close to local eateries.
L Villas Kalimba, T2656-0929, www.villas
kalimba.com. A gorgeous place with 6 fully
equipped, 2-bedroom, Italian-designed villas
surrounding a pool, jacuzzi and *rancho* with
BBQ. Each villa has a/c, a hand-crafted wooden
window system, hand-made furniture,
warmly painted, luxurious farmhouse-style
kitchen and 2 bathrooms (1 en suite).
Delightful Italian owners. Recommended.

B Belvedere, sloping up the hill, T2656-0213, www.belvederesamara.net. 10 double rooms sleeping 2-4 people, all with private bath and solar-heated hot water, a/c and cable TV. Swimming pool, jacuzzi and a comfortable family atmosphere with very friendly German owners. Also has a couple of flats sleeping up to 4 for longer stays. A small restaurant serves breakfast and light snacks overlooking the bay.

AL Giada, on the main road, T2656-0132, www.hotelgiada.net. 24 pleasantly decorated rooms with attractive bathrooms, hot water, a/c, cable TV and balcony in this Italian-owned hotel. Pool, laundry, internet, dolphin and horse tours. Restaurant and bar open from 1200-2200, serving pizza and pasta.

C Posada Matilori, T2656-0314, posada matilori@racsa.co.cr. 3 rooms with shared bath in a private house with fully equipped kitchen and communal chill-out area. All rooms are screened but let in loads of light and air; a very well constructed place and a great hidden spot, moments from the beach, perfect if you are travelling in a group – you can rent out the entire place . Bicycle rental for guests, washer and dryer with soap provided – even spices in the kitchen – a gem. **B Marbella**, T2656-0302, www.marbella. com. 10 rooms with private hot water bath, some with a/c, cheaper with fan, attractive building, German-run hotel, nice grounds, pool and good service. Breakfast included in the price, bar and restaurant open during high season.

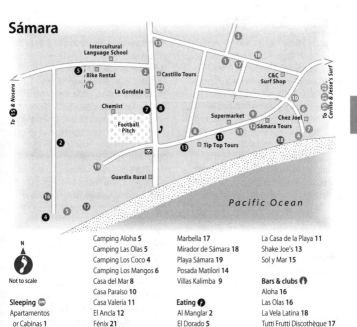

Sámara

Not to scale

Sleeping 🛏
Apartamentos
or Cabinas **1**
Arenas **2**
Bahia **23**
Belvedere **3**

Camping Aloha **5**
Camping Las Olas **5**
Camping Los Coco **4**
Camping Los Mangos **6**
Casa del Mar **8**
Casa Paraíso **10**
Casa Valeria **11**
El Ancla **12**
Fénix **21**
Giada **13**
Hospedaje Muñoz **22**
Las Brisas **15**

Marbella **17**
Mirador de Sámara **18**
Playa Sámara **19**
Posada Matilori **14**
Villas Kalimba **9**

Eating 🍴
Al Manglar **2**
El Dorado **5**
El Jardín Marino **8**
El Lagarto **4**
Las Brasas **7**

La Casa de la Playa **11**
Shake Joe's **13**
Sol y Mar **15**

Bars & clubs 🍸
Aloha **16**
Las Olas **16**
La Vela Latina **18**
Tutti Frutti Discothèque **17**

A-C Casa del Mar, T2656-0264, www.casa delmarsamara.com. French/Canadian-owned hotel near the beach with 11 simple rooms with bath, 6 with shared bath. Also a suite for 6 available. There's a safe, laundry, jacuzzi in gardens, tours. Prices are high in peak season, but the hotel has an exceptionally friendly and safe feel. A good choice. The cheaper rooms are an excellent deal off-season.

B-D Cabinas Acuario, next to the beach, T2656-0036. Clean and friendly chalet-style rooms with private bath.

B-C Casa Valeria, on the beach, T2656-0511, casavaleria_af@hotmail.com. Various different rooms, some with sea view, all nicely decorated, most with hot water and private bath. Friendly and good value, especially for 3 sharing. Breakfast included, kitchen and laundry available and a small bar. Tours, tickets and car hire arranged.

C Apartamentos or Cabinas, next to Hotel Marbella, T2656-0209. Catering for a predominantly *Tico* crowd and usually on a weekly or monthly basis, units have bath, fridge, fan and kitchen. No reception, telephone only. Good value and often full.

C Bahía, on the beach near Las Brisas. Tired-looking rooms with bath and fan sleeping up to 3. The *Tico* owner works in the post office – ask if there is room before trekking out there. Restaurant serves *típica* and Western food.

C Casa Paraíso. Several high-ceilinged, airy rooms with bath, hot showers and king-size beds. No-frills but friendly and well run by the French owners, seems reasonable compared to some, but better value if you are sharing with several people. Restaurant open for lunch and dinner serving typical food, seafood and meat.

E Arenas, in the centre of town, T2656-0320. 12 basic but clean rooms with bath, cold showers, fan, use of sink to wash clothes, friendly *Tico* owner and parrot. *Típica* restaurant in the high season, discounts for longer stays.

E-F Hotel Playa Sámara, T2656-0190. A large hotel with 84 grimy rooms, all with bath and fan, feels like a scene from *Escape from Alcatraz*. A last resort.

F Hospedaje Muñoz, opposite Arenas. 8 very basic rooms with shared bath and a very happy owner who loves his music.

F pp El Ancla, T2656-0254. Clean and simple rooms with bath and fan on the beach and restaurant. Friendly and good value.

Camping

On the eastern side of the village, on the beach, try **G pp Camping Los Coco**, T2656-0496, toilets, electricity until 2200. Slightly further from the beach is **Camping Los Mangos**. At the other end of the village, near El Lagartos disco is **Camping Aloha**, T2658-0028, with electricity and showers, and **Camping Las Olas**.

🍴 Eating

Nosara *p253, map p253*
Playa Pelada
North section 🍴 **La Luna**, slightly up the hill. Good food and ambience.

🍴🍴 **Hotel Almost Paradise**. Serves good food in high season with great view.

🍴🍴 **Lagarta Lodge**. Restaurant is worth visiting at least once, not just for the extensive menu, but the breathtaking views. They have a great selection of salads, pastas, meats and fish, treat yourself to a sunset and one of their excellent wines. Closed Tue.

🍴🍴 **Olga's**. Highly recommended for seafood on the beach and cheap, all-day breakfasts.

🍴🍴 **Pancho's Mexican Restaurant and Market**. A good place for *enchiladas* with the works.

Middle section 🍴 **Casa Romántica**. A good European restaurant.

🍴🍴 **Giardino Tropicale**. For pizza cooked in a wood-fired oven.

🍴🍴 **Gilded Iguana**. Good for gringo food and company. Open for all day.

🍴 **Blew Dogs**. Has a lively bar and restaurant offering American-style fast food, wings, jerk chicken, pizzas. Open every day until midnight.

Fooney's Mexican Restaurant, next to their surf school. A huge place with a few too many varnished tree trunks, but good food, friendly hosts and US$1 margaritas on Wed nights. Closes at 2100.

South section ¶¶ **Café de Paris**. Not cheap, but big plates. Recommended.
¶ **La Dolce Vita**. Good Italian food.
¶-¶ **Marlins Bill**, slightly off the road north. A good seafood option.
Casa Tucan, an outdoor option towards the beach. A popular spot with good local food and regular live music.
Pizza Restaurant Costa Mar, south along the road out of town.

In the village ¶ **Rancho Tico**, on the outskirts of the village. Popular and local.
Soda Vanessa. Good and very cheap. One of plenty of *sodas* in the village.

Refugio Nacional de Vida Silvestre Ostional *p254*
1 km south of Cabinas Guacamaya is **Mirador de los Tortugueros**, a good restaurant with coffee and pancakes, good atmosphere.

Sámara *p254, map p257*
There are several cheap *sodas* around the football pitch in the centre of town.
¶-¶ **El Jardín Marino**, on the main street. Serves seafood, as you would expect.
¶-¶ **El Lagarto**, on the beach, close to Camping Las Olas. A steak house and BBQ restaurant with a good bar.
¶-¶ **Las Brasas**, on the main street. A mid-scale Spanish restaurant and bar. Great food with ravioli, surf'n'turf and seafood, but somewhat overpriced.
¶ **Al Manglar**, towards the beach. Best pizza in town.
¶ **Bahía Restaurant**, on the beach. Has an extensive menu of local, seafood and pasta dishes.
¶ **Cabinas El Ancla**. Has a good restaurant with both local and some international food.

¶ **El Dorado**, a little way along the road to Cangrejal. *Tico*, good pastas and pizza.
¶ **Free Radical**, *soda* on main road, 1 km east of town centre. Offers fresh *ceviche*, delightful pastries, beer, wine, natural juices, local honey and unique hand-blown glass products.
¶ **Las Casa de la Playa**, opposite Hotel Casa del Mar. Good salads, fish or chicken coconut curries and specials, they also have a small art gallery.
¶ **Pizza delivery**, T2656-0926. An Argentinian business delivers pizzas to hotels or any-where else you fancy, on Sat only, standard pizza menu.
¶ **Shake Joe's**, next to Casa de la Playa, and located on the beach. Dutch Joe has a relaxing 'hang out' bar and restaurant open from 1000 that serves huge filled baguettes, eggs any style, and for dinner they make everything other than *casado*, including homemade pastas, mega-salads and steak, all dinners come with locally made baguettes, and a very friendly owner. Cocktails also on the menu.
¶ **Sol y Mar**, now located slightly out of town on the road to Nosara. A good *soda* serving a mixture of Costa Rican and Western food.

🎷 Bars and clubs

Nosara *p253, map p253*
Playa Pelada
In the village Some of the funkier nightlife is in the village as well including **Bambú**, **Disco Tropicana**, only open at weekends, and various other hang-outs lining the football pitch.

Sámara *p254, map p257*
There are a few bars in town.
Bar La Gondola, renowned for cocktails, is a good starting spot.
Bar Las Olas is currently the hippest place to be at the weekend. They have 2 pool tables and loads of beach to dance away the night hours.

Aloha, next to Bar Las Olas. With pool tables and serving bar snacks – a fine night can be had between these 2 places.

Bar La Vela Latina, on the beach by Casa de Latina. Good choice for a more sophisticated drink.

Shake Joe's, perfect for a totally chilled night.

El Lagartos, near Al Manglar. Disco on the beach with live music, BBQ and pool tables.

Tutti Frutti Discothèque, close to Las Olas. Open at weekends.

○ Shopping

Nosara *p253, map p253*

There are several *pulperías* in the village, and a supermarket just beyond the airfield as you drive into the centre.

Café de Paris has an excellent bakery. Past Café del Mar is a small stretch of very attractive and pricey boutiques and souvenir shops including **Arte Guay** and **Chenoa Handcrafts**. There are several surf shops on the Café de Paris Rd, **Coconut Harry's Surf Shop** is on the main road, **Surf Shack**, is alongside the boutiques, and further down is **Nosara Surf n'Sport** (www.nosarasurf shop.com) and **Safari Surf**.

Sámara *p254, map p257*

There are various small shops and stalls selling clothing and souvenirs on the main road. **Super Sámara**, supermarket, near Casa del Mar, is well stocked.

▲ Activities and tours

Nosara *p253, map p253*

Most hotels will arrange tours, but if you're not staying at one of them, **Casa Río Nosara** is recommended for horse or river tours, and **Captain Joe's Jungle Expeditions**, at the Gilded Iguana, for kayaking and fishing. You can also go fishing with **Captain Woody's** charters, T2682-0307. For turtle tours, try **Rancho Suizo** or **Lagarta Lodge**, which are both sensitive to the turtles and don't exploit or bother them. You can get a healing energy massage from **Betty Coe Reiner**, T2682-0082, by appointment only. **The Yoga Institute**, T2682-0071, www.nosarayoga.com, is a world-renowned yoga centre with courses occasionally blending yoga and surfing. They're south of town, but their offices are by the boutiques near Café de Paris. There is a gym at **Surf Till Ya Die**, they also offer various treatments for tired and injured surfers, T2682-0096 for more information.

Sámara *p254, map p257*

Most hotels will arrange tours for you. You can rent bikes from a hardware store on the road to Cangrejal.

Alexis y Marco Boat Tours, T2656-0468. Offer ocean safari and boat transfers, Italian, English and Spanish spoken.

C&C Surf Shop, located opposite Hotel Mirador, T2656-0628. Also offers lessons, board hire, leashes, and other gear.

Captain Francisco, T2656-0708. Sports fishing, dolphin spotting and snorkeling, also boat transfers.

Carrillo Tours, offices located in the internet café on the main street, T2656-0543, carrillotours@racsa.co.cr. Run all the local tours, dolphin watching, kayaking, snorkelling and fishing.

Chon Tours, T2656-6674. Run horse-riding trips over beach or through jungle – your choice.

Guanasport ATV Tour, on the road to Ananas, T8843-6057. Quad bikes for hire.

Jesse's Original Sámara Beach Surf School & Gym, T2656-0055, www.samara surfschool.com. Promises that you can learn to surf in just an hour, which could be true as this is not a surfers' beach so it's a good place to start.

Sámara Sub Sport Diving, T2656-0700. Offers 2- and 3-tank diving, night, shark and wreck courses.

Shake Joe's. Home to Joe who has a boat and runs informal tours for groups, US$25 per person, fishing, snorkelling, exploring, whatever takes your fancy.

◎ Transport

Nosara *p253, map p253*

Air SANSA and NatureAir have early morning daily flights from **San José**, 40 mins, US$89 and US$117 one way.

Bus A direct bus from **San José** leaves Av 5 and C 14 at 0500 and 1200, 6 hrs, US$7.10. The bus returns at 1200. Tickets available from Soda Vanessa. There are also 4 daily buses to and from **Nicoya** at 0500, 0700, 1200 and 1500, 1½ hrs.

Sámara *p254, map p257*

Air Daily flights to and from **San José** are operated by **SANSA**, US$89. Hotel Giada is a representative for SANSA and Interbus.

Boat In high season it is possible to charter a boat to **Montezuma**, US$250 for 4 people, call Captain Francisco, T2656-0131.

Bus There is a direct bus to **San José** at 0400 and 0845 on Mon-Sat, 1300 Sun, up to 6 hrs, US$6.60. A good paved road leads from Sámara to **Nicoya**, with 5 buses between 0530 and 1630, 1½ hrs. To get to **Nosara** take a taxi to Servicentre Sámara (a gas station on the edge of town) buses to Nosara pass at 1300 and 1700, make sure you wait opposite the gas station and allow a little extra time; the bus won't stop if the driver doesn't see you. A school bus makes the journey to Nosara at about 1600 – ask locally for information about how to get on it.

◎ Directory

Nosara *p253, map p253*

Banks Banco Nacional, behind Café de Paris, open on Tue and Fri (0900-1500, closed at 1200 for 1-hr lunch), for withdrawals, changing cash or TCs and basic transactions. Some hotels also change money.
Internet At **Café de Paris. Language schools** Rey de Nosara Escuela de Idiomas, in the village, T2682-0215, www.reydenosara. itgo.com. Also acts as an impromptu information office, with advice about other things to see and do in the area and can arrange tours. **Laundry** In the boutique mall near Café de Paris, US$15 for a service wash, do it yourself for US$10.
Telephone Nosara office centre, in the village offers email, fax, international calls and photocopies, although there are reports that it is closing down. Open 0900-1200, 1330-1700, Mon-Fri, 0900-1300, Sat.

Sámara *p254, map p257*

Banks There is a branch of Banco Nacional in Sámara. Larger hotels will change their guests' money. Super Sámara, will give cash back on Visa when you buy something in the store. **Internet** Tropical Latitudes Internet Café, in centre of town. The main Internet café is on the main street behind Dragonfly handcrafts, open 0900-2100. **Language schools** Intercultura, Centro de Idiomas, by the beach, 150 m from El Dorado restaurant (see Eating), T2656-0127, www.samaralanguageschool.com, beach campus of the Heredia-based language school. **Medical services** Dentist next to pharmacy by the football field, English spoken, call T2656-0236 or T2838-6885 in emergencies. **Medical clinic** just out of town on the road to Cangrejal, T2656-0166. There are 2 chemists in town, the larger on the north side of the football field, same day delivery for medicines ordered from Nicoya. **Post office** By the bus station. **Telephone** Card-operated public telephones are opposite the football field.

Southern peninsula

From Nicoya, Highway 21 continues southeast skirting close to the towns of Holancha and Carmona, before running along the eastern flank of the peninsula with fine views of the gulf and small villages with sodas and cafés for refreshment. Although the road is asphalted, it takes a fair pounding from traffic and there are some axle-crunching potholes that almost stops at Playa Naranjo. Ferries from Puntarenas provide an easier route to Naranjo, and to Paquera further round the peninsula, from where the road heads west to the popular destinations of Montezuma, Malpaís and Santa Theresa. ▸▸ *For listings, see pages 266-276.*

Ins and outs

Getting there and around Regular vehicle and passenger ferries leave Puntarenas for Playa Naranjo and further around the bay to Paquera. See Puntarenas transport, page 293 for details. Zuma Tours provide a taxi boat service between Jaco and Montezuma. Buses meet the ferries arriving at Playa Naranjo providing transport to Nicoya and the north of the peninsula, and west to Montezuma and Malpaís. Ferries also go to Paquera and head west which conveniently avoids the truly appalling dirt road that links Playa Naranjo and Paquera. ▸▸ *See Transport, page 276, for further details.*

Playa Naranjo → *Colour map 1, C5.*

Deceptive to the last, there are no oranges and only fair beaches in Playa Naranjo, which is little more than a ferry dock with a few overpriced *sodas*, a restaurant and a gas station.

Paquera → *Colour map 1, C5.*

A small village 22 km along the coast from Playa Naranjo, Paquera is reached overland along one of Costa Rica's more deceptive roads. Seemingly a natural connection to the southernmost tip of the peninsula, the road climbs and falls over and around the rocky headland for the mind-numbingly slow trip towards the main tourist areas. If you're out exploring, a 4WD is recommended for the bone-shaking journey. If you're coming from Puntarenas, get the boat to Paquera where there are a few shops and some simple lodgings, for example Cabinas Rosita, on the inland side of the village. It is separated from the quay by a kilometre or so, where apart from a good *soda,* one restaurant, a public telephone, a petrol station and a branch of Banco de Costa Rica, there are few facilities. You will, however, find transport heading west to Tambor and beyond.

Playa Tambor → *Colour map 1, inset.*

From Paquera the road improves. Once a quiet fishing village, Tambor makes for a pleasant and quiet stopping point, with a dark sand beach stretching for 6 km around Bahía Ballena. The town has a handful of shops and restaurants, but apart from that you'll be entertaining yourself all day lying on the beach and taking walks along the sand.

Refugio Nacional de Vida Silvestre Curú → *Colour map 1, C5.*

① *Access to this privately owned refuge is only with advance permission by phoning Doña Julieta, T2661-2392. Trips can be organized from Montezuma. The Paquera-Montezuma bus can drop you at the locked gate. Basic accommodation is available, but is often booked in advance.*

Between Bahía Ballena and Paquera the Curú National Wildlife Refuge vies for the title of smallest protected area in the country with a mere 70 ha which nevertheless packs an

Peninsula and Gulf islands

Drifting off the southeastern tip of the Nicoya Peninsula, a handful of sand-fringed islands are easily visited from the peninsula, Puntarenas or San José. By far the most popular is a luxury cruise to **Isla Tortuga**, a pair of small uninhabited islands just off the peninsula to the south of Curú with beautiful white sand beaches, crystal-clear water ideal for swimming, snorkelling and other aquatic malarkey and just a gentle hint of a desert island feel. As one of the most popular trips in Costa Rica – and marketed accordingly – don't expect to have the place to yourself. Day tours from San José are available with several companies, the most respected being **Calypso Tours**, T2256-2727, www.calypsocruises.com. Tortuga can also be visited with trips starting from Puntarenas or, if you're on the peninsula, from Tambor or Montezuma.

Travelling from Puntarenas, boats also sail close to the biological reserves of **Isla Guayabo** and **Isla Negritos**.

Guayabo, a huge slab of steeply angled sedimentary rock and cliffs, is uninhabited and uninhabitable – for humans at least. Fortunately the 200-300 brown pelicans that use the island as a nesting site don't seem to mind, neither do the several other marine birds and, in winter, the peregrine falcons. Access is also denied to Isla Negritos, which protects and supports more marine birds as well as some important fauna.

Isla Gitana, or Isla Muertos as it is also known, is 13 km southwest of Puntarenas, just off the tip of the Nicoya Peninsula. It's cut off, and the stuff that tropical paradise islands are made of, with white sand beaches, lots of wildlife and a couple of rustic cabins (A per person, including meals), T2661-2994, www.islagitana.com. Water activities are also possible, and the owners will arrange speedboat transfers from Puntarenas or meet the Puntarenas–Paquera launch.

impressively diverse punch. Rising from the three beaches, perfect for swimming and snorkelling, there are five different lifezones, including red mangrove swamps. Mammals are equally diverse with white-tailed deer, raccoons, pacas and capuchin monkeys visible to the patiently quiet.

Cóbano

Little more than a junction for travellers passing through, Cóbano can be reached by bus from the Paquera ferry terminal. Its primary interest to visitors to the area is a branch of Banco Nacional, a petrol station and road access, by 4WD and in only the best conditions, to the north of the peninsula if the rivers are low enough. Ask locally for conditions – and listen to the answer. Taxis from Cobano to Montezuma are around US$5.

Montezuma → *Colour map 1, inset.*

Once a quiet sleepy hamlet, Montezuma is a small village which has become one of the most popular budget traveller destinations along the coast. Montezuma made its way onto the tourist circuit by virtue of its reputation for having a laid-back alternative lifestyle. These days it is no longer a secret hideaway, attracting as many holiday makers as backpackers, and you shouldn't expect to see much of the *Tico* way of life. At busy periods, hotels fill up every day, so check in early.

Although it gets crowded, there are some wonderful beaches, rounded off by rocky points, great for exploring tidal pools. Go for beautiful walks along the tree-lined beach, visit impressive waterfalls and, further afield, Cabo Blanco Nature Reserve (see below), is an easy and enjoyable day trip.

Montezuma

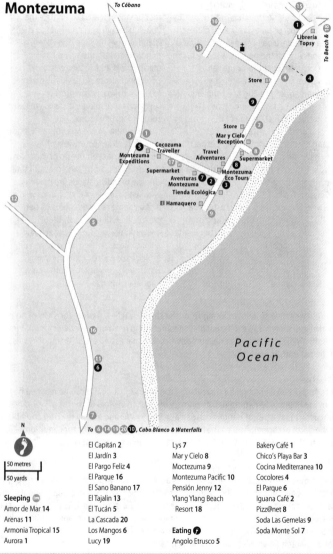

To Cóbano

To Beach &

Librería Topsy

Store

Store
Mar y Cielo Reception

Cocozuma Traveller
Montezuma Expeditions

Travel Adventures

Supermarket

Supermarket
Aventuras Montezuma
Tienda Ecológica
El Hamaquero

Montezuma Eco Tours

To 6 14 19 20 10, Cabo Blanco & Waterfalls

Pacific Ocean

N

50 metres
50 yards

El Capitán **2**
El Jardín **3**
El Pargo Feliz **4**
El Parque **16**
El Sano Banano **17**
El Tajalin **13**
El Tucán **5**
La Cascada **20**
Los Mangos **6**
Lucy **19**

Sleeping
Amor de Mar **14**
Arenas **11**
Armonia Tropical **15**
Aurora **1**

Lys **7**
Mar y Cielo **8**
Moctezuma **9**
Montezuma Pacific **10**
Pensión Jenny **12**
Ylang Ylang Beach
  Resort **18**

Eating
Angolo Etrusco **5**

Bakery Café **1**
Chico's Playa Bar **3**
Cocina Mediterranea **10**
Cocolores **4**
El Parque **6**
Iguana Café **2**
Pizz@net **8**
Soda Las Gemelas **9**
Soda Monte Sol **7**

Trips Tour operators in Montezuma offer a range of trips including kayaking and snorkelling at **Isla Cabuya** (US$25 per person), day trips to **Isla Tortuga** (US$40), horse tours to nearby waterfalls (US$25) and mountain bike rental (US$5 per day). Quad bike rental is one of the best ways to get around if you don't have a car and want to explore by yourself (US$60 per day). The canopy tour is one of the most popular in the area and takes place above the local waterfalls – the tour includes a cool dip (US$30). Other trips further afield include whitewater rafting, sunset and wildlife tours. For something more relaxing Hotel Los Mangos has yoga classes from US$12, www.montezumayoga.com. Diving is also possible (US$45 one tank, US$75 two tanks). *See Activities and tours, page 275, for further details.*

If you want to strike out on your own, 20 minutes up the Montezuma River, is a huge, beautiful **waterfall** with a big, natural swimming hole, beyond a smaller waterfall. Intrepid walkers can carry on up to further waterfalls but note that it can be dangerous and accidents have been reported – most of which have occurred when people have got too adventurous and have tried to climb up the waterfall rocks, slipped and fallen. North of Montezuma (6 km) is **El Chorro**, another waterfall with a pool right by the beach – follow the road out to the beach at the north end of town and keep going past three coves for about 30 minutes until you reach the trail off to the left (you can't miss it). Part of the pool beneath the falls has recently been filled with rocks from a landslide. There is concern that the land around here is still unstable and swimming could be dangerous. However, people do still swim regularly here, so ask around for advice locally and go cautiously.

Cabuya

A small town 9 km south of Montezuma along the coast road, Cabuya lies close to the southwestern most point of the peninsula, and 2 km from the entrance to Cabo Blanco Nature Reserve. It's a quiet spot and there's not much to do – and so it's fantastically relaxing as a result. At low tide, you can wade out to **Isla Cabuya**. A rough 4WD-only road leads west to Malpaís.

Reserva Natural Absoluta Cabo Blanco → *Colour map 1, inset.*

ⓘ *The park is closed Mon-Tue. Other days 0800-1600, US$10. Contact the ranger station on T2642-0093 or www.caboblancopark.com for more details. A shuttle service leaves Montezuma at 0800, 1000, 1400, 1700 and 1900 (although no reason to take later ones as nowhere to stay in the park) and picks you up outside the park at 0700, 0900, 1300 and 1600, US$1. Alternatively a taxi will cost in the region of US$7 per person.*

Neatly covering the southwestern tip of the Nicoya Peninsula, Cabo Blanco Nature Reserve is a precious reserve, both ideologically and biologically. Created in 1963, it is the oldest protected area in the country apart from the frontier corridor to the north with Nicaragua. The reserve is the legacy of Nicolás Wessberg and his wife Karen Mogensen who set out to preserve the stands of moist forest as development gradually denuded the surrounding area. The land was finally donated to the National Parks programme in 1994, when Doña Karen bequeathed the land to the state.

Today, the 1370-ha reserve is easily visited on short trips from nearby Montezuma. The reserve is home to tracts of evergreen and deciduous tree species in the beautiful moist forest that fringes the beaches and rocky headlands. With roughly 2300 mm of rain a year, this is one of the wettest spots on the peninsula.

A couple of trails lead through the park which, for its size, has a good variety of wildlife including porcupines, armadillos and three species of monkey. The reserve is also an important site for seabirds including brown pelicans, frigate birds and the largest nesting colony of brown boobies. Just beyond Cabo Blanco is beautiful **Playa Balsitas**, with lots of pelicans and howler monkeys; however, some reports say this area is closed. Ask at the ranger station before visiting.

Carmen, Malpaís and Santa Teresa → *Colour map 1, inset. www.malpais.net.*

From Cóbano a road leads west for 11 km to Carmen, splitting to head south for Malpaís, a rocky beach at the northern limits of the Cabo Blanco Nature Reserve. The right fork at Carmen leads to the beach at Santa Teresa, with long white beaches, creeks and natural pools stretching along the coast.

Once a quiet spot, the area is now buzzing with activity, from surfers, creative bohemians and conventional foreign families and investors; the growing community is strangely close-knit and very friendly. There is an organic market every Saturday morning at Playa Carman, and regular community beach clean ups. Unlike small villages packed with tourists, such as neighbouring Montezuma, life here is spread throughout the long stretch between Malpaís and Santa Teresa creating a great mix of both lively activity and empty pockets of beach and deserted hiking trails around the hills.

These two villages have expanded along the beach to meet in the middle. They have become a surf Mecca for all nationalities from the US to UK, or Switzerland to Sweden. There is a relaxed beach vibe, reminiscent of Kuta in Bali in the early days of surf exploration. It's also becoming popular for those seeking a yoga retreat. The Mal Pais crossroads has recently seen new developments including appartments and shops, now boasting a modern bank with ATM (open seven days a week). The road north to Santa Teresa is prone to flooding in the rainy season, and is bumpy and dusty during the high season. Rumours of a new tarmac road abound. Surfing in Malpaís is good for beginners and there are a number of surf camps and surf shops here, however, the surf to the north in Santa Teresa is best left to the more experienced. (Note that some European surfers find it cheaper to buy a surfboard in Santa Teresa (from US\$200), use it for a week, then sell it back to the shop, rather than pay board carriage on airlines.)

Due to the numbers of surfers drawn to the area throughout the year, accommodation can often be fully booked throughout the low season, so book in advance to make sure. Additionally, due to surfers' demands and propensity for longer stays, there is a good variety of fully equipped self catering accommodation. There are numerous cabins and rooms undergoing construction so take the time to explore if you are intending to stay for a while. Most places listed are around E-F in low season. Unless specified, most are within a five-minute walk from the beach.

The best way to get around is to hire a bike, but quads are available.

◉ Southern Peninsula listings

For Sleeping and Eating price codes and other relevant information, see Essentials, pages 44-47.

◉ Sleeping

Playa Naranjo *p262*

AL-A Bahía Luminosa, south of Naranjo on the road to Paquera, T2641-0386, www.bahia luminosa.com. 14 comfortable rooms with good views (or set round the pool) in a quiet spot of the Nicoya Peninsula. Great family atmosphere, not too slick, but good reports.

A-B Oasis del Pacífico, T2641-8092, www. costaricareisen.com/oasis. An old building on the beach with 36 rooms with a/c, hot water bath, a pool and good restaurant. Good discounts in the rainy season.

Cabinas Maquinay, 1.3 km northwest towards Jicaral, T2661-1763. Simple rooms, with a pool and the attached Disco Maquinay.
El Paso, T2641-8133. A clean, slightly cheaper option, with rooms with private bath, cheaper without, restaurant and a pool.

Playa Tambor *p262*
In town
L Tambor Tropical, T2683-0011, www.tambortropical.com. 12 luxury *cabinas* created from tropical hardwoods that glow in the golden light of sunset. Each cabin has a small kitchenette or you can dine in the hotel restaurant. There's a pool, gardens that lead to the beach, a jacuzzi and a positive attitude encouraging guests to do nothing … although activities can be arranged.
A-B Costa Coral, T2683-0105, www.costa coral.com. A blaze of colour throughout the 10 villas with fully equipped kitchenettes, private baths, a/c or fans, and terraces. Bright (just like the decor), attentive service with a pool and jacuzzi. Lively bar and excellent mid-range open-air restaurant. Good craft shop, a refreshing change from the norm.
C-D Cabinas Cristina, T2683-0028. Has 6 simple clean rooms, with fans, on the beach.
D Cabinas del Bosque, T2683-0039. One of the cheapest options in town.
C Dos Lagartos, T2683-0236. Good, clean rooms, some with private bath and fans. Small snack bar and flower-filled garden that leads to the beach. Good value and recommended.

Out of town
LL Tango Mar, south of town, T2683-0001, www.tangomar.com. Full-on comforts including their own golf course and a spectacular waterfall nearby that crashes directly into a coastal rock pool.
LL-L Tambor Beach, on the run into town from the north, T2683-0303, www.barcelo. com. A 5-star all-inclusive resort with almost every amenity available including a private airstrip. The focus is on beach life and water activities, there's also a 9-hole golf course in the neighbouring Los Delfines Golf and

Country Club. The Spanish Barceló group walked into a storm of controversy with the construction of the Hotel and Golf Club. Built around a former cattle farm, the resort is alleged to have encroached on the public beach and drained mangrove swamps and wildlife habitats.

Montezuma *p263, map p264*
In town
L-AL El Jardín, stretching up the hill behind the village T2642-0548, www.hoteleljardin. com. 1 fully equipped house and 16 cool, airy rooms, many with sea view and balcony, all with bath, hot water, 2 with a/c are less bright (the rest have a fan). Nice, private gardens, great pool with jacuzzi and waterfall, very friendly and well run. A small shop sells clothes, and tours can be organized.
L-A Ylang Ylang Beach Resort, T2642-0636, www.ylangylangresort.com. A range of accommodation from 8 private bungalows and 3 beach suites with kitchenettes to 3 beach rooms, all with hot water bath, fans, excellent restaurant, café, massage, gift shop, tours. Plush but informal. Book in advance.
AL-B Armonía Tropical, Playa Montezuma, on the beach to the north of town, T2642-0096, or enquire for Marilyn Rojas Delgado at Pizz@net. Currently she has 2 rooms and 1 cabin on the beach, a pool and gardens. All rooms are exceptionally well built and pristine inside, private bath with hot water, fridge and coffee maker. The cabin has a fully equipped kitchen and wooden shutters throughout to catch the sea breeze.
AL-B El Tajalín, beyond the church on the hill, T2642-0061, www.tajalin.com. 11 big rooms sleeping doubles and triples, with hot water bath, a/c or fans. Sparkling clean bathrooms and crisp white sheets, breakfast included in the price during high season only.
AL-B Los Mangos, a little further along the road from Hotel Lys, T2642-0384, www.hotel losmangos.com. A large site comprising 9 polished wood bungalows each sleeping 3 people with hot water bath, fridge, fan, private terrace and hammocks. Slightly cheaper are

the 10 brightly painted rooms, some with shared bath, some for 4 people. Swimming pool, jacuzzi, and lots of mango trees on site. Yoga classes take place in an open-air pagoda.

AL-C Amor de Mar, just past the river, T2642-0262, www.amordemar.com. Rooms carry different prices (not all have private bath or hot water) but all are bright and comfortable. Pleasant gardens lead to the beach via rock pools. Friendly, families welcome, breakfast and brunch served in a small terrace restaurant that is surrounded by flowers and pot plants. There's some great attention to detail here – this place is well run and well loved.

A El Sano Banano Village Hotel, above the excellent restaurant, T2642-0523, www.el banano.com. 12 rooms sleeping 2-5, with private hot water bath, a/c and cable TV. Also offer tours throughout the area, transfers to and from San José International airport, Tambor airport and local taxis. Different and fun.

A-C Aurora, at the top of the hill, T2642-0051, www.playamontezuma.net. A great atmosphere in this place with simple rooms, some with private bath, hot water and a/c, cheaper without. It's set back from the road in gardens and there's a communal kitchen, laundry service, books and games for everyone to use.

A-F Hotel Moctezuma, T2642-0058. A very central, main hub in town with 27 rooms ranging from budget with shared bath, to spacious fully equipped rooms with kitchen, private bath and a/c. Clean and helpful, the cheaper rooms look over the ocean but are located over the town's only 2 bars, so can be a bit noisy. Popular bar and restaurant downstairs serving selection of *típica* food – popular with *Ticos*.

B Hotel Montezuma Pacific, past the church in a quiet and pretty location against the hill, T2642-0204. Quiet rooms with private bath, hot water, a/c and carpets – rare in these parts. It gives the place a very cosy atmosphere, although perhaps not entirely necessary in the tropics. Communal fridge for guests, and friendly staff.

B Mar y Cielo, T2642-0261. 6 rustic rooms sleeping 2-5 people, on the beach, all with bath, fan and sea view. German-run, it's very clean and recommended. The reception is inside the souvenir shop on the corner next to the public phones.

B-C La Cascada, alongside the river and track to the waterfalls and canopy tours, T2642-0057. 18 pleasant, simple rooms for 1-5 people, with bath (cold water) and fan. A quiet spot, excellent for the price, rooms upstairs are most attractive and some have sea views. Large communal terrace with hammocks overlooking the ocean. Laundry service available, they are currently building a bar and restaurant. *Tico*-owned, ask for Doña Vicky. Recommended. Good deals in low season.

C El Pargo Feliz, on the beach, T2642-0065. 8 very clean, large and pleasant rooms, all with cold water bath and fan. Upstairs rooms have big windows and lots of light, but all are good value. There is also a large communal veranda with hammocks and a small bookshelf. No reservations – arrive between 1000 and 1200 to secure your room. The friendly owners do request quiet however – no visitors, and party-goers are not welcome.

C-D El Tucán, a short walk south of the centre, T2642-0284. Locally owned, basic, clean and friendly. Shared bath. Laundry service available.

D pp Arenas, on the beach, T2642-0649. Another budget option. Free camping.

D Hotel El Parque, fronting the beach, T2642-0614. 10 budget rooms, shared bath, in a fantastic spot for both beach and town, with a good restaurant serving excellent and very cheap *casados*.

D Lucy, opposite Los Mangos, T2642-0273. One of the oldest hotels in town with 19 very good, varnished wooden rooms with spectacular views over the beach and a very welcoming owner. Shared bath. Lucy's restaurant next door serves typical fare in high season.

D-E Hotel El Capitán, on the beach,
T2642-0069. A large rickety hotel with 30
rooms sleeping up to 4 people, with fan and
shared bath. Some are tiny and makeshift,
the party goers are accommodated on the
2nd floor, the 3rd floor is quieter. Outside
are some interestingly laid out rooms with
private bath. Great owners, very relaxed
atmosphere. Dollars changed and Visa
accepted.
E pp Hotel Lys, T2642-0642. 13 small,
and rather tatty rooms, the best of which
are upstairs. Shared bath.
E-F Pensión Jenny, up the path alongside
Soda Caracol, T2642-0306. 14 rooms sleeping
1-4 with shared bath. Budget but nice.
Laundry service available.

Out of town
AL-A Horizontes, 1.8 km north on the
road to Cóbano, T2642-0534, www.
horizontes-montezuma.com. 7 good
rooms with private bath and fine views
from this elevated spot. A good restaurant
serving local and international dishes open
in high season, but breakfast served to
guests throughout the year, a pool and
language school. No public transport out
here at night, but still highly recommended.
A Cabinas Las Rocas, 20 mins south of
Montezuma, T8842-4402. Good rooms
but quite expensive meals, small, seashore
setting, isolated.
A Linda Vista, T2642-0274. On the hill,
units sleep 6, with bath (cold water) and fan,
ocean views.
A Los Caballos, 3 km north on the road to
Cóbano, T2642-0124, www.naturelodge.net.
8 recently remodelled rooms with bath. Also
a pool, outdoor restaurant, ocean views,
5 mins from beach. Horse riding a speciality.
A-B Estudio Los Almendros, between
Montezuma and Cabuya, T2642-0378,
www.somaritmoscostarica.com. Beachfront
location with a handful of rooms and an
apartment, with a simple restaurant, all
dedicated to the practice and research
of somatic education and dance.

Camping
You can camp for free at **Pensión Arenas**
and there is also camping in the high season
at **Rincón de los Monos**, on the beach 300 m
north of the village – no prices available.
Clean, well organized with lockers for rent.
Several monkeys live here too.

Cabuya *p265*
L-AL Celaje, T2642-0374, www.celaje.com.
Thatched-roof cabins on the beach, with
private bath and hot water. Swimming pool
and very good Italian restaurant.
B-C Cabinas y Restaurante El Ancla de Oro,
T2642-0369, www.caboblancopark.com/
ancla. Cabins with private bath, cheaper
sharing. Seafood restaurant with lobster
dinners and filling breakfasts. Horses and
mountain bikes available for hire.

Carmen, Malpaís and Santa Teresa *p266*
Carmen
AL-B Frank's Place, at the road junction,
T2640-0096. Located by the bus stop and
opposite the short track to Playa Carman
(which is particularly good for beginner
surfers) Frank's is perhaps the best spot in the
area if you want to be close to activity. Has a
wide variety of rooms set in tropical gardens
with private or shared bath, and self-catering
options available. Swimming pool, internet,
bicycle and quad-bike rental, restaurant and
bar and loads of advice on the local area.

Malpaís
Hotels listed in order as you head south.
A Ritmo Tropical, T2640-0174,
ritmotropical_mp@yahoo.com. 7 pleasant
and clean cabins with terracotta-tiled roofs,
private hot water bath and fan, excellent
restaurant in well tended gardens open for
breakfast and dinner.
AL-B The Place, T2640-0001, www.theplace
malpais.com. 5 luxurious bungalows with
individual themes such as 'Africa' and 'Sea
Breeze'. All incorporate a stylish mix of stone,
wood and tiles. Also has rooms and a villa. The
pool and breakfast terrace is lit up at night.

A Oasis, T2640-0259, oasismalpais@racsa.co.cr. Three simple, clean, bright and spacious, fully equipped bungalows in elevated gardens with pool, and breakfast brought to your private terrace on request.

AL-D Mal País Surf Camp and Resort, T2640-0031, www.malpaissurfcamp.com. A variety of small budget rooms some with private bath others shared, dorms with shared bath and poolside house and villas, sleeping up to 5, to camping with all amenities included. Swimming pool, gym, massage (US$35), board rental (US$10-20 per day), surf lessons (US$40 including board), transfers from San José (US$35 per person), bar, restaurant, pool table, ping-pong, and a myriad of other games as well as live jam sessions on Wed nights. A great place to play. International and seafood served in the lively café-style restaurant.

AL Blue Jay Lodge, T2640-0089, www.bluejaylodgecostarica.com. Open-sided, screened bungalows elevated almost to canopy level with hot water bath and hammocks on private terraces overlooking the jungle. Stunning. Restaurant and bar is open for breakfast (included in the price) and dinner. Swimming pool, snorkelling, and canopy, birdwatching and horse-riding tours also arranged.

L-A Pachamama, T2640-0195, www.pacha-malpais.com. Colourful cabins in a relaxed environment with one bungalow with kitchen. Can arrange many activities including kitesurfing, surfing, canopy tours, diving and fishing. Has good restaurant/bar open at night.

LL-L Vistas de Olas, quite a hike up the hill but accessible by car, T2640-0183, www.bungalows-vistadeolas.com. 3 bungalows set in large grounds overlooking miles of coast, the view from the edge of their infinity pool is phenomenal. Watch the sunset while mist rolls up the mountains. Recommended. Bar, restaurant and jacuzzi.

B Bosque Mar, T2640-0074. Set in attractive grounds and run by very friendly, helpful owners. 9 cabins all with hot water private bath, 7 with kitchen. Pool and parking.

AL-B Star Mountain Eco-Resort, set back 2 km from the beach on the road to Cabuyo, T2640-0101, www.starmountaineco.com. 4 spacious rooms all with private bath set in a rustic *pueblo* setting and 2 *casitas* both sleeping 4, dorm-style or perfect for families (children under 3 free, under 6 pay 50%) and groups. In a wonderful, peaceful hillside setting surrounded by thick forest and natural springs. There are several recommended trails through their 86 ha, some taking you to points where both sides of the ocean are visible. The restaurant serves gourmet dining, including fresh fruits and home-baked breads.

AL Sunset Reef, located at the end of the Malpaís road, T2640-0012, www.sunsetreefhotel.com. A small resort with personal touches including fruit baskets, coffee makers and flowers placed in each of their 14 rooms, all of which have private hot water bath and a/c. Situated on the beach, hammocks are slung between palm trees and there is a swimming pool if the sea gets too rough. Their restaurant is open all day every day and they can organize tours and transfers. **Pura Vida Adventures**, in the US on T415-465-2162, www.puravidaadventures.com, runs from the hotel with a surf camp for women.

Santa Teresa

Playa Santa Teresa is further north along the coast from Carmen.

C-D pp Cabinas Arenas Blancas, T2640-0178. 4 small, dark and basic rooms, with fridge, fan and shared bath, tiny communal kitchen on the terrace. They also hire out quad-bikes (US$40 for 7 hrs, US$70 for 24 hrs).

F pp Cabinas Santa Teresa, T2640-0172. 8 basic, clean rooms with shared bath, there's also a small restaurant or *sodita* serving cheap *casado* (⋔).

L-AL Hotel Casa Azul, T2640-0379, www.hotelcasaazul.com. Painted inside and out in dark sea blue, this stylish house has 3 double rooms and a fully equipped, luxury 2-bedroom apartment with yellow sofas and a wrap-around balcony overlooking the ocean. It also has a roof top terrace where they plan to install a hot tub, a pool and a/c throughout. It feels more like a home than a hotel. Swish and recently built, a great spot, often booked up months in advance.

C-D Tranquilo Backpackers, T2640-0589, www.tranquilo.com (if they get the ink working). Dorms, private rooms, a kitchen, internet and general budget relaxation from the people who run Tranquilo in San José.

AL Ronny's Hotel , T2640-0301. 10 rooms in a block with tinted windows, cable TV, a/c, and private hot water bath in the rooms. Also parking, pool, and bar with pool table. Not unusual, but gets booked up quickly.

D pp Cabinas de Carman, T2640-0179. 10 very basic, cabins sleeping 2-4 with shared bath. Clean, fresh, fine.

LL-L Hotel Horizon, T2640-0524, www.horizon-yogahotel.com. Luxury in a hillside spot with superb views. Vegetarian restaurant and yoga classes. And relax.

A-B Surf Paradiso, T2640-0013. Has fully equipped bungalows with kitchen, private bath and 2 double beds in each. Locally owned and very local-esque – authentic Central American living. They have some great bargains in low season.

LL-A Trópico Latino Lodge, T2640-0062, www.hoteltropicolatino.com. 6 spacious, Italian-designed bungalows that use local materials, all with private bath and hot water, big ceiling fans and tiled floor leading to a private porch and hammock. The restaurant serves north Italian and local cuisine, using seafood for many dishes, in a thatched *rancho* overlooking the beach side. Also has a swimming pool and jacuzzi. Tours can be easily arranged.

L La Luz de Vida Resort, T2640-0319, www.luzdevida-resort.com. Run by some Israeli brothers and their families, who are all very passionate about their growing project. A resort of types, the bungalows all vary slightly in design and are mostly constructed with wood. Not totally unique, and yet the place has a great vibe. All rooms have private

hot water bath, a/c, coffee makers, fridge and private terrace, some have toasters. There is a terrace restaurant, with drinks served in the wet bar of the pool, which is free for non-guests if using the restaurant. Tours, surfing, board rental and lessons are offered, as are water skiing and diving. Situated in large grounds with loads of space to roam in or you can go for a wander on the beach. Kids welcome, cash exchanged, transfers and taxis can be arranged.

B-D Casa Zen, T2640-0523, www.zen costarica.com. A friendly meeting place is the idea here, with a selction of rooms and dorms to choose from. Small restaurant/bar on site.

D-E Cuesta Arriba, T2640-0607, www.santateresahostels.com. A straight down the line dormitory, with bar, communcal areas, hammocks for lazing in and it's all a short walk from the beach.

AL-A Ranchos Itauna, T2640-0095, www.ranchos-itauna.com. Run by a very friendly Brazilian/Austrian couple, 4 beautiful cabins close to the beach with hot water private bath with and without kitchen. Restaurant open to all serving Brazillian BBQ. Superbly located in the middle of 2 popular surfing spots.

E Wave Trotter, T2640-0805, www.wavetrotterhostel.com. Simple clean and spacious dorm with dorm rooms, shared bathrooms, kitchen and communal space.

AL-A Funky Monkey, T2640-0272, www.funky-monkey-lodge.com. Up a small hill behind Jungle Juice Café, a great spot. 3 wooden bungalows with 1 queen-size and 2 single beds, scenic private terrace and spacious private hot water bath. A further bungalow and rooms over their restaurant have dorm-style beds, sleeping 8 (**F pp**), a real bargain for the luxury setting and great for groups. Their laid-back bar and restaurant are open to non-guests and serve sushi, pizza, fish, *tacos* and other specialties, the owners are all for chatting with the guests to see what everyone fancies for dinner. A good atmosphere.

A-B Luz de Luna, T2640-0280. Another attractive set-up (people have style in this area) 4 bungalows sleeping 2-4 with roomy private hot water bath, mosquito nets, fan, 1 with kitchen, and split level design, terraces, and hammocks. Belgian-run, breakfast is available for a little extra.

B-D Zeneidas, T2640-0118. Camping, cabins and *soda*. Very friendly, clean rooms sleeping up to 3, some with private bath, others shared, 1 fully equipped with kitchen. Laid back place, breakfast is only served during high season.

B-C Cabinas Playa , T2640-0137. 9 German-run *cabinas*, 3 have kitchen (fridge in those without), all have private bath with cold water. It's all 150 m from the beach, with surfboard rental and horse riding.

B Santa Teresa Surf Camp, T2640-0469. Have cabins sleeping 2-4, fully equipped and by the beach. They have also constructed a hammock hotel, consisting of a number of hammocks with locker, shower and bathrooms facilities (**F**).

B Roca del Mar Cabins and Camping, very close to the beach, T2640-0250. Cabins sleep up to 5, some have private bath, some don't, camping (**G**) and a restaurant open for high season.

AL Milarepa, on beach, T2640-0023, www.milarepahotel.com. Great bamboo bungalows with Indonesian antique beds and furniture throughout, relaxing features, and open-air bathroom. Private yoga and massage available, they have a pool and families are very welcome. Their restaurant will serve breakfast, lunch and dinner, the chef creates a fusion of Latin and Asian cuisine – with a professional French touch.

LL Florblanca, T2640-0232, www.flor blanca.com. Florblanca is a stunning place. Dream sand-coloured stone bungalows with lounges, open terraces, luxurious 4-poster beds, CD players, Balinese-style open-air bathrooms with sunken stone pool and showers the size of the moon. There's also, of course, a pool, waterfalls, spa, gym, yoga

and pilates classes, gourmet open-air and ocean-facing restaurant and internet access. Private naturalist guides, kayaking, surfboard, bicycle rental are all also on offer. Bliss if you can afford it, but note that children under 6 are not permitted and a 5-night minimum stay is required in peak season.

L Trópico Latino, T2640-0062, www.hoteltropicolatino.com. 10 bungalows, a pool and a restaurant that open out onto the beach on the southern side of Santa Teresa. Each bungalow boasts a huge porch with hammocks, as well as a/c and fridges.

LL-L Casas Pura Vida, T2640-0511, www.casaspuravida.com. A choice of 4 excellent, clean and safe self-catering villas in the northern part of Santa Teresa ranging from the 2-bed Casa Iguana to the luxury Casa Yin Yang. They have beach access, private gardens and pools. Highly recommended.

🍴 Eating

Playa Tambor *p262*

Many of the hotels have their own restaurants including **Cabinas Cristina**, **Dos Lagartos** and the mid-range but stylish and excellent **Costa Coral**. The beachfront restaurant in Tambor is also very good, serving up big portions of seafood dishes and hamburgers at cheap prices. If you fancy a bit of a walk to the west of the bay, try the **Bahía Ballena Yacht Club** which has a restaurant and bar that has received recommendations.

Montezuma *p263, map p264*

♯♯ **Cocina Mediterranea** (also called Playa de las Artistas), about 5 mins south of town on the road to Cabuya, T642-0920. The best restaurant in town serving fantastic food in a beautifully adorned beach spot. We could recommend some dishes, but the menu changes daily, so just see what tasty offers come your way. Bizarre menu of beer cocktails including Leffe mixed with J&B and honey and Stella Artois with tequila, chili and lemon.

Cocolores on the beach behind El Pargo Feliz. Rustically adorned and serving excellent international fare. Sizzling fajitas, curries and outstanding salads, great service, a good place to eat. Closed Mon.

El Sano Banano. A health food restaurant, good vegetarian food, large helpings, daily change of menu, milkshakes, fresh fruit and home-made yoghurt, owned by Dutch/Americans, free movies are played every night with dinner (no entrance fee but minimum US$6 per person table charge), however, the place fills up quickly, the entire restaurant becoming a cinema – arrive on time or you will risk tiptoeing around people in the dark trying to find a seat. There's also a sports bar and disco.

Pizz@net, down on the beach. Popular, with jumbo-sized pizzas, good salads and free garlic bread.

Angolo Etrusco, opposite El Jardín. Serves great pizza, *calzone* and Italian sandwiches in Spanish-style restaurant.

Bakery Café, at the north end of town. Don't miss this place for breakfast. It serves bread and cakes as well as vegetarian food. Aside from the croissants, mango streusels and banana bread, the café has an excellent world cuisine menu. It's a great shame that it is not open for dinner (closes 1600). Home-made Indian Palak panir, tofu satay, jungle curries, *nachos*, pesto pasta and falafel. Recommended.

Chico's Playa Bar, behind Chico's Bar. A popular beach hang-out, opening early evening, serves bar snacks, excellent sushi and cocktails.

El Parque, on the beach next to Pensión Arenas. Best *gallo pinto* breakfast in town, try it with avocado, scrambled eggs and sour cream; a heavenly dish with a heavenly view.

Iguana Café, on the corner in the middle of the town by the bus stop. Serves fruit juices and healthy snacks and it is a good place to watch local life.

Pizzería Romana, on the main street. Small and central, good for pizza and home-made pasta.

There are also several *sodas* around town, including **Soda Monte Sol**, recommended for good-value Mexican *burritos*. **Soda Las Gemelas** serves simple, local food.

Cabuya *p265*
El Delfín. Restaurant, at the crossroads. Friendly, serving good value local food.
Cafetería El Coyote, on the road west out of Cabuya. Local and Caribbean dishes.

Carmen, Malpaís and Santa Teresa *p266*
In low season most restaurants in the area close in the afternoon, and early (around 2100) in the evening. Most hotels have restaurants and bars that welcome non-guests.

Carmen
Frank's Place. One of the best; additionally, it is open all day, every day, a rarity in the area. *Casados*, including a vegetarian option, they also have salads and sandwiches. At night the restaurant becomes far more fancy and a little pricier.
Pizzería Playa Carman, right on the beach, a short walk from Frank's. Serving excellent pizzas with all the usual toppings, (although there's also strange one involving Nutella and rum), also pastas with, among other things, gorgonzola and pesto.

Towards Malpaís
Mar Azul, situated on the beach. Serves local food and seafood specials, open till midnight.
Rest Mary, by the Cabuya turn-off. Serves pizza.
Ristorante Italiano La Bella Napoli, opposite Rest Mary. Also authentic pasta, cannelloni, lasagne, pizza, and good wines.
Malpaís Surf Camp. Has a small but great menu, creamy garlic pasta, fish *burritos* and Starvin' Surfer *casados*.
Ritmo Pizzería. Serves 4-cheese gnocchi, fish dishes, pizzas and salads.

Towards Santa Teresa

Santa Teresa has plenty of eating options ranging from good value sodas to high end luxury resorts, new ones opening up all the time.

ＴＴＴ-ＴＴ Florblanca. If you fancy something more upmarket, this is an unforgettable Balinese-style experience. A romantic, open-air restaurant decked with candles and great service. The Canadian-trained chef creates Asian-style cuisine and there is a full sushi menu between 1500 and 1800. Lunches cheaper than dinner.

ＴＴ Brisas del Mar. Just south of the soccer ground offers great local seafood – Tuna or Mahi Mahi straight from the boats at Malpaís. Great service and atmosphere. Highly recommended. From 5500 colones.

ＴＴ-Ｔ El Pulpo Pizzería. Next door to Brisas del Mar is this good-value pizzeria that will also deliver.

Ｔ Buena Luna Tourist Centre. Has a Middle Eastern café, good for falafel.

Ｔ Soda Los Piedras. Serves meat cuts BBQ'd Brazilian-style over a huge grill.

Ｔ Ranchos Itauna. Also serve Brazilian fare.

Ｔ Jungle Juice Café. Has a good menu with breakfast *burritos* and banana pancakes and veggie burgers.

Ｔ Funky Monkey, further up. Has a light everyday menu and specializes in sushi at weekends; they have Tuna Nigiri, various fish rolls and sake. Mid-week the food depends on their guests' requests, could be anything from pizza to Mexican.

⊙ Bars and clubs

Montezuma *p263, map p264*

Many of the hotels have also sedate bars in their restaurants.

Chicho's Bar is the most happening place in town. There are pool and football tables and the music is always loud. DJ's from San José appear regularly during high season. Chico's Playa Bar is slightly quieter and offers cocktails.

Bar Montezuma, opens even later than Chico's, but is slightly more sedate.

Carmen, Malpaís and Santa Teresa *p266*

For drinks there are a number of new bars opening up on the beachfront at Mal País each season.

Tabu, in Santa Teresa, a short walk from Frank's Place. The liveliest bar in the area – if there is a crowd in town this is where it will be. A good spot on the beach (not so great when it rains) with excellent tribal beats, DJ's on occasion and the odd flame thrower.

Funky Monkey, in Santa Teresa, behind Jungle Juice. Has a very relaxed bar in a seductive setting. It's a friendly and communal atmosphere.

Flor Blanca, at the northern edge of Santa Teresa. With a mojito in hand this place makes for a real treat.

La Lora. A big, mostly local bar with pool tables. Shows movies and occasional events.

Frank's Place, has a small bar but you can have a drink in the restaurant as well.

The Surf Camp, in Malpaís. Is great for drinking beers, chatting about waves or playing some of their entertaining games.

⊙ Shopping

Playa Tambor *p262*

Services in the village are limited, although there are a few shops, a public telephone, a supermarket and an agency for bicycle hire.

Tucán Boutique, sells a mix of goods including beachwear, and will help with inquiries.

Montezuma *p263, map p264*

There are several small souvenir shops in the town.

El Hamaquero, which sells locally made crafts and puts some of the profits back into the community.

Tienda Ecológica, international calls and money exchange.

Librería Topsy, sells books and maps, blank CDs, and also has a library service,

US$1.25 per book for 2 weeks, with deposit US$10). There's a good selection of travel books here and, for a small fee (cost of stamp plus US$0.07), they will stamp and take your postcards to the nearest Post Office in Cobano. Open Mon-Fri, 0800-1400, until 1200 Sat.
AKALA, Italian-owned glassworks selling unique selection of fine art, homeware, beads and jewellery. Also offers glasswork classes, T2642-0667.

Carmen, Malpaís and Santa Teresa *p266*
There are several boutiques, clothes shops and surf shops along the stretch from Malpaís to Santa Teresa.

▲ Activities and tours

Montezuma *p263, map p264*
There are several tour operators in town that offer day trips to Cabo Blanco National Park, tours and prices are standard. Additionally, all are more than happy to advise you on the local area. Tours include Isla Tortuga, canopy tours, snorkelling, diving, horse riding through jungle and beach, and the locally renowned waterfalls.
Aventuras en Montezuma, Travel Agency and Tourist Office, T2642-0050. Has very helpful staff and can also organize hotel reservations, plane tickets, tours and locals transfers.
Cocozuma Traveller, T2642-0911, www.cocozuma.com. A very friendly and reliable group with local guides. Other than the usual tour line-up they are the only operator to offer a full day trip to Cabo Blanco National Park, and take experienced guides. Daily boat service to Jaco, US$35. They also rent out motorcycles, quad-bikes, kayaks, bicycles, surf and snorkel equipment and change cash.
Montezuma Eco Tours, opposite Iguana Café. The friendly manager has lived in the

area for years so she's good to talk to if you are after local information. She is also very flexible with tour schedules and can provide discounts for students, families, groups and guests of Hotel Montezuma.
Montezuma Expeditions, T2642-0919, www.montezumaexpeditions.com. Extremely helpful people who offer a shuttle service throughout the country. They provide transport from Montezuma, Santa Teresa and Malpaís to San José Airport, Sámara, Tamarindo, Jaco, Manuel Antonio, Monteverde, Arenal and packages including Cahuita and Puerto Viejo on the Caribbean coast. Most trips are priced at US$35 per person one way. Packages are US$85.
Travel Adventures, T2642-0716, www.montezumatraveladventures.com. A professional outfit that runs all the usual tours. They can also book hotels in Malpaís and have information on local real estate.

Carmen, Malpaís and Santa Teresa *p266*
For information on the area and surfing, the owners at Buena Luna Tourist Centre, situated a few doors down from Frank's (towards Santa Teresa) are very helpful.
Malpaís Canopy Tour, by Sunset Reef Resort. Has 9 platforms, book with a tour operator, or call T2640-0091.
Paradise Reach Boat Charter, Malpaís, T2640-0431. Runs a surf express, fishing, kayaking, diving, snorkelling and boat transfers.
Sunset and Waves Tropical Tours, in the mini shopping mall in Santa Teresa, T2640-0384, tropicaltours@caboblanco park.com. They can organize shuttle transfers, tours to Curu Wildlife refuge, Cabo Blanco National Park.
Zuma Tours, next to the supermarket in the centre of town, T8849-8569, www.zumatours.net. With a wide range of services, tours including taxi boat service to Jaco for US$40.
Alex's Surf Shop, offers bike and board hire, board sales and advice.

☉ Transport

Playa Tambor *p262*
Air SANSA and Natureair have scheduled daily flights from **San José** to Tambor, US$71 and US$87.

Bus The Paquera-Montezuma bus passes through town, meeting the ferries to and from **Puntarenas**. If you want to get to **Montezuma** after the last bus, a taxi will cost you US$40, but you may find other travellers on the ferry to share the cost.

Montezuma *p263, map p264*
Boat Local boatmen can arrange transport further up the peninsula or to the mainland.

Bus Montezuma to **Paquera** 6 times a day, connecting with the ferry. Tickets available in advance from tourist information centre; be at bus stop outside Hotel Moctezuma in good time as the bus fills up quickly, US$3, 2 hrs. Daily shuttle bus to **Cabo Blanco**, departing 0800, 1000, 1400, 1700 and 1900, returning at 0700, 0900, 1300 and 1600, US$1.

There is no public transport heading up the coast. You need to go back to Paquera and take a taxi, or go back to Puntarenas on the ferry and get the next ferry to Playa Naranjo, from where a bus service connects to Nicoya. Shuttle transfers can be reasonable if you are not on a shoestring, or short of time. Prices start at US$35 per person (minimum of 3, but places fill up easily) to Sámara, Tamarindo, Monte Verde, Arenal and San José international airport.

From Montezuma to **Malpaís** take the 1000 or 1400 Paquera bus and change at Cobano for the waiting 1030 or 1430 bus to Malpaís (approx US$1.80).

Taxi Montezuma to **Cóbano** US$5; taxi **Paquera** to Montezuma US$40.

Carmen, Malpaís and Santa Teresa *p266*
Air SANSA and NatureAir fly twice a day to **Tambor** (US$71 and US$87) from where the mid- and upper-range hotels will arrange transport. Others will need to catch a bus.

Bus 2 buses run service between **Cóbano** and Malpaís at 1030 and 1430. Sunset and Waves Tropical Tours, T2640-0384, can organize transport to and from San José International Airport or Tambor Airport.

☉ Directory

Montezuma *p263, map p264*
Banks Change money at Hotel Montezuma, Cocozuma Traveller, Hotel El Capitan and sometimes in Aventuras Montezuma if they have enough colones. Otherwise go to the **Banco Nacional** in Cóbano. **Internet** Sano Banano have a flash, but very slow, all Apple Mac internet café next to their restaurant (20 colones per min). Also try **Montezuma Travel Adventures** and Pizz@net next to Hotel Montezuma. **Language schools** Horizontes de Montezuma, T2653-0359, www.horizontes-montezuma.com. 1-week Spanish survival course, 4 hrs a day, including accommodation and breakfast for a week, US$420. **Laundry** There is a launderette in Pensión Jenny. **Pharmacies** If you need a pharmacy, you will have to go to Cóbano.

Carmen, Malpaís and Santa Teresa *p266*
Banks No banks in the area, the nearest is in Cóbano, but some of the big hotels will change cash. **Internet** Frank's Place has an internet café located upstairs next to the restaurant. Several others in the area. Towards Santa Teresa, **Buena Luna Tourist Centre** has internet, so does Sunset and Waves tourist office and further along is **Amigos Café**. **Laundry** Cabinas Arenas Blancas, next to Frank's Place has a laundry service, US$1.50 per kg. Look for signs, there are several others in the area.

Contents

280 Puntarenas to Quepos
280 Ins and outs
281 Puntarenas
283 South to Jacó
284 Jacó
285 Around Jacó
287 Listings

295 Quepos and Manuel Antonio
295 Ins and outs
296 Quepos
299 Manuel Antonio
301 Listings

308 Southern costanera
311 Listings

Footprint features

278 Don't miss …
282 Parque Nacional Isla del Coco
300 Education in Manuel Antonio
309 Driving the costanera

Central Pacific

At a glance

☕ **Getting around** A regular and reliable bus service connects all major centres and by nature of the region, smaller areas can easily be reached by hailing down a passing bus.

🕐 **Time required** 3 or 4 days if staying in one place, but you could easily stay much longer if you like the beach.

🌤 **Weather** The dry season runs from Dec to Apr. For the rest of the year – the green season – the greatest rainfall is in Sep and Oct.

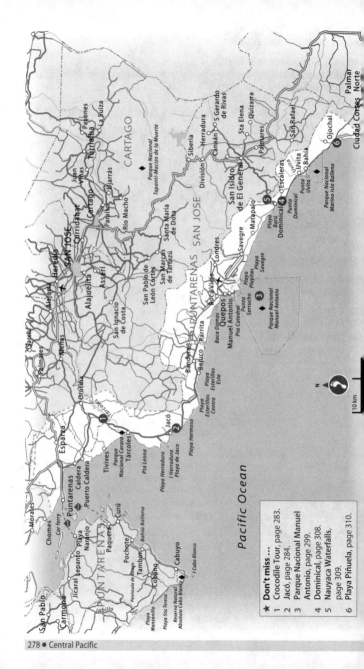

Pacific Ocean

★ Don't miss ...
1 Crocodile Tour, page 283.
2 Jacó, page 284.
3 Parque Nacional Manuel Antonio, page 299.
4 Dominical, page 308.
5 Nauyaca Waterfalls, page 309.
6 Playa Piñuela, page 310.

10 km

N

Hiding neatly between the peninsulas of Nicoya and Osa, the Central Pacific area is a well-defined lowland region hugging the western coastal lowlands from the extended sandy point of the Pacific transport hub Puntarenas in the north as far south as Palmar Norte. The last ripples of the Talamanca mountain range push up to the shore, creating a challenging blend of rocky outcrops and broad sandy beaches with the occasional fertile lowland used for plantation agriculture.

Much of the region's interest lies, literally, on the beach. The lively surf spots of Jacó and Playa Hermosa with their reliable waves, golden beaches and bustling nightlife, provide entertainment day and night for surfers and beach lovers. The hum of activity surrounding Quepos and Manuel Antonio is a little more swanky and upmarket. Further south are the quieter beach towns of Dominical and Uvita, with good budget accommodation and more exclusive and secluded hillside hideaways further south around the slowly developing Playa Tortuga.

Protected areas also entice visitors to the region. Carara National Park is a transitional zone between the dry forests to the north, and the humid tropics to the south. Its trails lead through an evergreen rainforest that teems with life. The palm-fringed sandy beaches separated by rocky peninsulas of Manuel Antonio National Park make it the most popular park outside those of the Central Highlands.

Beyond the beaches, hard agricultural living toils under the harsh tropical sun where endless lines of neatly planted African palms produce oil in plantations that are a world away – economically and socially – from the wealthy, vibrant tourist hot-spots of the region.

Puntarenas to Quepos

Puntarenas (population 22,009) is a strange place – the northern side of this long thin coastal sand spit is a bustling array of commercial fishing and ferry docks. The southern side – just six blocks away – is a coastal promenade and beach dotted with bars, cafés, restaurants and hotels. Neither aspect is particularly successful.

Traditionally, the town has survived on marine trade but these days the commodity is people. They come to bathe or to move. Ferries go to the Nicoya Peninsula and bus connections head north and south avoiding the capital to the east. With all this movement, Puntarenas achieves the impressive trick of appearing to be permanently on the move yet somehow stagnating at the same time.

Heading south to Quepos, the road is packed with options, including canopy tours, crocodile trips, isolated resorts and Carara National Park, before hitting the party town of Jacó. Puntarenas is also the setting-off point for keen divers travelling on liveaboard dive boats to Isla del Coco. ▶▶ *For listings, see pages 287-294.*

Ins and outs ▶▶ *Colour map 1, C5. www.puntarenas.com.*

Getting there

Puntarenas is the main transport hub on the Pacific coast. With the singular purpose of avoiding the two-hour journey to San José, buses from Puntarenas link with Liberia, Cañas, and Santa Elena/Monteverde in the north, and Jacó and Quepos to the south.

Passenger and vehicle ferries leave Puntarenas for Playa Naranjo and Paquera on the Nicoya Peninsula. ▶▶ *See Transport, page 293, for further details.*

Puntarenas

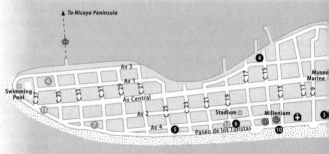

Sleeping	Helen **1**	Yadran **13**
Cabezas **2**	La Punta **6**	
Cayuga **3**	Las Brisas **7**	**Eating**
Gran Chorotega **4**	Río **11**	Arenas Chepes Bar **10**
Gran Imperial **5**	Tioga **12**	Casa de Mariscos **3**

;etting around

arely six blocks across, the walk from Puntarenas town to the beach is manageable. But t over 40 blocks from end to end, you may want to get a taxi if catching the ferry which eaves from the northwestern most tip of the peninsula. Apart from Avenida Central, the nain thoroughfare is the beachfront Paseo de los Turistas.

;est time to visit

/eather is reliably good from December to May. The main festivity of the year in Puntarenas is he Festival of the Virgin of the Sea in the second week of July. General revelry culminates n 16 July with a parade of brightly decorated boats sailing out into the gulf.

'untarenas » *pp287-294.*

or several centuries, Puntarenas has flourished and floundered with the rise and fall of er importance to trade routes. Once the town was the country's main port, until rail links etween Puerto Limón on the Atlantic coast and the Central Highlands moved the potlight. Her role was reduced still further with the construction of an international ontainer port in the 1980s at Caldera, a short distance to the south of the centre.

Puntarenas is like an old maid trying hard to retain her beauty. If the sun is shining, you an just see glimpses of her former glory, but with overcast skies the wrinkles appear and nly those closest to her feel any real affection. The northern side of the town has the typical haracteristics of many ports, with an edgy energy and carelessness that works and plays ard. Take a stroll around the market or the fishing dock on the north of the peninsula and his is *pura vida*. Not the sunset and beach type of holiday brochures, but the real life of hard raft and toil. Stroll a little further, preferably in the day, and you'll discover a world of orgotten, albeit grubby, architectural charms and more than a few follies. The neglect of the port is so great that someone forgot to pull down the older buildings, which now could be renovated to glorious effect. This is the heart of Puntarenas (around Calle Central), with its banks, the market, a few hotels and fishing docks.

The southern side is made up of the **Paseo de los Turistas**, drawing crowds to the hot, sometimes dirty beach, especially at weekends. It's a pleasant enough stroll down the promenade, which is home to several hotels, as well as restaurants, bars and has a generally laid-back seafront beach atmosphere. There is a public swimming pool at the western end of the point (US$1 entrance), close to the ferries. The **Museum of Marine History** in the Cultural Centre is by the main church and **tourist office**. ⓘ *Tue-Sun, 0945-1200, 1300-1715.*

Puntarenas's appeal is limited but with time a stay here would probably be more rewarding than more glitzy *Tico* towns.

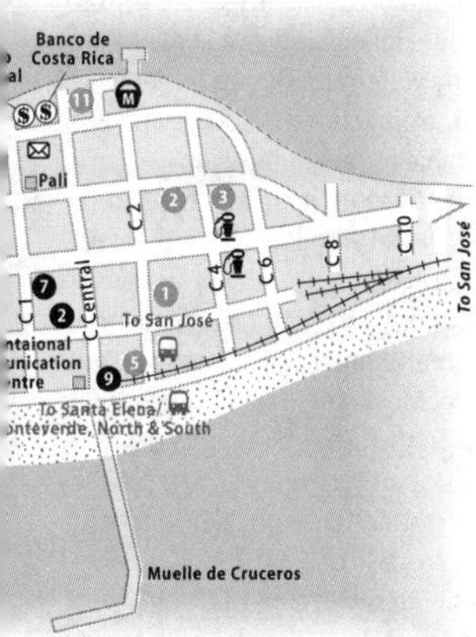

;ayte Negro **4**
gas **2**
erial **9**
dín Cervecero **5**
/unta **6**
Mandarín **7**
Mariscos Kahite Blanco **4**

Parque Nacional Isla del Coco

For distant island destinations the diving paradise of Isla del Coco – one of the largest uninhabited islands in the world – has to be the best option around. Over 550 km southwest of Costa Rica, the volcanic island rises from the sea floor at the western tip of the Coco Plate. With an area of just 14.5 sq km, most of the coast is lined with steep cliffs, rising to 634 m at Cerro Yglesias. The rugged terrain creates numerous watersheds and rivers, which in turn become waterfalls, some of which plunge directly into the ocean. Only the bays of Wafer and Chatham make the island accessible.

Temperatures of 30°C and annual rainfall close to 7 m guarantees almost permanent cloud cover over the islands and produces lush premontane rainforest. But while preserved as a National Park and a UNESCO World Heritage Site, the island is considered to be impoverished in terms of diversity when compared to the mainland, largely due to its isolation. But a number of endemic species exist here (of the 87 bird species, three – the Cocos Island flycatcher, cuckoo and finch – are endemic, as are two species of reptile). Insects proliferate and hawksbill, green and olive ridley turtles occasionally visit the undisturbed bays.

Offshore, the 97,000 ha of protected waters are rich with coastal reefs and emergent islands. Over 300 species of fish are found in these waters, hammerhead sharks school in their hundreds, and there's an abundance of white-tipped sharks, whale sharks and manta rays.

History has added spice to the islands which showed no signs of habitation prior to the arrival of the Spanish. Poorly marked on maps, only experienced sailors could find them. Myth and legend claims the pirates Benito Bonito, William Davies and Captain Thompson buried significant quantities of treasure here between the late 1600s and 1821, including the Lima Booty which is supposed to include a life-size statue of the Virgin Mary and Child in solid gold. Since then, over 300 expeditions have visited the island in search of the elusive 'X'. The island was also prison between 1872 and 1874. An exploratory trip in 1898 to reopen the penitentiary ended up being a scientific expedition which realized the importance of protecting the area.

Diving deals Marine life is the main draw and most people visiting are serious about diving and arrive on live-aboard dive boats. Trips normally last at least a week as the boat journey to the islands takes 36 hours. May-November is the rainy season and considered the best time of year for diving but conditions are generally good all year round. Once in the area, diving is guided and organized by the divemaster and subject to the weather. If conditions allow, there are trips to explore inland and visit some of the many waterfalls. Due to cooler waters and strong currents Coco Island is not suitable for beginners.

The *Okeanos Aggressor* is a 110-ft steel vessel with berths for 21 guests, all fully carpeted, with a/c and private bathrooms. The comfortable salon has an entertainment centre with TV and video. Meals are served buffet-style and on the top deck there is a wet bar. Departing from Puntarenas, the Aggressor offers eight-day charters with six days of diving and 10-day trips with seven days of diving, most guests making up to three dives a day. Prices start at US$2695 for 84 days, US$3095 for 10 days. T2228-6613, in the US toll free on T1-800-348-2628, www.aggressor.com.

Trips from Puntarenas

① *Prices are US$99, or US$150 from San José, transport and food included.*

Charter vessels and cruisers leave Puntarenas for day trips to **Isla Tortuga**, with most people starting out from San José (see page 263). Variations on the sailing theme are offered by **Calypso Tours** who take you out to **Punta Coral**, a small deserted beach on the eastern-most point of the Nicoya Peninsula. Here there are trails through dry forest and opportunities for snorkelling in the crystal clear waters or relaxing in a shaded hammock in the peaceful private reserve. An alternative trip sails the 60-ft catamaran *Lohe Lani* to **Isla San Lucas**, Costa Rica's own Alcatraz and described as the dreaded Devil's Island. It was eventually closed in 1991. Trips take in a visit to the cells, visits to the bird sanctuary islands of **Pan de Azúcar** and the **Reserva Biológica Isla Guayabo** and also stop at a couple of beaches.

South to Jacó ⬤❼▲ ▸▸ *pp287-293.*

Heading for the Central Pacific, Highway 27 links Puntarenas with the town of Orotina. At **Roble**, 10 km east of Puntarenas, there are a few quiet accommodation options.

On the old San José-Puntarenas railway, near the new port of Caldera is **Mata de Limón**. It's a simple resort with a beach and mangrove swamps nearby. The fishing nearby is reported to be good. Once a quiet spot, the peace has been shattered by the traffic from the nearby port.

Heading inland, the road from Caldera heads along the broad valley of the Cuarros and Tárcoles rivers. A dirt track leads to the coast at **Tivives** with mangrove swamps popular with birdwatchers and a good surfing spot.

Once an important rail road and transport junction, the 9000-strong lively town of **Orotina** still maintains a role as an important commercial transport hub with good links to the port at Caldera, the agricultural industry along the Pacific coast and the Central Highlands. A short 14 km south of Orotina, **Mahogany Park** is home to the **Original Canopy Tour company** ① *T2291-4465, www.canopytour.com, open 0800-1600, last tour leaves at 1330, US$45 plus entrance to Iguana Park*, with a tour going through three different lifezones. The third platform rests on a strangler fig over 30 m high which links to a fourth on a 44-m-high kapok tree. It's an entertaining way of learning about the rainforest. Tours last 3½ hours and an all-inclusive trip from San José costs US$60.

Orotina to Jacó

South from Orotina, the Central Pacific region becomes clearly defined. The predominant dry forest of the north gives way to moist forest, and Highway 34 becomes the coastal road proper, or *costanera*. The road is in good condition – maybe too good, watch your speed if driving.

If you're driving, one of the most popular free experiences in Costa Rica is to dangle over the side of the **Río Tárcoles bridge** to see the opaque, sediment-filled waters broken only by the bony backs of the somnolent crocodiles below. It's easy to find the spot to stop, as parked cars cram the roadside, especially at dawn and dusk when scarlet macaws can be seen returning to their roosts from Carara National Park on the southern banks of the river. You can get a closer look by taking a **boat tour** with **Jungle Crocodile Safari** ① *T2236-6473, www.junglecrocodilesafari.com*, or **Crocodile Man Tour** ① *T2637-0426, www.crocodilemantour.com. US$25-30 per person from the dock in Tárcoles, a little more on a round trip from Jacó.*

WARNING Regular letters appear in the weekly *Tico Times* recording the latest innovative scams of car thieves who empty vehicles while drivers watch the crocodiles from the bridge of the Río Tárcoles. Vehicles parked in the ranger's station have also been targeted. An increased police presence on the bridge has reduced the problem, but the police clock off at 1600! Make sure your vehicle is locked at all times, and avoid leaving valuables in the vehicle if possible.

Next to Carara National Park (see below) is **La Catarata** ① *0800-1500, Dec-Apr, US$15; there are signs on the main road, take the gravel road up the hill beside Hotel Villa Lapas, and it's 2.5-km hike to the falls and pools*, a private reserve with an impressive waterfall with a drop of close to 200 m with natural pools for bathing. You'll need to take food and refreshments but it's definitely worth the effort.

Parque Nacional Carara → *Colour map 1, C6.*

① *T2383-9953. The park is open daily from 0800-1600. Entrance is US$10. Tours in English available – reserve ahead if possible, T2200-5023. The entrance to the park is a couple of kilometres south of the Río Tárcoles bridge. Travelling by regular bus from San José or Puntarenas, ask the driver to drop you off at the entrance or the bridge, or if staying in Jacó, it's easy to get a bus back once you've sorted out accommodation.*

Incredibly close to San José (just 90 km away, or a couple of hours by road), Carara National Park provides some of the most accessible primary forest in the country and is one of the most popular protected areas. Lying in a transitional zone between the dry forests to the north and moist forests to the south, the average temperature of 27°C and annual rainfall of 2.8 m creates a staggering diversity of plants with over 750 species recorded to date in the park. The region was once part of Hacienda el Coyolar, one of the largest land titles in the country, before it was protected in 1978. The park also protects numerous **pre-Columbian archaeological sites**, some dating back to 300 BC.

A few trails lead through the park, which you can explore on your own or with a guide. Wildlife includes scarlet macaws, spider monkeys and the typically Costa Rican black and green poison arrow frog. A couple of trails just over 1 km leave from the ranger's station at the southern boundary of the park. The longest trail, at the northern boundary of the 5242-ha park, takes up to four hours and skirts the gallery forest along the Río Tárcoles passing an ox-bow lake carpeted with water hyacinths home to waterfowl, wading birds including the roseate spoonbill and dozing crocodiles.

Jacó ●◗◑▲◒◉ » *pp287-294. Colour map 2, C1.*

The original surf capital of Costa Rica, Jacó (population 3552) continues to be a major attraction as the closest real beach to San José. That proximity makes it a popular choice for *Ticos* and international visitors alike and the population feels far larger than official figures suggest. While the place is hardly paradise, the sandy beach is pleasant enough, and long enough for you to be able to find a relatively quiet spot.

Ins and outs

Getting there and around The town is a few hundred metres west of the *costanera*, some 117 km from San José. A good road links it to the capital making driving there simple. Buses (five daily) take just over two hours from the Coca-Cola Terminal. There are also services to Quepos, Puntarenas and Orotina. From north to south the bay of Playa Jacó is just over 3 km in length. Taxis, bikes and cars are all available for hire.

Best time to visit Temperatures and climate for the beach lover reach ideal from December to April with offshore breezes keeping temperatures in the mid 20s. The surf is best in the rainy season from May to November but is good all year round according to locals.

Sights and activities

Visitor numbers make sure that there are activities throughout the year and a fair amount of partying if you're looking to start your vacation with a bang or grab a few last rays of sunshine at the closest point to San José before heading home.

It's more 'do' than 'see' in Jacó, with activities mostly relating to water and therefore, naturally enough, **surfing**. Surf stores and schools exist in profusion to serve both the experienced and the rookie surfer. The Terraza del Pacífico, based in Playa Hermosa occasionally has international competitions.

Kayaks are available for hire for a different type of messing about on the water. Deep-sea **fishing** and sunset **cruises** are easily arranged. Beyond this, **horse riding** is also popular and can be organized through most hotels. You can get a bird's-eye view of the place with **paragliding** and the latest addition to the scene are **ultralight tours** and **boat-plane tours** with private beach drops.

If you are seeking higher levels of adrenaline head for **Waterfall Canopy Tour**, **ATV Tours**, or **paintballing**, all of which are about as far removed from the natural paradise that is Costa Rica as it is possible to be. For those seeking more gentle activity, there is the **Butterfly Fantasy** ⓘ *closed Mon, US$5*, which gives you the chance to observe the lifecycle of the butterfly.

Around Jacó

Tours to regional attractions – **Carara National Park**, **La Catarata waterfalls** and **Tárcoles crocodile tours**, and to nearby **Playa Hermosa** to the south – are easily arranged from Jacó. **Rain Forest Aerial Tram – Pacific** ⓘ *3 km from Jacó,*

Jacó

200 metres
200 yards

To San José

Sleeping 🛏
Alice 1
Apartotel Gaviotas 2
Best Western Jacó
  Beach Resort 3
Bohío 4
Cabinas La Cometa 6
Cabinas Las Palmas 7
Cabinas Tangeri 8
Camping El Hicaco 9
Club del Mar 18
Cocal 10
Copacabana 11
El Paraíso
  Escondido 12
Hard Rock Resort 13
Los Ranchos 14
Nathon's Surfer
  Hostel 5
Paraíso del Sol 15
Pochote Grande 16
ZabaMar 17

Eating 🍴
Aberdeen Angus 12
Bananas 1
Bubba's Tacos 14
Chatty Cathy's 2
El Barco de
  Marisco 13
La Hacienda 4
Pacific Bistro 10
Sunrise Grill
  Breakfast Place 7
Tsunami Suchi 11
Wahoo 3
Wishbone 8

Bars & clubs 🍸
Beatle 9

T2257-5961, www.rfat.com. US$55, children US$27.50. A short distance before Jacó, the younger relation of the Aerial Tram in Braulio Carrillo National Park, the Pacific version is set in 90 ha of transitional tropical rainforest linked to rare tropical dry forest, covering small waterfalls and good views to the Pacific.

Playa Hermosa → *Colour map 2, C1.*

A rocky headland and 3 km separate Jacó from Playa Hermosa, a far more sedate and arguably better surf hang-out – for both the surfing and the atmosphere if you like a quieter spot. The *costanera* skims the coastline where you'll see a huddle of hotels – check in and get your board out.

In 1998, 10 km of dark sand beach from Playa Hermosa south was declared a Wildlife Refuge to protect the nesting site of marine turtles which arrive on the beach between July and December. Ask at local hotels to see if night tours are available for visitors.

Playa Esterillos and beaches south to Manuel Antonio

South of Playa Hermosa, the *costanera* heads inland and the coastline is filled with row upon row of African palm. The dense plantations are dark and vaguely threatening, hidden from view and all but the most curious of drivers and surfers, it almost requires a leap of faith to take a turn and head through the dark to find a line of fine beaches stretching for some 20 km south of Jacó.

The secluded and sparse accommodation is available across a range of budgets – perfect for a quiet hideaway and definitely for those with the resources to keep themselves amused. While independent travellers can walk down any of the access roads and will love the seclusion, you will probably feel quite cut off once you get there and services are limited.

A popular choice with *Tico* families, **Playa Palma** is a surf beach with a gently humming village life that at some point as it heads south along the shore becomes the village of **Bandera**.

Parrita to Quepos

The first and only town of any real size between Jacó and Quepos is Parrita, a bustling low-level supply town serving nearby agricultural communities. There's not much to see but there's a Banco Nacional, a Banco de Costa Rica with an ATM, a gas station and a few basic hotels and stores – handy if you're staying at a nearby beach.

A road heads south at Parrita for 5 km to **Isla Palo Seco** with more fine sandy beaches, mangrove swamps and canals to explore. The road continues for about 22 km to Quepos down a mainly good but in places pot-holed road that travels through more endless stretches of African palm plantations, broken only by the occasional village of two-storey balconied houses laid out around a central football pitch and a church of normally Evangelical denomination. Most of the villages look tired, destitute and forgotten. Driving through, it would appear that some members of the community are getting their spirit from a different source, as the obligatory branches of Alcoholics Anonymous seem to suggest.

For Sleeping and Eating price codes and other relevant information, see Essentials, pages 44-47.

Sleeping

Puntarenas *p281, map p280*

AL Yadran, almost at the western limit of the peninsula at C 37, T2661-2662, www.hotelyadrancr.com. A mid-sized complex with comfortable rooms all with private bath and a/c. A couple of pools – for the kiddies, 3 restaurants and a disco.

L-AL Tioga, on the beachfront between C 19 and 21, T2661-0271, www.hotel tioga.com. 45 rooms, all with private bath, a/c, TV and telephone. The best hotel in town with a restaurant, swimming pool, the new Playa de Oro casino. Rooms with balconies are, of course, much better and have good views.

AL Las Brisas, on the waterfront between C 31-33, T2661-4040, www.lasbrisashotelcr.com. 20 smart motel-style rooms, with a/c and TV. Small restaurant serving Greek, Mexican and *Tico* cuisine and a pool. Small multi-lingual book swap. Price includes breakfast and tax. A little overpriced, but comfortable.

B La Punta, good position 1 block from the ferry dock to the Nicoya Peninsula at Av 1-3, C 35, T2661-0696. OK rooms with private bath and a/c, and a small pool out back. Mixed reports, at times surly service.

B-C Gran Hotel Chorotega, near the banks and market on the corner of C 1, Av 3, T2661-0998, www.granhotelchorotega.com. 38 clean rooms with private bath, cheaper if shared. Efficient and friendly service. Popular with Costa Rican business types, cheaper rooms are a good deal.

C Gran Imperial, on the beachfront, in front of the Muelle de Cruceros (dock), C Central-2, T2661-0579. Pleasant rooms in an old building, although a little dark, but clean, with private bath and fan. Small garden patio and a chilled atmosphere. Good spot and handy for buses.

C-D Cayuga, C 4, Av Central-1, T2661-0344. 31 rooms with private bathroom, a/c, some with TV and fridge. The rooms are pretty dark, as respite you can sit in the small patio garden but it's hardly paradise.

D Cabezas, Av 1, C 2-4, T2661-1045. 23 simple, no-frills rooms, but bright and clean, some with private bath, cheaper without. With friendly service this is a good deal.

D-E Río, down a side street off Av 3 between C Central and 2, near market, T2661-0331. Countless rooms with shared or private bath and fans. Friendly Chinese owners, very keen to help. Once a good backpacker choice, but as ferry services have moved, you'll need to get a taxi down the road.

E Hotel Helen, 150 m north of the buses, C2, Av C-2, T2661-2159. OK budget place with partioned walls which don't reach up to the ceiling, but handy for buses.

Out of town

On the neck of the peninsula at Cocal is the Yacht Club, T2661-0784, www.costa ricayachtclub.com, catering for members of international yacht clubs and the usual yachtie types.

A Portobello, Av Central, C 68-70, T2661-1322. With bath and a/c. Pool in pleasant gardens, clean and quiet with excellent food in the restaurant and a helpful Italian owner.

South to Jacó *p283*

B Casa San Francisco, near the regional hospital, Roble, T2663-0148, www.casa sanfrancisco.info. A friendly place run by a couple of Canadian women, with clean rooms, a pool, breakfast and laundry facilities.

B Villa del Roble, T2663-0447. By the sea, with 12 quiet rooms. A charming stop with a small pool.

E Casablanca, Av 14, C 2-4, T2222-2921, Mata de Limón. Can provide full board.

E Manglares, near the former train station, Mata de Limón. A reasonable option with a good restaurant.

Orotina *p283*

A-B El Rancho Oropendola, just north of Orotina in San Mateo, T2428-8600, www.ranchoropendola.com. Cabins with private bath or rooms with shared bath, rustic and peaceful, pool, nature trails.

B Las Candelillas, west of San Mateo, at Higuito de San Mateo, T2428-9157, www.lascandelillas.com. A 26-ha farm and reforestation project with fruit trees and sugar-cane plantation. There is also a **camping** area with showers, pool and horse riding.

C Cabinas Kalim, near the plaza in town, T2428-8082.

Orotina to Jacó *p283*

AL Villa Lapas, on the southern side of Carara National Park beside the Río Tarcolitos turn, T2637-0232, www.villalapas.com. 55 comfortable but uninspiring rooms, all with private bath and a/c. Each room has a terrace with views of the river, garden or pool and a jacuzzi. International and local dishes are served buffet-style in the Toucan Restaurant. Over 2.5 km of trails connected by hanging bridges meander through the hotel's own private reserve.

Playa Tárcoles

AL all-inclusive pp Tarcol Lodge, T2430-0400, www.costaricagateway.com. A handful of rooms in a small, rustic lodge with hot water shared bath, and meals using fresh seafood. Resident bird guide makes sure guests get the most out of spotting bird life which flocks to the mud flats as the tidal waters recede.

C Cabinas Carara, T2637-0178. Basic, 16 cabins with bath, small, simple restaurant, pool, superb birdwatching at mouth of Río Tárcoles about 5 km along this road.

Punta Leona

With dramatic scenery and sandy bays, Punta Leona is home to a number of top-end hotels and resorts.

LL-L Villa Caletas, T2637-0505, www.hotelvillacaletas.com. Perched high on a cliff above the ocean and surrounded by lush rainforest, this place truly is, as they claim, close to heaven. A combination of rooms, suites and villas, all luxuriously decorated throughout. Many of the rooms have views out to the Pacific, the villas and junior suites offer greater space, and the suites and master suite even have their own private swimming pools. Don't worry, the shared pool is no less elegant. A couple of restaurants serve international gourmet cuisine.

L Los Sueños Resort & Marina, T2630-9000, www.lsrm.com. Bahía Herradura is the next beach south before Jacó and you may know it better than you realize as it was used for location filming for the gloriously over-produced movie *1492: Conquest of Paradise* starring Gérard Depardieu. As part of the *Marriott* chain, you should expect the very best in standards and services. Over 200 rooms with apartments and a marina with moorings for 300 yachts. All the expected services, including the popular 18-hole golf course. Still evolving, there are plans for sportsfishing charters, international bill-fishing competitions, day and sunset cruises. See also Activities and tours below.

AL Punta Leona, T2231-3131, www.hotel puntaleona.com. A full service resort with over 200 rooms and apartments set in 300 ha of rainforest. All rooms have a private bath, a/c, TV, telephone, fridge and safety box. But it's the activities laid on that will appeal most: tennis, mini-golf, aerobics, dance classes and a wide range of nature tours and watersports provided by JD's Watersports. Ideal for families, the activity-obsessed and those who like an all-inclusive package vacation.

Jacó *p284, map p285*

Accommodation in Jacó is overpriced. Look for discounts May-Nov.

LL Club del Mar, at south end of the beach, T2643-3194, www.clubdelmarcostarica.com.

Casitas, rooms and suites with kitchen, fridge and ceiling fans all recently renovated. You can lounge by the pool, or set out on your own adventure with rented bikes, boards and cars.

L Hard Rock Resort, at the southern end of town, T2643-3147, www.hardrockresort casino.cr. Popular medium-size resort with comfortable rooms, 3 pools, tennis courts, pool tables, and countless other activities. Popular with groups, English, German and French spoken. Generous discounts (**A**) in the green season.

L-A Cabinas Tangeri, T2643-3001, www.hoteltangeri.com. 25 a/c chalets and villas (1 with capacity for up to 8 people) with private bath, TV and fridge. 3 pools – 1 for children – set in pleasant gardens leading to the beach. Good BBQ grill and restaurant with cocktails. Nothing special, but excellent value for groups.

AL Copacabana, on the beach just north of the centre, T2643-1005, www.copaca banahotel.com. Canadian-owned with 30-odd rooms all with hot showers and fans. Lively relaxation with a pool, complete with wet bar, open-air restaurant, access to the beach and gentle whoops of the howler *homo sapiens* in the sports bar. Popular choice.

L Best Western Jacó Beach Resort, at the northern end of town, T2643-1000, www.bestwestern.com. Big comfortable Best Western rooms with private bath and tub, cable TV but no awards for creativity. Large pool and beachfront bar and restaurant. Activities include tennis court and free use of bikes for guests.

AL ZabaMar, central and close to the beach, T2643-3174. 20 large rooms some with a/c, cheaper with a fan. A small pool which seems to be more popular than the beach. Helpful American owners, small restaurant and bar. Booking ahead is recommended.

L-A Paraíso del Sol, east of main street close to centre, T2643-3250, www.paraisodelsolcr. com. Apartments sleeping 2-6 people with kitchenette, swimming pool and parking. Recommended and good for groups.

AL-A Pochote Grande, north of town, T2643-3236, www.hotelpochotegrande.net. A simple 2-storey villa with 24 spacious rooms all with hot water, private bath and fridge, with a terrace or balcony. The fine tropical gardens include a pool partially shaded by an incredible 500-year old *pochote* tree, with direct access to the beach. Quiet little bar and restaurant, with good secure parking. A good choice in this price bracket.

A Cocal, on the beach near the centre of town, T2643-3067, www.hotelcocaland casino.com. Neat and tidy throughout, the 44 rooms have a/c and private bath. There are 2 pools, an open-air restaurant and claims to have the largest casino in Jacó.

A-B Apartotel Gaviotas, T2643-3092, www.hotelgaviotas.com. 12 self-catering apartments with kitchenette, TV, some with a/c, cheaper with fans. Big pool and easy-come, easy-go atmosphere. Parking.

A-B Cabinas Las Palmas, north end of town, T2643-3005. Simple tidy rooms, some with kitchenette, all with bath and fan, clean, set in pretty gardens – shame about the lime green colour scheme.

AL-C El Jardín, at the north end of town, T2643-3050. Close to the beach, 10 rooms in quiet spot, friendly with small pool.

AL-A pp El Paraíso Escondido, 150 m east of the Catholic church on C Los Cholos, T2643-2883, www.hoteljaco.com. All the tiled floor rooms have a private bath, patio and a/c – there are some cheaper rooms with fan. There is a swimming pool set in fine quiet gardens. Good service, attention to detail and the friendly owner often meets arriving buses.

A-C Los Ranchos, central and close to the beach, T2643-3070. 4 bungalows, complete with kitchenette and 8 rooms sleeping 4-8 people. Good for groups. Lively spot with a small pool, a short walk from the beach.

B-D Alice, south of centre, T2643-3061, cabalice@racsa.co.cr. Tidy rooms with private bath, small terrace and pool. Good spot, close to the beach.

C Bohío, central and near beach, T2643-3017. Simple accommodation with private bath, cold water and fan.

C Cabinas La Cometa, on the main street in the centre, T2643-3615, cometadejaco@ yahoo.com. Good rooms with fan, hot water shared bath, very clean.

C-E Nathon's Surfer Hostel, south end of town near the beach, T8355-4356, www.nathonshostel.com. Selection of dormitory and private rooms, It's all about surfing and partying at Nathon's.

Camping

G Camping El Hicaco, slightly south of the centre, T2643-3004, with Restaurant Los Hicacos nearby, both down same access route to the beach.

Playa Hermosa *p286*

L Terraza del Pacífico, T2440-6862, www.terrazadelpacifico.com. 62 big rooms with tiled floors, high wooden ceilings and private bathroom. The mid-price open-air bar and restaurant overlooks the sea. There's also a souvenir shop and internet service. Although it's a comfortable resort-style hotel, complete with a big pool and wet bar, the atmosphere is more genuine than most.

L-AL Hotel Sandpiper Inn, T2643-7042, www.sandpipercostarica.com. Popular surf place with 8 rooms, all with hot water private bath, a/c and ceiling fans. Lounge around the pool, the open-air bar and restaurant or stroll a short distance to the beach. Good for surfing and fishing trips, a good comfortable choice.

AL-A Fuego del Sol, T2289-6060, www.fuegodelsolhotel.com. 21 rooms and suites, with hot water private bath, a/c and telephone in a 2-storey villa overlooking the pool, gardens and to the beach. 4 suites have a kitchenette and fridge. The pool has a wet bar and the restaurant looks directly out to the beach and the coast.

AL-A Las Olas, T2643-7021, www.lasolas hotel.com. Cabins, with hot water and fridge, and *ranchos*, with a kitchenette, sleeping

2-6 people. Small pool and a beachfront café in a quiet if slightly cramped spot.

A Casa Pura Vida, T2643-7039. 4 apartments with a couple of rooms sleeping up to 4 people. A/c, hot shower and kitchenettes, but breakfast is also included. A graceful and quiet Mediterranean-style villa, with a pool with direct access to the beach – a good relaxing choice.

A-B Las Arenas, T2643-7013, www.cabinaslasarenas.com. 10 basic surf cabins with microwave and fridge – what else do you need? The *Tico* owner Chino speaks English and is a keen surfer and is happy to talk about local breaks. Good Jammin restaurant serving breakfast, lunch and dinner. Can help sort out transfers, and surfing tours.

C-D Ola Bonita Aparthotel, T2643-3990, www.olabonita.com. 6 basic rather uninspiring rooms sleeping 4 with a pool.

C-D Outback Hermosa, T2643-2575. 3 simple rooms, with fine views to the ocean. Good, friendly place to stay.

D-E pp Rancho Grande, T2643-7023, www.cabinasranchogrande.com. A funky wood and bamboo house, just renovated, that makes a home away from home run by the friendly Rhonda and Brian from Florida – get the top room if you're in a group. 7 rooms of varying size which fill up with surfers. Private baths have cold water, shared baths are hot.

Playa Esterillos and beaches south to Manuel Antonio *p286*
Playa Esterillos

LL Xandari by the Pacific, Este, T2778-7070, www.xandari.com. The Central Highlands Xandari experience comes to the Pacific, with villas opening up to great Pacific views, or onto the gardens, a couple of pools, full spa treatments and an excellent open-air restaurant, that emphasizes fresh seafood and produce.

AL-A La Felicidad Country Club, Centro, T2778-6824, www.lafelicidad.com. A low-key option with comfortable rooms with private bath, some with kitchens and balconies overlooking the endless beach. A private pool, comfy chairs and hammocks. There's a small bar and restaurant, and a couple of *sodas* and seafood restaurants on the beachfront.

A-B Pelican Hotel, Este, T2778-8105, www.pelicanbeachfronthotel.com. A very comfortable small hotel with 9 rooms all with hot water, private bath, cheaper if shared, and safe box. There's a small pool and a range of watersports activities for messing about on the beach, a good restaurant service and a small airstrip right on the doorstep.

Playa Bejuco

L Hotel El Delfín, T2770-8308, www.delfinbeachfront.com. With 15 a/c rooms with private bath, many with balconies. Has a small cheap restaurant serving seafood dishes. Playa Bejuco is an even quieter beach.

Playas Palma and Bandera

A-C Cabinas Maldonado, T2286-1116. 5 cabins sleeping 4-10 people, all with private bath. Facilities include fan, kitchen and fridge. Small pool, jacuzzi and BBQ grill just a few metres from the beach.

D Finca Don Herbert, T2779-9204. Good spot for families. 5 well-equipped cabins with a small pool with waterslides and a café snack bar.

E Rooms/Restaurant Alex, with simple rooms is 2.6 km south towards Playa Bandera.

Isla Palo Seco

AL-A La Isla, T2779-9393, www.laisla hotel.com. 16 furnished and fully equipped self-catering apartments complete with TV, fan. There's a pool and jacuzzi, and horses for riding along the beach, and canoes for exploring the mangroves.

A Beso del Viento, T2779-9674, www.beso delviento.com. A better choice, this French-owned hotel has large open villas, with stylish

decorative touches and 4 self-catering apartments sleeping up to 6. The pool is quiet and there are kayaks and horses for rent. The beach is close to paradise – stretching for miles into the distance.

🍽 Eating

Puntarenas *p281, map p280*
Paseo de los Turistas sparkles and twinkles in the evening breeze, inviting you to walk and explore the restaurants, bars and karaoke clubs. Explore until you find something that meets your mood.

🍴 **La Yunta**, at C 19. A good mid-priced steakhouse, with a selection of seafood dishes as well.

🍴-🍴 **Casa de Mariscos**, C 7-9. A popular mid-range seafood restaurant on the seafront.

🍴-🍴 **El Kayte Negro**, towards the north side of the peninsula on Av 1, C 17. Has cheap, good local seafood.

🍴-🍴 **Jardín Cervecero**, C 23-25. Big place good for snack sandwiches, hamburgers and a finely chilled beer.

🍴-🍴 **Mariscos Kahite Blanco**, next to El Kayte Negro, Av 1, C17. Excellent and locally renowned cheap seafood restaurant, popular dining spot for *Tico* families at weekends.

🍴 **Arenas Chepes Bar**, on seafront between C 13-15. Good, cheap seafood, where the locals eat.

🍴 **Gugas**, Av 2, C Central-1. Selection of meat and seafood dishes, close to the bus station so handy if passing through.

🍴 **Imperial**, opposite the Muelle de Cruceros. Bar-cum-restaurant, chilled by sea breezes, serving seafood and pasta. Quick service, come for a snack or a full meal. Open 0600-2200.

🍴 **Soda Macarena**, opposite the Muelle de Cruceros close to the bus stops. Makes good cheap *empañadas*, ideal when waiting for the bus.

There are a number of Chinese restaurants on Av Central and C 1 (eg **Mandarín**).

South to Jacó p283
¶ **María Vargas**, Roble. Good food and reasonable prices in a friendly setting.

Orotina to Jáco p283
El Tico, 3 km from Playa Tárcoles. A good seafood restaurant.

Jacó p284, map p285
Jacó is the classic stroll-and-discover resort. Meandering down the main street you'll find a restaurant or bar that takes your fancy and then move on. There are also many cheap *sodas* throughout town, and a number of international fast-food names down the main street.

¶¶ **Aberdeen Angus**, very good Argentine restaurant with great steaks, right on the main street.

¶¶-¶ **El Barco de Marisco**, north of Más x Menos. Seafood and shellfish, popular.

¶¶-¶ **La Hacienda**, northern end. Good bar and restaurant serving mid-priced snacks. There's a breezy balcony and gentle rock standards drifting through the background.

¶¶-¶ **Wishbone**, on the main street. Serving big plates of Mexican in a fine Tex-Mex *cantina* setting, with a small terrace.

¶ **Bananas**, international and local dishes.

¶ **Bubba's Tacos**, close to Más x Menos. New taco joint.

¶ **Chatty Cathy's**, on the main drag. Popular and long time favourite dining spots.

¶ **Pacific Bistro**, just north of the centre of town. Asian-fusion dishes, with great seafood.

¶ **Sunrise Grill Breakfast Place**, serves a good breakfast from 0600 until 1200. Closed Wed.

¶ **Tsunami Sushi**, good sushi if that's what you're looking for.

¶ **Wahoo**, just within the centre to the north. Simple decor without the razzmatazz of many places in town, with unassuming, cheap and mainly seafish *Tico* dishes.

Playa Hermosa p286
¶¶ **Costa Nera**, is a well thought of mid-range Italian restaurant serving Italian food cooked by … Italians.

¶ **Las Arenas**, is a good spot for an ice-cold beer and snack food.

¶ **Goola Café**, new vegetarian restaurant café on the beach, open for breakfast and with internet too.

¶ **Jungle Surf Café**. Has a chalked-up menu based on what's available but normally includes fish, burger snacks and a few cheap local dishes.

Bars and clubs

Jacó p284, map p285
Several bars rise and flow through the course of an evening including **Bohío**, **El Rincón del Mar**, **Jungle Bar**, and **Monkey Bar** to name but a few.

Beatle Bar, towards the north end of town. Open throughout the day, serves food and drinks, but gets going from 2100. Pool tables and oldies music as you'd expect.

Filthy McNasty's, has been described as over the top by some, fun by others.

La Hacienda, is a big hit at weekends.

Festivals and events

Puntarenas p281, map p280
Mid-Feb Puntarenas Carnival takes place over 10 days with decorated parades, wandering musicians, concerts and processions ending in bull fights and fireworks.
Jul Fiesta de la Virgen del Mar has a week of festivities leading to a carnival and regatta of decorated fishing boats and yachts on the Sat closest to 16 Jul.

Shopping

Jacó p284, map p285
Beach There are a wide range of shops down the main street selling everything you need for beach life. **Mother of Fear Surf Shop** and more enticingly **Cocobolo** provide for all your beach necessities including surf

gear, beachwear, oils and lotions. Around a dozen stores renting out boards, and they'll know how to get board repairs if needed.

Supermarkets There are several supermarkets in the centre for stocking up on basics and supplies if you're in self-catering accommodation. If your addiction is shopping malls, try Playa Jacó Plaza Mall to the north of town.

▲ Activities and tours

Puntarenas *p281, map p280*
Puntarenas is home to **Puntarenas FC**, a first division team that flirted with winning the championship over 20 years ago. Ask locally for details on matches.

See San José Tour operators, page 105 for cruises in the Gulf of Nicoya from Puntarenas.

Orotina to Jacó *p283*
Watersports
JD's Watersports, at Los Sueños, Punta Leona (see Sleeping, above), T2290-1560, toll free in the US on T1-800-477-8971, www.jdwatersports.com. JD's – who also have a base at Hotel Punta Leona – are watersports specialists. Wherever there is water they'll do something on, in or with it, from Jungle River Cruises up the Tárcoles River, sunset cruises, scuba diving courses and sportsfishing. Can also organize trips around the country.

Jacó *p284, map p285*
Several tour operators down the main street. **Green Tours**, T2643-2773, greentourscr@yahoo.com, arrange local and national tours. **Solutions Tourism and Services**, T2643-3560, www.solutionscr.com. Provide all local, regional and national tourism services. **Jaco Surf School**, T2643-1905, www.jaco surfschool.com; and **Vista Guapa Surf Camp**, T2643-2830, www.vistaguapa.com, are 2 of the companies in town offering surf lessons, and regional tours.

Playa Hermosa *p286*
Del Mar Surf Camp, T2643-3197, www.costa ricasurfingchicas.com. Surf school for women, getting you up on the board, enjoying the water and the workout.

◉ Transport

Puntarenas *p281, map p280*
Bus Empresarios Unidos (T2222-0064) between **San José** and **Puntarenas** leave San José from Terminal Puntarenas C 16, Av 10-12, 0400-2200. In Puntarenas the terminal is at C 2, Av 2-4, T2661-2158. Buses leave every 40 mins or so from 0415-1900, 2 hrs, US$3.20.

Buses to other locations leave from C 2 on the beachfront promenade, close to the terminal. Heading north there is a daily bus to **Santa Elena** for **Monteverde** at 1315, with an occasional bus at 1415, 5 hrs, US$2.30. Buses go to **Liberia** 8 times daily, first at 0440, last 1500, 2½ hrs, US$3.70. There are a couple of buses to **Tilarán** via **Cañas** leaving at 1145 and 1630, 3½ hrs, US$1.80. Heading south, buses leave for **Jacó**, 2 hrs, US$1.70, continuing on to **Quepos**, 4 hrs, US$2.80, at 0500, 1100, 1430 and 1630.

Boat There are ferry services across the Gulf of Nicoya to the Nicoya Peninsula from 2 docks. The most commonly used dock is at the northwestern end of Puntarenas, on Av 3, between C 33-35. Between **Puntarenas** and **Playa Naranjo** there is a passenger and vehicle service provided by **Coonatramar**, T2661-1069, www.coonatramar.com. Ferries depart at 0630, 1000, 1430 and 1930, returning from **Playa Naranjo** at 0800, 1230, 1730 and 2100, 1½ hrs, pedestrians US$1.70, motorbikes US$3.20, cars US$10.30. Buses meet the arriving ferry in Playa Naranjo providing connections to **Nicoya**, via **Carmona**, and beyond.

A couple of passenger and vehicle ferries also head for **Paquera** on the southern side

of the peninsula. **Ferry Peninsular**
(T2641-0515) services leave at 0830, 1130,
1330, 1600 and 2030, returning at 0500,
0730, 1100, 1400 and 1600, 1½ hrs,
pedestrians US1.40, cars US$9. Buses to
Tambor, **Cóbano** and **Montezuma**
meet the ferry.

Hotel Playa Tambor operates the Naviera
Tambor, T2661-2084, naviera@racsa.co.cr.
Primarily for guests. Non-guests can use the
service, subject to availability, which leaves
Puntarenas at 0500, 0900, 1300 and 1700,
returning at 0700, 1100, 1500 and 2100,
1½ hrs, pedestrians US1.40, cars US$9.

Jacó *p284, map p285*
Boat   **Zuma Tours**, based on the Nicoya
Peninsula, T8849-8569, www.zumatours.net.
Provide a taxi boat service between Jacó and
Montezuma on the Nicoya Peninsula, US$40.

Bus   The bus terminal is at the north end of
town by the Playa Jacó Plaza Mall, close to
Pizza Hut. From **San José** there are 5 direct
daily buses a day at 0730, 1030, 1300, 1500
and 1700, from the Coca-Cola terminal,
2¼ hrs, US$3. Buses return at 0500, 0730,
1100, 1500 and 1700. 4 buses a day for
Quepos to the south (0500, 1100, 1430
and 1630) and also for **Puntarenas** to the
north (0500, 1100, 1430 and 1630, 2hrs,
US$1.70). For information about services
call T2643-3135.

Jacó is also on the **Interbus** itinerary, with
a minibuses going north to **San José** and
south to **Quepos** and on to the rest of
the country.

Car hire   Economy, next to the Jacó
Best Western hotel, T2643-1719,
www.economyrentacar.com. **Elegante**,
T2643-3224, www.eleganterentacar.com.
Budget, T2643-2665, www.budget.co.cr.

① Directory

Puntarenas *p281, map p280*
Banks   Banco Nacional and Banco de
Costa Rica on Av 3, C 1-3 near the central
market, both change TCs and have ATMs.
Internet   Millennium Cyber Café on the
beachfront with C 15, open 0900-2200 daily,
US$1/hr, set up for Skype and VOIP. **Internet
Café Puntarenas**, near the Marine History
Museum, open 0930-2200, US$1/hr. Another
outdoor, probably seasonal, café nearby.
Laundry   Below Millenium Cyber Café,
US$6 for 5 kg wash and dry, open Mon-Fri
0830-1700. Fast turnaround time when
requested. **Post office**   Post office on
Av 3, C Central-1, close to the central
market. **Telephone**   ICE and Radiográfica
on Av C, C 2-4.

Jacó *p284, map p285*
Banks   Banco Nacional in centre of town.
Internet   Several options in town but
Mexican Joe's on main road at a couple of
places, US$0.75/hr, continues to provide a
reliable service, with international telephone
service. **Language schools**   Instituto
Pácifico de Idiomas, T2643-2244,
www.spanish-ipai.com, offers Spanish
classes 4 hours a day for 1 week at
US$470, including homestay, meals and
airport pick-up. Surfing classes included
for free. **Medical services**   Red Cross in
the centre of town, T2643-3090. **Post
office**   The post office is at the southern
end of town near the *municipalidad* offices.
Useful addresses   Chuck's Surf Repairs ,
T2643-3328 or 643-1308, www.surf
outfitters.com will sort out any serious
damage to your board.

Quepos and Manuel Antonio

Quepos pulsates with the crowds that converge on this small Pacific town, arriving in search of palm-fringed beaches and the wildlife encounters to be had at the end of a winding 7-km road that climbs and falls over the rocky Punta Quepos peninsula to arrive at the justifiably popular Manuel Antonio National Park. The town has successfully moved beyond a dependency on banana exports and is filled with lively bars and restaurants, sustained by a considerable expatriate community and visiting tourists, that buzz and hum in the warm ocean breeze. The road to Manuel Antonio is also lined with hotels and restaurants each offering comfort and relaxation in the tropical paradise. There's something for everyone here: many hotels are in the upper range, but a few mid-range and budget options are starting to open up, and activities abound from peaceful nature tours through to full on adrenalin pumping adventure. ▸▸ *For listings, see pages 301-307.*

Ins and outs ▸▸ *Colour map 3, B1.*

Getting there

There are several direct daily flights for the 25-minute journey from San José, with **SANSA**, locally on T8777-0683, www.flysansa.com, US$53, and **NatureAir**, T2220-3054, www.natureair.com, US$66. The flight takes just over 30 minutes. Taxis meet incoming flights for the 4-km journey to Quepos. There are nine buses a day from San José to Quepos. If driving, Highway 34 – the *costanera* – passes Quepos a couple of kilometres to the east – watch out for the signs or follow the traffic. From the north it's a good road for most of the 192-km journey. To the south, the road is in poor condition as far as Dominical. A regular bus runs from Quepos to along the 7-km road to Manuel Antonio National Park. ▸▸ *See Transport, page 307, for further details.*

Getting around

Quepos is certainly small enough to walk around without any trouble. If heading for Manuel Antonio, a half-hourly bus service makes the 7-km journey from town, US$0.40. The road is lined with hotels, bars, restaurants and stores – tell the bus driver exactly where you want to get off and he wil stop at the nearest safe point. Taxis to Manuel Antonio cost about US$3 on a good day and it should be a set fair of US$0.50 on the return journey.

Best time to visit

Ask a *Quepolandian* when is the best time to visit their town and their rose-tinted view of the world will usually incline them to say that any time is good, but the dry season runs from January-March, when clear skies and temperatures in the high 20s are guaranteed. For the rest of the year, life is still pretty good, with the heaviest rainfall between August and October.

Tourist information

There is no tourist information office but drop into **Lynch Travel Services** or **Iguana Tours** for a full run-down on the latest offerings and information. Keep an eye out for *Quepolandia*, www.quepolandia.com, a locally produced free English language magazine dripping with advice, tips and permanently positive quips. ▸▸ *See Activities and tours, page 306, for further details.*

History

The earliest interactions with the Quepo people of the peninsula took place in 1519, but it was not until Juan Vásquez de Coronado began his exploits in Costa Rica in 1563 that the Spanish conquerors got a foothold in the country. By 1570 the first mission in the country had been created in nearby San Bernadino. Fortunes waned for the *indígenas* and the population declined rapidly and the mission closed in 1747. Activity in the region recommenced with the small-scale planting of bananas in the area in the early 1900s, which was later adopted by the United Fruit Company who began plantation production in the 1930s. Development of the port and docks began at the expense of mangroves but sigatoka disease hit in the 1940s followed by Panama disease in the 1950s, which virtually wiped out the industry. Partial economic recovery came with the introduction of African palms which produce the oil used in margarine and soap. The seeds of tourism were planted in the 1970s and early 1980s when a few isolated cabins peopled by a lucky few enjoyed the unspoilt beauty of the area. Add word of mouth, passing on news of the beauty of the place, and a few decades of development and the rest is history.

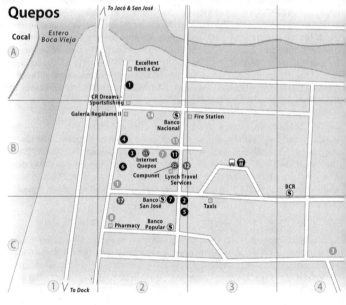

Quepos

N

100 metres (approx)
100 yards (approx)

Sleeping 🛏
Best Western Kamuk **1** *B2*
Cabinas El Cisne &
  Sensación Tropical **2** *A6*
Cabinas Hellen **3** *C4*
Ceciliano **5** *C4*
Doña Alicia **6** *B5*

El Malinche **7** *B2*
El Parque **8** *C2*
Hospedaje La Mancha **9** *B6*
Mar y Luna **11** *B2*
Sirena **14** *B2*
Wide Mouth Frog **15** *B5*

Eating 🍴
Café Milagro **1** *A2*
Dos Locos **2** *C2*
El Banco Sports Bar **3** *B2*
El Gran Escape **4** *B2*
Escalofrío **5** *C2*
La Lanterna **6** *B2*

Trips from Quepos

Beyond lazing on the beach, **surfboards** are available for hire from rental outlets in front of the beach near the park. You can hire a board, or have a lesson. US$30/hr and they guarantee to get you up on the board. Local tour operators can organize **surf taxis** to nearby locations on request. **Guided walks** of Manuel Antonio National Park lasting 2½ hours can be arranged through your hotel or at the entrance to the national park. Tours are available in Spanish, English and some guides speak German, T2777-4122, US$20. Wildlife tours head out to the mangroves of nearby **Damas Island**, with caiman, sloths, monkeys and many birds, from US$60. Or you can head out on tour by **kayak** from US$65.

Tours of the nearby forest are a popular activity. **Horse riding** gives you the best chance of seeing wildlife. One local option is **Rancho Marlboro** towards the end of the road to the park, T2777-1108. Trips lead inland to **Rancho Los Tucanes**, touring the quiet hills, valleys and waterfalls near Londres. Prices from US$60.

Canopy Tours are available in the area with the Titi Canopy Tour at Rancho Casa Grande, 14 platforms and 11 cables carrying you through the canopy for over a mile. Out of town there is Rain Maker (see below), and the Rain Forest Aerial Tram near Jacó (page 285).

Raising the heart rate slightly, **whitewater rafting** trips head out to the Class III and IV Naranjo and Savegre rivers, passing through serene jungle scenery that you will notice when not fighting the rapids. In addition to **Amigos del Río**, T2777-0082, Ríos Tropicales have opened an office in Quepos, T2777-4095. Prices from US$70.

Canyoning tours are one way of getting even more intimate with the rivers of the area, with rappels up and down the face of nearby waterfalls.

Noisy, and potentially dangerous, **All-terrain Vehicle (ATV) tours** are more exciting, but you'll only see wildlife if you run it over. Price from US$95, each ATV holds two people.

Finally take to the air with a spot of **parascending** or **hangliding** for the best imagineable views.

The best way to wind down at the end of the day is with a **sunset tour** of the coastal waters in one of the fine yachts that cruise the bay, sipping an ice-cold beverage as the sun sinks below the western horizon.

To Airport & Dominical

Alamo
Car Rental

Football Pitch

To Manuel Antonio

16 Blue Fin Sports Fishing Charters

Iguana Tours

5

6

anopy afari

2

l'Angolo **7** C2
Monchados **11** B2
Pan Aldo **16** C5

Bars & clubs
Pueblo **12** B2
Wacky Wanda's **17** C2

Rain Maker Nature Reserve

ⓘ *T2777-0777, www.rainmakercostarica.com. US$70. Open daily. Most people visit the reserve on trips from Quepos or Manuel Antonio. If you want to make your own way there, head for San Rafael Norte, leaving the costanera at Pocora, 10 km east of Parrita.*

High up in the treetops is where you'll find the real activity of the rainforest, and Rain Maker, a short trip northeast of Quepos, will get you there. A network of suspended cable bridges hung between trees and linking platforms affords a unique bird's eye view of the canopy and this fascinating world. Accompanied by a local guide the trip starts with a steep – but manageable – climb to the first bridge. The 540-ha reserve protects

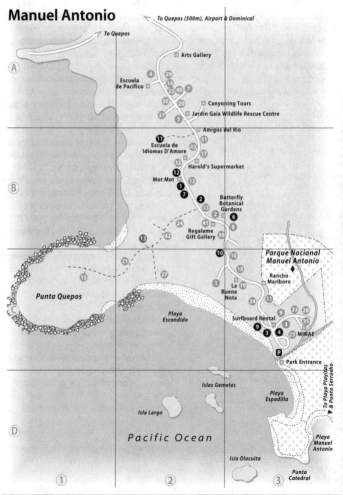

Manuel Antonio

To Quepos (500m), Airport & Dominical

To Quepos

Arts Gallery

Escuela de Pacifico

Canyoning Tours

Jardin Gaia Wildlife Rescue Centre

Amigos del Rio

Escuela de Idiomas D'Amore

Harold's Supermarket

Mot Mot

Butterfly Botanical Gardens

Regalame Gift Gallery

Parque Nacional Manuel Antonio

Punta Quepos

La Buena Nota

Rancho Marlboro

Playa Escondido

Surfboard Rental

MINAE

Park Entrance

To Playa Playitas & Punta Serrucho

Islas Gemelas

Playa Espadilla

Isla Largo

Pacific Ocean

Isla Olocuita

Playa Manuel Antonio

Punta Catedral

① ② ③

ecosystems ranging in altitude from 200-1100 m above sea level, and your guide will point out some of the 40 butterfly and 300 bird species found in the reserve.

Manuel Antonio ⊟🏨🍴🏠🏕️🅲 → *pp301-307. Colour map 3, A1.*

From the southeastern corner of Quepos, a road winds up, over and round the peninsula of Punta Quepos, passing the hotels, restaurants, bars and stores that have flourished along the length of this rocky outcrop. Travelling the road for the first time, you can't fail to be impressed by the beauty of the views. But if you happen to travel at night, you can't help being blinded by the neon and bright lights that speckle the hillside – evidence of the vibrant tourist trade. At times it is difficult to believe a national park flourishes on the other side of the watershed.

With the arrival of the Spanish, the threat to the region's natural wealth began in earnest. Long after the indigenous peoples had been sold off as labourers or wiped out by illness, the land was cleared for agriculture. While much of the region was used for banana plantations, the spectacular vistas of the peninsula were views acquired by foreigners. With the locals denied access, state authorities became aware of rumoured plans to clear the region for agriculture. In haste, the area was declared a national park in 1972.

Since then tourism development has been broadly limited to either side of the access road to the north and west of the national park. While there is no denying the fact that a flourishing tourist industry and a national park can make uncomfortable neighbours, the extent of the damage depends on your perspective. For the time being at least development is confined – and the future looks very different depending on who you talk to.

Parque Nacional Manuel Antonio
→ *Colour map 3, B1.*
ⓘ *T2777-4122. The park is open 0700-1600, US$10. The entrance to the park is across the tidal estuary of the Quebrada Camaronera. If the tide is too high to wade across, small boats will ferry you for a small fee. On the land side of the river, there is ample parking (US$3 for the day). The half-hourly bus from*

N
🧭

| 600 metres |
| 600 yards |

Sleeping 🛏️
Arboleda **1** *C2*
Byblos **2** *B2*
Cabinas Espadillas **3** *C3*
Cabinas Pedro Miguel **4** *A2*
Cabinas Piscis **5** *A2*
California **7** *A2*
Casa Buena Vista B&B **42** *B2*
Casa Costa Linda **9** *C3*
Casitas Eclipse **8** *B3*
Costa Verde **10** *C3*
Del Mar **11** *C3*
Didi's Charming B&B **20** *A2*
Divisamar **12** *B2*
El Mirador del Pacífico **14** *A2*
El Parador **15** *C1*
Flor Blanca **17** *B2*
Karahe **18** *C3*
Kekoldi Beach-Dorado
   Mojado **13** *B2*
La Colina **19** *C3*
Makanda by the Sea **21** *B2*
Manuel Antonio &
   Restaurant **23** *C3*
Mariposa **24** *B2*
Mimo's **25** *A2*
Mono Azul &
   Restaurant **26** *A2*
Nature's Beachfront **27** *C2*
Playa Espadilla **28** *C3*

Plinio **29** *A2*
Si Como No **30** *B2*
Tres Banderas **31** *B2*
Tulemar **32** *B2*
Vela Bar **33** *C3*
Verde Mar **34** *C3*
Villabosque **35** *C3*
Villas Mymosa **40** *A2*
Villas Nicolás **41** *B2*
Villa Teca **42** *A2*
Vista Serena **43** *B2*

Eating 🍴
Barba Roja **1** *B2*
Café Milagro **2** *B2*
Del Mar **3** *C3*
El Avión **10** *C2*
El Mono Loco **4** *C3*
Gato Negro **6** *B3*
Karola's **7** *B2*
Mar y Sombre **9** *C3*
Mirador Mi Lugar **11** *B2*
Salsipuedes **12** *B2*

Bars & clubs 🍸
Cave Bar at Mansion
   Inn **13** *B2*

Education in Manuel Antonio

At times the insatiable desire to make a fast buck is unpalatable, especially when it's made at the expense of the rainforest which is at the very heart of Costa Rica's appeal. Local and international residents – and visitors too, for that matter – all have their part to play in creating the demand for land and resources that involves the destruction of rainforest.

Breaking down the relationship between conservation, preservation and economic growth is a complex affair, fit for academia and its endless international conferences and papers, but you can be certain that youngsters will keep things simple.

Kids Saving the Rainforest is a non-profit association that was founded by a couple of elementary schoolchildren in Manuel Antonio. With the help of a variety of local charity events money has been raised with the simple goal of trying to save the local rainforest and the remaining squirrel monkeys that are found throughout the area. Funds raised have purchased monkey bridges which should help them move from one side of the busy main road to the other without having to cross by ground or resort to using the electric cables which straddle the road.

Donations are welcome: Kids Saving the Rainforest, Apdo 297, Quepos, Costa Rica, T2777-2592, www.kids savingtherainforest.org, or drop in at the Mono Azul.

Quepos ends at the parking area. Guides provide nature tours of the park in Spanish, English and some in German, lasting 2½ hrs, US$20 per person, T2779-1167. Arrange directly with the guides at the entrance to the park, call or make arrangements through your hotel.

Universally acclaimed as one of the most scenic landscapes of Costa Rica, Manuel Antonio National Park is a gem of tropical wilderness. Whether you are a lover of pristine sandy beaches and crystal-clear waters, or of wandering through tropical forests that are teeming with wildlife, you will find something in this park for you.

The park only protects 1625 ha (with a further 55,000 ha of marine preserve) but it nevertheless packs quite a punch. High annual rainfall (close to 4 m) makes this an area of humid forest with sections of untouched primary forest and secondary forest slowly under-going regeneration. The diversity is complemented by stands of red, white and buttonwood mangrove. Offshore, a dozen coastal islands provide refuge and nesting sites for seabirds.

Rocky outcrops feature strongly in the headland. **Punta Catedral**, once an island, is now connected to the mainland by a sandy link or tombolo, slowly deposited over time by opposing currents sweeping along the coastline. A **trail** climbs steeply around the point, with viewing stops conveniently placed so you can catch your breath. The former island is home to primary and secondary forest and a quiet early morning walk will find you face to face with surprisingly timid wildlife including pacas, agoutis and iguanas. As always, however, with a guide you'll see a lot more. A couple of longer trails head east along the coastline passing the tree-fringed beaches of Manuel Antonio, heading out to **Playa Escondido** and beyond to **Punta Serrucho** and **Playa Playitas**. The trails are the best place to see the monkeys, which are fairly easily seen in the park, including white-faced capuchins and the rarer and endangered squirrel monkey.

The second main attraction in the park involves strolling just beyond the entrance to the park and plonking yourself on a beach. There are five beautiful, sandy beaches here, each fringed with the attractive (but poisonous) **manzanillo** tree and with gentle gradients that are good for swimming (but do watch out for rip currents).

⊙ Quepos and Manuel Antonio listings

For Sleeping and Eating price codes and other relevant information, see Essentials, pages 44-47.

⊜ Sleeping

Quepos *p296, map p296*
It can be difficult to find accommodation on Sat, Dec-Apr and when local schools are on holiday. In general, accommodation in Quepos is cheaper than on the road south to Manuel Antonio. With regular buses to the park, you may want to base yourself in Quepos if you're on a tight budget.

L-AL Best Western Kamuk, T2777-0811, www.kamuk.co.cr. 44 uninspiring but comfortable rooms with a/c, cable TV and private bath. Some of the rooms have ocean views and there's a sports bar and restaurant at street level. Now has a pool.

L-AL Rancho Casa Grande, on the *costanera* close to the airstrip, T2777-3130, www.ranchocasagrande.com. Lovely yellow *casitas* in tropical gardens, with a/c, private bath and TV. Pleasant mosaic-tiled swimming pool with thatched *palapas* strewn around the sundeck. Good open-air restaurant and bar.

AL-A Hotel Sirena, T2777-0528, www.lasirenahotel.com. 10 fair-sized rooms, with a/c, hot water and private bath. Small pool, with restaurant and small bar.

A-C El Malinche, T2777-0093, hotelmalinche@hotmail.com. 24 clean, good sized rooms, simply decorated. Some new rooms with a/c but much cheaper without.

B Mar y Luna, T2777-0394. With or without bath, quiet, clean and popular place.

E pp El Parque, on the waterfront, T2777-0063. Clean and friendly place with private bath and fan. A bit rundown but good value.

Eastern side of town
The following places are east of the town centre but still within walking distance.

A-B Cabinas El Cisne & Sensación Tropical, T2777-0719. Has grown rapidly in the last few years, but still holds onto the motel-style accommodation in a family-run atmosphere. Some 70 rooms to choose from, many with a/c, cheaper without. Safe with secure parking. Plans to expand even more which should include a pool.

B Doña Alicia, T2777-0419. Big cabin with bath, friendly, quiet and parking.

B-C Wide Mouth Frog , T2777-2798, www.widemouthfrog.org. 8 rooms with private bath and hot shower, a couple are cheaper with shared bath. Relaxed spot with parking available.

C Cabinas Hellen, T2777-0504. 24 quite small but clean rooms with private bath and fan. Plenty of parking.

D Ceciliano, T2777-0192. Quiet, family-run hotel with small rooms and private bath.

E Hospedaje La Mancha, next to post office on walkway by the football pitch, T2777-0216. Cheapest place in town, basic but clean.

Manuel Antonio *p299, map p298*
Some hotels shut in the low season; those that stay open offer generous discounts – prices listed are for high season. Many of the hotels along the road are in the higher price bracket, but there are a couple of budget options. In high season, it is best to book ahead. The area is full to bursting at weekends, many locals camping on the beach. If you want to go to the beach every day, head for a hotel at the very end of the road. Hotels are listed in order from Quepos to Manuel Antonio.

A Cabinas Pedro Miguel, the first and one of the cheapest hotels in the area, T2777-0035, www.cabinaspedromiguel.com. 16 simple rooms in a *Tico*-owned hotel, complete with small pool. Credit cards accepted. The owners are down-to-earth and very helpful – a world away from the slick service up the hill.

AL-B Plinio, T2777-0055, www.hotelplinio. com. 12 suites and rooms of varying sizes, facilities and comforts and a jungle house, climbing up the hillside in a flourish of tropical hardwoods, with a nature trail leading to an observation tower. Comfortable restaurant specializing in Indian and Thai as well as *Tico*, Italian, German, North American dishes, open from 1700. Good bar and a pool set in shady tropical gardens.

AL El Mirador del Pacífico, T2777-0119, www.elmiradorcostarica.com. A total of 25 rooms and villas, all with private bath, fan, a/c and balcony, some with an ocean view. The popular Bambu Jam and restaurant has a range of lively dishes and offers, including happy hours and live music. The pool and jacuzzi mean you don't have to wander out to the beach unless you really want to. Happy to help book tours. No credit cards.

LL-A Mimo's, T2777-0054, www.mimos hotel.com. 10 big rooms sleeping up to 4 people in a large villa, with hammocks on the veranda. Pool with bar and Italian restaurant set in pleasant gardens.

L-A Mono Azul, T2777-2572, www.hotel monoazul.com. 32 rooms and villas with private bath, with a little extra for TV and a/c. Wide range of services including 3 pools, games room, small library and internet café. The full service bar and restaurant is open daily from 0600 until 2200 – 365 days a year. Actively involved in trying to limit further development in the region with 10% of profits going to Kids Save the Rainforest charity. For that very special holiday romance, co-owner Jennifer Rice is a minister – bring your passport and birth certificate just in case.

LL-AL Villas Mymosa, hidden up a side road, T2777-2454, www.villasmymosa.com. 10 airy villas with refreshing cross-ventilation, with fully equipped kitchenette. Big pool with moody dark-blue mosaic tiling. Good discounts in low season.

AL-A California, a little further up the same side road, T2777-1234, www.hotel-california. com. A fine view from the 28 rooms and a good-sized family villa, all with private bath, a/c, minibar and telephone. Great pool, with mini waterfall.

AL-A Villa Teca, T2777-1117, www.villateca hotel.com. 20 villas, each with 2 a/c rooms with a private terrace, pool, Italian restaurant and a useful free shuttle service to Manuel Antonio and the beaches.

A-B Didi's Charming B&B, T2777-0069. Italian-run B&B with 4 rooms, comfortably furnished with a pinch of Italian style. Pool and jacuzzi and small restaurant for dinner.

LL-B Tres Banderas, T2777-1871, www.hoteltresbanderas.com. 11 units with private bath and tiling throughout, finished off with local hardwood touches. All rooms have a balcony, some with a view over the big pool, others to the rainforest.

L-B La Colina, T2777-0231, www.lacolina. com. Rooms, apartments and suites, with garden terraces and fine ocean views. Relaxing 2-tier pool complete with waterfall and wet bar. Also have a popular place in Monteverde.

A-E Vista Serena, T2777-5162, www.vista serena.com. 12 comfortable rooms, some with double beds, others with dormitory bunk beds. Small restaurant, kitchen available and hammocks out on the balcony to watch the spectacular sunsets. Great value, busting the myth that good budget accommodation doesn't exist in Manuel Antonio.

A-B Flor Blanca, in the middle of town, close to the supermarket, T2777-5050, www.hotelflorblanca.com. 10 fairly pleasant rooms some with a/c, cheaper with fans, in a *Tico*-owned hotel.

LL Tulemar, T2777-0580, www.tulemar. com. Every luxury you can expect at this level, with villas and bungalows providing floor-to-ceiling windows and views. Beautiful pool, nature trails and an exclusive beach. Arguably the most luxurious option in the area.

L-AL Divisamar, T2777-0371, www.divisa
mar.com. A *Tico*-owned hotel with a couple
of dozen large rooms with private bath and
a/c. The popular casino is the main attraction.

Punta Quepos

A dirt road opposite Café Milagro leads to
Punta Quepos, which has some of the area's
most exclusive (and expensive) hotels.
LL-L Mariposa, T2777-0456,
www.lamariposa.com. A fine hotel with
62 rooms, suites and villas in a spectacular
setting on a cliff overlooking Manuel Antonio
beach and Punta Catedral. The restaurant is
set out with all the trappings of a Spanish
villa and the rooms are comfortably breezy.
B Casa Buena Vista B&B, T2777-1002,
www.casabuenavista.net. 8 comfortable
rooms, 6 with private bath, 2 sharing. Run by
Anita who also runs the Buena Nota store
near the beach. Not a hotel, more of a home.
L-B Nature's Beachfront, look for the sign
just past Casa Buena Vista and follow the road
for a couple of kilometres to the beach,
T2777-1473, www.maqbeach.com/
natures.html. The beachfront property has
large studios sleeping 7, a smaller studio for 4
and standard double rooms all right on the
beach. Great spot, discounts for longer stays.
LL Makanda by the Sea, T2777-0442,
www.makanda.com. Meandering paths lead
to private studios and villas fully equipped for
a stay of pure indulgence. With subtle
Japanese influences, conventions such as
walls, which restrict the view, are kept to a
bare minimum. What remains in the split-
level studios is a simply stunning view as the
day unfolds from dawn to dusk, seen from
the perfectly positioned sofa, hammock or
bed. In a doubtless dreamy haze, you can
wander to the infinity pool, jacuzzi, or the
nearby almost-private beach. Hopeless
romantics positively encouraged.
LL El Parador, 2 km from the main road,
T2777-1414, www.hotelparador.com. 78
rooms with all the expected comforts. The
success of the Parador lies in providing abject
luxury while keeping a happy fresh face on

the place. Chatty and always courteous staff
tend your every need, 4 dining rooms cater
for every mood and moment. Beyond are the
comfortable rooms with fine views of the
ocean and gardens. There's a pool, tennis
courts and a gym to keep you in fine trim.
There's a free shuttle bus to the beach and
even a helipad, but note that cross-winds
can make for a lively take-off.

Main road to Manuel Antonio
**AL-A Kekoldi Beach Hotel – Dorado
Mojado**, T2777-0368. Set back in the forest
with 8 rooms – 4 fully equipped villas and
2 studios and a couple of standard rooms
in this popular gay hotel.
L Byblos, T2777-0411, www.bybloshotel
costarica.com. Quirky little rooms with
some outrageous decor. Free-form pool
surrounded by rainforest and a rancho-
style bar and restaurant. Overpriced.
LL-AL Villas Nicolás, T2777-0481,
www.villas nicolas.com. 12 comfortable
and spacious rental suites. If the stylish
furnishings and relaxed touches feel homely
that's because all the suites are someone's
home, rented out when not used.
LL Si Como No, T2777-0777, www.sicomo
no.com. A wave of refreshing originality
greets the visitor staying in one of 58 rooms
with ocean or forest views. With more cool
touches than a polar bear on Christmas Day,
the hotel sparkles with the reflected light of
stained-glass windows. Comforts include a
solar-heated jacuzzi, a pool and the new Boca
Bar Mogotes wet-bar. Of course you can dine
as well at the Claro Que Si! seafood restaurant
or the Rico Tico bar and grill. And naturally a
small 48-seater cinema. Yes, why not. One of
the 'Distinctive Hotels of Costa Rica', with all
the best intentions to be environmentally
sensitive – expensive, but worth every cent.
LL-L Casitas Eclipse, T2777-0408,
www.casitaseclipse.org. Whitewashed villas
and suites drifting down the hillside, with
space for 2-5 people. All rooms equipped
with private bath, a/c and telephone and no
less than 3 freeform pools to choose from.

A-B Banana Tree Hotel, T2777-1585, www.bananatreehotel.com. One of the closest options to budget accommodation in this area. Basic rooms with a couple of beds, private bath and small pool. Price includes breakfast.

LL-AL Costa Verde, just past the El Avión bar/restaurant, T2777-0584, www.hotelcosta verde.com. Booking in at the train carriage reception you're led to one of 5 multi-storey apartment blocks with spacious suites all with ocean or jungle views. A couple of pools have sundecks with Pacific views, and trails lead through the nearby forest which apparently still has "more monkeys than people". Restaurants and bars equally charismatic.

AL-B Arboleda, T2777-1385, www.hotel arboleda.com. Cabins sleeping 2-3 with bath and fan. On the hillside leading right down to beach, there's a Uruguayan restaurant, swimming pool, squash court and 8-ha wood to explore. Beware snakes, crabs and monkeys in the yard at night, it's a jungle out there. Recommended.

L-AL Karahe, T2777-0170, www.karahe.com. *Tico*-owned and run, 32 pleasant rooms set in tropical gardens within walking distance of the beach. Set on a steep hillside, some of the cabins have lovely views. Fishing trips arranged using the 32-ft *Trinidad*.

B-C Cabinas Piscis, next to La Buena Nota store, T2777-0046. A dozen simple rooms, handily close to the beach.

A-B Hotel del Mar, T2777-2122, www.gohoteldelmar.com. A dozen simple rooms with private bath, a/c or fan.

AL Verde Mar, T2777-1805, www.verde mar.com. 20 rooms with kitchenettes, fridge, personable service and a funky little pool.

AL-A Hotel & Restaurant Manuel Antonio, at the end of the road, T2777-1237. Looking straight out to the beach, has a few simple rooms where location is more important than decor. You can camp in the parking lot next to the restaurant. A handy spot, but naturally you'll need to watch your gear.

A small side road – made prominent by a cluster of *sodas*, surfboard rental shops, tour operators and information kiosks – leads to a handful of popular hotels.

D pp Casa Costa Linda, T2777-0304, hirschmann_dieter@yahoo.com. Double rooms or in 6-bed dormitories with fan and cooking facilities, fan.

AL Cabinas Espadillas, T2777-0416, www.espadilla.com. A good family choice with fully equipped cabins sleeping up to 4 people, complete with kitchenette – a good deal if you can get the numbers together, shares the facilities of the Hotel Playa Espadilla.

A Hotel Vela Bar, T2777-0413, www.velabar.com. 11 rooms including a fully equipped house, with private bath, fans, porch and safe box. The restaurant is very good. Open all day serving a mix of international, Costa Rican and vegetarian dishes. At night, the bar is also a popular spot.

L-AL Hotel Playa Espadilla, T2777-0903, www.espadilla.com. 16 rooms in pleasant gardens, 12 with hot water bath, cable TV and a/c. 4 fully equipped rooms have a kitchenette and fridge. A wide range of activities including pool table, tennis, as well as a restaurant, bar, swimming pool and wet bar.

LL-L Villabosque, T2777-0463, www.hotelvillabosque.com. 16 comfortable but unexceptional rooms all with a/c, private bath and hot water. Good range of services including a pool, bar, restaurant and parking, but just a little too cramped.

🍴 Eating

Quepos *p296, map p296*

🍴🍴 **Dos Locos**, T2777-1526, popular place open to the street giving a *cantina* feel with big portions of Mexican food. Occasional live music which drifts towards impromptu karaoke.

🍴-🍴 **El Banco Sports Bar**, long bar dressed in bright neon and a good line in Tex Mex. TV screens for the all-important sports games.

🍴-🍴 **La Lanterna**, great Italian restaurant one block back from the sea front, serving great pasta and pizzas with seafood undertones.

El Gran Escape, takes up most of a block. On the one side Ciao Pizzeria with pasta in a chic setting, next door is the open surf'n'turf dishes, with the very popular Tropical Sushi next to that. All good food, with a bar squeezed in somewhere in between which happens to show movies every Mon at 2000.

Monchados, Mexican, Caribbean and seafood, with a Pacific-Caribbean feel. Add live music on Tue and Thu and you've got the lot.

Café Milagro, on the waterfront. Best espresso and coffees, cakes and shakes. Also sell Cuban cigars, souvenirs and freshly roasted coffee for sale.

Escalofrío. Pizza, pasta and ice cream to die for.

L'Angolo, opposite Dos Locos, excellent Italian delicatessen with pasta, cheeses, bread and meats – will make up subs … a little pricey, but good.

Pan Aldo, eastern end of town, T2777-2697. Bread and coffee to die for – flaky and light. Open Mon-Sat 0430-1800. Get there before 10 if you want to choose from the full range.

Manuel Antonio p299, map p298
There are also many good restaurants along the road towards Manuel Antonio. These are listed in order from Quepos to Manuel Antonio.

Mirador Mi Lugar, also known as Ronny's Place, about a mile down the side road opposite Amigos del Río. Cheap seafood in a simple open-air – a perfect spot to watch the sun go down.

Salsipuedes. Great ocean views in a lively cantina serving tapas.

Barba Roja. Restaurant and bar in a popular spot, with happy hour either side of sunset. Good mix of seafood, grills, burgers and snacks. Credit cards accepted. Open 0700 until 2300. Mid-range and up.

Karola's, T2777-1557. One of the best restaurants in the area with a mind-boggling international menu. Naturally seafood dominates, but there's something for everyone.

Café Milagro. Serves good coffee and homemade baked goods, with a selection of international newspapers and magazines.

The BS Bar & Grill, T2777-5280. Indeed a bar and grill with a fine view out west. Stop for a beer, a snack or, in the evening, choose one of the great hamburgers from the grill menu.

Tico Rico Bar & Grill, at Sí Como No. Fine outdoor dining as you'd expect at one of the area's best hotels, with live music to accompany seafood and meat dishes, and a children's menu too.

Restaurant Gato Negro. Worth a visit for the Italian and seafood dishes.

El Avión. Dining under the wing of an old military transport plane is a novelty for most people, but remarkably comfortable once you settle into the fine international food and drinks on offer.

La Cantina BBQ, at Costa Verde Inn, T2777-0384. Positively hums with activities. If you're keen on live music, it's worth stopping by for the lively atmosphere before heading elsewhere.

Bar & Restaurant Mar y Sombre, almost at the beach area, T2777-0003. Good *casado especial* and jumbo shrimps with shady tables on the beach and sun-loungers for hire.

Restaurant del Mar, T2777-0543. Rents surfboards, sells drinks and light meals and has a collection of English novels to read in the bar.

El Mono Loco, almost at the end of the road. Serving up a full menu of international dishes and lively in the evenings.

Bars and clubs

Quepos p296, map p296
Many of the restaurants above will be equally happy to serve you if you just want to stick around for a drink.
Restaurant Pueblo, is a lively bar with karaoke for the exhibitionist in you.
Wacky Wanda's, fully a/c bar serving chilled beers 'til the early hours.

Manuel Antonio *p299, map p298*
Bambu Jam, at the El Mirador del Pacífico, T2777-3369. Lively bar-cum-restaurant with jam sessions on Tue, live music on Fri and a DJ playing latin dance on Sats.
Cave Bar, at Mansion Inn, bar set in a cave. No sunsets here, just the electric sparkle of being underground. Mind your head.
El Avión, at the high point in the road, a Second World War aeroplane decked out as a bar and restaurant. Great idea, bizarre experience.

○ Shopping

Quepos *p296, map p296*
Try the municipal market for fruit and bread at the bus station, as the Super Mas supermarket is generally poorly stocked.
L'Angolo, serves an absolutely divine mix of breads, olives, hams and everything you'd need for self-catering in style.
Café Milagro, see above. Sells coffee to take home (or order online at www.cafemilagro.com).
Galería Regálame II, the gift store branch in Quepos of the excellent Sí Como No hotel in Manuel Antonio.

Manuel Antonio *p299, map p298*
La Buena Nota, on the road near the beach, T2777-1002, buennota@racsa.co.cr. One-stop shop for newspapers, magazines, books, beachwear, postcards, information and the odd bar of chocolate.
Mot Mot, next to Barba Roja, sells a good selection of souvenirs and original T-shirts.
Regalame, is one of the best gift shops in Costa Rica, with a great collection of souvenirs and goods, all made in Costa Rica and all made by genuine artists.
Supermarket, is pretty much in the middle between the national park and Quepos. Well stocked, in their own words "if we don't have it, you don't need it".

▲ Activities and tours

Quepos *p296, map p296*
Activities in the region are developing fast. Iguana Tours, Lynch Travel Services and your hotel will be able to arrange any of the trips mentioned on page 297).
Iguana Tours, close to the church on the football pitch, T2777-2052, www.iguanatours. com. Excellent local knowledge with all the locally available tours. Friendly and helpful.
Lynch Travel Services, right in the centre of town, T2777-0161, www.lynchtravel.com. Good information on local tours and the best one-stop shop for travel arrangements including SANSA and NatureAir flights, vehicle rental, and regional accommodation.

More specialist tours are available from:
Amigos del Río, T2777-0082, www.amigosdelrio.net. Tours and good guides. Provides full-day Class III-IV whitewater rafting on the nearby Savegre and Naranjo rivers and sea kayaking.
Avenatura, T2777-0973, www.avenatura. com. Nature tours – their one and only focus whether its the butterfly gardens, Las Damas mangrove or the National Park.
Blue Fin Sports Fishing Charters, T2777-1676, www.bluefinsportfishing.com. Offers sports fishing charters in Quepos from US$430 for a half day, also Playa Flamingo and Drake Bay, and local tours.
Canopy Safari, in the centre of town, T2777-0100, www.canopysafari.com. Operate the canopy tour and ATV rainforest adventures.
Canyoning Tours, T2777-1924, will send you down or up waterfalls trussed up in all the safety gear – refreshing exhilaration.
Costa Rica Adventure Divers, T2777-0234, www.costaricadiving.com. Local dives including resort dives and PADI certification from the Drake Bay specialists.
Sunset Sails, T2777-1304. Life on the ocean waves, for a half day, sunset or moonlight tour with food and drinks all included. Adults US$59, children US$49.

Manuel Antonio *p299, map p298*
Also see Quepos, page 297.
Horse riding **Equus Stables**, T2777-
0001. Beach (US$35) and rainforest (US$60)
trips. Also **Marlboro Stables**, T2777-1108.
Surfboard rental Available from several
beachside outlets down in Manuel Antonio,
including **Manuel Antonio Surf School**,
T2777-4842, info@masurfschool.com.

● Transport

Quepos *p296, map p296*
Air There are 8 daily flights from **San José**,
4 with **SANSA** (US$53 one way) and 4 with
NatureAir (US$66 one way). Book in advance
either with Lynch Tours, or direct. In Quepos
the SANSA office is under Hotel Quepos,
T2777-0683. Minibuses and taxis meet
arriving flights at the airport, which is about
4 km from Quepos.

Bus Buses leave the capital from the Coca
Cola Terminal. There are 4 express buses a
day leaving **San José** at 0600, 1200, 1800 and
1930, returning at 0600, 0930, 1200, 1500 (Sat
only) and 17001230, 1900, 3½ hrs, US$4.30,
book a day in advance, 4 regular buses, 5 hrs,
US$4.20. From **Quepos** there are buses
northwest along the coast stopping at **Jacó**
before continuing to **Puntarenas**, 0430,
0730, 1030 and 1500, return 0500, 1100, 1430
and 1630, 3 hrs, US$2.80. 2 daily buses via
Dominical to **San Isidro de El General**, 0500
and 1330, 3½ hrs, US$2.90, connections can
be made there to get to the Panamanian
border, return 0700 and 1330.

Car hire Alamo, 100 m north of the
post office, T2777-3344, www.alamo
costarica.com. **Excellent** have an office in
Quepos, T2777-3052, www.excellentcar
rental.com.

Taxi Taxis line up on the street opposite
the bus terminal, just up from Dos
Locos restaurant.

● Directory

Quepos *p296, map p296*
Banks Banco Nacional, Banco Popular
and Banco San José all have a Visa ATMs.
The best place to exchange TCs or US$ cash
is at **Distribuidora Puerto Quepos**, opposite
Banco de Costa Rica, open 0900-1700, no
paperwork, no commission, all done in 2
mins, same rate as banks. **Internet** Internet
Quepos, in the centre of town, T2777-4411.
Fast machines, a/c offices, good technical
knowledge. There is also an internet café at
the eastern end of town, near Iguana Surf.
Language schools There are a couple of
schools on the road out to the national park.
La Escuela D'Amore is in a great setting
overlooking the ocean, half-way between
Quepos and the national park. Focusses and
stresses the benefits of immersion learning,
T2777-1143, www.escueladamore.com.
US$845 for 2 weeks, US$995 with homestay.
Costa Rica Spanish Institute, T2777-0021,
www.cosi.co.cr. US$350 for 4 hrs a day,
US$495 with homestay. **Pacífico Spanish
School**, beside Cabinas Pedro Miguel,
T2777-0805. One of the oldest schools in
the area, currently undergoing a relaunch.
Sí Sé Spanish School, T2777-4642. US$630
for 2 weeks, US$830 with homestay.
Laundry Lavanderías de Costa Rica, near
the football pitch on the road out to Manuel
Antonio. **Medical services** The hospital
is out of town near the airstrip, call T2777-
0922, or the Red Cross on T2777-0118.
Post office Post office is on the walkway
by the football pitch, open 0800-1700.
Useful addresses Immigration: on the
same street as the *Banco de Costa Rica*.
Police: T2777-0196.

Manuel Antonio *p299, map p298*
Language Schools These include
Escuela de Idiomas D'Amore, T2777-1143,
www.escueladamore.com, which subscribes
to the immersion technique. See page 53.

Southern costanera

From Quepos the costanera continues its journey down the coast along a dirt road which is the last remaining stretch left to be upgraded. It's an interesting drive with very few tourist services for the 42-km journey to Dominical, just endless neat lines of African palms glistening and rustling in the coastal breeze. If you're driving, there are many single-width bridges that are not signposted and which have been the site of several accidents – drive carefully. Matapalo is a quiet beach resort – ideal if you want seclusion. Dominical is the surf hang-out, with enough people to make a party, and handy for trips to waterfalls, Baru Nature Reserve and south to Ballena before continuing on to Corcovado National Park. ➤➤ *For listings, see pages 312-315.*

Matapalo → *Colour map 3, B2.*

Matapalo, about 24 km south of Quepos – look out for the sign on the main highway, is a small, mainly Swiss, community that has seized on the beauty of this almost uninhabited stretch of fine sandy beaches, all of which are good for swimming. It's a great place to stop for truly quiet relaxation, yet it's close enough to visit attractions near Manuel Antonio to the north and Dominical to the south, albeit on a pretty painful road.

Dominical → *Colour map 3, B2. www.dominical.net.*

A small town of no more than a few hundred people just south of the mouth of the Río Barú, Dominical owes its success to the fine surf that pounds the coastline. If you want to surf, or learn, it's a great spot with classes available. Nearby breaks add a touch of variety and there are several locals who will happily offer advice and suggestions on places to go.

Beyond surfing, the beaches in the area are quite pleasant. There are also tours and trips to **Hacienda Barú** private reserve, complete with canopy tours and nature trails, nearby waterfalls, trails through the forest on foot or horseback and to the south at **Marino Ballena Parque Nacional** (see page 310).

Hacienda Barú

ⓘ *T2787-0003, www.haciendabaru.com. Open daily. Guided walks start at US$6 for the self-guided tours, US$35 per person for guided tours, rising to US$60 for a night in the jungle. Barú is about 2 km north of Dominical. Accommodation is available (A) in simple, fully equipped cabins. A pleasant open-air restaurant serves Tico dishes.*

Hacienda Barú is an eco-friendly adventure park set in a privately owned national wildlife refuge. The owner Jack Ewing and his wife arrived in the area in 1972 at a time when Costa Rican conservation was in its infancy. By the end of the 1980s, the cattle-man turned conservationist – a reasonably common conversion – had the opportunity and foresight to buy and formally protect the remarkably diverse property. In an area of just 3.3 sq km, 318 species of bird have been recorded – the whole of the United States has 996.

A sense of personal discovery is created by the use of interpretive pamphlets that allow you to wander through the trails alone. Going as slow as you like you can soak up the complexities of the rainforest at your own speed. Guides are also available if you prefer. A range of trails cover a total of 7 km leading through primary and secondary forest, to the mangroves along the beach and to an observation tower where you may see three-toed sloths, white-faced capuchin monkeys and peccaries.

Driving the costanera

From Orotina to the Pan-American Highway at Palmar Norte, Highway 34, colloquially known as the *costanera*, follows the coastline for 230 km. Serving popular beaches, agricultural industries and communities alike, it is a busy road and a crucial lifeline. It's a fascinating road, drawing a line through varied sections of Costa Rican life.

Considering the importance of the region, the paving of the *costanera* has been slow in coming. But now, only the 42 km section between Quepos and Dominical remains unpaved and that will completed at some point.

One word of warning if driving. While the roads – even the dirt ones – are good, many of the bridges in the middle section are single carriageway. More than one rented-vehicle driver fresh out of Quepos has misjudged speed and space, ending up crashing down to the riverbed below.

The road is not dangerous – but some of the drivers are. Drive with great caution at all times, especially at night.

Beyond the trails activities include tree climbing, trussed up in harness and safety gear, a full day guided nature walk through primary forest or a night spent in the jungle – an eerie experience under a dark moonless sky. The beach is also used by solitary nesting Olive Ridley, and increasingly rare hawksbill, turtles that arrive from July through to October.

There is a volunteer work programme run by the local conservation group **Asociación de Amigos de la Naturaleza del Pacífico Central y Sur (ASANA)** ⓘ *Contact ASANA on T2787-0254, asana@racsa.co.cr, or Jack Ewing on T2787-0001, jeewing@racsa.co.cr, for work on the turtle project,* which is working to develop the Tapir Biological Corridor between Manuel Antonio and the Osa Peninsula. Placements cost US$75 a week for food, working on trail maintenance, tree nurseries, planting and other tasks.

Waterfalls
ⓘ *Trips can be organized from Dominical or with Don Lulo, T2787-8013, www.cataratasnauyaca.com.*
Ten kilometres along the road to San Isidro, a road leads to a couple of waterfalls, the largest being the 50-m high **Nauyaca Waterfalls** reached by horse riding tours through the rainforest.

South of Dominical
Newly paved road stretches south to Uvita and beyond to Palmar opening up a number of comfortable roadside options and secluded hideaways to the privileged few who get this far south by road. The main appeal of the area is slowing down – venturing out to the few beaches found down the coastline when the mood takes you or to the undeveloped Parque Nacional Marino Ballena. As is true for much of Costa Rica's west coast, the sunsets are simply beyond words. Public transport is available to Uvita. Outside of this immediate area most – though not all – hotels are away from the main road making private transport a necessity. New hotels are opening so look out for any new and pleasant surprises.

On the east side of the road, 3.5 km south of Dominical, hills give way to a small, grassy area and a dirt road that climbs steeply to **Escaleras**. The road winds through good forests, ideal for a bit of independent exploring if you've got the confidence to strike out alone. While the gradient is challenging, 4WD will get through, and the road leads to a number of isolated rental properties including Finca Brian y Emilia (page 312).

Around the town of **Uvita**, a few small communities including **Bahía** provide simple budget accommodation popular with people seeking quiet and solitude on the Pacific coast. It's also a good base for exploring Parque Nacional Marino Ballena if you want to see whales and dolphins. The entrance to Pueblo Uvita is marked by the El Viajero restaurant. Uvita now has a bank **Coope Alianza** ① *open Mon-Fri 1300-1700, Sat 0800-1200.*

South of Uvita, **Rancho La Merced** ① *T2771-4582, www.wildlifecostarica.com, prices from US$25 for a half-day walking tour*, is a national wildlife refuge adjacent to the Marino Ballena National Park, with over 500 ha of primary and secondary tropical rainforest as well as mangrove estuary. The area can be explored easily, ideally on horseback, with trips going down the beach, to the mangroves or around the ranch as you get to be cowboy for a day, driving and roping cattle and checking calves and cows. There are also walking tours to nearby waterfalls. (Accommodation is available at Rancho La Merced on **A The Old Farm House**, with a capacity for 10 with five bedrooms, a bathroom and kitchen. Costa Rican country-style meals included in the price, with electricity provided by a generator from 1800-2100. Book through Selva Mar.)

Parque Nacional Marino Ballena → *Colour map 3, B2.*
The vast majority of Ballena Marine National Park is coastal waters – 5161 ha against 172 ha of protected land – which may go some way to explaining why there isn't a lot to see on land at this, one of Costa Rica's least-developed national parks.

The underwater wo rld is home to coral reefs and abundant marine life that includes common and bottle-nosed dolphins as well as humpback whales (*ballenas*), which at times you can see with their calves. The best time to see them is from December to April, and from August to October. Contact Chumi (see below) or ask at your hotel for details.

Offshore, **Las Tres Hermanas** and **Isla Ballena** mark the southernmost boundary of the park providing nesting sights for frigate birds, white ibis and brown pelicans. To the north, at **Punta Uvita**, sandy deposits have created a tombolo linking the former island with the mainland.

Although there is a rarely staffed ranger's station in **Bahía** (T2786-7161), and signposts line the *costanera*, the infrastructure in the park is non-existent. There is a nominal entrance fee of US$6 which is rarely collected. Along the beach at Bahía is a **turtle nesting** project administered by the local community. As with the park itself, the organization is very ad hoc – visitors and volunteers are welcome. **Beachcombing** is good, as is **snorkelling** when the tides are favourable. **Boat trips** to the island can be arranged from Bahía, and **diving** is starting up; the most recommended local being Máximo Vásquez, or Chumi as he is known.

Ojochal and around
The beaches continue south, sprinkled with the ornate shapes of bleached white driftwood. Currents are strong and ever changing due to tides and the influence of the Río Térraba with its main outlet to the south. The area around the town of **Ojochal** and **Playa Tortuga** has sprouted a modest harvest of comfortable hotel and dining options – many of them with French-Canadian owners. North of Posada Playa Tortuga a road heads inland to Ojochal, which by planning or default is overwhelmingly French-Canadian.

The *costanera* then continues south to join the Pan-American Highway at Palmar Norte. If you're feeling brave enough and suitably inclined, stop at **Playa Piñuela**, and taste some of the best *ceviche* in the country. You can't miss the place as cars and lorries are always parked up along the otherwise empty roadside.

For Sleeping and Eating price codes and other relevant information, see Essentials, pages 44-47.

Sleeping

Matapalo p308

AL Jungle House, T2787-5253, www.jungle house.com. 5 completely furnished cabins, each with bathroom, kitchenette and screened windows, and a private house.

A-B El Coquito del Pacífico, T2384-7220, www.elcoquito.com. 6 big bungalows and the same number of rooms, all kitted out to European standards. The bungalows, decorated with Latin American wall hangings, get fresh cross-ventilation from the sea breezes. The French-influenced Swiss restaurant serves excellent fresh food from a menu tailored to the guests' requests. Big pool and pleasant gardens right on the beach.

B Albergue Suiza, T2382-7122l, www.matapaloplaya.com. 3 big rooms with tiled floors and bamboo furniture plus terraces and private bath in a large villa. Quiet little balcony restaurant upstairs serves a fusion of reasonably priced European and *Tico* cuisine. Horses and mountain bikes available for rent.

B-C Piedras Blancas, T2771-3015. 5 reasonably comfortable wooden bungalows. Owned by one of the longest resident expats in town, the place is evolving slowly and with a chaotic charm. Good international menu at the restaurant and plans for a small beachwear boutique.

C Terraza del Sol, with a handful of beach-front cabins, a restaurant and a good range of activities.

Dominical p308

Also see **Hacienda Barú**, page 308.

LL-A Diuwak, T2787-0087, www.diuwak.com. Popular mini-tourist complex, comfortable rooms or fully equipped bungalows sleeping 2-6 people, which are smartly if rather unimaginatively decorated. Services include internet access, a small supermarket, and international telephone service.

A-B Río Lindo, at entrance to town, T2787-0078, www.riolindo.com. Clean, tidy rooms with a balcony or terrace, run by the affable Paco. Each room has a private bath with *agua natural*, fan or a/c. Big pool and sundeck.

B Posada del Sol, on the main street next to Diuwak, T2787-0085. Owned by local historian Mariela Badilla, 20 or so well-kept and tidy rooms, with bath, fan and a small patio with hammocks. A quiet spot.

B Tortilla Flats, a stone's throw from the beach, T2787-0033, www.tortillaflats dominical.com. 18 rooms, sleeping 3 people, private bath and hot water. Overpriced in high season, but good discounts for rest of the year.

C-E Cabinas San Clemente, on the beach next to Green Iguana Surf Camp, T2787-0026. 12 *cabinas*, both with and without a/c, sleeping 3-5 people. Also 6 surf rooms, where your interests should lie beyond where you're sleeping. Friendly US-owned place, with same owners as the restaurant on the main street. Cheaper rooms above the bar with shared bath and fan.

D-E Cabinas El Coco, at the end of the road, T2787-0235. 20 rooms, the 10 that are close to the beachfront are OK with private bath.

D-E Camping Antorchas, down the beach from Cabinas El Coco, T2787-0307, www.campingantorchas.net. Camping, and some lodgings with shared and private bath. Good deal if you're on a budget.

Outside the town

AL Hotel Roca Verde, on the beach 1 km south of Dominical reached along the main road, T2787-0036, www.rocaverde.net. Tropical rooms with a/c and a small balcony or terrace. Good quiet spot in a secluded cove, with a pool, big bar and restaurant.

AL Villas Río Mar Jungle and Beach Resort, about 500 m from the beach upstream along the Río Barú at the northern end of town and reached through the main entrance road, T2787-0052, www.villasriomar.com. 40 thatched-roof bungalows scattered on the hillside, with kitchenette, bathrooms and small terrace with hammock. The complex focuses on a big pool, with a wetside bar and a huge restaurant serving local and international specialties. There's a tennis court and it's a good spot for families and groups.

South of Dominical p309
Escaleras
LL Rancho Pacífico, T2825-8370, www.ranchopacifico.com. Super luxurious hotel, in one of the quietest, well-hidden parts of the country. Come for the privacy and comfort, the beauty treatments, or both.
L Villas Escalera, even further up the hill, (in the US on T 1-866-658-7796), www.villas-escaleras.com. Top-of-the-range comforts are available in this luxury, fully equipped house with 4 rooms large enough to take up to 10 people. Vaulted ceilings, beautiful hardwood flooring and white-wash walls decorated with fine textiles. Quiet and secluded, with a freeform pool, it's a great spot to hide away.
A Finca Brian y Milena, T2396-6206, Apdo 2-8000, San Isidro de El General, Costa Rica, for a 2-day minimum, all meals included. A working farm with simple accommodation that has been "making paradise a reality" for 25 years. A couple of cabins and some rooms set in a forested area. Good hiking in the grounds. Also a volunteer programme which you can work on for a week or even longer.
A-B Bella Vista Lodge, a little further up the hill with unbelievable views, T2787-8069, www.bellavistalodge.com, or through Selva Mar. A handful of rooms and fully equipped *casitas* in a large wooden house with broad balconies perched on the edge of the forested escarpment looking out to the Pacific. Filling national dishes keep the energy levels up for the moments of exertion which naturally include hiking and birdwatching, and further afield horse riding to the Barú River falls.

Uvita
In order going up the road.
D-E pp Steve's Toucan Hotel, on the right, T2743-8140, www.tucanhotel.com. Basic, but comfortable and pleasant budget accommodation. Space for preparing food, and plenty of hammocks for relaxing in on the patio shaded by fruit trees. Good place to hang out.
B-C Cabinas Los Laureles, a short distance up on the left, T2743-8235, www.cabinasloslaureles.com. 3 *cabinas* with private bathroom, simple and quite good value.
E-G Cascada Verde, up a steep signposted hike of a couple of km, T2743-8191, www.cascadaverde.org. An educational retreat and permaculture farm with a variety of accommodation, including beds, hammocks and camping. You can actually work on the farm to offset your accommodation expenses. Vegetarian meals work out at US$4 a day, and every 7th night a meal is free. Mixed reports, however, and not much permaculture going on.

Bahía
LL-A La Cusinga, 5 km south of Uvita Bridge, between KM166 and 167, T2770-2549, www.lacusingalodge.com. A welcome private hotel to the area, looking to benefit from the coastal and rainforest location with natural tours in the surrounding area. Good private and group accommodation rooms.
AL Canto de Ballenas, T2743-8085, www.turismoruralcr.com. A dozen comfortable wooden cabins, set in pleasing landscaped gardens in this cooperatively run hotel. Simple but good traditional *Tico* dishes served in the restaurants. Attracts guests who want to see whales.
E Cabinas Punta Uvita, closest to the beach opposite Restaurant Los Almendros, T2770-8066. Simple, basic *cabinas* with private bathroom. Also provide tourist information, arrange horse riding and snorkelling and scuba diving.

D Villa Hegalva, T2743-8016. In a permanent state of evolution, the 14 basic rooms are clean and a good deal. Camping is permitted for a small fee, and hammocks rock gently in the breezy shade of the pleasant gardens. Small bar and restaurant to keep you going and there may also be a kitchen by the time you get there.

Ojochal and around *p310*

AL Villas Gaia, a little further on, T2244-0316, www.villasgaia.com. A Dutch-run hotel with 14 colourful wooden cabins perched up on the hillside. Each cabin has private bath, orthopedic beds for 3 and a superb view from a balcony that looks straight out to the forest. The restaurant is a colourful scene of murals and plants with good food at reasonable prices. A big pool has beautiful views across the Pacific to the west and a drink from the bar will finish off what is certain to have been a perfect day.

A Paraíso del Pacífico, about 12 km south of Uvita, T2788-8280. 11 comfortable, if slightly sparse cabins with private bath and hot water and small balcony set on the hillside. Excellent views with an open-air restaurant to watch the setting sun, and a pool and sundeck. A slightly livelier option than most places nearby.

AL Villas El Bosque, T2398-2112, www.villasel bosque.com. Also with a fine view from the bluff overlooking the beach below, with just a couple of cabins surrounded by forest sleeping 4 and a double room. Private bath, hot water and kitchenettes are available. The balconies look directly over the cliff – giving a bird's eye view of the birds' eyes. A small pool and a small trail make this a great, intimate little spot.

B Posada Playa Tortuga B&B, just south of the turning to Ojochal, home of 'Gringo Mike', T2384-5489. 10 elegantly decorated and spacious rooms, all with private bath, an air of relaxed sophistication and fine ocean views. Mike's genuine and apparently effortless charm blends excellent service with an inherent knowledge of the weakness in us all – the desire for fine food and good

times. A full breakfast starts the day, with evening dishes several nights a week if there's enough interest. With excellent local knowledge, Mike is one of the original expat arrivals to the area and one of the best hosts.

In town

AL-C Rancho ô Soluna, T2788-8351, solunacr@yahoo.com. A couple of rooms decorated with celestial influences, and a pair of small houses with kitchenette. Pleasant gardens are now home to a new swimming pool or take the more natural approach in the Río Balsa – an idyllic setting for swimming in the shallow pools or camping.

Several other good options in the region lead further inland – but many close or wind down for the rainy season so be sure to book in advance.

A-B El Perezosa, www.elperezoso.net. Wonderful comforts in the house and gardens of Perezosa, some of the rooms with spectacular views. Price includes breakfast.

🍴 Eating

Matapalo *p308*

🍴 **Express del Pacífico**, on the main road. A good stopping point for snacks if you're driving through town. International and local cuisine and ping pong … just what you need after driving down the response-testing *costanera*.

Dominical *p308*

🍴🍴 **San Clemente Bar & Grill**. A lively Tex-Mex sports bar with mid-range dishes and huge portions, a pool table and satellite TV. Recommended.

🍴 **Restaurant Coco**. End of the road café which relies on you not being able to go anywhere else. Food is OK, and a good variety beyond seafood.

🍴 **Soda Nanyoa**. Simple *Tico soda*.

🍴 **Sushi Bar**, just outside Thrusters. Great sushi. Owners about to change, but let's hope the place and the quality remains.

☗ **Thrusters**. Positively heaves – it's the hip spot for the surf crowd and the beautiful people. Pool table and TV.

☗ **Tortilla Flats**, restaurant and bar at Green Iguana Surf Camp is on the beachfront with divine gourmet sandwiches and other dishes. Great spot for topping up on energy before or after a stretch in the water. Great iced cocktails.

Ojochal and around *p310*

☗ **Gringo Mike's** (see Posada Playa Tortuga B&B, above). Apparently does some of the best pizza in the New World.

☗ **Ojochal Internet Café**. Has great food and internet. It is a bit pricey but you are a long way from anywhere and it's all done by a satellite sitting on the roof. The French-Canadian owners are also very helpful and can help with any inquiries.

▲ Activities and tours

Dominical *p308*
Green Iguana Surf Camp, T2787-0033, www.greeniguanasurfcamp.com. Long standing surf school with accommodation packages. Turn up and hire a board, book a couple of lessons or go for a multi-day package. A week of surfing, including accommodation, transport to local beaches and use of boards, is US$725 per person, min of 2.

South of Dominical *p309*
Ballena Tours, Uvita, T2818-4100. Run by the elusive Chumi who offers snorkelling, whale and dolphin watching tours in the area.

☺ Transport

Dominical *p308*
Dominical is a bit of a transport hub. Highway 34 meets the only good road from San Isidro de El General and the highlands for its entire length just north of the town.

There are 3 daily buses to **Quepos** at 0545, 0800 and 1430, with a 1300 on weekends and in the high season, 2 hrs. Heading south, 5 daily buses go to **Uvita** from 0950 to 2100, 45 mins. A other buses head south to **Ciudad Cortés** and **Ciudad Neily**, for connections to the Osa Peninsula, at 0420 and 1000.

Heading inland, there are 4 daily buses to **San Isidro de El General**, 1½ hrs, US$1.60, from where there are frequent buses to **San José**.

If driving, it is a good 34-km scenic road that climbs slowly through the mountains arriving eventually at San Isidro de El General.

Uvita *p310*
Bus services in the area are increasing as transport becomes easier. Buses leave from **San José** Coca-Cola Terminal at 0530 and 1500, returning at 0500 and 1300, 5 hrs, US$6.40.

From **San Isidro de El General** there are daily services at 0900 and 1600, returning at 0600 and 1400, 2 hrs, US$2.30. From **Dominical** buses leave at 1000 and 1700. From the south, buses leave **Palmar Sur** at 0700, 1300 and 1700, returning at 0430, 1100 and 1500, 2 hrs. Buses do a trawl of the area stopping close to Uvita and **Bahía**. Let the driver know where you are planning to stay and he will drop you off at the closest point.

☻ Directory

Dominical *p308*
Internet There are a couple of public telephone boxes in town, but for long distance calls visit **Diuwak** who also have an internet service. **Language schools** Adventure Education Center, T2787-0023, www.adventure spanishschool.com. A multi-campus school combing spanish language classes with adventure – other sites are in Arenal and Turrialba. 4 hrs a day for a week is US$315, with homestay US$440.

Contents

318 South to San Isidro
    318 Route of the Saints
    318 Pan-American Highway
         to San Isidro
    319 San Isidro de El General
    322 Parque Nacional Chirripó
    324 Listings

329 South of San Isidro
    334 Listings

Footprint features

316 Don't miss …
330 ARADIKES – supporting
    indigenous communities
331 Great Balls of Diquís Delta

Border essentials

Costa Rica–Panama
  332 Paso Canoas

Southern Region

At a glance

⊖ **Getting around** It's a long way
down here by bus, then moving
around can take time as well. You'll
need to plan your trip carefully
when travelling long distances.

◉ **Time required** A 3- to 10-day
trip would pass in no time.

☽ **Weather** Dec-Apr is good.
There are spectacular tropical
storms between Sep and Nov.

☻ **When not to go** Sep-Nov
if you're hoping to spend most
of the time outside.

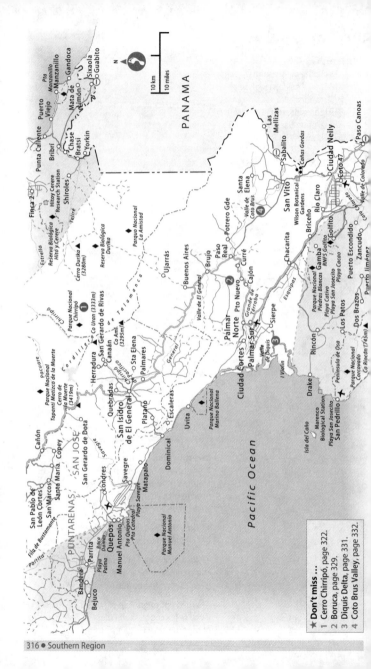

★ **Don't miss …**

1 Cerro Chirripó, page 322.
2 Boruca, page 329.
3 Diquís Delta, page 331.
4 Coto Brus Valley, page 332.

Tell a Tico you're going south along the Pan-American Highway through the Cordillera de Talamanca and the look of bewilderment that will spread across his face is unfailing and immediate. From south of Cartago to the Osa Peninsula, the central southern district of Costa Rica is almost an undiscovered, or more likely forgotten, region. Your journey takes you through Siberia and beyond to Cerro de la Muerte (the Mountain of Death) – hardly names to inspire a journey through paradise – before making a slow and steady descent through the valley of the Río El General.

But the southern zone has some very real charms, which may be the highlight of your visit. This is where the smart money goes for guaranteed quetzal sightings. The highest point in the country, Cerro Chirripó, at 3820 m, is a steady and rewarding hike from San Gerardo de Rivas, close to San Isidro de El General. For the entire length of the Talamanca Mountains, stretching beyond the border with Panama, a handful of opportunities exist to explore this vast protected area.

Further south, culturally depleted indigenous communities struggle to adapt to an ever-changing world. From San Vito in the far south, it's a short trip to the world famous Wilson Botanical Gardens, from where a spectacular road drops rapidly to the western lowlands around Ciudad Neily.

South to San Isidro

From San José, Highway 2 (Pan-American) heads southeast towards Cartago, veering south of the city and beginning the steep ascent through switchbacks, with only clouds and heavily laden trucks for company as you climb to the continental divide at almost 2050 m. Accommodation is dotted along the road although signposting – as in much of the country – is not necessarily a reliable indication of direction. In general hotels advertise their location in relation to kilometres from San José. While kilometre markers are erratic, the system does work, even if it does occasionally mean getting involved in advanced algebra as you try to work out precisely where you are. ▸▸ *For listings, see pages 324-328.*

Route of the Saints ⊙⊙ ▸▸ *pp324-328. Colour map 3, A1/2.*

Forgotten in time – and just over one hour's drive south of San José – the 'Route of the Saints' is a popular day-trip from the capital or an interesting detour if heading south. You can visit the area heading south from San José through Aserrí along Highway 209.

It's a curious collection of small towns and cut-off communities; some are set in broad valleys, while others cling to hillsides surrounded by neat lines of coffee bushes. Youthful streams have carved steep-sided valleys, often shadowed by challenging roads that provide spectacular scenery and the odd unexpected views – especially when lit by the soft light of dawn or dusk. As the name of the area suggests, saintly guidance is big here and the churches of the towns are as varied as Costa Rica's wildlife. They are not the kind of places you 'must see', rather a pleasant collection of experiences.

Taking the turning west at Km 51, south of Empalme, a winding road descends to the town of **Santa María de Dota** (population 4713). A simple lime-green church basks in the spacious main plaza. There is no shortage of *sodas* in town and if you are short of cash there's a Banco Nacional.

Sliding down the steep slopes of the Río Pirrís valley, a 6-km road leads to **San Marcos de Tarrazú** with its fine cream-coloured church perched on the hillside and a community that might be auditioning for a John Ford western. There are several *sodas* here too as well as the fine Pizzeria Las Tejas round the back of the church and branches of Banco Nacional and Banco de Costa Rica in town.

Further southwest **San Lorenzo** has a thoroughly modern church which, in a complete break with tradition, isn't on the main plaza. North of San Marcos, **San Pablo de León Cortes** has a modern, polygonal church with fine carpentry.

East of Santa María, the road climbs the Pirrís valley to **Copey**, 7 km from the Pan-American Highway at Km 58, with a fine, rickety old tin church that defies nature and the elements, and somehow remains standing.

Pan-American Highway to San Isidro ⊙ ▸▸ *pp324-328. Colour map 3, A2.*

At Km 56, you pass Jack's B&B (see page 325), and the Macizo de la Muerte Information Centre. Continuing south, there are a few points of interest worth stopping at. At Km 62 is the Tapantí Albergue de Montaña (see page 325). Further along, at Km 70, is **Finca Eddie Serrano Mirador de Quetzales**, more formally known as Mirador de Quetzales ⓘ *T2771-4582, tours take a couple of hours, US$6, accommodation also available, see page 325.* Here you are almost guaranteed to see the brilliant red and emerald green colours of the quetzal, as well as fine views down the Valle de los Santos. A short 3-km self-guided trail leads through forests of giant oak to a couple of waterfalls and a look-out point. The rather neglected **Casa Refugio de Ojo de Agua**, at Km 78, was once a historic pioneer home. The now creaking wooden building is certain to collapse under the environmental battering dealt out by the harsh climate of the region, but on a fine day, it's a good place to stop for a picnic or just to break the journey.

San Gerardo de Dota

A steep, dramatic and scenic road (4WD recommended) at Km 80 heads down the valley that gives birth to the mighty Río Savegre and leads to the small community of San Gerardo de Dota, on its way to the Pacific. If it were just a little warmer, the crashing waters of the Savegre and the lush forest of the narrow valley could be the Garden of Eden. Naturally the birdwatching is excellent, there is some fishing in the area and there are trails for walking and horse riding.

Cerro de la Muerte

Highway 2 continues the climb to the highpoint of the Pan-American Highway reaching its apex at **Km 89.5** and the nearby Cerro de la Muerte (3419 m) – which enticingly translates as the 'Mountain of Death'. Driving rain and mist often create the conditions that would clearly have been life-threatening when most transport was by foot. Barren *páramo* scenery dominates, stunted by the wet, windy and cold climate.

If you want to climb La Muerte, stop at Hospedaje Georgina at Km 95 (see page 325). Many of the buses making the journey between San José and San Isidro stop at the Georgina, which also serves good and hearty cheap meals.

The road then twists and turns to the broad Río General valley with sweeping views to the Talamanca Mountains and Cerro Chirripó to the east. Soak up the view at Km 119 the Restaurant Mirador Vista del Valle (see page 325).

San Isidro de El General ⊙🔗⊙▲⊙🄲 ▸▸ pp324-328. Colour map 3, B2.

Easily the largest town south of San José, San Isidro de El General (population 45,145) rests at the base of a broad fertile valley created by several rivers – the largest being the Río General. Completion of the Pan-American Highway in the 1950s has seen the quiet town grow as a service centre of the agricultural hinterland and a transport hub for journeys north, south and east. Tourism has seen the town develop as the departure point for ascents of Costa Rica's highest peak, Cerro Chirripó, and descents of the Río General rapids. Happy to wear several hats, the town also has several names – San Isidro is a useful contraction of the full name, and Pérez Zeledón is the name favoured by bus companies.

Ins and outs

Getting there San Isidro is the main transport hub for the southern region, making it a good place to change buses. The Pan-American Highway slices through, draining and supplying the town with a constant flow of produce and people from the north and south. A road heads west to Dominical and the Pacific coast. Regular buses ply all routes with terminals on or close to the highway. ▸▸ *See Transport, page 328, for further details.*

Getting around The main areas of interest in the town – hotels, restaurants and bus terminals – are within a seven-block square, all easy walking distances.

Best time to visit The skies are clearest from December-April. If you're in town in February you may catch the livestock and agricultural festival. On 15 May the death of San Isidro Labrador, the patron saint of the town and agricultural workers, is celebrated. The anniversary of the city's founding is celebrated on 9 October.

San Isidro de El General

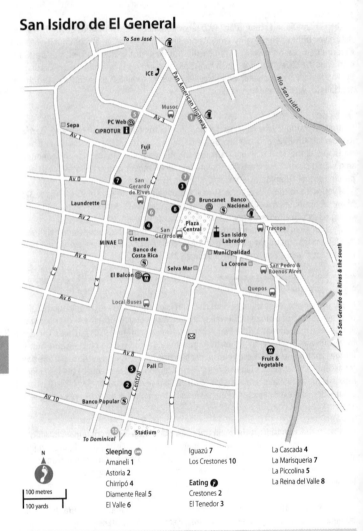

N	Sleeping	Iguazú 7	La Cascada 4
	Amaneli 1	Los Crestones 10	La Marisqueria 7
	Astoria 2		La Piccolina 5
	Chirripó 4	Eating	La Reina del Valle 8
100 metres	Diamente Real 5	Crestones 2	
100 yards	El Valle 6	El Tenedor 3	

History and sights

The rapid but low-key growth of recent years would have given the town a blank historical slate bar one major and highly significant event. According to the Museo Nacional in the capital, **José María Figueres** used the town as a foothold from which to launch the short civil war of 1948. The events of that year led to the creation of the modern political era in Costa Rica and to the abolition of the nation's armed forces.

From the 'provoke a response' school of architecture, the startling mid-1950s **cathedral** in honour of San Isidro Labrador, was for some a bold statement, for others nothing short of sacrilegious. Inside the temple is light, bright and breezy with a few refreshing approaches to religious iconography.

Trips from San Isidro

An interesting trip that involves a short hike goes to **Centro Biológico Las Quebradas**, ① T2771-4131, or contact Ciprotur, T2771-4131, www.ecotourism.co.cr, Tue-Fri, 0800-1400, Sat and Sun, 0800-1500. US$4, take the bus or drive to Quebradas (5 km) from where it's a 2.5-km walk to the centre, there is accommodation available, see page 326. This 750-ha community-protected reserve is host to mosses, bromeliads, butterflies and birds of the Quebradas River basin, which ranges from 1000 to 2500 m above sea level. It is this river basin that supplies San Isidro with drinking water, so while the development of the park and almost 3 km of trails is useful for educational purposes, there is a genuine interest in protecting the reserve.

Rancho La Botija ① T2770-2146, www.rancholabotija.com, weekdays 1400-1700, weekends 0900-0500, US$5 adults, US$3 children, head south before taking the road to San Gerardo de Rivas and keep an eye out after about 6 km, see page 326 for details of the hotel's facilities, is more than just a hotel. Trails lead from the main building through grassland and forest to **pre-Columbian petroglyphs** and the mysterious **Rock of the Indian**, which the owner believes was etched from the stone by the Chirripoyas.

Los Cusingos ① T2253-3267, www.cct.or.cr, 30 mins' journey southeast of San Isidro in Quizarrá de Pérez Zeledón, is a small but highly significant bird reserve which was home to one of the best known ornithologists in Costa Rica, Dr Alexander Skutch, co-author of the seminal field guide A Guide to the Birds of Costa Rica. The reserve of 76 ha was threatened with encroaching deforestation when the Tropical Science Center purchased the land from the late Dr Skutch. Visits by appointment only are limited to researchers, students, naturalists and birdwatchers.

Whitewater rafting is a popular pastime round these parts. The El General river is widely recognized as the largest whitewater river in Costa Rica, with over 100 miles of paddleable streams according to the experts Mayfield and Gallo. While the valley is scenic, the novice rafter tends to head for the spectacular forested sections of the **Pacuare** and **Reventazón**, leaving the Class III to V rapids of the General, ideal for playboating, to the specialists. Trips can be organized locally through Selva Mar (page 327) or from San José with Ríos Tropicales or Costa Rica Expeditions (page 106).

San Gerardo de Rivas

Of the myriad small communities that dot the General valley, San Gerardo de Rivas stands out as the entrance to Chirripó National Park and the base for hikes to the summit of Cerro Chirripó Grande (3820 m). Situated in a cool, pleasant spot at the confluence of the Río Blanco and the Río Pacífico Chirripó, the town is spread up a steep slope that only gets steeper once you start the climb proper. The surrounding scenery is impressive with whitewater streams crashing and tumbling over huge boulders in the steep-sided valleys pocked with agricultural smallholdings (where gradient allows). But in all honesty, you wouldn't visit the place unless intent on hiking, birdwatching, or more specifically conquering the summit of Cerro Chirripó. That said, there's a growing range of activities including waterfall tours and horse riding. There are also some **hot springs** ① *US$3, before crossing the new concrete bridge at the bottom of town, turn left towards Herradura, after a 10-min walk, look for the sign after Parqueo Las Rosas, go down the suspension bridge, cross the river and continue for 10 mins to the house where you pay*, rather handy for weary legs after the stiff climb if you're planning to stay in town an extra night.

Parque Nacional Chirripó ▸ *Colour map 3, A3.*

Chirripó is the icing on the cake that is Costa Rica. For seekers of the highest spot or even just in search of a good, hard walk, a two- or three-day trip to Chirripó National Park (50,150 ha) is just the ticket. As far as boot-busting, foot-blistering walks go, it's a pretty tough number. It's up all the way up and down all the way down – and there are very few flat bits to break the slope. Make sure you use a good pair of hiking shoes. Climbing steadily from a starting altitude of 1400 m, the path skirts through evergreen forest, floats among cloudforest, and eventually leads to the barren open *páramo* savannahs. Along the length of the route the fauna and birdlife is constantly changing and the views from the top to the Atlantic, the Pacific and down the spine of the Talamanca range are spectacular.

Parque Nacional Chirripó

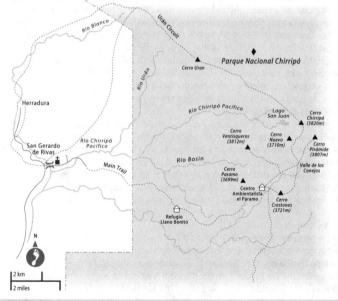

Ins and outs

Admission and accommmodation Entrance to the park is US$15 for a day, US$10 for each extra day. Accommodation at the refuge costs US$10 a night, and is booked through **MINAE** which has offices in San Isidro (T2771-3155) and San Gerardo (T2200-5348 or T2770-8040). The refuge does fill up, particularly in the dry season from January to April and at weekends, so book in advance at San Isidro if possible. To conserve the area, there is also a limit of 35 people a day permitted into the park. While no shows are common and the trip is usually possible, book in advance if you can. Sleeping bags and small gas stoves are available for hire at a small fee. You can hire horses to carry your equipment to the refuge in the dry season. Bags for two people costs US$20 – but you will still need to carry a day pack. Make arrangements in your hotel.

Finding out more Chirripo is a well-kept secret because there's not a great deal of information freely available. That's changing courtesy of a great new community website: www.sangerardocostarica.com. There's also information on tour operator sites (see below) – most have links on this website.

Tour operators If all you want to do is climb the peak and let someone else do the organization, most tour operators in San José will arrange it, costing around US$500 for the four-day round trip. Alternatively contact the regional specialists Selva Mar (page 327) who will organize your trip, T2771-4582, www.chirripo.com, US$440 for two people. They also have trips up Mount Uran and into Tapanti National Park.

Maps A simple map of the park is available from MINAE for US$0.75. While interesting, it is not appropriate for walking off the main path. It is possible to complete a circuit of the park but you will need a guide or good topographical maps, available from the Instituto Geográfico Nacional and Lehmann book store in San José (page 103).

The national park

Chirripó National Park is Costa Rica's second largest national park. With neighbouring La Amistad International National Park (the largest) Chirripó protects the Talamanca Mountains from south of Cartago down to the border with Panama. In a world of subtle tropical variations, the presence of classic glacial formations – u-shaped valleys, moraine deposit and glacial lakes – appear out of place. The barest hint of an ice-age remains with bitter winds and temperatures that drop, at their lowest, to -9°C. From around 3000 m, the barren *páramo* landscape is of stunted forest and savannah covering broad open plateau. The dominant oak landscape just below the summit area is severely scorched and slowly recovering from a fire in 1992. Around the summit, trails lead to **Cerro Crestones** – a rocky outcrop slowly developing spiritual significance as a site of pilgrimage – the **Valle de los Conejos** (Valley of the Rabbits) and the **Sabana de los Leones** (Lions' Savanna).

At lower altitudes, and warmer temperatures, cloudforest dominates with incredible diversity of flora and fauna – in particular the birdlife, of which there are over 400 species. For those that like to get engrossed in their landscape, it's a mind-expanding journey that could take a very long time.

Climbing Cerro Chirripó Grande Technically and navigationally the climb up Cerro Chirripó Grande is straightforward. A well marked trail leads to the **Centro Ambientalista el Paramoa** or *refugio* at 3400 m above sea level. It's between eight and 10 hours for the average trekker to the *refugio*, from where it's a couple of hours, mostly on the flat, to ascend the last 400 m of the hike. Other trails in the area are easily navigated, although you may feel more comfortable with maps or a guide.

Organizing the two- or three-day trip is straightforward. The *refugio* has around 80 dormitory rooms with four beds, and a kitchen for preparing food. You'll need food for the trip depending on how many days you plan to take. Temperatures at the refuge and the summit are close to freezing around nightfall and warm clothing is essential, as is rain gear from May to December.

Day 1 Start the trek at the gate just past El Urán on the left around 0600, earlier if possible, and aim to get to the refuge in one day. It is a long, uphill trek with barely any level, let alone downhill sections to break the monotony. While the scenery compensates, you don't want to be struggling towards the top with nightfall approaching so keep going at a reasonable pace.

Water is available at the very basic, open-air Llano Bonito lodge at 2500 m reached after about three hours. It is possible to stay at Llano Bonito but the conditions vary and are not reliably clean.

Day 2 Another early start, leaving the refuge around 0330, goes through the mainly flat terrain passing through the Valle de los Conejos to the final summit push – a rock scramble of a couple of hundred metres – reaching the peak for sunrise. If short of time and keen to move on, head downhill and you should be able to make the 1600 bus to San Isidro. If not, take things a little slower, spending another night at the refugio and enjoy the simple trek to Cerro Crestones and other peaks and valleys in the area. Most people follow the main trail.

◉ South to San Isidro listings

For Sleeping and Eating price codes and other relevant information, see Essentials, pages 44-47.

◉ Sleeping

Route of the Saints *p318*
Santa María de Dota
B-C Cecilia's Cabinas, 15 mins' walk southeast from the plaza T2541-1233, cabinasdececicia@gmail.com. 7 simple, clean cabins with hot showers. Incredibly friendly and highly recommended.
E Hotel and Restaurant Dota, 25 m north of the plaza, T2541-1026. Without bath.
E Hospedaje Fonda Marieuse, by the bus stop, T2541-1176. Shared bath, clean but very basic. Has seen better days, but still OK.

San Marcos de Tarrazú
Accommodation here is generally pretty unappealing.

D-E Tarrazú, close to the main square, T2546-6022. Simple rooms with private bath, hot water and parking.
E Continental, T2546-6225. With shared bath and cold water.

Copey
AL El Toucanet Lodge, just outside town, T2541-1435, www.eltoucanet.com. 8 rooms sleeping 3, in a beautiful wooden stilted house built by the owner Gary Roberts. Each room has a private bath, hot water and a small terrace. After a day exploring the nearby *páramo* and cloudforest biological reserve looking for quetzals and other birds you can feast on international and *Tico* dishes before resting by the fireside to ward off the chill that accompanies the night at 1950m. Opportunities for horse riding vary from a couple of hours to two days down to the coast.

Pan-American Highway to San Isidro *p318*

Listed in geographical order heading south.

B-C Cerro Alto, at Km 48, T2551-1010, www.cerroaltolodge.com. Simple A-frame alpine cabins sleeping up to 4 people with kitchenette and a café-style restaurant. It's a bit cold at night so light a fire and talk until dawn. Popular with *Josefinos* at weekends, you'll have the place and views of the volcanoes and valleys to yourself in the week.

C Cabañas de Montaña, at Km 51, set back 1.6 km off a 4WD road, T2382-4148. Very quiet and basic cabins with real fires at a chilly 2200 m above sea level. Beautiful cloudforest with several trails leading through the moss-laden trees.

C-D Jack's B&B, Km 56, T2823-7906. Has a couple of cabins and some trails. Handy place to stop if passing through. Also has a souvenir shop selling hammocks and other crafts.

AL Tapantí Albergue de Montaña, Km 62, T2290-7641. Spanish-owned, 10 quite good, large rooms sleeping up to 5, all with private bathrooms, hot water and some with balconies. It's a good choice for groups, with a fireplace in the cosy restaurant and fine views across the nearby hills.

B Finca Eddie Serrano, Km 70, T2771-4582, www.exploringcostarica.com/mirador/quetzales.html. 8 cabins and 4 rooms in the main lodge, with fine traditional food in the restaurant. Great views and trails, and one of the best sites to spot quetzals.

San Gerardo de Dota *p319*

A Restaurant Mirador Vista del Valle, Km 119, T8384-4685, www.vistadelvalle.com. 8 wood-framed rooms, each with private bath and hot water. Great views down the El General Valley and to the Pacific. Prices include breakfast – great place to stop if heading north or south.

LL-AL pp Hotel de Montaña Savegre, T2741-1028, www.savegre.co.cr. "The best place in Costa Rica to see the quetzal". 26 rooms are fairly simple and the buffet restaurant reminiscent of a college café, but you'll be outside most of the time walking trails, birdwatching, riding horses, fly-fishing for trout or on the coffee tour.

L-AL Trogón Lodge, T2293-8181, www.grupomawamba.com. 16 fine wooden cabins each with private bath, small balcony set in beautiful landscaped gardens connected by paths frequented by dive-bombing hummingbirds. International and national dishes served in the wood-panelled restaurant. There are 3 trails – the longest lasting 2 hrs 30 mins – fanning out from the lodge, as well as a waterfall tour, birdwatching and horse riding. Bilingual guides available on request.

L Dantica, T2740-1067, www.dantica.com. A handful of double and family-sized rooms with terraces looking out to the valley, with a beautiful gallery in this Dutch-run hotel. Breakfast and lunch included, dinner at nearby restaurant. Focus on quetzal spotting, but all local tours available.

Cerro de la Muerte *p319*

C Hospedaje Georgina, Km 95, T2770-8043. This is Costa Rica's highest hotel, and has simple double rooms.

B Restaurant Mirador Vista del Valle, T2771-4582, www.vistadelvallecr.com. Predominantly a restaurant serving fine food amid lovely scenery, this place also has some accommodation as well.

San Isidro de El General *p319, map p320*
In town

A-C Diamante Real, 100 m west of Musoc, T2770-6230, www.hoteldiamantereal.com. Smart business-style hotel, a comfortable mid-range choice with private bath, a/c TV and Wi-Fi. Secure parking.

B-C Hotel Los Crestones, a few blocks south of the plaza, T2770-1200, www.hotelloscrestones.com. 27 tidy rooms, comfortably decorated, with TV and a/c. Good mid-range choice, and popular with the business traveller.

Small pool out back and plenty of parking. A good efficient choice.

D Amaneli, T2771-0352. 41 quite good rooms with private bathroom, fan, a little more with TV. Also has a diner-style café. Some rooms close to the main road are quite noisy.

D Astoria, on north side of square, T2771-0914. Expansive impersonal hotel with 50 tiny but clean rooms. Some rooms have private bath.

D Iguazú, above Alacén Super Lido, C Central, Av 1, T2771-2571. 20 or so smart rooms with just a hint of interior design. Hot water, private bath, clean rooms with cable TV, safe place with secure parking.

C Chirripó, south side of Parque Central, T2771-0529. Plenty of rooms in this multi-storey hotel, which is bright and airy. It's nothing special but the odd plant and picture make the world of difference. Many combinations of rooms sleeping up to 4 people, with or without bathroom. Very good restaurant downstairs, free covered parking. Popular choice.

E El Valle, C 2, Av Central-2, T2771-0246. The 32 rooms, each with private bath and TV, are certainly better than most in town for this price.

Trips from San Isidro *p321*

A Rancho La Botija, on the road to San Gerardo de Rivas, 6 km east of San Isidro, T2770-2146/7, www.rancholabotija.com. 4 comfortable cabins with private bath and hot water sleeping 4 people. The rustic style of the restaurant, decorated with agricultural implements and shards of *botijas* around a central *trapiche* or sugar mill, serves a mix of Mexican and national dishes. Small pool overlooking the forest in a fine setting, very friendly owners. Several interesting tours – see below. Recommended.

A-B Talari Mountain Lodge, near to La Botija, T2771-0341, www.talari.co.cr. 9 rooms, each with private bath and hot water, set on an 8-ha farm with trails leading

through virgin, regenerated forest and fruit orchards. The mid-range restaurant serves healthy and varied dishes with fresh fruit from the daily harvest. There's also a couple of pools – one for kids. They close for 2 weeks every year, usually in Oct.

A Hotel Country Club del Sur, 6 km south on the Pan-American Highway, T2771-3033. A mini-resort-style complex with almost 60 rooms, suites and cabins. Some rooms are very spacious, with bath, hot water, telephone and TV. Others are distinctly unkempt but are in a process of being redecorated. Large pool, tennis courts and other activities. Reasonable restaurant.

C-E pp Centro Biológico Las Quebradas, 2.5 km from Quebradas (5 km from San Isidro), T2771-4131, www.ecotourism.co.cr. A wood-frame lodge sleeping 30 in bunk beds, with shared baths, hot water, meal service and laundry. Slightly cheaper for students with ID.

San Gerardo de Rivas *p321*

Starting at the bottom of the hill on the right just after the cemetery.

AL Chirripó Pacífico, T2771-7065, www.riochirripo.com. 8 comfortable rooms in bamboo buildings and a vast conical-roofed, thatched *palapa* communal space with restaurant and fireplace. Mainly a yoga and Watsu retreat, guests welcome when workshops have not taken all the rooms.

B-C Albergue de Montaña el Pelicano, perched on a steeped-sided hill, T2742-5050, www.hotelpelicano.net . 11 rooms in a large wooden lodge, with shared bathrooms. Loosely decorated with idiosyncratic wooden creations. Now has a pool, making a fine setting with trails leading to the nearby mountains, good for birdwatching.

D Marín, next to the MINAE national park office, T2742-5099. 8 basic, rather dark, but OK rooms, with shared bath and hot water. Simple dishes in the hotel restaurant.

D-E Cabinas Bosque, opposite the MINAE national park office, T2771-4129, elbosque@gmail.com. Scruffy-looking from the outside, the 8 rooms – 1 large enough for a group of 7 – are spotless. Some rooms have a balcony with hammocks overlooking the River Chirripó Pacífico and down the valley – a divine spot especially at sunset.

E pp **Cabinas El Descanso**, over the bridge, home of local hill-running legend Sr Francisco Elizondo Badilla, T2742-5061, hoteldescanso@hotmail.com. 10 clean and tidy rooms, 6 doubles and 4 singles. A few hammocks for hanging around and a cosy restaurant complete with fireside for late night tale telling.

C-E Roca Dura, opposite the football pitch, is the highest point you can reach by bus, T2742-5071, rocadurasangerardo@hotmail.com. Built on a huge boulder, this is the original 'hard rock' café with 10 rooms a little on the dark side, but popular (the strange foundations form a rather dramatic feature in at least one of the rooms). Rooms are for 1, 2 or 3 people, some with private bath, others shared, all with hot water. Also has a good café.

D El Urán, at the very top of the road and a good spot for the early morning start, T2742-5003, www.hoteluran.com. The closest hotel to the park entrance just a few metres from the start of the trail. Rooms are basic with shared bath, but friendly staff will send you up the hill with a hearty breakfast at some unearthly hour.

🍽 Eating

San Isidro de El General *p319, map p320*
†↑-† El Tenedor, C Central, Av Central-1. A popular choice for pizzas and a selection of traditional dishes.
† Chirripó, south side of the main plaza. Gets the vote from the current gringo crowd, with a patio terrace for people watching.
† La Cascada, on Av 2 and C 2. Balcony bar where the bright young things hang out.

† La Marisquería, Av 0, C 4, T2771-3614. Divine ceviche and a host of other fish dishes served fresh in front of you.
† La Piccolina, T2771-8692, www.piccolina pizza.com. Good pizza, to eat in or delivered to your door.
† La Reina del Valle, on the corner of the plaza. Good restaurant serving *Tico* dishes and fast food. Restaurant downstairs, open 0600-2130. Bar upstairs serving cocktails open 1000-2400.
† Restaurant Crestones, a few blocks south of the main plaza. Nothing special, but serves a good mix of snacks and drinks. It's popular with locals and makes for lively company at night.
† Soda J&P, in the indoor market south of the main plaza. The best of many sodas in town.

🛍 Shopping

San Isidro de El General *p319, map p320*
Supermarkets La Corona supermarket has a good selection of food, good for stocking up for the Chirripó summit, as does **Pali** a few blocks south of the main square.
For fruit and vegetables try the fruit and vegetable **market** on the south side of town on Thu and Fri.

⛰ Activities and tours

San Isidro de El General *p319, map p320*
CIPROTUR, the Centro de Información y Promoción Turística del Pacífico Sur, C 4, Av 1-3, T2771-2003 , www.ecotourism.co.cr. A regional tourist board working hard to promote the attractions of the south. A good source of information.
Selva Mar, C 1, Av 2-4, T2771-4582 , www.exploringcostarica.com. General tours and the main contact for out of the way destinations and hotels in the southern region.

⊖ Transport

Route of the Saints *p318*
There are 6 daily buses from San José to
Santa María via **San Marcos**, US$1.80, 2 hrs,
from Av 16, C 19-21, Terminal Los Santos.

San Isidro de El General *p319, map p320*
Buses from **San José** with Musoc,
T2222-2422 or T2771-0414, leave the
capital from C Central, Av 22-24, every hr
on the ½ hr from 0530 to 1830, 3 hrs,
US$3.80. Return buses from 0500-1730.
Most buses for destinations south of San
José pass through San Isidro so try **Tracopa**,
Av 5 and C 14, T2222-2666, as well.

Buses heading west from San Isidro go
to Dominical then north to Quepos and
south to Uvita from the **Transportes
Blanco** terminal, T2771-2550. To **Dominical**
at 0700, 0900, 1330 and 1600, 1½ hrs,
US$1.50. To **Quepos** at 0700 and 1330,
3½ hrs, US$2.50. To **Uvita** at 0900 and 1600,
passing through Dominical, 2 hrs, US$1.90.

Local buses tend to leave from the
newish bus terminal to the south of the
main plaza. Buses to **San Gerardo de Rivas**
and **Cerro Chirripó** leave at 0530 (from
the main plaza) and 1400 (from the bus
terminal), returning at 0700 and 1600.

Continuing south, buses leave from the
Tracopa terminal, T2771-0468. You can
either turn up and wait for the next hourly
bus passing through or get the precise times
from your hotel. Timetables vary depending
on road conditions and it is normally not
possible to buy tickets in advance as buses
may be full. **Tracopa** have services heading
south to **Buenos Aires**, 4 daily, 4 hrs, US2,
Palmar Norte, **Ciudad Neilly** and **Paso
Canoas**, 0830, 1600, 1930 and 2100, 4 hrs
to Paso Canoas, US$6.80. **David, Panama**,
at 1030, 5hrs. **Golfito**, at 1000 and 1800,
4 hrs, US$6.30. **Puerto Jiménez**, 0500 and
1300, 5 hrs, US$4.50, and **San Vito** 0900,
1100, 1430 and 1745, 3 hrs, US$5.70.

San Gerardo de Rivas *p321*
Buses to San Gerardo leave **San Isidro**
at 0500 and 1400, returning at 0700
and 1600, US$1.40. If driving, the 20 km
route to San Gerardo leaves the Pan-
American Highway a short distance
south of San Isidro.

4WD **taxis** cost around US$20.

⊕ Directory

San Isidro de El General *p319, map p320*
Banks Banco Nacional, on north side
of plaza, Mon-Fri, 0830-1545. Banco
Popular, Mon-Fri, 0815-1700, with a
Visa ATM. **Internet** Bruncanet, on the
north side of plaza, US$1.25/hr, also Net 2
Phone service. Open Mon-Sat 0800-2000,
Sun 0900-1700, T2771-3235. Internet el
Balcón, Av 4, next to BCR, T2771-6300.
New place, new machines. PC Web,
US$1/hr, open Mon-Fri 0800-2200, closes
at 1700 Fri. **Language schools** SEPA,
5 blocks west of the main plaza, T2770-1457,
www.spanish-school-costarica.com, has
Spanish language classes. It's a far quieter
option than San José and recommended
by several volunteer organizations. From
US$195 a week for 20 hrs of classes a week,
US$333 staying with a local family. They
also provide classes by the hour, US$18.
Laundry There's a launderette a couple
of blocks west of the main plaza.
Post office The post office is 3 blocks
south of the church. **Telephone**
ICE office on C 4, Av 3 – Pan-American
for international calls. **Useful addresses**
The MINAE office, a couple of blocks west
of the main plaza, T2771-4836 or T771-3155,
is useful for booking accommodation
and making reservations to climb Cerro
Chirripó. Open Mon-Fri 0800-1200.
Emergencies: T911.

South of San Isidro

A slow descent on the Pan-American Highway from San Isidro meanders gently through the broad valley – this is possibly the best bit of road in Costa Rica, permanently dominated by fine views of the Cordillera de Talamanca. Coffee plantations merge with eucalyptus groves giving way, close to Buenos Aires, to the distinct sweetness and aroma of pineapples that cover vast fields as far as the eye can see. If driving, there are plenty of side roads to explore. ▸▸ *For listings, see pages 334-338.*

Buenos Aires → *Colour map 3, B4.*

Buenos Aires (population 15,577), owes its prominence to the huge Del Monte cannery that sits at the junction of the town and the Pan-American Highway. The town itself is a few kilometres off the main highway. It's the main place to stay if heading for the Durika Biological Reserve further east in the Talamanca mountains, seeking a bus to the Boruca Indian Reserve to the southwest, or changing for a bus south to San Vito.

Reserva Biológica Durika

ⓘ *17 km east of Buenos Aires, reached by 4WD along a dirt track, T2730-0657, www.durika.org. Accommodation available, see page 334.*

One of the few places where you can spend time in the depths of the Talamanca mountains is in the Durika Biological Reserve, a private reserve of almost 800 ha. The community aims to encourage conservation and reforestation of the region and ecotourism plays a part in that process. Good trails through the area and to the nearby Cerro Durika (3280 m) give an insight into this rarely visited part of Costa Rica. Don't expect pristine wilderness – deforestation has led to serious erosion in the rainy months. But according to the Durika Foundation the environmental education programmes are beginning to reap rewards.

Boruca → *Colour map 3, B4.*

The small community of Boruca is the focal point of the Boruca people. For much of the year, the small village of several hundred people is almost lifeless – a loose collection of simple homes scattered around dusty lanes that twist and wind around the elevated and rather scruffy church. The steady erosion of the traditional culture in the region began in earnest with the arrival of the Jesuits in 1649. Today a simple cultural museum, sitting in the shadow of the church, is a sad (and true) reflection of the value placed on indigenous people in the country. Black and white photographs with peeling edges, desiccated by the wind blowing through the dilapidated structure, show of a steady decline in traditional life.

But each year on the last day of December and the first two days of January the hardships of agricultural life are discarded in the colourful celebrations of **La Danza de los Diablitos** – the Dance of the Devils. Dressed in fine masks and colourful costumes an elaborate game of tag sees the bull destroy the devils. On the third day, the devils rise again to stalk and eventually kill the bull. The bull symbolizes the colonization and persecution of the lands and indigenous people at the hands of the Spanish, offering the hope that, one day, the indigenous communities will be victorious. The festival sees the continuation of a tradition that has lasted for centuries, and is the culmination of months of quiet, behind-the-scenes preparation. If you can time your visit to coincide with the festival, visitors are welcome. If not, a visit is still worthwhile. There are waterfalls nearby and several villagers still carve masks, bows and arrows which you can buy.

ARADIKES – supporting indigenous communities

The latest estimates put the Amerindian population of Costa Rica at just 1% of the total. Consistent with tendencies worldwide, the plight of indigenous groups has not been uppermost in the minds of government officials. While the government ratified the international agreement for the rights of indigenous people in 1992, indigenous communities believe that as a minority, their rights are constantly being infringed – with the invasion of their private property, illegal logging and unauthorized cattle roaming. Other projects like the proposed hydro project on the Río General put more pressure on communities to sell land and slowly relinquish the few ties that still exist with their history.

The six communities close to Buenos Aires – Térraba, Boruca, Rey Curré, Salitre, Ujarrás and Cabagra – have created the Asociación Regional Aborigen del Dike (ARADIKES) a non-governmental organization that aims to strengthen indigenous communities in the region, working on natural resource conservation and management, social assistance in terms of housing, education, training and health, legal support defending indigenous rights, credit for small business activities and other programmes such as ecotourism, infrastructure and land recovery.

ARADIKES has a small office in Buenos Aires if you are interested in their work and there's a programme for volunteers genuinely interested in the rights of indigenous peoples, conservation developments and community programmes. Applications should be made in advance to Aradikes, Apdo Postal 24-8100, T2730-0289, aradikes@racsa.co.cr.

Paso Real → *Colour map 3, B4.*

Most of the rain that falls on the western side of the Talamanca mountains from División to the north and the Panama border to the south is channelled through Grande de Térraba river valley that cuts through the coastal mountain range to Palmar Norte. The Pan-American Highway follows the north bank heading west to the Pacific. A large bridge over the River Térraba provides access to the valley of the River Coto Brus leading to San Vito and the Wilson Botanical Gardens – see page 333. Just after the junction, on the northern river bank, is Restaurant Hilda, a classic *Tico* transport café with wholesome dishes and fast service. There are great views of the Térraba river from here.

Palmar Norte and Palmar Sur → *Colour map 3, B2.*

At a major junction on the Pan-American Highway, Palmar Norte is of particular interest to people fascinated by big trucks. The whole town, tucked in the elbow behind a right-angled sweep in the highway, is one big truck stop. Roads lead southeast to Golfito and the Panama border, south to Sierpe – for boats to Drake Bay on the Osa Peninsula – northwest to follow the Pacific coast and east to head inland, eventually reaching San José. Such convenient access makes this an important transport hub and it should be used accordingly. If passing, one regional curiosity is the impressive, mysterious and perfectly spherical **stone carvings** left by the Diquis culture (see box). The region is littered with these curious objects which you can see most easily from outside the

Great Balls of Diquís Delta

First discovered in the 1930s when the United Fruit Company began to clear thick jungle for their banana plantations, these mysterious stone objects continue to intrigue and fascinate. Since word got out, hundreds have been found throughout the Diquís Delta which is fed by the Río Terrabá from Palmar Norte.

Ranging in size from a few centimetres to up to 2.4 m in diameter, the objects are almost perfectly spherical and made from granite, despite the fact that there is no obvious quarry for the material in the area. The largest weighs in excess of 16 tonnes – suggesting that they carried great importance, as they clearly required a great deal of labour. As for their use, the theories range from their being grave markers or symbols of physical perfection through to possible representations of the planets. Their creators are also still a mystery.

Instituto Agropecuario in the Palmar Norte or in the central square of Palmar Sur – on the opposite bank of the Térraba river, a couple of kilometres to the south.

As with much of Costa Rican archaeology, the construction and purpose of the *esferas piedras*, believed to be around 2000 years old, is still very much open to debate. Significant detail relating to the Diquis culture is lacking and the subject is desperately in need of detailed and dedicated study. If you want to visit, the gravel track leaves the Pan-American Highway opposite the entrance to Palmar Sur. After about 4 km, just before the second concrete bridge, an overgrown path leads for a hundred metres to the sphere. If you get lost, ask in the local smallholdings – no one knows where it is, but you'll make some good friends along the way and get there eventually.

South from Palmar Norte

At **Chacarita** the only access road to the Osa Peninsula heads southwest. Ten kilometres further on, at **Briceño** a barely noticeable junction leads to Esquinas Rainforest Lodge in **Parque Nacional Piedras Blancas** ① *4 km to Esquinas from the Pan-American Highway, or you can approach from Golfito from the south along a hairy and occasionally impassable road – especially in the wet season.* One of the few remaining areas of moist tropical forest on the Pacific, the park was created in 1991 by presidential decree. As with many parks, legal protection did little to stop the reality of private landowners selectively logging the area – so the land needed to be purchased. As the local communities realized the newly created park challenged their way of life, the growth in interest in the region's preservation saw the Austrian government, with particular support from the well known classical violinist Michael Schnitzler, a part-time resident of Costa Rica, begin to purchase land, creating the 'Rainforest of the Austrians'. By 2007, Austrian individuals had donated more than US$4.2 m, enabling the purchase of over 146 sq km of rainforest. The property, most of which had exploitation permits for logging, has been donated to the Costa Rican government and become part of new Piedras Blancas National Park. Sixteen park rangers now patrol the park and scarlet macaws, spider monkeys, peccaries and even jaguar have returned to the area. The park can be explored along a 10-km network of paths that lead from the Esquinas Rainforest Lodge, see page 335.

Border essentials: Costa Rica–Panama

Paso Canoas
Customs and immigration is on the left side of the road as you enter town.
Border opening hours The border and immigration are open 24 hours.
Border formalities Formalities are straightforward and completed in one stop.
The crossing is quick and painless for international buses. For private vehicles,
there are maps of Panama available at the IPAT tourist office on the Panamanian
side. Don't forget Panama is one hour ahead of Costa Rica. Private vehicles should
be able to cross the border fairly easy, as long as all your paperwork is in order.
You will need to get the vehicle fumigated.

Ciudad Neily → *Colour map 3, C5.*

About 15 km from Río Claro and the turning for Golfito, and 16 km from Paso Canoas on
the Panama border, the town of Ciudad Neily sits in a broad valley created by the River
Corredor. Easily missed from the Pan-American Highway, the small-town agricultural feel
of the place, supporting the banana and African oil palm plantations to the south, belies a
district population of almost 22,000. Close to sea level, the town is uncomfortably hot and
humid in the wet season. Bus travellers will be more likely to see Neily, as it's an important
transport hub for bus services linking all points on the compass.

Paso Canoas → *Colour map 3, C5.*

If you could stereotype a border town, Paso Canoas would probably be the outcome. A
few thousand people, scratch out a living from any cross-border differential (in this case
the price of goods such as CDs, sunglasses and other items) and live huddled together in a
town that feels like it could be dismantled at a moment's notice. But it is a long way to
come for CDs which are neither good nor, in most cases, current, so you'll probably only
end up here if you're heading for Panama or entering Costa Rica. If circumstances find you
seeking a bed, there are some surprisingly acceptable options. See page 335.

Valle de Coto Brus → *Colour map 3, B4.*

The sharp bend in the Pan-American Highway back up at Paso Real (see page 330) marks
the confluence of the El General river to the north and the Coto Brus river to the south, to
form the Río Térraba which turns west to join the Pacific near Sierpe. Highway 237 crosses
the Térraba and climbs slowly towards San Vito (see below). If driving towards the
southernmost point of the country with a little time to spare, this route – as opposed to
the Pan-American Highway – is considerably more enjoyable. The journey takes longer
even though the distance is shorter, but the views of the Talamanca mountains are
impressive, particularly in the early morning, and the dramatic descent from San Vito to
Ciudad Neily is nothing short of spectacular with fine views across the southern lowlands
to the Osa Peninsula.

The good road south towards San Vito is dotted with the occasional hamlet – often
little more than a few houses and sometimes a simple café. This is probably one of the few
main roads in Costa Rica no tourism presence. There are some serious pot holes – some
even have plants growing out of them – so keep the speed low and enjoy the views.

San Vito → *Colour map 3, C5.*

Climbing close to a vertical kilometre from Paso Real or Ciudad Neily, San Vito (population 14,732, altitude 970 m) has a distinctly comfortable climate compared to the lowlands to the south – one of the reasons Italian settlers founded the town in the 1950s. Today, it's a regional commercial and agricultural centre of limited interest to the casual visitor (aside from some craftwork, see page 336). The main centre of the town is a two-block long street running downhill from the triangular plaza. South of town towards Cuidad Neily, are the world-renowned Wilson Botanical Gardens. A good gravel road, paved in places, also runs east via Sabalito to the Panama border at **Río Sereno**. There are buses from Sabalito to San José.

Las Cruces Biological Station, Wilson Botanical Gardens → *Colour map 3, C5.*
① *T2524-0607, www.esintro.co.cr. 0800-1600 daily. Prices from US$18. 6 km south of San Vito, easily reached by car, bus or taxi.*

In 1961 Robert and Catherine Wilson moved here from their botanical gardens in Miami with the aim of setting up a botanical garden and a commercial nursery. Almost 50 years later, the legacy of that vision has created the Wilson Botanical Gardens – one of the world's premier collections of tropical plants open for day visits, overnight stays and research.

The 10-ha gardens have a network of trails and paths designed by the Brazilian landscape architect Roberto Burle Marx. The success of the gardens lies in their location. At an altitude of 1100 m, they receive around 4000 mm of rain a year from May to December when the area can be shrouded in heavy fog and is regularly watered by afternoon clouds.

A number of self-guided tours lasting from 20 minutes to 2½ hours provide snippets of information allowing you to wander aimlessly at your own pace. Alternatively you can use a guide on a two-hour tour who will point out some of the 700 species of palms found in the garden – there are a total of 1000 in the neotropics. Resident birds species total 331 and mammals are also found in the gardens. A short well maintained trail takes you to the Java River, and night tours are available. All guided tours should be booked in advance if possible, US$18-38 per person, cheaper in a group.

The Wilson Gardens are part of the Las Cruces Biological Station, owned and operated by the Organisation for Tropical Studies. As with La Selva and Palo Verde, the station is a focus for biologists, students, birders and naturalists keen to take advantage of the phenomenal diversity of the region.

Parque Nacional La Amistad → *Colour map 3, B4.*

La Amistad National Park protects the Talamanca Mountain range of south-central Costa Rica – and at 199,147 ha is easily the largest park in the country. In some respects La Amistad is the perfect national park: secluded, difficult to reach and lacking significant services, it's a hothouse of diversity which goes beyond national boundaries and receives very few visitors.

Ins and outs Visiting the park is difficult to say the least. There are three rangers' stations at Tres Colinas, Estación Pittier and Altamira. Access to them is tricky and there is no guarantee that the stations will be manned when you arrive. When you get there, you will find a few paths that are only occasionally used. If exploring, you should be competent at navigation, carry all equipment and supplies you might need and get hold of a topographical map. Your best bet is to contact the park services in San Isidro de El General,

T2771-4836, for the latest information. For serious trekkers, ATEC, based in Puerto Viejo on the Caribbean coast, have a strenuous and extremely memorable trans-Talamanca trek taking 10 days (see box, page 392). You will be carrying your own food and equipment, so hope the weather is bearable and book at least a week in advance.

The park La Amistad National Park is the cornerstone of the International Amistad Biosphere Reserve, created by the United Nations in 1982. The reserve includes Tapantí-Macizo de la Muerte National Park (just south of Cartago), Chirripó National Park, four indigenous reserves and several other protected areas. When Panama created the neighbouring La Amistad National Park across the border in 1990, the entire Talamanca Mountain range became a World Heritage Site creating a protected area slightly larger than the state of Delaware in the USA.

The park is the very epitome of the convergence of North and South American flora. Its varied climate and soils create an inventory of species that reads like a What's What of the neotropics.

The **Talamancas** are the highest non-volcanic mountain range in Central America, created by uplift of the earth surface which was subsequently eroded by glacial activity and heavy rainfall. That rainfall – up to 6 m a year in places – has created steep-sided slopes that have left some areas of the park devoid of any human intervention. Temperatures range from 25°C down to -9°C. Eight of the 12 lifezones found in Costa Rica are present in the park, including lowland tropical rainforest, cloudforest and *paramo* forests. Altitudes range from 3820 m (Cerro Chirripó) down to 50 m above sea level. Over 9000 flowering plant species are found in the park, as well as all six species of feline occurring in Central America, the quetzal, the three-wattled bellbird, the umbrella bird and the harpy eagle. In the words of the United Nations, "it has been suggested that no other park in the world possesses as many species and such a wealth of fauna".

◉ South of San Isidro listings

For Sleeping and Eating price codes and other relevant information, see Essentials, pages 44-47.

◉ Sleeping

Buenos Aires *p329*
F Cabinas Mary, 800 m south of the centre close to the ARADIKES office, T2730-0187. A quiet spot which at least tries to be clean.
F Cabinas Violeta, next to the fire station 200 m west of the plaza, T2730-0104. Clean, simple and central. It's OK if you're stuck for the night.

Reserva Biológica Durika *p329*
B Reserva Biológica Durika, roughly 17 kms northeast of Buenos Aires, T2730-0657, www.durika.org. Accommodation is in 5 comfortable but rustic cabins and the price includes 3 vegetarian meals a day. All sorts of healthy pursuits for mind and body with short hikes to *campesino* and *indígena* communities, longer hikes to the mountain peaks and yoga and meditation classes, adding around US$10 per person to the daily rate.

Boruca *p329*
F Boruca, with basic rooms, a small restaurant and bar with a pool table. It's the only option in town.

Palmar Norte and Palmar Sur *p330*
C-D Hotel y Cabinas Casa Amarilla, a couple of blocks back from the highway, T2786-6251. 16 *cabinas* and 19 single rooms in a big yellow clapboard house

on the west side of the park. The service is largely indifferent but the rooms are clean and well kept.

D-E Cabinas Tico Aleman, on the Pan-American Highway, just east of the gas station, T2786-6232. Has 25 rooms, each with private bath and if you pay a little more and you also get hot water, a/c and TV.

South from Palmar Norte *p331*

AL Esquinas Rainforest Lodge, at Briceño, T2741-8001, www.esquinaslodge.com. Rooms and cabins, with tiled floor, ceiling fans and private bath (plus hot water) and verandas overlooking the tropical gardens and forest. The large thatched bar and restaurant serves local and Austrian dishes and there's a pool for cooling off after a day's hiking. As part of the programme to alleviate the economic pressures for logging, the lodge employs local people, and uses all profits to support projects in the small community of nearby La Gamba, such as the repair of the water system, roads and bridges, planting of cash crops, reforestation or environmental education.

Ciudad Neily *p332*

C Hotel Andrea, in front of the *ICE* office, T2783-3784. Some 50 clean *cabinas* with private bathroom, a/c or fan and TV. Pleasant open-air bar and restaurant serving mid-price dishes. Parking available. Popular place with *Ticos*, handy for the bus terminal and the best place in town.

C-D Centro Turístico Neily, T2783-3031. 69 reasonable rooms sleeping 5, with hot water private bath, a/c and TV. There's a couple of pools and a small disco – probably the best choice for a family if you have to stay in town.

D Cabinas Helga, T2783-3146. 13 spotless *cabinas* sleeping up to 4 people, each with fan. Well maintained, and with friendly owners.

D-F El Rancho, T2783-3060. 50 uninspiring rooms with private bath, a/c and TV.

E Elvira, T2783-3057. Offers the curious luxury of parking despite being very grim.

E-F Cabinas Heileen, T2783-3080. 10 simple *cabinas* with private bath and fan.

Paso Canoas *p332*

All south of the main road into town.

B-C Real Victoria, T2732-2586. 33 rooms with a/c or fan, and cable TV throughout. Credit cards accepted and a swimming pool open to the public.

D-E Cabinas Jiménez, T2732-2258. 18 quiet good *cabinas* with private bath, fan, a/c and TV. Very clean.

E Cabinas el Interamericano, T2732-2041. A good choice with big, clean rooms – upstairs rooms even have windows.

F Cabinas Jiménez Annexe, T2732-2258. A scruffy option if the rest are full.

San Vito *p333*

B-C El Ceibo, just off the main plaza, T2773-3025. Easily the best place in town, 40 or so neat rooms with hot water private bath and TV. Good, mid-range restaurant, serving Italian and local dishes. Parking available.

C-D Cabinas Rino, right in the centre of town, T2773-3071, hotelrino@hotmail.com. 13 clean, well-kept rooms with a few simple touches, hot water private bathroom, cable TV and secure parking.

F Colono, in the centre of town facing the plaza, T2773-4543, grubby looking but essentially clean place, although some of the beds are a bit lumpy. Also has a cheap restaurant.

F Las Mirlas, on the opposite side of the road to Hotel Pitier, T2773-3714. Slightly more attractive with half a dozen small cabins overlooking woodlands.

F Hotel Pitier, 0.5 km out of town on the road to Sabalito, T2773-3027, clean with bath.

Las Cruces Biological Station, Wilson Botanical Garden *p333*
L-AL Accommodation is available at the reserve. 12 beautiful airy cabins with hot water private bath and a small balcony. The price includes 3 meals at the fine café-style restaurant with a small balcony and library and one guided walk.

🍴 Eating

Buenos Aires *p329*
🍴 **Soda Kriss**, on the east side of the plaza. A popular spot, one of several *sodas* in town.

Palmar Norte and Palmar Sur *p330*
Several *sodas* and Chinese restaurants in town and close to the various bus stops.
🍴 **Restaurant Diquis**, opposite Banco Nacional. Concrete seats in an open area restaurant, full-on mix of fast food, *Tico* dishes and seafood.
🍴 **Marisquería**, opposite the gas station. For hearty portions of fairly simple cuisine.

Paso Canoas *p332*
Several other options close to the hotels.
🍴 **Brunca**, serves fairly unappealing but filling and cheap meals if you're waiting for a bus out of town or with a hole in your stomach.

San Vito *p333*
🍴🍴 **Hotel El Ceibo**, good Italian food in the hotel's large restaurant.
🍴🍴-🍴 **Liliana's**, close to the plaza. True to the Italian heritage of San Vito, Liliana's serves good, cheap pasta dishes. Very nice little balcony at the back if the weather is warm enough. Open daily 1030-2200.
🍴 **Jimar**, has a pleasant spot with a small patio on the road out to Paso Real serving cheap food.
🍴 **Restaurant Nelly**, near the gas station on the west side of town. Serves good wholesome truck drivers' fare *Tico*-style complete with a smile.

🍴 **Riobamba**, popular and lively bar with locals and other people passing through. Also has a good selection of *casadas*.

🛍 Shopping

San Vito *p333*
Finca Cántaros, on the road south out of town towards Ciudad Neily, T2773-3760. Specializing in local arts and crafts, including Chorotega pottery and more modern pieces from the capital. Woven textiles and hand-crafted wooden products from the Guaymi and Boruca and coffee fresh from the harvest in the Coto Brus valley. With carvings and *molas* (brightly coloured appliqué embroidery) from neighbouring Panama adding an international flavour, Cántaros is one of the best craft shops in Costa Rica – worth a look even if you don't buy anything.

▲ Activities and tours

Palmar Norte *p330*
Osa Tours, in the shopping mall on the Pan-American Highway, T2786-7825, www.osacostarica.com. Good regional tour operator who can organize activities and accommodation throughout the region as well as running the Osa Chamber of Tourism.

🚍 Transport

Buenos Aires *p329*
Regular **Tracopa** buses from San José heading south to **Ciudad Neily** and **Paso Canoas** pass through town or the *bomba* on the highway. Buses head inland to **Ujarras** at 0600 and 1200, taking 2 hrs. Buses to **Boruca** leave at 1100 and 1530, 1½ hrs, US$0.75.

Boruca *p329*

Buses from **Buenos Aires** depart at 1100 and 1530. If driving, take the road east from the Pan-American Highway at Brujo, or from Puerto Nuevo on the section connecting Paso Real and Palmar Norte.

Palmar Norte and Palmar Sur *p330*

Air SANSA, T2221-9414, www.flysansa.com US$81, and **NatureAir**, T2220-3054, www.natureair.com, US$110. Both have 2 daily return flights from **San José** to Palmar Sur.

Bus There are several daily express buses to and from **San José** with Tracopa from Av 5, C 14, T2222-2666, between 0525 and 1645, 6 hrs, US$8.35. Regular buses also pass through from **San Isidro de El General** throughout the day. 6 daily buses go to **Sierpe** leaving at 0430, 0700, 0930, 1200, 1300, 1420 and 1650, 45 mins – you'll need to get an early one if you're trying to get the regular boat from Sierpe to Drake. Heading south there are buses to **Ciudad Neily** (over 20, 1½ hrs), **Golfito** (1230, 1½ hrs) and **Paso Canoas** (1100 and 1900, 1¾ hrs). Heading north a bus leaves Ciudad Neily for **Dominical** at 0600 and 1430, passing through Palmar around 0730 and 1600.

Ciudad Neily *p332*

Air SANSA, US$89, T2221-9414, www.flysansa.com, has a daily return flight to **Coto 47**, a few kilometres south of town, from San José.

Bus 5 daily buses from **San José** head for **Ciudad Neily** and on to Paso Canoas from 0500 to 1800, 7 hrs, US$10.70 with **Tracopa** T2783-3227. Hourly buses leave for **Paso Canoas** from 0500-1800.

Heading towards the Osa Peninsula buses to **Golfito** leave every 30 mins from 0600-1930. **Transportes Térraba**, T2783-4293, have a service to **Puerto Jiménez** at 0700 and 1400, 3 hrs, US$0.70.

Heading north, buses head for **Palmar** and **Dominical** at 0600 and 1430, 3 hrs. Inland of Neily is **San Vito**, served by 9 daily buses between 0600-1730, 1½ hrs, US$1.20.

Paso Canoas *p332*

Tracopa buses to **San José** leave at 0730, 0900 and 1500, 8 hrs, US$11.20. There is reported to be a bus at 0400, but don't count on it.

An hourly service goes to **Ciudad Neily** where there are many more transport options with connections to **Golfito**, 0500-1830, 2 hrs, US$1.20, the **Osa Peninsula**, north to the **Pacific Coast** and inland to **San Vito** and the **Talamanca Mountains**.

San Vito *p333*

Air No direct flights to San Vito, although there is an airstrip. The closest would be Coto 47, just outside Ciudad Neily, SANSA, US$89, T2221-9414, www.flysansa.com.

Bus Long distance buses leave from the **Tracopa** terminal in the centre of town, T2773-3410. Buses from **San José** leave at 0545, 0815 and 1130 (8 hrs) with a direct bus at 1445, 6 hrs, US$10.11. Return buses run at 0500 (direct), 0730, 1000 and 1300. Services leave **San Isidro** at 0530 and 1400, returning at 0645 and 1330, 3 hrs, US$5.70.

Local buses leave from a separate, but fairly close terminal. There are 7 buses a day to **Ciudad Neily** taking all sorts of circuitous routes via **Sabalito** and **Cañas**, leaving from 0530 to 1700. Take a direct bus for **Wilson Botanical Gardens**. If travelling San Vito–Ciudad Neily by bus sit on the right going down, the left going up to get the best of the wonderful views.

Buses head north for villages including **Santa Elena**, **Roble**, **Guinea** and **Mellizas.**

❶ Directory

Buenos Aires *p329*
Banks A large concentration of banks with branches of **Banco Nacional**, **Banco de Costa Rica** and **Banco Popular** (open Sat mornings), all with ATMs.

Palmar Norte and Palmar Sur *p330*
Banks Banco Nacional on the main road, with ATM. **Internet** Centro de Computo, a couple of blocks back from the main road, US$0.70 for 15 mins. Open Mon-Fri 0800-1900, Sat 0900-1800.

Ciudad Neily *p332*
Banks Banco de Costa Rica has an ATM as does the branch of **Banco Nacional** and the **Banco Popular**. **Internet** Techno Planet, US$1.10 per hr, open Mon-Sat, 0900-2130. Also **Neurotec**, open Mon-Fri, 0800-2000.

Paso Canoas *p332*
Banks Services are limited to the branch of **Banco Nacional**, although dollars can easily be changed around the border with money changers. **Post office** Close to the border crossing.

San Vito *p333*
Banks Surprisingly good selection of banks to choose from with branches of **Banco de Costa Rica**, **Banco Nacional** and **Banco Popular**, all with ATM, in a line just south of the plaza. **Hospital** New hospital on the road out to Sabalito, only one for miles. **Internet** Neurotec, close to Bar Restaurant S'Hogar. **Post office** The post office is at the northern end of town. **Telephone** ICE telephone office is a few metres west of the main plaza, open 0730-1700.

Contents

342 Sierpe and Bahía Drake
   342 Ins and outs
   342 Sierpe
   342 Bahía Drake
   343 Reserva Biológica Isla del Caño
   344 Listings

347 Around Puerto Jiménez
   347 Ins and outs
   347 Rincón and La Palma
   347 Puerto Jiménez and around
   349 Parque Nacional Corcovado
   351 Listings

356 Golfito and the beaches
   356 Ins and outs
   356 Golfito and around
   359 Listings

Footprint features

340 Don't miss …

Golfito & the Osa Peninsula

At a glance

◎ **Getting around** It's a long trip from San José, so consider getting a flight down if the budget can cope. There are boat services between Sierpe and Drake Bay, Golfito and Puerto Jiménez. Once there, it's slow moving on jeeps and 4WDs; or even slower on the best rainforest treks in the country.

◉ **Time required** 3 or 4 days, add another 5 if trekking through Corcovado National Park.

☼ **Weather** Driest from Dec to Apr, with light rains building to spectacular torrential storms in Sep and Oct.

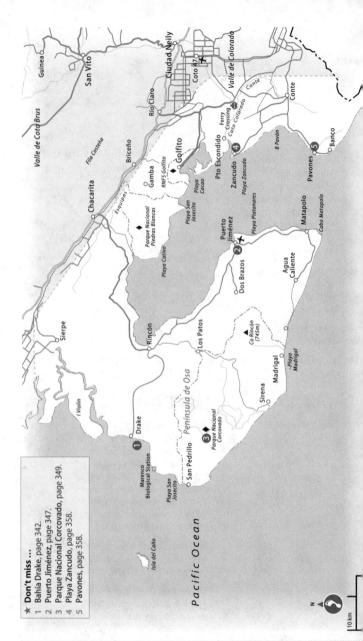

★ **Don't miss ...**
1 Bahía Drake, page 342.
2 Puerto Jiménez, page 347.
3 Parque Nacional Corcovado, page 349.
4 Playa Zancudo, page 358.
5 Pavones, page 358.

Pacific Ocean

Isla del Caño

Guinea

San Vito

Valle de Cota Brus

Ciudad Neily

Coto 47

Valle de Colorado

Río Claro

Conte

Briceño

Fila Costeña

Coto Colorado

Ferry Crossing

Chacarita

Enquivas

GOLFITO

RNFS Golfito

Gamba

Parque Nacional Piedras Blancas

Pto Escondido

Conte

Banco

Pavones

Playa Cativo

Playa San Josecito

Zancudo

Playa Zancudo

B Pavón

Sierpe

Rincón

Puerto Jiménez

Playa Platanares

Matapolo

Cabo Matapolo

Los Patos

Dos Brazos

Agua Caliente

Península de Osa

Cº Rincón (745m)

I Violín

San Pedrillo

Parque Nacional Corcovado

Madrigal

Playa Madrigal

Sirena

Drake

Marenco Biological Station

Playa San Josecito

Playa Cacao

N

10 km

The Osa Peninsula is the smaller of Costa Rica's two Pacific protuberances and while broadly similar in shape, the landscape could hardly be more different. All lush, verdant tropical exuberance – Corcovado National Park is the place to visit in Costa Rica if you're looking for a rainforest wilderness experience. On the western side of the peninsula, Corcovado makes you work for your pleasure and requires a demanding trek which you can do on your own or as part of a group. Beyond rainforest hikes, there's kayaking, diving and surfing on offer at several points around the peninsula, including the budget option of Puerto Jiménez or the more comfortable base of Bahía Drake.

On the mainland, the regional centre of Golfito is an important town, flourishing as a tax-free trade centre and the stepping-off point for beaches around the Golfo Dulce to the north and south. Heading south it's increasingly remote. Zancudo is a fine beach and base for chilling out and some of the best deep-sea fishing in the country, while Pavones further south still provides the ultimate surf experience with one of the longest lefts in the world.

All around the gulf and the peninsula, hotels and lodges hide in exclusive bays basking in comfortable temperatures for much of the year.

Sierpe and Bahía Drake

Sierpe is the stepping-off point for a boat journey to the secluded and comfortable Bahía Drake. From the highly active to the super laid back, the bay blends the wildlife of the rainforest and the ocean in one, normally luxurious, location. It's also a good access point for the northern section of Corcovado National Park.➤➤ *For listings, see pages 344-346.*

Ins and outs

Getting there
Daily flights from San José go to Drake Bay with **SANSA**, T2221-9414, www.flysansa.com, US$91, and **NatureAir**, T2220-3054, www.natureair.com, US$120, although flights are not always scheduled for September and October. Flights to Palmar Sur/Dominical with SANSA, US$81, and NatureAir, US$106, are good for boats from Sierpe connecting to Drake Bay. Regular buses from San José to Palmer Norte take six hours. Driving to Drake Bay is an option in the dry season.

Getting around
Moving around the region is easiest using local boats, taxis and bus services. Many of the more expensive lodges provide transport from the nearest airport by boat and/or taxi to whisk you to comfort with the least possible inconvenience. Those on a tighter budget will need to use local bus services which are limited but get you to most places eventually and reasonably economically. Osa Tourism Chamber is at www.osacostarica.com.➤➤ *See also Transport, page 346, for further details.*

Sierpe ●❷▲●❻ ➤➤ *pp344-346. Colour map 3, B3.*

A maze-like gravel road leads south for 12 km from Palmar Sur to Sierpe through lines of banana plantations and African palms that produce a natural oil for cooking, sunblock and skin cream. The small town on the banks of the Río Sierpe, with a population of around 4000, is pleasant in a laid-back, indifferent way. The flux of people passing through has seen a few basic services crop up – two restaurants, a tour operator and internet café – but most people are normally just passing through en route to Drake.

Keen to capitalize on regional attractions, trips to nearby Isla Violín, Isla del Caño and Corcovado can be arranged from here. **Isla Violín** is home to some beautiful beaches and a couple of treks. Further, **Isla del Caño** is a popular destination for divers and snorkellers, with several *esferas de piedra* (rock spheres) to beguile the onlooker. It is also possible to visit the **Térraba-Sierpe Mangrove Forest Reserve**, at 27,065 ha the largest area of mangrove swamps in the country, and an internationally protected RAMSAR wetland. It's a good place to see birds and crocodiles, snakes and other wildlife. For more information contact the Osa Conservation Area office in Palmar Norte on T2786-7161.

Bahía Drake ●❷▲● ➤➤ *pp344-346. Colour map 3, B3.*

A crescent shaped bay on the northern end of the Osa Peninsula, Drake (pronounced *dra-kay*) Bay is named after Sir Francis Drake, the English bucaneering seaman who in March 1579 careened (deliberately beached) his ship on Playa Colorada in Bahía Drake. A plaque commemorating the 400th anniversary of the nautical event was erected in Agujitas. Going ashore these days no longer requires such drastic action, the alighting point of preference now being the landing stage at Aguila de Osa Inn.

The main attraction of Drake is trips into Corcovado National Park, jungle activities including treks and night tours, and trips on or in the water including diving off Isla del Caño – where the water is exceptionally warm (around 25°C). Life in the bay is quite pricey and once you include transport you're looking at US$100-140 for one night without including any tours. Good regional information on the web at www.drakebay.info.

Local trips and activities Drake is good for swimming, but the beach is pebbly and lots of hotel boats use the water. Day trips to **Isla Caño**, **Corcovado National Park** and the mangroves of the **Sierpe-Térraba estuary** cost around US$80 per person but prices fall considerably if travelling in a group. **Diving** in the area is mainly to view fish rather than coral and you may well see white-tipped sharks, manta and sting rays (for Dive operators, see page 346).

Day tours into **Corcovado National Park** can be organized with trips to San Pedrillo costing US$70, and round to Sirena around US$100.

The continuous research of the Vida Marina Foundation (part of the Delfín Amor Eco Lodge, see page 345), who hope to set up a marine reserve here, has recorded 25 species of **dolphins** and **whales** in Drake Bay, including humpback whales, bottlenose dolphins, pilot whales and sea turtles. The lodge offers tours and packages to see dolphins and whales, T8847-3131, www.divinedolphin.com. Green and hawksbill **turtles** nest to the north and south of Bahía Drake in the green season, but egg-poaching is a problem – ask locally for tour information.

Several hotels arrange **sportsfishing**. Prices starting at US$350 per person for inshore fishing, US$600 for deep sea.

Away from the water the latest small big thing is **The Night Tour**, a night trek through the rainforest that takes in all that the Tracie 'The Bug Lady' can spot when the animals of the forest are far more active. The walks last about 2½ hours, T2382-1619, www.thenighttour.com, US$35.

Up in the air the **Canopy Tour** operates out of the Jinetes de Osa. Nine platforms with six cables zip through the primary rainforest and there's a 20-m-high observation bridge you can stop at to take in the views, T2371-1598, US$55.

Reserva Biológica Isla del Caño ▸▸ *Colour map 3, C2.*

Some 20 km west of the Osa Peninsula, Caño Island Biological Reserve, with a single path on the island and good opportunities for snorkelling close to the coast, is a popular day trip from Sierpe. The 300-ha island rises to a height of barely 110 m above sea level with much of the coastline made up of high cliffs. Wildlife is relatively scarce on land although you may see bird species such as osprey and brown booby, and pacas, four-eyed opossums and boa constrictors are also present.

The island's main interest – on land at least – is archaeological. There is evidence that the island was used as a pre-Columbian cemetery. The perfectly round stone spheres found throughout the Diquis Valley on the mainland (see page 330) are also present on the island, adding to the mystery of how and why these stone spheres were created.

The 2700-ha marine portion of the reserve protects marine platforms of low coral reef, large pelagics (fish) and the regionally endangered lobster and giant conch.

For Sleeping and Eating price codes and other relevant information, see Essentials, pages 44-47.

Sleeping

Sierpe *p342*
A-B Oleaje Sereno, one block west of the park, T2788-1103, www.hoteloleaje sereno.com. Neat and tidy place with 10 good rooms with private bath, hot water and a/c. The best option in town. The small restaurant overlooking the river is a fine spot to relax. Also provides extensive tour options.
F-G Margarita, 2 blocks north of the park, T2786-7574. 5 clean and simple *cabinas* with fan and private bath, or 13 bright and breezy rooms with windows. Friendly owners.

Out of town
A-B Eco Manglares Sierpe Lodge, 2.1 km across a rather hairy suspension bridge T2786-7414, www.ecotourism.co.cr/ ecomanglares. 10 rustic cabins for 3-4 people, with private bath and hot water. Pleasant gardens and an open-air restaurant serving mid-priced Italian and *Tico* dishes. Good range of tours including day trips to Corcovado, Drake and Caño Islands.
L Río Sierpe Lodge, T2384-5595, www.riosierpelodge.com. 14 rustic but comfortable rooms with private bath near the mouth of the Sierpe river. Good spot for nature tours of the mangrove swamps and an ideal location for billfish and wahoo fishing in Pacific and snook and roosterfish in the tidal basin.

Bahía Drake *p342*
Hotels in Bahía Drake are hugely overpriced in comparison to the rest of the country. Prices quoted are **per person** not per room and include 3 meals unless otherwise stated. It's a good idea to book, especially in the high season from Jan-Apr. Some places offer discounts in the green season, most offer tours directly or can arrange them on request.

LL Aguila de Osa Inn, T2296-2190, www.aguiladeosainn.com. A very plush hotel set in tropical gardens on a bluff with fine views to Drake Bay. 11 spacious rooms and 2 suites, all with tiled bathrooms, fan and mesh windows to keep that tropical breeze moving through. Open-air restaurant and bar serving international dishes. Mainly US clientele for sports fishing.
LL Drake Bay Rainforest Chalet, T2382-1619, www.drakebayholiday.com. Good spot, with many personal touches. Comfortable rooms with Italian tiled bathrooms, and decks with hammocks. Home to The Night Tour.
LL Drake Bay Wilderness Camp, opposite Aguila de Osa, T2770-8012, www.drakebay. com. Large cabins, sleeping up to 5, with hot water, private bath and splendid ocean views. Generous discounts for children and package deals out of San José.
L La Paloma Lodge, next to Drake Bay Wilderness Camp, T2293-7502, www.la palomalodge.com. Perched up on the hill with magnificent views out to the Bay and Caño Island in the distance are 4 rustic but elegant rooms sleeping 3, and 7 bungalows sleeping 5, all have private bath and hot water and there's a fine tiled pool set in land-scaped gardens. Full service dive operations. The highlight of a trip to Costa Rica for many.
L-AL Pirate Cove, northern end of the beach, T2393-9449, www.piratecovecostarica.com. Very pleasant tent-like cabins, some with bath, emulate an outdoor experience minus the mud, as well as more conventional cabins and bungalows. Large open-air restaurant serving *comida típica* with a hint of Swiss. Also home to PADI-accredited **Caño Divers**.
AL-A Jinetes de Osa, T2231-5806, www.jinetesdeosa.com. A funky hotel at the southern end of the bay, run by brothers from Colorado. Rooms are spacious and airy, all have bath, hot water and fan, some practically have waves lapping at the door. Open-air restaurant serves family-style meals with fresh bread. PADI-accredited diver centre and canopy tour.

A-C Jade Mar, 5 mins up the hill along the road behind the *pulpería*, T2384-6681, www.jademarcr.com. Breezy simple rooms with bath and fan and much cheaper rooms without bath. Good open-air restaurant with views and tours available.

A Rancho Corcovado Lodge, roughly in the middle of the beach, T2241-7083, www.ranchocorcovado.com. Simple rooms, many with views, all with bath. Pleasant restaurant on beach serves *comida típica*. Good value tours offered. Friendly *Tico* owners.

B El Mirador Lodge, up the hill just north of Rancho Corcovado and follow the signs, T2387-9138, www.mirador.co.cr. Pleasant, airy and rustic rooms, all with bath. Restaurant serves *comida típica* using only fresh food (some good choices for vegetarians). The owner, José Antonio Vargas, is an ecologist and there are trails on the property for birdwatching. A good deal in an expensive town. Recommended.

Camping F pp **Rancho Corcovado** including use of electricity and bathrooms; **Pirate Cove** which has no fixed price but a small charge for use of baths; and **Poor Man's Paradise**, see below, page 345.

Out of town

LL Casa Corcovado Jungle Lodge, near the San Pedrillo park entrance to Corcovado National Park in a 69-ha private reserve, T2256-3181, www.casacorcovado.com. 14 luxurious thatched bungalows with tiled floors, ceiling fans and beds with mosquito nets. Perfect for honeymoons. Offers packages at US$855 per person, including transfers from and to San José, 3 nights' accommodation, all meals and tours to Corcovado and Caño Island.

LL Delfín Amor Eco Lodge, part of the Vida Marina Foundation, a short boat journey just over 1 km west of Drake, T2786-7636, www.divinedolphin.com. 5 simple screened cabins with a couple of double beds, set in lush jungle surrounded by wildlife. The set-up is guided by a passion for dolphins and whales that visit the Drake Bay. A 3-night

package from San José is US$592. Also has a well organized volunteer programme.

L-AL Campanario Biological Reserve, T2258-5778, www.campanario.org. Squeezing into the space between education and tourism, the reserve offers courses in ecology and rainforest conservation camps. There are 70 ha of rich humid tropical forest from sea level to 155 m, to explore and plenty of trails. A good spot for earthy tourism, also has a volunteer programme.

L-AL Guaria de Osa, T8358-9788, www.guariadeosa.com. A combination of conventional lodging and tents. A holistic experience: activities include yoga as part of **World Family Yoga** (www.worldfamilyyoga.com), t'ai chi, surfing, bird-watching and a spiritual activities program.

L-B Poor Man's Paradise, in Playa San Josecito southwest of Drake, T2771-4582, www.mypoormansparadise.com. 8 clean, rustic and pleasant cabins with bath provided by the Amaya family. Also provide tents so you can **camp** (**F**) or pitch your own. Prices include 3 meals served in the breezy, thatched roof restaurant.

AL-A Marenco Beach and Rainforest Lodge, in 600 ha of private reserve, T2258-1919, www.marencolodge.com. 17 rustic bungalows and 8 rooms, all with bath and sea view. Exploring the options for tourism and conservation working successfully side by side, the hotel supports students and research with discounted rates. Good range of packages offered from San José including guided tours. Very friendly. A good selection of meals served too.

AL-A Corcovado Adventures Tent Camp, set in forest right on Playa Caletas (4 km southwest of Drake), T8384-1679, www.corcovado.com. Large tents with comfortable beds complete with babbling brook. Great fun, lots of tours and snorkelling and boogie boarding from the beach.

AL-B Treetop Resort, T8844-7272, www.drakebayresort.com. Small resort with a handful of rooms all completely screened, set in the jungle and just a short 60-m walk from

the beach. Fresh fruit and seafood served in the open-air restaurant. Good, relaxed spot.
A Cabinas Las Caletas, T2381-4052, www.caletas.co.cr. A couple of rooms and a cabin sleeping between 2 and 5 people, all with private tiled bath. *Tico*/Swiss owners have merged cultures and kept the best bits of both in this growing ecotourism spot.

🍴 Eating

Sierpe *p342*
Many local hotels have their own restaurant including Oleaje Sereno (page 344).
♥ Las Vegas Bar/Restaurant, T2786-6682. Good traditional dishes and seafood with a breezy balcony out back looking across the river. Owner Jorge is very helpful. Open 0600 to midnight, daily.

Bahía Drake *p342*
Most hotel restaurants only cater for guests. Hotels that might make an exception if you give a little advance notice include: **Jade Mar, Rancho Corcovado, Mirador Lodge** and **Pirate Cove**. All food tends to be expensive because supplies have to come by boat from Sierpe. There is a *soda* on the beach in the village, but it's nearly always closed. Otherwise, the *pulpería* stocks a few basics.

As with dining, the nightlife is mostly arranged by the hotels, but you could try **Bar Mar y Sombra**, up some steps from the beach between Jinetes de Osa and Bella Vista Lodge.

🏔 Activities and tours

Sierpe *p342*
Ask at **Oleaje Sereno** or **Las Vegas** restaurant to organize local trips.

Bahía Drake *p342*
Caño Divers, at Pirate Cove Hotel, T2234-6154, www.canodiverscostarica.com. Charge US$130 for a 2-tank day's diving at Isla Caño.

Costa Rica Adventure Divers, at Jinetes de Osa, www.costaricadiving.com. Offer 4-day PADI courses (US$340), full-day 2-tank dive with lunch at Caño Island (US$105).

If you're not staying at either of these places, you can arrange your dive with them through your hotel. There is good snorkelling at several places in the area. From US$65.

🚌 Transport

Sierpe *p342*
Buses to Sierpe leave **Palmar Norte** at 0430, 0700, 0930, 1200, 1300, 1420 and 1650, 45 mins, US0.40. Buses to Palmar Norte leave Sierpe at 0530, 0800, 1000, 1300 and 1530. A taxi would cost around US$12. Most hotels in **Drake** provide transport from Sierpe. Space permitting, you may be able to hitch a ride – most leave in the morning. There is also a regular service leaving at 1000 and 1200, US$15 per person. If you have missed the boats or are travelling in a group, chartering a vessel is an option, US$80 for up to 6 people.

Bahía Drake *p342*
Most people arrive at Bahía Drake by boat from **Sierpe**, having got there from Palmar Sur on one of the daily SANSA flights. But **SANSA** and **NatureAir** now both also fly direct to Drake from San José, although services may not be scheduled in Sep-Oct. It is possible to drive to Drake leaving the Pan-American Highway at **Chacarita**, following the road to Rincón from where a right fork leads to Agujitas. This road is 4WD and passable only in the dry season.

📖 Directory

Sierpe *p342*
Internet Next to Marisqueria. A bit pricey but if you really need your cyber-fix they're open 0800-2200.

Around Puerto Jiménez

A good road leaves the Pan-American Highway at Chacarita, and quickly deteriorates as it climbs round the rocky headland to the towns of Rincón, La Palma and eventually the old mining centre of Puerto Jiménez. The dusty main street still has a frontier feel but the prospectors were slowly cleared out of town with the creation of Corcovado National Park in 1985. For many the Corcovado is the most precious protected area in Costa Rica. It preserves the lowland rainforest with just a few trails for the truly adventurous to explore. ▶▶ *For listings, see pages 351-355.*

Ins and outs

Getting there

Daily flights with Sansa (US$89) and NatureAir (US$120) connect Puerto Jiménez to San José and there's a regular, and long (eight hours), bus journey from the capital twice daily. Ferries cross the Gulf of Dulce to Golfito a couple of times a day. If you're driving, the 79 km road from the Pan-American Highway follows a good road to Rincón, from where the 35 km reasonable dirt road heads south to Puerto Jiménez. There are many bridge crossings so check locally for conditions. ▶▶ *See Transport, page 355, for further details.*

Getting around

If you're staying in Puerto Jiménez, you can walk everywhere without inconvenience. If your accommodation is out of town, make arrangements with the hotel to be picked up from the airstrip, ferry dock or bus station. *Colectivos* (pick-ups) at 0600 and 1330 make the journey to Carate from Puerto Jiménez, from where you can make trips to Corcovado. You can travel through the park using any combination of entrance and exit points. Entering through Carate and exiting through La Palma – or vice versa – is probably the simplest and cheapest option.

Tourist information

None officially, but you won't go wrong if you pop into Carolina's and talk to the people at **Escondido Trex**, see page 355.

Rincón and La Palma ⊜❼▲ ▶▶ *pp351-355. Colour map 3, C3.*

The small town of Rincón is marked by the stylish La Ventana restaurant (mid-range) and the author of the Southern Costa Rica Guide, Alexander del Sol lives next door. He's local, knowledgeable, passionate about southern Costa Rica and welcomes visitors. From Rincón it's 14 km along the now dirt road to the town of La Palma and the road heading west for access to the Los Patos ranger's station of Corcovado National Park.

Puerto Jiménez and around ⊜❼▲⊕❶ ▶▶ *pp351-355. Colour map 3, C4.*

Today, Puerto Jiménez (population 2500) is a popular destination which just holds onto its laid-back but occasionally lively atmosphere. Barely five blocks square it's relatively free from road traffic and there are some reasonable beaches nearby but it's the beautiful Corcovado National Park that is the main draw. There's some good budget accommodation but standards (and prices) are increasing. There are also interesting local walks to the jungle, beaches, and mangroves, where you will see monkeys and many birds, are only a couple of blocks from the main street. If you want to see wildlife you don't even have to go that far – scarlet macaws roost in the trees around the football pitch.

Playa Platanares

Outside Puerto Jiménez, 5 km south, behind the airstrip is the grey sand beach of Playa Platanares. Quiet and secluded with good swimming, it's a good spot for groups and

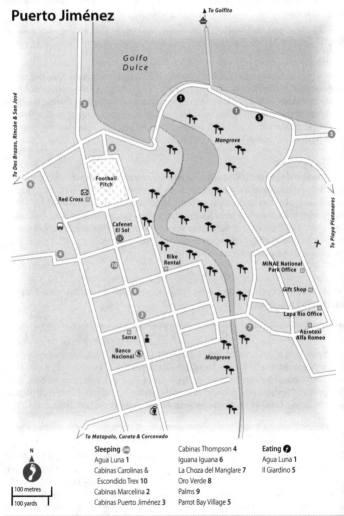

Puerto Jiménez

▲ To Golfito

Golfo Dulce

To Dos Brazos, Rincón & San José

To Playa Platanares

Football Pitch
Red Cross
Cafenet El Sol
Bike Rental
Sansa
Banco Nacional
Mangrove
Mangrove

MINAE National Park Office
Gift Shop
Lapa Rio Office
Aerotaxi Alfa Romeo

To Matapalo, Carate & Corcovado

N

100 metres
100 yards

Sleeping
Agua Luna 1
Cabinas Carolinas & Escondido Trex 10
Cabinas Marcelina 2
Cabinas Puerto Jiménez 3

Cabinas Thompson 4
Iguana Iguana 6
La Choza del Manglare 7
Oro Verde 8
Palms 9
Parrot Bay Village 5

Eating
Agua Luna 1
Il Giardino 5

particularly popular with Europeans. As part of the Preciosa Platanares National Wildlife Refuge, plans are underway to develop a turtle project and ensure the protection of the beaches used by olive ridley, hawksbill and green turtles.

Dos Brazos → *Colour map 3, C4.*

Out of town on the way out towards the mainland a road leads after 4 km to Dos Brazos. Local gold mine workings can be visited here by climbing the road that goes uphill beyond the town. In the wet season, the road has puddles the size of small lakes – call ahead for bookings and to enquire about road conditions.

Carate → *Colour map 3, C3.*

From Puerto Jiménez, a dirt road continues for 33 km to Carate, which gives the southernmost road access to the park. The route skims the coastline dipping and rising with the rocky outcrops and crossing a handful of streams that are normally passable in the dry season but rise quickly after rain. If driving, proceed with caution, take local advice and be prepared for delays. There's a clutch of good accommodation in the area which is great for simply relaxing in and equally good for use as a base for short trips to the national park and the surrounding rainforest.

Parque Nacional Corcovado ● ↠ *pp351-355. Colour map 3, C3.*

ⓘ *There are 3 ranger's stations providing access to the Corcovado National Park. San Pedrillo, to the north is reached through Drake from where you need to charter a boat or walk round the headland. Los Patos in the centre of the peninsula is reached from La Palma, accessed by buses travelling from the Pan-American Highway to Puerto Jiménez. The final option is through La Leona to the south, reached from Carate which in turn has road access from Puerto Jiménez. If the budget stretches that far you can get an air taxi from Puerto Jiménez to Carate, San Pedrillo and even La Sirena for as little as US$175 per person with 5 people (just think of the views). If short of time and/or money, the simplest way to the park is to take the pick-up truck from outside Carolina's in Puerto Jiménez to Carate, from where you can go on short treks in the south of the park. Entrance to the park is US$6 paid at the ranger's station.*

For many Corcovado National Park is the most magnificent jewel in the priceless green crown that is Costa Rica. The park protects roughly one third of the Osa Peninsula (42,469 ha). After Monteverde and Arenal, Corcovado National Park is probably the most recorded and researched part of Costa Rica. National Geographic called it "the most biologically intense place on the planet" (as everyone in the region is more than happy to remind you), and the BBC among countless other esteemed naturalists have filmed and written about the delights of the area, and with good reason. Although selectively logged until its creation in 1975, and only finally cleared of gold prospectors in 1985, the national park protects the largest area of humid tropical rainforest in the country.

For wildlife watchers the place is a paradise, for people who want to hike on their own it offers one of the few opportunities in Costa Rica for serious, long-distance treks through lowland rainforest that really stretch your legs. To follow the coastal path from San Pedrino to La Leona will take at least three days – without allowing for extra time spent exploring shorter trails close to La Sirena.

Wildlife

As ever it's the combination of temperatures, in the high 20s, and rainfall, up to 5.5 m annually, that has created eight different lifezones. Cloudforest on some of the higher peaks gives way to montane forest, which covers over half the park. With swamp forest around Corcovado lagoon and mangrove forests along the river estuaries there are over 500 species of tree in the park including the 70-m-high silk cotton or ceiba tree – probably the largest in the country.

Wildlife is equally diverse. Corcovado is home to the largest population of scarlet macaws in the country. All six cats in Costa Rica are found in the park, and the beach to the north at Llorona is used as a nesting site by four species of sea turtles. The wildlife inventory is staggering – 140 species of mammals, 367 of birds, 177 amphibians and reptiles and 40 freshwater fish – but you'll need a guide, patience and a good deal of luck to tick significant numbers off your list.

Trails

About 40 minutes beyond Carate is **La Leona** station. It's about 18 km (six hours) from Carate to Sirena which you can make in one day as long as the tides don't work against you – check with the wardens so you don't get stuck. From La Leona to the end of Playa Madrigal is another 2½-hour walk, part sandy, part rock with some rock pools and rusty shipwrecks looking like modern art sculptures. At points the trail rises steeply into the forest and you are surrounded by mangroves, almonds and coconut palms. A couple of rivers break the beachline. The first, **Río Madrigal**, is only about 15 minutes beyond La Leona. Clear, cool and deep enough for swimming about 200 m upstream, it's a refreshing stop if you're walking out and a good place to spot wildlife.

Parque Nacional Corcovado

The best place for viewing wildlife – although increasingly popular in the dry season – is **La Sirena**, where there are several short trails lasting from 30 minutes to a few hours exploring the network of paths inland and Corcovado lagoon. It's definitely worth staying a couple of nights at La Sirena ranger's station, if time allows. Several visitors to Costa Rica have said that staying here is the highlight of their trip.

From La Sirena you can head inland on a trail to **Los Patos** (20 km, six to nine hours depending on conditions) passing several rivers full of reptiles on the way. The ranger station at Los Patos has a balcony which is a great observation point for birds especially the redheaded woodpecker. From Los Patos you can carry on to the park border, before criss-crossing the Río Rincón to **La Palma**, a settlement on the opposite side of the Peninsula (13 km, six more hours). From La Palma there is transport to Puerto Jiménez.

Alternatively, from La Sirena you can walk north along the coast to **Llorona**, with waterfalls nearby, continuing north on a forest trail and then along the beach to the station at **San Pedrillo** on the edge of the park. You can stay here and eat with the rangers if you've made a reservation.

⊙ Around Puerto Jiménez listings

For Sleeping and Eating price codes and other relevant information, see Essentials, pages 44-47.

⬤ Sleeping

Rincón and La Palma *p347*
Chacarita to Rincón
B pp **Centro Juvenil Tropical**, along the road to Drake, run by Fundación Neotrópica, T2735-5522, in San José on T2253-2130, www.neotropica.org. Probably of only passing interest to ecotourists, if you're a teacher, however, you should go and explore this environmental education centre for Costa Rican kids. Good, simple dormitory accommodation and great access to the rainforest.
AL-A Suital Lodge, 28 km from Pan-American Highway in the elbow of the Peninsula, T2826-0342, www.suital.com. A handful of genuinely rustic, but clean, rooms and bungalows in a wonderfully secluded spot. Good wildlife in the lodge reserve, and options for horse riding, kayaking and other activities.

La Palma
B Albergue Ecoturístico Cerro de Oro, on the road towards Puerto Jiménez, T2290-8646, www.turismoruralcr.com. As part of the Cooprena cooperative, you'll be contributing to the grass-roots economy by staying in 1 of the 6 rooms with shared bath, or the cabins which sleep up to 6 people. A good spot for exploring the Río Rincón and surrounding area. Breakfast included.
AL-A pp **Danta Corcovado Lodge**, 3 km east from La Palma, T2735-1111, www.danta corcovado.net. Simple accommodation, well situated for entrance and exit to Corcovado through Los Patos station.
F Cabinas El Tucán, in La Palma town, simple cabins.

Puerto Jiménez *p347, map p348*
AL-A La Choza del Manglare, T2735-5002, www.manglares.com. 11 clean and well-maintained cabins with private bath, although some a little cramped. Big bar and restaurant area, close to the river. Capuchin monkeys visit for breakfast, scarlet macaws roost in nearby trees and the odd crocodile basks in the grounds by the river.
AL-C Parrot Bay Village, on the beach east of the dock, T2735-5180, www.parrotbay village.com. 7 private *cabinas*, and a couple of houses equipped with private bath and a/c. The beach is barely 30 m from the open-air restaurant. Set in beautiful gardens and with kayaks free for guests to explore nearby coves and the mangroves. Full tours available, and Wi-Fi too. Good for groups and families.

A-B Agua Luna, right in front of you if arriving by ferry, T2735-5393. 14 uninspiring but comfortable recently rooms equipped with TV, telephone, fridge and optional a/c. Good service and fishing tours arranged.

A-C The Palms, beside the soccer pitch, T2735-5012, www.thepalmscostarica.com. Renovated place with rooms in simple accommodation. A good range of tours.

B pp Cabinas Marcelina, T2735-5007, cabmarce@hotmail.com. A good choice, with 8 clean rooms leading to the patio looking out to the garden.

C pp Cabinas Puerto Jiménez, on the gulf shore with great views, T2735-5090, www.cabinasjimenez.com. 10 big, spotless rooms sleeping 2-4 people, with a couple of very well-appointed private bungalows with balcony looking out to the Gulf. Tiki bar and grill on the water's edge, and La Sirena boat for trips in the Gulf. Good spot, now has Wi-Fi.

C Cabinas Carolinas, on the main street behind restaurant, T2735-5696. 15 good rooms, with a/c or fan. Good, central choice.

E Oro Verde, T2735-5241. 10, big and comfortable rooms with bath and fan, some overlooking the street. Friendly efficient service and can arrange tours.

F Iguana Iguana, on the road into town, T2735-5158. Simple rooms with private bath. Has a small bar and swimming pool.

G Cabinas Thompson, T2735-5148. Quiet spot off the main street, dark rooms but essentially clean, with a small patio.

Playa Platanares p348

LL Iguana Lodge, T2735-5205, www.iguanalodge.com. Right on the beach, with luxurious *casitas*, and a villa, built from bamboo and local hardwoods complete with private bath in fine landscaped gardens. Business is booming so they've also taken on the place next door and renamed it Pearl of the Osa – call for details.

A Playa PreciOsa Lodge, T2735-5062, www.playa-preciosa-lodge.de. 4 funky round cabins with a double bed and a couple of singles. The restaurant has a fine panorama overlooking the gulf, and when not eating, you can hang in the hammocks and relax all day. Right on the beach, it's ideal for swimming and surfing.

Dos Brazos p349

L-AL Bosque del Río Tigre, T2735-5725, www.osaadventures.com. A small lodge set in the forest on the Río Tigre on the outskirts of Dos Brazos, with trails nearby. Targetting the traveller looking for a little luxury in the middle of the forest, the rustic and peaceful lodge sleeps a maximum of 10 people. The naturalist owners have quietly built up a reputation for a friendly atmosphere, good food and great guiding (about 300 bird species spotted within a 30-min walking radius of the lodge).

L-AL Río Nuevo Lodge, north of town close to the Dos Brazos turn-off, T2735-5411, www.rionuevolodge.com. Comfortable camping option with just a tent between you and the sounds of the rainforest outside. Meals included so you can stay around and explore local trails.

D Namu Woke, T2265-7475 (owner's sister in Heredia) or just turn up (if the road is good). 6 basic cabins sleeping up to 3 people with private bath. Restaurant serves basic meals.

South to Carate (Matapalo)

Around 17 km from Puerto Jiménez the road rises steeply to pass over Cabo Matapalo. **Osa Tropical**, T2735-5062, osatropical@ice.co.cr, in Puerto Jiménez acts as the booking agents for a number of lodges and cabins in the area. Many are aimed at the self-catering market.

LL Lapa Ríos, T2735-5130, www.laparios. com. A celebrated hotel, with 14 spacious thatched bungalows using hardwoods and bamboo furniture from top to bottom. Each bungalow has a private deck with views to the ocean or rainforest, and a private bathroom with solar-heated shower. Set in 400-ha private rainforest reserve, the open-air restaurant serves divine international cuisine, complete with a full bar providing cooled drinks you can sip from the observation deck with fantastic views. A full range of tours is available and a there's a pool to contemplate the paradise. All this comes at a quite a price, but the guiding principals for this eco-conscious hotel mean that only locals are employed. Too bad such relaxing natural comforts are not available for everyone – if they were, nature conservation would be a far easier nut to crack.

L Bosque el Cabo Rainforest Lodge, T2735-5206, www.bosquedelcabo.com. Whitewashed with terracotta tiles, each of the 10 breezy bungalow and 2 rental houses, has fantastic views out to the Pacific from the idyllic location perched on the cliffs of Cabo Matapalo. Set in beautifully tended gardens – with enough space to think you have the place to yourself – it would be easy to spend the days just lounging in the hammock listening to the sounds of the rainforest as the day slowly passes. But venture from such comforts and you'll find a pool and a fine open-air restaurant serving national and international dishes.

The places listed below are booked and managed by Osa Tropical.

AL pp Encanta la Vida, www.encantala vida.com. A range of options, including 3 thatched roofed cabins, comfortably furnished with tiled floors and hardwood furnishing, or a 4-bedroom, 2-bathroom house and new deluxe cabins. Privacy and seclusion for honeymooners and groups. The price includes 3 meals a day.

C pp Casa Tortuga de Oro, www.costa rica.com/tortuga. Sleeping up to 6 people, with a 2-day minimum stay. Good choice for surfing off Matapalo Point.

Carate *p349*
LL-AL Corcovado Lodge Tent Camp, 30 mins' walk west along the beach, T2257-0766, www.costaricaexpeditions.com. Part of the impressive Costa Rica Expeditions set-up, the camp is a creative and comfortable camping option. If camping isn't your style then you've clearly not seen the 16 walk-in tents, each with a couple of comfortable

camp beds and a small front porch, set in a beautiful coconut grove yards from the beach with the rainforest climbing up the hills nearby. Shared bathrooms are a short walk from the tents. Meals are served in a large thatched roofed dining room, and there's a hammock house for relaxing. As ever, the Costa Rica Expeditions team provide bilingual experts to guide you through their 161-ha private reserve and wildlife canopy viewing platform some 100 ft off the ground. You can follow trails to wonderful views of the bay or you can go on longer treks to and through Corcovado National Park. Multi-day packages available from San José or starting locally. Highly recommended.

LL-AL pp Lookout Inn, T2735-5431, www.lookout-inn.com. A growing array of comfortable tiled-floor rooms complete with bamboo furniture and nature scene murals on the walls have a fine breezy feel, with hot water private bathrooms. Also has *cabinas*, each with bathroom and hot water, large private balconies, hammocks and paths to the beach, pool and house, the secluded Monkey House and the Swing-Inn Cabina. International and local dishes (price includes all meals) naturally incorporate fresh fruit and lots of home cooking served on the rooftop observation platform with spectacular views of the rainforest and the ocean. Also has a swimming pool and spa.

L pp Luna Lodge, close to Carate, T2380-5036, www.lunalodge.com. A retreat for mind and body, complete with spa and yoga. 8 comfortable thatched roof bungalows climbing up the valley of the Carate River, each with a couple of double beds, private bath and a viewing deck. Set in gently landscaped gardens, over half the property is primary rainforest with trails leading to several nearby waterfalls. A fine *rancho* restaurant is the setting for international cuisine, views from the retreat centre are phenomenal. A great spot for mulling over the wonders of days past and yet to come.

AL-A La Leona Ecolodge, T2735-5704, www.laleonalodge.com. More funky, posh camping, with 13 tents, each for 2 people. The main lodge provides dining and relaxing areas, and the whole place is just in front of the black sand beach. Not the smoothest operation in the place, but a good price.

A Carate Jungle Camp, just before town. Has simple cabins and shared showers, meals included.

A pp Terrapin Lodge, T22278-1003, www.terrapinlodge.com. 5 wooden screened cabins, some with ocean views, surrounded by rainforest and powered by solar panels. Dining is in a wooden *cabana* with a bar.

The only 'budget' option available is to camp at the *pulpería* in town run by Gilberto Morales and his wife, who will let you camp for a small fee.

Parque Nacional Corcovado *p349*
F Basic accommodation is available at the ranger's stations in San Pedrillo, Los Patos, La Leona and, the most commonly used, La Sirena. Bring sleeping bag and mosquito net. **Camping** is possible at US$2 a night. Meals used to be available, but check locally and reserve in advance. You should be prepared to carry your own provisions. To get the very latest information contact MINAE office in Puerto Jiménez, T2735-5036. If trekking alone, get topographical maps from the IGM in San José, see page 103.

🍴 Eating

Rincón and La Palma *p347*
Chacarita to Rincón
🍴 **Soda El Puente**, at the southern end of Rincón just before the bridge over the Río Rincón at the junction of the road to Drake Bay. Good, basic dishes, open long hours.

Puerto Jiménez *p347, map p348*
🍴🍴 **Agua Luna**. Linen tablecloths and tiled floors. Overlooking the bay.
🍴🍴 **Il Giardino**. A refreshing addition to the Puerto Jiménez scene, a quiet little open-air

Italian place. Split bamboo walls add a hint of Asian, in keeping with the sushi on the menu.
🍴 **Carolina's**, on the main street. Good and cheap, recommended for fish and as a place to gen up on tour options with the guys at Escondido Trex at the back of the restaurant.
🍴 **Juanita's**, next to Café el Sol. Lively Mexican bar and grill with tasty *fajitas* and refreshing cocktails.

🔺 Activities and tours

La Palma *p351*
Quira Expeditions, T2365-6986. A *Tico*-owned tour operator with trips into Corcovado National Park, to nearby Guaymi Indigenous Reserve, as well as dolphin tours in the Gulf and trips by kayak and mountain bike.

Puerto Jiménez *p347, map p348*
Puerto Jiménez has worked hard to provide a host of adventurous trips to keep you in the place as long as possible – and it works. You could stay here for days trying to do everything. Trips to **Corcovado** can be arranged, and there are a variety of options from day trips to full hiking. Hiking from Los Patos to San Pedrillo, a 5-day trip including transport, meals and equipment, costs around US$450 with Osa Aventura. Cheaper, shorter variations are also available. Rainforest trails take in birdwatching, but for the more adventurous you can try **mountain biking**, **waterfall rappelling**, **horse riding** and even chance your luck with a bit of **gold mining**. Prices for tours range from US$20 up to US$100 for half or full day trips. You can a lso **rent bikes** in town if you want to explore at your own pace, US$10/day. **Kayaking** in the mangrove swamps or out in the Gulf is popular either in the day or at sunset. **Dolphin and whale tours** in the Gulf, with the chance of seeing black-spotted, spinner and bottle-nose dolphins and occasional whales, are also popular. Sticking on the water, you can head round to Matapalo and try a bit of **surfing**.

Tour operators

Escondido Trex, in Carolina's on the main street, T2735-5210, www.escondidotrex.com. Open daily and you'll normally find someone around in the evening. The original tour operators in Puerto Jiménez, they have a full range of tours on the Osa Peninsula and around the Dulce Gulf, know the region very well and have a small book swap.

Everyday Adventures, T8353-8619, www.psychotours.com. Agency with a good reputation for nature hikes, tree climbing and waterfall rapelling. Prices from US$45 upwards. (Don't let the website put you off!)

Osa Aventura, T2735-5670, www.osa aventura.com. Good tours run by the lifelong rainforest fanatic Mike Boston.

Osa Tropical, at the southern end of the main street, T2735-5062, osatropical@ ice.co.cr. Agents for SANSA and NatureAir in Puerto Jiménez. Can organize car rental, taxis and act as booking agents for several secluded and privately owned houses to the south of the peninsula.

MINAE, office facing the airstrip, T2735-5036. If planning to book accommodation in Corcovado National Park you will need to make reservations here.

Surfdog Tours, on main street, www.surf dogtours.com. A US couple with strong attachment to the area provide help with travel, accommodation and tours.

Toucan Travel, on the main street, T2735-5826, www.toucan-travel.com. New, Spanish-run agency in town that can sort travel, accommodation and tours and is getting good reports.

🚍 Transport

Puerto Jiménez *p347, map p348*

Air Daily flights with SANSA, T2735-5017, www.flysansa.com (US$89) and NatureAir, T2735-5062, www.natureair.com (US$120). The airstrip is at the southeastern corner of town. Alongside the airstrip are the offices of **Alfa Romeo Aero Taxi**, T2735-5112, which

provide alternatives to getting to out of the way places including Drake Bay and Carate.

Boat A boat leaves the *muellecito* (small dock) from **Golfito** for Puerto Jiménez at 1120, US$4, 1½ hrs. The ferry leaves Puerto Jiménez at 0600. Alternatively you can charter a boat – US$80 for up to 8 passengers.

Bus From **San José** buses leave the Terminal Atlántico Norte (C 12, Av 9-11) with Autotransportes Blanco Lobo and make the 8 hr journey to **Puerto Jiménez** at 1200, US$7, passing through **San Isidro**, **Buenos Aires**, **Palmar Norte** and **Palmar Sur**. The return bus leaves at 0500. Buses for **Ciudad Neily** leave at 0530 and 1400, 3 hrs, US$3.30. There's a café by the bus stop where you can get a good, cheap breakfast (opens at 0430).

A couple of *colectivos* depart daily for **Carate** from Soda Thompson at 0600 and 1330, returning at 0830 and 1600, US$8. Services may be restricted in the wet season. Transport services are also provided by many tour operators.

Car Leave the Pan-American Highway at Chacarita, 33 km south of Palmar Norte. The road is paved to Rincón – although there are some precipitous drops and horrendous potholes – and a fairly good gravel road for the remaining distance.

🅸 Directory

Puerto Jiménez *p347, map p348*
Banks There's a branch of Banco Nacional in town. **Internet** Café el Sol. **Post office** At the northern end of town opposite the football pitch. **Medical services** Emergency: T911. Red Cross, beside the football pitch. **Useful addresses** Police station is at the northern end of town on the main street. www.soldeosa.com is a source of Osa-related online news that has taken a few tentative early steps.

Golfito and the beaches

Tiny in comparison to the Golfo Dulce, the diminutive Golfito built its success on the long and sheltered bay that lines the town. These perfect conditions saw the town flourish as a major banana exporting port when the United Fruit Company set up operations in the 1930s. Bust followed boom and the company pulled out in 1985 leaving behind the skeletal remains of a once-prosperous town. Golfito (population 15,157), stretched long and thin between the coastline to the west and steep, forested hills to the east, still seems a little on the skinny side. With bare bones showing, it's difficult to warm to the place and you'll probably be just passing through to get somewhere else – the Osa Peninsula, northern beach resorts or Playa Zancudo and Pavones to the south. The affluence and services that do remain owe their success to the tax free zone or depósito libre set up in 1990. Ticos and resident expats travel half way across the country to get items at about 60% of prices in the capital – what a bargain! ▶▶ *For listings, see pages 359-362.*

Ins and outs ▶▶ *Colour map 3, C4.*

Getting there

Daily flights from San José with **SANSA** (US$89) and **NatureAir** (US$117) arrive on the airstrip at the northern end of town. If driving, the paved Highway 14 leaves the Pan-American Highway at Río Claro, 15 km north of Ciudad Neily. A daily bus service plies the Pan-American Highway from San José, with a more regular service between nearby Ciudad Neily. If you're out on the Peninsula at Puerto Jiménez you can catch a ferry across the Gulf. ▶▶ *See Transport, page 362, for further details.*

Golfito

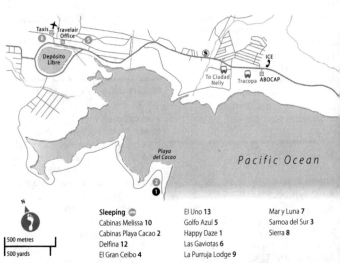

Sleeping 😴
Cabinas Melissa **10**
Cabinas Playa Cacao **2**
Delfina **12**
El Gran Ceibo **4**

El Uno **13**
Golfo Azul **5**
Happy Daze **1**
Las Gaviotas **6**
La Purruja Lodge **9**

Mar y Luna **7**
Samoa del Sur **3**
Sierra **8**

Getting around

Moving around Golfito without your own transport is tedious. It's almost 6 km from the first hotel on the sea front to the *depósito libre* and once you've done the journey you'll wonder why you did. Thankfully there's a local bus that commutes the main drag in a hail and ride system. Beyond that, taxis are readily available.

Golfito and around ›› *Colour map 3, C4.*

The United Fruit Company history of the town has left a distinctive mark on Golfito, which is strung out along the shore in clusters. Arriving from the south, you encounter a few of the better hotels in the area. Further north the administrative centre of the town, complete with rusting locomotive and a statue in weary tribute to a banana labourer, has a few old clapboard hotels. At the northernmost point, a few old management buildings of the United Fruit Company create a sense of elevated grace completely overshadowed by the gaudy nature of the rush to buy domestic appliances and Hi-Fi systems at the *depósito libre*.

Trips from Golfito

The steep slopes to the east of Golfito and the northern peninsula constitute the 1309-ha **Refugio Nacional de Fauna Silvestre Golfito** (Golfito National Wildlife Refuge) ① *book through Land Sea Tours, T2775-1614, entrance US$5 including a 3-hr tour, open Sun-Thu.* Created to protect Golfito's watershed, the tall evergreen forest receives heavy rainfall and is rich in rare, medicinal plants. Bird and mammal residents in the refuge include jaguar, coatis and peccaries but in reality, research in the refuge has been limited to date

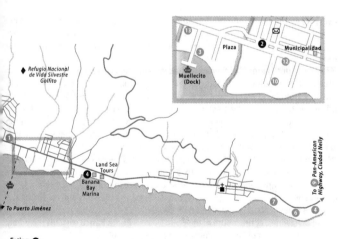

Eating 🍴
Bilge Bar **4**
Cubana **2**
La Eurekita **3**
Siete Mares **1**

and services are non-existent. On the positive side, this makes it a great place for surprises. Treks can be organized through **Land Sea Tours** (see page 361).

Thirty minutes by water taxi from Golfito at Playa San Josecito, you can visit **Casa Orquídeas** ① *T2829-1247*, a family-owned botanical garden with a large collection of herbs, orchids and local flowers and trees and an entertaining 2½-hour tour that explains all about the various edible, medicinal and ornamental plants and given you the chance to smell, touch and taste your way through the gardens.

Further north, **kayak** tours to the mouth of the **Río Esquinas** explore the mangroves and provide ideal conditions to see monkeys, dolphins, freshwater and sea turtles, and caiman. Trips also run south of the bay to the mouth of the **Río Coto Colorado**.

For serious **deep-sea fishing**, you're best off heading south to Playa Zancudo (see below) and making plans with the lodges there, but trips can be booked through **Banana Bay Marina**, see page 361.

Beaches north of Golfito

Golfito has little to offer in the way of beaches and genuine relaxation, but across the bay at **Playa del Cacao**, and just outside the bay on beaches to the north of Golfito, there are a number of small bays that break the line of rocky outcrops that make up this part of the coastline. While trips to the beaches can easily be arranged from Golfito, most are only visited by people staying in lodges nearby. It's just a small strip of sand but worth a visit if you are in town and need a few hours sun or sea. You can pop over on a taxi boat from Golfito or, road conditions permitting, follow the bay round in a 4WD. Beyond Playa de Cacao, the next beach north – and outside the protected bay is **Playa San Josecito**. A couple of activity jungle retreats occupy the rocky bay.

Beach south of Golfito

Leaving the bay of Golfito and heading south you cross the mangrove estuary of the Río Coto Colorado and eventually arrive in **Playa Zancudo**, with not only some fine beaches but great sports fishing facilties (the best in the country). Try www.zancudotimes.com for the latest updates.

Arriving at dusk along the overland route that meanders through endless groves of African palm, the setting sun shoots golden beams through the jauntily angled coconut palms that both blind and hypnotize simultaneously. For beach lovers Zancudo has a captivating charm that has attracted a mixed bag of expats who have created a fine balance of laid-back comforts while avoiding any complicated trappings. For fishing junkies, you probably won't mind which of the two top-notch fishing lodges you choose to take you to the deep waters which offer up world-record sized fish.

Moving further south, the sleepy little surf village of **Pavones** is growing quickly as surfers arrive in droves to ride the country's longest left-hander. The main activity in the area is surfing – trips can be arranged with Happy Daze in Golfito – but fishing, horse riding and hiking to waterfalls in the area can easily be arranged through local hotels. If you want a quiet beach, Zancudo is a better choice.

South of Pavones, at the mouth of the Golfo Dulce is **Punta Banco** with the incredibly remote tropical retreat of **Tiskita Jungle Lodge**, see page 361.

For Sleeping and Eating price codes and other relevant information, see Essentials, pages 44-47.

● Sleeping

Golfito *p356, map p356*

Hotels in the area don't exactly bend over backwards to win business – people visiting the town are here for the discounted goods. Although there are a couple of exceptions, don't expect too much in the way of service.

AL Samoa del Sur, T2775-0233, www.samoadelsur.com. Popular international choice, with waterfront rooms, and every imagineable entertainment.

AL Sierra, T2775-0666, www.hotelsierra.com. 72 double rooms with a/c, a couple of pools and a restaurant. Rooms are better than the place looks from the outside, but it's still overpriced.

A Las Gaviotas, T2775-0062, www.c-tales.com. One of the better places in town, it has 21 tidy cabins and rooms strung out along the waterfront, all with TV, telephone, fridge and safe box. Fine pool with sundeck and an open-air restaurant serving dishes (🍴🍴) and a bar to keep you entertained day and night.

B-D El Gran Ceibo, arriving at the coastline the first place in town, T2775-0403, www.hotel-elgranceibo.com. Reasonable rooms, some with a/c, some with TV, and cold water private bath. There is a small pool.

C Golfo Azul, T2775-0871. 20 comfortable and homely rooms with private bath, a/c and cable TV. Breakfast included.

C La Purruja Lodge, on the road to Golfito, 4 km before the coastal strip, T2775-1054, www.purruja.com. 5 simple duplex cabins with bath. There's also a small outhouse with a couple of hammocks, a restaurant, pool table, darts board and safe parking.

C-D Mar y Luna, T2775-0192. 8 good rooms sleeping 2-4, with bath and fan. Unassuming and simple, the restaurant sits on stilts above the sea. Quiet, friendly spot – a good deal.

D Cabinas Melissa, behind Delfina, T2775-0043. 4 simple, clean and tidy rooms, with private bath and small terrace with views of the bay and safe parking. A great bargain, although service varies.

E Happy Daze, T2775-0058, www.happydazecostarica.com. Basic, clean rooms, a good stepping stone for surfing trips further afield.

E-F Delfina, T2775-1274. Basic rooms with fans. Rooms with a private bath are much better, and rooms on the street can be noisy. Parking available.

G El Uno, above the restaurant of the same name, T2775-0061. Very basic, in a clapboard house from the 1940s. That said, it is friendly and probably the cheapest place in Costa Rica.

Beaches north of Golfito *p358*
Playa de Cacao
B Cabinas Playa Cacao, T2382-1593. 6 bright, conical thatched huts complete with hot water baths, fridge, kitchenette, hammocks and fan. Fine views across the bay in a wonderfully quiet and secluded spot. A good location for exploring other places in the area. In the same bay is the popular **Siete Mares**, a good, cheap restaurant.

Playa San Josecito
L-AL Golfo Dulce Lodge, T8821-5398, www.golfodulcelodge.com. Set in 300 ha of private reserve bordering the Piedras Blancas National Park. 5 spacious wooden bungalows, with fan and sun-heated water in the private bathrooms, each sleeping 3 people. There are also 3 rooms. Everyone gets a private veranda with hammock and rocking chair. European meals served in the thatched restaurant. An observation platform and self-guided tour are close and local tours easily arranged.

AL-B Dolphin Quest, T2382-8630, www.dolphinquestcostarica.com. A secluded rainforest retreat, with *cabinas*, thatched roof *ranchitos*, a room, dormitory lodgings and camping. Set in 280 ha of mountainous rainforest, with trails and waterfalls nearby.

A huge range of land- and sea-based activities and volunteer opportunities available.

Playa Cativo

LL Playa Nicuesa Lodge, between Casa Orchideas and Rainbow Lodge, T2735-5237, www.nicuesalodge.com. Eco-lodge with 4 cabins and 4 rooms in the main guesthouse all on the fringe of Piedras Blancas National Park. Wide range of activities on the Gulf or in the rainforest.

Beaches south of Golfito p358
Playa Zancudo

For anglers Most people staying at these lodges are on part of a fishing package.
LL Golfito Sportfishing, T2776-0007, www.costaricafishing.com. 8 screened cabins with a/c and tiled bathrooms in comfortable gardens backing on to the Río Coto Colorado so when you're not fishing out in the bay, you can drop a line out back.
AL-A The Zancudo Lodge, a short distance further south, T2776-0008, www.thezancudo lodge.com. 4 comfortable suites and 20 rooms, all with a/c and private bath, set around a floodlit swimming pool in pleasant gardens dotted with palms. Fine bar and restaurant serving all-you-can-eat meals. Plenty of stuffed fish just in case the fishing yarns are lacking – which is highly unlikely given that the lodge's guests have held over 60 fishing world records.
For the rest AL-A Oasis on the Beach, T2776-0087, www.oasisonthebeach.com. 3 cabins and a couple of rooms in a two-story villa. The spacious accommodation has a/c, private bath and the beautifully maintained cabins have fridge, microwave and coffee machine. Spectacular views from the rooms and restaurant look out to the beach. Good restaurant serves an extensive international menu. Tours available including horse riding through the forest to secluded beaches.
A-B Los Cocos, T2776-0012, www.loscocos. com. A handful of cabins – some of which were originally for banana plantation workers – with kitchen, decks with hammocks and big

'windows' to let the ocean breeze cool. On the beachfront, it's a very laid-back choice ideal for privacy. Bikes, boogie boards and beach chairs free for guests, kayaks available for rent. Andrew and Susan also run Zancudo Boat Tours with a taxi service to Golfito and local boat tours. Recommended.
B-C Coloso Del Mar, T2776-0050, www. coloso-del-mar.com. 4 all-wood cabins in a great little spot just a few metres from the beach. A big *rancho* in the beachfront garden serves local and Caribbean dishes and is ideal for watching the sun go down. Also has a house for long-term rentals.
B-C Sol y Mar, T2776-0014, www.zancudo. com. The 4 screened cabins, complete with private bath, and 3-story rental house are comfortable and relaxing. The restaurant serves meals from 0700 until 2200. The place is the activity centre of Zancudo. The beachfront is littered with sports equipment, the bar is the focus point of nightly gatherings and there's a gentle energy bubbling through the place. Free Wi-Fi. Highly recommended.
F Hotel Pitier, a cheap *Tico*-owned place in town, has some simple rooms.

Pavones

AL-B Cabinas La Ponderosa, T8824-4145, www.cabinaslaponderosa.com. Large cabins with a variety of options and comforts, including private bath and fan, owned by a couple of surfers. Fishing, diving and, naturally enough, surfing.
C Mira Olas, T2776-2006 www.miraolas. com. A handful of cabins with private bath and use of the kitchen. A pleasant jungle setting with good access to beach.
C Cabinas Willy, town centre across from the football field. Has clean rooms and private bath.
E Cabinas Mendoza, town centre. 4 rooms, cold water and shared kitchen.
E Esquina del Mar, town centre, above the lively bar, T2368-6920. Watch the magnificent left-hander out at sea from here.
F Cabinas Carol. Basic rooms with shared bathrooms.

Punta Banco

LL Tiskita Jungle Lodge, normally reached by chartered plane to the private airstrip, T2296-8125, www.tiskita-lodge.co.cr. A collection of 16 cabins and rooms set in 223 ha of private biological reserve. The ultimate escape-from-it-all lodge in Costa Rica, you can go no further south – in this country at least. Cabins have broad balconies and quite spectacular natural bathrooms. Hearty dishes using the freshest fruit and produce are served in the open-air restaurant. Activities include natural tide pools, trails leading through the nearby primary and secondary rainforest – and a home-made table-tennis table. Trips head further afield to Corcovado National Park and Sirena across the Gulf.

🍴 Eating

Golfito *p356, map p356*
♦♦-♦ Bilge Bar, in Banana Bay Marina, open 0700-2100. Good American, European and *Tico* food in the waterfront restaurant.
♦ Buenos Días, in the centre of town, T2775-1124. A great way to start your day, fine, cheap, fast food *Tico* style.
♦ Cubana, near the post office. Excellent local dishes at seriously cheap prices.
♦ Delfina Restaurant, in the centre. Cheap breakfasts from 0700, snacks and home-baked goods.
♦ El Uno. Serves good seafood.
♦ La Eurekita, a popular cheap place with locals in the centre serving a mean breakfast of *huevos rancheros* (fried or scrambled eggs served with chopped tomato, and a good place to watch the world go by.

Beaches South of Golfito *p358*
Playa Zancudo
♦♦ La Puerta Negra. Top-notch Italian dishes using fresh seafood.
♦♦ Macondo. Popular Italian restaurant.

♦ Bar y Restaurant Tranquilo. Lively, open-air spot between Oasis by the Beach and Coloso Del Mar.

Pavones
♦ Café de la Suerte, by the soccer field. A popular place to hang out with great baguettes and smoothies.
♦ Doña Dora. Cheap, traditional *Tico* fare.
♦ Esquina del Mar. Serves snacks through the day, beer at night.
♦ McRonalds, in the cantina on the beach side of the football field. More of the same.

🛍 Shopping

Pavones *p358*
Arte Nativo, T2383-6939, tomello@racsa. co.cr. A craft shop selling locally produced art with the eventual aim of creating art workshops. The owner Candyce Speck is the main communication link with the outside world, and a good source of information.
Sea Kings sells and rents everything surf related you could possibly need.

🏃 Activities and tours

Golfito *p356, map p356*
Banana Bay Marina, T2775-0838, www.bananabaymarina.com. Primarily marina service, but also sort out sports fishing and travel in and beyond Costa Rica.
Land Sea Tours, to the south of the centre of town, T2775-1614, www.marinaservices-yachtdelivery.com. Mon-Fri 0730-0500, Sat 0800-1300. Whether you're looking for local information, to organize a personalized local tour, book accommodation in some distant hideaway, marina services, to rent a car or arrange national or international flights, Tim and Katie and their team provide a one-stop shop. If you needed any other reason to drop by they also have a good book swap, internet service and fresh coffee permanently on the go.

Beaches South of Golfito p358
Playa Zancudo
Sportfishing Unlimited, T2776-0036, www.sportfishing.co.cr. Prices vary depending on the package, but a 5-day round trip from San José with 3 days fishing, accommodation, food, drinks and equipment included will set you back around US$2670 per person. Get a group together and prices fall considerably.

Zancudo Boat Tours run by Andrew Robertson at Los Cocos, has tours down the Río Coto Colorado behind town, and to Casa Orquídeas north of Golfito. US$45 for a 4-hr tour. They'll also take you to Golfito (US$20 per person, US$50 minimum) or to Puerto Jiménez for US$15 per person, US$60 minimum. No service down to Pavones – the big waves make the landing too hairy.

⊙ Transport

Golfito p356, map p356
Air Several daily flights, mostly in the morning, with SANSA and NatureAir (local agent **Land Sea Tours**, T2775-1614), also via **Coto 47** or **Puerto Jiménez**. The landing is reported to be a little on the tight side between the trees.

Boat A ferry (locally called *la lancha*) makes the 1½ hr journey across the Dulce Gulf to **Puerto Jiménez** leaving the *muellecito* (small dock) beside Restaurante El Uno at 1120, returning at 0600, US$4. There is also a launch service to **Playa Zancudo** leaving around noon, 40 mins, US$4 – check time at Land Sea Tours or the *muellicito*.

For boat journeys further afield ABOCAP (Asociación de Boteros), T2775-0712, opposite the ICE building, provide water taxis in and around Golfito. To **Puerto Jiménez** it's about US$80 for up to 6 people; US$45 to **Playa Zancudo**. Make enquiries for other destinations. **Froylan Lopex**, another water taxi, T2824-6571.

Bus Services to **San José** with **Tracopa**, T2775-0365, leave the capital from Terminal Alfaro at Av 5, C 14, at 0700 and 1500 (7 hrs), returning at 0500 and 1300, US$6.10. Buses travel down the Pan-American Highway through **San Isidro**. Alternatively, take any bus heading south, alighting at the junction at **Río Clara**. Hourly buses travel to and from **Ciudad Neily** and **Paso Canoas**, US$1.

Beaches south of Golfito p358
Playa Zancudo
The best way to town is by **boat**. Public service at noon from the *muellecito*, 40 mins, US$4. Private service provided by **Zancudo Boat Tours**, T2776-0012, US$15 per person, minimum US$40. **Land Sea Tours** in Golfito, T2775-0838, also arrange transport from town.

It is possible to **drive** to Zancudo from Paso Canoas, or by cutting through on the Golfito/Río Claro road 10 km from the Pan-American Highway, turning left at Bar El Rodeo and catching the ferry across the Río Coto Colorado. Either way be prepared to get lost as signposts are poorly marked.

A **bus** leaves **Golfito** for **Zancudo** at 1400, 3 hrs. Transport to **Pavones** can be arranged locally, US$50 for two.

Pavones
Driving is possible, but a **water taxi** from Golfito is eminently more convenient. A **bus** leaves **Golfito** for Pavones at 1400, returning at 0500, 3hrs, US$1.60.

⊙ Directory

Golfito p356, map p356
Banks Banco Nacional will change TCs, although the service can be slow. **Internet** Internet service at Golfito On Line in centre of town. Good machines with a/c, open 0800-2100 daily. Also a machine at Land Sea Travel. **Post office** In centre of town beside the football pitch. **Telephone** ICE office further up the street opposite the small dock.

Contents

366 Highway 32 to
Puerto Limón
366 Ins and outs
366 Heading west to
Puerto Limón
369 Puerto Limón
370 Listings

375 North Caribbean
375 Ins and outs
375 Parque Nacional
Tortuguero
380 Coast north and
south of Toruguero
381 Listings

386 South Caribbean
386 Ins and outs
386 South to Cahuita
387 Cahuita
390 South of Cahuita
394 Listings

Footprint features

364 Don't miss …
367 Costa Rican bananas,
a fair-trade cop
377 Independent travelling
to Tortuguero
378 A greener turtle harvest?
387 Raptor Watch – an aerial
freeway
392 Tough times in
the Talamancas
393 Riptides rumble
Russian reformer

Caribbean Lowlands

At a glance

◉ **Getting around** Driving in the region is easy by private vehicle and regular buses provide links up and down the coastal highway. Opportunities for moving inland are limited. North of Limón is a maze of banana plantations and waterways. Independent travel on boats is also possible.

◉ **Time required** Spend 3 or 4 days in Tortuguero, and then a few days at one of the beach towns in the south.

◉ **Weather** Temperatures are in the upper 20s for most of the year. Rainfall varies slightly from the Pacific coast, with rain throughout the year, but at its lightest in Feb, and Mar and Aug-Oct. Annual rainfall varies from 3-6 m, falling most heavily in the north.

★ **Don't miss ...**
1 Parque Nacional Tortuguero, page 375.
2 Cahuita, page 387.
3 Raptors, page 387.
4 Puerto Viejo de Talamanca, page 390.
5 Refugio Nacional de Vida Silvestre Gandoca-Manzanillo, page 392.

N

10 km
10 miles

Barra del Colorado

Caño Bravo

Isla Brava

Refugio Nacional de Fauna Silvestre Barra del Colorado

Llanura de Tortugueri

Co Tortuguero (119m)

① Tortuguero

Parque Nacional Tortuguero

Caribbean Sea

Cariari

LIMON

Llanura de Santa Clara

Parismina

Parismina

Guápiles

Guácimo

Pacuare

Siquirres

Matina

③ Barra de Matina Norte

Parque Nacional Vol Turrialba

Monumento Nacional Guayabo

Pacuare

Pavones

La Suiza

Parque Nacional Barbilla

Moín Puerto Limón

Isla Uvita

CARTAGO

Bananito Sur

Cerro Muchilla (911m)

Co Matama (2251m)

Penshurst

Parque Nacional Cahuita

Parque Nacional Tapanti Matizco de la Muerte

Atlántico

Estrella

Finca 2

La Estrella

Punta Caliente

② Cahuita

Playa Negra

Puerto Viejo de Talamanca

Chirripó

Reserva Biológica Hitoy Cerere

Hitoy Cerere Research Station

Bribrí

④

Cordillera de Talamanca

Pacuare

Co La Muerte (349m)

Co Urán (3333m)

Parque Nacional Chirripó

Co Durika (3280m)

Telire

Shiroles

Chase

Manzanillo

Pta Uva

Refugio Nacional de Vida Silvestre Gandoca-Manzanillo

⑤ Gandoc

División

Herradura

Co Chirripó (3820m)

Bratsi

Yorkin

Aralón

Canaán

San Isidro de El General

S Gerardo de Rivas

Co Amo

Co Ami (3295m)

Mata de Limón

Guabito

Sta Elena

Palmares

Reserva de la Biosfera La Amistad

PANAMA

Platarillo

General

Ujarrás

Uvita

Buenos Aires

Valle de El General

At times the Caribbean Lowlands of Costa Rica are like a different country. The cultural links with the *Ticos* of the Central Highlands and the Pacific are as minimal as the single road that now links the two regions. The area was closed to the rest of the country until the opening of the railroads in the 1890s and only creeping roads, electrification and telecommunication lines have slowly opened up the region to visitors.

Bananas (still the main source of employment round here) replace coffee as the temperature rises and the climate gets wetter. The Latino lifestyle gives way to Caribbean culture, the marimba is replaced by reggae, and the casaba is pushed out by the coconut as the rivers run steadily to the coast. Friendly informality is preferred over quiet courtesies – you will find the Caribbean *Tico* distinctly laid back compared with his western, highland compatriot.

After the chaotic charms of Puerto Limón, the northern lowlands of Tortuguero are a nature lover's paradise, remote and cut off, even from Limón. (Access is by the canal that was originally built for the transportation and export of bananas.) South of the city, beautiful beaches line the coast, with the settlements of Cahuita and Puerto Viejo drawing visitors into the relaxed atmosphere.

Highway 32 to Puerto Limón

From the misty ridges and peaks of the Braulio Carrillo National Park and beyond the rainforest aerial tram (see page 140), Highway 32 continues east along the flat lowlands towards Puerto Limón. The road is straight and the scenery has just a smattering of interest on a clear day with the profiles of Irazú and Turrialba breaking the skyline to the south. Just north of the main highway, the banana towns of Guápiles, Guácimo and Siquirres are hardly inspiring. As you head east, all this inactivity simply provides you with more time to contemplate the differences between the regions. Places of interest are dotted along the road, and outside the main towns, accommodation options require a vehicle – or energetic legs. ➤➤ *For listings, see pages 370-374.*

Ins and outs

Getting there and away
There are seasonal flights to Puerto Limón three days a week. From the Central Highlands, the main route to the Caribbean Lowlands follows Highway 32 from San José through Braulio Carrillo National Park and then directly east to Limón. Alternative routes join Highway 32 swinging round the northern flanks of Barva Volcano through Puerto Viejo de Sarapiquí, and from the south through Turrialba joining the highway at Siquirres. From Limón Highway 36 hugs the coastline heading south as far as Manzanillo. Regular buses from San José, some of which stop at the towns along the way, arrive and depart from Terminal Caribeño in Puerto Limón, a few blocks west of the centre. ➤➤ *For further details, see Transport, page 374.*

Getting around
Puerto Limón is small enough to walk round. But the beaches north of town and the docks at Moín for Tortuguero require transport. Regular buses leave from behind the cathedral for Moín and taxis cruise the streets looking for business. Only go with an official taxi – red with yellow triangle on the door – get a price before travelling and get the driver to use a meter.

Best time to visit
Allowing for seasonal variations, Carnival, culminating on October 12, is the best time of year to be in Puerto Limón.

Security
Limón has a history of causing problems for visitors. While care and sensible precautions should keep you out of most difficult situations, there is a 24-hour police booth on the main square if you have difficulties or undue hassle.

Heading west to Puerto Limón ⊖❼◷▲⊖ ➤➤ *pp370-374. Colour map 2, B4.*

West of Guápiles
On Highway 32, 6 km after the junction at Santa Clara which heads north to Puerto Viejo de Sarapiquí, **Río Danta Restaurant and Reserve** ⓘ *T2293-8181, www.grupo mawamba.com, US$4 for the trail,* is part of Grupo Mawamba, which also owns a lodge in Tortuguero. The 8-ha reserve is a fairly recent acquisition for the group and is currently a stopover for all-inclusive trips travelling to Tortuguero. If you want to stop, there are good birding trails pushing up to Braulio Carrillo National Park.

Costa Rican bananas, a fair-trade cop

Next time you're in the supermarket, look at the sticker on the label of the bananas and there's a one in five chance that they came from Costa Rica, the second largest exporter of bananas in the world. Bananas are the country's main agricultural export, earning it US$674 million in 2007 for exports of two million tonnes – this despite a drop in the price of bananas (in real terms) by 35% in the last 15 years – a fall in price that has, naturally, not been reflected in supermarkets.

Ever since Minor C Keith founded the United Fruit Company at the turn of the 19th century and began growing bananas to pay for railroad expansion, Costa Rica's fortunes have been linked with the fruit.

Since those early days the industry has been in the hands of US-based international companies. The United Fruit Company has expanded and grown to become Chiquita, while the Standard Fruit Company is now commonly known as Dole. More recently Del Monte has also become a significant exporter. All of them have been accused of poor working conditions, confrontational labour relations, job insecurity and falling wages. But while workers fought to improve conditions, bureaucrats were meddling with the industry and trade lawyers on both sides of the Atlantic were having a field day.

In 1993 the creation of a single market in the European Union created a limit on imports of 'dollar' bananas from Latin America, in favour of producers with whom the EU has historical ties. The majority of bananas grown in Latin America are sold by Dole, Chiquita and Del Monte, and the cheapest come from the world's largest producer, Ecuador. The World Trade Organisation, formed in 1995, set out to liberalize and promote international free trade. Blocked from European markets Chiquita pressurized the US to take the EU to the World Trade Organisation for contravening the rules of international trade.

After a ruling against the EU and US$200 million in economic sanctions, the trade dispute in effect ended in July of 2001 after the EU came to an agreement with the US and Ecuador.

According to the National Chamber of Independent Banana Producers in Costa Rica, the cost of liberalizing and promoting international free trade in the industry in Costa Rica will be paid by finding a balance between the wages of labourers in Costa Rica and Ecuador. The hard fought-for minimum wage in Costa Rica is US$240 a month, while workers in Ecuador receive just US$90 a month – even though the official minimum wage is US$170.

The implications of the new regime are uncertain but the outcome looks bleak for independent producers. In 1999 and 2000 dozens had their contracts cancelled by multinationals. Then in 2001 the multinationals further reduced the price paid to Costa Rican growers.

It is still difficult to assess the implications of the global restructuring of the industry on Costa Rica specifically. The national response was to increase productivity to remain competitive. One thing is certain – the cost of liberalizing and promoting inte-national free trade will be met in the plantations.

Can you make a difference? Yes, as one UK newspaper put it, "Change the world with your shopping trolley". Buy fair trade bananas, buy fair trade coffee and everything else fair trade for that matter.

Guápiles → *Colour map 2, B4.*

A regional transport hub for travel to the network of banana plantations to the north, Guápiles (district population 19,686) is a lively centre but with little of specific interest for the visitor. The most budget-minded travellers stop here en route to Cariari, then take the GEEST Casa Verde or the La Pavona bus from where a regular morning boat makes the journey to Tortuguero village.

Guácimo → *Colour map 2, B4.*

Heading east for 12 km leads to Guácimo where rail and road merged at this once important town, with about 10,000 people in the surrounding district. Nearby is **EARTH** (Escuela de Agricultura de la Región Tropical Húmeda) ① *T2713-0000 ext 5006, www.earth.ac.cr.* This private international school with a natty acronym title receives graduates specializing in tropical agriculture from throughout Latin America.

Siquirres → *Colour map 2, B4.*

You'll be getting the idea by now when, after another 25 km, Siquirres (district population 29,781) marks another banana town. The largest town along the lowland section of Highway 32, and almost half way, it also marks the junction with the old Pacific Highway joining from the south and the route of the Pacific railroad.

Not normally a stopping point, you can nevertheless tour **La Esperanza Banana Plantation** ① *Banana Tours T2768-8683, www.bananatourcostarica.com, aimed primarily at groups, walk-ins are possible in high season on Thu and Sat, US$15 per person,* which exports Dole bananas, seeing the process from harvesting to packing. There is also talk of the introduction of the banana train from Siquirres to Matina.

Nearby is **Parque Nacional Barbilla** ① *T2768-8603,* with 11,944 ha of humid and premontane tropical forest. Created in 1982, the park has crept silently through the national park system. Services are beginning to open up with a couple of short trails.

For the car crazy, Siquirres is the access town for the closest point by car to Tortuguero. The route, according to residents of Tortuguero, is as follows: head north through Carmen and Maryland for 37 km to Caño Blanco marina where you can catch a boat to Tortuguero, and safely park your vehicle while you're away.

Matina → *Colour map 2, B5.*

Last stop on the banana train line before the coast is Matina, 26 km east of Siquirres, a short distance north of Highway 32 at the junction known locally as 'techo rojo'. Around 7000 people in the surrounding area, and Matina still has the air of a small town with the train station as the focal point of activity. Most all-inclusive trips to Tortuguero pass through, travelling to the docks before heading north through the canals.

A few kilometres east of Matina is the 800-ha **Pacuare Nature Reserve** ① *www.rainforestconcern.org, for volunteer work contact Carlos Fernandez, Av 10, C 21, No 1065, fdezlaw@racsa.co.cr. Minimum stay one week. Accommodation at the reserve is AL per person, including transport to the lodge and three meals. Book through Conselva in San José, T2253-8118, conselva@racsa.co.cr.* This privately owned reserve, run in conjunction with Rainforest Concern, protects the nesting sites of marine turtles: leatherbacks nest from March to June, with the green turtle arriving between June and August. Accommodation is available for volunteers in a fine lodge complete with balcony. Away from the beach, the reserve is a quiet and secluded spot for birdwatching and exploring nearby waterways.

Puerto Limón ⊖⊙⊙⊛⊙▲⊙⊙ ⇨ pp371-374. Colour map 2, B6.

Arriving in Puerto Limón (population 61,494), you can instantly feel the difference in atmosphere and it isn't just the high humidity or almost-daily rains. A rocky outcrop in a generally featureless coastline, Limón has born the brunt of its geographical prominence. With fortunes rising and falling, Limón had, and still has, all the problems and nefarious energy associated with the transient populations of port towns worldwide. Columbus dropped anchor on Isla Uvita off the coast and later waves of labourers arrived from the Caribbean and China to work on the railroads. They created a unique cultural diversity and a ready labour supply for the banana plantations and burgeoning eastern port. For most the town is tolerated at best and visited only in passing – if driving, you don't even have to do that if you are heading for the south Caribbean. But for all this negative talk, on the right day and with the right attitude, Limón is a refreshing change and a challenge. The town may care little for the tourist but it's a rare chance to slip into community life without being pampered for your precious tourist dollars – unless you arrive for carnival (see page 373).

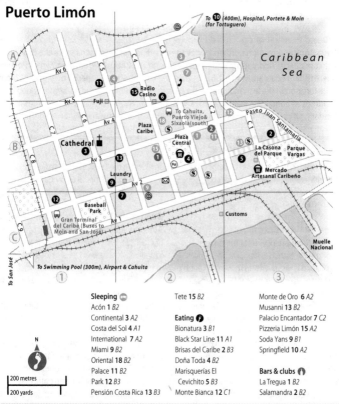

Puerto Limón

Sleeping
Acón 1 *B2*
Continental 3 *A2*
Costa del Sol 4 *A1*
International 7 *A2*
Miami 9 *B2*
Oriental 18 *B2*
Palace 11 *B2*
Park 12 *B3*
Pensión Costa Rica 13 *B3*

Tete 15 *B2*

Eating
Bionatura 3 *B1*
Black Star Line 11 *A1*
Brisas del Caribe 2 *B3*
Doña Toda 4 *B2*
Marisquerías El
  Cevichito 5 *B3*
Monte Bianca 12 *C1*

Monte de Oro 6 *A2*
Musanni 13 *B2*
Palacio Encantador 7 *C2*
Pizzeria Limón 15 *A2*
Soda Yans 9 *B1*
Springfield 10 *A2*

Bars & clubs
La Tregua 1 *B2*
Salamandra 2 *B2*

N

200 metres
200 yards

Sights

Parque Vargas is a tired old park of straggling palms and plants that barely muster up a rustle when a coastal breeze rolls in. Sadly run-down, a colourful mural depicts the town's turbulent history and woeful neglect while a peeling-paint pagoda stands waiting for the band that seems never to arrive. Craning the neck upwards through the trees, you may see the sloths that are said to meander their way through the upper reaches – but then that could be a town-wide joke at the expense of tourists. A promenade looks out to Isla Uvita where Columbus dropped anchor and you can't help thinking: why did he bother?

South of the park, the **docks** are busy with cargo vessels and international crews making regular journeys, as well as the pristine floating palaces that cruise the Caribbean.

The **central market** is the main focus of activity, with most Limeños drifting through the plaza several times a day. **Casa de Cultura** ① *Av 3, C3-4, opposite Plaza Central,* has occasional displays on local history and art exhibitions.

It's all rather boring, unless you happen to roll up when a drumming band is practising in the street. Three dozen young men will appear in their finest bandannas and crisp ironed shirts, a small crowd will join in and an impromptu street party kicks off. Even the trees seem to perk up and, refreshed by the vibrancy, the dreary cloud dissolves, replaced instead by the optimistic glow of dusk-lit neon.

Around Puerto Limón

Playa Bonita some 5 km north following the coastline, has the best beaches close to Limón if circumstances find you staying in town. A handful of houses form the town of **Portete** where fishing boats are moored in the protected little bay, and further on over the hill, **Moín** is the location of the international docks where modern-day banana boats are loaded with hundreds of containers used to export most of Costa Rica's 2.1 million tonnes of bananas annually. Of passing interest if you like big boats, dull as ditchwater if you don't.

◉ Highway 32 to Limón listings

For Sleeping and Eating price codes and other relevant information, see Essentials, pages 44-47.

● Sleeping

West of Guápiles *p366*

A Casa Río Blanco, west of the bridge over the Río Blanco, 6 km west of Guápiles. Río Blanco is just over 1 km down the pebble-dashed road from Restaurant Ponderosa, T2382-0957, www.casarioblanco.com. Space for 6 guests in rustic, comfortable cabins. Each cabin has a small terrace and looks over the Río Blanco, which creates a cool microclimate and a bird list of over 300 species. Old jars collecting dust exhibit several other deceased local inhabitants – many of which you'd probably rather not see. Vegetarian meals, with breakfast

included in the price, and supper optional. A good place to stop for a few days' genuine relaxation.

Guápiles *p368*

AL Hotel Suerre, at eastern end of town, T2710-7551, www.suerre.com. A large country club hotel with 55 spacious tiled rooms and wooden decor. TV, safebox, telephone and a/c. There's an Olympic-size pool, indoor tennis courts, a casino, conference rooms and open-air restaurant.
C Cabinas Car, 50 m west of the church in the centre of town, T2710-0035. 10 clean, tidy rooms with hot water private bath, fan and TV.
E Cabinas de Oro, northeast of the bus terminal, T2710-6663. Clean rooms with a/c, cable TV and hot water private bath, even cheaper without and a restaurant downstairs.

G Hotel Alfaro (El Tunél), 50 m west of the bus terminal, T2710-6293. Clean, simple rooms, reached by way of a rather funky aluminium stairway – open 24 hrs! Good value and best budget deal in town.

Guácimo *p368*

B Río Palmas, 1 km east of EARTH, T2760-0330, riopalmas@hotmail.com. The only real choice in the area. 30 rooms all with private bath and hot water. A good restaurant and relaxing pool add to the pleasures of a 200-ha property that includes an ornamental plant farm with a few trails through rainforest.

Siquirres *p368*

C-D Centro Turístico Pacuare, on the main road, T2768-6482. Some rooms with a/c, renovated with large pool.
F Alcema, 50 m east of the market, T2768-6004. Clean rooms with fan and shared bath.

Puerto Limón *p369, map p369*

Hotels fill up at carnival – book in advance.
A-B Park, Av 3, C 1-2, T2798-0555. Overlooking the bay with 34 rooms, all with cable TV and safebox, this is a neat hotel with a luxury feel. Sea-facing rooms are quiet, cool and a little more expensive. Room service from their excellent mid-range restaurant is available but downstairs you get occasional live music and sea views. Recently renovated.
B-C Acón, on northeastern corner of the main square, C 3, Av 3, T2758-1010. 39 big, clean rooms with private bath, a/c, telephone and safebox. Good restaurant downstairs and popular Aquarius disco. In need of sprucing up and overpriced for Limón.
C Tete, overlooking the main square, Av 3, C 4-5, T2758-1122. Clean, bright rooms with good beds and private bath. Some sleeping up to 6 and some with balconies overlooking the street and the square. Good value and friendly, helpful staff; other than Park Hotel, one of the nicest options in town.
C-D Miami, next to King on Av 2, C 4-5, T2758-0490. Reliable hotel with 35 clean rooms with private bath. Some with a/c,

others with fans, some with hot water and TV. Secure and efficient. Credit cards accepted.
D Palace, C 2-3, Av 2, T2758-2604. Family-run hotel, with 33 mostly big rooms. Pretty clean, French doors open on to authentic balcony overlooking street, TV in many rooms, popular with travellers and a good place to make up groups for Tortuguero.
E Continental, a few blocks north of the centre, Av 5, C 2-3, T2758-0434. 25 big, clean rooms some good for groups, with private bath and ceiling fans. Safe parking outside.
E International, opposite the Continental, and under the same management, Av 5, C 2-3, T2758-0434. 24 tidy rooms with private bath, some with a/c, others with fan. Some rooms are a little dark, but a good, safe place and popular with travellers.
E Pensión Costa Rica, Av 2, C 1-2, T2758-0241. Very quaint on the outside, not so great inside. Small, dark rooms with a fan.
E-F Costa del Sol, Av 5, C 5, T2798-0808. Growing rapidly there are 30 rooms, some with a/c, telephone and private bath.
F Hotel Oriental, C 4, Av 3-4. Clean and fairly bright, despite the look from the street. Still, very basic rooms with fan and shared cold-water bath. Very lively local bar beneath – not recommended for lone women.

Around Puerto Limón *p370*
Playa Bonita

C Oasys del Caribe, at the eastern end of the beach, T2795-0024. 15 painted cabins, adorned inside and out with *caña blanca*, like Costa Rican-style gingerbread houses. A little warm and dark inside, but spacious, with cable TV, private bath and hot water. A pool and restaurant serving fried food and meats.

Punta Piuta

AL Maribú Caribe, T2795-2543. 50 comfortable rooms in thatched roof, circular bungalows, with fine wooden furniture. A couple of pools in the rather cramped grounds, but the Caribbean views from the buffet restaurant are dreamy. Close by is **Restaurant Placeres** (♜), a popular choice.

A Matama, further west, T2795-1123. Straddling the hillside this rather eclectic tourist complex has 16 comfortable, modern rooms, with a/c, cable TV and telephone. Price includes breakfast in the palm-roofed *ranchos* housing the bar and buffet-style restaurant, a couple of trails, a large botanical garden and a pool for a bit of activity. They can arrange trips to Tortuguero. Targeting large Costa Rican family gatherings, it's the best place in the area, and up for sale.
B Cocorí, across the road from Matama, T2795-1670. 25 darkish rooms, most with a/c, hot water private bath and cable TV. Price includes breakfast served on the pleasant balcony restaurant looking out to the beach and rocky headland, with endless tasty options on the menu, including Chinese, Mexican and local fish dishes. They've recently added a jacuzzi, play room for children and big screen TV. Looking far better on the outside than it is inside, but it's nothing a fresh coat of paint wouldn't put right.
B-C Cabinas Roca Mar, T2795-1504. 9 rooms in a very clean block, with great ocean views, private bath and TV. Good choice for those who prefer to avoid Limón.

Moín
D Turtle Relax, T2795-1533. *Cabinas*, bar and restaurant with 8 rooms each with private bath and fan, and swimming pool. The restaurant serves *típica Limonense* and BBQ, seafood a speciality. They run trips to Matina (US$50 for 6 people), Tortuguero, fishing trips and rent kayaks.

❶ Eating

West of Guápiles *p366*
❚❚-❚ **Rancho Robertos**, at the Santa Clara junction, T2711-0050. Fine old *rancho* serving grills and traditional dishes. Next door is a tropical frog garden, US$5, an interesting short stop if you have the time.
❚ **Restaurant Ponderosa**, west of the Río Blanco bridge. A recommended local choice.

Guápiles *p368*
There are several *sodas* and snack bars around town.

Siquirres *p368*
❚ **Café Restaurant Ellis**. Has a good local reputation for seafood, meat and pasta.

Puerto Limón *p369, map p369*
❚❚ **Park Hotel**, Av 3, C 1-2. One of the best dining options in town with a full menu, reasonable prices and a sea view.
❚❚ **Springfield**, a 15-min walk north of town opposite the hospital. A stylish restaurant serving a mix of *Tico* and international dishes.
❚ **Bionatura**, opposite the cathedral on C 6, next to Macrobiótica. Excellent vegetarian café, mostly light snacks and one plate of the day. Various cereals and fruits served with honey.
❚ **Black Star Line**, Av 5, C 5. A spacious cafeteria with basic Caribbean fare.
❚ **Brisas del Caribe**, facing Parque Vargas, Av 2, C 1. Wide range of dishes including noodles, meat, seafood. Good service and a popular drinking spot in the evenings.
❚ **Doña Toda**, near the market on the main square. A cheap, cheerful street *soda*, perfect for people-watching and hanging out.
❚ **Marisquerías El Cevichito**, Av 2, C 1-2. Fish and excellent *ceviche*. Good place to relax in the bamboo café chairs. Still a good choice.
❚ **Monte Bianca**, in front of Gran Terminal Caribe bus station. Handy for time killing.
❚ **Musanni**, on Av 3, opposite the cathedral. An excellent takeaway bakery. Next door is TCBY Treats, an ice cream café. Both cheap.
❚ **Monte de Oro**, Av 4, C 3-4. Good local dishes in a rough and ready atmosphere. Handy while waiting for buses going south.
❚ **Palacio Encantador**, 50 m east of baseball park. Good Chinese.
❚ **Pizzeria Limón**, on C4, Av 4-5, T2758-3341. Not so great pizza, but very cheap, including free soda.
❚ **Soda Yans** along Av 2, C 5-6. Popular spot.
❚ **Star Crème Express Restaurant**, opposite the Black Star Line. Good, fast, local food.

Cheap food is also available in the central market. **Milk Bar La Negra Mendoza** has good milk shakes and cheap snacks. *Pan bon*, is an extra special Limón-style spicy bread from a Creole recipe. There are two Pollazo kiosks next to the police booth in the main square selling fried chicken.

Around Puerto Limón p370
Playa Bonita
♜-♜ **Restaurant Placeres**. A popular local choice with lots of specialities like *fajitas Talamanca*, *croquettes de pollo*, platters for two. Credit cards accepted.

Punta Piuta
♜-♜ **Restaurant Joy**. A more formal eatery offering loads of fish dishes from *ceviche* to jumbo prawn cocktails.
♜ **Bar and Restaurant Quimamba**, across the road from Roca Mar. Offering beer and *casado* by the beach.

🔾 Bars and clubs

Puerto Limón *p369, map p369*
Aquarius, at the Acón hotel. Nightly disco that doesn't get going until around midnight.
Bar La Tregua, on C 4, opposite the Plaza. Unimposing local bar with friendly staff.
Brisas del Caribe, on Parque Vargas. A good spot for an drink early in the evening.
Salamandra, top floor of a colonial building on the corner of Av 3 and C2. Well designed bar and restaurant with a good ambience.

🏵 Festivals and events

Puerto Limón *p369, map p369*
12 Oct Carnaval. The preceding days build steadily to the big *Día de la Raza*. The town springs into action as sedate highlanders flock to the Caribbean to join the music, dancing and celebrations. The biggest celebration in Costa Rica, the costumes are out in full as the 2 sides of the country unite.

15 Sep Independence from Spain is celebrated locally with more marching by local schools and colleges.

🔾 Shopping

West of Guápiles *p366*
Patricia and Brian Erickson, 6 km from Guápiles on the western side of the Río Blanco, down the road beside Restaurant Ponderosa, T2710-1858. A renowned artist, Patricia Erickson produces some of the most vibrant images of Costa Rica in her studio. Brian Erickson also works from home on his bamboo furniture and sculpture. Call in advance if you can.

Puerto Limón *p369, map p369*
La Casona del Parque and **Mercado Artesanal Caribeño** are on the west side of Parque Vargas. They sell a mix of standard crafts. Upstairs at the Mercado Artesanal is an odd mix of crafts, from simple painted shells to excellent pre-Colombian pottery replicas.

🔺 Activities and tours

West of Guápiles *p366*
Veragua Rainforest, on the road to Siquirres, 12 km south of Liverpool, T2296-5056, www.veraguarainforest.com. Insectarium, butterfly garden, frog exhibit, reptiles, canopy tour and rainforest tours. Aimed at the cruise market from Limón.

Puerto Limón *p369, map p369*
There are few tour operators in town. If you want to arrange a boat out to **Isla Uvita** ask in your hotel, or local guide Bernard, based opposite Matama on the road to Playa Bonita, will take you to Isla Uvita in the morning and pick you up later for US$8 per person.
Trips to **Tortuguero National Park** can be usually be arranged through your hotel.
Tortuguero Odyssey Tours, T2758-0824, charges US$60 per person. The tour is unlikely

to get to Tortuguero proper – more likely a trip through some of the southern canals. **Viajes Laura**, T2795-2410, www.viajes tropicaleslaura.net. Have been recommended and provide a daily service with an open return by boat for US$60 from Moín. See also Tortuguero section (page 375).

⊙ Transport

Guápiles *p368*
The bus terminal is on the southeast side of town. Hourly buses pass through town going west to **San José**, 1½ hrs, US$2.20) and east to **Limón**, 2 hrs, US$2.80. Buses to **Puerto Viejo de Sarapiquí** leave every hour from 0530, 1 hr, US$1.50. Regular buses to **Cariari**, 45 mins, US$0.70, for connections to **GEEST Casa Verde**, leave from the old terminal in the centre of town.

Puerto Limón *p369, map p369*
Air The airstrip is about 5km south of town. Flights in high season 3 times a week with NatureAir, www.natureair.com.

Bus Regular buses travel Highway 32 from San José to Limón. Buses leave from the Gran Terminal del Caribe at least hourly, 0500-2000, 3 hrs, US$4.30. Buses are direct or stop off at **Guápiles**, **Guácimo** and **Siquirres**. Buses with Caribeños, T2222-0610 (San José), T2758-2575 (Limón), arrive and depart from Gran Terminal del Caribe – on Av 2, C 7-8.

For destinations south of Limón, buses leave from Av 4, C 3-4, close to Radio Casino, with **Mepe**, T2758-0618. The ticket office is on the opposite side of the street. There are 9 daily buses to **Sixaola** on the border with Panama, stopping at **Bananito**, **Cahuita**, **Puerto Viejo** and **Bribrí** en route.

Buses north to **Moín** to catch boats down the coastal waterways to **Tortuguero** leave every 20 mins from the San José terminal to the west of town.

Boat Boats for independent travel to **Tortuguero** leave the small canal dock (Terminal de Desarrollo) at **Moín**, at around 1000, US$60 return. You will have to pay for all accommodation, food and tours once you arrive in Tortuguero. Just turn up (30 mins in advance to ensure a place) or contact Sebastian Torres on T2798-6059, T8828-4787, or Alexis Soto Barrantes T2758-4279, T8829-0913. It's a 3½-hr journey with one stop for 10 mins at a small café and snack kiosk. This is a spectacular trip and at least one way the boat driver will stop periodically, explain some of the area's history and show you the wildlife; be prepared to see crocodiles close up, monkeys and river birds. You can also charter a boat to **Parismina** (US$25 per person one way, and to **Barra del Colorado** (about US$75), minimum 4 people.

⊙ Directory

Puerto Limón *p369, map p369*
Banks Usual banking hrs (roughly 0830-1500) and services and all with ATMs at Banco de Costa Rica, Av 2, C 1, Banco Nacional, Av 2, C 3, Banco Popular. C 3. Av 1-2. Banco San José, Av 3, C 3-4.
Hospitals The regional hospital is north of town on the road to Moín, opposite Springfield Restaurant, T2758-2222.
Internet Services are slow in arriving at Limón. Ask around for any new places. Sitec S.A. Internet, just outside town past the end of the *malécon*, less than US$0.75/hr, speedy service, a/c, recommended. Internet Café on C5 between Av 1-2. A/c and open daily until 2200, US$1/hr. Also internet service on upper level of the bus station, not open late, handy if killing time. **Post office** Opposite the central market, also has internet service.
Telephone Calls can be made from ICE on Av 2, C 5-6 and at C 3, Av 4-5, open Mon-Thu, 0800-1700, Fri 0800-1600. **Useful address** The police booth on the main plaza is open 24 hrs a day if you have problems to report.

North Caribbean

Tantamount to an offshore island, the north Caribbean area between Limón and the Río San Juan on the Nicaraguan border is an adventure to reach and a rainforest paradise to visit. Arriving by air, you skim over the Caribbean Lowlands or by river you travel through the inland waterways and canals to arrive at Tortuguero or Barra del Colorado. This is the largest area of tropical wet forest in Costa Rica. The coastal canals of the northern Caribbean were built in the mid-1960s to connect the indigenous communities living along the rivers and lagoons of the region. While the canal network dramatically improved access to the communities, this is still one of the least accessible parts of the country.

The beaches of Tortuguero, as some of the most important green and leatherback turtle nesting sites in the country, are a major natural attraction. Inland, the rivers and man-made channels draped with the dense growth of riverine forests are flooded with up to 5 m of rain a year and the buttressed root forest giants and stilted trees are home to abundant wildlife, all of which you can see from the comfort of a small launch drifting silently through the narrow creeks. ▸▸ *For listings, see pages 381-385.*

Ins and outs

Getting there

Most people visit Tortuguero as part of a two- or three-day package tour from San José, flying to the airport in Tortuguero, or going by bus and then catching a lodge boat from Matina. However, it is possible to travel to Tortuguero independently – see box, page 377. There are daily flights to Tortuguero and Barra del Colorado with **SANSA**, T221 9414, www.flysansa.com, US$72, and **NatureAir**, T2220-3054, www.natureair.com, US$96. Most visitors arrange accommodation before arriving and transport from the airstrip is provided. In Tortuguero SANSA offers a boat service to the town for US$3 per person. If flying with NatureAir, call the Tortuguero Information Centre or Ronald Artavia Corea T2223-3030 (beeper) to arrange a ride.

Transport by boat is also easily arranged. The simplest option is from Moín, a few kilometres north of Limón from where you catch a boat heading up the coastal canal. There are also a couple of routes from San José via Cariari. It is also possible to catch a boat from GEEST Casa Verde, a short bus ride from Cariari. Finally, you can charter a vessel from Puerto Viejo de Sarapiquí – the most expensive option. Most all-inclusive packages leave from a small private dock close to Matina. ▸▸ *For further details, see Transport, page 385.*

Tourist information

www.tortuguerovillage.com is a very useful site for travelling for the area. Keep an eye on tagged turtles on the net at www.cccturtle.org.

Parque Nacional Tortuguero ▸▸ *Colour map 2, A/B4.*

ⓘ *Entrance to the park is US$10 per person for 1 day, which is paid to the headquarters at the southern end of the town before beginning any trip through the waterways. The office can be a little difficult to find due to various concrete walls and piles of coconut shells blocking what looks like the end of the path – just skip over them! A few hikes lead out from the park office on 2.5 km of usually muddy trails. Night-time trips along the beach are co-ordinated through the lodges or individual tour guides. There is a small exhibition centre at the office, with* *information about wildlife and projects in the area. More information is available on T2709-8086, www.acto.go.cr.*

Tortuguero National Park is one of the great treasures of Costa Rica. The 31,187-ha area is made up of a network of flooded waterways that twist and meander through the vast alluvial plain created by rivers flowing off the Central Highlands' eastern slopes. By the time the rivers reach the coast they have slowed almost to a standstill and with high rainfall, the dense tropical forest is often flooded. Essentially flat, the landscape is bursting with vegetation and trees which crowd up to the edge of waterways, only occasional gaps providing a glimpse of the world within.

The main focus for visitors to the park is the small town of Tortuguero which lives, as it has for centuries, in co-existence with the turtles that nest on its beaches. According to guides, the community made a living selling turtles, a self-preserving, stay-fresh source of meat, to mariners that sailed the Caribbean. And indeed, Tortuguero – meaning 'turtle seller' in Spanish – still makes a living from its turtles. Conservationist Archie Carr, one of the park's main proponents, set out to encourage the local community to take a long-term view of the nesting turtles: that the welfare of the turtles will always be directly related to that of the community.

Best time to visit

With an average temperature of 26°C and rainfall between 4.5 and 6 m a year, Tortuguero is one of the wettest spots in the country. While there is slightly less rain in February and March, there is a high chance of getting wet throughout the year. According to the information centre, July to October is the best time to see green turtles nesting. The leatherback or *baula* nests between March and June.

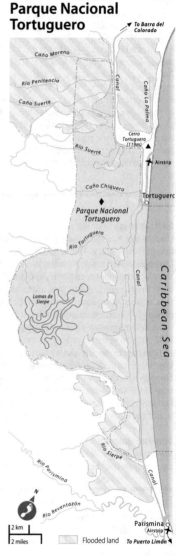

Parque Nacional Tortuguero

Wildlife

Tortuguero is one of the country's most diverse national parks and home to over half the bird and reptile species found in the country. It also just so happens to be the most important nesting site of the green turtle in the western Caribbean. The looping flight of the keel-billed toucan crossing the open waterways is a common site as are northern jacanas, oropendolas and herons. Less commonly spotted is the endangered green macaw which also resides in the park. Needless to say, wildlife viewing in the area is spectacular and best seen from a boat moving silently through the myriad channels. Mammals are also numerous, you'll find that howler monkeys and sloths a common sight, while hidden within the undergrowth the tracks of jaguar, ocelot and tapir go unseen by most, as does the endangered manatee that explores and grazes to beds of the watery channels. If you're particularly lucky you may see the fishing bulldog bat, a large bat with a 60-cm wingspan that hunts on the waters of the canals. Reptiles and amphibians are also on the scene, and in large numbers – you will very probably see crocodiles, and, if you are lucky, glass and poison-dart frogs and the bug-eyed gaudy leaf frog.

But the main reason for travelling to Tortuguero is to see nesting **turtles**. The green turtle uses the beaches in significant numbers, and there are also visits from leatherback, hawksbill and occasionally loggerhead turtles as well. As with much of Costa Rica, getting the timing right to see this natural phenomenon is essential. The green turtles lay their eggs at night between June and October, with the hatchlings emerging from the depths of their sandy nests until November at the latest. Leatherbacks can be seen between March and June. While access to the beaches is unrestricted, trips to look for nesting turtles are carefully monitored and you must be accompanied by a licensed guide at all times. For more information, see 'Turtle watching' below.

Tortuguero town → *Colour map 2, A4.*

The small town of Tortuguero on the southern tip of a sandy spit with a few hundred resident *Ticos* and no cars, is the main focus of the area. At the confluence of the Río Tortuguero and the coastal canal, the town pulsates to a distinctly Caribbean beat.

A greener turtle harvest?

First populated in the time of pirates when turtles provided a ready supply of stay-fresh meat for the ship-bound mariners, the turtle harvest supported the local community and continued for hundreds of years until research by Archie Carr, the founder of the Caribbean Conservation Corporation in the 1950s, suggested that the green turtle was probably heading for extinction.

Today the nesting grounds attract attention for a different reason, bringing tourists from around the world. Yet while some members of the community invariably benefit from tourism-related employment, others are having difficulties adapting to a new world which puts the conservation of the turtle above all other issues. The introduction of a recycling programme, for instance, probably seems like a good idea to the majority of visitors who stay in the all-inclusive lodges, but it looks rather out of place in Tortuguero (it's difficult not to see the big divide between the comfort of the tourist lodges and the basic lifestyle of the village community). It's worth bearing in mind when you hire your guide that sharing out the benefits of the region's attractions throughout the community is a greater priority for most locals.

Spread around the network of sandy paths and lush vegetation, the town itself has a creaking old church, a general store, football pitch, a couple of gift shops and half a dozen accommodation options (see page 381).

Flowing north from the town is the **Laguna de Tortuguero** which leads for 5 km to the Caribbean. On either side of the narrow waterway – and on the canal running parallel further inland to the west – comfortable, all-inclusive lodges have spread out along the river banks.

Turtle watching

For information on turtle and other tours and permits to enter the park, go to the National Park office at the end of the track south of town. There are a number of local guides and most work together to ensure that everyone gets an equal split of tourist revenue. Many have a speciality, whether it be a strong eye for camouflaged jungle wildlife, knowledge of turtle behaviour, or simply the right language skills. It's a good idea to get to know as many of them as you can first, ensuring that both you and the guides get the best deal (see page 384).

The Caribbean beaches of Tortuguero National Park protect the nesting sites of the green turtle and also, in smaller numbers, the hawksbill, loggerhead and the huge leatherback turtles. To see one of these magnificent creatures emerge from the ocean surf, haul itself up the beach and dig a nest in which to store its precious cargo is an unforgettable experience. Likewise, seeing the tiny, dazed hatchlings emerge from their sandy place of birth, before heading frantically for the ocean like wind-up mechanical toys is truly memorable. The palm-fringed beach, struggling under growths of icacao and sea grape and with nest craters everywhere and driftwood scattered around, looks more like a bomb-site than a sensitive nesting area.

The understanding of the beach and its importance to the green turtle began with the work of Archie Carr – a prominent figures in the Costa Rican conservation movement. The work and study that began with The Brotherhood of the Green Turtle continued with the creation of the **Caribbean Conservation Corporation** (CCC) ⓘ *Tortuguero, T2709-8091, San José T2297-5510, www.cccturtle.org, open daily, entrance US$1, turtle tours are arranged through your lodge or individual guides in Tortuguero village.* Carr's work and energy were crucial in the creation of Tortuguero National Park. Today the Corporation has a small exhibition centre to the north of town and continues tagging work, the tagged turtles being monitored by satellite (they can be seen on the CCC website). Despite the conservation activity, the number of nesting females visting the beach has fallen by 30% since 1995, although 2007 did show an increase on 2006. CCC's volunteers patrol the beach throughout the night, every night, during nesting season. CCC accepts, and needs, volunteers to help with turtle monitoring but they do not take walk-ins – all applicants must initially apply to their US (Gainsville) office. Check their website for details.

Tours to see nesting turtles take place at night and cost US$10. Strict rules govern the tours which are only carried out by authorized local guides. You must be accompanied at night. Torches, cameras, video cameras and smoking are prohibited. Tours last for a couple of hours (the elderly may find trudging blindly along the beach difficult after a while) and you are advised to wear dark clothes and closed shoes. This is designed to limit disturbance to any turtles. Naturally, being quiet is also advised.

Touring the waterways

From the Tortuguero Lagoon a network of smaller channels are accessible by launch. Two recommended canals are **Chiquero** and **Caño Mora**, both of which you can investigate on your own or with a guide. There are maps of the canals at the national park office. Kayaks and canoes are also available for rent around town, try Miss Junie's (page 381). You will of course be likely to see much more if you are accompanied by a guide, but expeditions on your own can also be fun, so take advantage of the opportunity and do both. Exploring these channels gives a window on the rainforest and if you travel in silence and with a good guide, you are certain to see much wildlife. Most tours leave early in the morning when birdlife is most in evidence and the chance of seeing mammals is higher.

Tours with lodges are normally included in the price. If you organize your own tour you have a slightly greater variety – the secret to a good tour is being quiet. On some self-organized tours you can take a guide that uses paddle power.

Note Most boats use petrol engines to get to the quieter channels. Once entering the park they are legally required to switch to electric engines to reduce noise and wave wash damage to the banks. Keen to maximize the clients' time spent viewing wildlife – and to keep tourists happy – many guides stay in the channels as long as they can, switching to petrol motors when they leave. Looking behind the boat you can see the waves crash against the banks. Only by visitors discouraging this will such misdirected good intentions be stopped – feel free to speak out.

Other tours

At the mouth of Tortuga Lagoon, **Cerro Tortuguero** rises to 119 m. While its height is not staggering, in an area that is overwhelmingly flat, the views from the top are spectacular. Walks up the hill can be arranged through lodges and local guides.

Less rarely visited, the **Lomas de Sierpe** lie to the west of Tortuguero – it's a good day trip for those wanting a more challenging trek. Tortuguero also has a zip wire canopy tour.

Coast north and south of Tortuguero ⬤⬤ ➡ *pp381-385.*

Parismina ➜ *Colour map 2, B5.*

ⓘ *To reach Parismina, take a ferry from Moín (see page 385). If you have booked accommodation, the lodge will arrange transport.*

Perched at the mouth of the Río Parismina, the small riverside hamlet of Parismina is just a passing glance for boats heading north to Tortuguero. The Parismina picks up the Reventazón and many other tributaries flowing off the slopes of Turrialba Volcano on its steady eastward journey to the Caribbean.

While Parismina is close to the southern limits of Tortuguero National Park, the riverside hamlet prefers to concentrate its energies on its reputation as one of the best places in the world to fish for tarpon and snook.

Barra del Colorado ➜ *Colour map 2, A4. The village telephone number is T2710-6592.*

Tucked up in the northeastern corner of the country, Barra del Colorado, one of the most isolated parts of Costa Rica, is reached by a couple of daily flights or a bumpy boat journey of several hours to the northernmost limit of the man-made coastal canal. Activity – if that's what life can be called in this relaxed, placid backwater – is based in the divided waterside hamlet which straddles the Río Colorado. Barra del Sur has the airstrip, lodges and the jaguar's share of available services. Barra del Norte enjoys the honour of being on Isla Calero – the largest island in Costa Rica. In addition to providing services for tourists, locals of Caribbean and Miskito origin (from neighbouring Nicaragua) make a living fishing for spiny lobster. Two major draws attract visitors to the region – excellent sports fishing for snook and tarpon and the Barra del Colorado Wildlife Reserve.

Refugio Nacionales de Vida Silvestre Barra del Colorado is a fair mouthful and at 81,211 ha is also one of the country's largest protected areas, much of it covering the border with Nicaragua along the Río San Juan. A drenching 6 m of rain a year in parts and temperatures averaging 26°C create conditions very similar to those in Tortuguero. Established in the mid-1980s much of the area had already been disturbed by logging but the potential for nature tourism in the area remains largely untapped. If you have the time and the money – Barra is more expensive than Tortuguero – the opportunities for exploring the quiet waterways and backwaters are exceptional.

Fishing is good all year round, but the best is from September to April. Accommodation (see page 383) is available at a number of lodges dotted throughout the area, some of them close to Barra del Colorado, some requiring a short boat ride.

Border with Nicaragua – Barra del Colorado

The Río San Juan – the southern bank of the river to be precise – marks the border between Costa Rica and Nicaragua. Technically, when travelling this route you are entering Nicaragua and should have your passport on you at all times. In reality, if you are simply travelling to Puerto Viejo de Sarapiquí you can travel without having to complete border formalities.

Crossing the Río Colorado to Barra del Norte (which in fact is the south arm of the Río San Juan delta), the truly adventurous can, in theory, walk to San Juan del Norte in Nicaragua along the coast. It is a 30-km-long beach walk, requiring food and lots of water. Seek advice from locals in Barra before setting out – you may be able to get a ride from a boat heading that way.

For Sleeping and Eating price codes and other relevant information, see Essentials, pages 44-47.

⊙ **Sleeping**

Tortuguero *p375 and p377*
Accommodation options have grown in the last few years. Lodges and hotels of varying comfort are scattered around the lagoon. For most lodges, with the exception of Mawamba and Laguna Lodge, you will require transport to and from Tortuguero. In Tortuguero village most accommodation options are perfect for the budget traveller.

In town
B Casa Marbella, in front of the church, T2709-8011, http://casamarbella.tripod.com. A B&B with 4 small but very well lit rooms, with private bath, solar assisted hot water and ceiling fans. Right on the river with a deck perfect for birdwatching and views of the setting sun over the forest. Run by local guide Daryl Loth who also provides tours and advice on local travel. It fills a great niche, providing comfort without having to go for an all-inclusive lodge option.
C Cabinas Tortuguero, T2709-8114, cabinas_tortuguero@yahoo.com. 8 exceptionally clean and bright little cabins, each sleeping 3 and with a private bath. Set in pleasant little gardens complete with hammocks – a good spot.
C Miss Miriam's, there are now 2 Miss Miriam's. The original and more basic rooms are north of the football field; the second location is south of the football field and fills up fast. Both have restaurants serving all the usual Caribbean fare, expertly cooked.
D Miss Junie's, also known as **Iguana Verde** T8709-8102. 12 good cabins with spacious rooms at the northern end of town and one of the town's old favourites. An excellent restaurant serves breakfast, lunch and dinner, see also page 379.

E Cabinas Aracari, T2709-8006. 13 rooms in a large lodge-style block, in slightly unkempt gardens. Thin walls, but hot water and a great communal vibe and security. Perfect for meeting other travellers.
E Meriscar, T2709-8132. 20 simple rooms with foam mattresses. Most have a shared bath, although there are a couple with private bath. There's a restaurant in the high season, friendly enough if other places are full.

Out of town
None of the lodges include entrance to the national park.
LL Tortuga Lodge and Gardens, at the northernmost point, T2257-0766, www.costaricaexpeditions.com. The most luxurious choice on the lagoon with 24 big, bright and breezy rooms, set in a couple of 2-storey lodges, each with hot water private bath, and a balcony or veranda complete with hammock overlooking the gardens and the lagoon. The restaurant is à la carte and there's a wine list worth exploring. On the quiet days you can relax around the pool that seems to blend into the river itself or wander at will round a couple of trails. Eco-touches include solar-heated water and a closed-water pool system. Expensive, but very comfortable. 3 days, 2 nights, US$379 per person; US$99 per person, based on double occupancy, per night, for lodging only.
LL Turtle Beach Lodge, T2383-1652, in San José T2248-0707, www.turtlebeach lodge.com. Further out in Caño Palma. Offers 32 luxurious rooms in 70 ha, an open-air restaurant, all the usual tours including kayaking, horse riding and birdwatching, TV in a communal bar, internet access and a turtle-shaped pool. Various packages start from US$210, per night, including meals.
L Ilan Ilan, through Agencia Mitur in San José, T2296-7378, www.ilan-ilanlodge.com. 24 rooms in a line, with private bath and slightly offensive decor. But the service is good and friendly, with big helpings served in

the screened buffet restaurant, and a pool, jacuzzi and riverside bar. Can also be arranged through Oasis Tours in Puerto Viajo de Sarapiquí, T2766-6108. 3 days all-inclusive US$215. Can arrange your trip to start in San José and continue on to Sarapiquí or Arenal (Fortuna).

L Jungle Lodge Hotel, north along the western bank of the lagoon, T2233-0133, www.grupopapagayo.com. 50 big, wood-panelled rooms with a small balcony and private bath. Meals are served buffet-style, there's a pool complete with wet bar, and a separate bar with a disco – a worrying development that hopefully won't be copied by all the lodges. Part of the large Grupo Papagayo.

L Laguna Lodge, a little further north, T2709-8082, www.lagunatortuguero.com. 80 rooms sleeping 2 or 3 people, each with private bath and a small balcony. The restaurant serving buffet meals has a fine view and location over the lagoon. There's a small pool and a bar, close to the garden which is planted to attract butterflies. A 2-night tour is US$259 to US$284 per person.

L Mawamba Lodge, the closest lodge to town, T2709-8181, or in San José on T2293-8181, www.grupomawamba.com. 50 or so rooms connected by covered and well lit walkways in fine gardens to lookouts over the lagoon. Rooms are wooden cabin-style with a fan, private bath, hot shower, and a small balcony and veranda. Tasty and healthy meals are served buffet-style in the restaurant and you can relax in the freeform pool. Dip through a little hole in the bushes and you're walking along the nesting beaches, or you can head south for the short walk to town – a good choice. Surrounding the pool the staff have created a red-eyed frog breeding programme. Visitors can see various stages of the frogs' development and there are lots around the gardens. Two nights and 3 days all-inclusive per person for US$330 high season, US$260 low season.

L Pachira Lodge, across the lagoon from Tortuguero, T2256-7080, www.pachira lodge.com. 34 comfortable rooms decorated with bamboo furniture and all with private bath and ceiling fans. Meals served buffet style, and a large sundeck surrounds a rather amusing turtle-shaped pool. 2 nights and 3 days package US$269.

B Samoa, one channel west from the lagoon, T2258-6137, www.samoalodge.com. Ecotourism and comfort combined in the only lodge actually in the Park. The 32 rooms are spacious and pleasantly decorated with fan, minibar and hot water private bath. The porch balconies look across a tended garden which has a natural feel and a stream complete with turtles and caiman, a butterfly garden and 1500 m of trails. 3 days, 2 nights, US$289 per person.

B-E Tortuguero Caribe Lodge, a little further north, T2385-4676. 10 simple cabins, friendly, *Tico*-run and owned. Breakfast and dinner available, cheaper without. Book direct or arrange a package through Ecole Travel in San José, T2223-2240, www.ecoletravel.com.

D El Manati, T2373-0330 and booked through Ecole Travel in San José, T2223-2240, www.ecoletravel.com. Just 10 simple budget cabins, with a homely atmosphere where you can truly relax without feeling the need to dress for dinner – because there is any unless requested in advance (breakfast *is* included). Boats are easily arranged if you want to pop over to town, and there's a small bar and thatched roof rancho overlooking the river for relaxing in the grounds. Kayaks and canoes available for hire. 3 days, 2 nights from Puerto Moín, US$135. Good value.

Volunteering

Caño Palma Biological Station, north of Tortuguero, run by the Canadian Organization for Tropical Education and Rainforest Conservation, T2381-4116, or in Canada T2905-831-8809, www.coterc.org. Aiming to provide leadership in education, research and conservation it has services and accommodation for visiting researchers, students and volunteers. **F** per person, including meals, minimum 2-week stay.

Parismina *p380*

LL Jungle Tarpon Lodge, locally on T2380-7636, in the US toll free on T1-800-544-2261, www.jungletarpon.com. Big rooms with beamed ceiling, tiled floors and private bathrooms. Catch-and-release tarpon are beyond doubt the target out in the ocean or in flat-bottomed boats in the jungle lagoons. 5 days and 4 nights start from US$2195, a full week is US$2995.

LL Río Parismina Lodge, T2798-0918, toll free on T1-800-338-5688, www.riop.com. A full comfort fishing lodge with 12 wooden cabins, restaurant and bar at the mouth of the Parismina. For added luxury there's a pool and jacuzzi in the hotel grounds. Weekend fishing packages start at US$1850 per person, a full week will set you back US$3100.

L Caribbean Expedition Lodge, T2232-8118, or in the US on T2361-884-4277, www.costaricasportfishing.com. A slightly less luxurious feel, but still very comfortable in the tiled floor cabins, with private bath. The screened dining room serves North American and local dishes, but as ever the action is out in the water with ocean and inland water vessels. A 5-day snook and tarpon package will set you back US$1700.

There are a few more choices, but they are certainly not budget, and the options for getting around are limited.

Barra del Colorado *p380*
In town

LL Río Colorado Lodge, T2232-4063, www.riocoloradolodge.com. One of the oldest lodges in the country and certainly in Barra. Comfortable rooms built in the early 1970s with private bath are connected by a maze of covered pathways. Happy hour at the bar, equipped with a TV and video, keeps the mood rolling along. The focus is on fishing but non-fishing guests are also welcome.

LL Silver King Lodge, T2381-1403, www.silverkinglodge.com. Widely regarded as the best and most luxurious lodge on the north Caribbean coastline, with big comfortable screened cabins and private bath with hot water. The food has been described as gourmet. Lots of little touches make it a great place to stay – an open bar, free laundry, a pool and jacuzzi. Hardly surprising that the fishing is equally impressive using 10 v-hull centre console boats in open water and unsinkable Carolina skiffs in inland waters.

B Tarponland Lodge, T2710-2141. The cheapest option in town with 12 basic rooms, a periodically neglected pool and a few fishing options available. It's also the closest to the airstrip.

Outside Barra

LL Casa Mar Lodge, a couple of km north of Barra del Colorado facing Laguna Agua Dulce, office in the US T2714-578-1881, toll free from the US on 800-543-0282, www.casamarlodge.com. 6 duplex cabins, each with private bath and showers, are set in 3 ha of tropical garden. Home-cooked north American buffet meals are served with a few local dishes for variety, and naturally plenty of fruit. Eddy Brown is a very experienced and well-known local fisherman, and there are 22-ft centre console vessels for inland water angling. 5 days' fishing will cost you US$2075.

LL Rain Goddess, T2231-4299, www.bluwing.com. Arguably the best way to find the best fish is to keep moving, which is easily done on the 65-ft customized houseboat finished with wood panelling in the 6 rooms. Meals are served with wine and the bar never closes in this 'flotel' which merges quality and comfort. What about the fishing? 16-ft Jon boats work the rivers and backwaters, with larger 20-ft vessels for fishing the river mouths. 5 days' and 3 nights' fishing will set you back US$2700 per person, non-anglers, US$1250.

⊙ Eating

Tortuguero town *p377*
Bear in mind that all lodges, apart from El Manati, provide 3 meals, usually all-inclusive.

¶ **El Muellecite**, next to La Caribeña.
Excellent *gallo pinto* and a breakfast
selection, in a welcoming family ambience.
¶ **Miss Junie's**, at the north end of town.
Good local Caribbean dishes. A reservation
is normally necessary.
¶ **Miss Miriam's**. 2 restaurants on either side
of the football pitch are very well thought of
locally. Serve very cheap and tasty *Tico* and
Caribbean dishes.
¶ **Dorling's Bakery**, bakery, coffee shop,
with tables looking out over the lagoon.
Open daily 0500-1900.

🎵 Bars and clubs

Tortuguero town *p377*
Nightlife in Tortuguero is limited, in part
due to tourists getting up early for tours,
but local bars are very relaxed.
El Colibre, by the main dock; and
Punto de Enquentro, a few metres to
the south are the two the main choices.
Both are on the water, the latter has a
younger vibe.
Bochinche, behind the football field, this
is the disco in town if you're up for making
a night of it. It's open most days during the
high season.

🛒 Shopping

Tortuguero town *p377*
Souvenir Pura Vida, to the north of the dock.
Sells a selection of souvenirs, T-shirts and
general goods. There are 3 small
general stores in this area.
The Jungle Shop, opposite the bakery.
Specializes in light clothes and swim wear,
local handicrafts some nature books
and postcards.
   Further north is a large store packed with
touristy souvenirs including hammocks,
wall hangings, coffee, handmade paper
notebooks and a myriad of other colourful
artefacts and handicrafts.

⛰ Activities and tours

Tortuguero town *p377*
Lodge bookings are generally arranged
through tour operators in San José – see
respeçtive lodges for details. Tours from
San José will include transport, meals,
guides and boat trips for between US$125
(from Moín) and US$450 per person.
Viajes Laura, in Puerto Limón, T2758-2410,
www.viajestropicaleslaura.net. Have been
recommended and provide a daily service
with an open return by boat for US$60
from Moín.

Local tour operators
If you want to arrange a guide for an
independent trip in advance try:
Tortuguero Safaris (Daryl Loth),
T2709-8011, safari@racsa.co.cr; or
Tinamon Tours (Barbara Hartung),
T8842-6561, www.tinamontours.de, an
English, German and Spanish-speaking
biologist who has been strongly
recommended for boat, hiking and
specifically turtle tours in Tortuguero.
A long-term resident in the area, Barbara
is a mine of information. Both Barbara
and Daryl are committed to keeping tours
environmentally and ecologically sound,
and try to make sure every guide gets an
equal share of tourists. Check who you
will actually be being guided by, however.
You may turn up and find yourself with
someone other than the guide you booked
with – if you want a specific guide, make
it known when you book.

Guides
Castor Hunter Thomas, T2709-8050 (or
enquire at Restaurant Caribeña opposite the
dock). Has 16 years of guiding experience and
his father was the first guide in Tortuguero.
Bonye Scott runs **Free Travel Information
Tours**, T8844-8099, bonyetravel2004@
yahoo.com. He organizes everything from
boat transport to canopy tours and is very
respectful of the area.

Anselmo Najarro a recommended guide (Spanish only). Find him at the Information Centre behind the basketball court.

There are many other good guides, ask around as much as you can; Tortuguero is a small and very friendly village, everyone knows each other. All guides charge roughly US$5 per person per hr.

● Transport

Tortuguero town *p377*

Air Daily flights from **San José** with SANSA, T2221-9414, www.flysansa.com, US$72, and NatureAir, T2220-3054, www.natureair.com, US$96. The airstrip is about 3 km north of the town. You will need to arrange transport from the airstrip to your hotel if it is not included.

Boat All-inclusive packages provide the transport links, normally by boat from a private dock near Matina. For independent travellers there are 2 main options. From Limón on the Caribbean coast take a bus to **Moín**. Tell the driver you are going to Tortuguero and he will drop you at the dock. An almost daily service is provided by **Alexis Soto Barrantes**, T2758-4279, T8829-0913, and **Sebastián Torres**, T2798-6059, T8828-4787, both are very helpful and run a reliable service to and from Tortuguero leaving at about 1000, charging US$30 one way, US$60 return. The boat returns from Tortuguero at 1000 providing plenty of time for an early morning trip before returning to Moín, arriving around 1300.

Alternatively, head for **Cariari** on the 0900 direct bus from Terminal Gran Caribe in San José. From Cariari there are two options, take a bus to **GEEST Casa Verde**, telling the driver you want to go to Tortuguero. For US$10 you get a gentle slow journey to Tortuguero arriving around 1500. Boats return at 0700 in the morning so you will probably need to stay 2 nights if you want to do an early morning tour. The GEEST operators are notorious for telling

travellers they provide the only route to Tortuguero from Cariari; this is not the case. An alternative route is via a bus from the local terminal, behind the police station in Cariari, to **La Pavona**. Buses leave at around 1145. From there a waiting boat will take you to Tortuguero. The price for the bus and boat is US$7-10. These services are subject to the vagaries of river level and cannot run if the water is too high or too low, however, this reputedly only occurs for a week or so each year. If in doubt, contact Tortuguero Information Centre on T2709-8047.

Transport can also be arranged from **Puerto Viejo de Sarapiquí**, see page 169.

If you need to charter a vessel there are several options. **Willie Rankin**, T2798-1556, travels from Moín to Tortuguero. **Ruben Bananero** also provides a charter service, T2709-8005.

Barra del Colorado *p380*

Air Daily flights from **San José** with SANSA, T2221-9414, www.flysansa.com, US$72, and NatureAir, T2220-3054, www.natureair.com, US$87.

Boat Boats can be arranged from **Tortuguero**, taking 1½ hrs. Costs vary widely ranging from US$35, if arranged by a lodge you're staying at, to around US$100. It makes sense to ask around, therefore. It is also possible to arrange a boat from **Puerto Viejo de Sarapiquí** – see page 169.

● Directory

Tortuguero town *p377*

Bank and post office There are no banks or other significant services in the town apart from
a quiet old **post office** which opens sporadically. **Internet** Access is available at the SANSA office, next to Casa Marbella, US$4 per hr, or US$1 for 15 mins.

South Caribbean

From Limón to the border with Panama, the southern Caribbean coast is dotted with quiet beaches and small communities that until relatively recently have been cut off from much of the rest of Costa Rica. Once the preserve of Bribrí and Cabecar people who lived in the southern Talamanca mountains, the indigenous populations were joined by Afro-Caribbean groups who built the railroad and worked on banana plantations in the early 1900s. This single means of transport was the only line of communication until the late 1970s when the road from Limón crept south slowly linking the isolated villages. The tarmac road finally reached Manzanillo in 2001.

The slow advance of progress has had some benefits, limiting the voracity of coastal development, retaining an element of cultural diversity and keeping a generally relaxed and laid-back atmosphere. Of course, this being Costa Rica, natural events always have a part to play. On the 22nd April 1991 an earthquake hit the area, raising some parts of the southern coastline by over a metre. Rivers were re-routed and temporary crossings replaced the bent and broken bridges ruined by the tremors. The bridges have been replaced now but at points along the coast you can still clearly see the 'shelf' on the land.

Accommodation is focused in the quickly growing towns of Cahuita and Puerto Viejo de Talamanca but a particular appeal of the region is the (generally pleasant) sprawling of individual lodges in quiet hideaways filled with a character and imagination as varied as their owners – many of them expatriates from around the globe who have fallen for the south coast's idyllic charms.
➤➤ For listings, see pages 394-408.

Ins and outs

Getting there and around
There are four buses a day to and from Puerto Limón and Puerto Viejo de Talamanca from San José and an almost hourly bus service between the two coastal towns. One express bus a day serves Manzanillo from San José. Area websites include: www.greencoast.com, www.puertoviejo.net. ➤➤ See Transport, page 406, for further details.

South to Cahuita ● ➤➤ p394-408. Colour map 3, A5/6.

Highway 36 begins its coastal journey south to Cahuita just west of Limón. A thin line of palms breaks the view of the beautiful beaches which hide dangerous currents. Hidden in the mountains is the incredible ecotourist destination of Selva Bananito Lodge and further down the road is Aviarios del Caribe animal reserve (for both, see page 394).

Reserva Biológica Hitoy Cerere
① Reserve office, T2798-3170. Getting to the park involves 4WD. Buses leave Limón for the Estrella Valley, but you are still 15 km short of the ranger station. The easiest and simplest way to visit is on a tour from Cahuita or Puerto Viejo.

From Penshurst, a road heads inland climbing the Estrella Valley, eventually arriving at Hitoy Cerere Biological Reserve. The 9950-ha reserve has some of the greatest wildlife diversity in Costa Rica, a fact that has created an interest in natural remedies from the park's flora. The reserve also offers some tough day-hikes.

Rainfall in the park is a steady 3.5 m a year, with temperatures in the mid to high 20s creating perfect conditions for wet and premontane tropical forest. Three basic trails lead

Raptor Watch – an aerial freeway

If travelling through the southern Caribbean between September and November cast your eyes to the sky and look for a steady stream of raptors moving south along an imaginary aerial freeway. In the autumn of the northern hemisphere over one million raptors migrate from North America to over-winter in South America. A bird count instigated by Pablo Porras of ANAI at the KeKöLdi reserve in the autumn of 2000 counted more than 1.3 million turkey vultures, broad-winged hawks, Swainson's hawks and Mississippi kites passing through the skies. This makes the watchsite one of only three in the world – the others being Elat in Israel, and Veracruz in Mexico – to record more than a million migrants in one season. The birds return from their winter break in the Amazon and throughout South America, reduced by as much as 30% due to mortality rates, between March and April.

A volunteer programme was developed by ANAI and is now managed by the KeKöLdi Indigenous Reserve. Contact ATEC (www.ateccr.org) for details. More information available at www.kekoldi.org – although the website is frequently not working.

from the rangers' station through the spectacular forest rich with epiphytes and many streams, rivers and waterfalls. Wildlife is profuse, with sloths, howler and white-faced monkeys to be seen. On the ground you may see otters, peccarys, and even jaguars and tapirs. Over a hundred birds have been spotted in the park.

Cahuita ⬤🐢🏠⛰️⬤🌊 ➤ pp394-408. Colour map 3, A5.

Blink and you'll miss Cahuita which is hidden a few hundred metres down an unassuming road off Highway 36, 10 km south of the petrol station at Penshurst. The small town (district population 4200) epitomizes the south Caribbean – laid back but with just enough energy to keep things ticking along. Don't rush, don't hibernate, do something in-between. The predominantly Afro-Caribbean town sits on a small rocky peninsula – the first protuberance of any significance south of Limón – and is barely larger than a football pitch. Heading north out of town, a bumpy dirt road shadows the dark sand beach of Playa Negra, drifting past quiet hotels and lodges. South of town, a small creek leads to the golden sands that mark the northernmost point of Cahuita National Park (see page 389), home to some of the best coral reefs in the country. If the Caribbean means beaches to you, these palm-fringed golden sands will be tough to beat. They are postcard perfect, shaded by jauntily angled coconut palms reaching out to the ocean, and a very short walk from the southern end of Cahuita town.

Warning Cahuita and Puerto Viejo de Talamanca have suffered from a lack of support and investment from the central government, a fact which has led to some social problems, in particular drugs. You may well be hassled by people selling drugs. You should also be aware there have been some violent attacks in the area. Local communities and the government have made efforts to reduce and isolate the problems, however, and the atmosphere of the area is reported to be improving.

Local trips

One of the main attractions in the area is Cahuita National Park which meets the sea at a fine stretch of golden sand. Locally there are several popular tours. It is easy to rent mountain bikes to explore on your own, or go horse riding. Contact **Centro Turístico Brigitte's**, along Playa Negra, T2755-0053, www.brigittecahuita.com.

Reef snorkelling trips leave town for three-hour tour trips to see the corals off Cahuita National Park. US$25 per person. A one-day trip to **Hitoy Cerere Biological Reserve**, promoted as the 'Pharmacy of the World', can be arranged. It's a 1½-hour drive for three hours walking to waterfalls and includes food and entrance fee. The latest adventure

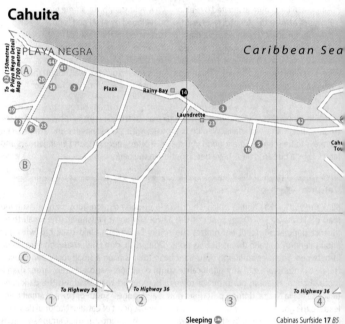

Cahuita

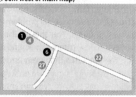

Playa Negra detail
(700m west of main map)

Sleeping
Albergue Mina's Room **1** *C6*
Alby Lodge **33** *C6*
Atlantida Lodge **2** *A1*
Belo Horizonte **3** *A3*
Bobo Shanti **36** *B5*
Bungalows Aché **35** *C6*
Cabinas Algebra
 Playa Negra detail **4**
Cabinas Arrecife **29** *A5*
Cabinas Caribe Luna **5** *B3*
Cabinas Iguana **8** *B1*
Cabinas Nirvana **12** *B1*
Cabinas Safari **14** *B5*
Cabinas Smith **16** *B5*

Cabinas Surfside **17** *B5*
Cabinas Tito **18** *B3*
Camping Kontiki **20** *A1*
Centro Turístico
 Brigitte's **38** *A1*
Chalet y Cabinas Hibiscu
 Playa Negra detail **22**
El Encanto **23** *B3*
Jardín Tropical **25** *B1*
Jenny's Cabinas **9** *B6*
Jungle House **39** *A1*
Kelly's Creek **26** *C6*
La Piscina Natural **32** *A*
Linda's Secret
 Garden **40** *C6*

sport is **body rafting** on the Class I Río Sixaola, which is also easily combined with a trip to the **KeKöLdi Indigenous Reserve** and the **Green Iguana Farm**. US$55 per person.

Trips further afield go up to **Tortuguero** for a two-day, one-night trip staying at Laguna Lodge (see page 382), and cost around US$160 per person, or you can just arrange transport. Most tour operators in town will organize this – only trips to Tortuguero, US$55 one way, US$110 round trip, or US$100 Cahuita-Tortuguero-La Fortuna. Likewise, you can head south to the clear waters and sandy beaches of **Bocas del Toro** in **Panama** for a couple of days, US$155 including accommodation. ➤ *See Activities and tours, page 405, for further details.*

Magellan Inn *Playa*
Negra detail **27**
National Park **28** *C6*
Reggae Bar & Cabins **41** *A1*
Restaurant & Bungalows
  Bluspirit **42** *B4*
Restaurant Chao's
  Paradise **44** *A1*
Riverside Cabinas **43** *C6*
Sol y Mar **31** *C6*
Spencer's Seeside
  Lodge **15** *B6*
Vaz Cabañas **19** *C6*

Eating 🍴
Banana *Playa*
Negra detail **1**
Café del
  Parquecito **16** *B5*
Cha Cha Cha **3** *B5*
El Palenque **5** *B5*
La Casa Creole *Playa*
Negra detail **6**
Miss Edith's **8** *A4*
Roberto's **13** *C6*
Sobre las Olas **14** *A2*
Soda Caribbean
  Flavour **17** *B5*
Vista del Mar **15** *C6*

Parque Nacional Cahuita
→ *Colour map 3, A5.*

ⓘ *There are 2 rangers' stations giving access to the park. At the southern end of Cahuita town, Kelly's Creek station works on a voluntary donation system designed to limit the cost of visiting the beach area of the national park. Puerto Vargas rangers' station at the southern end of the park charges the usual national park entrance fee of US$6. Entering the park from Cahuita gives good access to the beaches, but be warned that valuables go missing if left unguarded. As tedious as this is, either leave all your belongings apart from essentials in your hotel, or have them watched by someone you can trust.*

Cahuita National Park was created in 1970 to protect the coral reef that lies off Punta Cahuita. As the best example of coral in the country, snorkellers who swim or join a tour to the reefs will see brain coral and leafy sea fans in the crystalline waters, and colourful coral fish darting nimbly among through the reef. However, the reef has suffered as a result of the earthquake of 1991 as well as from chemical run-off from banana plantations and increased sediment run-off due to deforestation. The marine portion of the protected area covers over 22,400 ha, the land portion is much smaller measuring just 1106 ha.

You can stroll through a small area of the park by entering from Cahuita, turning around after you've been far enough. Or, if you walk through, which makes for a comfortable day's walk, you eventually arrive at Puerto Vargas and the junction with Highway 36 from where you can catch a bus back to Cahuita. There is also a small tourist complex here with a couple of *sodas* and a simple restaurant. Alternatively, take an early morning bus south, ask the bus driver to drop you at Puerto Vargas and walk back to Cahuita. A 7-km path follows the coastline around Punta Cahuita moving through the coconut palms and entering the mixed forest where you have a good chance of seeing howler monkeys, coatis, raccoons, snakes and butterflies. Areas of swamp are good places to see green ibis, yellow-crowned night herons and northern boat-billed herons.

Turtle volunteers are needed at Cahuita. Contact **Latin American Sea Turtles** ① *T2261-3814, www.latinamericanseaturtles.org*. The season runs from July to September.

South of Cahuita

South of Cahuita, Highway 36 loses interest in the coastline and heads inland at Hotel Creek travelling through Bribrí for Sixaola and the Panamanian border. Energetic travellers will head straight on for Puerto Viejo de Talamanca, those of a calmer disposition should consider following the signs to Samasati Nature Retreat (see page 397).

Puerto Viejo de Talamanca → *Colour map 3, A5.*
Puerto Viejo de Talamanca, 17 km south of Cahuita, is a popular spot where the laid-back relax and surfers seek out the glorious **Salsa Brava** reef break which peaks from December to February. Out of the water, a dark sand beach stretches to the west. To the east the more enjoyable golden beaches of **Playa Cocles**, **Playa Chiquita**, **Punta Uva**, and **Manzanillo** offer a quieter retreat along a road blessed with countless hotels and restaurants. Onshore and away from the beach, botanical gardens invite you to explore: you can visit the nearby KeKöLdi Indigenous Reserve or enjoy countless other activities.

An early morning stroll through the streets puts you face to face with sleepy individuals dazed by the bright sunshine scuffling along scratching ruffled hair. Whether they are hyperactive surfers who have risen too early or late night wanderers who forgot to go to bed is unclear. As you will soon find out, Puerto Viejo, with its good beaches, surfing and energy has become the main party town of the Caribbean coast. With the steady arrival of expatriates setting up homes in quiet backwaters, the Afro-Caribbean feel of the town is slowly being diluted – the town is changing, and changing fast.

Sights A popular trip goes to the **KeköLdi Indigenous Reserve** just east of Puerto Viejo. You can visit the reserve on your own, paying a small fee to see the Green Iguana Farm or join an ATEC-organized tour that includes a four-hour guided hike through the reserve and a traditional meal. Twitchers can join **birdwatching** tours in the surrounding hills and further south in **Gandoca-Manzanillo Wildlife Refuge**.

The **Botanical Garden** ① *open Fri to Mon, 1000-1600, US$5 for the trail, US$10 for a tour (minimum 3 people), T2750-0046, www.greencoast.com/garden.htm*, just a few hundred metres west of the town is a fascinating experience with self-guided jungle trails that loop through a forest filled with flowering and medical plants, and over 60 kinds of fruit trees. In addition to learning about the forest pantry, there's a good chance of seeing toucans, sloths and butterflies from the treehouse and four different species of poison-dart frog that live naturally in the area. Peter and Lindy are incredibly knowledgeable and genuinely passionate about their work.

If you're based in the area for a while, most tour operators can organize trips to **Tortuguero** and **whitewater rafting** around Turrialba, or trips south for a few days to **Bocas del Toro** in **Panama**. ▶▶ *See Activities and tours, page 405, for further details and information about watersports including diving.*

Puerto Viejo de Talamanca

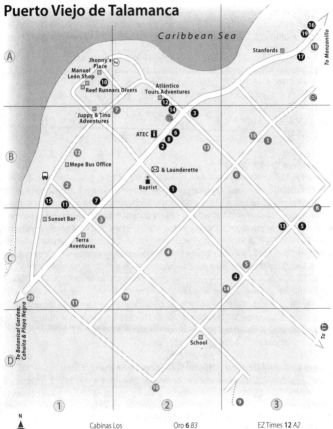

Sleeping
Cabinas Casa Verde 1 B3
Cabinas Diti 2 B1
Cabinas Grant 3 C1
Cabinas Guaraná 4 C2
Cabinas Lika 19 C2

Cabinas Los
  Almendros 7 B2
Cabinas Tropical 8 C3
Cashew Hill Jungle
  Lodge 9 D3
Coco Loco Lodge 10 D2
Jacaranda 5 C3
Kaya's Place 20 C1
Kiskadee 17 D3
Lizard King Resort 18 A3
Los Sueños 11 C1
Maritza 12 B1

Oro 6 B3
Puerto Viejo 13 B2
Pura Vida 14 C3

Eating
Amimodo 16 A3
Café Pizzería Coral 1 B2
Chili Rojo 8 B2
El Dorado 2 B2
El Loco Natural 7 B1
El Parquecito 3 B2
Esmeralda 4 C3

EZ Times 12 A2
Hot Rocks Café 14 B2
Lidia's Place 5 C3
Lotus Garden 17 A3
Pan Pay 10 A1
Peace & Love &
  Bread & Coffee 11 B1
Red Stripe Café 15 B1
Salsa Brava 19 A3
Soda Miss Sam 13 C3
Tamara 6 B2

Tough times in the Talamancas

Asociación Talamanqueña de Ecoturismo y Conservación (Talamancan Association of Ecotourism and Conservation, ATEC) have developed a couple of interesting and challenging activities. One- or multi-day trips head by motorized dugout canoe up the Río Sixaola to the indigenous community of Yorkin, some 20 km west of Puerto Viejo on the Costa Rica–Panama border. Trips longer than a day involve hiking through the forest learning about indigenous lore, handicrafts and staying in simple lodgings.

The ultimate challenge is a no-frills transcontinental crossing of the Talamanca Mountains. It's a tough trek, lasting between six and 15 days, and you carry all your own gear, but recent reports say the crossing has a very high success rate. It's only a hunch, but this has the potential to become one of the great hikes in Costa Rica. For the time being, it's possible to do it for just US$750 for up to three people. Contact ATEC or visit www.ateccr.org for details.

Puerto Viejo to Manzanillo

Heading east from Puerto Viejo the road to Manzanillo provides a wide range of accommodation (see page 400) – seclusion, family homes and must-avoid resorts. The strip is developing quite quickly, despite the restriction of the Gandoca-Manzanillo Wildlife Refuge (see below). About 4 km away through **Playa Cocles**, which has some of the best surfing on this coast, is **Punta Cocles**. A further 2 km is **Playa Chiquita** with many places to stay. Next is **Punta Uva**, which translates as 'Grape Point', and eventually **Manzanillo**, followed by the white sand beaches and rocky headlands of **Punta Mona** and the **Gandoca-Manzanillo Wildlife Refuge**.

Manzanillo → *Colour map3, A6.*

Locally simply known as the 'End of the Road', Manzanillo is little more than a turning circle for buses, but there are good opportunities for laid-back and adventurous activity, including diving – in open sea or the lagoon – surfing, kayking and dolphin watching. **▶▶** *See Activities and tours, page 406, for further details.*

Refugio Nacional de Vida Silvestre Gandoca-Manzanillo

ⓘ *Visiting the park is easy enough and can be arranged through the park offices in Manzanillo, T2754-2133. While exploring the coastline is pretty straightforward, a guide is strongly recommended if you intend to go inland. Trips to the land sections of Gandoca-Manzanillo can be organized through ATEC, see page 406.*

At the southeastern corner of Costa Rica, Gandoca-Manzanillo National Wildlife Refuge protects some of the country's most important wetlands. While many areas in the country suffered from intervention before their value was realized, it looks as if Gandoca-Manzanillo's wealth has been recognized before much damage occurred. A combination of geographical, historical and cultural factors have limited human impact on the moist tropical forest and the inland and coastal waters have been left largely unscathed.

The 5103-ha land portion of the refuge protects creeks, lagoons and the only natural population of mangrove oysters in the Central American Caribbean. The inland waterways are home to manatee, crocodile and caiman, while the forests provide a refuge for jaguar and tapir, howler, capuchin and spider monkeys. Over 300 bird species have been recorded in the area including the vivid green emerald toucanet.

The coastal waters are equally diverse. White sandy beaches to the south of Punta Mona are used by nesting leatherback, loggerhead, green and hawksbill turtles. Below the surface, the 4436 ha of marine reserve protects large areas of coral, including 11 species of sponges endemic to the area.

Marine and freshwater fish species throughout the reserve are estimated to number over 500 and mammals are topped off with three species of resident dolphins – the bottlenose, Atlantic spotted and the little-known tucuxi. All in all, Gandoca-Manzanillo is a natural wonderland and a magnet for wildlife lovers.

Volunteer programmes Several organizations work in the area to ensure that tourism and nature interact with minimum impact. The Talamanca Dolphin Foundation, T2759-9115, www.dolphinlink.org, was established to create a greater awareness of the dolphins in the area and has subsequently developed guidelines for interaction between dolphins and people. The TDF and Aquamor (see page 406) have trained local captains and guides in dolphin etiquette with the aim of keeping the impact of dolphin watching to a minimum. Likewise, the nesting sites of the leatherback turtles are overseen by Latin American Sea Turtles ① T2261-3814, www.latinamericanseaturtles.org. Volunteer programmes exist with both organizations between the end of March and July. They require a commitment of at least 1 week, and charge from US$6 per night camping in the community of Gandoca. Lodging with local families is also available.

Bribrí → Colour map 3, A5.

At Hotel Creek, north of Puerto Viejo, the paved road heads through the hills to the small village of Bribrí, the municipal hub of the region and really only of interest to the visitor because it has a bank.

The town is at the foot of the Talamanca Mountains and the Talamanca Indian Reserve. Access to the park is limited, the most viable option being to plan a trip in conjuction with ATEC in Puerto Viejo (page 406).

Sixaola → Colour map 3, A6.

From Bribrí Highway 36 struggles valiantly through the potholed road that passes through line after line after line of banana plantations. Company villages of clapboard houses, with schools, football pitches and playgrounds for the children spring up from time to time between the banana packing plants and the churches of the Seventh Day Adventists. It's a funny old road that leads you to Panama.

The **border crossing** at Sixaola is straightforward. Immigration is on the Tico side of the bridge, open from 0700 to 1700, closed for an hour at lunch. Cross over the bridge, and Panamanian formalities are immediately on your left. Don't miss them. There is some simple accommodation, but you'd be better off timing your journey to pass straight through.

◉ South Caribbean listings

For Sleeping and Eating price codes and other relevant information, see Essentials, pages 44-47.

◉ Sleeping

South to Cahuita *p386*
LL Selva Bananito Lodge and Reserve, head inland on the challenging road at Bananito, T2253-8118, www.selvabananito. com. A family-run rainforest lodge that is probably winner of the 'Most Difficult Lodge to Reach' award, Selva Bananito is beautifully remote, on the border of La Amistad Biosphere Reserve. It's also ecologically very considerate. More than a holiday stop, it's a place for body, mind and soul. 11 exquisite cabins are made from earthquake-salvaged hardwoods. Tiled bathrooms with solar heated water, lead from terracotta-tiled rooms with a balcony complete with hammock, opening onto spectacular views of the mountains. Without electricity, the evenings are lit by candles and the days start with the sun and the dawn chorus from the surrounding rainforest. Meals cater for vegetarians and non-vegetarians, taking influences from the highlands and the Caribbean. Beyond the tree-hugging calmness, you can also enjoy some serious activities if you're up to it: tree climbing and rappelling, mountain biking, hiking, waterfall swimming, horse riding, or the more sedate pleasures of birdwatching. Getting here can be amusing and involves crossing 4 rivers – 4WD is essential, but Selva Bananito will pick you up or provide a map if you want to drive yourself.
AL Aviarios del Caribe, a few kilometres north of Penshurst, T2750-0775, www.ogphoto.com/ aviarios. 6 spacious rooms and suites, with private bath and hot water, with breakfast included. Beyond the comfortable lodging Aviarios has become the main sloth rescue centre in the country. Buttercup is the first among equals of a cherished family of 2- and 3-toed sloths that turn up through various tales of misadventure to be nursed back to health and then, with a bit of luck, returned to the wild. Judith and Louis are passionate about sloths, which are just crying out for serious research. Beyond getting up close and personal with one of the deadly sins, the 60-ha island delta of the Estrella River has created a tropical paradise alive with otters, monkeys, caiman, poison-dart frogs and butterflies. The bird species list has topped 318. A 3½-hr tour of the Wildlife Sanctuary is US$30 and worth every cent. There's a volunteer programme as well – contact Aviarios for details.

Cahuita *p387, map p388*
Hotels and lodges, especially those out of town, will give discounts for stays of over a week. If you want a little more life in the evenings, choose somewhere central. The quieter, and generally more expensive places, are on the road north out of town along Playa Negra.

In town
AL La Casa de las Flores, T2755-0326, www.lacasadelasfloreshotel.com. Centrally located, this Italian-run hotel is new, modern and very clean. However, the black and white minimalism is quite harsh in the bedrooms.
A Siatami Lodge, down the road from Kelly's, taking the right fork, T2755-0374,

www.siatami.com. A 5-min walk from town but the surroundings are so tranquil it is worth it whether you decide to stay or not. Also accessible from the main road. Siatami (Bribrí for 'sacred stone') offers exceptionally reasonably priced bungalows, attractively painted in different colours, in stunning garden surroundings. One of the best spots in Cahuita.

A-B Alby Lodge, T2755-0031, www.alby lodge.com. Austrian-run with 4 bungalows, styled in a cosy Alpine lodge-meets-thatched Caribbean *cabaña* effect. In a well tended tropical garden, all come with mosquito nets, hot water, and private terrace with a table, chairs and hammock, perfect for lying back listening to the howler monkeys in the surrounding canopy.

A-B Bungalows Aché, down the left fork, T2755-0119, www.bungalowsache.com. Very highly polished wooden cabins neighbouring the national park, with mosquito nets, private hot water bath, fridge, coffee maker and hammocks. Exceptionally clean and pleasant in a great location, one cabin has wheelchair access.

B Kelly's Creek, right on the border of the national park at the southern end of town, T2755-0007, www.hotelkellycreek.com. 4 big rooms in an old plantation-style wooden house complete with broad eves and shaded veranda. Decorated with colourful textiles, the bathrooms are spacious with lots of light, and the ceiling fan and louvred windows are perfect for getting a sea breeze moving through. You can also see caiman and alligators in the neighbouring creek.

B-E Villa del Mar, T2755-0392. 9 cabins of varying specs, 2 with fully equipped kitchen at a bargain price; all have private bath and most have hot water. Very friendly local owners intending to add internet facilities and breakfasts in the future.

B-F pp Cabinas Safari, opposite Cabinas Palmar, T2755-0405, safari@racsa.co.cr. Presentable rooms with fan, cold water (hot water on the way – honest!). Friendly

owner, clean and good value. They also have one larger, more expensive room with kitchen, and a block of cheap, very basic rooms around the corner, with shared bath.

C Cabinas Arrecife, right on the coast, close to Miss Edith's, T2755-0081, www.cabinasarrecife.com. Rooms with private bath, hot water and ceiling fan could be a little bigger, but OK for the price. Mini pool, tiny bar and breakfast now served. A good, quiet spot with good views from the restaurant.

C Jenny's Cabinas, T2755-0256, jenny@ racsa.co.cr. Canadian-owned *cabinas* for singles, doubles and triples, in a quiet spot with sea views. Upstairs is more expensive, but roomier, with private terraces, worth the extra. Breakfast is served from the seaview terrace and they specialize in kayaking trips down the Río Sixaola.

C Spencer's Seaside Lodge, on the beach close to Jenny's, T2755-0027. A lively spot, with brightly decorated rooms, 2 of which come with kitchen, another is available for monthly rental. Rasta Spencer offers local guided tours, accepts credit cards and TCs. Internet use on site. You'll either love it or hate it.

C-D Linda's Secret Garden, T2755-0327. Canadian Linda has designed and built the house herself and the 4 rooms she offers are cool, bright and inviting, with hot water showers behind simple screens, wall murals, and vases of flowers. Small communal kitchen in the garden.

C-D National Park, T2755-0244, www.cahuita nationalparkhotel.com. 14 rooms with just a bit too much plastic. Some rooms upstairs have good views, but the grudging friendliness with poor service ruins a good spot. The restaurant on the beach is just enough to compensate.

D Vaz Cabañas, T2755-0218. 24 rooms, with private bath, hot water and ceiling fan, laid out in a big garden. Nice bright rooms and an easy-come, easy-go atmosphere. Also have 2 suites with cable TV (**A**), not so attractive, but fine. Same owners have now opened more *cabañas* (**C**), under the same name, in front of the bus station. Clean and bright with private hot water showers.

D-E Cabinas Surfside, facing the school, T2755-0246. Clean rooms, good value and with safe parking.

E Bobo Shanti, close to Cabinas Safari. Colourful block of apartments, with a clearly, publicly stated love of Bob Marley, hot water and a communal kitchen.

E Cabinas Smith, T2755-0068. Simple clean rooms, with hot water private bath, fridge and ceiling fans. Not much better than basic, but good for the price.

E Riverside Cabinas, very basic, but clean and private in a quiet location. Enquire at Sol y Mar for information.

E Sol y Mar, T2755-0237. 10 big rooms with ceiling fans and hot water, the ones upstairs have lots of light. Clean, friendly and family-run – good for the price.

F Albergue Mina's Room, T2755-0192. 12 basic rooms owned by Carlos who permanently laments the absence of business. The rooms are basic but clean – enough said.

North along Playa Negra

Places listed in the order that you come across them.

D Restaurant and Bungalows Bluspirit, T2755-0122. 3 very attractive bungalows with hot water private bath and mosquito nets. The bedroom is on an upper level, with a single sofa bed below. An idyllic pathway from the bungalow doors winds through the garden to the beach. Breakfast and dinner are also available in the stylish restaurant.

C Cabinas Tito, T2755-0286. With a distinct Hansel and Gretel feel to the place, these 'little houses' are clean, safe and quiet, with hot water, private bath, fans and some pleasant personal touches. Breakfast is available, as is a laundry service, bike hire, even Spanish lessons. Quiet spot, good for families.

L-C Cabinas Caribe Luna, opposite Cabinas Tito, T2755-0131, www.caribeluna.com. Offers a range of cabins in coloured houses that sleep couples and up to 8 people, in a very large quiet garden. Internet service also available; Catalan, Spanish, French and English spoken.

L-AL El Encanto, T2755-0113, www.elencanto bedandbreakfast.com. 3 beautifully decorated cabins with choice textile hangings, an apartment and a 3-bedroom house in immaculate, well-tended gardens. You will be well taken care of with yoga and massage available in this serene environment. The open-air restaurant is in a Spanish-style villa with breakfast included in the price, and the owners are French.

A Atlantida Lodge, T2755-0115. 30 rooms with private bath, terrace and ceiling fans in what is the closest thing to a resort Cahuita has to offer. Big restaurant and bar, pool and jacuzzi, massage rooms, gym, all in over-tended gardens. Safe parking. Popular with groups. Very pleasant, but not very Cahuita.

C-D Reggae Bar and Cabins, T2755-0515. 4 rooms and a small apartment with kitchen, sleeps 3, all with private bath, a lively bar and restaurant and very friendly owners.

C-B Centro Turístico Brigitte's, T2755-0053, www.brigittecahuita.com. 2 small cabins, 1 with kitchen, sleeping 2 and 3 respectively, but the place is more about providing excellent local information. There's also a good small restaurant for breakfast snacks. Arrange lots of tours on bikes and horses, and provide surf board and snorkel rental. There is also internet and laundry. Recommended.

D Cabinas Nirvana, T2755-0110, nirvana99@ racsa.co.cr. 7 simple wooden cabins sleeping 2-4 people, some with shared bath, others with private bath, balcony and hammock. Pool in the garden.

A-B Jardín Tropical, T2755-0033, www.tropical.ch. Looks can be deceptive, but deep within the undergrowth are some fine self-catering *cabinas*, and a couple of simple, but well-equipped rooms. Seeing a couple of poison-dart frogs and agoutis running about like pet rabbits on leaving, the penny finally dropped – this is a tropical garden. They also have a small bar with pool table. Not so tropical, but worth mentioning.

B-C Cabinas Iguana, T2755-0005, www.cabinas-iguana.com. Swiss-owned with a selection of houses and rooms to rent, some with fully equipped kitchen and balcony. All very neat and tidy with a mosaic-tiled waterfall-fed pool and probably the best book swap in the country with every conceivable language on offer. Credit cards accepted. Very good value, recommended.

C Jungle House, opposite Brigitte's down a small path, T2755-0105. Offers 1 small and simple thatched cabin with private bath, mosquito nets and fan, in exceptionally wild jungle gardens. There's also a restaurant on site. A good spot.

F Restaurant Chao's Paradise, back on the main road, T2755-0261, right opposite the beach. An excellent surfers' budget choice.

D La Piscina Natural. A place so laid back it's horizontal. 5 simple rooms, with a small patio. A sea-fed lagoon creates a natural swimming pool, and tables and hammocks are dotted round the rocky coastline and garden. Sounds good enough to make a reservation. However, Walter the owner is not going near that telecommunications stuff.

AL Magellan Inn, T2755-0035, www.magellaninn.com. 6 comfortable carpeted rooms offer the most luxurious relaxation in Cahuita. The garden is filled with the perfume of bella dona by day, ylan ylan at night and there are plenty of birds. The unimposing pool is a mere 10,000 years old, courtesy of some fossils that have been uncovered. Recommended.

C Chalet y Cabinas Hibiscus, T2755-0021, www.hotels.co.cr/hibiscus.html. A mini-resort with a handful of fully equipped cabins, a small pool, pool table and volleyball court. Popular with families.

C Cabinas Algebra, T2755-0057. 1 big and 1 small fully equipped house, each sleeping

up to 4 people. Nothing fancy, but full of character and a quiet spot.

Camping

G pp **Kontiki** T2755-0261, opposite Centro Turístico Brigitte, with laundry, showers and toilets, and **Paradise Colibris**, out of village close to Playa Negra. Camping is also possible in Cahuita National Park (see below).

South of Cahuita *p390*

L Samasati Lodge and Retreat Center, T2224-1870, www.samasati.com. Filled with enough healthy options to send the caffeine addict packing, Samasati is a genuinely relaxing lodge perched on a hill overlooking the Caribbean. It has 3 houses and 9 beautifully constructed hardwood bungalows with private bathrooms, all with balconies looking across to the ocean or to the rainforest. The real focus of the retreat is yoga, meditation, massage and other therapies given in the wonderful setting of the meditation hall – deep within the privacy of the rainforest. Price includes breakfast, lunch and dinner.

Puerto Viejo de Talamanca *p390, map p391*
In town

AL-A Cashew Hill Jungle Lodge, at the south end of town, T2750-0256, www.cashewhilllodge.co.cr. Quiet and clean cabins in a great escape location, kitchen facilities available, a variety of options, perfect for families. Stunning mirador overlooking jungle and sea, absolutely lovely owners.

A-E Cabinas Los Almendros, T2750-0235, www.cabinaslosalmendros.com. Offer clean chalet-style rooms for pretty much every budget, and they accept credit cards and change cash.

B Coco Loco Lodge, at the southern end of town, T2750-0281, www.cocolocolodge.de. 7 thatched cabins spread out in expansive garden. The cabins are well fitted out, comfortable and in a great spot.

B-C Cabinas Casa Verde, T2750-0015, www.cabinascasaverde.com. Comfortable rooms with hammocks, private bath, ornate cracked-tile showers in beautiful gardens, swimming pool and hot tub. Ask to see the frog gardens. All very pleasant and far too relaxing.

B-C Cabinas Guaraná, T2750-0244, www.hotelguarana.com. 12 rooms all with private bath and hot water overlooking a small patio garden.

C Cabinas Tropical, T2750-0283, www.cabinas-tropical.com. Spotless rooms, with good mattresses, private bath and hot water. Pleasant gardens with a shaded *rancho* in the garden for relaxing, small bar/café. The German owner, Rolf Blancke, is a tropical biologist and runs tours. Recommended.

C Jacaranda, T2750-0069. A very relaxed place set in beautiful gardens with coloured mosaic pathways. Some rooms have a private bath but some of the mattresses are a bit on the thin side. In the garden there are 2 cabins each with a couple of rooms, private terrace and hammocks. A perfect private space for couples and groups travelling together. Shared kitchen, on-site massage service.

C Maritza, T2750-0003. Simple rooms in cabins with private bath, hot water and fans. Affiliated to the Youth Hostel Association. English spoken. Recommended. In front of the beach and next to Maritza bar that hosts live music on Sun nights.

C-D Pura Vida, T2750-0002. Spotlessly clean Swiss-run hotel, with hot water and private bath. A quiet spot with plenty of shade, although lacking in character.

D Los Sueños, T2750-0369, www.costarica guide.info/lossuenos.htm. A great little spot with just 4 rooms sleeping 2-3 people, shared bath and laundry facilities. Brightly painted with a couple of windows in each room. A good choice.

E Cabinas Diti, T2750-0311. 4 rooms with private bath, cold water and ceiling fan. Credit cards accepted. Enquire at Café Stop opposite cabins.

E Cabinas Grant, T2752-0292. 10 large clean rooms, with private bath, fan and a small terrace with a fine view of the parking lot. Most reliable bike rental in town, and good restaurant upstairs.

E Cabinas Lika. 9 rooms and dormitory for 8, friendly, locally owned, good for backpackers, with communal kitchen and lots of hammocks.

E Hotel Oro, T2750-0469. Budget rooms in a convenient, central location.

F Kiskadee, about 200 m south of football field, from where it is signposted, take torch and rubber boots, T2750-0075. Small jungle lodge with 2 dormitories, kitchen available, American-run. Recommended.

F Puerto Viejo, T2750-0620. The most popular backpackers'/surfers' spot in the centre of town. American owner Kurt, resident in Puerto Viejo for 18 years has created a mini-village of coloured cabins and rooms sleeping 1-5. Communal kitchen, surfing information, boards rented, bought and sold. Food available.

F Tamandua Lodge, in a back side road to the east of town, T2750-0298, tamandualodge@yahoo.com. *Tico*-owned with very basic rooms; shared kitchen and free laundry facilities for guests.

Out of town (west)

AL-A El Pizote, T2750-0227, www.pizote lodge.com. 18 cabins and bungalows, many with kitchen. Nice gardens with a couple of pools. Good mid-range restaurant if you want to stop. A comfortable choice and close to town. Credit cards accepted.

AL-C Kaya's Place, the first accommodation you come to heading west along the black sand beach (right opposite the beach, the bus will drop you off at the door if you ask), T2750-0690, www.kayasplace.com. Proudly constructed with an eye on conservation, they have used reclaimed wood throughout; the chunky beds are great, as are the wide lounge areas on the upper balcony.

A-C Chimurí Beach Cottages, turning north on the road on the opposite side of the river to Puerto Viejo, T2750-0119, www.chimuribeach.com. 3 fully equipped bungalows in a wonderfully quiet setting 1.5 km from Puerto Viejo. A good place to check in and be left to your own devices. They have created basic rooms (and 1 dormitory) with thatched roofs that mimic an authentic indigenous village. Shared bath, breakfast included and communal kitchen.

C Cabinas WB, T2750-0413. Basic rooms with private bath and hot water.

Out of town (east)

AL Jordan's Jacuzzi Suites, within easy walking distance of town, T2750-0232. 2 exceptionally smart apartments complete with jacuzzi and indoor Zen garden; perfect for those after inner calm and not on a budget.

AL-A Banana Azul Guest House, Playa Negra, T2750-2035, www.bananaazul.com, New accommodation offering neat and comfortable rooms with private bath as well as beach houses. Breakfast included.

A Calalú, slightly off the main road, T2750-0042. Private bath and hot water, with thatched cabins, some have kitchen, there's also an attractive pool and butterfly gardens.

B Lizard King Resort, T2750-0614, www. lizardkingresort.com. 12 rooms sleeping 2-7, all with private bath, swimming pool, superb restaurant, also disco and bar – don't expect early nights.

B-C Alalunga, T2750-0800, jmmuntada@ mundivia.es. Run by a fantastic Catalan couple. They currently have 2 fully equipped bungalows, both including kitchen and a/c, in peaceful grounds and they plan on several more in the future. There's a pool and restaurant but still has a secluded, tropical atmosphere.

C Agapi Apartments, T2750-0446, www.agapisite.com. All with private bath and some with kitchen and TV. A great spot overlooking the beach.

C Cabinas David, T2750-0542. Clean, tidy rooms within walking distance of

town, they offer breakfast and dinner for a little extra.

C Cabinas Kire, back on the road to Manzanillo, T2750-0448. Has 3 cabins with private shower, 2 with kitchen.

C Hotel Casa Blanca, 10 mins' walk from town, T2750-0001. Simple rooms cooled by ceiling fans, hot water private bath, hammocks on the terrace and snorkelling gear and boogie boards for hire.

C Monte Sol, T2750-0098, www.monte sol.net. A selection of rooms and cabins in very relaxed surroundings, with mosquito nets, terrace and hammocks that back on to a private garden, most with private bath, breakfast US$5. Credit cards accepted, German, English, Spanish and French spoken, internet access available.

D Escape Caribeño, 500 m along road to Punta Uva, T2750-0103, www.escape caribeno.com. Well-furnished bungalows set in pleasant gardens sleeping 2-4. Very small and pretty tiled communal breakfast area, overlooking cascading flowers and exotic bird feeder.

D Vista Verde, T2750-0014. In wild garden surroundings, clean rooms, hot water and shared kitchen.

F Cabinas Talamanca, T2750-0425. Very basic rooms with private shower, pool table and communal kitchen.

F Corazon Caribe, T2250-0617. 17 beds in dormitories, nice restaurant and an owner keen on fishing trips.

F pp Rocking J's, T2750-0657, www.rockingjs.com. A quite unique backpackers' resort by the beach. Rooms with or without fans, camping, communal kitchen, storage lockers and the locally infamous 'hammock-hotel' which is, literally, a hotel of hammocks. Attracts a fun, 'good vibrations' crowd; fronted with bright orange walls and interesting statues at the gate – you can't miss it.

Puerto Viejo to Manzanillo *p392*

Playa Cocles

Places are listed in order as you head south along the beach from Puerto Viejo towards Manzanillo.

B La Isla Inn, T2750-0109, www.laislainn.com. A stone's throw from the beach in front of Cocles Island, 12 comfortable rooms with great views from the balcony. Breakfast, sandwiches and light snacks available at a small extra charge. German, Spanish and English spoken and the owners are more than happy to help you organize trips in the area.

C Beach Break, T2750-0326. Perfect for down-to-earth surfers, all the rooms overlook the ocean. They offer breakfast and lunch, hire out, buy and sell boards and organize lessons.

A Totem Cabinas and Restaurant, T2750-0758, www.totemsite.com. For the more upmarket surfer, an impressive hotel painted almost entirely in purple. Spacious rooms have a terrace overlooking the ocean and are decked out in bamboo – the beds are particularly smart. They also have a very hip and pleasant restaurant serving Italian-style pasta, salads and grilled meats (♈-♈). Swimming pool and surf shop on the way.

L-A Cariblue, T2750-0035, www.cariblue.com. Beautiful gardens surrounded by rainforest are home to 16 Italian-style bungalows, some made of dark hardwoods, and all with thatched roofs. They are spacious inside and out and have balconies. The private bathrooms are all decorated with colourful cracked-tile mosaics. One of the bungalows is fully equipped with kitchen. The restaurant has a Swiss chef and breakfast is included in the price. Swimming pool and bikes available for hire.

D Cabinas Garibaldi, T2750-0101. A cheap option with 7 rooms to choose from (with private bath).

A Azania, T2750-0540, www.azania-costarica.com. 8 well-presented thatched bungalows, in picturesque grounds with hammocks, pool and a jacuzzi. Truly relaxing and they are currently building a restaurant.

A La Costa de Papito, T2750-0080, www.lacostadepapito.com. 10 rustic but elegance bungalows each individually designed with touches you'll barely notice (such as the grain and cut of the wood). The spacious cabins all have cracked-tile bathrooms and a small balcony complete with hammock. Papito is all about good service and the staff go out their way to make sure you get what you need with the least inconvenience. Breakfast is available, and brought to your door if requested. Genuinely very friendly and welcoming, and great for families. There's a minibar in the communal area, a swimming pool and gym, a book exchange and internet available. Relax – your host Eddie Ryan knows exactly what he is doing.

C Olé Caribe, T2750-0455. 8 simple cabins that sleep up to 4 people in a quiet family home.

L-A Aguas Claras, T2750-0131, www.aguasclaras-cr.com. 5 quaint cottages, all brightly painted in pinks, greens and aquas with picturesque white gables in trim surroundings. Fully equipped with everything you will need from a kitchen to mosquito nets and hot water.

AL Villas del Caribe, T2233-2200, www.villasdelcaribe.com. 2-storey apartments looking out to the sea, with fully equipped studio kitchens and a lounge for relaxing in. Not as special, but very friendly and just moments from the beach.

A La Caracola, hidden down a small driveway, T2750-0135, http://lacaracola-cr.com. 14 brightly painted and *Tico*-owned rooms all with hot water private bath, and access to the sea. It's a quiet spot and a good choice.

Playa Chiquita

AL Hotel Kasha, 6 km from Puerto Viejo, T2750-0205, US toll free 1-800-521-5200, www.costarica-hotelkasha.com. 10 quiet bungalows surrounded by landscaped gardens and tropical forest. Satellite TV, very luxurious pool, open-air gym and jacuzzi if the relaxation gets too much. Packages include private airport shuttle, gourmet meals and drinks, tours available.

A-B Miraflores Lodge and Restaurant, T2750-0038, www.mirafloreslodge.com. Clearly the home of an artist and someone seeking to find a genuine affinity with nature. 10 rooms throughout the spacious lodge, with shared bath. Beautiful rooms with loads of natural light and decorated with tropical flowers. Upstairs a visionary shared area looks out directly onto the rainforest and you just have to relax. Pamela Navarro is making all efforts to support the ideals of sustainable tourism and it shows. Check the botanical gardens. While it may be a little too rustic for some, it's a great spot and recommended.

A Playa Chiquita Lodge, T2750-0062, www.playachiquitalodge.com. 12 tranquil cabins and 3 fully equipped houses nestled in superb tropical gardens, each with screened windows, ceiling fan and hot water private bathroom. The open-air restaurant serves local dishes, breakfast is included in the price and you're just a short walk from the beach. Naturalist guides available for tours. The lodge is also home to the South Caribbean Music Festival which takes place every year in the weeks before Easter.

AL Shawandha Lodge, T2750-0018, www.shawandhalodge.com. A luxury complex designed and laid out like an old village, with 11 refined and comfortable bungalows in a neo-primitive style. The bathrooms are particularly appealing and decked out with fantastic mosaics and loads of space. Shawandha have created a truely luxurious experience while managing to hold onto the sense that you are in the thick of the jungle. Well worth treating yourself. Wonderful ambience from the restaurant at night with dishes created by a French chef. The place positively oozes comfort. It's pricey, but worth it.

Punta Uva

L-A Costa Rica Tree House, T2750-0706, www.costaricatreehouse.com. Tree house and beach house accommodation sleeping 2-5 people, equipped with kitchen and close to the beach. A great experience especially for groups and families. Part of the Iguana Verde Federation, www.iguanaverde.com, which runs a conservation project to protect the endangered green iguana which may be wiped out if hunting continues. Visitors permitted on a limited basis, so call first – check the website for more information.

D Sloth Club Cabinas, T2750-0358. Basic cabins and a kitchen, just mins away from the beach.

A-B Pachamama Bungalows, T2759-9196. Fine wooden cabins, with balconies, hammocks and other good comforts.

E Walaba Travellers' Hostel, T2750-0147. Good choice for budget travellers with simple dormitory accommodation.

AL Almonds and Corals Tent Camp, T2759-9056, www.almondsandcorals.com. Brings a warm glow to the soul. Luxury camping in screened, elevated cabins with private bath and hot water – it's like camping without the mud, think 5-star hotel room in a large tent. To be woken by the hum of the jungle in the morning but knowing it can't get in is a special feeling that should be compulsory for all visitors to Costa Rica. Excellent open-air restaurant serving filling, tasty local seafood meals. Many activities available and the elevated walkways lead to a beautiful beach. They have been awarded a certificate for sustainable tourism. They prefer you to book through their San José office – walk-in vacancies rarely available.

B Arrecife, T2759-9200, jorge_puntauva@ yahoo.com. 8 rooms in a large, well built wooden house, private bath, fan, laundry service and can arrange tours. Caribbean food is cooked in their restaurant and it's 2 mins to the beach. There's also a language school here that offers some environmental, cultural and historical programmes.

Manzanillo *p392*
C Pangea B&B, behind Aquamor,
T2759-9204. 2 clean, simple and perfect
rooms, set in a quiet tropical garden. Both
have private hot water bath, mosquito net
and ceiling fan and open on to a spacious
veranda with tables, flowers and shells. The
Californian owner is a chef and will cook
dinner for guests on prior request. He has
also explored every inch of the surrounding
jungle, rivers and ocean and can organize
tours to relatively undiscovered areas.
He uses local guides and takes no
personal commission.
D Cabinas Manzanillo or **Cabinas
Something Diferent** (sic), 100 m or so south,
T2759-9014, T2759-9097. Offers 14 rooms,
small but clean, with cold or hot water, some
have kitchen, fridge and direct TV (**C**). Set in
a private courtyard, friendly owners.
A Colibrí, T2759-9036, www.elcolibri
lodge.com. 5 lodge-style rooms amid the
Manzanillo jungle with all the usual
trimmings, private hot water shower, fans,
hammocks, terraces, breakfast, and tropical
gardens in a perfect escape spot. Parking
and tour information also available.

Bribrí *p393*
D-F Cabinas El Piculino, T2751-0130.
14 clean and tidy rooms, some with a/c
and TV, cheaper without.
F Bar Restaurant El Mango, T2751-
0054. Have a simple room when the
mood takes them.

Sixaola *p393*
F Hotel Doris, T2754-2207. 4 very basic
rooms, each with 2 beds with fan in a rickety
old house, parking and bar beneath.

🍴 Eating

Cahuita *p387, map p*
In town
🍴🍴 **Cha Cha Cha**, T2750-0191. International
menu, great food and service, refreshing chic

decor, very good pasta, bruschetta, tapenade
and hummus. Dinner only, closed Mon.
🍴🍴 **Kelly's Creek** (see page 395). The hotel
restaurant serves authentic Spanish cuisine.
🍴 **Café del Parquecito**. Lives up to its good
name, pancakes, *gallo pinto* or simply toast
and jam, Cahuita's best breakfasts.
🍴 **El Palenque**. Has a distinctly tropical feel
with spilt bamboo walls, sand floors and a
good menu.
🍴 **Miss Edith's**. Almost legendary delicious
and totally authentic Caribbean and
vegetarian food, nice people, good value,
no alcohol licence (bring your own), many
recommendations for breakfast and dinner,
but don't expect quick service. She now
also has a restaurant on the main street.
🍴 **Restaurant Le Fe**, opposite Coco's Bar.
Has an extensive, cheap menu and a
good lively atmosphere.
🍴 **Roberto's**. Open for breakfast, lunch and
dinner. The rustic ambience is particularly
nice in the evening when it's decked out
with candles. Good Caribbean food.
🍴 **Soda Caribbean Flavour**, between
Willie's Tours and Safari Cabins. Has a
variety of mainly rice and beans options.
🍴 **Sol y Mar**, see page 396. Open 0730-1200,
1630-2000. Need to arrive early and wait at
least 45 mins for food. Red snapper and
volcano potato are especially goof. For
breakfast, try cheese, egg and tomato
sandwich. Very good value.
🍴 **Vista del Mar**, facing entrance to
Park. Good fish and Chinese dishes.

Playa Negra
🍴🍴 **Bluspirit**. A small, well-designed
restaurant serving only fish, which is
cooked on the grill to order, alongside
a selection of exotic salsas and salads.
Very relaxed atmosphere.
🍴🍴 **La Casa Creole**, next to the Magellan Inn,
2 km north of Cahuita, call T2755-0104 for
reservations. Open 0600-0900, closed Sun.
A culinary feast of French and Creole
creations and the best restaurant in the
area. Recommended.

Pizz 'n' Love, Cahuita. Excellent new restaurant run by a Dutch hippy. The pizzas are named after celebrities with loads of good toppings such as ricotta, parmesan and ginger prawns, served on tables painted with slogans such as 'give pizza a chance'. Recommended.

Pizzería and BBQ Grill El Cactus. Good pizzas in an open-air restaurant.

Restaurant & Marisquería Tío Cayman, Cahuita. Fish and seafood, as the name suggests.

Restaurant Relax, Cahuita. Over Rikki's Bar. Fantastic pizzas, pastas, some Mexican and fish, plus good Italian wines.

Sobre las Olas, right on the beach serving *Tico* and Mexican food. Loads of seafood, from midday and a popular bar in the evening.

Chao's Paradise. Good little reggae bar looking out to the beach, with oropendola nests hanging out too. Excellent food cooked by Chao himself, including a very saucy vegetarian plate.

Jungle House Restaurant, a little way past Brigitte's place. An impressive open eating area owned and run by a pleasant German couple who cook delights such as goulash, bolognese and Berlin-style liver as well as fish and meat on a charcoal BBQ. A great experience.

Reggae Restaurant. Laid back bar serving a mixed bag of Caribbean dishes, including fish curry and *rondón*.

Restaurant Banana, at the top of Playa Negra. Has a good restaurant and bar popular with the semi-resident gringo crowd with good rice and beans with chicken and salad. Recommended and worth the walk.

Puerto Viejo de Talamanca
p390, map p391

Café Viejo. The town's classiest restaurant and lounge bar. The Italian chef's speciality is Strozzopreti, a mix of aged Italian cheeses, another speciality is the ravioli; all the pasta is home-made.

El Loco Natural. Has an exotic and wholesome menu with special seafood and vegetarian plates. Live music on Thu and Sat.

Salsa Brava. Spanish food and seafood. Recommended, closed Mon.

Café Pizzería Coral, south of centre. Does good breakfasts from 0700, and good pizzas and meals for the rest of the day. Not cheap but recommended.

Chili Rojo. Cosy place that specializes in Middle Eastern vegetarian delights, very reasonably priced with cocktail happy hours every night 1800-2000.

Peace & Love & Bread & Coffee, south of centre. Does good breakfasts from 0700, and good pizzas and meals for the rest of the day. Not cheap but recommended.

El Dorado Restaurant and Bar. Stylish Mexican and Caribbean dishes.

El Parquecito, facing sea in the centre. Nice breezy atmosphere, a lively hub in town, specializes in cheap fish and seafood dishes.

Esmeralda, opposite Jacaranda. Has a well recommended cook (for those in the know, she used to cook for the Garden Restaurant) serves excellent, cheap *comida típica*.

EZ Times. Serves pizza cooked in a wood fire, also a good selection of salads, pasta and bruschetta, in a chilled and stylish bar.

Hot Rocks Café, T2750-0525, www.hotrockscafe.com. Large restaurant/ bar hang out overlooking the sea, offers the only performing stage in the area. Live bands feature regularly, and the friendly American owner wants to introduce theatre. Every night she plays 2 or 3 movies and also football when it's on. Pizzas, steaks and fajitas cooked on volcanic rocks. Good community people.

Lidia's Place. Has good, cheap typical food, including an excellent vegetarian rice and beans, and to-die-for chocolate cake that does not hang around for long.

Oro, close to Miss Sam. Budget Mediterranean-style seafood café serving pastas and paellas.

Pan Pay. Fresh daily croissants, sandwiches and cakes on beachfront. Closed Wed.

Red Stripe Café, opposite the bus stop. Eclectic budget stuff, worth checking out.
Soda Miss Sam, south of the centre. Good local food piled high, seriously cheap.
Tamara, on main street. Open 0600-2100. Local good fish dishes, excellent *patacones*, popular throughout the day, bar upstairs always packed at weekends – the life and soul of the place.

East of town
There are a handful of great *sodas* between Neptune Sports Bar and Bambu.
Stanford's. The restaurant upstairs offers excellent Caribbean cuisine, laid-back breakfasts and good service in a fantastic location. Usually music coming from somewhere.
Amimodo, within easy walking distance of the centre, T2750-0257. Stylish Italian restaurant with fresh bread and pasta.
Lotus Garden. Serves Asian fusion – Japanese, Chinese and Thai, an elegant restaurant complete with oriental garden and waterfall.

Playa Cocles
Jaco's Pizza, in a very pretty little restaurant shortly before Cariblue. Perfect to visit if you are staying in the area. Very friendly staff and a varied menu.
Café Internet Río Negro, further down the road. A vibrant *soda* with online access.
El Rinconcito Peruano. A small Peruvian seafood restaurant serving a mean *ceviche* at good prices. Some rumours that it is closing down, however.

Playa Chiquita
Café Negra another option nearby.
Elena's Restaurant, T2750-0265. Serving Caribbean traditional-style food washed down with cool beers to the sounds of reggae.
Magic Ginger. French food with a great reputation.
La Casa del Pan. Serves freshly baked delights, and breakfast and lunch.

Punta Uva
Ranchito Bar and Restaurant. Have a daily aperitif special between 1600 and 2000; they also hire kayaks and snorkel equipment and offer some local tours.

Manzanillo *p392*
Restaurant Maxi's. Well known in the area for very good seafood and Caribbean dishes, but locals say the prices have been bumped up too high and few people eat there these days. Seems the most popular tourist choice for food, mainly because it is bigger and brighter than anywhere else – in fact there really aren't many other restaurant options. The bar has the potential to be lively when everyone's notglued to the TV, or slightly inebriated. 9 double rooms (**E**) including fan and bathroom, ideal for beach lovers.
Soda Rinconcito Allegre, opposite the entrance to Pangea. Highly recommended by locals who rave about the home-made soups.

Bribrí *p393*
There are several restaurants and *sodas* around town.

○ Bars and clubs

Cahuita *p387, map p388*
Ricky's Bar and **Cocos Bar** are right in the centre of town. Both offer daily treats such as cocktail night, karaoke night or ladies' night, both are open fronted and so close together you can chose the liveliest and always swap if things change. Along the main street **Hannia's Bar** also fills up.

Out of town, the places to get a drink include: **Sobre Las Olas**, the **Reggae Restaurant** and **Chao's Paradise**. **Bluspirit**, has a small bar and plays good chill-out stuff, but closes early.

Puerto Viejo de Talamanca

p390, map p391

Partying is a profession in Puerto Viejo – not for wimps or for those who like an early night.

Stanford's, right on the beach. This is the place to end up at the end of the night when the reggae and dancehall continue well into the early hours. It's also a good spot to mill around and enjoy the music and ambience if you don't actually want to be right in the thick of it.

Dubliner Irish Bar, past Salsa Brava. Don't get too excited – they're apparently often out of Guinness and there's nothing in the way of traditional ale, but there *is* an Irish flag on the wall and lots of Irish music. Good if you fancy something, er … not very tropical.

Zarpe Bar, further east along the seafront. Featuring – reggae mainly – what else?

EZ Times. Offers loaded cocktails and good-time relaxed vibes.

On the main street are **Tamara** and **El Dorado**, with a pool table next door. Both are good places to start the evening with a drink or two, as is the lounge bar at **Café Viejo**, where the chef is a DJ, so the crowd usually always knows where to locate the late-night party. **Neptune Sports Bar** on the ocean corner off the main street also gets lively.

⊛ Festivals and events

Puerto Viejo de Talamanca

p390, map p391

Feb/Mar South Caribbean Music Festival is an annual event in the calendar bringing together both local and national musicians and performers in the weeks leading up to Easter. Ask locally for further details or you could contact Playa Chiquita Lodge, T2750-0062.

⃝ Shopping

Puerto Viejo de Talamanca

p390, map p391

For a wide range of books, check out **David's Library**, above Lotus Garden.

▲ Activities and tours

Cahuita *p387, map p388*

There are a number of tour operators right in the centre of town.

Turística Cahuita, T2755-0071, dltacb@ racsa.co.cr. Long-established Tommy Thompson is a mine of information about the area and now a representative for Interbus. He also arranges sea-fishing trips, US$35 for 4 hrs, dolphin watching, canopy tours and snorkelling.

Willie's Tours, just about to move office but still central, T2755-0267, www.willies-costarica-tours.com. Willie is an excellent and renowned tour operator. He prides himself on good service and uses experienced local guides. Tours include whitewater rafting at Río Pacuare and Reventazon, Tortuguero, visits to the Bribrí people, butterfly and iguana gardens, canopy tours, Bastimentos Panama and, most intriguingly, overnight trips to a healing Bribrí shaman. Can sort out most transport challenges in the country (including Cahuita-Tortuguero-La Fortuna for US$100! Also has high-speed internet access.

None of the following places stands out particularly but they are all close to each other, so walk around and see which one takes your fancy.

Cahuita Tours, T2758-0000.

Mister Big J Tourist Service, T2755-0328.

Roberto Tours, T2755-01178.

Puerto Viejo de Talamanca
p390, map p391

Growth in recent years has seen rapid changes in activity opportunities the area.

Diving
Aquamor, based in Manzanillo, see below, have now established over 100 dive sites in the surrounding waters.
Reef Runners Divers, T2750-0480, www.reefrunnerdivers.com, in Puerto Viejo. Offers full PADI courses and 'discover scuba', temporary 2-week certificates for unqualified divers to experience the underwater scene. A 2-tank boat dive costs about US$80 with at least 2 people.

Other watersports
Naturally, a lot of activities in the area involve water. **Surfing** is best from Nov to Mar. You can also rent **snorkelling** gear, sea **kayaks**, **boogie boards** and **mountain bikes** from several places in town.

On land
You can also rent **scooters** from **Natural Born Riders**, 25 m south of the bus stop in Puerto Viejo, T8841-5578. Great for independent travel. You can visit Manzanillo, Cahuita, Bribrí or simply explore the area. They also hire **quad-bikes** for more adventurous excursions. Scooters are also available at **Amimodo**, T2750-0257.
Dragon Scooter Rental, T2750-0728, sales@dragonscooterrentals.com, in Puerto Viejo.

Tour operators
ATEC (Asociación Talamanqueña de Ecoturismo y Conservación), T2750-0398, www.ateccr.org. Set up in 1990 to tackle some of the issues caused by rapid growth and now provides advice and organizes many trips in the area and has by far the broadest offering (see box, page 392).

Atlántico Tours Adventures, T2750-0004. Offers a range of trips, building on the popularity of the area.
Terra Aventuras, T2750-0750, www.terraventuras.com.
Puerto Viejo Tours, T2750-0411, www.ptoviejotours.com. Offer a full list of adventures, including such diverse combinations as the indigenous reserve and body rafting.
Juppy & Tino, opposite Maritza Bar, T2750-0621, juppytinoadventures@yahoo.com.

Manzanillo *p392*
Aquamor, T2759-9012, www.greencoast.com/aquamor.htm. Have been operating a **diving** and **kayak** centre out of Manzanillo since 1993 and have now established over 100 dive sites in the surrounding waters including diving trips to the Gandoca lagoon by kayak. While the general criticism of poor visibility in Costa Rica stands true, there are times when the diving can be world-class, the reef diving in particular. In general the diving is best in Sep and Oct, Apr and May, although opportunities always arrive outside these months. 2-tank dives start at US$55, a beach dive is US$30. A full PADI course is US$300. When not playing with tanks, the Aquamor team are **surfing on sea kayaks**, something they claim they'll have you doing in no time. More genteel kayak adventures can be found in small rivers and lagoons. Kayak rental is US$6/hr or US$15 for 2 hrs guided.
Dolphin-watching trips in Gandoca-Manzanillo Wildlife Refuge using local captains and guides can also be arranged through Aquamor. US$35 or US$30 for more than 2 people.

⊙ Transport

Cahuita *p387, map p388*
A direct service from **San José** Terminal del Caribe with **Transportes Mepe**, T2257-8129, at 0600, 1000, 1330 and 1530, return 0730, 0930, 1130, 1630, 4 hrs, US$6.80, and

from **Puerto Limón**, in front of Radio Casino, T2758-1572, almost hourly from 0500-1800, returning 0630-2000, 1 hr, US$1.80. Both continue to **Bribrí** (US$0.60) and **Sixaola** (US$1.80) on the Panamanian border.

Puerto Viejo de Talamanca
p390, map p391

There are 4 daily buses from **San José** from Gran Terminal del Caribe at 0600, 1000, 1330 and 1530, returning at 0700, 0900, 1100 and 1600, 4½ hrs, US$7.90. **Transportes Mepe** in Puerto Viejo, T2750-0023. 10 daily buses from **Limón** between 0500-1800, 1½ hrs, US$2.60. **Cahuita**, US$0.65, 30 mins. 3 daily buses to **Manzanillo** at 0730, 1200, 1630 and 1930, 30 mins, US$0.65. 5 daily buses to **Sixaola** 0545-1915, 1½ hrs.

Amimodo rents scooters by the hour, day or overnight, T2750-0257.

Manzanillo *p392*
Express to Manzanillo from **San José**, Terminal Sixaola, daily, 1600, returning at 0630. Buses travel between **Puerto Viejo de Talamanca** and Manzanillo. They leave Puerto Viejo at 0730, 1600 and 1930, returning at 0500, 0830 and 1700, 30 mins, US$0.80.

Bribrí *p393*
Local departures for **Shiroles** 4 times a day, providing transport to the villages of **Chase** and **Bratsi**.

Sixaola *p393*
Direct buses leave Terminal del Gran Caribe in **San José** at 0600, 1000, 1330 and 1530, 6 hrs, US9.80, returning at 0500, 0700, 0930, and 1430. You can join this bus at **Limón**, **Cahuita**, **Puerto Viejo** and **Bribrí**. Additional options from Limón.

ⓘ Directory

Cahuita *p387, map p388*
Banks There is a branch of **Banco de Costa Rica** on the main entrance road into Cahuita. **Cahuita Tours** change dollars and TCs. But it's wise to take plenty of colones from Limón, although several places accept credit cards. **Internet** Willie's Tours, opposite Cabinas Palmer, US$2 per hour. Spencer's Seeside Lodge, enquire for rates. **Laundry** There is a launderette in town and also on the Playa Negra road. **Language schools** Caribe Spanish Language and Cultural Centre, T2775-0417, operates a language school in the area. Call or make inquiries at Belo Horizonte. The friendly owner of **Cabinas Tito** is a professional teacher and offers groups and individuals Spanish lessons, around US$5 per person per hr. **Post office** Next to police station at northern end of town. **Useful addresses** The police are at the northern end of town.

Puerto Viejo de Talamanca
p390, map p391

Banks There is a branch of Banco Costa Rica in town. The alternative is to change cash and TCs at Manuel Leon's general store on the beach, although commission on TCs is high. **Cabinas Los Almendras** change cash and accept credit cards. **Post office** The post office is half a block south of ATEC. **Telephone and internet** ATEC is the communications hub of the town. You can visit them for international telephone calls, faxes and internet. There are also a couple of public telephones outside their office. **Video Mundo**, a few doors down from ATEC, offers internet access, along with DVD and video rental. **Cibercafé** just south of Stanford's, has a couple of internet connections. **Useful addresses** Police can be contacted on the seafront.

Sixaola *p393*

Banks There are no banks in Sixaola. It is possible to change money in the supermarket, but rates to the US dollar are very poor. Shops near the border in Panama will accept colones but shops in Changuinola and beyond do not. If heading to Bocas del Toro the bank there does not accept colones.

Immigration The border is open 0700-1700. The immigration office is just before the railway bridge over the Sixaola river which marks the border with Panama. All formalities are quick and straightforward.

Contents

410 History

421 Modern Costa Rica
421 Government
421 Economy

424 Culture

428 Land and environment
428 Geography
431 National parks
431 Wildlife of Costa Rica

452 Books and websites

Footprint features

413 The Walker affair
422 Costa Rica's provinces
427 Francisco Zúñiga

Background

History

Pre-Columbian history

Population of the Americas began somewhere between 40,000 and 15,000 years ago, when mankind first crossed the Bering Straight from Asia. A slow southerly migration steadily peopled the continent, and evidence suggests that humans first appeared in what is now Costa Rica roughly 10,000 years ago.

Early human settlement developed in this intermediate zone without a single dominant cultural group. The region was very much at the boundary of a north-south divde, taking its influences from both the Maya civilizations of modern-day Mexico and from several smaller groups in South America.

Farming, which began in earnest around 1000 BC, is the greatest indicator of this division. The Chorotega people, who lived in the northwest of Costa Rica on the Nicoya Peninsula, present day Guanacaste, were the largest and most advanced tribe in the country at the time of conquest. Arriving from Chiapas in southern Mexico around the 13th century, they cultivated beans and maize and developed a tradition of ceramics influenced by the Mesoamerican cultures of the Maya and later the Aztec. However, people on the Caribbean coast and in southern regions were more influenced by South American cultures, leading to the dominance of tuber cultivation, in particular yucca or manioc. Likewise, the dominance of jade, an influence from the north, waned with the decline of the Maya between 500-800 AD, allowing the influence of gold from cultures of the south to emerge.

With increased food supplies, social organization and hierarchy developed to manage the increased populations. Regions of Costa Rica were divided into *cacicazgos* which were the basis for exchange of goods within the country and further afield. Rivalry and competition were intrinsic to the hierarchy, and dominance of an area was directly related to military ability and population. Likewise, dominance relied on the creation and development of strategic alliances to overcome and dominate the enemy.

Archaeological evidence of early settlements in the country are scarce. The largest single pre-columbian site in the country is the Guayabo National Monument, close to Turrialba, which is believed to have been ruled by a *cacique* or shaman. Inhabited from 1000 BC to 1400 AD, the economy of Guayabo was based on agriculture, hunting and fishing. The reasons for abandoning the site remain a mystery, as do explanations of the country's other main archaeological remains, the stone spheres found dotted around the Diquis Valley in the south of the country.

Population estimates for the country prior to the arrival of the Spaniards vary dramatically. Early studies put the population as low as 27,000, but these estimates are almost certainly made after the first wave of diseases impacted on the region. More recent studies put the figure somewhere between 250,000 and 400,000.

The Spanish arrive

The Genoese explorer Christopher Columbus introduced European influences to the country when he dropped anchor off the coast of Puerto Limón at Isla Uvita on 18 September 1502. After 17 days exploring the coastal area, teased by the prospect of Indians decorated in gold, Columbus and his men moved south, calling this section of the coast of 'Veragua' *costa rica* – the rich coast. The precious metal never materialized in significant quantities but rumours travelled far and fast at the turn of the 16th century.

For almost 60 years the Spanish made half-hearted attempts to settle the region, with the primary intention of taking rich pickings of gold and easy labour, only to be hampered by difficulties. The conquest of Central America was launched from Panama to the south, and following Cortés' successful defeat of the Aztecs, from Mexico to the north. Using Panama as a base **Diego de Nicuesa**, appointed governor of Veragua in 1508, launched the first attempt to establish a settlement in Costa Rica on the Caribbean coast. Nicuesa's expedition foundered off the coast of Panama and ground troops attempting to march north endured sickness, hunger and encountered hostile tribes who denied the Spaniards food and slaughtered the invaders when the opportunity allowed, eventually forcing them to retreat. In 1513 the governor of Darién in Panama, **Vásco Núñez de Balboa**, led his forces across the isthmus and became one of the first Europeans to see the Pacific Ocean. Following the difficulties of colonizing the Caribbean, the focus now shifted to the Pacific coastline. Coastal explorations of the Pacific coastline reached the Nicoya Peninsula and by 1522 **Gil González Dávila** had established good relations with the Chorotega people. After a foray that continued further north to Nicaragua and Honduras, Dávila returned to Panama with a cargo of gold and equally importantly, the souls of several thousand converted Chorotegas. However, a couple of years later, when Francisco Fernándo de Córdova established the first Spanish settlement of **Villa Bruselas** to the north of present day Puntarenas, the site had to be abandoned within three years as a result of starvation and further attacks from the Chorotega.

Despite the successes, the pattern of exploration, settlement and desertion continued as Spanish attempts at forced colonization met with resistance. Not until 1561, under orders from King Philip II of Spain, was an attempt at conquest successful, when **Juan de Cavallón** managed to cross the territory from east to west for the first time, establishing a permanent settlement in the northwest of the central highlands at Garcimuñez. But it is **Juan Vásquez de Coronado** who receives the credit for establishing the first truly permanent settlement in the central highlands. Forging temporary alliances and utilizing rivalries between different indigenous groups – a technique that proved successful for Cortés in Mexico and Pizarro in Peru – Vásquez de Coronado founded Cartago in 1563. He established a settlement of reasonable size in the relative comfort of Cartago which had plenty of fresh water and fertile volcanic soils for agriculture and was away from the sweltering heat and fetid coastal waterways of the Caribbean.

Despite Vásquez de Coronado's less bellicose approach to settlement, he too faced problems of indigenous uprisings. The energy and resources of the governor was all but depleted and the city nearly abandoned in 1568, when the next governor **Perafán de Ribera** arrived with extra supplies, manpower and enthusiasm for the pursuit of precious metals and conquest. The Talamanca people resisted his attempts at pacification, and plans to settle in the southern region were quickly abandoned.

With Cartago finally secured, the division of land between settlers began. While land was divided between Spanish gentry and commoners, the relatively low indigenous populations and the absence of mineral wealth in any substantial quantity denied the landholders many of the comforts afforded those in other parts of the Spanish empire. While the gentry provided leadership in municipal government, the reality was that most settlers were simple farmers, forced to work the land themselves. Some historians suggest this is the bedrock of the liberal sentiments that created the social advances and democratic traditions of modern Costa Rica.

The absence of labour was partly the Spaniards' own doing. First, the indigenous population was decimated by smallpox, measles and a host of other new diseases introduced to the new world by the Europeans against which the indigenous people had no immunity. They were then reduced still further by the discovery of gold and silver in South America. A heavy demand for labour in the ports of Panama meant many men of working age were sold to work as slaves. Once the conquerors had settled, the *encomienda* system, which allowed the new landlords to extract labour and produce from the indigenous population in return for protection and religious guidance, lacked enough labour to fuel the system. By the 1560s, the indigenous population had been reduced by as much as 95 and the indigenous people that remained had already demonstrated their resistance to the Spanish.

Europeans settling the land

The new settlers had hardly made an encouraging start and the absence of labour and mineral wealth placed Costa Rica in a colonial no-man's land. The Spanish system of administration was both regional and tiered. Costa Rica answered first to the Audiencia of Guatemala which included land from Chiapas in Southern Mexico to the southern border of Costa Rica and ultimately to Spain. Costa Rica's size did not warrant her involvement in the detailed financial administration of empire and the province deemed too remote to manage at distance. Apart from taxes and salaries, which were collected and paid from Nicaragua, Costa Rica was left to govern herself without much interference.

Left to her own devices and to fend for herself, the small size of the Costa Rican population limited the development of an internal market and the aspirations of settlers were quickly lowered. Brief moments of optimism broke the gloom. Mules bred in the north were fattened in the Central Valley before heading to Panama to shift cargo across the isthmus supply route. In Guanacaste, cattle were raised and slaughtered for tallow and leather, planting the seeds of ranches throughout the region. Small concentrations of cacao plantations rose up around the Caribbean port of Matina, responding to a demand around the Caribbean and in Venezuela, and were actually encouraged and promoted by the governor Diejo de la Haya Fernández (1718-1727). But in general opportunities were rare and the outlook bleak. For a brief time in 1709, money was so scarce that the cacao bean was temporarily used as currency.

A two-pronged military missionary expedition to the Talamanca region to extract forced labour from the remaining indigenous population culminated in the last significant indigenous uprising in 1709 and the eventual execution of the leader **Pablo Presbere**. The absence of labour, the growth in cacao production and trade with the Caribbean created the first wave of Afro-Caribbean migration as slaves were imported from Jamaica. However, by the 1750s, the demand for cacao, and consequently slave labour, had fallen due to increased competition from regions throughout the Caribbean.

The slow growth and brief periods of prosperity through the 1700s saw the founding of the fledging settlements of Heredia (1706), San José (1736) and Alajuela (1782). The award of a monopoly to Costa Rica for tobacco production for the whole of Central America in the late 1700s was the catalyst for the growth of smallholdings in the central highlands and the first signs of an internal economy. San José grew too, with the establishment of the trading centre for tobacco there, and this was to prove significant when a second crop introduced at the turn of the 18th and 19th centuries also played a significant role in the nation's development. That second crop, coffee, was introduced from Cuba in the late 1700s – although the official date for introduction is often reported as 1808 – and planted in the volcanic soils of the Central Valley. The sleepy colonial territory was finally waking up, and a new phase of Costa Rican history was just beginning.

The Walker affair

In 1855, at a time when Costa Rica was beginning to enjoy the fruits of her independent labours during the presidency of Juan Rafael Mora Porras, one William Walker entered the Central American stage from the United States. Driven by the Monroe Doctrine which made all Latin American developments to be the business of the US, a thinly veiled attempt to protect US business interests and reintroduce slavery, Walker made a belated and ambitious attempt to reunite Central America.

His academic record was impressive: medicine, law then finally journalism before embarking on his ill-fated adventures to the south.

Arriving in Nicaragua in 1855 at the invitation of the Liberals, Walker declared himself President and set about implementing his expansionist plans. The Central American nations took up arms.

When news reached Mora Porras that a small band of Walker's forces had taken La Casona ranch in the northwestern province of Guanacaste, he hurriedly gathered together his armed forces, swelled by volunteer peasants and labourers, to lead a victorious assault in March of 1856. Costa Rican forces marched on to Rivas in southern Nicaragua where Walker's troops were defeated in a bloody battle during which the young Alajuelan drummer boy Juan Santamaría rose to the status of national hero by torching the mercenaries' military headquarters.

Walker eventually surrendered to British forces in 1857, and after several attempts at talking his way out of his predicament, colonial powers, tired of his meddling, handed him over to Honduran authorities who tried and sentenced him to death by firing squad in 1860.

For Costa Rica, the Walker affair proved a defining moment. The country lost one tenth of its population from the battle and the cholera epidemic brought in with the army, but the Battle of Rivas distilled a sense of nationalism in what was still a young state.

Independence from Spain by post

On the eve of independence the population of Costa Rica had grown to 63,000 – still easily the smallest of the provinces of the Audiencia de Guatemala and just one 20th of the total. (The province amounted to little more than the principal settlements of Cartago, Heredia, San José and Alajuela.) Following the near decimation of the indigenous populations, the mixed race *mestizo* population of Costa Rica had more Spanish blood than those of neighbouring countries with less than 10 of Costa Ricans being able to trace a pure Spanish heritage, the friction between the Costa Rican born and the Spanish born and bred authorities lacked the heat found in some Latin American countries. This mutual disinterest between ruler and ruled could hardly be illustrated better than when independence for the nations of the Central American isthmus was granted on 15 September 1821. Such was the significance of the lost to the motherland and the importance to Costa Rica, the notification of independence is reported to have taken a month to arrive from Guatemala City.

Independence created problems for Costa Rica which were to impact on the country for almost 20 years. Mexico declared independence a few weeks before the Central American provinces. **General Agustín de Iturbide** invited the provinces to join a Mexican Empire, which sent the four towns of Costa Rica into a tailspin. Cartago and Heredia favoured joining the Empire, while San José and Alajuela preferred federal relations with the Central American provinces or better still, complete independence. A brief civil war broke out in late 1822 in which the republican forces of San José and Alajuela emerged victorious, and domination by Mexico was rejected. While the fighting was in vain, as Iturbide's imperial aspirations collapsed in early 1823, it did expose the rivalry between the towns of the Central Valley.

With the disintegration of the Mexican Empire, Costa Rica joined the newly formed Central American Federation. As the prospects for peaceful integration through this fledgling Federation waxed and waned with varying degrees of violence, the people of Guanacaste chose to secede from Nicaragua in 1824. Meanwhile in Costa Rica the conservatives of Cartago and Heredia resented the recent victory of San José and Alajuela, and the rivals fought over the dominance of the nation in a series of regional quarrels. In desperation, in 1834 the head of state **José Rafael de Gallegos** approved the somewhat bizarre Law of Movement which rotated the capital seat every four years. But the conflicts continued and Gallegos resigned to be replaced by the forceful leader **Braulio Carrillo Colina**, who firmly established San José as the capital.

Disgruntled by the imposition of a liberal, Cartago, Heredia and Alajuela rose up against San José in a league of capitals. The **War of Leagues** in 1835 was victorious for Carillo and eventually put an end to the rivalry for the capital seat.

The golden bean and social progress
Elected as the first head of state by Congress in 1824 **Juan Mora Fernández** governed over a period of economic stability which saw the construction of state schools and houses, the founding of the national mint and government promotion of coffee cultivation. Following the introduction of coffee at the end of the 18th century its importance to the economy grew steadily and by 1829 coffee had overtaken cacao, tobacco and sugar to become the nation's major source of foreign revenue. When Braulio Carrillo Colina became head of state in 1835, he encouraged cultivation of the coffee industry still further, donating publicly owned land to anyone who would plant it with coffee trees, and constructing roads to bring coffee to market.

The breakthrough for Costa Rican coffee occurred in 1843, when an English captain, seeking ballast for his return journey to Liverpool, took on board sacks of coffee beans. The cargo was well received in England and Costa Rican coffee no longer stopped in Chile to be blended with inferior beans, but was shipped direct to Europe. This boom in coffee production and exports to Europe funded social developments for much of the 19th century.

When Carrillo declared himself dictator for life in 1841, his conservative opponents sought out the Honduran General **Francisco Morazán Quesada**, the former leader of the Central American Federation, to remove Carrillo from office. Morazán's tenure as head of state was briefly popular until he imposed direct taxes with the aim of funding a Costa Rican army and relaunching his ideal of the regional federation. He was overthrown and later executed in San José's Central Park.

Morazón's execution cleared the way for a number of developments which were a result of liberal enlightenment that balanced the vested interests of the coffee elite, with a belief in improved education, public works and more efficient government.

A new constitution in 1844 unsuccessfully attempted to introduce direct election, removing the process from the meddling of a Congress dominated by influential families. In 1847 Congress named the youthful 29-year-old **José María Castro Madriz** the first president of the republic. Castro officially declared Costa Rica a republic in 1848, drawing a line under the perennial discussions amongst the ruling classes on the subject of joining the Central American Federation. Castro's wife, Doña Pacifica, is credited with designing the national flag. As a co-founder of the University of Santo Tomás in 1843, Castro stressed the importance of education and, as a believer in democracy, encouraged free speech and freedom of the press. But while his achievements appear noble, his reforms eventually trod on the toes of the barely established coffee elite and he was replaced.

When **Juan Rafael Mora Porras** rose from the coffee aristocracy to become president in 1849, the role of the coffee elite in society and the economy was established and influenced the development of the nation through the defining years of the 19th century.

The growth of the nation was facilitated by the excellent reputation of Costa Rican coffee in Europe. While the majority of smallholdings were family owned – a fact that is still true today – a brief crisis between 1847 and 1849 assisted the coffee barons to add to their wholesale role by acquiring property. Simple economies of scales exacerbated the differences with every trade cycle and an ever stronger coffee elite increasingly influenced society. The arrival of Porras as president in 1849 marked the beginning of the rule of the coffee barons which lasted until 1870. Liberal government policies continued to improve the general well-being of the nation while nurturing the coffee industry.

With every shipment of the golden bean to Europe, vessels returned from Europe with an increasing supply of European goods. Styles of fashion, entertainment, architecture and culture – exemplified in the extravagance of the Teatro Nacional paid for by a direct coffee tax and inaugurated in 1897 – all took their lead from Europe. For Iván Molina and Steven Palmer, contemporary Costa Rican-US historians, it is the 'European disposition' of the new coffee elite that saw the introduction of liberal ideals to Costa Rica.

However, the continued domination of the political and economic future of the country by the coffee families led to the coup of 1870 which gave **General Tomás Guardia Gutiérrez** the presidency. Guardia ruled as an authoritarian dictator determined to break the power of the coffee barons, redistributing land from some of the larger landowners and introducing taxes on personal wealth. He introduced a new constitution in 1871 which extended the voting to an electoral college and abolished the death penalty. But his programmes continued the liberal tradition of extending education, stimulating trade and encouraging greater production of coffee and sugar. Guardia also initiated the construction of the **Atlantic railroad**.

Guardia succeeded in breaking the power of the coffee families, only to replace them with his own nepotistic successions. On Guardia's death in 1882 his brother-in-law **Próspero Fernández Oreamuno** ruled as president until his death in 1885, when his brother-in-law **Bernardo Soto Alfaro** took the presidential position. But despite continuing the dictatorial style, Soto introduced **free and compulsory education**, the national library, the Red Cross and promised to abide by congressional elections at the end of his term in 1889. With freedom of the press, the first truly honest and open election in Costa Rica's history took place. Soto set himself up as the victor, but lost.

The 1890s marked a shift in the political and economic landscape of the country beyond the introduction of a considerable improvement in the democratic process. The church tired of the consistent undermining of its role as the educators and moral guides of society also re-entered the political arena. As early as 1825 the income of the church through state-collected taxes had been cut, then abolished, and eventually the clergy were demanded to pay taxes on their income. In the presidency of Fernández civil marriage and divorce had been introduced, religious instruction in schools prohibited and the Jesuits expelled from the country. The creation of the Partido Unión Católica (Catholic Union Party) in 1891 was intended to defend the interests of the church.

The banana boom

When Guardia instigated the construction of the railroad link from the Central Valley to the Atlantic coast, the simple logic was to speed up and reduce the cost of transporting coffee to European markets. Guardia contacted **Henry Meiggs** who had experience of railroad building in Chile and Peru. Almost £4 million was borrowed from British banks to finance the construction.

The first tracks were laid in 1872, but due to mismanagement and corruption, construction was regularly delayed. The task actually fell to Meigg's nephew **Minor Cooper Keith** who completed the line in 1890, having managed to secure some generous concessions along the way in return for taking on the debts of the railroad. Keith moved in political and social circles that enabled him to negotiate a 99-year lease on the railroad, purchase land for banana cultivation alongside the track and marry the daughter of former president Castro Madriz. In the process of construction over 4000 workers died and labourers from China, Italy and then from Jamaica were recruited to work on the railroad. By the time the railroad opened in 1890 foreign capital had gained a strong foothold in the Costa Rican economy, the economic profile of the country had shifted and the social make-up of the country had been dramatically altered.

With the completion of the railroad a permanent link to the Caribbean was established and the banana industry grew rapidly. In 1899 Keith created the *United Fruit Company* (today known as *Chiquita*) and many of the labourers that worked on construction of the railroad moved to work in the port of Limón or the banana plantations. The coffee elite of the highlands avoided investing in bananas, leaving the industry and the lowlands to develop in almost complete isolation. Between 1910 and 1920, banana exports had grown to equal coffee in value and control of the Caribbean lowlands was almost entirely in the hands of the company which colloquially became known as *Yunai*.

Seeds of democratic reform

On the back of the prosperity of the late 19th century and the increased affluence for the agricultural elites, an increasingly educated populace enlarged by considerable migration from Spain, Germany and Italy, and ever-greater hardships for plantation workers and the urban working class sowed the seeds of resentment in the early years of the 20th century. The constitution was nudged gently towards direct elections and eventually produced President **Alfredo González Flores** (1914-1917). When he proposed the liberal reforms of a state bank and direct taxes as gestures towards reducing growing inequalities and tackling problems with the public finances produced by falling coffee prices, González lost popular support and was ousted in the military coup of **Federico Tinoco Granados** in 1917. Events conspired against Tinoco as the US withdrew support for the regime and loss of German markets due to World War I crippled public finances still further. By popular consent he was removed from power in 1919.

Protest movements and revolutions springing up around the world in Russia, Mexico and closer to home in neighbouring Nicaragua added strength to the ever-louder cry for better working conditions. Economic hardship between the two world wars, culminating in the depression of the 1930s led to greater social conflict. The broadening influence on the political process exerted by the educated and opinionated population, introduced the notion of ideology into the Costa Rican political process. The **Reformist Party**, which promoted unions, an end to state monopolies and control over foreign capital, was created in 1923, founded by Jorge Volio, a politician and priest credited with the introduction of the Christian Socialist policies to national politics. The **Communist Party** was founded in 1931, and under the leadership of Carlos Fallas led strikes that in 1934 paralysed the banana plantations of the *United Fruit Company*. One outcome of the strike was the introduction of a minimum wage. However, economic recovery towards the end of the 1930s was abruptly halted by the outbreak of war in Europe and once again the immediate loss of markets for bananas and coffee. But despite the economic problems, government investment in health and education continued to improve health provision and reduce levels of illiteracy.

Civil war

In the 1940s tensions between agricultural and urban forces rose to boiling point and the eventual outbreak of civil war. The elections of 1940 awarded the presidency to **Rafael Angel Calderón Guardia** of the Partido Republican Nacional (PRN). Calderón favoured government intervention in social and economic affairs and marked a slight shift in the liberal tradition. His early reforms were unsuccessful but raised the suspicions of many landowners, and in a small band of modernizing liberals that prompted the idea it was the structures and institutions of governments (not just the policies) that needed to be changed for the good of the country overall. Costa Rica's early declaration of war against the Japanese and shortly after with Germany and Italy earned Calderón the greater criticism that he had overstretched the position of a country without the means to defend itself. One vocal critic of Calderón was **José Figueres Ferrer**, a landholder with sympathies towards the modernizing factions, who denounced the president. Figueres was promptly exiled to Mexico. Calderón's social intervention increased with a swathe of reforms called the 'Social Guarantees' which improved job security, proposed health insurance and introduced a moderate series of land reforms. With the criticism of Calderón's opponents escalating and with elections approaching in 1944, Calderón tried to shore up his political support. The church gave tacit support to his social reforms and the reintroduction of religious instruction in schools. An unholy alliance was created when rumours of a coup pushed Calderón into the arms of the renamed and toned down Communist Party, thus gaining valuable support of labour movements which promptly led to the introduction of a minimum wage, an eight-hour working day and trade union rights for workers. While the reforms further ostracized the ruling elites, young professionals and liberal modernizers, opposition to communism was widespread and growing.

After two years in exile in Mexico the vehemently anti-communist **Figueres** returned in 1944 to find the Communist Party still playing an increasingly significant role in national politics and with no direct political heritage of his own, he formed an allegiance with Calderón's adversaries.

Calderón himself was constitutionally barred from standing as president for a second term in the election that same year, but his PRN puppet candidate, **Teodoro Picado Michalski**, was voted in, and held the presidency till 1948. Civil liberties were increasingly restricted through the Picado presidency and unrest rose to new heights when government forces killed two protesters. Picado promised to abide by the outcome of presidential elections in 1948, but few were convinced. **Figueres**, calling on Central American allegiances he had made while in exile, planned for military intervention if democratic elections failed.

The elections of 1948 set Calderón against **Otilio Ulate Blanco** who occupied the anti-Calderón ticket. The election produced a victory for Ulate but, as feared, alleged voting irregularities led Congress to award the presidency to Calderón.

Figueres decided a military uprising in defence of democracy was justified and began a brief but bloody civil war. His **Army of National Liberation**, supplemented with soldiers and weapons flown in from Guatemala, made rapid progress from San Isidro de El General, via Limón and eventually to Ochomogo, outside Cartago. The decisive five-week battle resulted in 2000 deaths before government troops surrendered in April 1948.

'**Don Pepe**', as Figueres later became known, assumed the position of head of state for a period of 18 months leading the Junta of the Second Republic. Against expectations, he retained many of the reforms of Calderón and extended them further. Power was prised away from the ruling elites by nationalizing the banks controlled by the coffee oligarchy, creating the Costa Rican Electrical Company, public bodies to administer health insurance, public utilities and social security and increasing taxes. The army was abolished and a new constitution extended suffrage to women, blacks and *indígenas* and created the Supreme Electoral Tribunal to remove the possibility of electoral fraud. With the new constitution designed to redistribute power away from established elites and eliminate institutional corruption, Figueres stood down in 1949, peacefully handing power to the elected president Ulate.

Historians continue to explore different interpretations of the reforms of the 1940s, but the legacy of a nation without armed forces has been enduring. The shift of political power away from social elites combined with improved education fuelled the growth of an urban middle class. The post-1949 era was to be defined by the acceptance of public involvement in the economy, an informal acceptance of centrist politics and the introduction of free and open democratic elections.

The birth of modern Costa Rica

Following the divisions of civil war and global economic expansion after the Second World War, Costa Rica enjoyed a period of extended growth. Ulate's presidency set the country on a sound economic footing and embarked on infrastructure developments. With the unifying anti-Calderón forces removed, Figueres founded the *Partido Liberación Nacional* (PLN).

The strength of Figueres' character, and the absence of any meaningful opposition handed Don Pepe the presidency with an overwhelming mandate. Investment in public bodies and services was funded by increased taxes on the *United Fruit Company* and individuals with higher incomes. However, the tax increases lost Figueres popularity and finally the presidency to **Mario Echandi Jiménez** (1958-1962) of the *Partido Unión Nacional* (PUN), but the PLN still strongly influenced congress and Echandi was unable to reduce the spending deficits incurred by Figueres on the programmes.

Through the 1960s and 1970s, despite healthy growth in the economy, successive governments battled to balance the books which needed to fund a burgeoning welfare sector and social security system. Investment in education, health and infrastructure saw the number of public sector employees expand to 33 of the working population, making the state the single largest employer and fuelling the development of an increasingly urban society. Banana exports and coffee prices grew rapidly, providing increased tax revenues through the state banking system. Tax incentives incubated a domestic manufacturing industry, to move away from the vulnerable exposure to commodity prices.

Beyond the city, small farmers struggled to adopt the efficient technologies of larger landholdings and many left the land for the bright lights of the city, focusing even greater pressure on the provision of public services in the city. At the same time, agricultural expansion led to widescale deforestation with the loss of almost 50,000 ha annually between 1963 and 1973 – the highest rates in the world at the time outside the Amazon Basin.

The return of Don Pepe to the presidency from 1970-1974 saw the continuation of PLN policies to invest in public services. The oil crisis of 1973 deflated the economic growth bubble of Costa Rica and after a brief rise in coffee prices in the mid-1970s, the drop in revenues from poor commodity prices and the global economic recession exacerbated the difference between public spending and income. The presidential term of **Daniel Oduber Quirós** (1974-1978) marked not only the first continuation of power within the same party but a continued deficit in public finances. Under the presidency of **Rodrigo Carazo Odio** (1978-1982), the economic crisis worsened as annual inflation reached 90, the economy shrank and relations with international lending agencies were stretched to the limit. During Carazo's administration public foreign debt rose to US$3 billion. In September 1981, with debt repayments already suspended, Carazo reluctantly agreed to austerity measures imposed by the IMF in return for a reduction in public spending and price controls.

With the Nicaraguan revolution to the north, **Luis Alberto Monge Alvarez** (1982-1986) was able to negotiate a financial aid package from the ally-seeking US that trod the difficult line between structural adjustment of the economy and avoiding complete social meltdown. First attempts at reducing the large number of public employees made minimal inroads. Despite pressure from the US which came with large sums of money to prop up the economy, Monge declared Costa Rica's neutrality in the Nicaraguan conflict and managed to avoid being drawn directly into events north of the border. With increasing pressure from the US, **Oscar Arias Sánchez** (1986-1990) proposed and successfully negotiated a Central American peace plan between Nicaragua, Costa Rica, Honduras, El Salvador and Guatemala. It seems entirely appropriate for a country that had disbanded its army almost 40 years before to be the seedbed for a regional peace process that eventually led to elections in Nicaragua, and discussions between governments and rebels in El Salvador and Guatemala. Arias Sánchez received the Nobel Peace Prize in 1987 for his efforts.

By 1987 the country's burgeoning national debt had risen to US$4.7 billion – more than the country's gross domestic product. The challenge facing governments of the 1990s was to reduce public spending and reschedule debt repayments while somehow managing to hold on to the education, health and social security benefits that made Costa Rica stand out from most countries in Latin America.

In 1990 **Rafael Calderón Fournier** of the *Partido Unidad Social Cristiana* (PUSC), the son of the 1940s reformist president Calderón Guardia, won the presidency and introduced austere measures that restricted public spending and introduced limited trade liberalization. One casualty was the closure of the Atlantic railroad 100 years after it had first opened, although any debate on the subject was finally terminated by the huge earthquake which hit the Caribbean lowlands in 1991, taking the railroad permanently out of action. The broader social impact was dramatic, and with some 38 of Costa Ricans judged to be living below the poverty line in 1993, labour protests increased accordingly.

The early 1990s also marked a greater focus on the potential for tourism, and the introduction in 1993 of quotas for banana exports to the European Union began a trans-Atlantic trade dispute that set Brussels and Washington on an economic collision course at the cost of uncertainty and job losses in the Costa Rican banana industry and other global producers (see box, page 367).

José María Figueres Olsen of the PLN, continued the difficult readjustment from 1994-1998, repeating history by following a Calderón administration as his father Don Pepe had done almost 50 years previously. Plans to minimize the pain of restructuring were quickly shelved by the collapse of the *Banco Anglo Costarricense*, the country's oldest bank. The loss of confidence rocked the economy, which drifted into recession in 1996. Figueres proposed a new range of reforms which tinkered with the restructuring of debts, the sale of two state banks and the privatization of RACSA, the state-owned telecommunications company. Most reforms never materialized due to Congressional obstruction and Figueres left office with some of the worst popularity ratings in Costa Rican history. However, he is credited with the stabilizing impact of removing the link between the economic and electoral cycle and attracting the US microprocessor *Intel* which opened a manufacturing plant in the central highlands in 1998 with an investment totalling US$500 million.

In 1998 a politically disillusioned electorate handed the presidency to the US-trained economist and lawyer **Miguel Angel Rodríguez** of the PUSC. Economic progress continued in the first two years, with the number of tourists exceeding one million for the first time in 1999, and the benefits in the growth of high-tech manufacturing beginning to filter through. A programme of reforms pursuing the opening up of the telecom, electricity and insurance sectors to private investment was initially supported by Congress but eventually led to widespread public protest and the plans were shelved. Traditional products of coffee and bananas also took a battering as commodity prices and industry developments dramatically reduced the value of exports. Global factors also highlighted the frailty of the economic market with the brief surge in the price of oil in 2000 threatening to crush economic progress, the global downturn in the high-tech market threatening to undermine the recent successes of the fledgling industry in the country, and the unpredictable impact of events in New York and Washington on 11 September 2001.

One political success of the Rodríguez government (1998-2002) was the resolution of an ongoing border dispute with Nicaragua. A long history of problems created a heightened sense of tension along the San Juan River, with Costa Rican police forces patrolling the river. The solution states the southern bank of the San Juan River is the boundary, with Costa Rican officials having right of navigation.

The 2002 elections had a similar feel to 1998, with the mainly two-party system of the PLN and PUSC running on poverty busting tickets disrupted by the Citizen's Action Party candidate Otton Solis. With no candidate getting at least 40 of the vote, the run-off election saw **Abel Pacheco** elected with 58 of the votes, in a historically low turnout.

President Pacheco's election promise to continue with free market reforms and create at least 40,000 jobs a year struggled as the low coffee and banana prices and economic slowdown in the US and the wider world continued to create problems at home. Pacheco pointed to inefficiencies and a lack of coordination in the public sector as the main problem. A three week strike in May 2003 highlighted the problems facing the country as energy and telecommunications workers striked over privatization plans which seem set to be an obstacle to significant changes in the sector. Teachers joined the strike and three ministers ended up resigning.

Regionally, Costa Rica signed up to the principles of the Central America Free Trade Agreement (CAFTA) in January 2004 which will see duties on trade reduced. While politicians and economists believe CAFTA will improve trade, local objections built steadily in Costa Rica with large rallys and campaigns setting out the views that US products would undermine the Costa Rican economy. In October 2007 a national referendum narrowly decided in favour of ratifying the treaty. Internationally Pacheco's presidency also broke the Costa Rica's peaceful traditions supporting the 2003 military intervention in Iraq. Popular protests eventually forced Costa Rica to withdraw its name from the list of countries supporting the war.

Having successfully convinced Costa Rica's Congress to change the constitution and allow re-election, Oscar Arias was elected president in 2006, 16 years after serving his first term. The election was extremely close, and only decided after several recounts. President Arias, a strong supporter of the Central America Free Trade Agreement, has promised to stabilize the economy and to make Costa Rica one of the Latin America's most developed countries. In a struggling economy, his privatization and tax reform plans have already met with strong opposition.

Modern Costa Rica

Government

The president is the head of state and government, elected for a four-year term. Two presidential terms must pass before re-election is permitted. Legislation is passed through the single-chamber Legislative Assembly with 57 deputies who, like the president, hold their positions for four years.

The current president, Oscar Arias, of the Partido Liberación Nacional (PLN – National Liberation Party) assumed the presidency in February 2006. The next elections will be held in February 2010.

Administratively the country is divided into seven provinces, 81 cantons and 449 districts. Over half the population lives in the central highlands which includes sections of the provinces of San José, Alajuela, Cartago and Heredia.

Government reforms

An ongoing government priority has been the reform of the telecommunications, insurance and energy sectors. Observers believe Arias will be more successful in achieving these objectives, gaining important efficiency reforms, while still maintaining a strong state role in these sectors to manage the impact of economic downturn and high oil prices.

Economy

Economically the country is undergoing a slow revolution, with every year bringing a steady shift away from traditional agricultural production, and a move towards tourism, the electronic services economy and manufacturing.

The national economy experienced strong growth in the last years of the 1990s with growth of 8.4% in 1999 and an average of 4.6% from 1992-2002. Global economic downturn produced growth of just 1.1% and 2.8% for 2001 and 2002 respectively. GDP growth of 5.9% and 8.2% in 2005 and 2006, are expected to be followed a slow down to 4% in 2008 and 3.1% in 2009.

The picture is dampened even more by inflation, which hovers around 11% and foreign debt, in 2006 totalling US$6.8 billion, continues to be a big drain.

Costa Rica's provinces

Province	Size – sq km	Population	Density/sq km
San José	4959	1,356,442	274
Alajuela	9753	716,935	74
Cartago	2657	432,923	163
Heredia	3125	354,926	114
Guanacaste	10,141	264,474	26
Puntarenas	11,277	358,137	32
Limón	9188	340,756	37
Total	**51,100**	**3,824,593**	

Figures from 2000 Census. Current estimates put the total population at 4.47 million.

Coffee

Coffee, which stimulated the growth of the nation through most of the 19th and the early 20th century, continues to be an important part of the economy, but a drop in commodity price at the turn of the millennium saw the value of exports fall by to US$165 million in 2002 compared to US$409 million in 1998. The rise in commodity prices in 2007/2008 has pushed the current prices up to US$130 a bag, from US$70 a bag, providing an income of US$254 million in 2007. The *Costa Rican Coffee Institute* (ICAFE) estimates prices need to be around US$100 a bag to break even.

Costa Rica is one of the largest producers of arabica coffee in Central America, with cultivation concentrated in the central highlands. The industry is made up of over 78,000 coffee growers cultivating an area of roughly 100,000 ha. Over 90 of smallholdings cover less than 5 ha and are owned and farmed by approximately 125,000 families, giving the industry considerable significance beyond its presence in the national identity.

Bananas

As with coffee, bananas are an intrinsic part of the national economy and identity. Exports of 2.2 million tonnes in 1999 earned US$629 million by 2002 that figure had fallen to US$478 million for exports of 1.87 million tonnes. Against expectations, exports in 2006 had risen to 2.19 million tonnes, providing income of US$645 million.

An ongoing trade war between the US and European Union over opening up access to European markets for banana producers has impacted banana production in the country. In the trans-Atlantic trade war, the certain losers in the global market for greater competition are the independent growers of Costa Rica who sell to the multi-national companies *Chiquita*, *Dole* and *Del Monte*. Hard fought for, and reluctantly given, concessions have slowly improved working conditions and job security for banana industry workers. At present, banana labourers account for 14 of agricultural labour, but just three of the total work force. After the industry has readjusted to the new trade regulations, employment figures are expected to be substantially lower. For more detailed information on the banana wars see page 367.

Other agriculture

Many traditional industries have also suffered with recent economic developments. The contribution of cattle rearing to the national economy has dwindled to just US$20 million, creating additional problems of increased unemployment in Guanacaste.

However a rising star in the agricultural sector is pineapples, which have grown from exports of 177 million tonnes with a value of US$58 million in 1995 to 504 million tonnes valued at US$174 million in 2002. The growth continued and by 2006, exports of 1183 million tonnes were valued at US$434 million.

Manufacturing

An unquestionable economic success has been the attraction of *Intel*, the US microprocessor manufacturing to the central highlands with a start-up investment of US$300 million. The plant, which opened in 1998 with the creation of 2000 jobs, is believed to have made a significant contribution to the surge in economic growth in 1999. Recent studies have shown that the overall investment is around US$770 million. The success in attracting this major high-tech company owes much to the country's education system. The arrival of *Intel* will reap multiple rewards, encouraging high-tech employment opportunities, and early signs already indicate that other companies are considering opening plants in Costa Rica. By 2004, approximately 12,000 people were employed in the electronics cluster, exporting products valued at US$1.65 billion. If the trend continues, it marks a shift from the golden bean (coffee) to the golden chip as the leading product in the national economy.

Tourism

Equally spectacular has been the growth in tourism. In 1999 more than one million tourists visited Costa Rica for the first time. Despite the global downturn in travel, visitors in 2002 were over 1.1million contributing almost US$1.1 billion to the country's finances. By 2007 tourism had risen to over 1.9 million, creating revenues of US$1.89 million. Recent growth has been attributed to a number of logistical improvements including improvements at Juan Santamaría near San José and Daniel Oduber airport in Guanacaste which has stimulated growth in frequency and origin of flights, as well as the construction of the Tempisque Bridge which improves access to the Nicoya Peninsula.

The rate of construction of hotels in beach locations appears furious in places, and land prices have soared, driven up by foreign (mainly US) purchasers. Conservation groups have criticized larger developments due to environmental impact, the proximity of national parks and reserves and the destruction of ecosystems.

According to the *Cámara Nacional de Turismo de Costa Rica* (CANATUR), the tourism industry employs around 140,000 people. Overall, the industry is structured towards the better-off traveller with all-inclusive resorts. The creation of the large scale Papagayo project on the northern coast of the Nicoya Peninsula has been widely criticized for damaging environmentally sensitive areas and promoting the kind of tourism that relies on large scale foreign investment, creating very little internal wealth for the country once the projects are operational.

Energy production

Over 80% of the country's electricity is produced by hydroelectric power, at 19 plants, with the latest addition to the installed capacity of 734 megawatts being the 177-megawatt **Angostura Dam** south of Turrialba, which was completed in early 2001.

Many of the country's hydroelectric projects are initially obstructed by locals and users before construction, on the grounds of loss of valuable natural resources. One such project is the possible development of a dam on the lower reaches of the El General river, south of San Isidro de El General, which is strongly opposed by indigenous groups in the area, or plans for a new plant close to Poco del Sol, near Fortuna.

Costa Rica has no viable oil reserves and imports its supplies from Mexico and Venezuela. In the early 1990s, concessions were granted for exploration in the southern Caribbean area, the government being keen to see appropriate development of oil reserves to offset the current spending of US$500 million on petroleum imports. This start-stop exploration is being fiercely contested by local residents who believe that it will damage the environmentally sensitive area.

Society
Government-led social investment between the 1950s and 1970s, has pushed Costa Rica to the top of regional league tables in terms of service provision. Education is free and compulsory up to the age of 15, with overall literacy rates of 95% against a Latin American average of 90%. There are three state universities which produce roughly 18,000 graduates each year, and several private universities. Health provision is also a high priority with the social security system providing effective health care to roughly 95% of the population. Infant mortality rates – at 11 deaths per thousand a year – are some of the lowest in the region, and life expectancy is 79 years, compared with a Latin American average of 73. Access to improved water supplies has now reached 95% of the population, which is also a significant improvement compared with the regional average, although the extent of drinking water supplies is estimated to reach only around three quarters of the population.

With the best education and social security system in the region, at current population growth rates of 1.9% a year, the provision of health and social security is seen as unsustainable. The welfare system is very important to the Costa Rican people. Government proposals to privatize some state-owned bodies were designed in part to fund necessary reforms. Limits on current financial spending combined with resistance against privatization mean reform is likely to be a long and difficult process.

Culture

Pinning down the culture of any nation is always difficult and runs the inherent risk of distilling traits and behaviours down to a single common denominator, taking the ever-elusive 'normal' person as your guide. With an amiable toleration of life, *Ticos* suffer more than many in this respect and risk being misjudged. And yet, to say that there is no culture in Costa Rica is bordering on the absurd. There are many low-key and highly localized indicators of culture. On the whole, what you find is all-encompassing and such an intrinsic part of life as to go almost unnoticed. (The universal reference to Costa Ricans as *Ticos*, for example, is almost second nature. The term is believed to derive from the Costa Rican tendency to use the diminutive Spanish *ito* at the end of the noun.)

The cultural foundations of Guanacaste to the northwest lie close to the land and the hardy existence of life on the ranch. The skills and style of the saddle-bound and somewhat endangered *sabanero* are still tried, and tested at rodeos with ironically pacifist non-fatal bull fights. The regional music – if such a thing exists – is the staccatoed percussion of the marimba, a xylophone-type instrument which, despite being technically impressive, is rarely relaxing and almost intrusive as it struggles for harmony. Yet a short flight east to the Caribbean lands you in a world that could not be more different. The energy to work and control the land is replaced by the more compliant and accommodating laid-back rhythms of the Caribbean where calypso and reggae are washed down with a diet of coconut and rum.

And in the heart of the country, *Ticos* perched up in the capital and the central highlands move to the beat of urban life. Patriotism comes out on national holidays and special occasions, but take away the number plates, currency and people, and you could almost be in any major city in Latin America.

People and language

The 2000 census put the national population at 3.82 million, latest estimate put the population at over 4.47 million – an annual increase of 2.1% – with the overwhelming majority (94%) considered to be white of mixed **Spanish** descent. The next largest single group is Afro-Caribbeans making up 3%, Amerindian 1%, Chinese 1% and 'others' the remaining 1%. Roughly one third of the population lives in the Greater San José metropolitan area and close to half of all *Ticos* live in the central highlands.

The **Afro-Caribbean** population is almost entirely concentrated on the Caribbean coast, in particular in Puerto Limón and the towns to the south. Originating in the Caribbean, most arrived from Jamaica to build the railroad and later found work on plantations. Likewise, the **Chinese** community can trace its Costa Rican roots to the period of railroad construction in the late 19th century.

Estimates for the number of **Nicaraguans** living in the country either as refugees or temporary economic migrants is as high as 400,000, or 10% of the population. Following Hurricane Mitch in 1998, the Costa Rican government announced a general amnesty to all illegal Central American immigrants living in the country. By June of 2000, 156,000 people had qualified for legal residency papers and 95% of them were Nicaraguan. The policy is intriguing and on the face of it a very generous one since most *Ticos* blame illegal Nicaraguans in Costa Rica for every affliction to beset the country, from theft and crime to extended periods of unseasonal rain. (The suspicion is mutual, and Nicaraguans believe that Costa Ricans have an elevated sense of self-importance and superiority.)

A significant but unquantifiable influence on the country is the large number of **'Western' expatriates** who have retired or emigrated to Costa Rica to work. Residency rules stipulate that retired persons need an income above US$1000 a month and that business investment requires a minimum start-up capital of US$50,000. The transportation of ideas, lifestyles and standards of living has an obvious effect in tourist areas. Throughout the Pacific coast, enclaves of German, Italian, Swiss, Canadian and, the most popular, US communities have sprung up, bringing with them all the traits of home – good and bad – and a few new ones that have evolved locally.

The **indigenous population** has been in steady decline ever since the arrival of Europeans. Those that did not succumb to new diseases, being sold to work in other parts of Central America or subjected to forced labour, retreated to the highland areas of the south. Today there are eight recognized indigenous cultures or tribes: Huetar, Bribrí, Cabécar, Guaymí, Chorotega, Boruca, Guatuso and Térraba, with land protected in 22 reserves, covering 1240 sq miles – just over 6% of the national territory.

The indigenous population has five recognized languages. The northern Chorotega culture were greatly influenced by Mesoamerican cultures and spoke the Nahuatl language of the Maya and Aztecs. The Boruca, Bribrí, Cabécar, Guaymí, Huetar and Guatuso spoke a language with its roots further to the south, which became more complex as the Arawak and Caribe cultures moved in to permanent settlements on the Caribbean coast adding their sounds.

The Bribrí and Cabécar are the only cultures that have been able to keep religious myths pure, outside of major influences from social and cultural changes, with the Sibú being the supreme god and creator of their world.

The *Comisión Nacional de Asuntos Indígenas* (CONAI – National Commission for Indigenous Affairs) is a government institution created in 1973 to uphold indigenous law. Indigenous affairs should have taken a turn for the better in 1977 when the government created the system of Indian reserves, but the government has retained the land titles and consequently the upper hand whenever an issue relating to land use has arisen. Several hydroelectric projects on indigenous land are in a permanent state of reappraisal. In 1992 the government went one step further, signing the International Labour Organization which ratified the constitutional rights of indigenous people. However, disenchantment is widespread. While the government provides education and health to many indigenous communities, the services are generally provided in Spanish by teachers from other cultures which automatically undermines the fabric of community life.

Indigenous communities are realizing that their best hope of retaining a sense of cultural identity is through fighting for their rights politically. Organizations like *Aradikes* (see page 330), in the Buenos Aires area of the western Talamancas, fight for the rights of indigenous communities on several fronts, although it must be said that progress is limited and painfully slow.

Several indigenous groups contribute to keeping their cultures alive by continuing to produce goods as they have for hundreds of years. In the north it is still possible to buy ceramics in the Chorotega style and Guatuso stonework. In the south you can buy the textiles of the Guaymí, and the *jícaro* engraved gourds of the Bribrí.

Sport

Nothing reflects better the ability of Costa Ricans to adapt their interests to the moment than sport. **Claudia Poll** made Olympic aficionados of Costa Ricans overnight after winning the country's first gold medal in the pool at the Atlanta Olympics in 1996. Although she was unable to repeat the feat at Sydney 2000, she returned home with a couple of bronze medals won in the 200-m and 400-m freestyle and still had the streets lined with welcoming crowds. Disappointingly Athens and Beijing failed to produce any medals. And by the way, don't tell the Costa Ricans, but Poll was born in Managua, Nicaragua.

Football, however, is the greatest passion, and many a *Tico* still gets starry eyed thinking about Costa Rica's qualification to the final stages of the World Cup in 1990, and even more incredibly progressing to the second round, taking Scottish and Swedish scalps on the way and making it to the last 16. For a country the size of Costa Rica, this was an impressive achievement which had the nation's football fans dancing in the streets. Qualification in 2002 and 2006 will, hopefully, be followed up by qualification for 2010 in South Africa.

Francisco Zúñiga

Francisco Zúñiga is the best known Costa Rican sculpture. Born in San José, in 1912, he left for Mexico in 1936 where he began to develop his skills including metal smelting and stone carving and polishing. Zúñiga was most influenced by modern European masters such as Brancusi, Giacometti and Moore. Like Diego Rivera, Zúñiga's drawings and sculptures of individuals symbolize the strength of the human spirit and reveal in a broader context the history and psychology of culture and society.

The triumph of the human spirit finds its most powerful symbolism in his sculptures of women, who are portrayed as both ethereal and resilient mother earth figures. Each female form appears with the imposing serenity of an ancient goddess contemplating the daily reality of existence and mother-hood. They are staunch and monu-mental females, madonnas with indigenous features, solemnly poised and harmoniously positioned within their environment.

Arts and crafts

Those looking to find a country draped in colonial creative arts will leave Costa Rica disappointed. Lovers of contemporary expressionism, however, are quite spoilt for choice with the capital in particular being an outpouring of individualism, or an eclectic mess, depending on your point of view.

Painting and sculpture The first Costa Rican sculptures emerged in the 19th century and, using wood as their medium, mainly worked on religious themes. Francisco Zúñiga is the best known artist in this field and achieved international fame after a period living in Mexico.

Painting blossomed from the 1930s and by the 1960s was taking its influence from Western abstract painters. Reflecting the concerns of the left, most painters at the time were politically and socially conscious and some, including Manuel de la Cruz González, Loda Fernández and Juan Luis Rodríquez, achieved international recognition for their work.

More recently, the 1980s saw the creation of the Bocaraca school of *Tico* painting influenced by Francis Bacon and informal Catalan art. For a more detailed look at Costa Rican art, get a copy of *Historia Crítica del Arte Costarricense* by Carlos Francisco Echeverría (Editorial Universidad Estatal).

Literature

Literature in Costa Rica is still relatively young and lacks the struggles and challenges that inspired many Latin writers. Carlos Fallas is perhaps the best known author: his work *Mamita Yunai* looks at life on the *United Fruit Company* banana plantations.

Contemporary writers include **José León Sánchez** and **Carlos Cortez Fernando Contreras**, and poetry lovers should seek out **Jorge de Bravo**.

In Costa Rica, the **Librería Internacional** in the Multiplaza in Escazú has a section dedicated to Costa Rican writers. Internationally, *Costa Rica – A Traveler's Literary Companion*, by Barbara Ras, is a good starting point.

Theatre and dance

What Costa Rica lacks in literature it makes up for in a thriving theatrical and contemporary dance scene. The golden age of the theatre was the 1970s, when Chilean and Argentine playwrights lived and worked in Costa Rica to escape the right-wing regimes of the time. Their influence on professional and amateur groups in San José has helped them reach some of the highest levels in Central America, a tradition maintained by the requirement for local theatres to perform at least two plays a year written by local playwrights. Some of the best theatre productions are performed by the **Compañía Nacional de Teatro**, but also keep a look out for smaller amateur productions which tackle every subject from classics to contemporary comedy.

For dance, see the **Compañía Nacional de Danza**, which performs in the Museum of Contemporary Arts and **Danza Universitaria** and **Danza Una** in the Universidad Nacional de Heredia.

For events and listings look in the 'Viva' section of *La Nación* on Thu or the *Tico Times*.

Religion

It is said that around 90 of *Ticos* would consider themselves as **Roman Catholics**, and a small survey of taxi and bus drivers, hotel staff and chance encounters does little to change this perception. Certainly the churches are packed to bursting on Sundays.

A particular feature of the *Tico* Catholicism is the annual pilgrimage on 2 August to the Basílica de Nuestra Señora de Los Angeles in Cartago to see the revered image of the Virgin Mary. Around 600,000 pilgrims are estimated to make the journey each year.

Moving away from the central highlands, the rise and rise of **evangelism** of varying denominations is apparent, with small churches often evident in quiet roadside communities.

Land and environment

Geography

The Republic of Costa Rica covers 51,100 sq km (19,730 sq miles), roughly half the size of the state of Kentucky in the United States, or one 10th the size of Spain. The country is part of the Central American isthmus ranging from 8° to 11° longitude north of the equator. The international boundary with Nicaragua to the north covers 309 km and is marked for much of the Caribbean slope by the southern bank of the Río San Juan which flows from Lake Nicaragua. To the south the boundary with Panama stretches for 330 km.

Geology

Geologically the region from southern Nicaragua to Colombia is the bridge between North and South America. The archipelago that stretched through the region was forced upwards by the subterranean forces of plate tectonics around 5 million years ago creating a land bridge between the north and south. These tremendous forces continue to affect the country, as the Cocos Plate to the west is forced eastwards against the Caribbean Plate which holds the land mass of Costa Rica. Moving at different speeds and in different directions, tension builds to breaking point between the two plates, eventually shifting and creating earthquakes. Massive pressures can force land upwards, as happened with the Talamanca Mountains to the south of the country. Likewise, one block of land may be forced below another creating a subduction zone. Release of pressure causes earthquakes and the super-heated friction forces molten rock to the surface, most visible as volcanoes and in some areas producing mudpots and hot springs as with Volcano Arenal and Rincón de la Vieja.

Tectonic events continue to affect the country, and low magnitude earthquakes are reasonably common, the vast majority having no damaging effects. Naturally, there are occasionally devastating exceptions. A large earthquake hit Cartago in 1910, leaving the church in ruins. It was the third and latest time the city was destroyed by earthquakes and the church ruins stand more or less as they were left after the last tremors. To the north of Cartago, Irazú volcano erupted with such force in 1963 that it showered San José with volcanic ash. Later that decade Arenal volcano woke from its slumber to begin an active phase which continues today with devastating effect – in August 2000 two people were killed by an unexpected lava flow, and further unexpected eruptions occurred in September 2003.

In April 1991, an earthquake measuring 7.5 on the Richter scale hit the Talamanca Mountains, resulted in 58 deaths and raised large sections of the Caribbean coastline by around 1.5 m.

Climate

In brief, the Costa Rican climate is tropical in the lowlands and temperate in the central highlands. Lowland temperatures drift around the mid-20°Cs, with slight seasonal variations taking the temperature higher in March and April. In the central highlands, day time temperatures are in the low 20°Cs cooling off slightly in the evenings. The dry season runs from December to April, with slight variations on the Caribbean coast which has a brief dry period in September and October.

In reality, the Costa Rican climate is a complex mosaic linking altitude, rainfall and local factors. Rainfall varies considerably throughout the country. Precipitation is heaviest close to Cerro de la Muerte and Tapanti-Macizo de la Muerte National Park where rainfall can exceed 6 m annually. On the Pacific coast rainfall is heaviest around the Osa Peninsula to the south, while on the Caribbean the northern region around Barra del Colorado is the wettest point. However, moving south from Barra del Colorado rainfall tails off down to around 2.5 m at Puerto de Viejo de Talamanca. On the Pacific side, moving north from the Osa Peninsula, the rainfall is even lower with northern parts of the Guanacaste province receiving just 1.5 m a year.

Variations in temperature are less complex; changes in temperature being directly affected by altitude with a change of between 4°C and 7°C with every thousand metres' shift in altitude.

This complex relationship between rainfall and altitude (and consequently temperature) directly affects the plant and wildlife found in any one area. In the late 1940s L.R. Holdridge developed a system of classification which divides regions into life zones. Widely used by botanists, biologists, field workers and probably your guide, Costa Rica has 12 so-called lifezones, the most significant, in terms of area, being **tropical dry forest** (10.3), **tropical moist forest** (24.2), **tropical wet forest** (22.6) and **tropical premontane wet forest** (13.6) (see page 433).

The central mountains

The creation of a land bridge between North and South America also created a land barrier between the Caribbean and the Pacific. The **Talamanca mountain range** in the south of the country stretches from southwest of San José to beyond the border with Panama and incorporates the highest peaks in the country including **Cerro Chirripó** at 3820 m where temperatures frequently fall to freezing point. Produced by the uplift of marine areas injected with localized volcanic events, the Talamanca range is geologically the oldest part of Costa Rica. There are extreme variations in the region, the higher altitudes home to the northernmost occurrence of Andean paramó above the treeline and with only sparse shrub cover.

A smaller coastal range – the **Fila Costeña** – runs parallel to the Talamancas separated by the El General and Coto Brus river systems, which merge to join the River Térraba.

To the east of San José, a line of volcanic peaks stretch northwest to the border with Nicaragua, incorporating three mountain chains: the **Cordillera Central**, **Cordillera de Tilarán** and finally the **Cordillera de Guanacaste**. Seven active volcanoes are found in the region including Arenal, one of the most active in Central America.

The central highlands

Nature didn't quite manage to join the mountain ranges, and the small gap between the Talamancas and the northern volcanic ranges creates a highland plateau. Detritus from volcanic eruptions and river run-off built up over millennia have formed a broad fertile plain at an altitude ranging between 1000 m and 1500 m which happens to be perfect conditions for growing coffee. Once Europe had perked up to the taste of coffee in the early 19th century, the central highlands became the economic powerhouse and foundation for the development of modern Costa Rica. The republic's four main cities – San José, Alajuela, Heredia and Cartago – are all in the Central Valley and all owe their origins, in part, to coffee.

The Caribbean lowlands

East of the continental divide – as the line dividing east from west is called – the Pacuare, Reventazón and Sarapiquí are three of many rivers that feed through the lowlands to the Caribbean. To the north, the extensive lowland plains stretch further inland created by vast alluvial deposits from the many rivers flowing off the eastern slopes of the northern volcanic ranges. Naturally the area would be subject to extensive flooding but banana cultivation has led to controlled irrigation of the area. To the south, the Talamancas push east almost to the coastline creating a thin coastal strip broken only by a few river valleys.

Much of the Caribbean coast remains undeveloped, compared with the Pacific, with unspoilt areas being the stereotypical image of rainforest or in terms of Holdridge's life zones, Tropical Moist Forest and to the north, Tropical Wet Forest.

The Pacific coastline

The Pacific coastline is far more varied than the Caribbean although, removing the complications, it is possible to see a thin coastal plain running the length of the country. To the south the **Fila Costeña** runs parallel to the coastline broken only by the Río Térraba, which, having collected most of the rainfall on the western slopes of the Talamancas, flows out to the Pacific, close to Palmar through the Diquis Valley and the extensive mangrove swamps around Sierpe. The rocky Osa Peninsula and Dulce Gulf are areas of high rainfall with tropical moist and premontane rainforest. To the south the **Coto Colorado Valley** is extensively farmed – mainly with African Palm.

Moving north, rainfall drops rapidly, with the Río Tárcoles just north of Jacó marking the dividing line between wet forest to the south and dry forest to the north, produced by the rain shadow created by the northern volcanic ranges and strong seasonal trade winds from the Caribbean southeast. The **Tempisque basin** which feeds into the Gulf of Nicoya is the main drainage system of the area providing extensive wetlands for seasonal and resident birds.

Within the **Nicoya Peninsula** the south receives slightly more rain, but essentially extends the ecosystem of the dry forest across its rocky peninsula, although extensive farming and human intervention has altered the region considerably from its natural state.

National parks

Costa Rica is promoted as a model of conservation with national parks protecting 11 of the country and just over one quarter of the national territory falling within a protected status category of some kind.

The country has undergone a dramatic turnaround within recent decades. From the 1940s to the 1970s it had some of the highest rates of deforestation in the world, clearing at a rate that would have stripped the entire country by early in the 21st century. Fortunately the efforts of a dozen or so national and international individuals – among them such guiding lights as Mario Boza, Archie Carr, Leslie R Holdridge, Daniel Janzen and the Organization for Tropical Studies (OTS) who have been successful in highlighting the extraordinary nature of Costa Rica's flora and fauna. Coupled with some rather timely falls in commodity prices, the government moved away from state-sponsored land clearance for ranching and agriculture, favouring instead the creation of the national parks system.

The evolution of protected parks began in 1970 with the creation of the National Parks Service (SPN). The latest reorganization completed in 1995 divided the entire country into 11 regions creating a National System of Protected Areas (SINAC – Sistema Nacional de Areas de Conservación), which is administered as part of the Ministry for the Environment and Energy (MINAE – Ministerio del Ambiente y Energía).

In addition to national parks, the National System protects land within a range of categories including biological and forest reserves, wildlife refuges and a few smaller categories. The goals are to consolidate and guarantee the conservation of the protected areas as integrated regions within the national territory, as well as protecting the national biodiversity and to control and manage its sustainable use. Many of the national parks have the combined purpose of protecting watersheds which feed the country's essential hydroelectric power system and protecting areas of particular biological interest.

Wildlife of Costa Rica

Costa Rica, considering its size, contains more species of plants and animals than any other country in the world. Indonesia holds the world record for the number of mammal species (515) in any one country, as Colombia, with 1721 species, does for birds. However, these two countries are, respectively, around 37 and 22 times the size of Costa Rica, so you would have to travel a lot further to see the same number of animals than you will in tiny Costa Rica. With around 12,000 plant species, 870 bird species (600 or so resident), 205 species of mammals, 215 reptiles, 160 amphibians, 130 species of freshwater fish and some 360,000 insects, the country is home to between four to five per cent of the world's terrestrial species.

In comparison, the USA, about 183 times the size of Costa Rica, has a total of only 996 species of birds and mammals combined, while the UK (about five times the size of Costa Rica) has a mere 284 species of mammals, birds, reptiles and amphibians combined.

Costa Rica's amazing biodiversity is partly due to its geographical situation in the centre of the two huge continental masses, partly because it is a barrier between two oceans, and also due to its wide variety of landscapes, including mountains, valleys, coastal plains and prairies. In addition, though wholly within the tropics, Costa Rica has a climatic diversity.

Much of the country's wildlife remains only in the small, but numerous, national parks and reserves which protect over 25 of the country. Elsewhere, most of the forest, home to the majority of the animals, has been cut down and replaced by agricultural land.

A brief description of the major forest habitats in the country and some of the more striking flora and fauna you may see will help with a broader understanding of the ecology of the country.

National parks & protected areas

NICARAGUA

○ Liberia

○ Puntarenas

SAN JOSE □

Pacific Ocean

20 km
20 miles

N

♦ **Parques nacionales**
1 Arenal
2 Braulio Carrillo
3 Juan Castro Blanco
4 Volcán Turrialba
5 Volcán Poas
6 Barra Honda
7 Marino Las Baulas de Guanacaste
8 Guanacaste
9 Rincón de la Vieja
10 Santa Rosa
11 Tortuguero
12 Corcovado
13 Piedras Blancas
14 Marino Ballena
15 Manuel Antonio
16 Cahuita
17 Chirripó
18 Internacional la Amistad

19 Barbilla
20 Isla del Coco
21 Palo Verde
22 Volcán Tenorio
23 Volcán Irazú
24 Tapantí - Macizo Cerro de la Muerte
25 Carara
26 Gandoca - Manzanillo

♦ **Reservas biológicas**
27 Isla del Caño
28 Hitoy Cerere
29 Lomas de Barbudal

♦ **Refugios nacionales de vida silvestre**
30 Barra del Colorado
31 Golfito
32 Caño Negro
33 Peñas Blancas

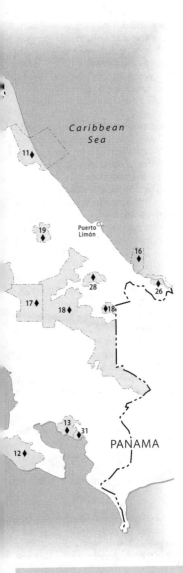

Caribbean
Sea

Puerto
Limón

PANAMA

Habitats

Of the many different systems used for the ecological classification of Costa Rica's vegetation, the most widely used is the system of 'Life Zones' devised mainly by L.R. Holdridge, based on a complex inter-relationship between rainfall, temperature and altitude. Under this system, Costa Rica's forests are divided into **tropical lowland**, **tropical premontane**, **lower montane** and **tropical montane**, with each category subdivided into moist, wet and rain forest types; also included are the dry forests and mangrove swamps. The forest habitats described below have been much simplified and do not follow Holdridge's system.

Lowland wet forests The lowland wet forests in Costa Rica, found in the northern and southern Caribbean lowlands and in the southern Pacific lowlands, are the classical tropical forests. Tall, semi-deciduous and evergreen trees reach to a height of 40-55 m and even taller; emergent evergreen trees soar above this canopy. A sub-canopy of lower trees is often present, while the ground may be bare or have a sparse shrub layer. While walking through the forest some of the most commonly seen plants in the understorey and shrub layer are members of the genus *Piper*. There are over 90 species in this genus within Costa Rica. All are small trees or shrubs characterized by their erect, candle-like flowering structures, which are generally pollinated by bats. Buttress and stilt roots are common features in these forests. Buttress roots appear as broad ridges attached to the side of a tree trunk and acting as support for the tree, to account for the minimal sub-surface root system. Stilt roots come off the side of a tree trunk, growing down and entering the earth some distance from the trunk to anchor the tree more firmly in the soil.

Palms are common in this type of forest and one species you may well see is *Welfia georgii*, which bears its fruit on its trunk.

Vines are also numerous; quite common is the passion flower (*Passiflora foetida*), with bright red flowers, and the Swiss Cheese plant (*Monstera deliciosa*), a large-leafed climber in these wet forests and commonly seen as a house plant in European and North American homes. **Epiphytes**, plants that grow on other plants, are frequent in the lowland wet forests and large trees such as the **kapok** (*Ceiba pentandra*) are often heavily laden with them. This tree is massive, often emerging above the surrounding canopy, with a broad, flat crown and a seed that produces a fibrous material often used to stuff cushions and furniture. Epiphytes include mosses, ferns, orchids and bromeliads. The **orchids**, with over 1000 species in Costa Rica, can be spectacular when in flower – indeed Costa Rica's national flower is an orchid, the *guaria morada* (*Cattleya skinneri*). **Bromeliads** typically have fleshy, often spiky leaves formed into a rosette with a central 'well' that holds water, which is often used as a small pond by a host of animals including snails, worms, insects and even tadpoles and adult frogs.

The driving force for change in the lowland wet forest is forest gaps. Clearings created by a tree fall produce a sudden availability of light and various plant species rush to colonize the area, before being gradually replaced by more mature, slower growing species. Within the lowland forest, pioneer species such as the **balsa tree** (*Ochroma lagopus*), grow rapidly in these gaps to reach a height of 30 m. Its light, soft wood is used for making many of the wooden souvenirs available to tourists in Costa Rica. *Cercropia obtusifolia* is another pioneer species, frequently found in lowland forests. Thriving on the light of forest gaps, it has large, umbrella-like leaves, which are a favourite food of sloths. Also found in disturbed areas of the forest, in clearings and along streams, are species of *Heliconia* which have large leaves resembling those on banana trees and striking red, orange and yellow flowers, shaped rather like lobster claws, pollinated by humming birds.

Lowland dry forest This type of forest once covered extensive areas of Costa Rica's northern Pacific coastal plain, but most has now been cleared for agriculture. The rainy season in this region is only six months in length (May-October). By comparison, rain falls year round in the Caribbean lowlands, hence the difference in forest type. The dry forest is semi-deciduous, with a canopy at 20-30 m, an understorey of trees 10-20 m tall and a 2-5 m high, dense shrub layer. **Vines** are present, but epiphytes are generally rare. Common or conspicuous plants include the **gumbo limbo tree** (*Bursera simaruba*), which is recognizable by its smooth, red/orange bark. The *Crescentia alata*, a fairly common,large, shrub-like tree, has conspicuous hard fruits or gourds growing from its trunk which are eaten by rodents and also used for decoration. **Corteza** trees, in the genus *Tabebuia*, are commonly seen but stand out most when in flower as all members of a species flower simultaneously towards the end of the dry season, though for only four days, so you'll have to be lucky to catch them. The flowers are either yellow or pink. **Palms** are not as frequent in the dry forests as they are in the wetland forest, but one palm, *Acrocomia vinifera*, is fairly common; it has long, sharp spines on its lower trunk and occurs particularly in swampy areas and along roads.

Wildlife is often easier to see in these more open, less dense forests than in the thicker, wetter forests, though biodiversity is lower.

Premontane and montane forest In the forests at higher elevations, the hot stickiness of the lowland forest areas is replaced by a cooler dampness. The cooler climate is due to the temperature dropping, on average, by 0.4-0.7°C for every 100 m gained in altitude. Mists of cloud or fog enshroud the forest canopy for much of the time, hence the evocative name 'cloudforest' which is often applied to these forests. Light levels tend to be reduced at higher elevations and the foliage drips with water that condenses out of the atmosphere. These forests are less diverse than those in the lowlands, but they are often home to endemic species – ones that are found nowhere else in the world.

These forests occur on the slopes and upper areas of Costa Rica's mountains. In the lower areas the cloudforest is mixed deciduous and evergreen, while at higher elevations it is uniformly evergreen. There are frequent strong winds in the higher forests so the tops of the trees become more even and flat compared to those in the lowland forests. In addition, the trees tend to become gnarled, twisted and multi-stemmed and the leaves are much smaller, narrower and leathery. Canopy height at lower levels is around 30-40 m, declining as elevation increases. There is usually a subcanopy and dense undergrowth. **Vines** and **epiphytes** grow profusely, especially in the evergreen cloudforests; indeed **lichens** can be hanging in curtains from many of the trees. Though also found at lower elevations, **tree ferns** are especially common in the higher forests. Quite a number of the trees and shrubs found at these higher elevations are ones from genera that may be found in temperate regions such as **oaks** (*Quercus*), **buddleia** (*Buddleja*) and **magnolia** (*Magnolia*). Also found in these high forests is the **Winter's bark** (*Drimys winteri*). Growing to about 15 m in height, it has aromatic bark, large, leathery oval yellow-green leaves with a waxy white underneath and clusters of fragrant, small, white flowers and dark purple berries. So attractive is it that it has been introduced as a garden plant to temperate gardens.

Páramo This treeless, subalpine habitat predominates at the highest elevations in Costa Rica. Only grasses and shrubs are found in these areas. Chirripó National Park contains some areas of páramo.

Terrestrial mammals

Primates Costa Rica has only four of the 70 or so species of monkey that are present in the New World. The three larger ones are quite common in many protected areas, while the squirrel monkey is found in only a few lowland wet forests of the southern Pacific slope of the country. **Red-backed squirrel monkeys** (mono titi, *Saimiri oerstedii*) are small (0.6-0.9 kg) monkeys, with a golden orange back, hands and feet, a black crown and muzzle and a white mask. Moving in groups of 10-20 individuals, they run and jump through the trees feeding on fruits, seeds, leaves and insects. The groups contain several adult females and males, with juveniles and infants. The birth season is in July and the young remain on their mother's back for the first month of their life; after that they spend an increasing numbers of hours away, exploring and playing, until they are finally weaned at 11 months. This species is found only in Panama and Costa Rica and is considered to be in danger of extinction. **White-faced capuchin monkeys** (mono carablanca, *Cebus capucinus*), are medium-sized monkeys weighing between 2.5-4 kg. They have a white throat, head and shoulders, while their back and prehensile tail are black. They forage over all levels of wet forests, including mangroves, and may even be seen on the ground. Their diet is mostly fruit, but also includes leaves, nuts, flowers, insects, small birds, reptiles and young mammals. Group size is around 10-20, consisting of several males and females, usually more of the latter. These monkeys are probably the most commonly seen in Costa Rica as they occur in dry and wet forests and are active and noisy throughout most of the day. Their threat display includes jumping up and down and shaking branches, which makes them quite difficult to miss! **Geoffroy's spider monkeys** (mono colorado, mono araña, *Ateles geoffroyi*) are definitely the most elegant of Costa Rica's primates. They weigh between 6-9 kg and their coat colour varies from light buff to black, usually with black hands and feet. They use their prehensile tail as a fifth limb, swinging, climbing and hanging mostly in the upper canopy of the forest, preferring the wet, evergreen forests to the dry forests. They eat mainly fruit, though include seeds, flowers, leaves and insects in their diet. There are usually around twice as many females as males in a group, though the number of monkeys moving together is very variable (between four and 35) as the troops tends to divide into small foraging parties, especially if food is scarce. Spider monkeys are active during the day, though, like many monkeys, they tend to be less active at midday when temperatures are highest. **Mantled howler monkeys** (mono congo, *Alouatta palliata*) are black except for a fringe of long, gold to buff hairs on their sides. Adult body weight is variable, from three to almost 10 kg, males are heavier than females. Even if not seen, these monkeys will certainly be heard by anyone visiting the lowland evergreen forests or the dry forests, though they are also present in montane forests. The males, in particular, give loud roaring vocalizations, most frequently at dawn and in the late afternoon, which can easily be heard 3 km or more away. Howlers move relatively slowly and deliberately high in the forest and may well be passed by unnoticed, especially as over 70 of the day can be spent resting. Leaves are the main component of their diet, though flowers and fruits are also taken. Group size is usually 10 to 20, made up of several adult males, females and offspring.

Opossums There are nine species of these marsupials in Costa Rica, occupying all habitats except high mountain areas. Most likely to be seen is the **common opossum** (zorro pelón or zarigüeya, *Didelphis marsupialis*), which resembles a large rat, around 42 cm long, with yellowish face, blackish or grey-black body, black ears and a long, hairless, prehensile tail. They are mostly nocturnal, but can be seen active during the day, usually foraging on the ground for fruits, eggs, invertebrates and small vertebrates, though they are also good climbers. They frequent human habitations, foraging in rubbish dumps and eating fruit crops. The smaller **gray four-eyed opossum** (zorro de cuatro ojos, *Philander opossum*) is found in rainforest regions; it has a black face mask with large white spots over its eyes. The **water opossum** (zorro de aqua, *Chironectes minimus*) is also seen quite commonly, often by or in water. This species has a grey body with broad black/brown stripes.

Anteaters Costa Rica has three species of anteater. The most commonly seen is the **northern tamandua** (oso hormiguero or tamandua, *Tamandua mexicana*) which has a brown or yellowish head and legs with a black vest on its belly and back. Its body is 45-75 cm long with a prehensile tail of the same length. It can be found in trees and on the ground in wet and dry forests and in savannah habitats, feeding mainly on termites and mostly at night. The **giant anteater** (oso homiguero gigante, *Myrmecophaga tridactyla*), up to 2.1 m in length (including the tail) and weighing as much as 39 kg, is extremely rare, while the tiny **silky anteater** (serafin de platanar, *Cyclopes didactylus*) standing just 17 cm tall is arboreal, nocturnal and unlikely to be seen.

Armadillos Costa Rica has two of the world's 20 species of armadillos. The more common species is the **nine-banded armadillo** (Armadillo de nueve bandas, *Dasypus novemcinctus*). It has a grey to yellowish, armour-plated body, a long snout, large ears and scales on its head and legs. Around 60 cm in length with a long ringed tail, it is found on the ground in all but the most arid habitats. Its diet is also extremely variable, including insects and small vertebrates, fruit, fungi, tubers and even carrion. It digs to obtain food, to make burrows and to escape predators so it is common to see signs of its presence, even if the armadillo itself is not seen. It and Costa Rica's other species, the **naked-tailed armadillo** (*Cabassous centralis*, are nocturnal. Uniquely among mammals, the nine-banded armadillo regularly give birth to four genetically identical offspring.

Sloths Costa Rica has two of these strange, slow-moving, upside down creatures: **Hoffman's two-toed sloth** (perezoso de dos dedos, *Choloepus hoffmanni*) and the **brown-throated three-toed-sloth** (perezoso de tres dedos, perico ligero, cúcula, *Bradypus variegatus*). The former is generally a tan colour and has no tail, while the latter is greyish brown with a distinctive grey and white mask and a small, stumpy tail. In moist conditions, the coats of both species may be suffused with green, the colour coming from the blue-green algae that live on their fur and help camouflage them in the trees. Both have three curved claws, or 'toes', on their hind feet, while it is the claws on the forefeet that give them their common names. The three-toed sloth is active both day and night and may move through four or five trees in two days, whereas the two-toed is nocturnal and is often in the same tree for two consecutive nights. Both species eat only leaves and it may take a month for a full meal to be completely digested. As a result, they need to defecate only once a week and descend to the base of a tree to do so. Young are born throughout the year and are carried by their mother for six to nine months, so it's worth looking for an extra, smaller head when you see an adult animal!

Cats All six species of the cat family in Costa Rica are both nocturnal and rare, which makes it unlikely that they will be seen. The smallest, spotted species is the **oncilla** (tigrillo, *Felis tigrinus*), which is the size of a small domestic cat; next in size is the **margay** (caucel, *F. wiedis*) weighing 4-9 kg, followed by the medium dog-sized **ocelot** (manigordo, *F. pardalis*) at 11-16 kg, and then the large **jaguar** (tigre or jaguar, *Panthera onca*) weighing 57-113 kg. The two unspotted cats are the smaller **jaguarundi** (léon breñero, *F. yaguarondi*) at 5.5-10 kg, and the **puma** (léon montés, *F. concolor*), which is almost the same size as a jaguar. All species are found in forest, though some also occur in scrubland and even savannah. The diet of the smallest, the oncilla, includes large insects, frogs, birds, lizards and small mammals, while even the largest, the jaguar which also takes deer, tapirs, monkeys and peccaries, is not averse to small prey such as fish and frogs. Most climb trees as well as hunting on the ground and both the jaguar and ocelot are also excellent swimmers. Nocturnal activity is most common though some, for instance the jaguar and jaguarundi, may also be active during the day. Walking at night along trails cleared in the forest will give you the best chance of seeing one of these cats. Wear a headlamp, rather than carrying a torch, as then their eyeshine is reflected back to your eyes and even a brief glimpse of a cat's glowing eyes is exciting.

Dogs The **coyote** (coyote, *Canis latrans*) and the **gray fox** (zorro gris, *Urocyon cinereoargenteus*) are Costa Rica's two species from the dog family. The coat colour of the former, the larger species, varies from grizzled grey to brownish yellow, while that of the latter is silver grey with tawny legs, feet and ears. Both are active during the day and night and both are found in forest or, more commonly, open areas of the northern Pacific lowlands. Both species tend to eat whatever is available, from fruit and insects to small mammals or even deer, in the case of the coyote. The coyote's howl, consisting of high-pitched staccato yelps followed by a long siren wail, is quite likely to be heard.

Raccoons Of the six species of this family found in Costa Rica; the **white-nosed coati** (pizote, *Nasua narica*) is most likely to be seen; also quite common are the **northern raccoon** (mapache norteño, *Procyon lotor*) and the **kinkajou** (martilla, *Potus flavus*). The **crab-eating raccoon** (mapache cangrejo, *Procyon cancrivorus*), the **olingo**, (olingo, *Bassaricyon gabbii*) and the **cacomistle** (cacomistle, *Bassariscus sumichrasti*) are also present in the country. All but the coati are nocturnal and all are omnivorous, foraging in trees and, in the case of the raccoons and coatis, also on the ground. Generally, these species have pointed muzzles, short legs and long tails. The northern and crab-eating raccoons have a striped tail and a distinctive, black face-mask; the overall coat colour of the former is grizzled grey, while that of the latter is brown. The northern raccoon is more widespread in Costa Rica, the crab-eater being confined to the Pacific lowlands. Both are most commonly seen near water, indeed the latter is considered semi-aquatic. Unlike the other species, coatis are very sociable with the females and their offspring living in groups the adult males, though, are solitary. Coat colour is grey or brown and they have a long, ringed tail that is often held erect above the body and a highly mobile, upturned and elongated snout. Infants in these species are small and poorly developed when born and they spend their first five or six weeks in a nest built by their mother in a tree. The kinkajou is the only species uniform in colour (greyish or reddish brown) and without a ringed tail, it also has a shorter muzzle than the others and is decidedly more cute looking! Its tail is prehensile and it has a long tongue used for probing nectar from flowers and honey from bees' nests. The olingo is similar in habit and appearance, but is smaller with indistinct rings on its bushier (non-prehensile) tail and faint grey markings on its more pointed face, it is also rarer. The cacomistle is found in drier forests, is has a fox-like face, larger ears than the other species in this group and a bushy, ringed tail.

Weasel family There are three species of skunk in Costa Rica, all more likely to be smelled than seen. The **striped hog-nosed skunk** (zorro hediondo raya, *Conepatus semistriatus*) is found countrywide, in forests but more often in cleared areas including gardens and agricultural land, so it is the most liable to be seen. It is black, with a wide white stripe on its head and along its back and it has a large white, bushy tail. It has a bare, elongated snout. The **spotted skunk** (zorro hediondo encamanchado, *Spilogale putorius*), and the **hooded skunk** (zorro hediondo encapuchado, *Mephitis macroura*) are much less common. All three skunks are nocturnal and forage on the ground for insects and small mammals, though they also eat fruit, birds' eggs and the like. The smallest species, the spotted skunk (0.5 kg), readily climbs trees. The **tayra** (tolumuco, *Eira barbara*) is a long, slender animal that resembles a mink; it has a black or brown body with a tan head and neck and a yellowish patch on its chest. At 4-6 kg, it is a lot heavier than any of the skunks. Tayras are often seen in pairs, foraging in trees and on the ground during the day and night for birds, small mammals and fruit. Other species found in Costa Rica are the **grison** (grisón, *Galictis vittata*), which has a smoky grey back and tail, with black legs, underparts and face and a white stripe across its forehead; the **long-tailed weasel** (comadreja, *Mustela frenata*), which resembles the European weasel; and the **Neotropical otter** (nutria neotropical, *Lutra longicaudis*). All three are active both day and night.

Peccaries The **collared peccary** (saíno, *Tayassu tajacu*) and the **white-lipped peccary** (chancho de monte, cariblanco, *T. pecari*) both travel in groups, of up to 50 individuals in the case of the collared peccary and 100 or more for the white-lipped. The groups tend to divide into smaller family groups of adult males, females and their offspring. They are rather pig-like, in both activity and appearance. With a diet of mostly roots, seeds and fruit, signs of their rooting activities can often be found, as can their dung piles, which are used as territory markers, and their mud wallows. The collared peccary weighs about 17-30 kg and is black or grey with a band of lighter coloured hair around its neck. It is the more widespread species, occurring in all forest types at low and mid elevations, in shrublands and agricultural areas and it is active mainly during the day. The white-lipped peccary, weighing 25-40 kg, occurs only in forests and is active day and night.

Deer The **white-tailed** (venado cola blanca, *Odocoileus virginianus*) is the largest of the two species of deer found in Costa Rica, standing 1 m high at the shoulder, and is seen more commonly. It is a light-, dark-, or greyish-brown deer, with a white belly, white under the tail and often has a white throat. Males over a year old have branched antlers, which are shed and regrown each year. The smaller **red brocket deer** (cabro de monte, *Mazama americana*) is reddish brown, with white under the tail and the males have small, straight antlers. The white-tailed occurs in more open, drier forests and on forest edges, while the brocket deer tends to be in thicker, wet forests, both are active day and night. Both deer species graze on grass and browse on leaves and twigs from trees and shrubs, with the brocket deer also taking fruit and flowers. Brocket deer live singly or in very small groups, while the white-tailed deer are in larger, usually single-sex, groups. When alarmed, both species flee with their tail raised, displaying its white underside. This is the most frequent sighting of the deer – a disappearing rump!

Tapirs **Baird's tapir** (danta, *Tapirus bairdii*) is the only tapir occurring in Costa Rica. It is a large, stocky mammal, weighing 200 kg or more. Its coat is sparsely furred with reddish brown hair and it has a short, bristly mane extending along the back of its neck. The tapir has a short, fleshy trunk, derived from the nose and upper lip, which is used to pull leaves and shoots into its mouth. Its sense of smell is excellent and its hearing is good, but its vision is not. It is found in wet forests and swampy areas, where it is active mostly at night, feeding on leaves, twigs, fruit and grass. The most likely clue to its presence to be seen is its characteristic three-toed track, but tapirs are uncommon and rarely seen in the country.

Rodents There are 50 or so rodent species in Costa Rica, including mice, rats, pocket gophers and squirrels and others such as the **paca** (tepezcuintle, *Agouti paca*) and **agouti**, (guatusa, *Dasyprocta punctata*). The agouti, a reddish brown creature which looks rather like a large, long-legged guinea pig, is quite likely to be seen moving on the forest floor during the day searching in particular for fallen fruit but also seeds and flowers. It may become nocturnal in areas where it is hunted. The paca is quite similar in shape, but, at around 10 kg in weight, is twice the size of an agouti with white spots on its body. It too feeds on fruit, seeds, nuts and other vegetation, but is nocturnal.

Of Costa Rica's five squirrel species, the **red-tailed squirrel** (ardilla roja, *Sciurus granatensis*) and the **variegated squirrel** (chiza, *S. variegatoides*) are the ones most likely to be seen. The former tends to be in wet forests, while the latter is found on forest edges, in drier forests and more open areas including close to human habitations. Both are diurnal, actively foraging for fruits, nuts, insects, leaves and flowers in the trees.

Porcupines The **Mexican hairy porcupine** (puercoespin, cuerpoespin, *Coendou mexicanus*), spends most of its time in trees, using its prehensile tail to help climb and hang on to branches, though it does come to the ground occasionally to feed and to move from tree to tree. Porcupines are nocturnal, spending the day on a branch or in a hollow tree. Their diet consists mainly of leaves but also includes fruits, seeds, roots insects and small vertebrates.

Rabbits Two or three species are present in the country, including the **eastern cottontail** (conejo cola de algodón, *Sylvilagus floridensis*) and the **forest rabbit** (conejo de bosque, *S. brasiliensis*). The former is found on the forest edge and in more open areas, while, as expected from its name, the latter lives inside forests.

Bats With over 100 species in the country and all just glimpsed as they swoop past at night, it is very difficult, if not impossible, for the casual visitor to identify the species seen. The smallest bat in Costa Rica, the **black myotis** (murciélago pardo, *Myotis nigricans*), weighs just 5 g, with a wingspan of 5 cm, while the largest, the **false vampire bat** (vampiro falso, *Vampyrum spectrum*), weighs 200 g with a 80-cm wingspan. Food items include pollen, nectar, fruit, insects, small vertebrates (including fish, frogs, birds, rodents or other bats) and blood, different species specializing in different items. Daytime roosting sites include hollow trees, caves, tree branches, rock crevices, under bridges and in buildings. The **sucker-footed bat** (murciélago de ventosas, *Thyroptera tricolor*) most commonly roosts in small family groups in rolled up banana or *Heliconia* leaves; unlike most species, they rest head upwards.

Birds
Though the mammals in Costa Rica might be elusive, you can guarantee that you will see birds, and lots of them. They'll vary from all those little brown jobs (LBJs for short) to comparatively massive, colourful macaws and toucans. For anyone with more than a superficial interest, a good bird book is a must as this guide can only touch on a few of the more outstanding or conspicuous species.

Sea and shore birds Very obvious by the sea is the **magnificent frigate bird** (rabihorcado magno, *Fregata magnificens*), a large (2 m wingspan), soaring, black bird with pointed wings and forked tail. Males have red throat pouches that they inflate during courtship displays. Seeing these frigatebirds stealing fish and nesting material from other seabirds and eating cute young sea-turtles, which have just hatched and are making a dash for the relative safety of the sea, makes you realize that their habits do not live up to their elegant appearance. The **brown pelican** (pelicano moreno, *Pelecanus occidentalis*) is a much sturdier bird, easily recognizable by its big throat pouch, which it uses as a net to scoop up fish underwater. Though somewhat ungainly-looking when on the ground, a group of them flying in formation slowly and silently low over the water or beach is an impressive sight. Less impressive are the many species of shorebirds – plovers, sandpipers, etc, that can be seen scuttling along the beaches. Though not necessarily small, they still tend to be classified as LBJs, of real interest only to ardent birdwatchers!

Waterbirds, herons and egrets Also seen by the sea, as well as in freshwater areas, are anhingas and cormorants – quite similar-looking birds, very often seen standing with their wings spread out to dry in the sun. The **olivaceous cormorant** (pato chancho, *Phalacrocorax brasilianus*) is a black/brown bird with a wingspan of 1 m, a longish tail and a long bill ending in a down-curve. The **anhinga** (pato aguja, *Anhinga anhinga*) has a longer neck and a long, pointed bill without a hook; the female has a brown neck. Many other birds, including storks, ibis, herons, egrets and spoonbills can be seen in aquatic habitats. Perhaps most desirable to spot is the **roseate spoonbill** (espátula rosada, *Ajaia ajaja*), a large, pink wading bird with a white neck and distinctive spoon-shaped bill that it opens and swings about underwater, snapping it shut when it feels a frog, fish or other such prey enter. Also very distinctive is the **jabiru stork** (galán sin ventura, *Jabiru mycteria*), a very large, white wading bird standing 1.4 m high, with a black bill, a huge black beak and a red area at the base of its neck.

Cattle egrets (garcilla bueyera, *Bubulcus ibis*) precede any river safari through open savanna, taking to the air in flocks in a blaze of feathers, only to roost. The **bare-throated tiger-heron** (garza-tigre, *Tigrisoma mexicanum*) is a far more impressive bird, standing 80 cm tall. The juvenile has tiger-like stripes, which blend perfectly against the alternating shade and sunlight. These grow out at adulthood.

Marsh and stream birds Included among Costa Rica's marsh and stream birds are such species as the jacana, several rails, crakes, coots and gallinules and the sun bittern. The **northern jacana** (gallina de agua, *Jacana spinosa*) is seen in marshes, wet pastures and on ponds, often walking on top of lily pads or other floating vegetation, its incredibly long toes spreading its weight and preventing it from sinking into the water. It feeds on insects, snails, frogs, fish and some vegetable matter. The adult has a black head, neck and chest with bright brown wings, belly and back and a yellow beak and forehead; the yellow under its wings is very noticeable as it flies off. More colourful is the **purple gallinule** (gallareta morada, *Porphryula martinica*) with its bluish, violet head neck and chest, green wings, red and yellow beak, light blue forehead and yellow legs. It too is found in marshes and around lakeshores.

Ducks Costa Rica's 15 or so species of ducks includes the **Muscovy** (pato real, *Cairina moschata)*, mentioned here as you may well have seen its domesticated form in a farm in your own country. The wild bird is mostly greenish-back, with white patches on its wings and the male has a feathered crest and red warts on his face and beak. It is no longer very common due to hunting pressure and habitat destruction.

Vultures Not beautiful, but conspicuous and commonly seen are Costa Rica's vultures. There are four species in the country. The more sociable **black vulture** (zopilote negro, *Coragyps atratus*) and **turkey vulture** (zopilote cabecirrojo, *Cathartes aura*) are a frequent sight round towns and villages. Both are large black birds, the former with a bare, red head and neck and the latter with a featherless, black head and neck. Larger than either of these, with a wingspan of 2 m, is the **king vulture** (zopilote rey, *Sarcoramphus papa*), which is white with black wings and tail and has a featherless, black, orange and yellow head. It usually hunts over forest and wooded areas. Least common and smallest is the **lesser yellow-headed vulture** (zopilote cabecigualdo, *Cathartes burrovianus*). All are carrion eaters, though the king and black vulture do sometimes take live prey.

Raptors Also known as birds of prey, raptors mostly hunt living animals. They include hawks, kites, eagles, falcons and caracaras; there are about 50 species of them in Costa Rica. Though often quite difficult to identify as they soar far overhead, above all types of habitats, some more conspicuous ones can be picked out. The **osprey** (aquila pescadora, *Pandion haliaetus*) is unusual in that is feeds on fish, grabbing them with its sharp claws from fresh or saltwater. White below and brown above, it is found more or less worldwide.

The American **swallow-tailed hawk** (elanio tijereta, *Elanoides forficatus*) can be distinguished from other raptors by its deeply forked, long black tail. It feeds on the wing, grabbing flying insects and snatching small prey such as lizards from trees. The **harpy eagle** (aguila arpía, *Harpia harpyja*) used to be widespread in Costa Rica, but is now very rare – possibly extinct. It is a large, spectacular bird standing around 1 m tall, which can grab small monkeys and other mammals from the tree tops as it flies above them. The **crested caracara** (caracara cargahuesos, *Polyborus plancus*) is a large (wingspan up to 1.3 m) black bird, with a barred black and white neck, a black, white and red head and yellow legs, found over open areas and quite commonly seen in groups eating carrion, along with black or turkey vultures.

Owls You might be lucky and see one of Costa Rica's 15 species of owl during the day, especially if a local guide knows a roosting site that a particular owl regularly uses, but, as they are mostly nocturnal hunters, you are more likely to just hear them. However, both the **spectacled owl** (buho de anteojos, *Pulsatrix perspicillata*) and the **ferruginous pygmy owl** (mochuelo común, *Glaucidium brasilianum*) can sometimes be seen hunting in the day or at dusk. The former is a large owl, 46 cm high, with a dark brown head and back with a lighter chest and, as indicated by its name, white 'spectacles' and white on its throat. It is found in forest and in more open areas. The pygmy owl is just 16 cm high, commonly hunting during the day, it is a reddish or greyish brown owl with white streaks on its front.

Goatsuckers or nightjars Nine species of these nocturnal birds are found in Costa Rica, the most common is the **pauraque** (tapacaminos común, *Nyctidromus albicollis*). They inhabit open areas such as farm- and parkland, thickets and forest edges but are most commonly seen as they fly up directly in front of one's car, their eyes flashing a bright red in the headlights. Indeed, their Spanish name means 'common road blocker'. Their mottled brown, black and white colour is an excellent camouflage, and they are almost impossible to spot roosting (on the ground or along tree branches) during the day. The **common potoo** (nictibio común, *Nyctibius griseus*), unlike most other nightjars, adopts a vertical roosting posture, often perching during the day in the open on a dead tree stump, looking very much like an extension of the stump.

Swifts and swallows There are 12 species of swallow and 11 swifts in Costa Rica. Though not closely related groups, they do superficially resemble each other being slender streamlined birds seen swooping through the air catching insects while on the wing. This group will be familiar to most visitors, indeed the **barn swallow** (golondrina tijereta, *Hirundo rustica*) is a common species more or less worldwide.

Hummingbirds Hummingbirds are wonderful little creatures that are a delight to watch and Costa Rica has over 50 species of them. Though easy to recognize as a group, they are actually quite difficult to identify as they dart past at high speed or hover briefly at a flower extracting its nectar. So tiny are some of the species, mostly weighing between 3-6 g, that they can become entangled in spiders' webs or be eaten by praying mantises and frogs. The major part of their diet is nectar, but they also feed on insects to obtain protein. The largest hummingbird in Costa Rica is the **violet sablewing** (ala de sable violáceo *Campylopterus hemileucurus*), which is 15 cm in length with a down-curved bill and white patches at the end of its tail. The male has a violet head and front with a dark green back and wings, while the female has a violet throat but a grey front. Although the **long-tailed** hermit (ermitaño colilargo, *Phaethornis superciliosus*) also measures 15 cm in length, much of this is, indeed, its tail. It is a greenish brown hummingbird, with a long white tipped tail, a down-curved bill, black and light coloured eye stripes and a light brown front and is found in forests and on forest edges. Most 'hummers', including the **crowned woodnymph** (ninfa violeta y verde, *Thalurania colombica*), are less than 10 cm long. The male of this species has a glossy green throat, chest and rump, with a purple head and belly and a dark forked tail and dark wings, the female is greenish with a light grey throat and chest. Both have a straight bill, only slightly curved at the tip. Many hummingbirds act as pollinators for flowers, the flowers generally being red, pink or orange, thereby indistinguishable to insects, and odourless so as not to attract nectar-feeding insects. The flowers also tend to be shaped into long thin tubes adapted to fit the birds' bills.

Trogons Of the 10 trogon species found in Costa Rica, the resplendent quetzal is the one most people want to see. However, all species are spectacular, particularly the males. They have metallic green, blue or violet heads and chests, with contrasting bright red, yellow or orange underparts. They usually sit erect in the forest with their distinctive tails (long, with horizontal black and white stripes on the underside and a squared off end) pointing downwards. The spectacular male **resplendent quetzal** (quetzal or fénix del bosque, *Pharomachrus mocinno*), is a bird of the cloudforests with an emerald green head, a crest of green feathers and long trailing green plumes extending 45 cm or more beyond his white tail. In spite of their bright colours, trogans can be quite difficult to spot in forests as they blend into the dark green foliage and tend to sit silently waiting to catch passing insects. They also feed on small lizards and frogs as well as fruits, especially figs. Other trogons found in Costa Rica are the **slaty-tailed trogon** (trogón coliplomizo, *Trogon massena*) and the **violaceous trogon** (trogón violaceo, *Trogon violaceus*), the latter being found in dry as well as wet forests at low elevations.

Kingfishers There are six species of kingfisher in Costa Rica, mostly seen perched on branches while they scan the water beneath them for fish, though they also seem to favour telegraph lines as perching sites. All have large heads, with long, straight, quite sturdy bills and fairly stubby bodies but they vary in size from 12 to 40 cm. The bigger species eat larger prey and hence avoid competition with the smaller ones. They lay their eggs in burrows dug in the banks of rivers or streams. The **ringed kingfisher** (martín pescador collarejo, *Ceryle torquata*), a blue-grey bird with a brownish front, white neckband and throat, is the largest kingfisher in the country. The smallest is the American **pygmy kingfisher** (martín pescador enano, *Chloroceryle aene*), which has a green back and head, a reddish brown neck-band, throat and chest with a white lower front. The female of this species has a green bar across her chest.

Motmots The motmots, relatives of the kingfisher, are very handsome birds, brightly coloured with distinctive, long, racquet tails. Perhaps the most attractive of the country's six species is the **turquoise-browed motmot** (momoto cejiceleste, *Eumomota superciliosa*), a green to brownish green bird, with a black throat, a small black mask round its eyes and turquoise bar above the eyes, its tail and wings are also turquoise. All motmots are more common in low and mid-altitude forests, but they can also be seen in parks, orchards and drier scrub areas. Like the kingfishers, they tend to sit and wait for their prey, mostly insects, but also frogs, snakes and lizards, then swoop down, grab it and return to their perch to beat it to death. Motmots will also eat some fruit.

Toucans The toucans are a quite unmistakable group – all bearing large, brightly coloured bills that look more plastic than real! There are six species in Costa Rica, two toucans, two aracaris and two toucanets. The **chestnut-mandibled toucan** (dios-te-dé, *Ramphastos swainsonii*) is the largest; both it and the slightly smaller **keel-billed toucan** (tucán pico iris, *Ramphastos sulfuratus*) are mainly black with a yellow face and chest and red under the tail. The former has a bicoloured bill, chestnut below and yellow above, while the latter has an amazing multicoloured bill, red, orange, green and blue. The **collared aracari** (tucancillo collarejo, *Pteroglossus torquatus*) and **fiery-billed aracari** (tucancillo piquianaranjado, *Pteroglossus frantzii*) look somewhat alike, but the former is found on the Caribbean side of the country and in Guanacaste region and the latter on the south Pacific. Both have a black head and chest, a dark green back and a yellow belly with a central black spot, the bill in both is black below, but is bright orange red above in the fiery-billed and pale yellow in the collared. The **yellow-eared toucanet** (tucancillo orejiamarillo *Selenidera spectablis*) and **emerald toucanet** (tucancillo verde, *Aulacorhynchus prasinusare*) are smaller birds, the latter only 30 cm in comparison with the 56 cm of the chestnut-mandibled toucan. The emerald toucanet is mostly green, but has a blue throat and is chestnut below its tail. Its bill is black below and yellow above. All species are forest-dwelling fruit eaters and tend to be seen in small groups, mostly staying high up in the canopy. Toucans nest in hollow trees, often using holes that have been made by woodpeckers.

Pigeons and doves This group hardly needs describing, as its members will be more or less familiar in overall appearance, at least, to all visitors to Costa Rica. There are 22 species in the country. The most common ground dove is the **ruddy ground dove** (tortolita rojiza, *Columbina talpacoti*), the male of which is reddish brown with a grey head, while the female is duller. This species is usually seen feeding in open areas, pastures, fields and woodland clearings, searching the ground for food such as seeds, fruit and some insects. A slightly more unusual looking member of the group is the **Inca dove** (tortolita colilarga, *Columbina inca*), which is a small pale grey bird with black linings on its feathers that give it a scaly appearance, it has a longish tail with white edges and, in flight, its reddish brown wing patches can be seen. Its habitats are very similar to those of the ground dove. Pigeons' nests tend to be rather scrappy structures, built on the ground, rock ledges or in trees or bushes. Usually only one or two eggs are laid and the fledglings are initially fed on 'pigeon milk', a nutritious liquid produced in the crop of both parents.

Parrots Many of Costa Rica's 16 species are small and green and quite difficult to tell apart unless seen very clearly, but quite unmistakable and very spectacular is the **scarlet macaw** (lapa roja, *Ara macao*). It is a large bird, 84 cm long, with a bright red body, yellow and blue wings, a long red tail and a white face. Sadly, this species has become quite rare, devastated by habitat destruction and hunting for the pet trade. It is found mostly on the southern Pacific side of the country, whereas the similarly sized **green macaw** (lapa verde, *Ara ambigua*) is found on the Caribbean side; this species, too, is endangered in Costa Rica. Most of the parrots are noisy and sociable, feeding on fruits and seeds that they tear apart with their powerful, short, hooked beaks. Breeding usually takes place in hollow trees, with the young of the large macaw species remaining in the nest for three to four months and those of smaller species for three to four weeks. They are very vulnerable at this time as many nestlings are taken and sold as pets. Fairly typical of the smaller species is the **white-fronted parrot** (loro frentiblanco, *Amazona albifrons*), a green bird with red around its eyes, with a white forehead, blue on top of its head and red and blue patches on its wing.

Woodpeckers Two of Costa Rica's 16 woodpecker species, the **lineated woodpecker** (carpintero lineado, *Dryocopus lineatus*) and the **pale-billed woodpecker** (carpintero picoplata, *Campephilus guatemalensis*) look just like the cartoon character Woody Woodpecker! They both have a large, crested head with varying amounts of red on it (depending on sex and species), a large black body with white markings and a banded, black and white front, but only the lineated has white on its head. Both are found in wet forests in the country. Though insects make up most of the diet of the majority of the woodpeckers, fruits, nuts and nectar may also be taken, while the sapsuckers do just that – drill holes in trees and suck the sap. Even if you do not see a woodpecker, you may well hear them drilling for insects, excavating nests or communicating with each other by drumming. As with the kingfishers, the different-sized species avoid competition by taking prey of different sorts or sizes. The smallest of the woodpeckers in Costa Rica is the 9 cm long **olivaceous piculet** (carpenterito oliváceo, *Picumnus olivaceus*), which may be seen in gardens and plantations as well as drier woodlands and wet forests. It has a dull green back and lighter front, with the male having orange streaks on its head. The medium sized species, around 19 cm in length, include the quite similar **Hoffman's woodpecker** (carpintero de Hoffman, *Melanerpes hoffmannii*) and **red-crowned woodpecker** (carpintero nuquirroja, *Melanerpes rubricapillus*). Both have black and white bars on their backs and wings and light brown chests; the former has a yellowish belly and the latter a reddish one. The male Hoffman's has red on the top of his head, while both sexes of the red-crowned have red backs to their necks and the male, in addition, has a red crown while the top of the female's head is white. Both species favour open, wooded sites and are found on the Pacific slope, but Hoffman's occurs in the north and the red-crowned in the south.

Curassows This group, with 13 species in the country, contains the guans and chachalacas as well as curassows, with the larger members of the group weighing up to 4 kg. They are related to such birds as pheasants, partridges and quail – all called 'chicken-like birds', even by serious birdwatchers! Unfortunately, they taste good too so several species, including the **crested guan** (pava crestada, *Penelope purpurascens*), **black guan** (pava negra, *Chamaepetes unicolor*) and the **great currasow** (pavon, *Crax rubra*) are becoming uncommon outside protected areas. They are quite heavily built birds, with long sturdy legs and often a long tail. They tend to be brown, black, grey or olive though might have some brightly coloured patch such as the red dewlap in the crested guan or yellow knobs on the bill of the male great curassow. Guans and curassows live in forests, the former mostly staying in the trees and the latter on the ground. The chachalacas are aboreal, but are more common on forest edges and clearings. The arboreal birds eat fruit, leaves, buds and some insects; while the terrestrial currasows feed on fruit, seeds and insects, generally moving round in flocks of 10-20 individuals except during the breeding season.

Tinamous The tinamous, five species in Costa Rica, look rather like partridges; they have chunky bodies, with short tails and legs and a small head. All are terrestrial, feeding, sleeping and nesting on the ground, except for the **great tinamou** (tinamú grande, *Tinamus major*), which roosts in trees. Their flight is clumsy and they are more likely to run than fly from danger. Tinamous are brown, grey or olive, with darker spots or bars so they are well camouflaged as they scuttle through the forest searching for fruit and seeds, but also taking insects and even small vertebrates. Females lay their eggs in indentations in the ground, generally hidden under a bush. Several females may use the same nest and then it is the male that incubates the eggs and looks after the chicks. They feed themselves as soon as they hatch, but he leads them round the forest and protects them from predators. In spite of being hunted by humans, tinamous appear to be quite common, perhaps because they are so secretive and also because they are adaptable, able to survive in forest that has been partially logged.

Cuckoos and anis Most commonly seen among the 11 species in this group are the **squirrel cuckoo** (cucu ardilla, *Piaya cayana*), the **smooth-billed ani** (garrapatero piquiliso, *Crotophaga ani*) and the **groove-billed ani** (garrapatero piquiestriado, *Crotophaga sulcirostris*). Unlike the European cuckoo, none of these three lays its eggs in the nest of another species. The squirrel cuckoo, which is a large (48 cm) reddish brown bird, with a bright yellow bill, a grey belly and a long tail with black and white stripes on its underside, is found in wooded areas across Costa Rica. It tends to be quite a secretive bird, feeding off insects and pairing up just for the breeding season. Both sexes build the nest, incubate the eggs and feed the young. In contrast, the anis are noisy, conspicuous, gregarious birds, living in flocks of eight to 25 individuals in bushy scrub and open areas, often around human habitation. They are often seen foraging on the ground around cattle, eating the insects flushed up by the cows. Both species are black with a large, almost parrot-like grey bill, the smooth-billed being found on the southern Pacific slope and the groove-billed in the northern Pacific and the Caribbean.

Passerines The groups mentioned above include fewer than half of Costa Rica's birds. All the others are passerines, with feet specialized to grasp and perch on tree branches. They tend to be small land birds, many are LBJs but some are very bright and conspicuous. Included among the passerines in Costa Rica are 16 species of **woodcreepers**, all looking and acting rather alike. They are slender brown birds, with longish beaks and stiff tails, most often seen moving up tree trunks probing under bark and in plants looking for insects. The **antbirds** (30 species), though a more variable group, are not seen often as they are inclined to skulk in the shade low down in the forest. Most males come in shades of black or brown with some white, while the females tend to be olive or brown. Their name comes from the habit that some of them have of following marching columns of ants eating the insects and other small prey that the ants flush out of hiding. Costa Rica's 22 species of **wren** are all smallish (10-20 cm), mostly brown or reddish brown. Their most distinguishing feature is their tail – usually held stiffly upright. They are found in forests, thickets, grassland and marshes, usually hopping or flitting low down searching for insects. Many of Costa Rica's 50 species of **warblers** are migrants from North America. They are small birds, commonly found flitting round gardens and plantations often in the company of other birds such as tanagers and honeycreepers. They can be quite brightly coloured, usually yellowish or greenish with varying amounts of black, grey and white and maybe patches of red orange or blue. They mostly forage for insects but also take some nectar and juice from fruits. The **gnatcatchers**, 11 species in Costa Rica, are small, predominantly grey birds that are very similar in habit to the warblers. Although common and frequently seen, the **sparrows** and **grosbeaks** of Costa Rica are mostly rather dull brown or grey little birds, not a group that most visitors would be particularly interested in searching out. Indeed, most people will be very familiar with one of them, the **house sparrow** (gorrión común, *Passer domesticus*), which arrived in Costa Rica in 1974 having spread from North America, where it was introduced by European settlers in the 1800s.

The **thrushes**, 11 species breeding in Costa Rica, also tend to be rather drab birds but you will almost certainly see and can easily recognize the **sooty robin** (mirlo negruzco, *Turdus nigrescens*), as it looks and acts much like the **blackbird** (*Turdus merula*) common across Europe. The male is black and the female dark brown and both have an orange beak, legs and eye-ring. One member of this quite diverse group, the **black-faced solitaire** (solitario carinegro, *Myadestes melanops*) is famed for its singing and consequently its numbers have declined as it is caught for the pet trade.

In another diverse group are the **blackbirds** and **orioles**, included with them are the caciques, cowbirds, grackles, meadowlarks and oropendolas. Around 20 species occur in Costa Rica, distributed through all elevations and most habitats including human settlements and agricultural areas. They vary in size (15-56 cm), colour, ecology and behaviour. Widely distributed and conspicuous in the country is the **great-tailed grackle** (clarinero, *Quiscalus mexicanus*); the male is a large black bird with a purple gloss to its foliage and a long black tail. Both sexes have yellow eyes and black bills. The male, reaching 43 cm, is quite a bit bigger than the brownish female (33 cm). They occur at low and middle elevations on both the Caribbean and Pacific slopes of the country, mostly in open habitats. The large groups they form outside the breeding season can cause damage to agricultural areas and their roosting sites. Much more spectacular to look at is **Montezuma's oropendola** (oropéndola de Montezuma, *Psarocolius montezuma*), which has a large (50 cm) brown body, with a black head and chest, a yellow-edged tail, an orange tip to its large black bill and a blue patch under its eye. The oropendolas breed in colonies, weaving large bag-like nests, many of which hang from the branches of each tree. Montezuma's oropendola is quite strange in that 3-10 males establish a colony in a single tree and then defend the 10-30 females that join them to mate and nest there. The dominant male tends to mate with most females, but there is much competition with aggressive displaying and fighting between the males. The **bronzed cowbird** (vaquero ojirrojo, *Molothrus aeneus*) does not bother to make any form of nest; instead, the female lays her eggs in the nest of another species and leaves the other bird to rear her young.

Jays, which are members of the crow family, are some of the largest passerines, reaching up to 71 cm in length. Most are brightly coloured, such as the **white-throated magpie-jay** (urraca copetona, *Calocitta formosa*), which is found in open wooded sites and around human settlements on the northern Pacific slope. This is a large bird, up to 46 cm, brilliant blue above and white below with a conspicuous crest and a long blue tail. In contrast, the slightly smaller (40 cm), more widely distributed **brown jay** (urraca parda, *Cyanocorax morio*) is, as you might guess, brown! It has a pale brown to white chest and belly and its tail is white-tipped. Jays are omnivorous, eating just about anything and everything. Their diet includes eggs, nestlings, carrion, insects, fruit and nuts, which are foraged for on the ground and among trees. Both species live in small groups of related individuals and jointly defend a territory. The oldest pair mates, while the others help to nest build and feed the young. There are five species of jay in Costa Rica.

The American **flycatchers** are a very large and diverse group of birds with about 75 species in Costa Rica. Many of the small drab species are difficult to identify but the **scissor-tailed flycatcher** (tijereta rosada, *Tyrannus forficatus*) is both handsome and easily seen as it adopts the typical flycatcher technique, perching motionless on a fence to dart out and grab a passing insect and then return to the same perch to eat it. This flycatcher is a non-breeding migrant found in open areas such as fields, marshes and human settlements on the northern Pacific slope. It is a medium sized, silver-grey bird, about 20 cm in length, with a long (15 cm) black, forked tail, black wings with reddish patches under them and a white chest. Another bright and frequently seen flycatcher is the **great kiskadee** (bienteveo grande, *Pitangus sulphuratus*), which is a medium-sized (23 cm) bird, with an olive brown back, chestnut wings, a bright yellow chest and belly, a white throat and a black and white head. It tends to be found in trees in quite open sites such as in gardens, along the forest edge and in grassland. Along with catching insects, the great kiskadee also eats frogs and lizards and even small fish.

Some of the most colourful of Costa Rica's passerines are the 50 or so species of **tanagers** found there; included in this group are honeycreepers and euphonias. They are found in forested and shrubby areas over a wide range of elevations, tending to be in more open places and often seen near human habitation in mixed-species flocks foraging for fruit. Most tanagers are arboreal and eat small fruits and berries, though some are ground foragers and some eat insects. The honeycreepers feed on nectar, which they suck out after making holes at the base of a flower with their bill; they also take insects and fruit. The **blue-gray tanager** (tangara azuleja, *Thraupis episcopus*) is abundant and found over most of the country at all elevations, often near towns and villages, in parks and along forest edges. As its name implies, it is a blue-grey bird, with a darker blue back and bright blue wings and tail, the female being duller in colour. The male **scarlet-rumped tanager** (tangara lomiescarlata, *Ramphocelus passerinii*), is about the same size (16 cm) as the blue-gray tanager, but is black with a conspicuous red rump and pale blue-grey beak. The female is yellowish-olive with a grey head and throat and a yellow-orange rump, chest and belly. Euphonia males are typically blue-black above, with yellow foreheads, breasts and bellies, while the females tend to be olive-green with duller yellow fronts. Many of the male honeycreepers are brilliantly coloured. Typical of these is the **red-legged honeycreeper** (mielero patirrojo, *Cyanerpes cyaneus*), which is a bright blue bird with a black back, wings, tail and eyestripe, a turquoise patch on top of his head and red legs. The female is overall yellowish green, but also has red legs. This species may well be seen in gardens and plantations and also on the edges of drier forests in the north of the country.

Though they are small (9-19 cm), stocky birds, male **manakins** are noted for both their colourful plumage and their elaborate courtship diplays. They are very active, forest dwelling birds, foraging in the understorey for small fruits and some insects. One very attractive species is the **long-tailed manakin** (saltarín colilargo, *Chiroxiphia linearis*), which is found in forests on the northern Pacific slope. The male is black with a bright blue back, a red crest on his head and two very long, black tail feathers. The female is olive green, with a more yellow-green front and orange legs and she lacks the long tail feathers. The female **white-collared manakin** (saltarín cuelliblanco, *Manacus candei*) is also a small olive-green bird, but the male has a bright yellow belly, black on his wings and on the top of his head, an olive rump and a white throat and chest. This species is found in low elevation, wet forest on the Caribbean side of Costa Rica. During the breeding season, from February to July, manakin males display at particular sites in bushes, on tree branches or on the forest floor; generally several males display in the same area – the lekking site. They try to attract females with both visual and vocal displays, involving elaborate courtship dances, the movements in which are species specific. In some species, including the long-tailed manakin, two or three males do a coordinated dance on the same perch. Once a female has selected the male she considers to be the most spectacular and has mated with him, she goes off to nest-build, incubate and rear the young on her own.

Closely related to the manakins are the **cotingas**. This is a very diverse group containing bellbirds, umbrella birds, phias and fruit crows as well as typical cotingas, though there are only 10 species in Costa Rica. The cotingas eat mainly fruit, finding it high up in the canopy of the forest, though some eat insects as well. The bellbirds, though, stick to a strictly frugivorous diet, even, unusually, feeding fruit to their chicks. The nestlings, consequently, take longer to develop as their diet is low in protein. The male **three-wattled bellbird** (pájaro campana, *Procnias tricarunculata*) is a medium-sized (20 cm), brown bird with a white head and three odd-looking, worm-like appendages or wattles, hanging from its bill. The female is olive-green with a yellow-streaked front. Also strangely ornamented is the male **bare-necked umbrella bird** (pájaro-sombrilla, *Cephalopterus glabricollis*), a mostly black bird with a large red throat sac that is inflated during displays and also an umbrella-shaped black crest. This umbrella bird is only sparsely distributed and is threatened by habitat destruction as it breeds in highland forests, but overwinters in lowland forests, so requires both habitats in the same area and a forest corridor connecting them. Somewhat more common is the **snowy cotinga** (cotinga nivosa, *Carpodectes nitidus*), which is found in wet forests at low elevation on the Caribbean slope and in more open wooded areas. The male is pale grey above and white below, while the female is overall more grey.

Reptiles

Snakes Among Costa Rica's reptiles there are 127 snake species. The best place to see the snakes is in a zoo or snake farm – they are not often seen in the wild. Indeed, there are some of them that you will be very glad not to meet at close quarters! The **bushmaster** (matabuey, *Lachesis muta*), for instance, is the New World's largest venomous snake which can reach 3.5 m in length. It is an aggressive, slender, large-headed snake with a yellowish to tan body with black or brown blotches along it. Another large (up to 2.5 m), poisonous snake to be avoided is the **fer-de-lance** (terciopelo, *Bothrops asper*) as it too can be quite aggressive. It has a triangular head and a patterned olive, beige, black and brown body. Both this species and the bushmaster tend to be found on the ground, though young fer-de-lance may be found in trees. The **eyelash viper** (toboba de pestaña, *Bothriechis schlegelii*) is much smaller, reaching only 75 cm in length and is arboreal. It is very variable in colour: grey, olive, through reddish yellow, to bright golden yellow with or without markings on the body. Its name comes from the two or three horny spine-like scales that jut out above each eye. The last of the poisonous snakes to be covered here is the Central American **coral snake** (coral, *Micrurus nigrocinctus*), which may be found on the floor in forests, but also in more open areas. It is very colourful, with a small, black and yellow head and red and black rings along its body, which may or may not have narrower yellow rings as well. Given just a quick glance, it is quite easy to confuse the non-poisonous **harlequin snake** (coral falsa, *Scolecophis atrocinctus*) and the **tropical kingsnake** (coral falsa, *Lampropeltis triangulum*) with the coral snake. Both have bodies with bands of yellow, red and black, thereby mimicking the coral snake's colouration, perhaps in an attempt to deter predators. It should be noted that the vast majority of Costa Rica's snakes are not venomous and those that are tend to be nocturnal and secretive, so it is really not necessary to worry about being bitten. However, it is still not advisable to poke under rocks and logs or into bushes and pay attention to where you are putting your feet.

Lizards Perhaps the most conspicuous and certainly the largest of Costa Rica's 68 lizard species are the **green iguana** (garrobo, *Iguana iguana*) and **black iguana**, (iguana negra, garrobo, *Ctenosuara similes*). The former reaches up to 2m in length and the latter just over 1 m. The green iguana is more widespread, found in wet forests at low elevations and along streams and rivers in drier areas on both the Caribbean and Pacific slopes. It can often be seen sunbathing high in trees, especially early in the morning. The black iguana is found only on the Pacific slope, often in drier areas and on the beach, but also in forests. Considerably smaller, but very commonly seen at night in houses are **geckos**, usually grey or brown with large eyes and toes that appear to have little pads on them. Unlike most lizards, they make quite audible squeaks.

Of the two crocodilians, the smaller **spectacled caiman**, (caiman, *Caiman crocodiles*), is more common, but the American **crocodile** (cocodrilo, *Crodylus acutus)* is also found in the country. The caiman can reach 2.5 m in length, while the crocodile can be up to 7m long, though 4 m is more usual. The crocodile has a longer, more slender and more pointed snout than the caiman and also, unlike the caiman, has a tooth on each side of its lower jaw, projecting upwards, that is visible when the mouth is closed.

Turtles Freshwater turtles, (there are eight freshwater and six marine species) such as the **white-lipped mud turtle** (tortuga caja, *Kinosternon leucostomum)* are quite a common sight, sunning themselves on logs along rivers. Six species of marine turtles nest on Costa Rican beaches and with luck and planning you may get to see one or two come ashore to nest on either the Pacific or Caribbean beaches. The small **Olive Ridley** (lora, *Lepidochelys olivacea*) arrives on the beach of Santa Rosa in spectacular *arribadas* with many thousands of turtles arriving to nest over a few consecutive nights at certain times in the year. The hook beak of the **hawksbill turtle** (carey, *Eretmochelys imbricata*) is a distinctive characteristic of the species, as is the treasured tortoise-shell carapace prized for its subtle patterns and once used for engravings. Green turtle soup is fortunately on fewer menus, improving the survival rates of the **green turtle** (tortuga verde, *Chelonia mydas*). The largest reptile in the world is the **leatherback turtle** (baula, *Dermochelys coriacea*) which can grow to over 2 m in length and weigh over 500 kg. All marine turtles are endangered and protected, along with their nest sites and eggs, by international law.

Amphibians

Around 35 salamander, 3 caecilian, 14 toad and about 105 frog species are found in Costa Rica. **Salamanders**, which look rather like wet lizards, tend to be nocturnal and secretive, hiding in damp places. **Caecilians**, which are legless and resemble earthworms, are even less commonly seen as they mostly live underground. The largest toad in the country is the huge marine or **cane toad** (sapo grande, *Bufo marinus*), which reaches up to 20 cm in length and 1.2 kg in weight. These toads can be found in forests, in more open areas and in and around buildings. In contrast, Costa Rica's **golden toad** (sapo dorado de Monteverde, *Bufo periglenes*), is only 6 cm in size, the males are golden while the females are black with red spots ringed with yellow. It was found only in the Monteverde Cloud Forest Reserve and now believed to be extinct, has moved largely in to the realm of legend. The reason for its decline, and that of 20 or so other species in the reserve, is unclear. The amphibian that is probably the best known and most sought after by visitors is the beautifully coloured **red-eyed** or **gaudy leaf frog** (rana calzonuda, rana verde de arbol, *Agalychnis callidryas*). This is 5-7 cm in size with a pale or dark green back, blue-purple patches both on the underside of its limbs and vertical bars on its side, orange fore and hind feet and ruby red eyes. When resting or dormant, only the green colouring shows making the frog virtually invisible. Also much sought after are the brightly coloured poison-dart and poison-arrow frogs. These include the **strawberry poison-dart frog** (ranita roja, *Dendrobates pumilio*), which is bright red with varying quantities of black flecks on its body and with red, blue, green or black limbs, the **orange and black poison-dart frog** (rana venenosa, *Phyllobates* vittatus), which is small (2-3 cm) and black with a wide pair of orange stripes on its back and turquoise mottling on its limbs and the **green poison-dart frog** (rana venenosa, *Dendrobates auratus*). This species can be up to 4 cm in size and is very variable in colour – bright blue, turquoise, green or dark green with brownish or black patches. It is found on the forest floor or in low vegetation, mostly in forests at lower elevations. While the sensational name suggests otherwise, there is no evidence that the toxic secretions of the poison-dart frogs have ever been used by the local people to tip darts for hunting in Costa Rica, unlike in western Colombia where they are used by the Choco people.

Insects
There is no space in this guide to cover Costa Rica's invertebrates, but try, at least, to visit a butterfly farm and keep your eyes open to search out the smaller creatures in the forests. You might well, for instance, see long marching columns of **leaf-cutter ants** (*Atta* spp.), each carrying a piece of leaf back to its nest. These can be very large structures – a mound of leaf mulch surrounded by a considerable area of forest floor cleared of all green vegetation. Probably most impressive of the many butterfly species is the **morpho** (*Morpho peleides*), which has a 15 cm wingspan. The upper side of its wings are bright, shiny blue with a brown edge marked with white, but once it settles and closes its wings, the dull brown underside ensures that it is almost invisible.

Books and websites

Books

Natural history

Beletsky, Les *Costa Rica: Traveller's Wildlife Guide* (2004, Interlink Books). A fine overview of the natural health and heritage of the country, with colour drawings covering all wildlife – a good all-in-one choice.

Boza, Mario *Costa Rica National Parks* (1999, Incafo). Take the small, handy option, or the glossy coffee table one – both filled with good information and pictures compiled by the founder of the national park system.

Carr, Archie *The Windward Road: Adventures of Naturalist on Remote Caribbean Shores* (1979). Tales of Archie Carr's experiences on the north Caribbean shore and the turtle nesting beaches of Tortuguero.

Emmons, Louise and Feer, François *Neotropical Rainforest Mammals: A Field Guide* (1997, Press). The neotropical rainforest mammals spotter's guide.

Janzen, Daniel *Costa Rica Natural History* (1983, University of Chicago Press). A glorious, weighty book, packed with highly accessible information edited by the 'grandfather' of Guanacaste National Park.

Kricher, John *A Neotropical Companion* (1999, Princeton University Press). A detailed guide neatly situated in the grey area between academic study and keen interest. A great introduction to the neotropics – now available in paperback.

Stiles, Gary and Skutch, Alexander *A Guide to the Birds of Costa Rica* (1989, Cornell University). *The* guide to the birdlife of Costa Rica – accept no imitations.

Travel guides

Baker, Bill *The Essential Road Guide to Costa Rica* (Baker, Apartado 1185-01011, San José, T2220-1415.) Detailed strip maps, kilometre by kilometre road logs, motoring information plus San José map and bus guide.

Gallo, Rafael and Mayfield, Michael *The Rivers of Costa Rica: A canoeing, kayaking and rafting guide* (1988, Menasha Ridge Press, Alabama). A punchy little guide to the rivers of Costa Rica.

Tico Times *Exploring Costa Rica*, updated annually. Produced and published by the staff of the *Tico Times*, Costa Rica's English language newspaper.

Koutnik, Jane *Costa Rica – Culture Smart!*, (2006, Kuperard) a quick guide to the customs and etiquette of the country written by resident expat.

Christopher Howard *The New Golden Door to Retirement and Living in Costa Rica*, (2007, Costa Rica Books, 15 Ed). Good on-the-ground advice about what you need to consider before taking the plunge.

Fiction

Ras, Barbara *Costa Rica: A Traveler's Literary Companion*, (1994, Whereabouts Press). A much-loved collection of 26 stories drawn from across the country.

History, culture and politics

Palmer, Steven and Molina, Iván *The Costa Rica Reader: History, Culture, Politics* (2004, Duke University Press). Good, authoritive and up-to-date historical overview of the country.

Daling, Tjabel *Costa Rica: A Guide to the People, Politics and Culture* (1998, Latin America Bureau, www.lab.org.uk). A pocket history and overview of the country, picking up on the main themes that make up modern Costa Rica. A little dated now, but still good.

Molina, Iván and Palmer, Steven *The History of Costa Rica* (2007, University of Costa Rica). A brief, up-to-date and illustrated history of Costa Rica in a highly manageable little package.

Palmer, Pauline *What Happen: A Folk History of Costa Rica's Talamanca Coast* (2005, Zona Tropical). The hardships of life in Costa Rica's southern Caribbean and meaning of progress to these coastal communities.

Biesanz, Mavis Hiltunen, et al *The Ticos: Culture and Social Change in Costa Rica* (1998, Lynne Rienner Publishers). Insights to everything on Tico life from health, religion, family, education, place in the world and more.

Colesberry, Adrian, et al *Costa Rica; The Last Country The Gods Made* (1993, Globe Pequot Press). A history-cum-coffee table book telling Costa Rica's story in a collection of well-written essays.

Echeverría, Carlos Francisco *Historia Crítica del Arte Costarricense* (1986, Editorial Universidad Estatal). Overview of Costa Rican art.

Fallas, Carlos *Mamita Yunai* (2000, Editorial Costa Rica). A look at life on the United Fruit Company banana plantations.

Costa Rica on the net

The presence of Costa Rica on the internet is positively daunting. Most hotels – even the cheapest – and organizations can be contacted by email, many have their own website and try to include far too much information in their keenness. Despite the vagaries of the economy the use of the internet is the same as ever – if the site is up-to-date it serves its purpose.

Government and conservation
www.visitcostarica.com The official *Costa Rican Tourist Board*. It's as good a place as any to start your surfing.

www.turismo-sostenible.co.cr The Tourist Board's *Certification for Sustainable Tourism* site, providing options to search for hotels by level of sustainability.

www.tourism.co.cr The *Costa Rican National Chamber of Tourism* site, with good hotel and background information.

www.ticotimes.net The *Tico Times* website, very useful for catching up on the latest. For a daily hit you can try www.amcostarica.com from *AM Costa Rica*.

www.costarica-embassy.org The *Costa Rican embassy site in Washington*, useful information and links.

www.usembassy.or.cr The *US Embassy* site in Costa Rica with good travel information, and some interesting background on projects. Good information and up-to-date links.

www.imn.ac.cr Instituto Meterorológico Nacional, full of fascinating bits on the weather, Spanish only.

www.rree.go.cr The *Costa Rican Ministry of Foreign Affairs* website with all the information you could need on visas, embassies, residency and so on.

www.minae.go.cr The *Ministry for the Environment and Energy* which has overall control for *SINAC*, the national park programme, and energy development. Strange bedfellows and clearly uncomfortable on the same website.

www.sinac.go.cr The *Sistema Nacional de Areas de Conservacion* website. Has the core of what could eventually be a very comprehensive site.

www.inbio.ac.cr Bilingual *INBioparques* site, with access to the conservation organization's databases.

www.intnet.co.cr Home page of many cultural organizations covering the arts and sports, with some general information on National Parks.

General information
www.yellowweb.co.cr A good overall site with good information and links although not always up to date.

www.infocostarica.com Another good general site.

www.costaricaoutdoors.com Good general information and packed with snippets of background information and stories.

www.centralamerica.com/cr Also a good base to start looking around.

www.costaricaexpeditions.com The website of one of Costa Rica's best tour operators, but with up-to-date news, information and weather, and which isn't always just trying to get you to spend more money.

Contents

456 Basic Spanish for
travellers

461 Index

466 Complete title listing

469 Advertisers' index

469 Acknowledgements

471 About the author

472 Credits

Footnotes

Basic Spanish for travellers

Learning Spanish is a useful part of the preparation for a trip to Latin America and no volumes of dictionaries, phrase books or word lists will provide the same enjoyment as being able to communicate directly with the people of the country you are visiting. It is a good idea to make an effort to grasp the basics before you go. As you travel you will pick up more of the language and the more you know, the more you will benefit from your stay.

General pronunciation

Whether you have been taught the 'Castilian' pronounciation (*z* and *c* followed by *i* or *e* are pronounced as the *th* in think) or the 'American' pronounciation (they are pronounced as *s*), you will encounter little difficulty in understanding either. Regional accents and usages vary, but the basic language is essentially the same everywhere.

Vowels
a	as in English *cat*
e	as in English *best*
i	as the *ee* in English *feet*
o	as in English *shop*
u	as the *oo* in English *food*
ai	as the *i* in English *ride*
ei	as *ey* in English *they*
oi	as *oy* in English *toy*

Consonants
Most consonants can be pronounced more or less as they are in English. The exceptions are:

g	before *e* or *i* is the same as *j*
h	is always silent (except in *ch* as in *chair*)
j	as the *ch* in Scottish *loch*
ll	as the *y* in *yellow*
ñ	as the *ni* in English *onion*
rr	trilled much more than in English
x	depending on its location, pronounced *x*, *s*, *sh* or *j*

Spanish words and phrases

Greetings, courtesies

hello	*hola*	I speak Spanish	*hablo español*
good morning	*buenos días*	I don't speak Spanish	*no hablo español*
good afternoon/		do you speak English?	*¿habla inglés?*
evening/night	*buenas tardes/noches*	I don't understand	*no entiendo/ no comprendo*
goodbye	*adiós/chao*	please speak slowly	*hable despacio por favor*
pleased to meet you	*mucho gusto*		
see you later	*hasta luego*	I am very sorry	*lo siento mucho/ disculpe*
how are you?	*¿cómo está? ¿cómo estás?*	what do you want?	*¿qué quiere? ¿qué quieres?*
I'm fine, thanks	*estoy muy bien, gracias*		
I'm called...	*me llamo...*	I want	*quiero*
what is your name?	*¿cómo se llama? ¿cómo te llamas?*	I don't want it	*no lo quiero*
yes/no	*sí/no*	leave me alone	*déjeme en paz/ no me moleste*
please	*por favor*		
thank you (very much)	*(muchas) gracias*	good/bad	*bueno/malo*

Questions and requests

Have you got a room for two people?
¿Tiene una habitación para dos personas?
How do I get to_? *¿Cómo llego a_?*
How much does it cost?
¿Cuánto cuesta? ¿cuánto es?
I'd like to make a long-distance phone call
Quisiera hacer una llamada de larga distancia
Is service included? *¿Está incluido el servicio?*
Is tax included? *¿Están incluidos los impuestos?*

When does the bus leave (arrive)?
¿A qué hora sale (llega) el autobús?
When? *¿cuándo?*
Where is_? *¿dónde está_?*
Where can I buy tickets?
¿Dónde puedo comprar boletos?
Where is the nearest petrol station?
¿Dónde está la gasolinera más cercana?
Why? *¿por qué?*

Basics

bank	el banco	market	el mercado
bathroom/toilet	el baño	note/coin	le billete/la moneda
bill	la factura/la cuenta	police (policeman)	la policía (el policía)
cash	el efectivo	post office	el correo
cheap	barato/a	public telephone	el teléfono público
credit card	la tarjeta de crédito	supermarket	el supermercado
exchange house	la casa de cambio	ticket office	la taquilla
exchange rate	el tipo de cambio	traveller's cheques	los cheques de viajero/
expensive	caro/a		los travelers

Getting around

aeroplane	el avión	insured person	el/la asegurado/a
airport	el aeropuerto	to insure yourself against	asegurarse contra
arrival/departure	la llegada/salida	luggage	el equipaje
avenue	la avenida	motorway, freeway	el autopista/la
block	la cuadra		carretera
border	la frontera	north, south, west, east	norte, sur, oeste
bus station	la terminal de		(occidente), este
	autobuses/camiones		(oriente)
bus	el bus/el autobús/	oil	el aceite
	el camión	to park	estacionarse
collective/		passport	el pasaporte
fixed-route taxi	el colectivo	petrol/gasoline	la gasolina
corner	la esquina	puncture	el pinchazo/
customs	la aduana		la ponchadura
first/second class	primera/segunda clase	street	la calle
left/right	izquierda/derecha	that way	por allí/por allá
ticket	el boleto	this way	por aquí/por acá
empty/full	vacío/lleno	tourist card/visa	la tarjeta de turista
highway, main road	la carretera	tyre	la llanta
immigration	la inmigración	unleaded	sin plomo
insurance	el seguro	to walk	caminar/andar

Accommodation

air conditioning	el aire acondicionado	power cut	el apagón/corte
all-inclusive	todo incluido	restaurant	el restaurante
bathroom, private	el baño privado	room/bedroom	el cuarto/la habitación
bed, double/single	la cama matrimonial/ sencilla	sheets	las sábanas
		shower	la ducha/regadera
blankets	las cobijas/mantas	soap	el jabón
to clean	limpiar	toilet	el sanitario/excusado
dining room	el comedor	toilet paper	el papel higiénico
guesthouse	la casa de huéspedes	towels, clean/dirty	las toallas limpias/ sucias
hotel	el hotel		
noisy	ruidoso	water, hot/cold	el agua caliente/fría
pillows	las almohadas		

Health

aspirin	la aspirina	diarrhoea	la diarrea
blood	la sangre	doctor	el médico
chemist	la farmacia	fever/sweat	la fiebre/el sudor
condoms	los preservativos, los condones	pain	el dolor
		head	la cabeza
contact lenses	los lentes de contacto	period/sanitary towels	la regla/ las toallas femeninas
contraceptives	los anticonceptivos		
contraceptive pill	la píldora anti- conceptiva	stomach	el estómago
		altitude sickness	el soroche

Family

family	la familia	boyfriend/girlfriend	el novio/la novia
brother/sister	el hermano/la hermana	friend	el amigo/la amiga
daughter/son	la hija/el hijo	married	casado/a
father/mother	el padre/la madre	single/unmarried	soltero/a
husband/wife	el esposo (marido)/ la esposa		

Months, days and time

January	enero	Monday	lunes
February	febrero	Tuesday	martes
March	marzo	Wednesday	miércoles
April	abril	Thursday	jueves
May	mayo	Friday	viernes
June	junio	Saturday	sábado
July	julio	Sunday	domingo
August	agosto		
September	septiembre	at one o'clock	a la una
October	octubre	at half past two	a las dos y media
November	noviembre	at a quarter to three	a cuarto para las tres/ a las tres menos quince
December	diciembre		
		it's one o'clock	es la una

it's seven o'clock	*son las siete*	in ten minutes	*en diez minutos*
it's six twenty	*son las seis y veinte*	five hours	*cinco horas*
it's five to nine	*son las nueve menos cinco*	does it take long?	*¿tarda mucho?*

Numbers

one	*uno/una*	sixteen	*dieciséis*
two	*dos*	seventeen	*diecisiete*
three	*tres*	eighteen	*dieciocho*
Four	*cuatro*	nineteen	*diecinueve*
five	*cinco*	twenty	*veinte*
six	*seis*	twenty-one	*veintiuno*
seven	*siete*	thirty	*treinta*
eight	*ocho*	forty	*cuarenta*
nine	*nueve*	fifty	*cincuenta*
ten	*diez*	sixty	*sesenta*
eleven	*once*	seventy	*setenta*
twelve	*doce*	eighty	*ochenta*
thirteen	*trece*	ninety	*noventa*
fourteen	*catorce*	hundred	*cien/ciento*
fifteen	*quince*	thousand	*mil*

Food

avocado	*la palta*	garlic	*el ajo*
baked	*al horno*	goat	*el chivo*
bakery	*la panadería*	grapefruit	*la toronja/el pomelo*
banana	*la banana*	grill	*la parrilla*
beans	*los frijoles/ las habichuelas*	grilled/griddled	*a la plancha*
		guava	*la guayaba*
beef	*la carne de res*	ham	*el jamón*
beef steak	*el lomo*	hamburger	*la hamburguesa*
boiled rice	*el arroz blanco*	hot, spicy	*picante*
bread	*el pan*	ice cream	*el helado*
breakfast	*el desayuno*	jam	*la mermelada*
butter	*la manteca*	knife	*el cuchillo*
cake	*la torta*	lemon	*el limón*
chewing gum	*el chicle*	lobster	*la langosta*
chicken	*el pollo*	lunch	*el almuerzo/la comida*
chilli or green pepper	*el ají/pimiento*	meal	*la comida*
clear soup, stock	*el caldo*	meat	*la carne*
cooked	*cocido*	minced meat	*la carne picada*
dining room	*el comedor*	onion	*la cebolla*
egg	*el huevo*	orange	*la naranja*
Fish	*el pescado*	pepper	*el pimiento*
fork	*el tenedor*	pasty, turnover	*la empanada/ el pastelito*
fried	*frito*		

pork	*el cerdo*	soup	*la sopa*
potato	*la papa*	spoon	*la cuchara*
prawns	*los camarones*	squash	*la calabaza*
raw	*crudo*	squid	*los calamares*
restaurant	*el restaurante*	supper	*la cena*
salad	*la ensalada*	sweet	*dulce*
salt	*la sal*	to eat	*comer*
sandwich	*el bocadillo*	toasted	*tostado*
sauce	*la salsa*	turkey	*el pavo*
sausage	*la longaniza/chorizo*	vegetables	*los legumbres/vegetales*
scrambled eggs	*los huevos revueltos*	without meat	*sin carne*
seafood	*los mariscos*	yam	*el camote*

Drink

beer	*la cerveza*	hot	*caliente*
boiled	*hervido/a*	ice/without ice	*el hielo/sin hielo*
bottled	*en botella*	juice	*el jugo*
camomile tea	*la manzanilla*	lemonade	*la limonada*
canned	*en lata*	milk	*la leche*
coffee	*el café*	mint	*la menta*
coffee, white	*el café con leche*	rum	*el ron*
cold	*frío*	soft drink	*el refresco*
cup	*la taza*	sugar	*el azúcar*
drink	*la bebida*	tea	*el té*
drunk	*borracho/a*	to drink	*beber/tomar*
		water	*el agua*
firewater *el aguardiente*		water, carbonated	*el agua mineral con gas*
fruit milkshake	*el batido/licuado*	water, still mineral	*el agua mineral sin gas*
glass	*el vaso*	wine, red	*el vino tinto*
		wine, white	*el vino blanco*

Key verbs

to go	**ir**	there isn't/aren't	*no hay*
I go	*voy*	**to be** **ser** (permanent state) **estar**	
you go (familiar)	*vas*	(positional or temporary state)	
he, she, it goes,		I am	*soy* *estoy*
you (formal) go	*va*	you are	*eres* *estás*
we go	*vamos*	he, she, it is,	
they, you (plural) go	*van*	you (formal) are	*es* *está*
to have (possess)	**tener**	we are	*somos* *estamos*
I have	*tengo*	they, you (plural) are	*son* *están*
you (familiar) have	*tienes*		
he, she, it,			
you (formal) have	*tiene*		
we have	*tenemos*		
they, you (plural) have	*tienen*		
there is/are	*hay*		

This section has been assembled on the basis of glossaries compiled by André de Mendonça and David Gilmour of South American Experience, London, and the Latin American Travel Advisor, No 9, March 1996.

Index → Entries in bold refer to maps

A

accommodation 44
Aguacalientes 147
Aguas Zarcas 166
air travel 39
airlines 35
Alajuela 120, **120**
Alto Pacuare 156
amphibians 450
Angostura Dam 423
Arenal (Nuevo) 176
Arias Sánchez, Oscar 419
art 427
Atenas 123

B

Bagaces 210
Bahía 312
Bahía Drake 342
Bahía Herradura 288
Bahía Salinas 223
bananas 416, 422
banks 56
bars 47
Barva 137
bed and breakfast 46
birds 440
boat travel 37, 39
boat travel, Tortuguero 379
Boca Tapada 166
books 452
border crossing
    Costa Rica–Nicaragua
        Barra del Colorado 380
        Los Chiles 186
        Peñas Blancas 223
    Costa Rica–Panama
        Paso Canoas 332
        Río Sereno 333
        Sixaola 393
Boruca 425
Bosque de Paz Rainforest
    Reserve 126
Bratsi 407

Braulio Carrillo National
    Park 162
Bribrí 425
Briceño 331
bus travel 37, 42

C

Cabécar 425
Cabo Matapalo 352
Cabuya 265
Café Britt coffee
    plantation 137
Cahuita 387, **388**
camping 46
Caño Negro Wildlife
    Reserve 184
car hire 40
Caribbean Lowlands 430
carnival
    Puerto Limón 366
Carrillo Colina, Braulio 414
Cartago 145, **146**, 411
Casa del Soñador 149
Central Highlands 430
Centro Biológico
    Las Quebradas 321
Centro Costarricense de
    Ciencias y Cultura 83
Cerro de la Muerte 319
Cerro Tortuguero 379
Chacarita 331
Chachagua 178
Chase 407
children 50
Chirripó Indian Reserve 156
Chorotega 410, 425
Ciudad Quesada
    (San Carlos) **170,** 171
climate 429
clothing 35, 51
Cóbano 263
coffee 422
Columbus, Christopher 410
conduct 50

Cooprena 46
Copey 318
Corobicí 209
cost of living 56
Costa Rican Tourist Board 60
crafts 427
credit cards 55
crime 58
currency 55
customs 51
cyber cafés 53
cycling 44

D

Damas Island 297
dance 427
Daniel Oduber Quirós
    International Airport 36
dengue fever 52
departure tax 36
disabled travellers 51
Dominical 308
Drake 342
drink 47, 51
driving 37, 41, 58
drugs 51
duty free 51

E

eating 47
economy 421
eco-tourism 46
El Bosque Eterno de los
    Niños 195
El Mundo de la Tortuga 239
embassies
    Costa Rican 51
    foreign 114
Empalme 318
Escaleras 309
Escazú 84
    sleeping 95
Esparza 208
Estación Biológica La Selva
    164

Esterillos 286
expatriates 425

F
fauna 435
fax services 60
ferries 39
festivals 48
Finca La Central 154
fishing 232
flight agents 36
flora 433
food 46-47
Fortuna 171, 171
Frajines 124
frogs 450

G
Gandoca 393
Garcimuñez 411
gay travellers 52
geography 428
geology 428
Golfito 356, 356
government 421
Grecia 125
Guanacaste Conservation
    Area 220, 221
Guatuso 425
Guayabo 210
Guayabo National
    Monument 410
Guaymí 425

H
Hacienda Barú 308
health 52
Heliconia Island B&B 164
Heredia 135, 135
history 410
hitchhiking 44
holidays 48
hotels 44
Huetar 425
Hummingbird Gallery 203
hummingbirds 442

I
immigration 64
INBio Parque 136
independence 413
indigenous population 425
inoculations 53
insects 451
insurance 53
internet 53
Isla Ballena 310
Isla Cabuya 265
Isla del Caño 342
Isla Gitana 263
Isla Guayabo 263
Isla Negritos 263
Isla Palo Seco 286
Isla San Lucas 283
Isla Tortuga 263, 283
Isla Uvita 373

J
Jacó 284, 285
José Figueres 417
Juan Santamaría
International airport 36, 70
    accommodation 89
Junquillal 242

K
Keith, Minor Cooper 416
KeköLdi Indigenous
    Reserve 390

L
La Casona 218
La Catarata 284
La Esperanza Banana
    Plantation 368
La Guácima de Alajuela 123
La Leona 349
La Palma 347, 351
La Sierra de Abangares 209
La Sirena 349, 351
La Virgen 165
Laguna de Fraijanes 124
language 53, 456
language schools 54

Lankester Botanical
    Garden 147
Las Nubes 141
Las Pumas 210
Las Tres Hermanas 310
lesbian travellers 52
Liberia 212
Limbo Lagoon 219
literature 427, 452
Llanos de Cortés
    waterfall 210
Llorona 351
Lomas de Sierpe 379
Londres 297
Los Angeles Cloudforest
    Reserve 127
Los Cusingos bird
    reserve 321
Los Patos 349

M
Mahogany Park 283
malaria 52
Malpaís 266
Manuel Antonio 298, 299
maps 55
Mata de Limón 283, 287
Matapalo 308, 352
media 55
Moín 370
money 55, 58
monkeys 435
Monte de la Cruz 141
Monte Sky 149
Montero 164
Monteverde 194, 194
Monteverde Cloud Forest
    Reserve 190, 191, 192
Montezuma 264
Mora Porras, Juan
    Rafael 415
Moravia 104
Moravia del Chirripó 156
motorbike rental 42
Murciélago Sector 220
Museo de Ciencias
    Naturales 83

N

Nacascolo 233
Naranjo 126
national parks 431, **432**
    information sources 57
    volunteering 66
National System of
    Protected Areas 431, **432**
NatureAir 39
Nauyaca 309
newspapers 55
Nicaraguans 425
Nicoya 250, **250**
Nosara 253, **253**
Nuevo Arenal 176

O

Ojo de Agua 122
Ojochal 310
opossums 436
Orosí 149
Orosí Valley 148
Orotina 283, 288
Ostional 254

P

packing 35
Pacuare Nature Reserve 368
Palmar Sur 330
Palmares 127
Pan de Azúcar 283
Paraíso 148
Páramo 435
Parque Nacional Arenal 173
Parque Nacional Barbilla
    368
Parque Nacional Braulio
    Carrillo 139, **163**
Parque Nacional Chirripó
    322, **322**
Parque Nacional Corcovado
    349, **350**
Parque Nacional Isla del
    Coco 282
Parque Nacional Juan Castro
    Blanco 126
Parque Nacional Manuel
    Antonio 299

Parque Nacional Mario las
    Baulas de Guanacaste 238
Parque Nacional Piedras
    Blancas 331
Parque Nacional Santa
    Rosa 218
Parque Nacional Tapantí-
    Macizo de la Muerte 149
Parque Nacional Tenorio
    181
Parque Nacional Tortuguero
    375, **376**
Parque Nacional Volcán
    Poás 124
Parque Nacional Volcán
    Turrialba 154
Parrita 286
Partido Liberación Nacional
    418
Paso Canoas 332
Pavones 358
Peñas Blancas 223
Penshurst 394
people 425
Pital 166
Playa Bandera 286
Playa Bejuco 291
Playa Bonita 370
Playa Brasilito 238
Playa Cativo 360
Playa Chiquita 400
Playa Conchal 238
Playa del Coco 230, **230**
Playa Escondido 300
Playa Esterillo Centro 290
Playa Flamingo 238
Playa Hermosa 231
Playa Langosto 245
Playa Nancite 219
Playa Naranjo 219
Playa Negra 396
Playa Ocotal 231
Playa Ostional 254
Playa Palma 286
Playa Pan de Azucar 239
Playa Panama 232
Playa Platanares 348
Playa Playitas 300

Playa Potrero 239
Playa San Josecito 358
Playa Tamarindo 240, **241**
Playa Tárcoles 288, 292
Playa Tortuga 310
Playa Zancudo 358
Pocosol 172
politics 421
Portete 370
post 57
pre-Columbian history 410
Presa de Cachí 149
primates 435
prostitution 59
Pueblo Antiguo 85
Puerto Jiménez 347, **348**
Puerto Limón 369, **369**
Puerto Viejo loop 162, **163**
Puerto Viejo de Sarapiquí
    164
Puerto Viejo de Talamanca
    390, **391**
Punta Banco 358
Punta Coral 283
Punta Leona 288
Punta Serrucho 300
Punta Uva 401
Punta Uvita 310
Puntarenas 280, **280**

Q

Quebrada Grande 225
Quepos 295, **296**
Quizarrá de Pérez Zeledón
    321

R

radio 55
railroad construction 416
Rain Maker Nature Reserve
    298
Rainforest aerial tram 140
Rancho La Merced 310
Rancho Las Botijas 321
Rancho Los Tucanes 297
Refugio de Fauna Silvestre
    Isla Bolaños 223

Refugio Nacional de Fauna Silvestre Golfito 357
Refugio Nacional de Vida Silvastre Caño Negro 187
Refugio Nacional de Vida Silvestre Gandoca-Manzanillo 392, 406
Refugio Nacional Silvestre Peñas Blancas 208
Refugio Nacionales de Vida Silvestre Barra del Colorado 380
religion 57, 428
reptiles 449
Reserva Biológica Bosque Nuboso Monteverde and Santa Elena 190
Reserva Biológica Bosque Nuboso Santa Elena 196
Reserva Biológica Durika 329
Reserva Biológica Hitoy Cerere 386
Reserva Biológica Isla del Caño 343
Reserva Biológica Isla Guayabo 283
Reserva Sendero Tranquilo 197
restaurants 47
Río Corobicí 209
Río Sereno 333
Río Tárcoles 283
rip tides 58
road travel 39
road travel to Costa Rica 37
Roble 283, 287, 292
Rosario de Naranjo 131

S
Sabalito 333
Sacremento 137
safety 57
Sámara 254, **257**
San Carlos (Ciudad Quesada) 170, 171
San Gerardo de Dota 319
San Gerardo de Rivas 321

San Isidro de Coronado 141
San Isidro de El General 319, 320
San José 67, 68, 72, 80
  activities and tours 105
  Amón 79
  Auditorio Nacional 83
  Barrio Tournón 83
  bars 100
  bars and clubs 100
  car hire 70, 112
  Centro Comercial El Pueblo 83
  directory 113
  easy trips from the city 85
  eating 96
  entertainment 101
  Escazú 84
  festivals 102
  Galería Nacional 83
  history 75
  hospitals 115
  ins and outs 70
  language schools 115
  medical services 115
  Mercado Central 82
  Museo de Arte y Diseño Contemporáneo 78
  Museo de Etimología 84
  Museo de Jade Fidel Tristán 79
  Museo de Niños 83
  Museo de Oro Precolombino 76
  Museo Dr Rafael Angel Calserón 78
  Museo Nacional 77
  Museo Nacional de Ferrocarril 78
  Museo Numismático 77
  nightclubs 101
  Otoya district 79
  Palacio Nacional 77
  Parque Zoológico Simón Bolívar 79
  Parque Central 79
  Parque España 79

  Parque Morazán 79
  Paseo Colón 82
  Plaza de la Cultura 76
  Plaza de la Democracia 77
  San Pedro 84
  shopping 103
  sights 76
  sleeping 88
  Spirogyra 84
  Teatro Nacional 77
  tour operators 105
  tourist office 74
  transport 107
  See University of Costa Rica
  vegetarian restaurant 98
  Western Central 82
San José de la Montaña 137
San Juan de Chicuá 150
San Juan de Valverde Vega 130
San Lorenzo 318
San Luis 201
San Marcus de Tarrazú 318
San Mateo 288
San Pablo de León Cortés 318
San Pedrillo 349, 351
San Pedro de Poás 124
San Rafael de Guatuso 186
San Rafael de Heredia 141
San Ramón 127
SANSA 39
Santa Clara 366
Santa Elena 190, 194
Santa Elena Cloud Forest Reserve 196
Santa María de Dota 318
Santa Teresa 266
Santo Domingo 213
Sarchí 49, 125
security 57
self-catering accommodation 46
Selva Verde Lodge 165
sex tourism 59
shopping 49

Sistema Nacional de Areas de Conservación 431
sleeping 44
sloths 437
Spanish conquest 410
sport 426
student travellers 59
swimming 58

T

Tabacón Resort 173
Talamanca mountains 334
Tamarindo **241**
taxis 43
telecommunications 59
television 55
Tempisque ferry 209
Tenorio volcano 209
Térraba 425
theatre 427
time 50, 60
tipping 59
Tirimbina Biological Reserve 165
Tivives 283
toucans 444
tour operators 61
tourism 423

tourist information office 60
tourist offices (overseas) 60
trade war 422
train travel 44
transport 34, 39
traveller's cheques 55
Turrialba 153, 154
turtle watching 378
turtles 450
    Tortuguero National Park 378

U

Ujarrás 148
United Fruit Company 416
University of Costa Rica 84
Upala 186
Uvita 310

V

vaccinations 52
Vara Blanca 124
Vásquez de Coronado 411
Venado Caves 173
Venecia 166
visas 64
Volcán Arenal 173, **174**

Volcán Barva 137
Volcán Irazú 147
Volcán Miravalles 210
volunteer projects 66
volunteer projects, Monteverde 193

W

Walker, William 413
websites 453
what to take 35
whitewater rafting 210
wildlife 431
Wilson Botanical Gardens 333
Witches' Rock 219
women travellers 58, 65
working in Costa Rica 65

Y

yoga 397
youth hostels 46

Z

Zarcero 126
Zoo Ave 123

Complete title listing

Footprint publishes travel guides to more than 150 destinations worldwide. Each guide is packed with practical, concise and colourful information for everybody from first-time travellers to travel aficionados. The list is growing fast and current titles are noted below.
Available from all good bookshops and online
www.footprintbooks.com

(P) Denotes pocket guide

Latin America and Caribbean
Antigua & Leeward Islands (P)
Argentina
Belize, Guatemala &
  Southern Mexico
Bolivia
Brazil
Caribbean Islands
Dominican Republic (P)
Chile
Colombia
Costa Rica
Costa Rica, Nicaragua & Panama
Cuba
Cuzco & the Inca Heartland
Ecuador & Galápagos
Mexico & Central America
Nicaragua
Patagonia
Peru
Peru, Bolivia & Ecuador
South American Handbook

North America
Vancouver (P)
Western Canada

Africa
Cape Town (P)
Egypt
Kenya
Morocco
Namibia
South Africa Handbook

Middle East
Dubai (P)

Australasia
East Coast Australia
New Zealand
Sydney (P)
West Coast Australia

Asia
Borneo
Cambodia
India
Laos
Malaysia & Singapore
Northeast India
Rajasthan
South India
Sri Lanka
Southeast Asia Handbook
Tibet
Thailand
Vietnam
Vietnam, Cambodia & Laos

Europe
Andalucía
Antwerp & Ghent (P)
Barcelona (P)

Bologna (P)
Cardiff (P)
Costa de la Luz (P)
Croatia
Madrid (P)
Naples (P)
Northern Spain
Scotland Highlands & Islands
Seville (P)
Siena (P)
Tallinn (P)
Valencia (P)
Verona (P)

Activity guides
Diving the World
Mountain Biking the World
Skiing Europe
Snowboarding the World
Surfing Britain & Ireland
Surfing Europe
Surfing the World

Lifestyle guides
Body & Soul Escapes
Body & Soul Escapes:
   Britain & Ireland
European City Breaks
Travel Photography
Travel with Kids
Wine Travel Guide to the World

Also available: Traveller's Handbook
(WEXAS)

Notes

Advertisers' index

Europcar, Costa Rica inside back cover
Intercultura, Centro de Idiomas, Costa Rica
  inside back cover
Galápagos Classic Cruises, UK 61
Last Frontiers, UK 62
Reef and Rainforest Tours, UK 62
Select Latin America, UK 63
Steppes Travel, UK 63

Acknowledgements

In some ways this third edition of the Costa Rica Handbook has been the easiest and most difficult to write. You can't ignore the impact of the internet on our world: as a research tool for travellers and writers it is powerful, frustrating and, at times, amusing. Costa Rican sites win, in my opinion, several awards including most annoying website music award. Such is the speed of change that use of the internet is an essential part of any serious research project and this handbook is no different.

For all the value of the internet, you can't beat on-the-ground research. On my most recent visit to Costa Rica I was staggered by the pace of change in parts of the country, and pleased about how much stayed the same.

Sections of Costa Rica were updated by Jane Koutnik and Heloise Crowther. We carry over the specialist contributions made in this or previous editions, in particular to: Dr Caroline Harcourt for the wildlife section, Simon Ellis for birdwatching, Jerry Rujlow for details on inland and ocean fishing. Surfing came from Phil Miller (www.dreamingfish.co.uk).

Thanks also go to Caroline Sylge, Chris Nelson and Demi Taylor, authors of Footprint's *Body & Soul escapes* and *Surfing the World*, for contributing to the front colour section of this guide.

Finally after all the research, tapping, head-scratching and writing, all the text and maps are checked in the office. So big thanks to the patient crew down in Bath, and in particular to Sarah Thorowgood and Alan Murphy.

Travellers' letters

Many thanks to the following readers who have taken the time to write notes as they travel and to share their experiences with us by post or, increasingly, by email. It's great to receive letters, from short pithy corrections to colourful, sometimes humorous descriptions of personal journeys. Special thanks to those who managed to get in all the details.

Carlos Agudelo (Costa Rica); Allan Ament; Bob Bacher; Adam Beals (US); Daniel Besser (Costa Rica); Rosanne Beukeboom (The Netherlands); Clint & Carly Blackbourn; Howard Buck (US); Francis Chambers (Belgium); Rebecca Craske (UK); Karen Schulpzand & Rudy Cruysbergs (Belgium); John Denham (UK); Sarah Dohle (USA); Hanno Eckstein (Germany); Arnold Flather (Costa Rica); Simon Gandolfi (UK); Megan Gross (US); Udi Gur (Israel); Viviana Gutierrez (Costa Rica); Lisa Helberg (Germany); Rebecca van der Horst (The Netherlands); Lachance Isabelle (Canada); David Jackson (Australia); Jesper König (Sweden); Richard La Val (Costa Rica); Marijke Lamers (Netherlands); Geoff Ledgerwood (US); Jean-Sebastien Leduc (Canada); Ina Lockau-Vogel (Germany); Jean Pierre Martin (Canada); Leslie McGinnis (US); Jacques Modiano (Costa Rica); Karol Pastorek (Slovakia); Heloise Plumley (UK); Shirley Price (USA); Alex Putt (Costa Rica); Lars & Marco Raedisch (Germany); Andrew Raffo (Costa Rica); Andrew Rhee (US); Johanna Riber (Costa Rica); Orlando Rivera (US); Volkmar Schuster (Germany); Anja Seidel (Costa Rica); Silvia Senger (Switzerland); Ree Sheck (Costa Rica); Ton de Snoo (The Netherlands); Alejandro Solano (Costa Rica); Geraldine Swartz (Switzerland); Katharina Vater & Gabriel Tecklenburg (Germany); Dana Verstappen (Costa Rica); Gordan & Sue Vint (UK); Clive Walker (Costa Rica); Steve Waller (UK); Willi Waschull (Germany); Cara Waters (Australia); Karyn Wesselingh (UK); Gerrit Wilmink (Netherlands); Steffan Wofford (Costa Rica); Nadja Wuest (Switzerland); Franziska (Czech Republic).

About the author

Peter Hutchison first travelled through Central and South America between 1993 and 1995 after gaining a degree in Development Studies, specializing in Latin American Studies, from Reading University. During his travels he used both the Mexico and Central American Handbook and the South American Handbook to guide his path. It wasn't all moving about and he stopped for almost two years to work on the *Bolivian Times* in La Paz. Since then regular trips to Latin America, travelling popular routes and journeying roads less travelled, have kept the passion alive.

In February and March 2002 a team of five, led by Peter, made the first recorded descent of the River Parapeti in Bolivia (www.coursingtheparapeti.com) with the support of the Royal Geographic Society and funding from a Travelling Fellowship provided by the Winston Churchill Memorial Trust. River travel by canoe continued in Belize 2003 when Peter entered the Macal River Race in Belize. Paddling the Devizes Westminster Canoe Marathon (www.dwrace.org.uk) down the River Thames in 2004, 2005 and again in 2008 kept the long-distance connection with water going. Peter is currently looking for a new river to explore, preferably in Latin America.

Peter now lives in Hanwell, West London, using this base to work as a freelance journalist and travel writer. Having trained on the kayaking course used in the Mexican Olympics in 1968, he is keen supporter of the London 2012 Games and very excited about watching developments in his home city.

Credits

Footprint credits
Editor: Sarah Thorowgood
Map editor: Sarah Sorensen
Colour section: Kassia Gawronski

Managing Director: Andy Riddle
Publisher: Patrick Dawson
Editorial: Felicity Laughton, Nicola Gibbs,
Sara Chare, Ria Gane, Jen Haddington,
Alan Murphy, Alice Jell
Cartography: Robert Lunn, Kevin Feeney,
Emma Bryers
Cover design: Robert Lunn
Design: Mytton Williams
Sales and marketing: Liz Harper,
Zoë Jackson, Hannah Bonnell
Advertising sales manager: Renu Sibal
Finance and administration:
Elizabeth Taylor

Photography credits
Front cover: Giovanni Simeone/4 Corners
Images (Isla Tortuga)
Back cover: age footstock/SuperStock
(Wooden toucans at the Volcán Poás
Visitor Centre)

Manufactured in Italy by LegoPrint
Pulp from sustainable forests

Footprint feedback
We try as hard as we can to make each
Footprint guide as up to date as possible
but, of course, things always change. If you
want to let us know about your experiences –
good, bad or ugly – then don't delay, go to
www.footprintbooks.com and send in
your comments.

Publishing information
Footprint Costa Rica
3rd edition
© Footprint Handbooks Ltd
December 2008

ISBN: 978 1 906098 37 7
CIP DATA: A catalogue record for this book
is available from the British Library

® Footprint Handbooks and the Footprint
mark are a registered trademark of Footprint
Handbooks Ltd

Published by Footprint
6 Riverside Court
Lower Bristol Road
Bath BA2 3DZ, UK
T +44 (0)1225 469141
F +44 (0)1225 469461
www.footprintbooks.com

Distributed in the USA by Globe Pequot Press,
Guilford, Connecticut

Every effort has been made to ensure that
the facts in this guidebook are accurate.
However, travellers should still obtain
advice from consulates, airlines, etc about
travel and visa requirements before travelling.
The authors and publishers cannot accept
responsibility for any loss, injury or
inconvenience however caused.